THE WINES OF THE SOUTH OF FRANCE
From Banyuls to Bellet

Rosemary George is one of the country's leading wine writers and currently chairman of the Circle of Wine Writers. Her interest in the wine trade began in 1972 and in 1979 she was one of the first women to pass the Master of Wine examinations. Her first book, *The Wines of Chablis and the Yonne*, won both the André Simon Award and the Glenfiddich Prize. Her other books include *French Country Wines*, *The Wines of New Zealand* (both published by Faber and Faber), *Chianti and the Wines of Tuscany* and *Lateral Wine Tasting*. She is a regular contributor to wine magazines in both Britain and the USA. She is married and lives in London, but travels extensively.

FABER BOOKS ON WINE

Series Editor: Julian Jeffs

Barolo to Valpolicella, The Wines of Northern Italy by Nicolas Belfrage
Bordeaux (new edition) by David Peppercorn
Brunello to Zibibbo: The Wines of Tuscany, Central and Southern Italy by Nicolas Belfrage
Burgundy (new edition) by Anthony Hanson
Champagne by Maggie McNie
Drilling for Wine: From Dentist to Wine Merchant - A Metamorphosis by Robin Yapp
French Country Wines by Rosemary George
Haut-Brion by Asa Briggs
Madeira by Alex Liddell
Port and the Douro by Richard Mayson
Sauternes by Stephen Brook
Sherry (new edition) by Julian Jeffs
The Wild Bunch: Great Wines from Small Producers by Patrick Matthews
The Wines of Alsace by Tom Stevenson
The Wines of Australia by Tim White
The Wines of Austria by Philipp Blom
The Wines of Britain and Ireland: A Guide to the Vineyards by Stephen Skelton
The Wines of California by Stephen Brook
The Wines of Greece by Miles Lambert-Gocs
The Wines of Latin America by Christopher Fielden
The Wines of the Loire by Roger Voss
The Wines of New Zealand by Rosemary George
The Wines of the Rhône (new edition) by John Livingstone-Learmonth
The Wines of South Africa by James Seely
The Wines of the South of France: from Banyuls to Bellet by Rosemary George
The Wines of Spain by Julian Jeffs
Wine-Tasters' Logic: Thinking about Wine – and Enjoying It by Pat Simon

THE WINES
OF THE SOUTH
OF FRANCE

From Banyuls to Bellet

ROSEMARY GEORGE

faber and faber

LONDON·NEW YORK

First published in 2001
by Faber and Faber Limited
3 Queen Square London WC1N 3AU
Published in the United States by Faber and Faber Inc.,
An affiliate of Farrar, Straus and Giroux, New York

Typeset by Steven Gardiner Ltd, Cambridge
Printed in England by Clays Ltd, St Ives plc

A CIP record for this book
is available from the British Library

ISBN 0–571–19267 X

2 4 6 8 10 9 7 5 3 1

Contents

CONTENTS

CONTENTS

Acknowledgements

It is quite simple. I could not have written this book without the enormous help provided by two people. They are Christine Behey-Molines of the Conseil Interprofessionnel des Vins du Languedoc in Narbonne and Catherine Manac'h of Sopexa in London. As will be seen, the Languedoc takes up the greater part of this book, and so it was Christine who organised most of my programme of visits. She has ambitious ideas as to what constitutes a full day of meetings and kept me fully occupied, with barely a moment for a reviving tea or coffee between wine cellars, sending me to talented wine-growers who were ready to air their views on their appellation. From her office in London, Catherine Manac'h provided the link with all the other parts of the Midi, contacting the local *syndicats* and dealing with bureaucratic complications with limitless patience, paving my way for trouble-free visits.

Numerous other people and organisations have helped in their way: Virginie Robert and her colleagues from the Fédération des Interprofessions des Vins du Roussillon in Perpignan with visits in the Côtes du Roussillon and adjoining appellations; Christophe Logeais from the Syndicat de l'AOC Corbières and Christine Ontivérot from the Union des Crus Signés guided me through the Corbières; Michel Nozeran from the Syndicat du Cru Fitou organised an entertaining afternoon in Fitou; Yves Castell and his colleagues from the Syndicat du Cru Minervois; Marie-Noëlle Grojean of the Syndicat du Cru Malepère for a day in the Côtes de la Malepère; Claudine Merhle from the Syndicat des Vins AOC de Limoux; Adrian Mould, the expatriate Brit who runs the Syndicat du Cru Cabardès; Françoise Ollieux from the Syndicat du Cru Faugères; Natalie Seva and then Axel de Woillement from Syndicat du Cru St Chinian; Michel Rousset of the Office National

Interprofessionnel des Vins and Jacques Boyer of Domaine la Croix Belle for arranging a day in the Côtes du Thongue; Sylvie Ellul of the Syndicat des Producteurs de Vin de Pays d'Oc for organising visits to numerous producers of Vin de Pays d'Oc; Jean-Philippe Granier for further help with visits in the Languedoc; the Syndicat des Costières de Nîmes; the Syndicat des Vignerons des Baux; the Syndicat Général des Coteaux d'Aix-en-Provence and Marie-Jeanne Double of Aix en Vignes; Philippe Bréban of the Syndicat des Vins Coteaux Varois; Bruno Bouscarle of the Syndicat des Vignerons AOC Coteaux de Pierrevert; Natalie Epercieux of the Syndicat Général des Côtes du Lubéron; Catherine Frugière and François Millo from the Comité Interprofessionnel des Vins Côtes de Provence, for organising numerous visits in their appellation; François Millo also deserves a second thank you, for the cover photograph of the Mont Ste Victoire. Mireille Brun of the Association Les Vins de Bandol arranged an enjoyable few days in Bandol, Jéromine Paret of Domaine la Ferme Blanche chauffeured me round Cassis and Ghislain de Charnacé of the Château de Bellet organised an afternoon in Bellet; and last but not least, Charles Morazzani of Domaine de Musoleu arranged the backbone of a week's island tour around Corsica. All these people in their own way facilitated the organisation of intensive days of research.

But wine books are above all about people, so it is all the wine-growers who feature within these pages who must be thanked, for allowing me to impose upon their time, for their readiness to answer questions and explain their appellation, for sharing their concerns and problems as well as their enthusiasm and passion, and for their willingness to open bottles and tap vats in the desire to illustrate the wonderful originality and intricacies of their appellation and *terroir*. There were some wonderful moments of hospitality, too many to single out, with lunches and dinners of regional flavours accompanied by lively conversation. I would also like to thank my great friends, Daniel and Patricia Domergue from Clos Centeilles in the Minervois, who have helped more than they realise in the formation of this book.

I am enormously grateful to the series editor at Faber and Faber, Julian Jeffs, for giving me the opportunity to explore yet more of my favourite part of my favourite country. Friends who came on various research trips with me – namely Monique Dorel, Aileen Hall, Margaret Harvey and Miyoko Stevenson – provided extra observations and encouragement. Back in London, Julia Wilkinson, who knows the Midi better than most, gave constructive comments on the contents of my manuscript and Aileen Hall provided further valuable advice. Last but certainly not least, I must thank my husband, Christopher Galleymore, who has encouraged and supported me through a lengthy gestation period, while retaining his own enthusiasm for the wines of the south of France.

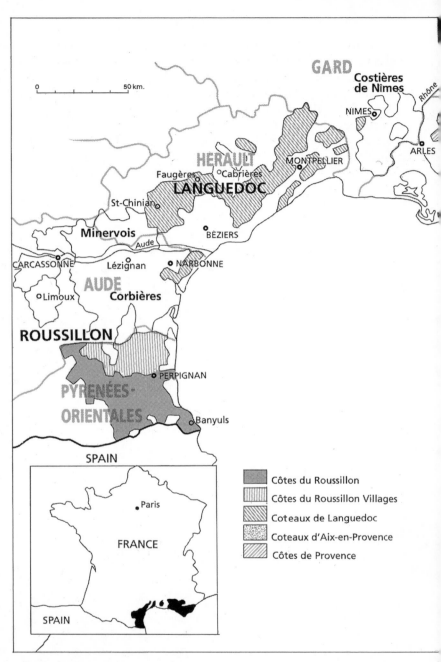

General map

xii

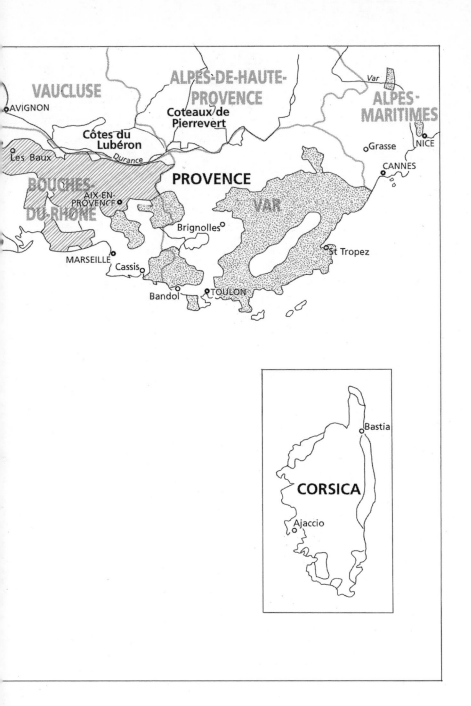

Introduction

The seeds of this book were first sown more than a dozen years ago. I was just completing the research for a previous book, *French Country Wines*, in which the vineyards of the south of France feature largely. It was the final day of an intensive fortnight of visits before I caught the night train to Paris, and an appointment with one of the big players in the Languedoc, the Vignerons du Val d'Orbieu, led to lunch with their then export manager, Claude Vialade. Over a cheerful *steak frites* and a bottle of Vin de Pays Nouveau – it was late October and the new wine had just been released, a month ahead of Beaujolais – the conversation naturally turned to the tremendous changes in the Languedoc. This was 1987 and already the contrasts and developments since my first visit to the Midi, almost ten years earlier, were palpable.

The transformation of this extraordinary region had started; the first stirrings towards quality were apparent. The most adventurous, innovative producers had not only planted the classic *cépages améliorateurs*, Syrah and Mourvèdre, but were trying out grape varieties with little or no tradition in the Midi – not just the more obvious choices, such as Cabernet Sauvignon and Chardonnay, but also Viognier and Chenin Blanc. The first *barriques* were appearing in cellars amid a prevailing spirit of adventure and discovery. The whole region vibrated on the edge of an explosion of progress. 'There is a book to be written,' one of us said. 'The Midi deserves a book of its own.' And the idea was planted. Since 1987 other books have intervened, but the seeds merely lay dormant.

Meanwhile, in the Midi the pace of change has increased breathtakingly. Existing vineyards have been replanted, and new ones have been created where once there were only scrubland and *garrigue*. New viticultural techniques have been tested; new grape

I

THE WINES OF THE SOUTH OF FRANCE

varieties introduced. You are never quite sure what you will encounter, from Petite Arvine in the St Chinianais to Pinot Noir in the Alpes-de-Haute-Provence. In the cellar, the improvements and innovations have to be seen, with all the latest modern equipment from pneumatic presses and sophisticated filters to computerised means of temperature control. Suddenly the south of France has captured the imagination of the wine world: its coming of age as a producer of top quality and original wines makes it without question the most stimulating region to visit.

What is exciting, too, is the wave of new people. So many of the producers I visited for this book have made their first wines within the last ten years. Long-established families may have tended their vineyards for generations but had the grapes vinified at the local co-operatives. Others may be newcomers to the world of grape growing and wine making, seized by an enthusiastic desire to create something from the land. They are people who have come from all walks of life, many struggling to make ends meet, some the lucky ones with money to invest and the wit to spend it profitably. Ask the wine growers why they do what they do. I have lost count of the number of times when, without a moment's hesitation, the reply was '*C'est ma passion.*' It is not just a living, but a passion. And these are the people that you will encounter on the pages of this book. As will be seen, in some instances they have flouted officialdom and challenged the sometimes restrictive bureaucracy of the INAO, with its regulations that often determine what you may or may not do in your own vineyard or cellar. In other instances, they are simply intent on making the best that their area can offer.

Rather than *The Wines of the Midi*, I have preferred to call this book *The Wines of the South of France*. Conveniently, Banyuls is the first appellation after the Spanish border, just as Bellet, on the outskirts of Nice, is the last appellation before Italy. Both illustrate the richness and diversity of this vast region: Banyuls' originality of flavours in a stylish *vin doux naturel* and Bellet's unexpected evolution of a dry white wine made from Rolle alongside the curiosities of red grape varieties, Folle Noir and Braquet. The term *Midi* does indeed describe the south of France and, in some parlance, specifically the Languedoc and Roussillon; but it can also more broadly include Provence and Corsica, and even parts of the vineyards of the South West. However, there is no escaping the fact that the term does have a pejorative ring to it, a reflection of the previous vocation of the region for producing enormous quantities of worse than ordinary *vin ordinaire*. These appellations merit a more specific description than the all-embracing *Midi*.

The book is the fruit of sixteen trips between April 1997 and September 1999. Some were no more than two-day flying visits to the recently developed biennial wine fair in Montpellier, Vinisud, which is increasingly providing a comprehensive showcase for the region. Others were two weeks of solid exploration of several appellations. The research had an inauspicious start. As I left the Gatwick Express to catch the early flight to Montpellier on an April Monday, the first words I heard, coming over the station loud-speaker, were 'Please evacuate the station immediately.' This was the morning in 1997 when the IRA brought most of central London as well as the capital's airports to a standstill. The next five hours were spent sitting on my luggage by a roundabout somewhere near the entrance to Gatwick's South Terminal. Fortunately it was a sunny morning and the novel in my hand luggage proved to be a good read. Things went much more smoothly the following morning: by midday I was driving out of Montpellier, down the *Languedocienne*, with yellow flowering gorse bushes resplendent in the spring sunshine, heading for my first meeting in the little town of St Chinian.

It has been a wonderful period of discovery. The French Mediterranean is rich in colour and flavour. It is the sea that provides a common link between these regions. Roussillon has strong associations with Catalonia, across the Pyrenees, for it shared a common history until well into the seventeenth century and its capital Perpignan has a Spanish flavour. There is a strong tradition of *vin doux naturel* here, with Rivesaltes, Banyuls and Maury, all based on Grenache Noir, Blanc or Gris, while the table wines, Côtes du Roussillon and Côtes du Roussillon Villages, as well as tinier Collioure, are establishing separate reputations.

Moving north across the departmental boundary, you come to the large appellation of Corbières covering the hills to the south of the valley of the Aude. Rivesaltes also makes an appearance here, as well as Fitou, the oldest table wine appellation of the Midi. This is wild, rugged countryside, with the hilltops dominated by the remains of Cathar castles. Narbonne is the nearest town, an agree-able centre with Roman origins. The unfinished cathedral of St Just merits a visit. Climb to the roof, admire the gargoyles close up and look over the roofs to the Montagne de la Clape, the vineyards of the Languedoc and the coastal plains with the large *étangs*, the inland saltwater lakes. The Canal du Midi, separating Corbières from Minervois, was a lifeline for the region before the development of the railways. Today it is populated by pleasure boats for tourists and provides pleasant walking along its towpath, under shady trees and past the locks to the animated little port of Homps with its canalside restaurants.

The medieval city of Carcassonne, turned into a fairy tale site by the restorations of Viollet-le-Duc, in some ways constitutes the western edge of the Languedoc. The watershed between the rivers of the Atlantic and the Mediterranean lies some twenty-five miles further west at Castelnaudary. The recently promoted appellation of Cabardès and the aspiring appellation of the Côtes de la Malepère are where the grape varieties of the Midi meet those of the south west, producing wines with both Syrah and Carignan as well as Merlot and Cabernet Sauvignon. The animated town of Limoux is the centre of an isolated appellation for sparkling wine that claims an even older history than Champagne. The Minervois is another lively appellation intent on improvement, establishing a series of *crus* with a strong emphasis on Syrah in preference to the oft decried Carignan.

The Coteaux du Languedoc is also undergoing considerable transformation. When the appellation was created in 1985, it incorporated a number of VDQS of greater or lesser importance; now it is working towards a scheme of *terroirs* and *crus*. Wines like La Clape, Picpoul de Pinet and Pic St Loup are likely to gain in importance, while village names like St Drézery, St Christol and Vérargues, once VDQS in their own right, are tending to fade into insignificance. As will be seen, administratively the Coteaux du Languedoc is very much in a state of flux, but that does not hinder the amazing creativity of its most innovative producers.

The Coteaux du Languedoc covers a large part of the department of the Hérault, with its enormous production of *vin de pays*. Here a second strand of viticulture coexists happily with the appellations that encapsulate the tradition of *terroir*. Many of the *vins de pays*, most notably Vin de Pays d'Oc, are increasingly based on varietal wines, a concept that is foreign to many a Midi wine maker. The classic wine of the Midi implies an *assemblage*, a blend in the cellar of different grape varieties. The monocepage *vins de pays*, on the

4

other hand, provide a powerful means of tackling the competition from the New World – the wines of Australia, Chile and South Africa. And a third strand of the Hérault viticulture is *vin doux naturel*, this time based on Muscat, with appellations like Frontignan and Lunel.

There is a wealth of history in the villages and towns of the Languedoc, the most important being Béziers and Montpellier. Béziers has the broad square of the Allées Paul Riquet and several Romanesque churches, while Montpellier has an attractive old quarter and lively squares, as well as the new buildings of the Antigone (though I would like it more if it were not a driver's nightmare). Much more accessible and friendly is Pézenas, once called the Versailles of the Languedoc, for it was an important cultural centre under the reign of Louis XIV, with visits from Molière in the 1650s. The elegant town houses and narrow streets remain today. In the region there are old abbeys such as St Guilhem-le-Désert and Valmagne, the ruins of Fontcaude and countless little towns and villages that merit a detour or a brief visit. Some only seem to come to life on market day; in others, hardly a dog stirs, and in summer the most demanding activity is the game of *boules* in the village square under the shade of the plane trees. Sometimes the most imposing building is the village co-operative, usually in the standard architecture of the 1930s. Some villages are worthy of note for their circular design, initially a means of fortification in the troubled times of the twelfth and thirteenth centuries. The countryside becomes wilder and more rugged the further you venture inland, away from the coastal plains and the gaudy resorts like la Grande Motte and Cap d'Agde.

The Camargue is where the vast River Rhône flows out into the Mediterranean. It is an extraordinary expanse of marshland, the home of pink flamingos, white horses and black bulls – a reminder that southern France shares the Spanish enthusiasm for bull fighting. Here, vines grow in the sand. On its edge is that jewel of a town, Aigues-Mortes, built by Louis IX as a port for the departure of the eighth and final crusade in 1270. The city walls are still intact and their circuit makes a pleasant walk, looking out over the russet roofs – and the forest of television aerials that abruptly remind you of the twentieth century. The Tour Constance dominates the horizon for miles around. After your walk, settle in the square, with its statue of St-Louis, for an aperitif as the sun sets and all will seem right with the world. The nearby Costières de Nimes, south of the Roman city of Nîmes with its magnificent arena and temple, is where the Languedoc meets the Rhône. Administratively it is in the Rhône valley, but I see it as part of the Languedoc in attitude, for it shares the pioneering spirit of that region.

The nearby town of Arles, which also has Roman vestiges, is the gateway to Provence, whence it is a short drive to the vineyards of Les Baux-en-Provence, the westernmost appellation of Provence. The dramatic jagged outline of the Alpilles dominates the skyline, and beneath these bauxite hills you encounter the first appellation of the south that permits – indeed, demands – the presence of Cabernet Sauvignon. Alternatively, if you approach Provence from the north, driving south from Orange, you will come first to the Montagne du Lubéron, where the vineyards of the Côtes du Lubéron provide another transition from the valley of the Rhône to Provence. Again, in terms of viticultural administration they are in the Rhône but historically this region is very much a part of Provence. Apt, the main town of the appellation, is an attractive market town with a Provençal atmosphere. To the east, close to the valley of the Durance, is the small and relatively unknown appellation of the Coteaux de Pierrevert, while if you cross the Montagne du Lubéron and head south, you come to the sprawling appellation of the Coteaux d'Aix-en-Provence. The city of Aix-en-Provence provides a charming centre to the appellation, with its tree- and café-lined boulevard Mirabelle, its narrow streets, memories of Cézanne and, on a Saturday morning, quite one of the best markets in the whole of Provence.

The Coteaux Varois, a relatively compact appellation sandwiched between the Coteaux d'Aix-en-Provence and the Côtes de Provence, is steadily and determinedly creating an identity and a reputation for its wines. The large Côtes de Provence, with its many different *terroirs*, is still a byword for *rosé*, but a *rosé* that is so much more appealing in flavour than it was even ten years ago, having benefited from the enormous technological progress of the region. St Tropez, for all its glamorous associations, is a pretty pleasure port and resort at the coastal centre of the appellation, while the Ile de Porquerolles is a delightful backwater. There are other, more compact appellations: Cassis, around another lively port, has a reputation for white wine; Palette is a tiny area just outside Aix-en-Provence whose reputation, and indeed continued existence, have been maintained for many years by just one family; Bandol is where that temperamental grape variety Mourvèdre is at its ultimate best, on steep, terraced vineyards; and finally, on the outskirts of Nice, a handful of wine growers save the tiny appellation of Bellet from disappearing under tarmac and concrete. Here the Italian influence is apparent, for this was part of Italy until 1860.

From Nice or Marseilles it is but a short flight across the water to the island of Corsica, with breathtaking views of Cap Corse as you fly into Bastia. Corsica too was Italian until a few months before the birth of Napoleon. However, it retains a fierce island individuality, firmly referring to mainland France as *le continent* and continuing to cultivate grape varieties like Nielluccio and Vermentino that have more to do with Italy than France. An island it may be, but the enormous technical progress of the last few years has not passed it by. There are growers in Patrimonio or Calvi as committed to the improvement of their wines as anywhere in the south of France.

The changes in the Midi over the past ten years have been enormous and the rate of change looks set to continue unabated. There are still many unanswered questions. Will a new, all-embracing appellation of Languedoc come into existence? Will the Coteaux du Languedoc be separated into several different *terroirs*, such as Terrasses de Larzac and Terres de Sommières? Will white appellations be developed for Faugères or Fitou? This book sets out to describe the wines of the south of France as they are at the end of the second millennium. As their history over more than two thousand years has shown, nothing ever stands still or can be taken for granted. This also applies very much on a personal level. Wine is essentially about people. It is people who create a vineyard and an appellation, encapsulating and absorbing the best that their *terroir* and climate have to offer. But people change: they move on and are replaced. Those who are noteworthy today may still be leaders in their appellation in ten years time, or they will have been superseded by newcomers. Only time will tell. In the meantime, I have attempted to visit most of the producers of note, over 360 in all, as well as talking to many others, and tasting their wines at the various fairs in Montpellier and Paris. Inevitably, I will have missed out people who should have been included. Space is one limitation and availability another, for, quite simply, they were away when I was in their area and there was nothing to be done.

I am also very aware that I was steered towards the *crème de la crème*, the people who are striving for their region, who are intent on creating wines that merit a reputation. Beneath this layer of quality you can still find the complacent co-operative member who is interested in nothing more than picking his grapes at the minimum acceptable level so that he is then free to spend the early autumn *à la chasse*. You still find the conservative thinker who does not understand the need to plant Syrah or Mourvèdre, who still produces badly vinified *vin ordinaire* and, more amazingly, finds a market for it. Unfortunately there are still cellars where volatile acidity is rife and oxidation the order of the day; and sadly the wine you find in the average village café in the south of France can still leave much to be desired. But this book does not concern these. It is about the people who are creating the Midi of the twenty-first century, an energetic, vibrant vineyard from Banyuls to Bellet, with intriguing and original flavours that offer enormous drinking pleasure, be it on the port at St Tropez or at one of the best tables in the area, Les Mimosas in the village of St Guiraud.

From the sixth century BC to the twenty-first century AD: history and trends

The four broad regions covered in this book, Roussillon, Languedoc, Provence and Corsica, have enjoyed quite a different political history over the last two millennia or so, but nonetheless there are common threads in their viticultural development as well as a diversity that originates from different external influences. Corsica was Italian until 1769, while Nice did not become part of France until 1860. The rest of Provence, the former Provincia Romana, was ruled by the Counts of Provence until it came under the French crown in 1486. In contrast, Roussillon has enjoyed a strong Catalan influence, with the Pyrenees providing a point of contact rather than a natural barrier. It was finally incorporated into France with the signing of the treaty of the Pyrenees in 1659. As for the Languedoc, the mountains of the Massif Central formed a substantial frontier, firmly separating the northern and southern parts of the country. Links with Paris were non-existent and the south enjoyed a rich cultural life, speaking a different language, the *langue d'oc*, as opposed to the *langue d'oil* of the north, until the area was torn apart by the Albigensian Crusade. The Languedoc was under the control of the Counts of Toulouse until the last of the line, Alphonse of Poitiers, died after a childless marriage in 1271; his heir was Philippe III of France. From then on, the Languedoc would be gradually assimilated into France.

THE GREEKS AND ROMANS

The viticultural history of the south begins with the Greeks. It is agreed that they brought vines with them when they founded Marsilia, on the site of the modern city of Marseille in the sixth century BC. There is evidence of viticulture and the remains of amphorae, indicate Marsilia's importance as a trading post – what Marcel Lachiver in his fascinating history of French viticulture, *Vins, Vignes et Vignerons*, describes as a point of anchorage for the Hellenic world in Gaul.

A few years later the Greeks had settled further along the coast around Agde, and there is again evidence of viticulture, but not necessarily of wine making. Excavations at Lattes outside Montpellier have uncovered a large quantity of grape pips from the fifth century BC, thus indicating with certainty the existence of vineyards in the Languedoc before the arrival of the Romans, who founded a colony at Narbonne in 118 BC. They built a thriving port and opened up the south with the Domitian Way, which linked the Rhone Valley to Spain. You can see today an original part of the road in the centre of Narbonne.

Viticulture flourished under the Romans. Domitian's edict of AD 92 ordering many existing vineyards to be pulled up, in an attempt to ensure that land suitable for the cultivation of wheat retained that purpose, had a temporary braking effect throughout Gaul, but only until the Emperor Probus repealed the edict in 276. Meanwhile there are records of wine being imported from Gaul to Italy, and ever since then viticulture has been a vital part of the agricultural activity and economy of the whole region, despite a brief period of Arab rule in Roussillon. The Saracens took Narbonne in 719 and it was recaptured by Pépin le Bref forty years later.

THE MIDDLE AGES

The collapse of the Roman Empire in the fifth century heralded a period of instability. Vandals and Visigoths, as well as Saracens, contributed to the upheavals until Charles I, soon to be known as Charlemagne, was crowned Emperor of the Romans by Pope Leo III on Christmas Day 800 at St Peter's in Rome. His rule brought some much-needed stability to the region.

The increasingly powerful Catholic Church also contributed to the development of viticulture throughout the region during the Middle Ages. There were Benedictine abbeys such as Saint Guilhem-le-Désert and Lagrasse, as well as the later Cistercian abbeys of Fontfroide and Valmagne, to mention just four that are still standing and which very much merit a visit. At one time, in fact, there were as many as fifty Benedictine abbeys in Languedoc–Roussillon, for all of which the production of wine was an essential part of monastic life. It was needed not only for the eucharist but also for hospitality, for the monasteries were the four-star hotels of the medieval traveller. They played a vital role in maintaining and expanding the viticultural traditions of the south throughout the Middle Ages, especially during the periods of social upheaval caused by the Albigensian crusade and the Hundred Years War.

The recurrent outbreaks of bubonic plague also had an effect, devastating the population and causing a sharp drop in the area of vineyards. The records of the village of Alignan-du-Vent near Béziers illustrate this sharp decline and subsequent revival. In 1353 there were forty vineyards out of a hundred fields. By 1378 the number had fallen to thirty-three and by the turn of the century to just six. It would seem that a revival began in the fifteenth century, with twenty vineyards by 1520 and a lively expansion during the middle of the sixteenth century. Vineyards competed with olive trees and with wheat. Once the Languedoc was assimilated into France, wine from the region began to travel north, and there are records of Languedoc wine being enjoyed at the Valois court of Charles V towards the end of the fourteenth century. Nonetheless the Massif Central represented a substantial barrier throughout the Middle Ages and difficulties of transport would ensure that the wines of the south remained unknown.

Viticultural fortunes continued to fluctuate. The ending of the Wars of Religion with the accession of Henri IV in 1589 offered a hope of prosperity. Vineyard plantings increased enormously in the first half of the seventeenth century as a result of the clearing of scrubland in the hills, while the plains remained indispensable for the production of wheat. Taverns flourished, trade developed and the market opened up towards Italy and Catalonia, with Agde and Béziers becoming important commercial centres.

THE CANAL DU MIDI

Nonetheless the region remained relatively isolated from the rest of the country, with poor communications, until the building of the Canal du Midi in the seventeenth century under the impetus of Colbert. The reputation of virtually every wine has depended upon ease of transport. Most great vineyards are close to river systems, which were vital in the days of impassable roads before the invention of railways. The Canal du Midi was opened in 1681. It is also appropriately called the Canal des Deux Mers, for it links the Mediterranean and Sète, a new port that had opened a few years earlier, with the Atlantic. To appreciate this colossal feat of engineering, it is worth taking a detour to see the locks of Fonséranes, just outside Béziers. This is a series of eight locks, one after the other like a flight of steps, that changes the water level by twenty-five metres. Pierre-Paul Riquet, the engineer who master-minded the whole project at great personal cost, is commemorated in the Allées Paul Riquet, the broad promenade in Béziers that has his statue in its centre.

However, the Bordelais maintained their privileges and during the eighteenth century only five per cent of the wines and *eaux de vie* of the Languedoc were exported along the Canal du Midi. Bordeaux did not want the Languedoc as competition. In 1742 a royal decree allowed the sales of wines from the Languedoc from the feast of St Martin on 11 November until 8 September, when any unsold wine would have to be returned to its source for distillation. Transport was expensive and so were the tolls. Although the port of Sète provided another opportunity for trade, it was only accessible to merchants from northern Europe, notably the Dutch, through the Straits of Gibraltar.

THE WINTER OF 1708–9

The terrible winter of 1708–9, with severe cold that lasted from the middle of October until the end of the following February, caused untold damage to agriculture all over France, and particularly in the northern part of the country. Many vineyards were devastated by frost, and only those near the sea in the south, with their more equable climate, particularly those of the Languedoc and Provence, survived. None the less, temperatures of $-17.5\,^{\circ}$C were recorded in Marseille and $-16.1\,^{\circ}$C in Montpellier, while in Paris they fell to $-23.1\,^{\circ}$C. A royal edict of 1710, intended to facilitate the transport and sale of wine from the south to the capital, caused friction with the Bordelais, who struggled to maintain their privileges. The south was able to benefit from the shortage of wine in the north.

THE PROSPERITY OF THE NINETEENTH CENTURY

It was not until the nineteenth century that the vineyards of the Midi experienced a period of major prosperity. The period of industrialisation after Napoleon's reign brought an immense demand for the wines of the Midi, for with the Industrial Revolution came a new clientele, the factory workers and miners of the north, who wanted a cheap, energy-inducing drink, namely wine. The Midi adapted itself to this demand and created an industrial vineyard for the production of thin, acidic wine that barely reached 7° or 8° alcohol and which was further watered down by its consumers. Today it would be considered quite undrinkable. However, it was on this that the economic and agricultural success of the Midi was built. This was the period that saw the building of many fine châteaux, with immense cellars that catered for enormous quantities of wine. A building such as the Château de Grézan in Faugères may look from a distance like a medieval edifice, but in fact it dates from the nineteenth century and is one of many such designed by a Bordelais architect, Monsieur Garosse, who offered potential clients a catalogue of different buildings.

The Midi, not Bordeaux or Burgundy, was where the greatest technical progress in wine making took place in the nineteenth century. In a vineyard near Mauguio in the Hérault, Henri Bouschet created a new grape variety, the Alicante Bouschet, by crossing Grenache Noir with a hybrid of Aramon and Teinturier du Cher developed by his father Louis, a few years earlier. Louis Bouschet de Bernard, known as 'the father of hybrids', lamented the demands of the market, which chose wine by colour, irrespective of taste: 'If I chose grape varieties like Aspiran and Terret, which give me fine delicate wines, why would I not fear that the *négociants*, although recognising the quality of the wine, would not want it. We know that these wines are neglected and despised. Colour is everything for trade. That the wines are bitter, hard and green, so long as they are deep in colour, it is all the same.' Alicante Bouschet was to become one of the most widely planted varieties of the Midi in the years following the phylloxera crisis.

At the beginning of the nineteenth century France had the largest vineyard in the world. The Gironde was the most productive department, followed by the Charente and Charente Inférieure (as the Charente-Maritime was then called) and then the Hérault. Lachiver asserts that in the early nineteenth century the viticultural fortunes of the Languedoc were based on *eau de vie*. In 1820 sixty per cent of the production of the Hérault was distilled. Lachiver sees 1850 as the year that brought the end of the traditional vineyard all over France, for within a few years it was to be transformed by cryptogrammic disease, notably oidium, as well as by the consequences of the railways and of phylloxera, which meant that the Languedoc would be replanted as a *vignoble de masse*, completely changing its traditional practices of cultivation and production.

The nineteenth-century authorities wrote of the wines of the Languedoc with varying degrees of enthusiasm, sometimes singling out specific *crus*. Jullien said that the red wines of the Languedoc generally had body and alcohol and that some were very good. He designated three categories, in addition to the *vins de chaudière* or wines for distillation.

By 1862 Rendu was more precise. He too classified the wines of the Languedoc into three categories: the vines of the hills or the *garrigue*, a term describing the wild scrub of the foothills of the Massif Central, which provided wines for export; the vines of the terraces, where the soil consisted of pebbles mixed with iron, which gave wines suitable for commerce; and finally the vineyards of the plains, planted with Aramon and Terret Bourret, that produced wines for distillation.

In the 1860s Guyot undertook a very detailed report on the vineyards of France for Napoleon III. He enthused about the quality of the Mourvèdre, called Espar in the Midi, and regretted the development of what he called the 'common' grape varieties. In the Hérault he found wines for distillation, ordinary wines and great wines, as well as fortified wines and brandy. As today, the surplus wine production was destined for distillation. He also mentioned that some eminent wine growers of the Hérault were experimenting with Pinots, Cabernet, Syrah, Cot, Sauvignon and Sémillon, as well as Spirans, Espar, Carignan, Grenache, Morastel and Clairette, which gave some very superior wines and drinks that were much in demand. There were apparently as many as 150 different grape varieties grown in the south. Sadly, many of them were to disappear completely in the aftermath of phylloxera.

Yields increased enormously in this period. In 1848 the Hérault overtook the Gironde as the department with the largest area of vines. Between 1861 and 1867, the six years during which Guyot was preparing his report, production in the Hérault rose from nine to fourteen million hectolitres. The all-time record harvest was 1869, when the Hérault produced a breathtaking 15,236,000 hectolitres from 226,000 hectares of vines. The average yield per hectare works out at almost 68 hectolitres, which is enormous for the period. The year 1875 saw the record harvest of France, with 84 million hectolitres. Between 1878 and 1899 there was never a harvest larger than 50 million hectolitres and consumption was always greater. However, in 1900 production soared to 68 million, dropping again to 58 million hectolitres in 1901.

The development of the railways in the second half of the nineteenth century coincided with the period of industrialisation and encouraged the growth of the Languedoc vineyards, providing an easy means of transport to the capital and the industrial north. The Paris–Lyons–Marseilles railway opened in 1856 and links were also provided with Sète, Montpellier, Béziers and Narbonne. The charges for the transport of wine dropped significantly. In 1840 it had cost 50 francs to send a cask of wine from Montpellier to Lyons, a price that fell to 10 francs by 1858.

PHYLLOXERA

But there were problems too. A severe attack of oidium in the 1850s led to a change in the composition of the vineyards, for Carignan and Aramon became the principal grape varieties when replanting took place. Then in 1863 the phylloxera louse was found at the village of Pujaut in the Gard, in the vineyards of a grower who had imported some American vines. The louse began its steady munch westwards and northwards, although it did not reach the Aude until 1885 and Chablis in northern France until 1887. People hoped to escape its devastating effects, but its progress was relentless.

In the later part of the nineteenth century enormous energy was devoted to finding a remedy for phylloxera. The louse was identified by Emile Planchon, professor in the school of chemistry at the University of Montpellier. His statue stands in front of the railway station in Montpellier. As well as identifying the dreaded louse, he made the connection between it and the American vines that had been brought into France. The effects of phylloxera were instantaneous. Plantings in the Hérault fell from 222,000 hectares in 1872 down to fewer than 90,000 in 1881, and in the Gard from 88,000 in 1871 to 15,000 in 1879. The French government offered a reward of 300,000 francs to whoever discovered a remedy. The Hérault alone produced some 696 different suggestions, of which about half were tried out in an experimental vineyard near Montpellier. Suggested remedies included the flooding of vineyards on the coastal plains, for the life cycle of the louse includes forty days underground. The soil around the roots of vines was injected with carbon bisulphide; occasionally you still see the piece of equipment used, carefully preserved as a museum piece. Gaston Bazille from Montpellier was the first to experiment with the grafting of European vines on to American rootstocks, but this procedure was not initially seen as the sought-after remedy and the reward was in fact never paid. Eventually, however, it was realised that this was the only viable solution. Already by 1879 there were four hundred and fifty hectares of grafted vines in the region.

Vines adapt more easily to grafting on the more fertile, less chalky soil of the coastal plains, and as the vineyards of the Midi were replanted in the last years of the nineteenth century, there was a definite shift away from the hillsides towards the coastal plains, leading to a neglect of many of vineyards of quality, of the *coteaux* and *terrasses* mentioned by the nineteenth-century authorities, that was to endure until almost the end of the twentieth century. When it was noticed that phylloxera did not survive in sandy soil, vineyards were developed on the coastal sand dunes, notably under the impetus of the Compagnie des Salins du Midi. These are now the vineyards of Domaines Listel.

In 1900 there were 200,000 hectares of vines in the Hérault, while between them the three departments of the Languedoc, the Aude, Hérault and Gard, produced 21,346,000 hectolitres from 384,560 hectares. The average yield of the particularly prolific vineyards of the Hérault was 66 hl/ha, which was enormous for the time, when the national average was only a meagre 29 hl/ha. In 1899 these three departments, which had twenty-three per cent of the country's vineyards, accounted for forty-four per cent of the total French production. Although for most of the nineteenth century vines had been grown alongside wheat and olive trees, by the turn of the century the Midi had become a region of monoculture. It was the reaction to phylloxera and at the most basic level.

TRADE AT SETE

During the same period the vineyards of Algeria, then a French colony, were being developed, with a phenomenal increase in production from 338,000 hectolitres in 1878 to 22,762,000 ten years later; in 1938 21.5 million hectolitres were produced from 400,000 hectares of vines. Wine growers from the Gard, Hérault and Aude, as well as from Spain and Italy, settled in Algeria and planted the grape varieties of the Midi, namely Grenache Noir, Cinsaut, Carignan, Aramon and Alicante Bouschet. The wines of Algeria soon became known as *vins de médicin* and the port of Sète developed a lively trade with Oran. Not for nothing is the railway station at Sète called the Gare du Maroc. The rich, full-bodied wines of Algeria had the necessary low acidity and deep colour to complement the pale, thin wines of the Midi.

This was the period when Sète, or Cette as the English writers of the time called it, developed a flourishing trade in all kinds of spurious wines. Writing in 1877, Charles Tovey describes a six-week tour through the vineyards of France with his friend T.G. Shaw, an active campaigner for the reduction in the duty on wine. He writes:

Fifteen miles S.W. Montpelier is the port of Cette. Here are extensive manufactures of wines of all countries – Port, Sherry Madeira, Claret Burgundy, or any other known wines. Mr Shaw is an apologist for Cette fabrications. He says: Cette is a by-word for adulteration, but its bad name is not deserved. Adulteration means the admixture of foreign matter with the juice of the grape. This is practised in Cette as well as in many other places, but probably comparatively little there, because there is such an ample choice of every description of grape juice for honest blending that some of the kinds are cheaper and more suitable for imitations desired than anything else. It is alleged that if you tell a Cette merchant at 9 a.m. you wish to have 50 pipes of Port, 50 butts of Sherry, and 50 hogsheads of Claret, he will promise to deliver them at 4 p.m. There is a good deal of (exaggerated) truth in this, but he can accomplish it, because he possesses an almost unlimited supply of a great variety of wines, with body and flavour, which his experience has taught him how to use, so that by certain combinations he will produce a remarkably close resemblance to that of any other quality or country.

Tovey goes on to say that he has 'records of tastings innumerable' of the wines of Cette, but:

> I condemned the whole, saving a really fine Muscat Frontignac, vintage 1861, some hogsheads of which I was tempted to purchase and which turned out most favourably. I believe that most of the concocted wines are shipped to the Brazils and all parts of America; some to India and Australia; but I do not think much is imported into England . . . I was shown Oporto Port and Burgundy Port, Madeira, and white wines which treatments would in a few hours convert into either Chablis or Sherry, Champagne, or sparkling Hock of Moselle. Houdin, the great conjuror, would not be equal to such transformations.

The process of fabrication was described in what seems to have been a best-seller of the time, a book by Joseph Audibert called *L'Art de faire le vin avec les raisins secs*, which first appeared in 1880 and sold out of five editions, each of a thousand copies, in six months. A sixth edition appeared in 1881 and a twelfth in 1886. Audibert explained how to make a wine from raisins soaked in *eau de vie* and hot water, recommending mixing this so-called wine with wine from the Languedoc or the Var. It is impossible to know just how much spurious wine was fabricated in this way. There were wines on the market that had never been near a grape, coming from glycerine, sulphuric acid and some colouring matter, while the most common process was simply to use sugar and raisins.

ECONOMIC AND SOCIAL FRICTION

But underneath the apparent prosperity and the recovery from the phylloxera crisis there were economic and social problems. The

Languedoc had become such an important source of supply that a bad harvest in the region automatically meant a wine deficit for the whole of France, while an abundant crop resulted in a surplus on the market. With the large vintages of the turn of the twentieth century, the price of wine fell and in 1901 supply exceeded demand by about 10 million hectolitres. Prices collapsed. In the 1880s a hectolitre of Languedoc wine cost 30 francs and in 1900 10 francs, while the cost of production was 15 francs. Prices picked up temporarily with the smaller crops in 1902 and 1903, but then the crisis reappeared with the large crop of 66 million hectolitres in 1904, which sold at an average price of between 6 and 7 francs per hectolitre. Things came to a head in 1907.

The viticultural community blindly refused to see that the root of the crisis lay in over-production, but insisted that the fault lay with fraud of the type practised in Sète and also with the incompetence of the French authorities. The large viticultural estates, such as the Compagnie des Salins du Midi, which had greatly extended their land holdings in the preceding years, were seen as symbols of the capitalist exploitation of the small wine grower, who was powerless against the commercial clout of the *négociants* paying derisory prices for their wine.

MARCELIN ALBERT AND THE REVOLT OF 1907

The inspiration for the revolt came from a humble wine grower, Marcelin Albert, who was born in the village of Argeliers in the Aude, a few kilometres north of Narbonne, in 1851. It seems that he was a simple man, but possessed of a powerful command of words, who inspired others to follow him in what he hoped would be peaceful demonstrations. He began with a petition in his village. In 1905 four hundred signatories refused to pay their taxes and asked for the resignation of the local council, united under the cry of '*Vive le vin naturel! A bas les empoissoneurs*'. The village council did resign. A commission given the task of investigating the crisis stated clearly in May 1907 that the viticultural crisis was not due to overproduction as the vineyard area was smaller than thirty years earlier. What they had simply failed to recognise was that the average yield was much higher. Obtusely, the commission proclaimed that the natural production of wine was insufficient to fulfil demand. And what seems curious today is that the wines of Algeria were not seen as contentious, but were accepted as French.

Meanwhile, the tide of protest swelled. On 24 March there was a demonstration of three hundred people in the village of Sallèles d'Aude; on 31 March six hundred people at Bize; on 14 April five thousand at Coursan; then ten thousand at Capestang on 21 April and twenty thousand at Lézignan on 28 April. The momentum gathered. On 5 May eighty thousand people swarmed to Narbonne. The demonstrators demanded: '*Que le vin se vende et se vende à un prix rémunerateur*'. Their banners cried '*Pas de revenu, pas d'impôts. Mort aux fraudeurs, le Midi veut vivre. Nous voulons du pain. Pas de politique*'. *Les Vignes de Sainte-Colombe* by Christian Signol provides a colourful, if somewhat romanticised, account of these turbulent times through the eyes of the heroine Charlotte, who runs her family's wine estate near Narbonne at the turn of the century

The demonstrations continued in the larger towns – Perpignan, Carcassonne and Nîmes – and culminated with six hundred thousand people collecting in Montpellier on 9 June, the day before the expiry of an ultimatum to the government to the effect that if it did not take the necessary steps to redress the wine market, a *grève d'impôts* or tax embargo would be declared. The expiry date passed with no action from the government, and in the days that followed, some 618 town councils resigned, indicated by the dramatic gesture of a black flag hung outside the town hall. Meanwhile, the Chamber of Deputies voted for an increase in the tax on sugar from 25 francs to 45 francs; the government had wanted it fixed at 60 francs and the sugar beet producers of the north had lobbied for a reduction to 15 francs. It was seen as a small gesture of appeasement, but meanwhile Clémenceau had called in the troops, albeit a local regiment sympathetic to the demands of the wine growers. Things came to a head in Narbonne on 19 June. More troops, this time from outside the region, were deployed against the demonstrators and the situation deteriorated, resulting in one death and nine injuries, with more people wounded or killed the following day.

Meanwhile Marcelin Albert, in hiding to avoid arrest, managed to reach Paris and surprise Clémenceau in his office. He was not, however, equal to the politician's cunning and was duped.

His fellow demonstrators accused Albert of being bought, for Clémenceau gave him a hundred-franc note to buy a train ticket home. Back in his village, ostracised and ridiculed, he gave himself up, although he was released a few weeks later. From a redeemer and a saviour, he became a traitor in the eyes of his fellow wine growers.

The demonstrations of 1907 were not in vain, however. A law, hastily passed on 29 June in an attempt to appease the situation, laid down some sensible measures, instituting the system of the *déclaration de récolte*, the declaration of the harvest, alongside the *déclaration de stocks*, which together gave an idea of the availability of wine for sale during the following twelve months. These two measures remain in force today. Action was also taken against fraud, by imposing some control over the sugar producers and taxing sugar destined for the wine industry. The following month saw the creation of the Répression des Fraudes and in September the legal definition of wine, as coming 'exclusively from the alcoholic fermentation of fresh grapes or from the juice of fresh grapes'. This was certainly a step in the right direction, but the real problem remained: the overproduction of mediocre wine. It was a problem that was to remain with the Languedoc for most of the twentieth century, lying dormant most of the time but erupting periodically and often violently.

THE FIRST CO-OPERATIVES

The creation of *caves coopératives* or co-operative cellars was put forward as a possible solution to the problem of overproduction. The idea was not new. The very first village co-operative had been set up in the Ahr valley in Germany in 1868 and others had followed in Catalonia, Hungary and in Alsace at Ribeauvillé in 1895. The concept appealed to the socialist unions, who saw co-operatives as an opportunity to resist the large *négociants* and landowners. The first co-operative of the Languedoc appeared in the village of Mudaison in the Hérault in October 1901, followed by that of Maraussan, which took the stirring name of Les Vignerons Libres. The first Provençal co-operative was set up at Néoules in the Var in 1908 and went under the name of l'Indispensable. By 1914 there were seventy-nine village co-operatives, of which twenty-seven were in Languedoc-Roussillon and thirty-five in the department of the Var alone.

The first co-operatives were intended to help sales while each wine grower made his own wine. It was only gradually that they began to produce wine as well and to share equipment and cellars. The development of the co-operatives was braked by the First World War, although sales and consumption of wine increased, with the daily ration of wine to the troops bringing new drinkers. The French army consumed 12 million hectolitres of wine in 1916, although the harvests of the war years were relatively modest. It was really only in the 1920s and 1930s that the movement took off: 750 co-operatives were founded between 1919 and 1939, of which 340 were in Languedoc-Roussillon alone. At the same time French consumption per capita increased from 103 litres in 1904 to 136 litres in 1926.

The co-operatives remain a strong force in the viticulture of the Midi today. They operate with varying degrees of competence, some actively promoting the quality of their appellation, encouraging their members to think of quality in terms of the condition of the grapes they deliver, the degree of ripeness, the importance of the vineyard sites and so on, in contrast to the conservative attitude still prevailing in some quarters that quality equals quantity. The fact remains that, for most wine growers during most of the twentieth century, the philosophy of *le père* Séchard in Balzac's *Les Illusions Perdues* held true. Balzac may have been writing in the 1830s but the sentiments expressed by Séchard – '*Pour moi, la qualité, c'est les écus*' – were still relevant 150 years later. Quite simply, the more wine they produce, the more money they make and the more money they have in the bank. Things are now changing as the more forward-thinking co-operatives are instituting systems of remuneration that take the quality of the grapes into consideration, and not just the number of hectolitres they produce.

DEPRESSION AND OVERPRODUCTION

The 1930s were another difficult time, with the worldwide depression and further overproduction caused by the two enormous vintages of 1934 and 1935. France and Algeria between them produced almost 200 million hectolitres of wine in those two years, at a time when the average annual consumption in France was 70 million hectolitres and the export market was moribund after the loss of traditional markets following the First World War. The problems were not confined to the Midi, however, and the French government had already attempted to resolve the situation with the Statute de la Viticulture in 1931. This contained four important principles: it limited yields; restricted new plantings; blocked stock at the property in order to regulate the market and introduced the obligatory distillation of part of the crop in order to reduce the excess. *Primes d'arrachages* were introduced and various hybrid varieties were forbidden, although they often remained in the small family plots destined for personal consumption. The much lower crop of 1936 and the outbreak of the Second World War relieved the situation to some extent. Meanwhile, 1936 saw the creation of the first appellations, among them Cassis in Provence, Rivesaltes in Roussillon and Muscat de Frontignan in Languedoc. However, it is also significant that the two Languedoc-Roussillon appellations were for *vin doux naturel*, rather than for table wine. The Midi had to wait until 1948 for its next table wine appellations, namely Fitou and Clairette du Languedoc in the Languedoc and Palette in Provence.

The Midi continued to be a vineyard of mass production and mass consumption, but changes were necessary. These have not been easy to achieve, and there have been casualties along the way. Marc Dubernet, one of the region's leading oenologists, explained. Superficially, 1956 was a year like any other, but a turning point had been reached, in that national consumption of wine fell for the very first time. In 1956 France was emerging from the austerity of the post-war years and barely perceptible changes in social habits were occurring. The French were beginning to drink less but better, and so the demand for the wines of the Midi, which was purely national at the time, began to fall. That year also saw the creation of the Common Market with the signing of the treaty of Rome, and a very hard winter that destroyed vineyards in northern France and olive trees in the Midi. The region was unprepared for change. Many of the landowners were complacent in their monoculture and the wine industry was out of date at all levels, both in its co-operative systems of production and in its methods of distribution through the *négociants* who dominated the market.

THE NEGOCIANTS

Probably the first to suffer were the *négociants*, for their systems of production and distribution had originally been established to meet the demands of the nineteenth century. I talked to Jean-Pierre Bonfils, who began working for his family company in 1952. He is now president of the professional body that includes *négociants*, the Association Française des Eleveurs, Embouteilleurs et Distributeurs de Vins et Spiritueux. First I asked him to reminisce. How were things back in 1952 for a *négociant* in Sète? Essentially, the *négociants* dominated the marketplace, for there were numerous small *cavistes* or wine shops but no large, serious wine merchants, and the production of the Languedoc and Roussillon was concentrated in *vin de table*. *Vins de pays* did not exist and appellation wines, or more often *Vins Délimités de Qualité Supérieure*, or VDQS wines, accounted for just five per cent of the region's production. There were two types of *négociant* at the time, those who practised the traditional trade and those who specialised in aperitifs, people like Noilly Prat, St Raphaël, Dubonnet and others, whose source of base wine was the Languedoc.

For the traditional *négociant*, trade with Algeria was still important. The port of Sète owed its prosperity to that trade, receiving wines from Algeria and also Tunisia. The high-yielding, low-degree wines of the Midi desperately needed a boost of alcohol and flavour, from the so-called *vins de médicin*, to make them acceptable to the consumer in northern France. Sète was at the heart of it all. Bonfils learnt his wine making skills in Algeria. He went there for what the French call a *stage*, a period of apprenticeship, where today he might well have gone to California. After all, Algeria was a part of France. And Bonfils was insistent that the wines for blending were chosen with care, just as you would make an *assemblage* of different vineyards today.

CHANGES IN THE TWENTIETH CENTURY

But things were beginning to change. Algeria was moving towards independence, with disastrous consequences for the so-called *pieds noirs*, many of whom found themselves obliged to leave the country. However, their expertise has helped the Midi. Many of them had considerable experience of wine making in a warm climate. The Midi *vigneron* was really only interested in his vines, whereas the *pieds noirs* were very much concerned with their cellars.

A contemporary account of the viewpoint of the twentieth-century wine grower comes from Emmanuel Maffre-Baugé, who was president of the Fédération Nationale des Producteurs de Vins de Table et de Vins de Pays for a number of years. In his book *Vendanges Amères* he relates the changes in the vineyards of the Languedoc over those years, describing the problems, the confusion and the lack of understanding of the growers and the inability of the government to improve the situation.

At the same time, the systems of commercialisation were beginning to change, with the development of the large supermarkets and a drop in the number of *marchands de vins en gros*, or wholesalers. In 1968 there were twelve thousand all over France; today there are just twelve hundred. The first Carrefour opened in 1962, and by 1992 supermarkets like Carrefour and Auchan controlled seventy per cent of the market. The number of *négociants* has dropped sharply too. In 1962 there were seventy in the port of Sète alone, but today there are just ten, and only five of any size.

How have they survived? Quite simply, according to Bonfils, by playing the card of quality. You must believe in the quality of the Midi. It can be difficult to convince people of regional identity. The wines need to evolve. You need to make an effort in the cellars, to believe in the appellations and to promote a regional identity. Some *négociants* have bought vineyards and become producers. Others have completely changed the emphasis in their business, so that appellation wines are important. *Vins de pays*, which were first created in 1973, are also significant, for they gave the *vin de table* some regional identity. The development of Vin de Pays d'Oc in 1987, with its emphasis on varietal wines, has also helped. This has all required a considerable modification in people's attitudes, taking thirty years.

ETS HERPE

Paul Herpe from the Narbonne company of Herpe has a similar point of view but approaches the subject from a different angle. The family company was founded in 1919. His grandfather, also Paul, had been responsible during the First World War for keeping the soldiers in the trenches supplied with wine, and after the war ended he carried on the business, selling to private clients by mail order, delivering the wine in barrel. Traditionally, many French wine drinkers have bottled their own wine, a procedure described as a *métier de barricailleur*, and until 1980 Ets Herpe sold only to private clients. They still maintain tiny sales in barrel, which are gradually diminishing as their traditional customers disappear. It is a complicated business. The wine is sold by the kilo, to assess the precise contents of the barrel, which is weighed both full and empty. The barrels need to be cleaned meticulously when they are returned. Herpe remembers that plastic appeared in the mid-1960s, for when he joined the company in 1975 they were already selling what are called *cubitainers*, plastic containers holding five, ten or thirty litres.

Ets Herpe then began looking for other markets, which led to the opening of twelve shops, mainly in northern France as well as Paris and Béziers. They have developed a successful trade with local restaurants and more recently an export market, although, as *négociants*, their role was different from the traditional one of companies like Bonfils. Herpe discussed how the means of supply has changed. Fifty years ago, all the little wine makers with a small plot of vines made their wine and sold it *en vrac* to a local *négociant*. It was the role of that *négociant* to blend the different wines according to the requirements of his customers. Now it is the co-operatives that have taken over that responsibility, as they have become a more powerful force in the marketplace. The traditional *négociants* have disappeared, to be superseded by what are called the *groupements de producteurs*.

Ets Herpe has survived, as the company has known how to adapt. Between the two world wars there were a hundred *négociants* in Narbonne. Today Ets Herpe is the sole survivor; the second longest survivor, Mercier, closed its door ten years ago. Paul Herpe insists that thirty or forty years ago they had quality criteria that were unusual for the time. They would choose the best vat at the co-operative and pay a little more for it. Now their sources of supply have evolved into partnerships with various producers scattered over the Languedoc, between the Corbières and Pic St Loup. They have agreements with their various partners concerning the vinification and blending. It is 'our' wine, made *chez le producteur*. From some they buy wine without using the name of the estate, and for others they have an exclusivity similar to the relationship between a Bordelais *négociant* and a classed growth château in the Médoc. In addition, the family also has vines of its own in the Corbières.

There has been a huge increase of sales in bottle: abroad, to the restaurant trade and to their mail order customers, who remain faithful but now of course also buy from supermarkets. Also, consumption has changed in that fewer people are drinking wine every day. For Herpe, the future lies in sales in bottle, with an increasing number of wine producing partners. Quality is the only way to survive for a small business looking for a niche. What Herpe called the policy of vintages is a new concept too for the region. The vintages in the Midi may be relatively regular, but there are differences. You only have to compare 1997 and 1998. Herpe is insistent that there have always been good wines in the Languedoc, but very few of them, so you had to look hard to find them.

A tasting of a small range of Herpe wines illustrated their sound quality, notably those from Château Auris in the Corbières. And we finished with a 'mystery' wine that turned out to be a pure Mourvèdre from the 1988 vintage, made from the 35 ares of Mourvèdre vines in Herpe's garden just outside Narbonne. Technically it is in the appellation of Corbières. The wine had spent six months in new wood and had a deep colour with a rich chocolatey nose, a rich, mature palate and a long, dry finish.

THE GROUPEMENTS DE PRODUCTEURS

The *négociants* have competed with the *groupements de producteurs*, but for Paul Herpe there was one significant difference. The *groupements de producteurs* concentrate on the supermarket custom, whereas for Ets Herpe that represents only four or five per cent of their turnover. In reality, you cannot compete with these monsters. The associations of producers were born out of the inability of the co-operatives to market their own wine and in order to meet the urgent problem of the fall in sales of the region's wines. They are all based on co-operatives, but the co-operatives on their own were not able to satisfy the requirements of large-scale distribution and the needs of supermarkets such as Auchan and

Casino. The associations of producers have their supporters and their critics. In many respects they perform the same role as the regional *négociants*.

LES VIGNERONS DU VAL D'ORBIEU

The most important of these groups is Les Vignerons du Val d'Orbieu, founded in 1967 by eight particularly dynamic wine growers based in the Corbières. The leading light, Yves Barsalou, is now president of the Crédit Agricole, the bank favoured by most wine growers. The group's objective was to give a new importance to their vineyards and to recover their prosperity. Today it includes seventeen co-operatives in Corbières, Minervois, St Chinian and the Coteaux du Languedoc, and in addition some two hundred independent producers in the Aude, Hérault and Pyrénées-Orientales, representing all the appellations of the region. It also owns the Château de Jonquières outside Narbonne in the Corbières, which is used as an experimental vineyard. Any producer who wishes to join the group buys a share value that relates to his production in hectolitres. In theory, you are not allowed to compete on the same market. However, there are growers who sell privately under one label and to the Vignerons du Val d'Orbieu under another.

The role of the Vignerons du Val d'Orbieu is essentially a commercial one. Its members make and mature their own wine, while the group is responsible for any blending and also for the bottling and sale of the wine. Although the vinification of its members' wine is not the group's responsibility, it still plays an important role as adviser and consultant, and it has instigated changes in the vineyards and improvements in the cellar. Marc Dubernet is the oenologist with overall responsibility for the wines.

In recent years, however, the group's role has changed. Not only has there been a distinct shift from sales in bulk to sales in bottle, with a greater emphasis on individual estates, but its horizons have expanded considerably. In 1994 it bought Domaines Listel, the large producer of Vin de Pays des Sables du Golfe de Lion; in 1997 it moved outside the Languedoc to acquire the Bordeaux *négociant* house of Cordier, with its estates in the Médoc; and in 1998 it bought Pradel in Provence. The group now boasts a FF 2.4 billion turnover. In reality, the Vignerons du Val d'Orbieu today consists of several limited companies.

One important reason for the development of these groups is that they have been able to receive the government and European subsidies available for what is called the *restructuration* or replanting of the vineyards. When in the mid-1970s the French government finally recognised the need to change the wine economy of the Midi, after yet another bout of demonstrations, and indeed violence, from angry wine growers, it chose the producers' associations rather than individual co-operatives as the main vehicles for the transformation. Many of the new plantings are linked to producers' associations. A group of producers would submit a planting schedule to the government for approval and subsidy, for you cannot obtain a subsidy as a private producer unless you are a particularly large private company. Indeed, many producers' associations were formed with the specific aim of acquiring subsidies and will eventually disappear. The associations are also able to offer guidance on vinification methods and market strategies; in theory, they are able to ascertain market demand and plan accordingly in vineyard and cellar.

This may all sound a little too optimistic. The producers' associations have certainly provided outlets and sales where none existed before, but they have also been criticised for the effect they have had on the region and have been accused of keeping prices unnaturally low. Currently there are about eighty such groups in Languedoc-Roussillon, but only about twenty do any serious marketing – others are more concerned with planting vineyards and with vinification. Some have already disappeared, and others will go in the few years as the market evolves. Certainly they are less important than they were ten years ago.

Ask the Vignerons du Val d'Orbieu who their competitors are, and the answer will hardly include any of the producers of the Midi. With the drop in wine consumption and the shift towards soft drinks, you could say that Coca Cola is a competitor, or perhaps the wine producing countries of the New World, such as Chile and Australia. The biggest wine brands in France are Georges Duboeuf, Piat d'Or, Mouton Cadet and the large champagne houses, none of which are really in direct competition in the market-place. In the Midi they compete with Skalli on varietal wines. Other big players in the Midi include the large *négociant* house of Jeanjean, run by two brothers who have also known how to adapt to the evolving market. UCCUOR – the Union des Caves Cooperatives de l'Ouest Audois et du Razès – is another *groupement de producteurs* based in the Côtes de la Malepère, but concentrating mainly on *vins de pays*. Chantovent, and the Vignerons Catalans, the key *groupement de producteurs* of Roussillon, are also significant.

THE 'WINE LAKE' AND THE DROP IN PRODUCTION

In the mid-1980s the European 'wine lake' was a cause for concern. It was the result of the enormous over-production of *vin de table* from the Midi and *vino da tavola* from southern Italy. Distillation was one answer to the problem, which resulted for a short time in an 'alcohol lake'. A sliding scale was introduced to determine how much of the production should be sent to the distillery. If a grower's vines produced only a very modest 45 hl/ha, two per cent of his production, which could mainly be accounted for by lees, went to the distillery. If his yield reached 90 hl/ha, which is considered reasonable for a *vin de pays* in the Midi, the grower had to send eleven and a half per cent of his production. However, once he exceeded the yield for a *vin de pays*, he was severely penalised, so the short-sighted grower who still thought it worthwhile to *faire pisser* his vines, in the mistaken belief that it would earn him more money, was discouraged. If he produced as much as 135 hl/ha, he simply did not obtain enough money to make it remunerative, for what he received for distillation was less than the price of *vin de table*. The more reasonable attitude to yields has also brought a significant drop in the liberal use of fertilisers, and today the 'wine lake' is a thing of the past.

In the last twenty years the production of Languedoc–Roussillon has almost halved, for not only have yields decreased, but the vineyard area has declined and at the same time the production of appellation wines has increased fivefold. At the beginning of the 1990s the total vineyard area of the Languedoc-Roussillon was 300,000 hectares, but this had fallen to nearer 250,000 hectares by the end of the decade, which still makes it the largest vineyard area of France and three times larger than that of Australia. This sharp drop has resulted from the policy of *arrachage*, of pulling up the vineyards that never produced anything but inferior *vin ordinaire*.

Primes d'arrachage have encouraged the disappearance of some vineyards, but they were not always a strong enough incentive when more money could be earned by sending wine to the distillery. And if vines are pulled up, what will the land be used for instead? Cereals are a possibility on the fertile coastal plains, except that you need more hectares to make a living from wheat or maize than you do from vines.

There is no doubt that a considerable proportion of the vineyards of the Midi will continue to disappear simply with the passage of time. At the same time there has been a shift in the location of the vineyards, with a much greater emphasis being placed on the low yielding quality hillsides of the hinterland. The average age of a co-operative member is over fifty. In fact, in Roussillon twenty-five per cent of all *vignerons* are over sixty-five, thirty-seven per cent are between fifty and sixty-five, twenty-one per cent between forty and fifty, thirteen per cent between thirty and forty and just four per cent are under the age of thirty. It seems that viticulture is an activity for the older generation, and people are gradually giving up their vines as they retire. Often the succeeding generation has no interest in them, so that they are simply abandoned or pulled up.

However, with the revival in the fortunes of the Midi, there has recently been a change in the attitude of the upcoming generation. Whereas ten years ago young people were probably regarded as mad to take over their parents' vines – a safe office job was considered more appealing – now they favour viticulture. Their decision may be partly influenced by the threat of unemployment and the fact that the vines do provide a ready activity, but amongst many a young wine grower you sense an ambition to create something with their vines. In many instances this may mean withdrawing from the village co-operative or simply putting their wine into bottle for the first time. It all augurs well for the future.

FINANCIAL VIABILITY

I asked Marc Dubernet what had been the most striking change in the Midi since we first met fifteen years ago. He did not hesitate over his answer. Viticulture in the Midi is now financially viable in a way that was simply not envisaged in the mid-1980s. At that time the French government and the officials in Brussels believed that viticulture in the Languedoc would disappear. The *primes d'arrachage* and social security payments would allow the wine growers to withdraw from the land. The viticultural population was elderly and people would simply retire. At that time thirty-five per cent of the income of Languedoc viticulture came from the French government or from Brussels. But it did not happen. In complete contrast, viticulture is today very buoyant, with only five per cent or less of its income coming in the form of subsidies. Ask most co-operatives how they paid for impressive new investments and they will say *autofinancement* above all. Maybe the Crédit Agricole has helped, but it is a loan, not a handout from the Government. There has been a clear shift from what Dubernet called *viticulture assisté* to *viticulture autonome*. Also, young people are returning to the land or remaining on their parents' land, which has made a considerable difference to the dynamics of the region.

Dubernet sees various reasons for this dramatic transformation. In the period of decline, when the only option was to disappear or to start afresh, people did not know what to plant instead. In so many areas, vines were the only viable agricultural choice. A few key producers had a vision that could change the perception of the region, and others followed in their wake. These producers began to consider what the market really wanted, realising that the demand was for better quality wine, as the French consumer was tending to drink less but better – people's standard of living had improved and lifestyles had changed. The market wanted wines with a more individual identity. In France, that means appellation wines and *vins de pays*, but not anonymous *vin de table*. There was a wave of new appellations in the Midi in the mid-1980s that has helped to give a greater sense of identity to the region. The development of the Vin de Pays d'Oc, with its emphasis – unusual for France – on varietal wine, also gave the region something with a more international dimension, providing consumers abroad with the ubiquitous but much in demand Chardonnay or Merlot.

THE NEW LANGUEDOC

Now the debate is about the meaning of the Languedoc, an argument that Roussillon and Provence ignore. The plan is to create an overall appellation Languedoc, in the same way that

Bordeaux is the basis of the appellations of the Gironde. Languedoc would form the base of the pyramid and above it there would be a hierarchy of more specific appellations. In the case of the Coteaux du Languedoc, for instance, that specific appellation would probably disappear and in its place a series of *terroirs* would be formulated, such as Terrasses de Larzac, Terres de Sommières and so on, and above those there would be *crus* or separate appellations, such as La Clape and Picpoul de Pinet. There is much talk about what is called *hierarchisation* from Carcassonne to the outskirts of Nîmes. The protagonists of this broad concept foresee that Corbières and Minervois would also feature in the overall appellation, but for the moment things are very much in a state of flux, with ferocious opponents as well as ardent supporters.

The advantage of such a system is the strength of a collective identity. As Jean-Pierre Bonfils said so firmly, '*L'union fait la force*,' and the Languedoc could really mean something. A federation of the various appellations, as well as the *vins de pays*, would have a powerful voice with which to communicate to the world outside the Languedoc. Languedoc could become a 'brand' almost in the same way as Bordeaux or Burgundy can be seen as brands, with an identity that can be promoted collectively. You need to convince people of the regional identity and invest in that.

As Bonfils put it, the Languedoc needs a single banner, *un seul drapeau*. That is the message. It was first voiced about fifteen years ago by Jean Clavel, then director of the Syndicat des Coteaux du Languedoc, but it is beset with problems. Local rivalries abound, and the French wine grower is an individualist who is often reluctant to join up with a large group, even if it may help him in the long run. There is a feeling, however, that things are beginning to change. The idea of a federation can now be voiced in a way that would have been impossible five or ten years ago. Others feel, however, that the use of Languedoc as an all-embracing description of the region will debase the meaning of the word. This is one reason for the existence of two *syndicats* in the Corbières. The smaller Union des Crus Signés des Corbières fears that Corbières will be declassified into the bottom end of the market, amidst the co-operatives and *groupements de producteurs*, and will lose any image of quality and real identity. There is no doubt that a lot is at stake and that vested interests and jealousies, big and small, abound.

Even more far-reaching is the suggestion, mentioned to me by Bernard du Tremblay of Château de Belle-Coste in the Costières de Nimes, to group the whole of the Rhône and the Mediterranean into one large administrative entity. It would encompass twelve departments in all, not just the vineyards covered in this book but also those of the whole Rhône Valley. That, I could not help thinking, sounded rather impractical. If the Languedoc cannot yet agree, what hope is there for Provence and Roussillon as well as the Rhône valley and Corsica?

OUTSIDE INTERESTS

Meanwhile, the economic buoyancy of the region is there for all to behold. Even five years ago it would have been inconceivable for a Midi group to buy a Bordeaux company, but that is what the Vignerons du Val d'Orbieu have done with their purchase of Cordier. And the interest in the region from outside has been palpable. A conservative estimate is that there are now at least two hundred Australian wine makers producing a vintage in the south of France each year. For them, it is an important learning process, an encounter with a wine culture that puts a strong emphasis on the importance of *terroir*, even in the production of varietal *vins de pays*, and in turn the French have benefited from an exposure to New World wine making processes and attitudes. An improvement in cellar hygiene has been fundamental, for the New World seems to be more clinical in its approach. It also strives for longer ripening periods, picking grapes at phenolic ripeness. The average French co-operative member likes to feel that his grapes are safely in the cellar by the time of the equinoctial rains, while the New World is a little more cavalier and demanding in its attitude towards the elements.

There is also more concrete investment in the region from outside. Bordeaux *négociants* such as Sichel have vineyards in the Corbières. The Rothschilds of Mouton have bought land in Limoux. Burgundians such as Moillard, Louis Latour, Domaine Dujac and Domaine Laroche have all invested in the region as an extension of their *négociant* businesses. Others have left their regions: there are numerous examples of Burgundians and *champenois* who have preferred to settle in the warm south and make wine there in less climatically taxing conditions. And there is investment from abroad. Some comes on a small scale, such as that by the English who have fallen in love with the area, as did Peter and Susan Munday at Domaine des Chandelles in the Corbières, or Robert and Kim Cripps at Domaine du Poujol in the Coteaux du Languedoc. Robert Eden operates on a larger scale and has bought vineyards in several different appellations. Australians have invested in Domaine de la Baume. BRL Hardy has created the brand of Laperouse, initially with the Vignerons du Val d'Orbieu, but found its attitudes and objectives to be so different that the Australians are now working without any French involvement. As for Americans, Robert Mondavi is leading the way with Vichon Méditerranée and John Goelet, owner of the Napa Valley winery Clos du Val, has bought the run-down Coteaux du Languedoc estate of Château Nizas.

This very positive approach augurs well for the future. As will be seen in the next chapter, there has been a huge development in technology in the cellar, while efforts are now being made in the vineyards, with improved methods of cultivation and the intro- duction of more rewarding grape varieties. For the consumer, who is always looking for something new, there is little left to unearth in Bordeaux and Burgundy, whereas there is great excitement in the new discoveries of the Midi, with an emphasis on the *côté jeunesse*. Each year brings new producers to the fore, keeping the surprise factor and the power to astonish very much alive. For the moment, it is the foreign consumer, rather than the French wine drinker, who is most enthusiastic about the Languedoc. More than once the observation was made that we are discovering our own region as a result of its appreciation from abroad.

Developments in the vineyard and cellar

The same broad lines of development in both vineyard and cellar are to be found all along the Mediterranean coastline of France, from Banyuls to Bellet – and the last two decades of the twentieth century have seen breathtaking progress.

The standard co-operative cellar contained concrete vats, a continuous press and badly maintained oak *foudres*, the enormous oak barrels that were the traditional containers of the Midi. Worst of all, given the warm conditions in which the grapes were usually picked, there was no means of controlling fermentation temperatures. Nor were private cellars likely to be better equipped. Today, by contrast, cellar hygiene is all-important and some means of temperature control utterly imperative. There is a much better understanding of what the vines need in the vineyard and of the techniques of vinification and *élevage* in the cellar, all contributing to enhance the flavour and individuality of the wines of the south.

GRAPE VARIETIES

Before 1900 there were as many as 150 different grape varieties in the Midi, most of which have sadly disappeared in the face of oidium, phylloxera and the industrialisation of the vineyards, resulting in a concentration on high-yielding Aramon and Carignan. Grape varieties determine the fundamental flavour of a wine, and when it was realised that Aramon and Carignan left much to be desired, the move towards *cépages améliorateurs*, 'improving grape varieties', gathered momentum. Grenache Noir has long had a presence in the Midi, especially in Roussillon for Rivesaltes and other *vins doux naturels*, but it has been joined by Syrah and Mourvèdre as essential *cépages améliorateurs*. Carignan remains the base in many areas and does indeed have its supporters. There is Cinsaut too, one of the old varieties of the region, present before phylloxera, which some people decry, using it for *rosé* and to dilute excessively concentrated or alcoholic red wines, while others such Daniel Domergue in the Minervois show just what can be achieved when it is vinified correctly, with the talented artist's touch.

Syrah has had the greatest impact on flavour, performing well in the cooler regions inland. It is much more easily adaptable to different sites than Mourvèdre and now features significantly in many appellations. Mourvèdre, by contrast, is more problematic, being a late ripener that demands both heat and humidity. It really comes into its own in the coastal appellation of Bandol. There is no denying that these five grape varieties present a pretty limited choice that people would like to broaden. There are wine growers and research organisations conducting experimental plantings of varieties like Counoise, Calitor, Muscardin, Monastrell, Oeillade, Picpoul Noir and Terret Noir, all of which were grown in the Midi before phylloxera wrought such havoc.

The process of what is called either *restructuration* or *re-encépagement*, the replanting of the vineyards, applies to white wine too, but was begun a few years later. The basic white varieties of the Midi are Grenache Blanc, Terret Blanc, Picpoul Blanc, Macabeu, Bourboulenc and Ugni Blanc, as well as Muscat. None of these impart much flavour, with the exception of Muscat, which was used primarily for *vins doux naturels*, such as the Muscats of Lunel and Frontignan. More often than not, the grapes were badly vinified and in any case destined for the vermouth industry, for which flavour was not a prime consideration. Even if some attempt at quality was made, it was thwarted by an insufficient understanding of the need for clean juice and a controlled fermentation. Consequently, recent years have seen the amendment of appellation regulations to include more aromatic varieties like Marsanne, Roussanne and Rolle, which is also called Vermentino, particularly in Corsica.

There has of course been an enormous amount of experimentation with grape varieties from other regions, Cabernet Sauvignon, Merlot, Chardonnay, Sauvignon and Viognier being the most obvious examples. In the mid-1980s, in the absence of serious research on indigenous varieties, Cabernet Sauvignon was considered to be 'the least bad solution' to the search for grape varieties with more flavour and it may well have been discreetly included in an appellation wine. Today that is less likely, and these varieties have now found their place among the *vins de pays*, notably the varietal Vin de Pays d'Oc. Others too are the subject of investigation and experimentation, such as Chenin Blanc, Riesling, Gewürztraminer, Petit Manseng and Petite Arvine, all from other parts of France or, in the case of Petite Arvine, from across the border in Switzerland. Some of these may be discreetly incorporated into the *vins de pays*, but when they come from regions with political clout, like Alsace or Bordeaux, vested interests are seen to be at stake and the repercussions can be considerable. The examples of Jean-Louis Denois in Limoux and Domaine de Bachellery outside Béziers illustrate the point.

RESEARCH ORGANISATIONS

Various government-funded research organisations have contributed to the development of viticulture in the Midi. There is ANTAV, for example; the French love acronyms and this one stands for the Association Nationale Technique pour l'Amélioration de la Viticulture, which does exactly what its name implies, namely improve viticulture. ANTAV was founded in 1963 and runs an experimental vineyard of 114 hectares at Domaine de l'Espiguette at Grau du Roi in the department of the Gard. It carries out work on the health of vines and on the viruses that attack them, as well as conducting research into clones and rootstocks.

The second organisation is SICAREX, the Societé d'Intérêt Collectif Agricole de Recherches d'Expérimentation, which came into existence in the end of the 1960s with broader responsibilities than ANTAV. It operates on a regional basis, with experimental vineyards all over the south of France. I met Philippe Gauthier, who talked about its work in the Aude, for which he is responsible. SICAREX has an experimental vineyard at Domaine de Cazes in the Côtes de la Malepère and two vineyards in the Corbières, at Domaine de Moux and at Domaine de Jonquières, which belongs to the Vignerons du Val d'Orbieu. Vinification practices come within its responsibility too.

Gauthier talked about the evolution of SICAREX's work. During the 1980s it looked at improving the traditional grape varieties of the Midi, working particularly on Syrah and Mourvèdre and considering methods of pruning and of *palissage* – the training of the vines on wires – as well as site selection and the choice of the most suitable *terroirs*. During the 1990s the consumer began to demand wines with more finesse and less of the rusticity that was commonly associated with the Midi. This has led to more work on carbonic maceration and the development of the process of *éraflage*, the destalking of the grapes. There has also been greater interest in white varieties, with the possible development of new appellations such as Collioure Blanc in Roussillon, Fitou Blanc in the Aude and St Chinian and Faugères Blanc in the Hérault.

PLANTING DENSITY

The producers too are involved with experimental vineyards. The density of planting is an important consideration. Mechanisation demanded rows wider apart, but now the trend is towards a greater density, with most appellations demanding a minimum of four thousand plants per hectare, whereas 3300 was the norm a few years ago. At Moux they have experimented with Grenache Noir planted at different densities, 2500, 3500, 5000 and 7000 plants per hectare, and have proved quite conclusively that you obtain a greater concentration of flavour at five thousand vines, with the same yield per hectare. However, seven thousand vines is best of all, giving even more flavour, but there is a loss of yield and the narrower rows can present problems for vineyard machinery.

ROOTSTOCKS AND CLONES

Rootstocks are also being examined. Twenty years ago, people wanted rootstocks that would provide quantity. Today they require those that will enhance quality. Twenty years ago, S04, R110 and R140 were the most popular rootstocks of the Languedoc for that reason, whereas today there is a definite move towards the better quality 3309, which is widely used in the northern Rhône. Tolerance of drought is also a consideration in the choice of rootstock.

As for clones, some fifteen different clones of Syrah and also of Mourvèdre have been identified and their behaviour has been tracked in the vineyard and then in the cellar with numerous micro-vinifications. However, as one grower observed, you really have to have an enormous amount of confidence in your vine nursery that it will give you exactly what you have asked for. When you take delivery of bunches of little twigs, you have few means of checking.

PRUNING METHODS

The common pruning method of the Midi was the *gobelet*, the low, stubby bush vines that covered the arid hillsides. Syrah, however, has fragile branches that need support, so initially it was the only variety trained on wires. Today, Carignan and Grenache Noir tend to remain as bush vines, but mechanisation has influenced their shape, altering the amount of aeration of the leaves and bunches. The *gobelet* used to be much more open, but now, with mechanis-ation, the arms of the vine are much closer together.

Cordon de royat, with one branch along a supporting wire, is slowly becoming the standard way of training most varieties apart from Grenache Noir and Carignan. The vine has longer arms, which gives better ripeness and sugar levels in the grapes. There is also a better circulation of air, which helps to combat disease and makes for an improved foliar surface, with fewer leaves in the shade and less shading of the bunches of grapes. This is a new system for many *vignerons* and so SICAREX organises training sessions for them.

There is an occasional example of lyre trellising, where the canopy is split into two curtains of foliage, supposedly resembling a lyre in shape. This is used particularly for Mourvèdre, as its exponents believe it enables this difficult variety to ripen more easily because of the larger leaf surface and better light exposure.

YIELDS

With the disappearance of the view that quality is synonymous with quantity, yields have fallen considerably in the Midi. The appellations and the *vins de pays* regulations limit yields, but most growers will tell you that they rarely, if ever, reach the permitted 45 or 50 hl/ha allowed by their appellation. They prune more strictly, for one of the principal purposes of pruning is to regulate the crop, to ensure that the vine is in balance, producing neither too few nor too many grapes. The Midi generally suffers from fewer climatic disasters than the more northern parts of France, but spring frosts are not unknown. The temperature fell sharply on the night of Easter Monday, 13 April 1998, and many people in the higher altitude vineyards of the Languedoc lost a significant proportion of their potential crop.

Flowering is another critical moment for determining the quantity of the harvest, although the weather is usually kind. But not always: the most dramatic and potentially disastrous hazard is the hailstorm that can happen almost without warning at any time during the growing season. In April 1999 the growers in the Côtes du Roussillon suffered a very severe hailstorm and have initiated legal proceedings against the French weather forecast service for its failure to issue an appropriate warning, when the Spanish authorities had managed to warn farmers south of the Pyrenees.

GREEN HARVESTING

If the growing season is fruitful and the vines have too large a crop, the latest solution to the problem is green harvesting or *vendange verte*. Opinions vary as to when is the best moment. Too early, and the exercise fails, for the vine simply produces even larger grapes in the remaining bunches; too late and it is pointless. It is best to wait for the *nouaison*, the moment when the grapes have formed and are the size of tiny peas, just before the *véraison*, when they begin to change colour. That is the moment when you can really judge the potential of the crop. Others firmly opine that if you prune properly in the first place, the vine will be in balance and there should be no need to 'green harvest'.

ORGANIC AND INTEGRATED VITICULTURE

Organic viticulture was already under discussion in the 1980s, as a reaction against the widespread use of artificial fertilisers, chemical weed-killers and insecticides. It has its ardent supporters, and those who are even more committed follow the biodynamic methods of Rudolf Steiner. In a climate with generally warm sunshine and drying winds during the growing season, wine producers here are fortunate compared with those in northern France. The prevailing winds, above all the Mistral, provide a healthy environment in which grapes can grow without developing disease or rot. This enables many producers to practise organic viticulture in everything but name, while reserving the right to apply a treatment as an emergency measure.

A practice that is becoming more widespread is *lutte raisonnée*, which probably best translates into English as integrated or sustained viticulture. It implies a reasoned consideration of the conditions of the vineyard when deciding whether a treatment is really necessary, and it favours preventative measures where possible. It represents a reaction against the tendency to apply treatments regularly as a matter of course, whether the vines really need it or not. With *lutte raisonnée*, in an average year, significantly fewer treatments are necessary, maybe six or eight as opposed to twelve or fifteen in Bordeaux; the usual remedies for mildew and oidium are copper and sulphur, which are acceptable to organic viticulture.

FLAVESCENCE DOREE

The main viticultural problem that preoccupies the Midi is the presence of *flavescence dorée* in the vineyards. This is a disease, spread by leaf hoppers, that infects the sap of the vine so that the wood goes rubbery and the plant dies. Unfortunately, once the problem is visible, it is often too late for treatment and the only solution is to pull up the vine. Others suggest that if you find *flavescence dorée* in summer you should prune the vine severely, as if you were giving it a winter pruning, and it will grow normally the next year. *Flavescence dorée* is widespread throughout south west France. It was first discovered in Armagnac in 1949, and has been present in the vineyards of Bordeaux for many years. Now it is spreading into the vineyards of the Midi. Some areas have it and some do not. Some consider it to be potentially as serious as phylloxera. Preventative measures can be taken and in some areas this is a legal requirement. A spray much stronger than sulphur is applied just once a year, in June. In Banyuls and Collioure, all the vineyards have been systematically sprayed by helicopter every year since 1995, but this poses problems for anyone wishing to pursue organic viticulture. Apparently if you treat regularly against *flavescence dorée* for four or five years, you will kill the vector, so that the infected vines can be pulled up.

DROUGHT AND IRRIGATION

Drought can be a factor in the vineyards of the Midi. In normal years there is enough rainfall to sustain vines, with the heaviest rains occurring in the late autumn and early spring. However, the rainfall can vary significantly from one year to the next. When I was in the Languedoc in March 1999, there had been fewer than 100 mm of rain since the previous harvest, and the grass on the roadsides was the yellowy-brown colour you would expect to see in late summer. There was widespread fear of drought, but in fact the rains came in May and later, more devastatingly, in November. Drought-resistant rootstock is therefore a consideration, as irrigation is not allowed for appellation vines, with the possible exception of very young vines. It is permitted in *vin de pays* vineyards, but not after the end of July. But, as James Herrick irreverently observed, the inspectors are on holiday in August. The usual method is drip irrigation, which allows for an accurate distribution of water.

MECHANICAL HARVESTING

Mechanical harvesting has become more widespread, particularly on the flatter coastal areas. For example, Domaines Listel picks just about all its 1400 hectares of vines in the sand dunes by machine, and works in close co-operation with Braud, the largest manufacturer of mechanical harvesters, to develop more refined techniques. Mechanical harvesting also makes it easier to pick at night, or in the very early morning before dawn, when the grapes are cool. However, there are situations where mechanical harvesting is not possible. The technique of carbonic maceration demands whole bunches, and in the hilly terrain of the inland appellations of the

Languedoc and Roussillon, mechanical harvesters would be quite impractical, as the vineyards are too small and too steep. There is also an underlying feeling that, although mechanical harvesters may in the long run make for cheaper and more efficient harvests, and do not have the irritating habit of asking for a pay rise on the eve of the vintage, they are not as gentle to the grapes. However, they can replace about fifty pickers and all the organisation that fifty people entail. A new machine costs about FF 600,000 and on an average size estate could probably be amortised in about five or six years. But as Guy Vanlancker from the Minervois observed, 'There are no great wines made in the Midi that are mechanically harvested.'

SITE SELECTION

Perhaps the greatest change in the vineyards of the Midi concerns site selection. There is now a much greater awareness of the individuality of different sites. The very positive shift away from the coastal plains for appellation wine has brought about a considerable amount of *défrichement*, the clearing of the scrub or *garrigue* that covers the hills, leaving open expanses of very stony, arid soil. New vineyards of Syrah, Mourvèdre and Grenache Noir are planted here on land that will support nothing else but vines, or maybe the occasional olive tree.

Many of the forward-thinking co-operatives now have a much clearer idea of the composition of their members' vineyards, of just what is planted where and how, taking into account not only the grape variety, but also the type of soil, the age of the vines, their density and, at the moment of harvest, the *état sanitaire* or condition of the grapes, as well as their yield and ripeness level. The ripening of the grapes is carefully monitored, with regular checks on the sugar levels in the vineyards in the days before the vintage, looking not just for the statutory alcoholic ripeness, but for the all-important phenolic ripeness, which means that the flavours and tannins are fully ripe. As a result, alcohol levels tend to be higher than was usual ten or twenty years ago, but this all makes for more concentration and flavour in the glass. Those who buy in grapes will often pay for their crop before the vintage and then ask the anxious grower, who is eager to see his grapes safely harvested, to wait. The risk is borne not by the grower but by the producer, who has already paid for a crop that may ultimately be spoilt by rain – or may prove even better because of the extra ripening time.

Those who select grapes for their wine ranges, such as James Herrick, Skalli or Domaine Laroche, go to great lengths in their search for the different components of their blends. They are very much aware of the enormous variations in the different zones of the Midi. James Herrick sources fruit from as many as thirty or forty different vineyards, and employs a dedicated viticulturalist who spends two-thirds of the year 'being nice to farmers'. At Skalli, their oenologist Philippe Tolleret explained how since 1996 they have operated a three-tier system of remuneration, depending not only on the quality of the grapes, but also on the characteristics of the vineyard. They look for sites that have a longer ripening period, observing differences from area to another and one grape variety to another. For instance, Syrah grown in the cooler areas of Gard will make lighter, fruitier *primeur* wines, while Syrah from the warmer, less fertile areas behind Montpellier will be riper and richer. He gave me the heat summation figures listed on page 707 below which illustrates the considerable differences in temperature, ranging from 1883 in Perpignan down to 1450 at St Martin-de-Londres on the edge of the Pic St Loup and Limoux at 1345. Altitude also makes a significant difference here: St Martin-de-Londres is at 200 metres, Limoux higher still, and Perpignan is almost at sea level.

THE OENOLOGIST'S WORK

All good wine makers will tell you that quality is achieved in the vineyard. With healthy grapes grown in the right conditions and *terroir*, you can make great wine. However, the evolution of cellar techniques in the Midi has dramatically changed the flavours of the south in recent years. Gone are the dilute, rustic tastes that were commonplace twenty years ago. White wines are now fresh and lively, with a balanced level of acidity, whereas not so long ago they were flabby and oxidised. Numerous factors have contributed to this transformation, not least the improvement in the quality of the grapes brought into the cellar. But that aside, developments in vinification have had their impact.

Marc Dubernet has worked as an oenologist in the Midi for over thirty years and I asked him to look back over this period. He studied in Paris and then at the University of Bordeaux at Talence under Ribereau-Gayon. In the mid-1960s people simply did not understand what a malolactic fermentation was, and carbonic maceration, *débourbage* and temperature control were all just developing. The Languedoc was the first region to have a system of consultant oenologists who follow vinifications, rather than simply carrying out basic analysis. At the beginning it was very difficult to gain access to a grower's cellar. To ask him to show you where he made his wine was a gross invasion of privacy, or worse – it was tantamount to committing rape. Today, there are few wine growers who do not have an oenologist on whom they call for advice. The exceptions are those who have actually studied oenology themselves, but those who are self-taught or have limited studies and have been guided by a parent feel reassured to know that there is someone to advise them. Good oenologists do not stamp their own personality on a producer's wine. On the contrary, they allow the producers their own self-expression, but prevent them from making unnecessary mistakes. The first time I met Marc Dubernet at his laboratory in Narbonne, I had to wait a few minutes and I felt as though I was sitting in an eminent doctor's waiting room. The vintage was nearing its end and samples of wine were awaiting the pronouncement of the oenologist. Their lives were in his hands. He was responsible for their future well-being.

Today, Dubernet is the man behind what must be the most technically advanced oenological laboratory in Europe. Everything is fully computerised and automatic. A scanner can make ten analytical readings on a wine in just thirty seconds, processing a total of 120 wines an hour. Other machines check colours and enzymes, managing a breathtaking 600 readings an hour. Virtually all the developments in routine analysis in the last twenty or thirty years have come from the Languedoc, and more precisely most of them came from Ets Dubernet. The laboratory developed the techniques of automatic analysis, giving virtually instant readings of the must and providing a wealth of information. But Dubernet is adamant that the technical tool is not an end in itself: fine wine is made in the cellar, not in the laboratory. It is a work of sensibility. Of artistry? No, he would not go that far. There are no two vineyards, no two cellars, no two wine makers that are the same. The good oenologist must bring out the quality and character of the product, and that is what Dubernet does for some 250 estates throughout the region. In sharp contrast to someone like Michel Rolland who, as a consultant oenologist, has given his wines, irrespective of their provenance, a very particular character, you would be hard pressed to say that a wine had received the ministrations of Marc Dubernet. And that is what a good oenologist should achieve.

WHITE WINE MAKING

Many of the recent changes in wine making are worldwide, involving developments in basic techniques that have taken place in numerous vineyards throughout the world, a process that has perhaps been accelerated by the interchange of wine makers: the 'flying wine makers' who come to the south of France for a season from the Antipodes and the increasing proportion of the new generation of French wine makers who seek broader horizons than their parents ever knew. Australian wine makers would say that they can make the greatest impact on white wine, and in just one harvest. The effect can be quite dramatic, as the procedure for making white wine is very straightforward. It is sufficient to have the appropriate equipment, notably for cooling the grapes and juice. Best of all is a pneumatic press, the latest bladder press, which will treat the grapes very gently and give clearer juice than a Vaslin hydraulic press. The juice needs to be chilled so that it will fall clear in the process of *débourbage*. Then the fermentation starts. Cultured yeast may be added, or the wine grower may rely on the natural yeast on the grapes. It is a question of efficiency. With natural yeast there is always the risk of a rogue yeast spoiling the quality of the wine, whereas cultured yeast – either an international brand or, even better, selected yeast from the region – is much more reliable. Essentially, good yeasts are neutral and should not in any way modify the flavour of your wine; they certainly do not improve the quality.

Once the fermentation starts, the temperature is closely monitored. Too cold and the flavours are more akin to boiled sweets, with notes of amylic acid; too hot and the wine will lose freshness and flavour. For white wine, stainless steel vats are preferable to concrete vats as they enable a more stringent control of temperature, while barrel fermentation is another recent development of the Midi. Other permutations include a few hours of *macération pelliculaire* or skin contact, which is done to enhance the flavour of more neutral grapes. It does not contribute anything to Chardonnay, but can make a considerable difference with Marsanne and Roussanne. It must be done in cool conditions and in a reductive, oxygen-free environment.

The malolactic fermentation is now understood and, depending on the style of wine, is allowed to happen or not. It depends upon whether the grower wishes to retain acidity or is looking for additional weight and complexity. More layers of complexity can also be added by lees contact, either in barrel or vat. Sometimes the lees are left undisturbed, or the wine may be given a regular *bâtonnage*. In a barrel, this is done by literally stirring up the wine and the lees at the bottom of the barrel, so that they remain in suspension for a few days. In a vat, nitrogen can be pumped into the bottom of the vat, which has a similar effect of circulating the lees in the wine. Filtering, fining and the moment of bottling are further considerations.

SWEET WINES

Sweet wines are now the subject of exploration, with a growing number of experimental late harvest wines, particularly in the Minervois, where some of the producers are working on the revival of an almost lost appellation, Minervois Noble. Unfortunately, the political clout of Alsace within the INAO is such that it has not been possible to use the words *vendange tardive;* Marc Benin of Domaine Ravanès faced legal proceedings for having the temerity to label a wine Vendange Tardive. That would be enough to deter even the most pig-headed of producers, so for the moment bottles of late harvest wines are condemned to bear the unsatisfactory description of *moût partiellement fermenté, issu de vendanges passerillés*, and most of these wines do not have official status, not even that of *vin de table*. However, that position may change, as the Syndicat des Producteurs du Vin de Pays d'Oc has taken up the challenge to obtain a category of Vendange Tardive.

Despite the problems of nomenclature, most producers remain undeterred, making wines that are often given a picturesque name, such as Douceur d'Automne, which more than adequately implies its late picking. Vinification methods for these wines have improved in line with the latest developments, so that overly-sulphured wines are a thing of the past. The quantities are usually minuscule, so the wine is often fermented in barrel, perhaps with some lees contact, and carefully nurtured through a slow, gentle fermentation and into bottle.

VINS DOUX NATURELS

The *vins doux naturels* based on Muscat have also improved enormously in quality. They are no longer tired and oxidised, but have a ripe freshness of flavour, resulting from cooler fermentations and impeccable cellar hygiene. Again, the better producers of appellations like Muscat de Frontignan and Muscat de Lunel are experimenting with various means of extracting the best from their grapes, altering the balance of sugar and alcohol in their wines and experimenting with late harvest wines that do not require *mutage* and the addition of alcohol.

ROSÉ

Rosé wines involve some of the same considerations as white wines, with temperature control a significant factor. That aside, the key question with *rosé* is colour and how to obtain it. The choice is between *pressurage direct*, the pressing of ripe grapes, or what is called *saignée*, the bleeding or running off of juice from a red vat. Pressing the grapes usually results in the most delicate, palest of pinks, as in elegant Côtes de Provence, while juice from a wine that is *saignée* is much deeper in colour. The juice has remained in contact with the skins for a few hours, so that it has inevitably absorbed much more colour. The timing is crucial. Leave the juice too long and the wine will look like a light red rather than a *rosé*; run it off too soon and the wine will be pale and insipid. The *saignée* method also has the potential benefit of concentrating the flavours of the red wine by reducing the proportion of juice to skins. Some consider *saignée* to be better than *pressurage direct*, as the maceration process results in a better diffusion of aromas.

CARBONIC MACERATION

The most striking development in red wine vinification is carbonic maceration, which, although used in other parts of France, has become very much a feature of the Midi. You cannot say the 'tradition' of the Midi, as it is a procedure that was only developed after the Second World War and really only gained popularity during the 1980s. Carbonic maceration has improved beyond recognition the quality of the ubiquitous Carignan, helping to mask some of its defects while giving character to the wine. Gérard Ploy, director of the Cave Pilote of Villeneuve-les-Corbières, explained how the co-operative acquired its name, for it was indeed one of the pilot cellars for this process of vinification, which had been instigated by Professor Flanzy, professor of oenology at the University of Narbonne. In the immediate post-war years Flanzy was looking for a cellar where he could develop the technique on a larger scale. Villeneuve-les-Corbières in the Aude became one, along with the co-operative cellar of Aspiran in the Hérault and Galissan in the Gard.

The technique of carbonic maceration involves putting whole bunches of grapes into a vat filled with carbon dioxide, which, as it is heavier than oxygen, will displace the oxygen in an open vat. A small amount of juice is inevitably released as the grapes at the bottom of the vat are crushed. This may be run off and heated, with cultured yeast added, before it is returned to the vat. Meanwhile, the intact grapes are heated to the desired temperature, usually around 30°C, and an intracellular fermentation starts inside the berries themselves. The process lasts for between eight and twenty days: it is shorter for wines intended for earlier drinking as they require less tannin, while wines destined for a longer life spend longer in the fermentation vats. The juice is then run off, the grapes pressed and the fermentation finished in the normal way. However, with a carbonic maceration, unlike a classic fermentation, the less free-run juice there is, the better the wine. The quality lies in the pressed juice, which began its fermentation inside the grapes. With a traditional vinification the pressed juice should constitute as little as twenty per cent of the whole, while with carbonic maceration it should be as much as sixty to seventy per cent. Partisans of carbonic maceration consider that it makes for fruitier, more intense wines, while the biggest difference in taste comes in the tannins, which are softer.

Opinions vary on the effectiveness of carbonic maceration. Some say that it is only suitable for *vin de primeur*, while others insist that the wines can age. There is no doubt that with Carignan it can make a silk purse out of a sow's ear, and some like it for Syrah too. At the co-operative of La Lavinière in the Minervois, where they took a decision back in 1978, when their cellar was built, to vinify their best grapes by carbonic maceration, they describe the differences in flavour thus: Syrah made by carbonic maceration tastes of violet and liquorice, while with a traditional vinification from destalked grapes it tastes more of raspberries and blackcurrants. Some criticise carbonic maceration for producing flavours that are short-lived, and most agree that it does nothing for Grenache Noir, which has skins that are too fragile, so that the grapes burst and release too much juice.

OTHER DEVELOPMENTS

Guy Bascou at Domaine de la Condamine l'Evêque near Pézenas is a wine maker with a clear vision of the evolution of the Midi. He studied oenology at the end of the 1960s and worked for the ICV, the Institut Coopérative des Vins, until he bought his own estate in 1980. He still continues his consultancy work with the ICV and has seen what he described as the 'technological revolution' of the Languedoc. One aspect of this has been the advent of cooling equipment. The Midi has the great advantage that most varieties ripen easily here, but this means that it is often quite hot during the vintage. Initially, people did not know how to cool the inside of a concrete vat, so stainless steel vats became popular; with their easy thermic exchange, you could cool them by running cold water over the sides, a process the French call *ruissellement*. Vats with double walls containing cooling fluid were also developed and concrete vats fell from favour. Next came the development of *drapeaux* or flags, which are large metal sheets containing cooling fluid that can be suspended inside a fermenting vat to cool the juice. This has led to the reinstatement of concrete as the preferred medium for red wine fermentation. With concrete, fermentation temperatures are much slower to rise and remain more constant, whereas stainless steel is very sensitive to the slightest climatic change and really needs to be housed in an insulated cellar. And cellars do vary considerably, from the very simple – the spacious buildings of the nineteenth century housing enormous *foudres* and stone vats – to the streamlined, state-of-the-art facilities of the twenty-first century. One consideration is the need to work by gravity: grapes arrive at a higher level and are dropped directly into the fermentation vats, and the wine is then run out into barrels in the cellars below, thus avoiding unnecessary pumping of juice and grapes.

Ten years ago few people had an *égrappoir* or *érafloir*, and indeed some of the big names, a notable example being Trévallon, still do not have one. The removal of the grape stalks, which could impart bitter, unripe, tannic flavours to the wine, has had the effect of considerably lengthening the maceration time or length of *cuvaison* in a classic vinification, as opposed to one by carbonic maceration. Now you will find wine growers pushing to the limit the length of their *cuvaison*, the neat French word that describes the length of time that the juice remains with the skins, irrespective of the actual fermentation time. In the attempt to extract the maximum that the grapes have to offer, prolonged maceration times of four or even six weeks are not unusual.

REMONTAGE, PIGEAGE AND DELESTAGE

There are other processes to facilitate the extraction of flavour, such as *remontage* and *pigeage*, which can be translated rather clumsily as 'pumping over' and 'pumping down' respectively. Then there is a newer procedure, *délestage*, for which I am unable to find the English translation in the context of wine making: one dictionary definition mentioned a power cut and another the removal of ballast! *Remontage* and *pigeage* are much as they sound. With *remontage*, the juice is run out of the bottom of the vat and pumped over the cap of grape skins in order to submerge it in the juice. *Pigeage*, which may now be mechanical, as opposed to the time-honoured use of the wine grower's own feet, is preferred by some because they consider it to be a softer, more gentle process: the wine is not disturbed by pumping and feet do not crush the grape pips, thereby imparting additional undesirable tannins to the wine.

With *délestage*, all the fermenting juice is run out of the vat so that the cap of grape skins is held away from the juice for about ten hours, then the juice is returned to the vat. The cap will take two or three days to rise slowly to the top of the vat again, thereby improving the maceration effect. You should try to extract the most amount of flavour before the alcoholic fermentation is finished, for once there is a significant amount of alcohol present, this can act as a solvent for colour and tannins. In the course of an average fermentation there may be three or four *délestages*, and its protagonists believe that it gives better results than *remontage*, although one does not necessarily exclude the other.

Post-fermentation macerations are another way of enhancing flavour and body. At Château de Viranel in St Chinian, once the fermentation is complete, the wine is left for three weeks *sous marc*, or on the skins. The closed vat is filled right up so that the cap is submerged, but contrary to what you might expect, it seems that the ripe tannins soften and lose any aggressiveness. A long post-fermentation maceration makes for a longer-lived wine, which brings us on to *élevage*.

ELEVAGE

Elevage is an elegant French term that is somehow impossible to translate into English. It can be used to describe the raising of children or the breeding of cattle, and in wine terms refers to the period after fermentation and before bottling. In English, one might use the word ageing or maturation, but somehow that has a ring of premature ageing about it, in that the wine is being rendered unnaturally old before its years, whereas in fact it is having its adolescent edges polished by a period of *élevage* in vat or barrel, large or small, new or old. The traditional wooden vessel throughout the Midi was the *foudre*, the magnificent giant barrels used for the storage of wine. Originally there was no concept of *élevage* in the Midi, for no one had the underground cellars needed to protect the wine from the heat of summer. As Guy Bascou explained, when people talked of *vieillissement* or ageing, this was not a notion of quality but referred to the process of modified oxidation involved in the production of a *rancio vin doux naturel*, as in Rivesaltes or Banyuls or in the once flourishing vermouth industry.

Barriques arrived in the Midi gradually. People often did not have the capital necessary to buy new barrels, so they bought second-hand ones from more or less reputable sources. Often the cellars where the barrels were kept were not insulated and the wines themselves lacked sufficient structure and quality to merit barrel ageing. But gradually people have begun to understand the process of *élevage* in *barrique*. They have found more suitable storage conditions for their barrels. They have begun to appreciate the nuances of different qualities of wood and of different levels of toasting or charring when the barrel is made, be it low, medium or high, and the effect these have on the taste of the wine. They have realised the need to rotate barrels, using barrels of one or two wines, and not just new barrels. And with confidence in the use of barrels comes a greater perception of which cooper suits their wines.

Another contribution to the potential of *élevage* is the improvement in the quality of the *vin de presse*, the pressed wine, especially as continuous presses disappear from use. The pneumatic press may be the ultimate in presses, but the popular Vaslin press still does an excellent job; as Guy Bascou put, you can still make quality wine without a Ferrari. And the judicious addition of some *vin de presse*, while perhaps compensating for the initial *éraflage*, can add some extra structure and tannin to the wine.

Some wine growers find the effects of a small *barrique* of 225 litres too marked, and are looking at slightly bigger sizes, from 400- to even 600-litre *demi-muids*. Another possibility is the small *foudre* of 30 or 40 hectolitres in size, rather than the giants of 200 hectolitres or more. Those who favour the small *foudres* consider that the ratio of wine to wood is more satisfactory than with either small barrels or very large *foudres*. Often it is a case of finding out what suits your particular wine, which is not something that can be done in just one vintage, but over the years as the region evolves.

Different sources of wood are also being considered, with experiments in Russian and American oak, as well as French oak. French oak is generally considered to give the most complexity, while American oak is more eye-catching and flattering on the palate; and curiously, Russian oak seems to taste more toasted, even with an identical level of toasting. It has also been found to be more watertight than French oak, consuming less wine and needing less topping up, but the oak effects are more intense and less subtle.

Economic factors govern the choice of barrels, for French wood is more expensive and the depreciation is not dissimilar to that of a motor car. A new barrel costs about FF 2200. Use it once and you can sell it for about FF 1300. If you use it again, its value drops to FF 750. Two wines later and at a second property, it is worth only FF 100–200.

Initially, owing to a lack of experience, the use of wood was somewhat excessive, but now there is a more reasoned approach, with wines less marked by wood, that results in a more harmonious marriage of flavours. However, Marc Dubernet issues a word of caution: *élevage* in wood is very much a current fashion, especially with new wood, but it is perfectly possible to have quality without wood. The taste of wood gives consumers a hook, a flavour that is reassuringly familiar, so that they automatically associate it with quality, which is not necessarily the case.

Most producers put their wine into wood when the malolactic fermentation is over, but some are now carrying out a malolactic fermentation in barrel, which they claim makes for more harmonious flavours. It is, however, quite tricky to control, and then you have to decide whether to leave your wine on the lees for its *élevage*. Current research on the subject produces contradictory results: sometimes it is better, sometimes not. Similarly, *élevage* in wood may have improved some wines, but by no means all.

MICROBULLAGE

Another technique relating to *élevage* is *microbullage*, or micro-oxygenation, first developed in Madiran in south west France by Patrick Ducorneau of Domaine Mouréou. The process involves the gentle addition of a tiny amount of oxygen, an almost imperceptible 5 ml per litre of wine per month, which goes into wine that has finished its alcoholic fermentation but is still *sous marc*, in contact with the grape skins, or else in a vat for *élevage*. The process helps the integration of the tannins. It will be carried out on wine that is destined to remain in vat before bottling, but it should not be seen as a substitute for *élevage* in barrel.

In fact, *microbullage* is a misleading term, for you do not actually obtain bubbles of oxygen. None the less the oxygen works on the anthocyanins, not reducing them in quantity but rendering them more intense. *Microbullage* is also useful in preventing odours of reduction and herbaceous tastes if the wine is in a closed container and has not been racked. Indeed, it can remove the need for frequent racking and *remontages* and thereby avoid unnecessary pumping, which can disturb the wine. Essentially, the purpose of *microbullage* is not to reduce the length of *élevage* but to improve the evolution of the wine during *élevage*. At its simplest, some would say that it is like an *élevage* in wood, but in vat, with a similar amount of oxygenation, but without the effect of oak.

INRA

Another organisation working away behind the scenes, conducting systematic research into various aspects of viticulture and vinification, is INRA, the Institute de Recherche Agronomique. INRA was created in 1946 and at Narbonne was incorporated into a much earlier research station that had been in existence since the end of the nineteenth century. As well as the Narbonne research station, which I visited at Domaine la Pech-Rouge on the edge of the Montagne de la Clape, there are similar stations in Bordeaux, Angers, Colmar and Montpellier. The government funds their basic overheads and salaries, but they raise money for future research by selling patents and licences on new techniques. The Narbonne station has a vineyard, but is primarily concerned with research into the niceties of vinification rather than work on grape varieties in the vineyard. Jean-Claude Boulet, one of the technicians, explained how INRA has helped to solve many of the small but problematic details of vinification. For example, it is working on the extraction of aromas in red wine, for there is still a lot of substance left in the skins after fermentation. White and *rosé* fermentations that stop without reason are another subject of investigation, perhaps caused by the yeasts' need for oxygen. INRA is also looking at the stabilisation of wine and for a less brutal way of removing tartrate crystals than by cold treatment, as well as at other methods of filtration, such as 'tangential micro-filtration', which is proving more efficient than the traditional filter pads. Various aspects of *élevage* and *microbullage* are also subjects of their research. This collection of details adds up to a significant whole and over the years INRA has contributed significantly to the development of the Midi – it was already working on Syrah and fermentation temperatures in the 1960s.

Such has been the development of the Midi in the past twenty years. There are now so many wine growers who are putting all these innovations into practice, drawing on what has gone before them, breaking new boundaries and questioning preconceived ideas. When I first met Marc Dubernet in 1987, he used the image of a virgin forest to describe the Midi: it has beautiful flowers, but you have to look for them among the trees. I think the analogy still holds. Some of the blooms of fourteen years ago are still flowering brightly; others have faded and there are growing number of new flowers to discover. What follows is what I found during a couple of years spent exploring the vineyards from Banyuls to Bellet at the close of the twentieth century.

ROUSSILLON

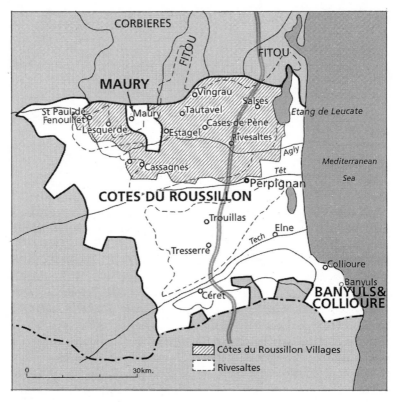

Roussillon

Roussillon is often grouped with the Languedoc, and the Languedoc is often used as an all-embracing term to describe the south of France. However, Roussillon is as different from the Languedoc as is Provence – and as justifiably proud of its separate identity. The vineyards of Roussillon cover a substantial part of the department of Pyrénées-Orientales. They are bound by the Albères, the foothills of the Pyrenees, to the south and west and by the mountains of Corbières to the north, so that the hills of Roussillon seem to form an enormous amphitheatre around the fertile plain surrounding Perpignan.

Perpignan is a lively town. The ancient capital of the counts of Roussillon and the kings of Majorca, it has preserved a Catalan atmosphere. The old quarter has narrow, twisting streets and colourful squares with animated cafés and bustling markets, while the sombre cathedral and the palace of the kings of Majorca are the principal historical monuments. The fertile plain around Perpignan supports orchards of fruit trees, peaches and apricots, standing out in sharp contrast to the wild dramatic scenery of the surrounding hills. Three river valleys break up the countryside, the Agly, the Têt and the Tech, twisting and turning their way to the Mediterranean. The Canigou, at 2784 metres the highest peak of the Pyrenees, snow-capped even in June, dominates the horizon. Little will grow on these arid hillsides apart from vines and olive trees, so that viticulture is and always has been a vital part of the region's economy.

There is an extraordinary variety of different soils. No other French vineyard, with the exception of Alsace, is as complicated geologically. Broadly speaking, the soil is based on limestone, clay and schist, but there are countless variations and permutations, with quartz, granite and gneiss as well. Visually the soil colour can change from one hillside to another, from black schist to red, iron-laden clay. The simplest way to appreciate this diversity is to invite yourself to a tasting at the head office of the Vignerons Catalans in Perpignan, for there in the floor of their tasting room, attractively displayed under glass, are samples of all the dominant soil types.

Present-day Roussillon is synonymous with the department of the Pyrénées-Orientales. The principal appellations for table wines are Côtes du Roussillon and Côtes du Roussillon Villages. However, this region also has a long tradition of producing *vin doux naturel*, of which Rivesaltes is the largest appellation. The *vin doux naturel* of Maury, with its stricter production regulations, forms an enclave within Rivesaltes, while to the south, towards the Spanish border, are the twin appellations of Banyuls and Collioure. Banyuls is the *vin doux naturel* while Collioure is the table wine, or *vin sec*. In addition, there are various *vins de pays*, not to mention table wines that do not conform to any recognised regulations.

Vin de Pays des Pyrénées-Orientales covers all the vineyards of the department, while Vin de Pays Catalan designates a large area south of the Têt river, more or less corresponding to the appellation of Côtes du Roussillon. Vin de Pays des Côtes Catalanes is smaller, centred on Rivesaltes and Salses, north of the Têt. Vins de Pays des Vals d'Agly covers sixteen villages in the valley of the Agly, including St Paul-de-Fenouillet and Latour-de-France, but is rarely used; nor is Vin de Pays des Coteaux Fenouillèdes, from a hilly area in the north west of the department. Finally, the evocative Vin de Pays de la Côte Vermeille is synonymous with the coastal appellations of Banyuls and Collioure.

The wines of Roussillon have a long history, as does the region itself. The earliest remains of European man, some 450,000 years old, were found near the village of Tautavel in 1971. In the eight and seventh centuries BC the Greeks came here to mine iron ore, and it is claimed that some of Hannibal's warriors settled at Maury, becoming the first wine growers of the region. The wines of Roussillon were praised by Pliny the Elder, who enthused over the Muscats and mellow sweet wines that were gathered on the hillsides and in the gorges of the area, producing a wine comparable to Falernian, Caecuban or the best *crus* celebrated by Horace.

After the Romans came the Visigoths. Then came the Saracens, whom Pépin le Bref defeated in 759, so that Roussillon was joined to Aquitaine for the next few centuries. In the thirteenth century it became part of the kingdom of Majorca, which in turn passed to the kings of Aragon, so that the province remained under Spanish rule, apart from one brief interlude in the fifteenth century, until it conclusively became part of France with the Treaty of the Pyrenees in 1659. The Spanish influence has remained strong, distinguishing it from the Languedoc; the local language is Catalan.

The region's greatest contribution to wine making was the discovery at the end of the thirteenth century that the addition of alcohol to fermenting grape juice brings the fermentation process to a halt. This was the work of Arnau de Vilanova, a doctor of medicine from the University of Montpellier, who is also credited with the introduction of the still into France from Moorish Spain. The word alembic, or still, is of Arab origin. This discovery was to have a marked effect on the viticultural development of the region.

Viticulture has always been the dominant agricultural activity, with table wine and *vin doux naturel* flourishing together – that is, until the recent fall from favour of *vin doux naturel*. By 1868, Guyot recorded sixty thousand hectares of vines in the department of the Pyrénées-Orientales, observing that the hotter climate, caused by the fact that the land was more sheltered from the wind than in the Hérault, gave wines that were richer, sweeter, more solid and with more colour than those of the Hérault. The vines were planted on terraces and mixed with olive trees. The main grape varieties were Grenache, Carignan, Picpoule Noir, Mataro (the Spanish and Australian synonym for Mourvèdre), Malvoisie, Clairette and Pampanal. Guyot particularly praised Banyuls and the Muscats of Rivesaltes, while he said that the ordinary wines had a very deep colour and the fine wines body, spirit, weight and vinosity. They travelled well and were worth as much as the best wine of Porto, either as a fortified wine or mixed with lighter wines.

Rendu described the wines of Roussillon, saying that the best-known vineyards were Banyuls-sur-Mer, Collioure, Port Vendres, Rivesaltes and Perpignan. The *vins doux naturels* received the most comment, but the table wines were credited with little distinction, for it seems that their role was one of blending. Favoured for their high alcohol and deep colour, they were destined to be mixed with lighter wines that were deficient in these qualities. Earlier in this century Morton Shand described them in very much the same way. Indeed, when the Algerian war of independence in 1962–3 meant that wine from North Africa was no longer available for blending with the lighter wines of the Languedoc, wine from Roussillon was used instead. It is only in the last twenty years or so that the table wines of Roussillon have acquired some separate and distinctive identity.

Côtes du Roussillon and other table wines

The wines of Roussillon are quite distinct from those of the Languedoc, even if the grape varieties are similar. The climate is generally hotter, and if the vines are not scorched by sunshine, they are burnt by the drying winds of the Tramontane, which blows hard one day in three. Even on a brilliant summer's day, you can feel your car buffeted by the wind, with leaves and even branches falling on to the road in front of you. Rainfall can be low too, averaging 500–600 mm a year. The consequence of this dry, sunny climate with some 2530 hours of sunshine is lower yields than from vineyards further east, but with higher levels of alcohol and a greater concentration of flavour – hence the original suitability of the wines for blending.

Roussillon also made its first tentative steps towards an image of quality a few years earlier than the Aude or Hérault. The very first moves away from the production of 'le gros rouge' were made in the early 1960s, and by 1970 three Vins Délimités de Qualités Supérieures, or VDQS, were recognised, namely Corbières du Roussillon, Corbières Supérieures du Roussillon and Roussillon des Aspres. In 1973 these were grouped into one VDQS, Coteaux du Roussillon, to which a village name could be added. Then in 1977 the two appellations of Côtes du Roussillon and Côtes du Roussillon Villages were created, and two villages, Caramany and Latour-de-France, were allowed to add their names to the appellation of Cotes du Roussillon Villages. Two more villages have subsequently followed suit, Lesquerde in 1996 and Tautavel in 1997.

Côtes du Roussillon Villages is made up of the former Corbières du Roussillon and Corbières Supérieures du Roussillon and consists of twenty-five villages in the northern part of the department, to the north of the river Têt, adjoining the appellation of Corbières. Côtes

65

du Roussillon covers 117 villages in the former Roussillon des Aspres, in the southern part of the department. Côtes du Roussillon Villages can only ever be red, while Côtes du Roussillon allows for white and pink wine. There are also differences in the production regulations, with a maximum yield of 45 hl/ha for the village appellation, as opposed to 50 hl/ha for the larger appellation. It was determined as early as 1977 that Côtes du Roussillon Villages must be made from a blend of at least three grape varieties, whereas this regulation has only applied to Côtes du Roussillon since 1985. The two most important varieties must not exceed ninety per cent of the blend, thereby ensuring that the third variety does make a contribution to the taste of the wine.

Producers of Côtes du Roussillon feel somewhat disadvantaged, for the underlying implication is that Côtes du Roussillon Villages is a better wine, in the same way that Côtes du Rhône Villages singles out the better villages. Consequently, there is now a move afoot for the reclassification of the appellation with the introduction of a superior level for Côtes du Roussillon, which might be called Premières Côtes du Roussillon. Yields would be restricted to 45 hl/ha, specific vineyards, grape varieties and *élevage* would all be taken into consideration and there would be a second *labelle* tasting to verify the quality. A minimum price would be set and the wine would have to be bottled by the producer, so that there would be no bulk sales. Work began on the dossier in 1989, to determine the ground rules and enlist the concerted support of the various producers. It has been a time-consuming process, fraught with bureaucratic machinations, to persuade the INAO to accept the argument, but for the moment nothing has been conclusively decided.

When the appellations were first introduced, not every producer had the requisite three grape varieties in his vineyard. The area was, and still is, dominated by Carignan, but that is now losing ground to Grenache Noir and is restricted to a maximum of sixty per cent in the blend. It is really Grenache Noir, the Garnacha of Spain, that accounts for the typicity of the red wines of Roussillon, providing the essential fruit and flavour. It produces wines that are high in alcohol and deep in colour, but often deficient in acidity. In other words, they benefit from blending, especially as yields can often be adversely affected by *coulure*, to which Grenache Noir is particularly prone. Lladoner Pelut, which is very similar to

Grenache Noir, is also allowed in the appellation, but in practice is rarely planted. Cinsaut is too and is included, as well as the two key *cépages améliorateurs*, Syrah and to a much lesser extent, Mourvèdre.

The first plantings of Syrah were at the end of the 1960s, so that it is now well established in the region, usually replacing Carignan and contributing significantly to some wines. Twenty per cent is the current minimum, which increases to thirty per cent in 2002. However, Syrah is not always planted in the most suitable sites, and if yields are too high, gives distinctly unsatisfactory results. Mourvèdre can be even more problematic. It is a late ripener that really likes to be near the sea rather than on inland hillsides, and with as much as one month's difference between the ripening time on the plains and in the hills, it is rarely found in the vineyards of Côtes du Roussillon Villages. Carignan has its supporters here, who argue that the variety is much better in Roussillon than anywhere else in the Midi, for on these sun-soaked hillsides it ripens well and give low yields of ripe grapes to make warm, red wine with soft tannins.

As for white wine, Macabeu, known as Macabeo across the border in Spain, and more specifically as Viura in Rioja, provides the base of most of the dry wines, while Grenache Blanc was initially grown for Rivesaltes, along with Grenache Gris and Malvoisie, also called Torbato. Macabeu provides acidity, Grenache Blanc body and structure and Malvoisie some discreet flavour. Now, in the quest for more aromatic wines, Rolle, Roussanne and Marsanne are becoming more widespread and have been allowed in the appellation since 1988. Chardonnay remains firmly excluded from the appellations, featuring only in *vins de pays*, as do Viognier, Cabernet Sauvignon and Merlot.

Whereas Grenache Noir, Gris and Blanc are grown for both table wine and *vins doux naturels*, Muscat – both Muscat *à petits grains* and Muscat d'Alexandrie, also known as Muscat *à gros grains* – was originally destined exclusively for Muscat de Rivesaltes, but is now increasingly vinified as a dry white wine, a Muscat Sec, *vin de pays*.

It is perhaps surprising that the villages of Caramany and Latour-de-France should have initially been singled out within the appellation of Côtes du Roussillon Villages. When the appellation was created in 1977, the wine from the co-operative of Latour-de-France was bought and bottled in large quantities by the French wine merchant Nicolas, so that name, with its memorable ring, already had a large following. Subsequently, however, the village co-operative has rested on its laurels, producing old-fashioned wines based on Carignan and Grenache Noir, without any improvement in flavour or technique. The wine does not really deserve its distinction. Caramany, on the other hand, may owe its status to a qualitative decision back in 1964, when it became one of the very first co-operatives to use carbonic maceration. The co-operative was already well organised for this purpose, as the cellars are built on a slope, enabling the vats to be filled easily by gravity without the need to pump the grapes. Since 1996 the neighbouring village of Cassagnes, which has some of the highest vineyards in the appellation, at 500-600 metres, has been entitled to inclusion in Caramany. The wines here are characterised by a distinctive pepperiness, originating from the schist soil.

Tautavel and Lesquerde were given appellation status in 1997 and 1996 respectively. The village of Tautavel nestles in the harsh, dramatic countryside of the northern part of the appellation. The adjoining village of Vingrau is also included in the appellation, for both have soil based on schist, which gives the wines a robust sturdiness, Lesquerde is based on granite and the village co-operative also has a reputation for its Muscat de Rivesaltes, as well as producing characterful Côtes du Roussillon Villages.

Now the president of the co-operative of Cases-de-Pène is working to obtain recognition for the black schists of his village, which are similar to those of Caramany and stretch along the river valley to the neighbouring village of Espira d'Agly. The proposed area would include two co-operatives as well as about twenty private producers. The area has been agreed and the dossier submitted to the INAO, but no firm decision has been made, for these things take time. For Tautavel, it was apparently a fifteen-year struggle. The aim at Cases-de-Pène is to establish the wine as a more expensive *haut de gamme*, with a minimum price of FF 50 to the French consumer, compared to the average price of a Côtes du Roussillon in Auchan, one of the largest supermarkets, of FF 22.50. The co-operative's flagship wine Château de Pène, provides the benchmark. It comes from old Carignan, with some Syrah and Grenache Noir, and since 1994 has been aged in barrel. Syrah was first introduced into the village some twenty-five years ago, when it was seen as the saviour *cépage améliorateur*, but now, although

68

Syrah continues to be planted, it is very much the third grape variety of the blend.

The 1995 vintage, which was being sold in the spring of 1999, was rounded and harmonious.

THE VIGNERONS CATALANS, PERPIGNAN

The appellation of Côtes du Roussillon is dominated by co-operatives, for nearly every village has one. Some are more successful and dynamic than others, and many of them in turn belong to a *groupement de producteurs* or producers' union, of which the Vignerons Catalans is by far the most influential in Roussillon. In 1998 it was responsible for sixty per cent of the total production of Roussillon, ranking fourth in order of size in the Midi after the combined Vignerons du Val d'Orbieu and Listel, the Union des Caves Coopératives de l'Ouest Audois et du Razès, more succinctly known as UCCUOR, followed by the family *négociant* house of Jeanjean, with Skalli in fifth place. The Vignerons Catalans was founded in 1964 as a consequence of the Algerian war, with the main object of providing wine for blending with the wines of the Languedoc. At that time it was well-nigh impossible for a wine grower in Roussillon to earn a living from his vines, when the average Roussillon vineyard yielded 35 hl/ha at 14°, while those of the Languedoc easily reached 200 hl/ha – though at only 8°.

Sales only really began to develop in the early 1970s, largely thanks to the French supermarket Carrefour, which started up at the same time. The two companies have grown together and Vignerons Catalans now bottles some 35 million bottles a year. It covers twenty-eight villages, with the village co-operatives of twenty-five of those villages as shareholders. Altogether the group takes wine from some 2500 people or around fifteen thousand hectares of vineyards. The average individual holding is between two and six hectares, but some of the co-operative members have very much less, just a few ares. Six oenologists advise on vineyard treatment and replanting, and as a producers' union, Vignerons Catalans is also responsible for the distribution of subsidies from the French government or from Brussels. In addition to Côtes du Roussillon and Côtes du Roussillon Villages, the group produces *vin de pays*, mainly Vin de Pays d'Oc and also some *vin doux naturel*. You will find its wines under a variety of labels. Saveurs Oubliés, P'tit Bonheur and Mediterroir are the key brands on the French market, and in addition there are the numerous individual estates whose wines it markets, even if it does not actually make them. Everything is centralised in the Vignerons Catalans offices and warehouse, with its brand new bottling line, on the industrial estate in Perpignan, and it also has two ageing cellars in the villages of Vingrau and Estagel.

For Emmanuel Montès, the genial export director of Vignerons Catalans, fruit summarises the style of the wines. That is what the group seeks, seeing the typicity of Roussillon in its warmth, with sufficient tannins to allow the wines to age. Nor is the group a champion of single varietals, for it likes to blend, emphasising that the character of the south is based above all on an *assemblage*. Even the rare varietal wines will include wines from different vineyards.

CAVE COOPERATIVE DE TROUILLAS

The co-operative at Trouillas was founded in 1927 and is now the largest in the southern part of the Côtes du Roussillon, with 136 members working eight hundred hectares. The young director, Thierry Cazech, is an enthusiast, utterly committed to his village and to the appellation. He explained that Trouillas was the first co-operative to have its own bottling line, as early as 1960, and today its prime concern is the organisation of its vineyards.

For Trouillas, as for all the villages in the area, grapes are the principal crop. In total the village covers eighteen hundred hectares, of which twelve hundred are vineyards, two-thirds of them cultivated by the members of the co-operative. The vineyards present a real patchwork of twelve or so different soil types, all originating with the major geological upheaval of the creation of the Pyrenees. Within the eight hundred hectares there are 1684 different plots, all of which have been classified, not only according to grape variety but also by zone, age of vines, method of pruning, average yield, the health of the vines, average ripening time and average sugar level in the grapes. This makes the task of blending easier, as similar parcels can be put together to provide an element of homogeneity within such diversity. And from those blends Trouillas will produce as many as twelve or fourteen different Côtes du Roussillon, as well as Rivesaltes and a small amount of *vin de pays*.

The co-operative is encouraging the planting of Syrah and Mourvèdre with planting subsidies, as part of a programme that is gradually reducing the proportion of Carignan. It also pays according to the quality of the grapes. Syrah and Mourvèdre are considerably more remunerative, at FF 500–1000 per hectolitre, than Grenache Noir at FF 500–700 and Carignan at a mere FF 300–320. The first Syrah was planted in the village in 1974, and Mourvèdre followed in 1979. The co-operative conducts numerous experimental micro-vinifications. For example, it has four plots of Mourvèdre, each with a different *terroir*, but planted with the same clone, with identical trellising and pruning, each of which is given the same vinification in order to see the effect of *terroir*. Cazech observed how sentimental people are about their land, for they will keep a small plot of vines even if they have a full-time occupation in quite a different field. One problem is the age of the co-operative members, for they tend to be elderly and therefore conservative. In the department of the Pyrénées-Orientales the average age of co-operative members is sixty-three, whereas in contrast at Trouillas itself it is only fifty-one. Young wine growers are starting up, as many as eight in 1998, with holdings varying between twenty and forty hectares. The ideal is twenty hectares, from which one man can earn a decent living without engaging much extra help.

At Trouillas they have worked with oak since about 1988, using several different coopers and experimenting with varying degrees of toasting. The 1994 Cuvée du Gouverneur, from forty per cent Syrah, with twenty per cent each of Mourvèdre, Grenache Noir and Carignan, of which one third had spent a year in wood, tasted of well integrated oak, with quite a firm structure and good fruit. The 1996 Pierre des Aspres, with the same blend, of which sixty per cent spent twelve months in new wood, was solid and rounded, and again the oak did not mask the fruit too much. A 1997 Côtes du Roussillon, with no oak, made from twenty per cent each of Grenache Noir and Carignan vinified by carbonic maceration, and forty per cent Syrah and twenty per cent Mourvèdre, destalked for a classic fermentation, had some appealingly supple fruit, with a backbone of tannin, and illustrated a co-operative that is working well for its members.

CAVE COOPERATIVE DE BAIXAS

The co-operative de Baixas is one of the shareholders of the Vignerons Catalans, with 380 members producing some 85,000 hectolitres from 2,100 hectares of vines. This is an impressively well-equipped establishment, with stainless steel vats and, unusually for Roussillon, an underground cellar for barrels, virtually all of French oak, that are used for Côtes du Roussillon Villages. Red and white wine vinifications are kept apart in two separate buildings. Reds are fermented by carbonic maceration or in the traditional way, with destalked grapes, and the recent purchase of pneumatic presses has had a significant impact on quality. The money for new equipment comes from the co-operative's own profits, with some help from local government and the Crédit Agricole. Members are encouraged to deliver the best raw material possible, with bonuses and also penalties, and are paid incentives to green-harvest Syrah and Mourvèdre, if necessary.

We tasted a range of wines, some sold under the Don Brial label. Don Brial was a priest from Baixas who became Marie-Antoinette's confessor and introduced his village's wine to the court of Versailles, and who subsequently left money for the building of a school in the village. Don Brial dry Muscat was fresh and pithy and the Muscat de Rivesaltes, from eighty per cent Muscat *à petits grains* and twenty per cent Muscat d'Alexandrie, was light and lemony with a honeyed finish. In contrast, the Château les Pins Muscat de Rivesaltes is made from seventy per cent Muscat d'Alexandrie and thirty per cent Muscat *à petits grains*. The grapes are destalked and the skins macerated with the alcohol, which makes for a much more solid, substantial wine than if the alcohol is added to fermenting juice. For red Côtes du Roussillon Villages, the co-operative selects the best plots and oldest vines, including as much Syrah as possible. Two wines are aged in oak, Dom Brial and Château les Pins, a château in the village that now belongs to the town council, while the co-operative runs the vineyards. The 1996 Château les Pins, from forty per cent

Syrah and thirty per cent Mourvèdre and Grenache Noir, had spice and structure, with well integrated oak and some ageing potential.

CAVE COOPERATIVE DE PEZILLA-LA-RIVIERE

The village co-operative at Pézilla-la-Rivière also ranks among the more forward-looking of the appellation, and once again is a member of the Vignerons Catalans. Its white wines have improved enormously in recent years. Whereas ten years ago the white Côtes du Roussillon would have been pure Macabeu, a grape variety distinctly short on flavour and aroma, it is now blended with Marsanne and Rolle, which were first planted in 1993. The difference is quite dramatic, with more aroma, structure and body. Chardonnay too is a recent arrival, with the first vinification in 1995 for a Vin de Pays Catalan. This is lightly fruity and refreshingly free of oak. This co-operative also has new pneumatic presses, which have contributed to the improved quality of its wines. However, the demand for white Côtes du Roussillon is insignificant and it prefers to concentrate on red wines. Syrah was first planted about 1983 and the co-operative now has fifty hectares out of a total of 780 hectares. There is some Mourvèdre too, but that is more problematic. If the yields are too high, you are better off with Carignan.

Although Pézilla-la-Rivière lies within the appellation of Côtes du Roussillon Villages, some of its wines, notably the oak-aged Château de Blanes, a property that belongs to the president of the co-operative, are simple Côtes du Roussillon. The reason is a question of revenue. Yields for Côtes du Roussillon Villages are lower than for Côtes du Roussillon, but the price differential does not compensate for the lower yield. Things are now improving, with a greater demand for Côtes du Roussillon Villages, encouraged partly by the marketing emphasis of the Vignerons Catalans on that appellation. The blend for Château de Blanes varies from vintage to vintage, with a high percentage of Syrah and old Carignan, as well as Grenache Noir, and spends ten to twelve months in wood, a proportion of which is new. It was well made, but did not greatly excite.

DOMAINE GAUBY, CALCE

It has to be said that the most inspiring wines come from the private producers, of whom there are a growing number. We visited estates that did not exist ten years ago, or older estates that were just beginning to break away from the custom of selling wine to *négociants* in order to start bottling their own wine and thereby create a reputation. One such is Domaine Gauby, a name that today would feature in any list of top Roussillon, or even top Midi, producers. However, when asked about the history of his estate, Gérard Gauby replied, *'L'histoire, c'est moi!'* His first bottling was as recently as 1985, which he described as a *sympa*, or nice, vintage. Until 1983 his grandfather had delivered grapes to the local co-operative and the estate only really took off at the beginning of the 1990s. Gauby now has forty hectares in the tiny village of Calce, having expanded from his grandfather's five, buying steep slopes that no one else wanted and replanting, using planting rights from a vineyard on the plain that had been pulled up.

We were treated to a tour of the vineyards. This is the Roussillon landscape at its wildest and most dramatic, with small plots of vineyards nestling amongst the garrigue. The remains of a Cathar tower that had served as a warning beacon stood on a hilltop, from where you would have been able to see the coast at Port Vendres and then signal to the nearby castle at Quéribus, and on as far as Toulouse. The north west wind, the Tramontane, was blowing hard, ripping leaves from the vines and even blowing some posts over. Apparently the wind is at its fiercest in June, the month that we were there. The soil is mainly chalk – hence the name of the village, for Calce originates from *calcaire* – and there is some schist too. Gauby's oldest vines are two hectares of Grenache Noir, planted in 1947 below an old iron mine that was in use up to the First World War, while his first Syrah was planted twenty years ago. Yields are low, 35 hl/ha at the very most, with as little as 19 for Syrah in 1997. Then we drove past the Mas de la Founs, an attractive old farmhouse belonging to the village co-operative, that sits perched on steep rocks outside the village.

Tasting gave Gauby an opportunity to expand on his thoughts. He is forthright and committed, describing the appellation of Côtes du Roussillon as a catastrophe, condemning its organisers for their complete lack of wine culture. They are all fifty years out of date. He himself is an example of one of the many producers in the south of France who question the appellation regulations, finding them much too restrictive and consequently preferring to label some of their wines as *vins de pays*. All Gauby's white wines are *vins de pays* for the simple reason that the white appellation has a maximum alcohol level of 13° and he invariably produces richer, more powerful wines, maybe by only a half a degree, but that is enough to make the difference. This restriction is a relic from the days when people had few means of controlling their fermentation temperatures and wines that were too alcoholic tended to oxidise quickly. Now that everything is more carefully controlled, higher alcohol levels, similar to those of Châteauneuf-du-Pape, are perfectly feasible. Gauby freely admits to being inspired by the wines of the Rhône valley and by Châteauneuf-du-Pape in particular.

The 1997 les Rocailles, Vin de Pays des Côtes Catalanes, is a blend of Macabeu, Grenache Blanc and Grenache Gris, all grown on schist, with yields of 40 hl/ha and an alcohol level of 13.5°. It is full and concentrated, with a hint of aniseed. A Viognier, from fifteen-year-old vines that produced only 12 hl/ha, was vinified mainly in new wood. It had the perfumed character of the grape, with well-integrated oak. Next came three different Grenaches from different vineyards, but all fermented in oak, in barrels from the Narbonne cooper Boutes. First there was a Grenache Gris grown on schist, which was going through a sulky phase and not showing well. Next came a Grenache Blanc from limestone and clay, with a powerful mouthful of flavour. Finally there was la Coume Ginestre, from very old Grenache Blanc vines that yielded just 20 hl/ha, which was fermented in new wood. It was long and concentrated, with herbal flavours.

As there is no alcohol limit for red wines, Gauby's are all Côtes du Roussillon for the moment. Les Rocailles, mainly from Grenache Noir with a little Mourvèdre and Carignan but no Syrah, spends the winter in vat and had some solid cherry fruit and spice. Cuvée des Calcinaires is mainly Grenache Noir, with a bit of Carignan and a drop of Cabernet Sauvignon, and has spent six months in wood. It was an appealing combination of smoke and spice with soft tannins. The Cabernet Sauvignon vines are about fifteen years old, planted at a time when Gauby was trying out all sorts of things. We continued tasting various barrels, combinations of Grenache Noir and Syrah, all promising well for future bottlings, with body and fruit, length and power.

Our tasting finished with a Muscat de Rivesaltes, from pure Muscat *à petits grains*, a wonderful combination of finesse and concentration, and the 1996 Vintage, which was kept in vat over the winter to be bottled in March. The old Grenache Noir vines yielded only 20 hl/ha and the palate was redolent of ripe cherries and spice. Gauby feels strongly that the development of table wine in Roussillon has been handicapped by the *vins doux naturels*. And when asked about the future, he declared himself super-optimistic!

DOMAINE FORCA-REAL, MILLAS

Jean-Pierre Henriques is the friendly owner of Domaine Força-Réal, which lies in a dramatic position on the hillside just below the Ermitage de Força-Réal. There are magnificent views from his vineyards below the cellar, stretching across the valley towards the Canigou and in the east to the Albères and the sea in the distance. This is another newly created estate. Henriques's father was a grocer in Perpignan who started a *négociant* business, while his son studied oenology at Dijon and dreamt of having his own estate. A few years later he was presented with a choice, to create his own estate or to extend the *négociant* business. He decided to take up the challenge of proving that you can make good wines here in Roussillon. When Henriques arrived in 1989, there was a plot or two of old Grenache Noir vines amidst the *garrigue* and an old building serving as a cellar with a press and some concrete vats. His first vinification, in 1991, was in a friend's cellar while his own was built for the 1992 vintage, and in 1993 he tried out his first small barrels. By 1998 Henriques felt that he had made a quantum leap in quality, partly because the vintage was very small – only half the normal size – as a result of drought.

Henriques explained how he has three different *terroirs* in his forty hectares. There is alluvium from the river for Syrah and Mourvèdre, a plateau of clay and limestone for Muscat and schist for Syrah and Grenache Noir. Each plot is vinified separately, as there are considerable variations in Syrah, depending on the depth of the soil and the altitude, which ranges from 100 to 400 metres. He has no problem in obtaining ripe Mourvèdre, as it likes the deep, cool, alluvial soil. He also has ten hectares of olive trees, reviving a tradition that died out when the great frosts and severe winter of 1956 destroyed not only vines but many of the olive trees of the region. The olives are sent to the co-operative in Millas; Henriques observed that there is as much to learn about them as about viticulture.

Henriques produces a convincing range of wines. The tasting room is decorated with a local artist's impressions of the Feria in Millas, for Roussillon, with its Catalan associations, is very much a bull-fighting region. Mas de la Garrigue, which Henriques described as *mon petit vin*, comes mainly from Grenache Noir, with some Syrah and Carignan. The vinification is traditional; he does not like carbonic maceration, as it makes the wine *'roussillonne'* as it ages. In other words, it becomes too warm and raisiny. The 1998, tasted the following June, had some appealing ripe fruit, with firm tannins. Domaine Força-Réal is a blend of Syrah and Mourvèdre, with a little Grenache Noir, making for warm liquorice flavours. Great attention is paid to the selection of the grapes at vintage time, with a preference for really ripe grapes and older vines, and also to the fermentation temperatures; the multitude of little details makes a convincing whole.

Les Hauts de Força-Réal is the barrel-aged wine. Henriques has tried several different coopers and finds that finely grained barrels from Taransaud suit his wine best. He replaces a third of the barrels each year. Syrah grown on schist forms the backbone of the wine, but in 1998 he even aged the Grenache Noir in oak, as it had so much more structure than usual. The oak in a young wine gives an impression of vanilla sweetness, but is well integrated with some ripe rounded fruit.

As with most wine estates in Roussillon, *vin doux* was the original vocation of Força Réal, and Henriques has continued it. His Vintage is a young wine that spends a few months in old wood, making for ripe, rounded fruit. He likes his Muscat with a little age rather than youthfully fresh, so his Muscat de Rivesaltes is rich and grapey. Best of all is the Hors d'Age, the base wine that he found in an old *foudre* when he bought the property. It is blended with younger wines in a variation on a *solera*, and spends time in old barrels under the eaves of the roof, where the temperature can fluctuate considerably. The resulting wine has a lingering, dry, nutty nose and palate.

MAS CREMAT, ESPIRA D'AGLY

Jean-Marc Jeannin at Mas Crémat, outside Espira d'Agly, is an example of a complete newcomer to the region. He and his wife are Burgundians. She is a Mongeard-Mugneret and he worked in the dairy industry. In 1990 they bought Mas Crémat, with thirty hectares of vines, for what would have been the price of just one hectare of Vosne Romanée *premier cru*, if you could have found it for sale. The farmhouse was in ruins and the grapes went to the co-operative. The vineyards had originally been planted for *vin doux*, but they will change the orientation to table wine. They have already pulled up the Macabeu and will concentrate on Syrah, Mourvèdre, Muscat and Grenache Noir. The first two years were very hard, for everyone said 'we would *casser la figure*, but we have proved what we could do in the bottle.' In fact, there are parallels between cheese and wine production, with the same insistence on hygiene and attention to temperature. In cheese you have sugar and acidity, as opposed to sugar and alcohol in wine, and there are yeasts – admittedly different yeasts – in both.

Jeannin finds Roussillon quite different from Burgundy, for here there is everything to achieve. Only about twenty estates are exporting seriously and creating a reputation for themselves, while most just sell to passing tourists. The climate is different, so are the grape varieties and the life style, for there is no wine culture as there is Burgundy. He admits that he has no real experience, but then neither has the region. Everything is possible, and as it is a region that is just beginning to take off, there is none of the complacency you can find in a region like Burgundy that has an established reputation.

Certainly Jeannin's wines demonstrate talent and commitment. A Muscat Sec from equal parts of *gros* and *petits grains* had a rich rounded nose with good body and fruit. Apparently there are as many as forty-eight different terpines, or aroma components, in Muscat. Grenache Blanc made from eighty-year-old vines, fermented and kept in wood for a total of eight months, had body with a herbal, nutty flavour. The variety is not popular in the region, particularly with co-operative members, as the yields are too low for it to be really remunerative. Jeannin obtains just 15–20 hl/ha from his old vineyard. A 1996 Côtes du Roussillon from equal parts of Syrah and Grenache Noir, kept in vat for twelve months, was solid and ripe, with the schist soil of Mas Crémat giving silkier tannins than from clay. The juice spends fifteen days on the skins, with a twice daily *pigeage*, in the original old stone vats. Mid-fermentation the cap is almost as solid as concrete, but you have to force it into the juice or else it will dry up and then it softens as the fermentation finishes.

A 1997 Côtes du Roussillon including twenty per cent Mourvèdre with forty per cent each of Grenache Noir and Mourvèdre spent twelve months in old wood. Jeannin buys barrels from a cooper who recycles one-year-old Burgundian barrels – but only from people he knows and whose wine he likes. This is a bit like buying a used car. You want to know where it has been, and the same applies to barrels. The wine was elegant and stylish, a marriage of schist and oak. The 1996, with similar production methods, had a balance of fruit and tannins, with concentration and length. Mourvèdre ripens well here, provided the yield is kept below 30 hl/ha. Eventually Jeannin will have four hectares of Mourvèdre in production and would like to try a pure varietal.

We talked about the work in the vineyards. Jeannin sees the wine grower as a farmer who has a responsibility for the upkeep of the countryside. Accordingly he follows the principles of *lutte raisonnée*, or sustained viticulture, trying to avoid any chemical products apart from minimal amounts of copper and sulphur. Most of his vineyards are planted in the traditional *gobelet* system. The problem with training vines on wires is that there is no protection for the grapes against the strong sunshine, whereas *gobelet* provides some shade, with the vegetation of the vine limiting evaporation; by retaining the humidity rather than keeping it out, it acts like an umbrella in reverse. Wires are useful for mechanisation and if the vine is particularly sensitive to wind. Jeannin also reproaches the nurseries. He has not yet tried taking cuttings from his own vines by *sélection massale*, but has bought vines from a nursery in the Vaucluse. You are, however, very much in the hands of the nurserymen – as with cork manufacturers and coopers, you do not really know what you are getting and you have to trust them. Certainly Mas Crémat will be a name to watch out for.

CHATEAU DE JAU, ESTAGEL

A more established estate is Château de Jau, which was bought by Bernard Dauré in 1974. He was already a *négociant* trading mainly in Rivesaltes, but wished to return to his roots, for his grandfather had been a wine grower and in addition he was convinced that the future of Roussillon lay very much with viticulture. When Dauré bought the estate, there were some ninety hectares of vines planted with varieties like Grenache Noir, Muscat, Carignan and Macabeu, all of which were sold to the *négoce*, mainly for *vin doux*. The early history of the property is monastic, and the monks remained there until the French Revolution. There is a tower that dates from the twelfth century and a magnificent mulberry tree that is over three hundred years old and classified as a historical monument. We sat under its shade in the attractive courtyard and talked to Dauré's daughter, Estelle, who now has responsibility for the wine making.

Over the last twenty years or so, most of the land has been replanted with varieties more suitable for table wine, notably Syrah and Mourvèdre, as well as some white varieties, and they now have vineyards in three main sites: in the valley close to the cellars; on some low-lying slopes nearby, and in a large plot of twenty-six hectares at an altitude of three hundred metres. The limestone soil there is very dry, retaining very little water. However, the Grenache Noir and Carignan vines benefit from the sea breezes that bring moisture from the Mediterranean. There are breathtaking views over the Agly valley to the Pyrenees beyond, while behind you is the ruined tower of Tautavel, part of the medieval system of watch towers.

As well as Château de Jau, the Dauré family also owns two other properties, Clos des Paulilles between Banyuls and Collioure and Mas Christine in Rivesaltes, which makes them one of the biggest landowners of the region. And so they produce a broad palette of wines. There is Viognier for a Vin de Pays de la Côte Vermeille, which is fermented in new oak and kept on the lees for a few months. The white Côtes du Roussillon is a blend of Rolle, Grenache Blanc and Malvoisie, with some delicate fruit, while the Côtes du Roussillon Villages, a blend of Syrah, Mourvèdre, Grenache Noir and Carignan, is quite firm with a spicy finish. Syrah and Mourvèdre were first planted when the Dauré family bought the property and make up the greater part of the blend. They are given a traditional vinification, while the Carignan is fermented by carbonic maceration in order to extract the maximum amount of fruit.

The Dauré family has always been aware of the possibilities for experimentation and innovation in Roussillon, and nothing has stood still in the twenty-five years that they have owned Château de Jau. Estelle Dauré would say that her ambition is to make a great wine – and not just one small vat but in a large quantity, as they do at Château Margaux. Meanwhile, her mother organises exhibitions of modern art at the château during the summer months and you can sample the wines with a simple lunch under the shade of the mulberry tree. Her father's ambitions are now set on Chile, for they bought land there in 1998.

DOMAINE PIQUEMAL, ESPIRA D'AGLY

Pierre Piquemal is a genial, welcoming character. We found his cellars in the back streets of the village of Espira d'Agly, with its fine Romanesque church. This is an estate that goes back several generations, but bottling is a recent development. Pierre's father died when he was fifteen, and he helped his grandfather run the family vineyards, from which all the wine was sold to the *négoce*. Today, by contrast, everything but a little Rivesaltes is put into bottle. We wandered around the slightly chaotic cellars, glass in hand, tasting the occasional vat. Like most Roussillon producers, Piquemal makes a varied range of wines. A dry, pithy Muscat followed a pink Côtes Catalanes from Merlot, Cabernet Sauvignon and Syrah, which was ripe and rounded. The market for *vins de pays* is buoyant and Piquemal is hoping to obtain a ten-year-old Chardonnay vineyard and extend his white range. Young red wines included Cuvée Justin Piquemal, named after his grandfather and made from equal parts of Grenache Noir, Cabernet Sauvignon and Syrah, and a Cuvée Pierre Andonnet, from his mother's side of the family, from seventy-five per cent Merlot with some Syrah and Cabernet Sauvignon. Côtes du Roussillon comes from equal parts of Grenache Noir, Mourvèdre, Syrah and Carignan, all vinified traditionally apart from the Carignan, resulting in some appealing smoky fruit, reminiscent of the *garrigue*.

In contrast, Piquemal's Côtes du Roussillon Villages has a much higher proportion of Mourvèdre, with less Syrah, some old Carignan and some Grenache Noir, and has spent twelve months in wood, which gives more tannin and concentration. He has worked with wood since 1989 and is convinced that it makes a considerable difference to the ageing potential of a wine. In 1997 he experimented with barrels, using a toasting process called *chauffe à coeur*, which he explained takes much longer, but is a lighter toasting so that the tannin of the oak is not burnt but lightly carbonised, thereby avoiding any bitterness and creating a fine aroma. Apparently the process is less traumatic for the oak. We tried a wine that had spent just one month in such a barrel and the flavour was a combination of silky oak and sweet fruit, but it was really too soon to tell. Then to illustrate his point about the benefit of wood for the ageing process, Piquemal opened a 1990 made from one quarter each of Syrah, Mourvèdre, Grenache Noir and Carignan. How right he was. The wine had an attractive, maturing nose with leathery fruit, liquorice and preserved cherries in several layers of flavour. Still very youthful, it was a good note on which to leave, with the long, lingering taste in our mouths.

DOMAINE DES SCHISTES, ESTAGEL

Jacques Sire at Domaine des Schistes in the small town of Estagel is another producer who decided, with his wife Nadine, to create his own estate. His family had owned vines for several generations, but his parents delivered their grapes to the village co-operative. It was not easy to extract his vineyards from the co-operative's grasp; it entailed endless negotiations and the payment of a forfeit, but he was not deterred and finally bottled his first wines in 1990. Sire has forty-five hectares, mainly between the villages of Tautavel and Maury in the foothills of the Corbières, on limestone and schist. Two-thirds of his production is Côtes du Roussillon Villages, and he could use the new appellation of Cotes du Roussillon Villages-Tautavel, but for the moment he wants to concentrate on creating a reputation for his own estate. He will wait and see whether 'Tautavel' on the label comes to mean something serious or not.

His white wine is a Vin de Pays des Pyrénées Orientales, for it is pure Grenache Blanc and you need a second variety to make an appellation wine. It was planted originally for Rivesaltes and its sensitivity to oxidation makes it problematic. Two-thirds of it is fermented in oak, half new and half one-year-old, and the wine is kept in wood on the lees until March, with a weekly *bâtonnage*. The wood gives more structure, as the wine is usually low in acidity, but it is none the less rich and full-bodied with a nutty finish. There is no tradition of ageing white wine in Roussillon, but the use of wood should counter that.

Sire's red wines are made from Carignan, Grenache Noir and Syrah, with the precise proportions depending on the vintage. He considers that he is too far away from the sea for Mourvèdre. There are two qualities of Côtes du Roussillon Villages, Cuvée Tradition and Cuvée les Terrasses, which does indeed come from vineyards on terraces. With the Cuvée Tradition he is seeking to express the terroir and the grape varieties. There are equal proportions of three varieties, and each is vinified separately and kept apart for as long as possible so that Sire can follow their evolution in vat. The 1996 was quite rugged, with peppery fruit, and the 1995 was dry and spicy, with the fruit of the *garrigue*, and went deliciously with some local black pudding. The Cuvée les Terrasses comes from fifty per cent Syrah with equal parts of Carignan and Grenache Noir. The Syrah has spent a year in wood and the oak was well integrated, with good tannins and longer ageing potential. Sire is cautious with new oak, putting no more than a quarter of the blend in new wood. A loudspeaker intruded on our conversation, broadcasting incomprehensible village news, and Sire said that, as a boy, he remembered the town crier pedalling round on his bicycle, which had much more charm that the modern loudspeaker.

The expression of *terroir* is Sire's main objective. In any case, in vineyards like these, which are impossible to mechanise, you cannot make what he called 'technological wines'. Production costs are high because of the steep slopes and low bush vines, 'so we have to remain with our typicity', which he seems to do superbly well, producing wines reminiscent of the scents of the *garrigue*. He has some eighty-year-old Carignan vines and is convinced of the value of this variety, provided it is planted in the right place, picked fully ripe with at least 13° and with a low yield. 'You must not generalise about it. Nor can you say that Syrah is good everywhere, nor is carbonic maceration suitable for Syrah.' He would like to try a pure Syrah and also a pure Carignan, but only if it is really ripe. 'If you can take the risk of waiting a further week with Carignan, you can obtain really good results.' The decision about when to pick is all-important, for in the space of just three or four days there can be an enormous development in the ripeness of the grapes, not just the phenolics but the tannins too. The stalks turn from green to yellow and that can make all the difference. This is another domain to watch.

DOMAINE CASENOVE, TROUILLAS

Etienne Montès, at Domaine Casenove outside the village of Trouillas, has the harsh but realistic view of the region of someone who has seen other horizons. He was a photographic reporter until the mid-1980s and then returned to work on the family property, taking over completely in 1994. He now employs Jean-Luc Colombo, the highly acclaimed consultant oenologist of Cornas. His father Jacques was in, 1967, the first person to plant Syrah in Roussillon and his brother Emmanuel is the energetic export director of the Vignerons Catalans. We sat under the shade of a lime tree, in a garden containing colourful pots of geraniums and tall cypresses, while two dogs, Punch and Ernest, snoozed in the sun. The estate has a long history. In the thirteenth century it belonged to the Commanderie Majorquine des Templiers, who did much for agriculture in the region, notably draining the salt lakes of the plain. Then it passed to the Knights Hospitallers, and it was from them that a Monsieur Jaubert, from Montès's grandmother's family, bought the land in the middle of the sixteenth century. Once it was a very large property, but today it is reduced to a manageable fifty hectares.

The estate was planted with the traditional varieties, Carignan and Grenache Noir, Macabeu and Grenache Blanc, and then Montès's father added Syrah and Mourvèdre. Syrah performs well, relishing the heat and achieving good levels of ripeness. Mourvèdre, by contrast, is more problematic, with more discreet flavours compared with the much more immediate Syrah. In addition, Montès has Muscat and Malvoisie. This is indicative of the strong Catalan influence in the region, for you do not find Malvoisie anywhere else in France, although thanks to the Aragonese it grows quite extensively in the western half of Sardinia, as Torbato.

There is also just one hectare of Roussanne, which was not yet in production. The vineyards are on the plain and the first foothills of the Canigou, where the soil is basically clay, but very mixed, with some alluvium as well as glacial sediments and bands of pebbles.

Montès said that his aim was to make wines of good quality for everyday drinking. His white wine has the perennial problem of being too high in alcohol to be a Côtes du Roussillon, as it reaches 13.5°, so it is a Vin de Pays Catalan, made from equals parts of forty-year-old Macabeu and twenty-year-old Malvoisie vines. Both are fermented in wood and blended after fermentation, giving a solid, rounded mouthful with a nutty, almondy flavour. In a way the wine was quite old-fashioned, but very appealing. The *rosé*, La Garrigue de la Casenove, is also a *vin de pays*, from Grenache Noir, Carignan and Syrah, with delicate raspberry fruit and fresh acidity. A 1997 red *vin de pays* from Grenache Noir and Carignan, with just twenty per cent of Mourvèdre, was ripe and plummy, with sufficient tannin. 1997 was a difficult year: there was rain, which resulted in rot, and yields were high, so they needed to select the grapes very carefully as the ripening was very irregular. 1996 was also very wet, resulting in diluted flavours, while 1995 was very much hotter – too hot, in fact, as the grapes almost lacked flavour. 1994, which Montès described as very good, produced ripe, healthy grapes.

As for appellation wines, Montès makes a Côtes du Roussillon Tradition, la Casenove, from Grenache Noir, Carignan and Syrah, with the precise proportions varying from year to year. The 1996 was given what Montès called a relatively short maceration of twenty-one days. The wine is blended at Christmas, and although kept in cement vats, it did almost taste as though it had been in wood, with a great concentration of flavour. It was very plummy and full-bodied, with the herbal flavours of the *garrigue* and a good backbone of tannin. Montès explained that a long maceration does not give more tannin but different ones, a certain indefinable extra, making for concentration and richness. The best Syrah goes into the Cuvée du Commandant François Jaubert, named in memory of Montès's great-uncle, who rebuilt the house and enlarged the cellar when he owned the estate at the end of the nineteenth century. 1993 was the first vintage in which he used new wood, and 1994 was the first vintage of pure Syrah. Yields were low, at 30 hl /ha, and Montès gave the grapes over a month of maceration, putting a third of the wine into new wood for eighteen months while the rest was aged in vat. In the summer of 1998 it was still immensely youthful, with a sweet, oaky vanilla nose, great concentration and a firm tannin structure. The ageing potential could be considerable, but there is no real experience to draw on. On the day I preferred the 1995, which had a much shorter maceration but with more obvious Syrah flavours of pepper and violets and greater elegance. The 1991, made without wood from a blend of Syrah, Grenache Noir and Carignan, was ageing elegantly, with a meaty nose, warm, dry fruit on the palate and mature notes on the finish.

Asked about his future projects, Montès replied candidly, 'To survive and to become better known.' The position of a wine grower in Roussillon is not always easy. 'Rivesaltes is not selling and all people want is cheap wine at five or six francs a bottle. The restaurants are just as bad. There are only about twenty restaurants in the whole department that are really interested in wine.' He rightly resents the low prices, for the production costs of the wines are the same as for more expensive wines like Bordeaux. He also criticises his fellow *vignerons* for their lack of interest in each other's wines and for their general lack of wine culture. The Groupement Interprofessionel de Promotion (GIP), the promotional organisation for the two appellations of Côtes du Roussillon and Côtes du Roussillon Villages, should organise tastings for them and take its educational role within the department more seriously.

DOMAINE CAZES, RIVESALTES

Domaine Cazes, a family company now run by the third and fourth generations, is the largest private producer of Roussillon. Michel Cazes was a market gardener at the beginning of the twentieth century who grew vines as well as vegetables and made some wine for the local market. His son Aimé decided to expand, and his grandsons André and Bernard are now in charge. You will find their large cellars in a back street of Rivesaltes, and they now have a total of 160 hectares of vineyards in one large plot on the plain of the Agly. To achieve such a vineyard was no mean feat, necessitating no fewer than two hundred sales transactions for plots of land varying between fifty ares and five hectares in size. Their vineyards are planted with Muscat, both Alexandrie and *petits grains*, Chardonnay, Grenache Blanc, Macabeu and a little Rolle, and for reds, Grenache Noir, Syrah and Mourvèdre. There is still a little Carignan, and also a sizeable amount of Merlot and Cabernet Sauvignon that were first planted in the mid-1980s.

André Cazes has always had a healthy disrespect for authority, and is not alone in resenting the INAO's iron grip on grape varieties. 'The INAO exercises protectionism on a national scale, but is powerless internationally. As a result, Cabernet Sauvignon is grown all over the world, but in France the Bordelais and their neighbours have the monopoly of it in their appellations.' Yet the Cazes family is convinced that both Cabernet Sauvignon and Merlot are grape varieties for the south of France. They give the best results, for they are the least demanding in the vineyard. Cinsaut is too light and Carignan should be dismissed completely. The quality of Mourvèdre in the region is debatable, while Grenache Noir, although it is the mainstay of Côtes du Roussillon, has no staying power. Syrah can be good. In producing Le Credo, which young Bruno Cazes described as his father's protest about grape varieties, André Cazes demonstrates his case. It is a Vin de Pays des Côtes Catalanes made from equal parts of Cabernet Sauvignon and Merlot, which undergo a four-week maceration and are then aged for one year in vat, one year in small barrels and one year in bottle, before sale. Ideally, they would like their customers to keep the wine a further two or three years. We tasted the 1995, with its firm blackcurrant fruit and smoky elegant palate.

Cazes are also known for their main *vin de pays* brand, Le Canon du Maréchal, named after Marshal Joffre, who was born in Rivesaltes. They first produced a dry white wine, Muscat Sec, from both *gros* and *petits grains*, in 1980. Depending on the quality of the grapes, the juice is given twelve hours of skin contact in a pneumatic press, and the wine has some fresh, pithy orange fruit. These are grapes that would originally have been grown for Muscat de Rivesaltes, but with the decline in the Rivesaltes market, the *vin de pays* has been developed. The red Canon du Maréchal, first produced in 1984, is a blend of Syrah, Grenache Noir, Merlot and Cabernet Sauvignon. They are looking for fruit, and that is just what they achieve: ripe berry flavours with supple tannin from carbonic maceration. It is a wine that is best drunk slightly chilled on a warm summer's day.

The Cazes range of Côtes du Roussillon includes a white wine made from Rolle and Macabeu; in better vintages, half of each grape variety is fermented in new oak. They first began working with small oak barrels about ten years ago. The 1996 was full and rounded, quite nutty and solid. The *rosé* comes from Grenache Noir, Syrah and Mourvèdre, and its quality took a quantum leap in 1997, when a new pneumatic press enabled Cazes to macerate the juice in the press. Grenache Noir is always the dominant grape variety of the red wines. A basic 1994 was quite firm and rugged, while a Cuvée Spéciale, with a lower yield and no Carignan, was more meaty and rounded. The Côtes du Roussillon Villages Vieille Chêne spends a year in vat and a year in wood, of which a third is new. It was firm and structured with good fruit, and would greatly benefit from some bottle age. As well as table wines, Cazes are important producers of Rivesaltes, of which more on page 101.

CHATEAU DE CORNEILLA, CORNEILLA DEL VERCOL

Philippe Jonquères d'Oriola, at the Château de Corneilla in the village of Corneilla-del-Vercol, near the town of Elne, also has a much broader view of his appellation than many of his colleagues. Unusually for the Midi, he studied oenology in Burgundy and then worked in Stellenbosch in the Cape. From there he joined International Distillers and Vintners in London, selling and promoting French regional wines for Morgan Furze at a time when few people had ever heard of the likes of Fitou or Corbières des Roussillon. He returned to run the family property in 1970, and in 1992 set up his own company with sixty hectares of vines. The imposing red stone château was built by the Knights Templars at the end of the twelfth century. After the order was destroyed by Philippe le Bel, the château was bought by Philippe de Corneilla, and Philippe d'Oriola's family, who are of Catalan origin, came there in 1485. Imagine knowing that your family had lived in the same place since Henry VII came to the English throne after the battle of Bosworth Field!

D'Oriola's cellars are enormous for his level of production. They were built by his grandfather when the estate totalled some four hundred hectares and had a capacity of some twenty-five thousand hectolitres. Today d'Oriola's production is closer to three thousand hectolitres, half Côtes du Roussillon and half *vin de pays* sold as bag in box as house wine for restaurants. There is also a small amount of Rivesaltes and Muscat de Rivesaltes. There have been gentle changes in the wine making since my first visit here in 1987. D'Oriola experimented with *barriques* for the first time in 1997. Ten barrels gave him three thousand bottles, but he is not sure about the taste and rather feels that he is pandering to market demand. More positive quality improvements come from practices such as picking the different varieties separately and blending in a more rational way. Now that they have a Vaslin press, they sometimes include the pressed wine. Some Viognier has been planted, and also Rolle. Ten years ago the white Côtes du Roussillon was made solely from Macabeu, but now it is a blend of Grenache Blanc and Rolle. The red Côtes du Roussillon includes some sixty-year-old Carignan vinified by carbonic maceration, as well as Syrah and Grenache Noir and a drop of Mourvèdre. It was full and smoky.

DOMAINE SARDA-MALET, PERPIGNAN

Suzanne Malet is a friendly, vivacious woman who with her husband Max took over her father's estate, Domaine Sarda-Malet on the edge of Perpignan, in 1983. The first thing they did was to replant three-quarters of the vineyards, concentrating on Mourvèdre, Syrah, Viognier, Malvoisie, Roussanne and Marsanne. Sadly, her husband has since died and so Mme Malet now works with her son Jérôme. She has a total of forty-eight hectares, thirty-eight around the cellars and ten on terraces further south towards the Aspres. She explained how her father had been a marvellous gardener, but did not really have the culture of wine, whereas her husband had been passionate about wine. When they arrived here, there was not even any cooling equipment. They bought their first barrels in 1984, bottling the first white wine in 1985.

Mme Malet bubbled with enthusiasm as she gave us wines to taste. There were 1997s from barrel, a range of table wines and various experimental dessert wines, as well as some delicious Rivesaltes. Highlights included a white Côtes du Roussillon, Terroirs Mailloles, from a nearby vineyard that had already had a reputation for its wine in the seventeenth century. Made from equal parts of Roussanne and Marsanne, fermented in oak, half new and half one-year-old, with a further three months of ageing, it was obviously oaky on the nose and palate but had honeyed fruit and length too.

They made their first oaked white wine in 1988. There is also an unoaked white, from Grenache Blanc, Macabeu, Malvoisie, a tiny drop of Roussanne and Marsanne, with an attractive dry, herbal flavour. The red Terroirs Mailloles, half Syrah and half Mourvèdre, spends nineteen months in new oak. 1993 was the first vintage and we tasted the 1995, which was deep in colour, with a ripe, smoky nose and a firm structured palate, showing great promise. Côtes du Roussillon Réserve, from Syrah, Mourvèdre and Grenache Noir, with the exact proportions varying from year to year, is also aged in oak for twelve months, after which blending takes place. The 1994 had a solid, rounded nose, with good fruit and a structured palate with a long finish. A lighter Côtes du Roussillon comes from Grenache Noir with some Syrah, a little Carignan and, unusually, a little Macabeu, making a very drinkable wine with smoky fruit and soft tannins. Here the Macabeu is used to similar effect as Viognier in Côte Rôtie.

We concluded with various delicious Rivesaltes, as well as some dessert wines. L'Abandon is made from late-picked Malvoisie that has some botrytis. Yields are tiny and the fermentation is stopped when 80 gms/l of residual sugar remain. The 1995 was biscuity and honey, with a good acidity and length. The illogicality of French wine law forbids mention of the word 'wine' on the label, either as an appellation or plain *vin de table*, for which it must be under 14° (it is just over). Accordingly L'Abandon is described as the 'must of partially fermented grapes'. Another project is the same wine fermented in wood. We tried the 1997, which was still in barrel in June 1998, with rich apricot fruit combining with oak to fill out the palate. It was immensely appealing.

MAS ROUS, MONTESQUIEU

José Pujol, at Mas Rous outside the village of Montesquieu, took over his grandfather's property in 1979 when he was just eighteen. This is another fine example of the changes that come with the succession of generations. His grandfather, who had Carignan and a little Grenache Noir for red and Macabeu, Grenache Gris and Muscat for whites, had sold his wine to the local *négoce*. Pujol claims to be one of the first to plant Syrah in the department, and he waited until it was fully in production before bottling his first wines in 1985. Today he concentrates on red Côtes du Roussillon, as well as making a little Rivesaltes and Muscat de Rivesaltes, some white *vin de pays* and *vin de table* for a local clientele.

His Côtes du Roussillon comes in two styles; Traditionnelle from thirty per cent Syrah with Grenache Noir, Carignan and Mourvèdre, and Sélection with sixty per cent Syrah plus Grenache Noir, Carignan and Mourvèdre. Somewhat surprisingly, Grenache Noir does not ripen so well in the hills of the Albères: it dislikes the cool air currents from the mountains. Often Pujol finds that his Grenache Noir lacks colour, so he is gradually replacing it with Mourvèdre. That too can be quite problematic. He has it in two vineyards, one where the soil is dry and stony and the variety ripens well, with 35 hl/ha, giving good concentration of flavour, and another with alluvial soil where it simply does not ripen, even with the same low yield. Syrah does very well here. Pujol has also kept some sixty-year-old Carignan, which gives good tannin and colour, vinified either traditionally or by carbonic maceration.

His Côtes du Roussillon Sélection spends a few months in barrel, mostly second-hand ones from Château Grand Mayne in St Emilion. He may buy a few new barrels, but wants to avoid any excess of oak as he is looking for gentle oxygenation rather than a taste of oak. When it was a couple of years old, the 1996 Sélection had a hint of vanilla from the oak, with some soft tannin but not a lot of body. Pujol sees the Côtes du Roussillon as a young appellation that is still looking for its identity. He has had problems with the *labelle* tasting. One year two vats were rejected for being atypical: a blend of Mourvèdre and Carignan was deemed too *viandé* and an almost pure Syrah vat, partly made by carbonic maceration, was considered uncharacteristic of the appellation. They were declassified into *vin de table*. The problem lies with the people conducting the tastings – if they are not receptive to the developing styles of the appellation, innovative producers are likely to be discouraged.

It is inevitable that within the two appellations of Côtes du Roussillon and Côtes du Roussillon Villages, which had the quite large area of 7622 hectares in production in 1998, there will be variations in style. Soil changes from one hillside to another. The grape variety blends and the methods of vinification and *élevage* vary from one estate to another. Like most of the appellations of the south of France, this young appellation is still finding itself. Within the broad spectrum there is a diversity of style, ranging from wines that are rounded, fruity and eminently easy to drink within a year or so of the vintage, to others that are firm, structured and tannic, with considerable ageing potential. Both fit well with the appellation.

DOMAINE VAQUER, TRESSERRE

While some producers make both appellations and *vins de pays*, others for one reason or another refuse to conform to the appellations at all. There are two notable examples in Roussillon. First we visited the Vaquer family in the sleepy village of Tresserre, which does not even boast a café. In the mid-1980s Fernand Vaquer's wines were amongst the most expensive from the south of France on any restaurant wine list, and justifiably so, despite their humble category of *vin de table*, not even *vin de pays*. They were quite different from anything else in Roussillon, with an intriguing originality that defied definition. The estate is now run by Fernand's son Bernard and daughter-in-law Frédérique, who gave us a friendly tasting. She is a Burgundian, but from an agricultural rather than a viticultural part of the region, and she met her husband when they were both studying oenology at Dijon. He has had his own vineyards since 1984 and finally took over his father's vineyards in 1990. However, Fernand is still very much around. He is a chubby faced man with bushy eyebrows. On a previous visit, every question I asked about his wine making was countered with '*Ça dépend*'. This time I found myself engaged in a conversation about rugby, for which I am decidedly ill-equipped; it is Fernand's other enthusiasm, for he has been involved with the rugby club of Perpignan for over fifty years, first as a player and then as the manager. On this visit, Frédérique was much more forthcoming in her replies to our questions about the estate and generous with her tasting samples.

We began with a 1994 Blanc de Blancs, now labelled Vin de Pays Catalan, made from pure Macabeu that has been kept in vat. It was light golden in colour, with a firm but almost honeyed nose and a rounded mouthful of flavour, without obvious fruit but with considerable intensity and weight. Frédérique explained how people tend to pick Macabeu when it still too acid, while she prefers to wait until it reaches 13°. However, there is the snag that if there is too much rain, it can easily rot and they have to select the grapes in the vineyard. The wine making process is very straightforward, with a fermentation in vat at 18°C, no skin contact, no malolactic fermentation and no oak aging. The grapes, with an average yield of 30 hl/ha, come from vineyards around Tresserre, grown on soil that is a mixture of clay, pebbles and flint. She explained that there are years of honey and years of *garrigue*. I thought that the second wine, the 1985 that followed, had both, with a firm nutty nose, both honey and herbs on the palate, and good acidity and structure. With the 1980, a comparison with white Hermitage would not have been out of place, with lovely, lingering leafy, honey fruit. It was perfectly balanced and by no means tiring in flavour.

Next came the *rosé*, a non-vintage blend of 1995 and 1996. They like a mature flavour for their *rosé*, but do not want to challenge people's preconceived ideas about drinking only young *rosé*, hence the lack of vintage information. The colour, with an orange hue, certainly denoted a little age, and the palate had hints of orange fruit with a firm bite and a full-bodied finish. They now make two *cuvées* of red wine, the Bernard Vaquer label for early drinking and the Cuvée Fernand Vaquer that will age in bottle. The 1995 Bernard Vaquer, from a maximum of twenty per cent Syrah with some Carignan and Grenache Noir, had firm cherry, peppery fruit, but was also very supple, perfect for early consumption. The fermentation is short, a week at the most, with the wine kept in vat and bottled in June. The 1985 Cuvée Fernand Vaquer, from eighty per cent Carignan and twenty per cent Grenache Noir, is in quite a different class and demonstrates just how well Carignan can perform. The vines are an average of thirty years old. The wine enjoys a three-week *cuvaison*, with destalked grapes and regular *remontages*, and subsequently spends a couple of years in a cement vat. It has not been near a barrel. It was deliciously elegant while giving an impression of warmth and sunshine, with the spicy herbs of the *garrigue* and a firm backbone of tannin. Even more intriguing was the 1968, the first vintage that Fernand bottled. It almost defied description. The colour had evolved and on the nose there were hints of mushrooms, what the French call *sous bois* or undergrowth, as well meaty notes, and the palate was mature with vegetal hints and the warmth of scented herbs. It was almost sweet, with richness and elegance.

Rivesaltes and Muscat de Rivesaltes have also been added to the range, under the name of Bernard's sister Marie-José. They were good, but somehow seemed an anticlimax after the stature of the table wines. Bernard and Frédérique's little boy Julien is already taking an interest in the family activity. He was in the cellar one day and picked up a glass, swirled its contents round his mouth and then spat out, just as he had seen his parents do!

MAS CHICHET, ELNE

From Tresserre we headed towards Elne, a small town south of Perpignan which is worth a detour for its magnificent Romanesque cathedral. The cloisters are breathtaking, with a wealth of carvings on columns and capitals. And from there we went on to Mas Chichet, which lies on the plain not far from the sea. In 1987 I had met Paul Chichet, who had transformed the vineyards from Aramon and Carignan to Cabernet Sauvignon and Merlot. The estate is now run by his son Jacques, who like his father is not only a wine maker but also has a career in newspapers. He is friendly, enthusiastic and opinionated, with a keen sense of his objectives and a good sense of fun: '*Je ne suis pas sérieux*; I want to earn a living and enjoy myself.' Meetings with his oenologist usually happen on the golf course. 'That way I don't have to follow his advice.' We argued about *terroir*, with Chichet maintaining firmly that it was invented by the Bordelais and that it is the wine maker who counts. He has a point, for the soil at Mas Chichet is fertile alluvium with some clay and the area was once important for market gardening. In fact, the Chamber of Agriculture in Perpignan had declared Mas Chichet '*impropre à la vigne*', or unsuitable for viticulture. Fortunately, Jacques Chichet and his father were prepared to prove them wrong.

Chichet senior had planted a lot of different varieties in an attempt to see what did best. Subsequently his son has pulled up the Chardonnay, Viognier, Sauvignon and Malvoisie to concentrate on three wines, a *rosé* from Cabernet Franc, Cabernet Sauvignon, Merlot, Grenache Noir and Syrah, a pure Merlot, and a blend of two parts Cabernet Sauvignon to one part Cabernet Franc. As for white wine, Chichet would like to try some Gros and Petit Manseng which are not allowed in the department, but he has found a friendly nurseryman willing to sell him some 'Chardonnay'. His wines are labelled Vin de Pays Catalan and their typical property is above all, fruit. He makes wines to drink young, although they will age, as he demonstrated with a tasting of the 1989 Cabernet when it was nine years old, which was elegantly cedary. The pink is fresh and fruity, with hints of wild strawberries, ripe fruit and acidity. The Merlot, although quite light in colour, is plummy with a hint of green pepper. Vinification entails quite cool fermentation temperatures in order to avoid too much tannin extraction, and a daily *délestage* for about a week. The wine is kept in vat until bottling in January. In contrast, the Cabernet spends twelve months in wood and was more structured on the palate, with firm cassis fruit. Despite the oak ageing, fruit was still the dominant characteristic.

The wines are not typical of Roussillon, but they characterise the individuality of wine makers in the south of France who are intent on working out what does best for them, while proving the authorities wrong. We returned to Perpignan for a cheerful dinner of Catalan cooking – red peppers and Collioure anchovies followed by *fèves catalanes*, a copious broad bean stew containing not only beans, but black pudding, chorizo, onions and tomato, all washed down with a bottle of Collioure. Our conversation was interrupted by cheers from the adjacent bar, where the television was showing France winning her first football match in the 1998 world cup.

Key facts

Côtes du Roussillon: red, white and pink AC 1977 for 117 villages in southern half of department of Pyrénées-Orientales; 50 hl/ha.

Côtes du Roussillon Villages: red only, from twenty-five villages in northern part of department, plus Caramany, Latour-de-France, Lesquerde (1996) and Tautavel (1997); 45 hl/ha.

Grapes are always a blend of a minimum of three varieties:

RED AND PINK: Grenache Noir, Carignan, Cinsaut, Syrah, Mourvèdre, Lladoner Pelut.

WHITE: Macabeu, Grenache Blanc, Grenache Gris, Malvoisie (Torbato), Rolle, Roussanne, Marsanne.

A mixture of soils.

Average annual rainfall 500–600 mm; average annual sunshine 2350 hours.

Vintages

1995: A warm year, making for some rich, concentrated wines.

1996: Unseasonal summer rain caused rot, increased yields and diluted the crop.

1997: Another problematic year with rain and rot. Cooler weather made for lighter, fruitier wines.

1998: A year of drought, resulting in a small crop of well-structured wines with a good concentration of fruit and flavour.

1999: A severe hailstorm in April affected some growers; there was also some rain in August, but with a good end result.

Rivesaltes

Roussillon's vinous originality is really based on *vin doux naturel*. The largest appellation of this is Rivesaltes, which takes its name from a small town just north of Perpignan. The town's other claim to fame is as the birthplace of Marshal Joffre, who made his reputation as a general during the First World War and is commemorated by a tree-lined square containing his statue.

As mentioned in the previous chapter, the discovery of the process of making *vin doux naturel* is attributed to Arnau de Vilanova or Arnaud de Villeneuve, who was a doctor of medicine at the University of Montpellier at the end of the thirteenth century. He added *eau de vie* to some fermenting grape juice, with the result that the fermentation stopped. In 1299 he received a patent for his discovery from Jaume II, the king of Majorca and the ruler of Roussillon at that time. He is also credited with introducing the still into France from Moorish Spain.

The wines of Rivesaltes have a long history and have been appreciated over the centuries. Sadly, that is no longer the case today, as their reputation is for various reasons somewhat tarnished. The earliest documentary evidence comes from 1394 when, as the Vatican archives record, Benedict XIII, the last of the Avignon popes, purchased through his *collecteur* in the diocese of Elne in Roussillon six *charges* of Vin Muscat de Claira. Claira is a village close to Rivesaltes. Roger Dion discusses this evidence in his authoritative history of French wines, stating that evidently no wine of this type was made in the Rhône valley at that time and that hitherto this style of wine had come from Greece, Crete or, best of all, Cyprus.

During the fourteenth century, however, after Arnaud de Villeneuve's discovery, Grenache rather than Muscat had assumed prominence as the grape variety for *vin de liqueur* or fortified wine. The Spanish influence is very much in evidence here, for Grenache, or Garnacha, is Spanish in origin and Roussillon was under Aragonese rule – and remained so until the Treaty of the Pyrenees in 1659.

In a later century Voltaire sang the praises of Rivesaltes. He was the uncle of M. de la Houlière, governor of the fortress of Salses, the magnificent fortification, built by the Aragonese in the fifteenth century and subsequently modified by Vauban, that stands at a strategic point on the road between Perpignan and Narbonne. Voltaire wrote that 'he experienced great pleasure when he drank a cup of the Salses wine, although his frail human mechanism was unworthy of that liquor'. When travelling through France in 1787 and 1788, Arthur Young also enthused about Muscat de Rivesaltes. Rostand referred to it in Cyrano de Bergerac, while Grimaud de la Reynière, writing his *Journal des Gourmands et des Belles* in the early nineteenth century, considered it the best fortified wine of the kingdom.

All the nineteenth-century authorities rated it highly. Muscat seems to have superseded Grenache as the principal grape variety, for Jullien described it as the best Muscat, not just of France, but of the universe, when it came from a good vintage and had aged for ten years. James Busby visited Rivesaltes in 1833, during a journey to France and Spain to collect vine cuttings to take back to Australia, and described how the grapes were left to shrivel on the vines. Guyot rated the Muscats of Rivesaltes more highly than those of the Hérault, such as Frontignan and Mireval, describing how the wines were made from dried grapes with no addition of spirit. Cavoleau also enthused about the Muscat of Rivesaltes, explaining that there were three grape varieties, Muscat Alexandrin, Rond Blanc and, best of all, St Jacques, that were harvested in two pickings. The first grapes were left to dry until the others had been picked.

Rendu gave the most detailed appraisal, rating Rivesaltes as the most important wine of the department of the Pyrénées-Orientales, covering ten thousand five hundred hectares, of which half were on slopes. The grape varieties included Carignan, Grenache, Mataro, Picpoule Noir and Clairette. Carignan was planted in three-quarters of the vineyards and blended with Mataro, which gave body and colour, while Grenache contributed sweetness and vivacity. What he called 'vin de commerce' formed the principal income of Rivesaltes, while Salses and Baixas were also mentioned as other important parts of the vineyards. The wines with a universal reputation were Muscat, Macabeo, Malvoisie, Grenache and Rancio. The first four, of course, are grape varieties, while *rancio* describes a distinctive style of wine that has been oxidised during the ageing process. Rendu went on to explain how the Muscat was dried on the vine and in the first year was more like a syrup than a wine, and how the vinification for Macabeo and Malvoisie was slightly different, as they were not dried. He also mentioned the wines of Perpignan, including some excellent *rancios*.

In 1872 the so-called Arago Law recognised the existence of a style of wine making that was peculiar to Roussillon, and in 1898 the term *vin doux naturel* was given legal recognition. The impact of phylloxera was catastrophic, and although the vineyard was subsequently reconstituted, it never regained its former size. Nevertheless, fortified wines were popular enough in the pre-war years to make Rivesaltes one of the early appellations, in 1936, along with Banyuls and Maury, also Côtes d'Agly and Côtes de Haut-Roussillon, which was subsequently incorporated into Rivesaltes in 1972. A lesser appellation, Grand Roussillon, was created in 1938 as a secondary appellation for wine that was not of the quality of Rivesaltes, Maury or Banyuls. Today, although the appellation still exists on paper, it is rarely seen in the glass. Muscat de Rivesaltes, grouping the Muscats of Banyuls and Maury as well as Rivesaltes and covering ninety villages, became an appellation in 1956.

The present-day appellation of Rivesaltes covers a total of eighty-six villages, mostly in the Pyrénées-Orientales, but also in the Aude and extending into the appellations not only of Côtes du Roussillon and Côtes du Roussillon Villages, but also Fitou and Corbières. You will never find an estate that produces Rivesaltes alone. With the declining market for fortified wine, the parallel appellation for table wine is much more significant.

Muscat de Rivesaltes, unlike some of the other Muscat-based *vins doux naturel*, is made from two grape varieties, Muscat *à petits grains* and Muscat d'Alexandrie, which has larger berries and is therefore sometimes called Muscat *à gros grains*. It is less aromatic than the smaller-berried Muscat, giving a heavier palate and less finesse, and a more citrus lemony character, while Muscat *à petits grains* is more exotic in flavour, with more pineapple. The percentage of the two grape varieties may vary, depending entirely on the grower's whim. The appellation regulations do not impose any minimum or maximum percentages, so that some producers, such as Gérard Gauby, make their wine from only Muscat *à petits grains*.

There are various permutations in the vinification methods, which may include a period of skin contact or immediate pressing, and the fermentation is alway strictly controlled so as to retain the fresh fruit of the grape variety. *Mutage sur grains*, when the fermentation is stopped while the juice is still in contact with the grape skins, is less usual for Muscat de Rivesaltes. The occasional producer, such as Pierre Piquemal, is experimenting with Muscat aged in wood. After the first vintage in 1993, he realised that the wine needed to age for a couple of years before it became an enjoyable drink and his 1995 Coup de Foudre is rich and apricoty.

As for Rivesaltes itself, there are three or four main styles according to the colour, which is determined not only by the grape variety, but also by the length of ageing. Grenache Noir is the grape variety that is at the basis of all good Rivesaltes, along with Grenache Gris and Blanc, Macabeu and Malvoisie. In addition, ten per cent of complementary grape varieties such as Carignan, Syrah, and Cinsaut are permitted. Rivesaltes Ambré comes from the white grapes varieties, but develops an amber colour after a couple of years of oxidative ageing. Then there is Rivesaltes Rouge, made from at least seventy-five per cent of Grenache Noir, which is young and fresh, while Rivesaltes Tuilé, with a minimum fifty per cent of Grenache Noir, has developed an orange brick colour, with a minimum of two years in wood. Finally, Rivesaltes Hors d'Age denotes a minimum of five years *élevage*, but it could be much longer; this term can be attached to wines that are *ambré* or *tuilé*. In practice, these distinctions are very blurred and much depends on individual producers' preferences. The traditional taste of Rivesaltes is the *goût de rancio* of gentle oxidation. This may be achieved by keeping the wine in large oak casks for some years, as many as twenty, or the occasional producer may also keep the wine in large glass demijohns called *bonbonnes*, so that the wine is subjected to all extremes of temperature. They are not airtight, nor are they completely filled, so that the oxidation is even more marked. With time, the wine turns brown, and it begins to smell of rich Christmas cake and taste sweet and raisiny with a lovely long, nutty tang.

CAZES FRERES, RIVESALTES

Cazes Frères is a long-established family company in the centre of Rivesaltes. Contrary to the general trend, they find that their Rivesaltes is selling well, even to the point that they do not have enough stock to meet demand. After tasting their wines, I could quite appreciate why. They have ignored the fashion for producing very young wine, with the exception of Muscat de Rivesaltes. For them, Rivesaltes must be aged, for that is a tradition of Rivesaltes and one they have always maintained. They have some magnificent old barrels that were purchased in 1911 and were not even new then. The cellar exudes an intoxicating aroma of fruitcake, prunes and liquorice, rather like the wine.

They see Rivesaltes as being at the top of their quality range, not somewhere near the bottom. First we tried a 1988 Rivesaltes Ambré that was bottled in 1996 after ageing in large oak *foudres* varying in size from 50 to 300 hectolitres. As they were never completely full, the wine was always in contact with air, so that the Grenache Blanc turned brown with age, developing a lovely herbal, honeyed flavour with a note of oxidation and a long finish. 1984 Rivesaltes Tuilé, from Grenache Noir, has spent twelve years in *foudres* and lost its original deep red colour. It is sweet and rich with a firm finish. The 1993 vintage, which is bottled young and had therefore aged for five years in bottle, was not dissimilar to ruby port, with herbs and red fruit, but more spirity than the oak-aged wines. The concept of a vintage is an attempt to make Rivesaltes more fashionable and more approachable.

Best of all was the 1975 Cuvée Aimé Cazes, from ninety per cent Grenache Blanc and ten per cent Muscat, which had spent twenty years in *foudres*. Aimé Cazes was the son of the founder of the company, which is now in its fourth generation, and in 1998 he was still alive and very much taking an interest in things at the age of ninety-seven. His wine was firm and nutty with layers of flavour, and at £17 a bottle, grossly under-priced. This is one of the great bargains of the south. Where else could you find a twenty-year-old wine for less than £20?

Muscat de Rivesaltes from Cazes has some opulent Muscat perfume, honeyed oranges and well-integrated spirit. Bruno Cazes explained that it is the combination of three vinification processes. Forty per cent is pressed immediately, fermented and muted while another forty per cent undergoes skin contact for twelve hours and is then pressed; the remaining twenty per cent is treated like a red wine, in that the skins and juice are fermented together so that *mutage* takes place *sur grains*. This process makes for an enormous amount of extract and is much too powerful on its own, so it is blended with the other two components before the wine is given six months of ageing on the fine lees. The final wine has 15° with 115 gms/l of residual sugar.

DOMAINE DES SCHISTES, ESTAGEL

Jacques Sire at Domaine des Schistes in the village of Estagel is another producer who takes his Rivesaltes seriously, for it represents a third of his production. He made a vintage Rivesaltes for the first time in 1996 and explained how the Grenache Noir was macerated with the alcohol for three weeks. As alcohol dissolves the colour in the grape skins, it is not added all at once, but gradually over the day. The wine had a wonderfully ripe cherry flavour, with some spice and tannins and a streak of spirit. Usually his Rivesaltes is more oxidative in character, and he is wondering about giving it some barrel instead of bottle ageing. This style of Rivesaltes may attract new young customers. Traditional Rivesaltes requires oxidation, so Sire gives his a couple of years in vats that are never completely full and then ages the wine in 600-litre barrels, some older than others. He runs off one third for bottling after eight years and tops up the barrels with younger wine, making for a *solera* of sorts. The taste is dry, nutty and very appealing.

DOMAINE SARDA-MALET, PERPIGNAN

Suzanne Malet from Domaine Sarda-Malet, just outside Perpignan, also produces some delicious Rivesaltes, 6 Ans d'Age. The ageing requirements of Rivesaltes seem very flexible, depending on the producer's whim. Hers was amber in colour, with a honeyed, nutty nose and biscuity fruit with hints of marmalade. She is justifiably proud of her wine – but it was her father who, on a much earlier visit to Rivesaltes, invited me for an aperitif and then offered me whisky or Martini, rather than one of the delicious Rivesaltes that we had just been tasting. He was delighted that I insisted on drinking his twenty-year-old Rivesaltes, but his attitude was typical of the region. Rivesaltes has fallen so far from favour that most producers have lost their pride in their product. Efforts to promote the wine have failed, even though overall quality has improved. Much greater attention is now paid to temperature control; in the past, if the fermentation stuck because it was too hot, this was not considered a problem as the fermentation had to be stopped anyway. Muscat de Rivesaltes was often a deep golden maderised colour with a taste of caramel, while today it is almost invariably opulently redolent of the fresh flavour of the grape variety.

THE MARKET FOR RIVESALTES

It is the co-operatives that tend to paint a gloomier picture of the Rivesaltes market. They have stock to sell, and many of them have reduced prices to a derisory level. It is possible to find Rivesaltes for as little as FF 30 a bottle, and even the better Rivesaltes are grossly under-priced. The co-operative in Rivesaltes is currently selling a wine labelled Hors d'Age that is twenty years old. It is a blend of Grenache, Macabeu and Muscat, aged in both vat and wood of varying sizes. The colour is tawny and the wine has dry nutty flavours with length and elegance; it costs just FF 70 a bottle. No one is quite sure of what the solution to the problem is. Rivesaltes has fallen from fashion, and even people who do like it drink it in very small quantities.

At Pézilla-la-Rivière they too described Rivesaltes as being in a state of ill health and said that they simply do not know what to do about it. Traditionally, Rivesaltes has been sold under a brand name, so that people were loyal to a brand without really knowing that they were drinking Rivesaltes. The brand name was in large letters and the word Rivesaltes on the label was barely legible; it was just a cheap aperitif, of which consumption is now falling. Younger drinkers prefer Muscat, while old Rivesaltes demands a certain connoisseurship that they may not have – the producers of Rivesaltes themselves more often than not drink pastis!

Attempts have been made to regulate the market, but it is often a matter of politics rather than technique. The production of some of the Rivesaltes vineyards is blocked, so that it becomes Côtes du

Roussillon or *vin de pays*. For instance, if you produce 40 hl/ha of Muscat, you are only allowed to make Muscat de Rivesaltes out of 30 hectolitres and the balance must be turned into a *vin de pays* as Muscat Sec, for which there is a more buoyant demand. At the same time, this remedy creates a somewhat artificial situation of supply and demand.

Some success has come from the development of the vintage wines. The co-operative at Baixas first made this style of young Grenache Noir that spent just twelve months in vat in 1994, and they find that sales are beginning to grow, albeit slowly. Compared with port, it is lower in alcohol – 17° versus 20° – and has some attractive berry fruit. In 1986 I was told that Rivesaltes suffered from the lack of a pacemaker and the same is still true today. There are five or six hundred producers of Rivesaltes, including several co-operatives and *négociants* as well as individual estates, but no collective will. Rivesaltes, especially the cheaper sort, is poorly presented, while in sharp contrast France is one of the biggest consumers of port as an aperitif, when a vintage Rivesaltes would be equally suitable.

By comparison, the two smaller appellations of Maury and Banyuls seem much more flourishing.

Fortunately, Grenache Noir can equally well be used for Côtes du Roussillon as for Rivesaltes, and so with the lack of demand for the latter, production of the table wine has increased. However, although Rivesaltes can be made from Grenache Noir alone, Côtes du Roussillon requires three grape varieties, and a co-operative member must have three varieties in his vineyard to enable his Grenache Noir to be used for table wine. None the less, in the last twenty years there has been a distinct shift towards Côtes du Roussillon and away from Rivesaltes. Twenty years ago three-quarters of the vineyards of Roussillon produced Rivesaltes, while today the converse is true. Good Rivesaltes remains a wonderfully appealing drink, but it will need drastic measures, such as a severe reduction of the appellation, for it to recover the reputation it had in earlier centuries.

Key facts

Rivesaltes: AC 1936; eighty-six villages in Pyrénées-Orientales and Aude.

Grenache Noir, Gris and Blanc, Macabeu, Malvoisie; ten per cent of Carignan, Cinsaut and Syrah also allowed.

Mutage with neutral grape brandy accounts for five to ten per cent of the volume, giving a minimum alcohol level of 15°.

Rivesaltes Ambré: white varieties; two years' ageing.

Rivesaltes Rouge: seventy-five per cent Grenache Noir.

Rivesaltes Tuilé: minimum fifty per cent Grenache Noir; two years minimum in wood.

Rivesaltes Hors d'Age: minimum five years *élevage* in wood; can be Tuilé or Ambré.

Muscat de Rivesaltes: AC 1956; ninety villages.

Muscat d'Alexandrie and Muscat *à petits grains*

Maury

The appellation of Maury forms a small enclave within the larger appellation of Rivesaltes, while for table wine Maury is one of the villages of Côtes du Roussillon Villages. It lies in the valley of the Agly, where apart from vines nothing grows except a few almonds and olive trees. To distinguish it from Rivesaltes, the area of the appellation for the *vin doux naturel* is determined by schist. The vineyards of Maury are planted on an island of schist some seventeen kilometres by three in the midst of the sea of limestone and clay that make up Rivesaltes. The area of the appellation was slightly modified in 1995 with the elimination of some vineyards not planted on schist, so that it presents a homogeneous entity. Grenache Noir is the principal grape variety, and you may also find Grenache Gris and Blanc, as well as Carignan, Muscat *à petits grains* and Macabeu. It is above all low-yielding Grenache Noir that gives Maury its typicity and character.

MAS AMIEL

The appellation totals some seventeen hundred hectares, of which the village co-operative is responsible for eighty-five per cent. In addition there are about ten independent producers, of whom the biggest and most successful is undoubtedly Mas Amiel. Some only sell their wine *en vrac*, while others have a small production of bottled wine. Since a recent purchase of twenty-three hectares, Mas Amiel now totals 155 hectares, seventy-five of which are on the slopes behind the cellars at an altitude of 120–150 metres while the remaining eighty are a little further north towards the village of Tautavel.

The story goes that a certain Raymond Amiel won the title deeds of the property from the bishop of Perpignan at a game of cards back in 1816, when the estate consisted of some eighty hectares, mainly of *garrigue*-covered hillsides and some vineyards. At that time the property was mainly devoted to rearing rabbits that were sold at Perpignan market. The vineyards were replanted with grafted vines in 1894, after the phylloxera crisis, by the son of the card player and an associate, a *négociant* named Camille Gouzy, and at the same time they built the cellar. Gouzy was bankrupted by the viticultural crisis of 1907 and died ruined in 1910, so that Amiel was forced to mortgage the estate, which was then bought by Charles Dupuy. His son Jean did much to develop the wines, breaking a contract with Violet, a producer of Byrrh, in order to produce his own *vin doux naturel*, which he first bottled in 1924, in bottles displaying a stylish Art Deco label.

Charles Dupuy, Jean's son, died in 1997, and at the time of my visit there were rumours that the estate was for sale, and indeed it was bought by a M. Olivier Decelle in the autumn of 1999. Jérémie Gaïk, who had been the enterprising manager of the property since 1987 and had successfully developed the range of *vins doux naturel*, has also departed for pastures new since my visit in 1998. For the moment Mas Amiel produces only fortified wine, but Syrah and Mourvèdre have been planted with a view to producing some table wine too.

The most distinctive feature of Mas Amiel is the large *parc de bonbonnes*, the seventy-litre glass demijohns that have been abandoned by most other producers of *vin doux*. They have a total capacity of 2000 hectolitres and all the traditional Maury is aged for twelve months in these demijohns, so that it is exposed to the full range of seasonal changes. Otherwise the basic vinification process is the same as for any other *vin doux*. The traditional wines also spend several years in enormous 250 hectolitre *foudres*, of which they have seventeen, dating back to 1820. They are topped up every so often to compensate for the evaporation, or 'angels' share', but are never completely full, so that the oxidation process continues.

The Cuvée Spéciale undergoes ten years of ageing, one in *bonbonnes* and nine in cask. It is a blend of ninety per cent Grenache Noir with a little Macabeu and Carignan, and has a warm, nutty nose and palate with a long dry finish. The fifteen-year-old Maury spends fourteen years in cask and has a very intense flavour, maybe of caramelised prunes, with considerable intensity and the long, sweet finish of dried fruit. These are the traditional styles that Mas Amiel was making fifteen years ago, and a twenty-year-old wine, which spent nineteen years in wood, was produced for the millennium.

Under Gaïk's guidance and questioning attitude, Mas Amiel have developed other wines, looking at the potential and diversity of Grenache Noir. Since 1988 they have been studying the characteristics of their different vineyards, and now make a vintage wine, partly for its young sweet fruit and partly to see how Grenache Noir will age in bottle. The pure Grenache Noir is given a thirty-day maceration at fermentation and the wine is bottled in the May or June following the vintage. The 1996 had some wonderful ripe cherry fruit and was very rich and concentrated, but still a little spirity on the finish. It is either a wine to drink in its youth or to mature like a vintage port.

Mas Amiel began working with *barriques* in 1989, from a desire to see just what small barrels will bring, but only in the best years, such as 1989, 1991, 1993 and 1996, and not with new wood, but with *barriques* of two or three wines. Again, the wine is given a thirty-day maceration and always muted in contact with the grape skins, which makes for more concentration and weight. Ageing in small barrels was a new experience for them, and in the 1989 which we tasted, the oak seemed well integrated, with a concentrated flavour, but with less obvious red fruit, balanced with body and some tannin.

Mas Amiel have also been exploring late harvest wines since 1993, leaving the grapes on the vines until November or December so that they are truly *passerillés* and dehydrated by the autumn winds. The grapes need to be destalked by hand. The 1996 was given a two-week pre-fermentation maceration at a cool temperature, in an attempt to extract the maximum from the grapes, of which the yield is only six or seven hl/ha. Fermentation lasts a month, then a small proportion of alcohol is added and the wine is put into barrel – either new or one or two wines old – for a few months so that it is intense and chocolatey, in fact so ripe and unctuous that you could almost stand a teaspoon in it. This is handcrafted wine making, with a production of 2000 bottles at the most. With the 1998 vintage they planned to try the same pre-fermentation maceration on grapes that had not been late harvested, for they found that it added so much colour and body.

Another experiment, which produced just 200 bottles in 1995, comes from grapes picked at the beginning of the harvest and left to dry for more than a year in small boxes, outside in the wind and sunshine. If rain threatens, which it rarely does in the Agly valley, the boxes are brought inside. This could be a variation of the Italian technique of *passito* and would only be possible in a climate where wind is such a significant factor. The juice was fermented in vat, but not muted, so that the fermentation stops of its own accord in April or May. Gaïk made a comparison with the Essencia of Tokay. Certainly the taste was very intense, honeyed and rich, with both sweetness and balancing acidity, an intriguing flavour pushing the boundaries of Grenache Noir to the limits.

One of the problems with wines like Maury is when to drink it. The vintage wines, with their accessible ripe fruit, are aimed at younger consumers in an attempt to upset one of the preconceived attitudes about *vins doux naturels* in France, that they are an older person's drink. 'My grandfather liked it' is a not uncommon reaction. Maybe the vintage wines will effect a change in attitude. Gaïk has also been working with the Salon du Chocolat, which is an annual event in Paris. If you think a wine fair may have the potential for an orgy, it is apparently nothing beside the excesses of chocolate. And certainly some of the richer Maury would marry well with chocolate desserts, while the traditional *rancio* styles make a delicious after dinner drink, either on their own or with a bowl of walnuts.

VIGNERONS DE MAURY

The rather unprepossessing village of Maury is dominated by large co-operative buildings at either end, each in the traditional architectural style of co-operatives. This is the oldest village co-operative of the Pyrénées-Orientales, founded in 1910, after the agricultural problems of 1907, and now going by the name of Vignerons de Maury following the inclusion of two other cellars. The co-operative was a member of the Vignerons Val d'Orbieu but left at the end of 1999, as they felt that there was a divergence in their respective aims. The Vignerons Val d'Orbieu concentrate on table wines, not on *vins doux naturels*, so now the Vignerons de Maury are going it alone, with the creation of their own marketing arm, Maury Diffusion. The success of the entire appellation is at stake in this move, as the co-operative accounts for eighty-five per cent of it. Two hundred and fifty members cultivate eighteen hundred hectares of vines, of which 1472 are within the appellation of Maury. The rest produce Côtes du Roussillon Village and Muscat de Rivesaltes, as well as *vins de pays*.

For the assistant director of the co-operative, Patrick Dheilly-Vica, the typicity of Maury comes from a long maceration, which could last until Christmas. Vignerons de Maury want as much colour as possible and plenty of extract in their wines, which is achieved by numerous *remontages*, as well as *mutage sur grains*, which they consider gives much better results than *mutage sur jus* without the grape skins. You can taste the difference between the two, even when the wine is only six months old and still in vat. A *mutage sur jus* was pure fruit, while a long maceration with *mutage sur grains* gave much more body and substance, with more liquorice fruit.

The co-operative is well equipped with barrels of varying sizes – *foudres*, *demi-muids* and *barriques* – but does not have the glass *bonbonnes* of Mas Amiel. They consider that this technique gives the wine too much of a thermic shock, whereas wood provides a gentle oxidation. There is also a trend to age wine in bottle, making a vintage wine rather than a blend of vintages from an imitation *solera* system. Each year the co-operative chooses its best vat, which is labelled Maury Sélection. The 1997 Sélection Cabiron, named after a nearby *lieu dit*, had some concentrated flavours of prunes and liquorice and could certainly age awhile, not unlike a good ruby port.

Maury Doré, which comes mainly from Macabeu with a little Grenache Blanc, is rather soft and biscuity and generally lacking in definition. More interesting are the older wines, a 6 Ans d'Age with prunes and liquorice, a 1989 Vieille Réserve with dry, nutty fruit, and best of all the 1981 Chabert de Barbera, named after the last defender of the nearby castle of Quéribus, which was concentrated and intense, but with the same nutty flavours that characterise mature Maury.

DOMAINE LA COUME DU ROY

There are the occasional growers' signs in the village, advertising their wines. I stopped at Maurydoré, where Mme Corrado, an exotic Martiniquaise, gave me a tasting. She explained that the estate belongs to Mme Paule de Voluntat, a member of the Estève family which has owned the property since 1856. In fact, Maurydoré is somewhat unfortunate as a brand name. It was thought up by a great-grandfather before the reputation of the *doré* or white style of Maury had been tarnished. There are twenty-five hectares of vines, mainly Grenache Noir as well as a little Macabeu and Muscat, and they have also made a Côtes du Roussillon for the last three or four years. The cellars are delightfully higgledy-piggledy, with barrels and *foudres* of varying shapes and sizes, from sixty hectolitres down to just forty litres, and two old basket presses that can takes as long as two days to press a load of grapes. We compared two wines from the 1995 vintage: a traditional wine that was muted *sur jus*, making a wine that is lighter, fruitier and quicker to develop, and another one from the same vintage muted *sur grains*, which was more concentrated and youthful with some spicy fruit. The 1977 Cuvée Désiré Estève, which has spent twenty years in *foudres*, was for my taste buds the epitome of mature Maury, an amber colour with a dry walnut nose and wonderful long, walnut-flavoured palate. They also have stocks of even older wines, which I tasted at the Salon des Caves Particulières in Paris. This is a splendid wine fair that takes place in Paris in early December and in other cities in France at other times of the year, allowing members of the public the opportunity to make contact with private producers from all over the country. On the Maurydoré stand they were offering wines from 1925, 1939 and, best of all, 1948; this would have been difficult to distinguish from an oloroso sherry, with its rich but dry nutty flavours and long, lingering finish.

DOMAINE LA PLEIADE

The other serious producer of Maury is Jacques Delcours at Domaine la Pléiade. He was director of the co-operative for fifteen years and left to create an estate of his own based on his wife's four hectares. He now has thirteen hectares, mainly of Maury, but also makes a little Côtes du Roussillon Villages. We talked and tasted. I thought it courageous to start something new. He suggested that suicidal might be a more appropriate adjective, but said that he had wanted to leave something for his children. He is very competent and capable, with a clear sense of purpose, a thoughtful man with focused ideas about his appellation. He is building a cellar that, at the time of my visit, had a roof and some vats but no walls, and his estate is not yet sign-posted. My instructions were to take a dirt track under the railway line and follow the telegraph poles.

Delcours' Côtes du Roussillon Villages comes mainly from Carignan vines that are at least fifty years old, but with some Mourvèdre and Syrah too, making a rounded, fruity wine. Next came the vintage wines, which could certainly be seen as Maury's answer to young port. A 1996 was still structured and tannic, needing bottle age; the 1995 was redolent of ripe plums, while a 1994, matured in wood rather than vat, was developing flavours of nuts and prunes. The Hors d'Age, a category for which there are no specific regulations, currently comes mainly from the 1993 vintage. It had been aged in wood for about five years and was firmly nutty in flavour.

Delcours is very much aware of the problems that beset Maury. The appellation is relatively unknown and risks being affected by the general stagnation of the *vin doux naturel* market, and particularly of Rivesaltes. Some of these problems go back to the 1960s, when the French government became concerned about alcoholism in France and increased the taxes on aperitifs like Dubonnet and Byrrh, for which most of the production from the vineyards in this part of France had been destined. As the demand for those drinks fell, people turned to *vin doux naturel* instead, and in particular to Rivesaltes, which continued to enjoy a lower tax rate. Unfortunately more Grenache Blanc and Grenache Gris was planted than Grenache Noir, indisputably the grape variety that makes the most distinctive *vin doux naturel*, and with the easy market, no effort was made to improve the quality. 'And now, with the exception of Muscat, we are paying the price.' That would be sad. Maury is undoubtedly a distinctive drink, at its best in a 1948 Maurydoré or a fifteen-year-old Mas Amiel, providing an original alternative to port or sherry. It deserves more than just a local reputation.

Key facts

AC 1936; seventeen hundred hectares in one village; all on schist; 30 hl/ha.

Grenache Noir is the main grape variety, plus Grenache Gris and Blanc, also Macabeu, Malvoisie, plus Muscat d'Alexandrie and Muscat *à petits grains* for Muscat de Rivesaltes, and Carignan, Cinsaut and Syrah for table wine.

Similar variations in style to Rivesaltes, ranging from young red, with a vintage to Hors d'Age, with *mutage sur grains* or *sur jus*.

15–18°; minimum of twenty-four months' ageing.

Banyuls and Collioure

Banyuls is the first wine of France, for a few kilometres south, beyond Cerbère, you cross the Spanish border at the unprepossessing town of Portbou. The road south of Argelès-sur-Mer runs along the Côte Vermeille through the small towns of Collioure and Port-Vendres, hugging the coast and offering dramatic views at every stomach-churning hairpin bend. There are the remains of old watchtowers, part of the warning system of beacons to raise the alarm against invaders. The Tour Madeloc dominates the skyline above Collioure, and from Cap Réderis you can enjoy a magnificent panorama of the coastline on a clear day. Here the Albères, the foothills of the Pyrenees, fall into the Mediterranean and the vineyards of Banyuls and Collioure rise on steep terraces. The winds can blow hard and the vines cling tenaciously to the hillsides.

Banyuls is a cheerful seaside resort and fishing port, while the little town of Collioure possesses more intrinsic charm. Painters, notably Matisse and Derain, have worked here and the tradition has lasted, with artists' studios in the attractive old quarter. The walls of the restaurant, Les Templiers, are covered with paintings, as the Pous family has continued the custom of accepting canvases as payment for restaurant bills. There is a lively Sunday market with local produce, including the anchovies for which Collioure is known and which are an essential part of Catalan cooking, usually allied with red peppers to make a delicious *salade catalane*. The tradition of the preparation of anchovies in Collioure goes back to the days when there was no tax on salt and people were both fishermen and wine growers. The seafront is dominated by the imposing Château Royal, summer residence of the kings of Majorca before Collioure became part of the kingdom of Aragon. Vauban added further fortifications after the treaty of the Pyrenees. There is also an imposing fortified church and a tiny chapel on a small promontory.

The wines of Banyuls and Collioure come from the same vineyards, for the two appellations cover the four villages of Banyuls-sur-Mer, Collioure, Port-Vendres and Cerbère. The distinction is partly one of grape varieties, but mainly one of vinification. Banyuls is a *vin doux naturel* while Collioure is an unfortified table wine. Banyuls was one of the first appellations to be created, as early as 1936, while Collioure came much later, the red wine in 1971 and the pink as recently as 1990. Until the creation of the appellation, Collioure was often called Banyuls Sec, and even today, when you taste with a grower, they tend to make the distinction between wines that are *sec* or *doux*, in other words, table or fortified wines. In the nineteenth century the two names were almost interchangeable, for both Banyuls and Collioure were praised as smooth rich wines.

In the Middle Ages, when Banyuls was made by the Knights Templar, who had settled in the area and adopted the methods of Arnaud de Villeneuve, it was enjoyed at the Aragonese court. After that, it remained in something of a vinous backwater, receiving the occasional passing mention from the nineteenth-century authorities. Jullien cited Banyuls, Collioure and Port-Vendres in the second category of his classification of red wines, while Guyot described Banyuls as an exceptional wine and very much sought after. It was made solely from Grenache Noir, pressed immediately and muted with spirit. Cavoleau enthused about the good wines made from Grenache Noir in Banyuls, Collioure and Port-Vendres, which at eight to ten years were velvety and rich but delicate and very agreeable. The best wines were very dark in colour and could be very sweet. Rendu said of the wines of Collioure that they had a beautiful colour and body and a lot of richness, that they held the balance between fortified and dry wines and that when they aged, they acquired finesse and a pronounced bouquet. They should not be bottled for ten years, by which time they should have taken on a *rancio* character.

In the twentieth century Banyuls and Collioure remained largely ignored outside their own region, though there are now signs that things may be slowly changing. The production of both wines is dominated by a group of five co-operatives, the Groupement Interproducteurs du Cru Banyuls, created in 1950 in an attempt to improve the market demand for Banyuls and to protect prices. There are two other co-operatives, those of Collioure and Cave l'Etoile, and together these co-operatives account for at least seventy per cent of the production of Banyuls. Today, however, their position is being challenged by a growing number of independent producers; there are now fifteen private estates.

The total area of the two appellations is 1930 hectares, which could be increased only with difficulty. The Spanish frontier limits the appellation to the south. The northern edge is where the hills fall into the plain and the schist soil ends, while to the west there are mountains and to the east lies the Mediterranean. On the coast some vineyards have been lost to building land. You can still find traces of overgrown terraces at 600 metres, whereas today the vines only go up as far as 400 metres. There are also olive and almond trees, but little else apart from vines will survive on this rough terrain.

Bernard Saperas of Domaine Vial-Magnères took us for a walk through his vineyards. Some of the vines go right down to the sea while others may be fifteen kilometres away, so there is a significant difference in the degree of maritime influence. The dry stone walls retain the soil and prevent erosion. No one quite knows when they were first constructed, but they have always been an essential part of the landscape of Banyuls. The soil is schist through which the roots of the vines filter to find water, and drainage systems have been constructed to prevent damage from the occasionally excessive rainfall. The average annual rainfall is about 900 mm. Normally the summers are very dry, with maybe six months without rain, so that cactus grows well there. When the rain does come, it is often at the autumn equinox, right in the middle of the harvest. That is what decides the quality of the vintage, and the differences can be very marked. It is the sea and the mountains that determine the character of Banyuls and Collioure, with a multiplicity of sites, *terroirs* and grape varieties.

All the vines are *gobelet* or bush vines except for Syrah, which is trained on wires because its shoots are too fragile for the strong winds. Vines are replaced as they die. A rootstock is planted and the vine grafted two years later. They use weedkiller, as it is very difficult to till the vines and mechanisation is well nigh impossible on such narrow terraces. Outside Collioure we watched a helicopter spraying a hillside of vines against oidium. *Flavescence dorée* is another problem treated systematically by helicopter spraying; just once a year in mid-June, but this presents a dilemma for those who would like to practise organic viticulture. Nonetheless there are wild flowers, what the French call *immortelles* and the English more prosaically curry plant, giving out their strong odour in the warm sunshine. Originally donkeys were used for the harvest. Each beast could carry 160 kilos of grapes and earlier this century 150 donkeys worked in the vineyards of Banyuls during the vintage. People used to carry the sulphur sprays on their backs. Yields are low: thirty and forty hectolitres per hectare are allowed for Banyuls and Collioure respectively, but in reality these levels are never achieved.

Grenache Noir is the key grape variety of both Banyuls and Collioure. For Banyuls it is often blended with Grenache Gris and Grenache Blanc, and traditionally all three varieties were grown mixed up together in the same vineyard. Carignan and Syrah are also allowed, but are more likely to be used for Collioure, as are Mourvèdre and Counoise. Whereas the vinification process for Collioure is very much like that of any classic red wine, Banyuls entails the addition of alcohol at a key moment during fermentation, which has the effect of stopping the fermentation and retaining some natural sweetness. For most Banyuls this is done on the grape skins, so that a percentage of alcohol is absorbed by the skins, making for a much longer-lived and more substantial wine. If you simply mute the juice, the result is more like a pink wine than a serious red wine.

The other vital element in the character of Banyuls is the ageing in an oxidative environment so that the wine takes on a *rancio* flavour. Banyuls is very resistant to the extremes of the Mediterranean climate, and in particular to the heat of summer. Barrels were often left under the roof so that they were subjected to both the summer and winter extremes of temperature. One producer even keeps wine outside in large glass *bonbonnes*, so that it acquires the distinctive *rancio* taste of nutty, oxidised fruit. In contrast, however, a style called Rimage has recently been developed with the aim of appealing to modern tastes. *Rime* is the Catalan for grape, so Rimage literally means 'the age of the grape'; in other words, a vintage wine, whereas traditional Banyuls is a blend of vintages. Rimage is designed for early drinking, so that the nearest taste comparison is young ruby port.

DOMAINE DU MAS BLANC

The most traditional estate of Banyuls is Domaine du Mas Blanc. It was Dr André Parcé who did most to create the appellation of Collioure and is generally considered to be the father of the appellation. The estate is now run by his son, Jean-Michel, who has a somewhat ambivalent attitude tó the more modern developments in Banyuls and Collioure. He talked of his father's work in retaining Counoise in the area, explaining how people replanted very quickly after phylloxera. However, not every grape variety adapted well to grafting and some disappeared – Counoise was almost one of these. It provides finesse and acidity, which can be highly desirable, but is even more temperamental than Mourvèdre. Parcé is fervently against what he calls *'vin technique'* and *'la parfumerie'*. He views the trend for early-drinking vintage wines, or Rimage, with scepticism, pointing out that *rimages* have always existed, but were not sold as such. 'In Banyuls there is the *avant garde*, but fortunately there is also the old guard.'

Altogether Parcé has twenty-one hectares and makes three different Collioure, named after the various vineyards, as well as several different Banyuls. First we tasted the Collioure. The 1996 Cosperons-Levant is a blend of sixty per cent Syrah, thirty per cent Mourvèdre and ten per cent Counoise, which are all destalked and then fermented together, with a twice-daily mechanical *pigeage* over the fifteen-day period of maceration. These are the oldest vines on the estate, from a vineyard planted on clay and schist, even including some thirty-year-old Mourvèdre. The success of Mourvèdre depends on where it is planted, for it requires deep cool soil, otherwise the flavour is too hard. The wine spends twelve months in old barrels and the taste is elegant and full of ripe cherries, with great finesse.

Le Clos du Moulin, from a two-hectare vineyard on the bank of the river Baillaury where the soil is mainly gravel, consists of eighty per cent Mourvèdre and twenty per cent Counoise, given twelve months in wood. It was more solid and tannic, with good fruit. Parcé buys second-hand barrels from some of the best addresses in Bordeaux, which he uses for about six years. The final Collioure, Les Junquets, is mainly Syrah with ten per cent of white grapes, in the way of Côte Rôtie, but Marsanne and Roussanne rather than Viognier. Sadly, production is tiny and we were unable to taste it.

Parcé dislikes Collioure *rosé*, but would be in favour of an appellation for white Collioure. However, he is critical of the INAO, accusing them of rushing things; they had promised the appellation for 2000, when there was nothing concrete on which to build it. There is no tradition for dry white wine in the area, and you cannot create an appellation from the single grape variety, Grenache Blanc, that has always been in the vineyards. They need more experience of Marsanne, Roussanne and Rolle, the other varieties being considered for Collioure Blanc.

Then we moved on to a selection of his extensive range of Banyuls. First was 1996 La Coume, which accounts for about a quarter of his production of Banyuls. It is mainly from Grenache Noir, as are all good Banyuls, but with tiny drops of Carignan, Syrah, Mourvèdre and Grenache Gris, and it spends eighteen months in *foudres*. There was a ripe taste of red fruit and bitter chocolate with a concentration of sugar and alcohol not unlike young vintage port, and it will age in just the same way. However, the big difference between port and Banyuls is that the latter requires much less alcohol – only five to ten per cent of the total volume – and the grapes are then left to macerate in the alcohol, making a final level of about 17° or 18°, compared to 20° for most port.

The 1981 Cuvée de St Martin, from eighty per cent Grenache Noir with some Carignan and Grenache Gris, had undergone the traditional oxidative ageing in *foudres* for about fifteen years before bottling in 1996. It was deep in colour, with an orange rim, and had a wonderful aroma of prunes. There were prunes on the palate too and a long sweet finish. The Hors d'Age is aged in a *solera* that Parcé's grandfather began in 1955. Some wine is run off every three years and the barrels are kept topped up in a semi-oxidative way. The flavour is very rounded, harmonious and mellow.

DOMAINE LA RECTORIE

Marc Parcé from Domaine la Rectorie is a very distant relation of Jean-Michel Parcé. Their great-grandfathers were brothers, but then Parcé is a very common name in Banyuls. Marc Parcé has the perceptive view of his appellation that comes with experience in another field that has broadened his horizons. He worked with autistic children in Paris and came back to the south in 1976, but not with the intention of running the family vineyard. It was only when a job offer failed to materialise that he enrolled for agricultural college, and twenty-odd years on, he is firmly committed to his vineyards and his appellation. This does not stop him from searching, questioning and criticising, for he is a thoughtful man with provocative ideas.

Parcé has twenty-four hectares of vines, divided up into some thirty different plots scattered around outside the town of Banyuls. He favours an early harvest in order to avoid the equinoctial rains, for, as he explained, Grenache is badly affected by rain, though it can cope well with drought. He aims to obtain a natural ripeness as early as possible, for Grenache does not express its real character at less than 13°. It is always the principal grape variety in the blend. If it is picked too late, the grapes are *passerillés* and lack acidity, nor will the wine oxidise in the desired way. For this reason Parcé is critical of the current trend for late picking. Mourvèdre is even more difficult, as it needs both water and heat and can really accentuate the unevenness of the vintages. Syrah is quite the opposite and ripens early.

Marc Parcé too is highly critical of the policy of the appellation, blaming the dominant co-operatives for not consulting the small producers. He explained how they had modified the appellation decree for Collioure in 1997. Originally you had to have a minimum of sixty per cent of Grenache Noir, or Mourvèdre, but now eighty per cent is the minimum percentage for Grenache Noir, Mourvèdre or Syrah and there is nothing to stop you from making Collioure from just one variety. Collioure should be mainly Grenache Noir with some Carignan, Mourvèdre and Syrah, but the flavour must not be dominated by Grenache Noir, which is what the new regulations allow. For this reason Parcé may well label his red wine *vin de pays*, as he already does for his *rosé*.

Our tasting began with a pink Vin de Pays de la Côte Vermeille, made from Grenache Noir with a little Grenache Gris and Carignan. The wine spends just one night on the skins before pressing and is fermented half in new wood and half in concrete vat. Apparently the colour of the wine is not bright enough to conform to appellation regulations, for it is a delicate pink, with light fruit, a rounded palate, well-integrated oak and considerable length; it also has too much body to conform to the accepted idea of Collioure *rosé*. A white *vin de pays* made from Grenache Gris,

Cuvée Argile, is vinified partly in new wood, partly in one-year-old wood and partly in vat. Again it has good extract and mouth-feel, with some attractive rounded fruit. The early harvest gives the wine freshness. Next came a selection of red Collioure, first the 1996 Col del Bast, from sixty per cent Grenache Noir and forty per cent Carignan, which are blended before the wine spends twelve months in large casks. The taste is of ripe cherries and liquorice, with backbone and ageing potential. Le Séris, a similar blend from different vineyards, aged in both *barriques* and *foudres*, has more concentration, tannin and length. Coume Pascole includes Syrah as well as Grenache Noir and Carignan, and spends as long as eighteen months in wood, of which twenty per cent is new. The 1996 is even more concentrated, with oak and cherries, while the 1993 showed how it could develop elegance and complexity, with the warm herbs of *garrigue*, leaving no doubt that good Collioure is a wine to age.

Table wine now makes up two-thirds of Parcé's production, whereas as recently as 1985 it accounted for only a third. His own taste, as well as market demand, is the reason. He also explained that Banyuls is difficult to make every year, for if you are going to mute *sur grains*, your grapes must be very healthy without a trace of rot, and that may be problematic if it has rained heavily during the harvest. He makes a variety of different Banyuls, both vintage wines and blends, with the most concentrated wines kept for vintages. 1996 Cuvée Léon Parcé, named after his grandfather, is a mixture of Grenache Noir, Gris and Blanc that has spent twelve months in *barriques* and tastes of liquorice and prunes, with an elegant concentration of flavour. 1994 Parcé Frères spends a few months in vat and is fresh and fruity. It is either a wine to drink when it is young or to keep for ten years. To prove the point we were then given the 1989, which had developed some spicy cherries with smoky, cedary notes, length and concentration.

Cuvée Docteur Camou, aged in *foudres* for between three and five years in a *solera* system, was noticeably lighter in colour and had developed the traditional *rancio* flavour. Banyuls Brut, which is vinified *en blanc*, without contact with the grape skins, has an orange colour with a nutty flavour and orange overtones. The *mutage* takes place later, so the wine is much drier than some. Finally we tried a Vin de Pierre, a Banyuls that is not muted but made from late harvested grapes, mainly Grenache Gris, that were quite shrivelled. Parcé described the wine as the most simple expression of his terroir, for it was quite dry and austere, with a certain weight and notes of hazelnut. It was left in *foudres* without any topping up.

DOMAINE VIAL-MAGNERES

Bernard Saperas is a genial character who caught the *virus du vin*, as he put it, and did an oenology diploma after a career in chemical engineering. He took over his parents-in-law's ten hectares in 1986 and uses the cellar they built in the residential back streets of Banyuls. The name of the estate is a combination of family names, for Vial is his father-in-law and Magnères his wife's grandfather, the original founder of the estate. As we tasted, it was apparent that he too has the questioning attitude of someone with a broader experience who has come to wine later in life. His 1997 Blanc Sec, Vin de Pays de la Côte Vermeille, principally from Grenache Blanc, with some Grenache Gris and Rolle, is fermented in *barriques*. This is the wine that will be Collioure Blanc in three or four years time, but for the moment it remains a *vin de pays*. Saperas has also planted just fifty plants each of Marsanne, Roussanne and Clairette, on an experimental basis.

His red Collioure from Grenache Noir, with a small amount of Syrah and Carignan, has a firm cherry nose and is quite peppery with sour cherry fruit and some firm tannin. It has spent six months in wood. He does not make any *rosé*, as he prefers to concentrate on white wine, nor is traditional Banyuls his objective either. We tasted first a white 1995 Rimage from Grenache Blanc and Grenache Gris, which had spent six months in wood, of which one-third was new. It still tasted very oaky, with notes of aniseed as well as hints of herbs. By contrast, a traditional white Banyuls would be oxidised, as is his Rivage Ambré, made from a blend of four vintages from 1987 to 1990 that were kept in wood without any topping up and then bottled in 1997. It was not unlike like *fino* sherry, but a little sweeter, with a dry finish. The 1995 red Rimage from Grenache Noir, which has not been near a stave of wood, had the fresh fruit of cherries, with some liquorice and a backbone of tannin. It will age in bottle. Unusually, as few producers take this category of Banyuls seriously, Saperas also makes *grand cru*

Banyuls, a wine from his best *cuvées* in a given year, which is kept in *foudres* for three years. There are hints of oxidation on the nose, with a certain warmth and nuttiness, and dry prunes and figs. Finally we tried a 1976 Rancio, made by his father-in-law, which had been bottled only in 1996. The wine had been kept in old *foudres* for maximum oxidation, and it had the attractively dry, nutty notes of traditional Banyuls.

DOMAINE LA TOUR VIEILLE

The other independent producers of note are Vincent Cantié and Christine Campadieu, a husband and wife team who have amalgamated their family vineyard holdings, hers from Banyuls and his in Collioure, to make a total of twelve hectares. They have small cellars in the back streets of Collioure. Although she was born into wine, as she put it, she studied English and Chinese, and Cantié has worked in New Caledonia as an agricultural engineer. Their first vintage was 1982. We tasted in their little shop in the old quarter of Collioure, first a range of table wines, or *vins secs*, and then some *vins doux*. The 1997 Vin de Pays de la Côte Vermeille, Les Canadells, named after a rocky point south of Banyuls, is made from seventy per cent Grenache Gris and thirty per cent Grenache Blanc and Marsanne. Twenty per cent of the wine is fermented in new wood and the rest in vat, giving just a hint of oak on the palate with some ripe rounded fruit and a firm finish.

The 1997 Collioure Rosé des Roches, from Grenache Noir with thirty per cent Syrah, made by the *saignée* method, has quite a deep colour, with ripe fruit and body. They used to pick the grapes for *rosé* early in order to retain acidity, but realised this was a mistake as the grapes were simply not ripe. They produce at least three red Collioure with different blends of grape varieties. La Pinède, from Grenache Noir with twenty per cent Carignan, is smoky and quite rustic in flavour. Puig Ambeilles, consisting of Grenache Noir with some Mourvèdre and Carignan, is fuller and more rounded, with firm tannins. Syrah is used in yet a third wine. It is easy to cultivate and ripens easily, whereas Mourvèdre is much more of a challenge, but has a wonderful wild character. The typicity of Collioure comes from the schist, which makes wines that are strong but smooth.

Underground cellars do not really exist in Collioure or Banyuls, and the resulting fluctuations in temperature are perfect for the production of *vin doux*. For *vin sec* you need a quite different and much more stable environment. Campadieu explained how her grandparents used to begin the oxidation process in the vineyard, squashing down the grapes as they were picked. The grapes were pressed immediately and mutage took place on the juice, rather than the grape skins. It illustrates the very strong Catalan influence in Roussillon, for the *rancio* style of wine making is traditional to this part of France alone, in Maury and Rivesaltes as well as in Banyuls. In contrast with the Côtes du Rhône village of Rasteau, where they also produce a *vin doux* from Grenache Noir, the emphasis tends to be on fruit, not on oxidation.

The 1996 Vintage Brut made solely from Grenache Noir has ripe cherry fruit. It was muted *sur grains* and bottled early in order to retain its fresh aroma. This is very much the new style of Banyuls and a very successful example. The 1993 Cuvée François Cantié, named after Vincent's grandfather, is a complete contrast. Half the wine has aged in glass *bonbonnes* for a year, half is made like a Rimage, and the two are blended together and aged in 600-litre barrels for about five years, without any topping up. The emphasis is on fruit, a deliciously nutty, liquorice fruit, and the alcohol is well integrated, with a harmonious flavour and a note of *rancio* on the finish.

Cap de Creus, Rancio Sec made from Grenache Gris, continues an old tradition, when people would keep back some of their grapes to make table wine for family consumption. The wine was allowed to ferment naturally until the fermentation was stopped, leaving about 10 gms/l of sugar. It has a high alcohol level, tasting almost as though alcohol has been added, when in fact there is none. It cannot be Banyuls for it is not muted, and the alcohol level is too high for either Collioure or a *vin de pays*. It is a light orange-brown in colour, with lovely dry biscuity fruit, great length and intensity. We finished with a Vin de Meditation Solera, from a *solera* that Campadieu's grandfather had begun in 1952. The wine is pure Grenache, mainly Grenache Gris with a little Grenache Blanc, and it tasted full and nutty, with some sweetness. Sadly, there is a diminishing demand for Banyuls like these. Once it was popular with grandfathers all over France, but now it is becoming something of a speciality. For Campadieu the appeal is the magical variety of Grenache, the fact that you can make so many different styles of wine from the same grape variety – red, white and pink, fortified and dry. This is the challenge and it gives her enormous pleasure.

CAVE DE L'ETOILE

The Cave de l'Etoile in Banyuls is the oldest co-operative of the area, dating back to 1921. They specialise in old Banyuls, for they have not only the traditional large casks, but also what they call a 'park' of glass *bonbonnes* on a terrace outside, where the wines are exposed to the extremes of the Mediterranean climate, the heat of summer and the chill of winter as well as the differences between night and daytime temperatures. The oldest casks are as old as the co-operative, for each founder member contributed an example to the cellar. The glass *bonbonnes* each hold sixty litres of wine, but are only filled with fifty-five litres. This small air bubble prevents any reductive flavours and there is a tiny reduction in alcohol content, but not in volume of wine. The sugar and alcohol seem to protect the wine, producing a quite different aromatic development from ageing in wood. This wine is used for just one cuvée, the Banyuls Grand Cru Doux Paillé Hors d'Age.

The oenologist, Patrick Terrier, is a Parisian by birth, but he studied at Bordeaux and came to Banyuls some twenty-five years ago. He talked of the changes during that time. A considerable effort has been made to improve the composition of the vineyards, with a much greater emphasis on Grenache Noir. Previously there was more Grenache Gris, Grenache Blanc, Macabeu and Carignan. It is Grenache, and particularly Grenache Noir, that provides quality. Carignan can be very good if it comes from old vines, grown on slopes. Nowadays much more attention is paid to the grapes in the vineyard, in deciding the date of the harvest and in taking care over the condition of the grapes and their *état sanitaire*. Also, a more detailed selection is made of which grapes go into which wines. A relatively recent development is the control of fermentation temperatures, when it was realised that this is important for fortified wines in order to retain the fruit and aroma. The grapes are now all destalked to eliminate any green, herbaceous flavours, and *mutage* is with the grape skins.

The Cave l'Etoile produces a variety of different Banyuls, as well as red and pink Collioure. Terms like Extra Vieux, Grande Réserve and Sélect Vieux have no precise meaning, but depend upon the co-operative's own criteria of selection. In this instance, Extra Vieux is usually a minimum of ten years, Sélect Vieux comes from wines with the best ageing potential and Grande Réserve is the most traditional. The term *grand cru* is little used, but does form a category in the appellation, implying thirty months of wood ageing of wine made from a minimum of seventy-five per cent Grenache Noir. I particularly enjoyed the Cuvée 75 Anniversaire, bottled in 1996 from a blend of several casks. It had a lovely nutty flavour, made from wines that were at least ten years old. The Banyuls Grand Cru Doux Paillé, of which a third had been kept for twelve months in the glass *bonbonnes*, as well as undergoing about ten years of wood ageing, provides the traditional image of Banyuls. The taste was of preserved oranges. There was the structure of a white wine, with acidity, sugar and alcohol, but all the tannins had disappeared, leaving a nutty *rancio* flavour.

GROUPEMENT INTERPRODUCTEURS

The big player in Banyuls and Collioure is the Groupement Interproducteurs, a group of five co-operatives formed in 1950. Today they produce sixty per cent of all Collioure, seventy-five per cent of Banyuls and ninety-five per cent of Banyuls *grand cru*. They are the only producers to give the rather meaningless definition of *grand cru* any distinction. Their eight hundred members are responsible for twelve hundred hectares of vines, but only a small number of these actually earn a living from their vines. You will find their wines under various labels, including the Cellier des Templiers and La Cave de l'Abbé Rous. François Rous was a nineteenth-century priest in Banyuls who sold wine to raise money for restoring his church. Castell des Hospices is a single vineyard, as is Domaine de Baillaury, and there are also *cuvées* named after various notables. Domaine de Baillaury Collioure is a peppery wine without wood ageing, which compares favourably with Castell des Hospices, which has spent fifteen months in *barriques* with rather clumsy results. As for Banyuls, there are various vintage or Rimage wines, with the youngest not unlike a fresh ruby port, while the older wines have developed in cask or bottle. The various *cuvées*, Joseph Neidal or Christian Reyneil, have aged in large casks, resulting in nutty, oxidative tastes. They also produce Banyuls vinegar, which sadly is not an answer to sherry vinegar and lacks the expected concentration of flavour. With the wines too, I was left with a feeling that their size worked to their detriment, proving a handicap to quality.

The co-operatives may dominate the market for Banyuls and Collioure, but the more exciting wines, both dry and sweet, undoubtedly come from the independent producers. The style of red Collioure varies from producer to producer, depending on grape blends and ageing methods. White Collioure is yet to be decided, and the *rosé* enjoys the success of summer drinking. Collioure is a growing market, whereas Banyuls has declined with the fall from favour of these rather old-fashioned wines, which nonetheless have great charm. Once they were drunk in France as an aperitif. Marc Parcé remembered that his grandmother served Banyuls at five o'clock in the afternoon, but today their role is perhaps more as an after-dinner drink, as an alternative to port or sherry, with ripe liquorice or delicious nutty flavours that would complement walnuts or cheese at the end of a meal.

Key facts

Banyuls AC 1936; Collioure AC red 1971, *rosé* 1990 and white still under discussion; both ACs cover four villages, Banyuls, Collioure, Cerbère, Port-Vendres; 1930 hectares.

Grape varieties: Grenache Noir the main variety for both. Also Grenache Gris and Blanc, Macabeu, with Carignan, Syrah, Mourvèdre and Counoise more likely to be used for Collioure.

Banyuls: a *vin doux naturel*, style varies from a vintage Rimage to an oxidised Rancio of several years' ageing.

Banyuls grand cru: minimum of seventy-five per cent Grenache Noir and minimum of thirty months' ageing.

Schist soil.

Annual average rainfall 900 mm.

Vintages

Vintages of Collioure similar to those of Côtes du Roussillon.

LANGUEDOC

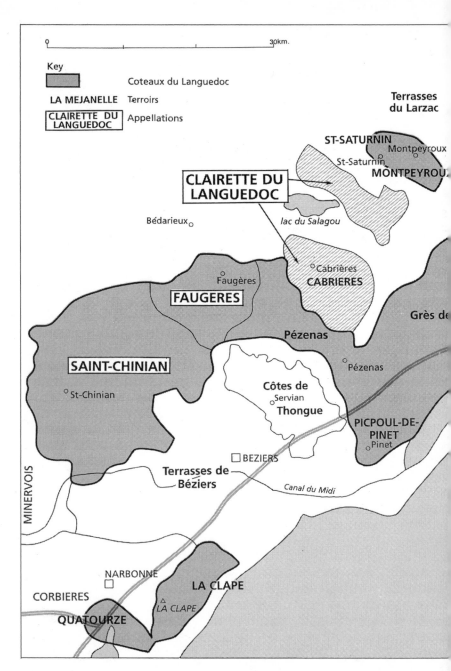

Languedoc

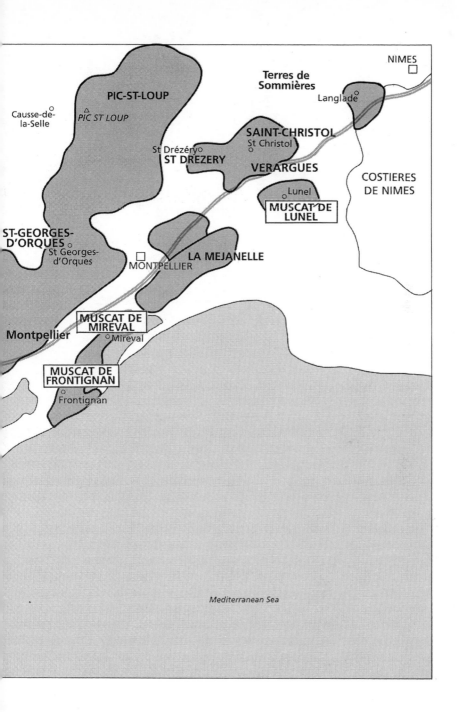

NIMES

Terres de
Sommières

Langlade

PIC-ST-LOUP

Causse-de-
la-Selle

PIC ST LOUP

St Drézéry
ST DREZERY

SAINT-CHRISTOL
St Christol

VERARGUES

COSTIERES
DE NIMES

Lunel
MUSCAT DE
LUNEL

ST-GEORGES-
D'ORQUES
St Georges-
d'Orques

MONTPELLIER

LA MEJANELLE

MUSCAT DE
MIREVAL

Montpellier

Mireval

MUSCAT DE
FRONTIGNAN

Frontignan

Mediterranean Sea

It was a landing with a view at Montpellier airport. The clouds cleared as we approached the Mediterranean. The plane circled and you could see the blue sea and the murkier water of the *étangs*, the inland salt lakes cut off from the sea by sand dunes, with their oyster beds and even the odd pink flamingo. From the airport, the motorway, La Languedocienne, that follows the old Roman road provides an easy access to the vineyards of the Languedoc. You pass the various *terroirs* of the Coteaux du Languedoc and the pockets of Muscat in Lunel, Frontignan and Mireval, and from Narbonne you can head either into the hills of the Minervois or towards the Corbières.

Alternatively, you can approach the Corbières from the south, from Roussillon. The two appellations, the Côtes du Roussillon and Corbières, are separated by an imperceptible departmental boundary that was once the frontier between France and Catalonia. Take the winding road from Estagel up past Tautavel. The next village, Paziols, is in the Languedoc and part of the appellations of Corbières and Fitou. From there the road takes you on past the ruined Château d'Aquilar to Tuchan and Durban in the heart of the Corbières hills.

On a summer afternoon in June, these villages are tranquil in their soporific warmth. Nothing stirs, and yet this calm appearance belies some dramatic and threatening weather conditions. During the day of 12 November, 1999 just as I was putting the finishing touches to this manuscript, the Corbières and Minervois received their annual rainfall in the space of twenty-four hours, with 50 centimetres of rain during Friday and a further 13.25 centimetres on Saturday, causing fast-flowing torrents of floodwater. More than fifteen hundred hectares of vines have been destroyed and several cellars devastated, with barrels and vats swept away in the water. The winery at Château Grand-Moulin in the Corbières collapsed – the building was unable to withstand the impact of floating barrels hitting the roof supports. A large vat from the co-operative of Cascastel was found in a vineyard ten kilometres away. Thirty people were drowned in the floodwater and the region is still counting the cost. It is a sobering thought that seemingly clement conditions can change so dramatically, and is something to be remembered as we wander through the vineyards of the Corbières.

Corbières

The vineyards of Corbières cover a large expanse of hilly land to the south west of the city of Narbonne. In the north the appellation is limited by the valley of the Aude and the Canal du Midi, while to the south the departmental boundary separates it from Côtes du Roussillon. The countryside is wild and scraggy, so that only vines and olive trees will grow here. Two mountains dominate the skyline, the Montagne d'Alaric in the north and Mont Tauch in the south. The wine takes its name from the region, the Corbières, which extends to the foothills of the Pyrenees. There are two theories about the origin of the name. *Corbe* in Occitan means a *corbeau* or crow, or alternatively *corbe* is the Celtic for a stone. The experts are undecided about which is correct.

The Romans, who settled in Narbonne in 125 BC, introduced viticulture to the area, but its development was interrupted by the invasions of the Visigoths and then the Saracens. It was only in the Middle Ages, with the foundation of the abbeys of Lagrasse and Fontfroide, that viticulture took a firm hold on the landscape of the region. This was also the period in which many of the Cathar castles, such as Aguilar, Tautavel, Quéribus and, most majestic of all, Peyrepertuse, were built on inaccessible hills. Their ruins still dominate the countryside, imposing reminders of those turbulent times.

Corbières, like so many of the wines of the Midi, has only recently acquired a distinctive identity. In the nineteenth century the Aude in general was described as an important wine producing department. Cyrus Redding, writing in 1833, referred to the indifference to quality, noting that quantity was principally regarded here and that the number of those who took a different view of things was small. Guyot gave the area of the vineyards in

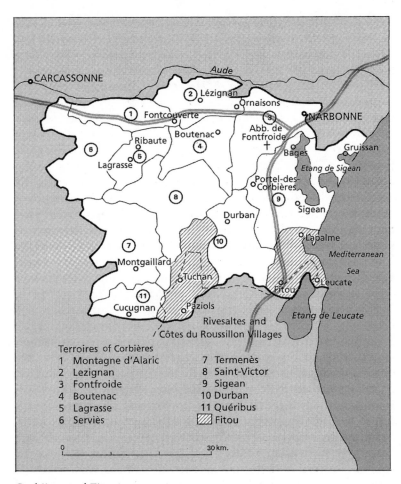

Terroires of Corbières

1 Montagne d'Alaric	7 Termenès
2 Lezignan	8 Saint-Victor
3 Fontfroide	9 Sigean
4 Boutenac	10 Durban
5 Lagrasse	11 Quéribus
6 Serviès	▨ Fitou

0   30 km.

Corbières and Fitou

1868 as eighty thousand hectares, stating that viticulture provided the wealth of the department and that Carignan was the most distinctive grape variety. In 1891 Corbières was described as having more stuffing than the wines of the Minervois and was consequently used for blending with lighter wines. The first *syndicat* of the Corbières was formed in 1908, and in 1923 the area of Corbières was defined for the first time.

Corbières acquired sufficient identity after the Second World War to make it one of the earlier VDQS of France in 1951, but it did not become an appellation until 1985. At the same time, the former classification of Corbières Supérieures, which was merely an indication of a higher alcoholic degree, was suppressed and the area of the appellation was drastically reduced from forty-four thousand hectares to twenty thousand in eighty-seven *communes*, or villages, between Narbonne and Carcassonne. Illogically, Gruissan, on the edge of the mountain of la Clape, is part of Corbières rather than la Clape, for reasons of local politics. Villages like Cucugnan, Paziols and Tuchan lie in the far south. With an average annual production of some six hundred thousand hectolitres, Corbières is the fourth largest appellation of France, after Bordeaux, the Côtes du Rhône and Champagne. The village co-operatives are important, with fifty-four of them accounting for over sixty per cent of the production of the appellation, while just over four hundred private estates make the rest.

Corbières is firmly red, with pink and white wine only accounting for five per cent of the appellation each. Red wine comes from the usual five grape varieties of the Midi, in varying proportions depending on the producer's whim and preference. The appellation regulations confirm Carignan as the mainstay of the appellation, with a maximum of sixty per cent, which must be reduced to fifty per cent by 2003. However, the region has undergone the same gentle transformation in the vineyards as elsewhere in the Midi, so that Syrah, Mourvèdre and Grenache Noir are taking the place of Carignan. Likewise, white wine now includes varieties such as Marsanne, Roussanne and Rolle as well as the more traditional Macabeu, Grenache Blanc and Bourboulenc (which is also called Malvoisie but, confusingly, is not the Malvoisie of Roussillon).

Within this large area there is an enormous variety of microclimate and soil. The altitude of the vineyards can vary from zero to six hundred metres, and inevitably there is a more Mediterranean influence in the east and an more oceanic influence in the north west. Consequently, different grape varieties do better in different areas. Mourvèdre likes the coastal areas, while Syrah performs better on higher, cooler altitudes inland. The prevailing winds also have a significant effect on microclimate. The Cers is a harsh, drying northern wind, while the Marin is a more gentle wind that comes from the sea and may bring rain, which usually falls in spring or autumn.

As a result of these differences, the appellation was further subdivided into eleven different *terroirs* in 1991. The indigenous vegetation provided some guidelines for defining the various *terroirs*, so that for example you will find *chêne blanche* in a cooler zone and mimosa where the climate is warmer. There are quite discernible differences within the various *terroirs*, from the point of view of soil and climate.

Sigean covers the coastal area, including part of the appellation of Fitou, with villages such as Bages and Leucate enjoying the influence not only of the sea but also the vast salt-water lakes. The soil is clay and limestone, and Mourvèdre is important here. Durban adjoins Sigean and is centred on the village of Durban, but also includes Tuchan, Embrès-et-Castelmaure and Paziols, villages that are included in the inland part of the appellation of Fitou. The *terroir* stretches down to the southern edge of the Corbières, covering a wild area that includes the hilltop castles of Durban and Aguilar. The soil is shallow and infertile and the summers are long and dry, with a long growing period for the vines.

Quéribus, in the south west corner of the appellation, is called after the ruined Cathar castle and includes the villages of Padern, which has another ruined castle, Duilhac and Cucugnan, whose *curé* featured in an Alphonse Daudet short story. The castle of Quéribus dominates the skyline, and the vineyards are at an altitude of between two hundred and fifty and four hundred metres, with Syrah and Grenache Noir enjoying the long dry summers. Termenès is on the western side of the appellation and contains the highest vineyards of the appellations, lying between four hundred and five hundred metres, sometimes reaching six hundred metres, on clay and limestone slopes. The weather pattern is predominately Mediterranean, but is also subject to some Atlantic influence as well as winds from the Pyrenees. Nights here are cooler than in vineyards at a lower altitude, which proves beneficial for white and pink wine.

Saint-Victor is right in the centre of the appellation, taking its name from a hermit's chapel at the top of the eponymous 420-metre hill, and covers seven villages including Albas and Tailaran. The soils here are a mixture of sandstone, clay and limestone with a little schist, and the vineyards lie at between one hundred and fifty and three hundred metres. There is little maritime influence and consequently very little Mourvèdre. Fontfroide, the north eastern *terroir*, adjoining Sigean, is centred on the village of Fontfroide with its magnificent Cistercian abbey. Only a low band of hills separates it from the sea. The climate is Mediterranean, but the hills afford some protection from the Marin and the sea breezes. Mourvèdre can ripen well here.

Lagrasse is another important *terroir*, with the valley of the Orbiel forming its centre. The Benedictine abbey of Lagrasse dominates the pretty village, with its Roman bridge over the Orbiel, attractive cobbled streets and old market hall. The vineyards here are at an altitude of between one hundred and fifty and two hundred and fifty metres, on predominantly red limestone.

Serviès forms the north western edge of the appellation, around the valley of the Dagne. The Montagne d'Alaric protects it from north winds, so the climate is both Mediterranean and continental, with vineyards planted on limestone clay. Syrah performs particularly well here, although it is often too cool for Grenache Noir and Carignan. The *terroir* of the Montagne d'Alaric covers the north slopes of the mountain overlooking the river Aude. The vineyards are on limestone terraces, in well-drained gravelly soil. Legend has it that Alaric, the king of the Visigoths, was buried on the mountain, and the drive over it from Montlaur to Capendu is certainly worth the detour for the breathtaking views. In June there are swathes of bright pink orchids.

Lézignan is on flatter land where the Aude and the Orbiel meet, around the town of Lezignan and other villages. This is a stony, well-drained plain lying at about fifty metres. And finally there is Boutenac, centred on one of the important villages of the appellation, to the east of Fontfroide. Carignan gives good results here on the low-lying hills, where the climate has a strong Mediterranean influence that also allows Mourvèdre to ripen well.

Of these eleven *terroirs*, four are likely to become *crus* in their own right, perhaps eventually without any reference to the overall appellation of Corbières. They are Sigean, Durban, Fontfroide and Lagrasse, but for the moment no *terroir* has any official recognition and their use on the label depends entirely on the producer's whim.

As there are nearly five hundred producers of Corbières, both private and co-operative, it is impossible to cover them in any great detail. What follows is a small selection of highlights, and even then I may have omitted names that merit inclusion. Constraints of time did not allow a visit to everyone who is anyone within the appellation. Many of the same themes recur, with improvements in the cellar and replanting in the vineyards.

DOMAINE LA VOULTE-GASPARETS, BOUTENAC

Domaine la Voulte-Gasparets in the hamlet of Gasparets, outside the village of Boutenac in the heart of the appellation, is now run by Patrick Reverdy. His father-in-law, Jacques Bergès, was one of the prime movers in the appellation, and also a founder of the Vignerons du Val d'Orbieu; when I met him the mid-1980s, he was a man of energy with firm ideas on the direction that the appellation should be taking. Young Laurent Reverdy showed us round. The estate now totals fifty-five hectares, mainly in Corbières, but also with nine hectares of *vin de pays*. They also have just two hectares for Corbières Blanc, Grenache Blanc, Rolle and Macabeu, for which their first vintage was 1991. Grenache Blanc provides body, which is balanced by acidity from the Rolle, and the wine is ripe and rounded. There is no skin contact and no malolactic fermentation, a simple cool fermentation, and the blending takes place just before bottling in the spring.

They make three grades of red Corbières, all by carbonic maceration. There is a basic unoaked wine, a *cuvée réservée* with six months of oak ageing, and their best wine is the Cuvée Romain Pauc, named after Jacques Bergès's maternal grandfather, which is given as much as thirteen months in oak. It was Romain Pauc who planted the first vines on the estate around 1905. Carignan, Grenache Noir and Syrah are the key grape varieties, grown on limestone and clay, while the vines for Cuvée Romain Pauc are the oldest of the estate, between forty-five and eighty years old, and are on much stonier soil – what the French call *galets roulées*, large round pebbles not unlike those of the vineyards of Châteauneuf-du-Pape. 1986 was the first vintage of Cuvée Romain Pauc, and since then only the 1991 vintage has lacked sufficient quality to make it.

The 1996 *cuvée réservée* was medium in weight with some peppery, raspberry fruit, while the 1996 Romain Pauc had a much greater concentration of flavour, with more tannin and body, as well as ageing potential. Corbières can vary enormously in style: there are wines that will age beautifully and rewardingly, while others are best drunk in their early youth.

DOMAINE DES CHANDELLES, MARSEILLETTE

The charm of the Corbières, as well as the potential of the rising appellation, attracts outsiders such as Susan and Peter Munday, who arrived here at the end of 1992. Peter did a year's wine-making course at Carcassonne and found some vines for the 1994 vintage, as well as a small cellar in the village of Marseillette on the northern edge of the appellation. It had a beaten earth floor, one small light socket and a couple of enormous concrete vats. The Mundays restored the roof and bought stainless steel and fibreglass vats. They now rent eight hectares of vines: four on the plain, from which the grapes go to the co-operative, and four on the slopes of the Montagne d'Alaric, which they vinify themselves. The difference in the yields is indicative of the contrast between quality and quantity so prevalent in the region: the average of 120 hl/h for the co-operative wines compares with 40 hl/ha for their own vinification. The Mundays make three wines, a red and a *rosé* called Chais Suzanne and an oak-aged red, Domaine des Chandelles. Syrah does best here. Mourvèdre will not ripen at all and Carignan can be a struggle. The yield must be low, with no more than 30 hl/ha from their fifty-year-old vines. They feel confident with a classic vinification, but are still mastering the technique of carbonic maceration. The Domaine des Chandelles is made from Syrah with some Grenache Noir, all of which is destalked. In 1995 they bought fourteen new barrels and have found that Syrah does well in wood, developing some attractive peppery and violet fruit. They have even tried what they call a two hundred per cent new wood on some 1995 Syrah, moving the wine into a second lot of new barrels after twelve months. It tasted very dense and structured, with some firm tannins, fruit and substance. The question is, how will it develop? *Elevage* in oak is something that not just the Mundays but the whole appellation is learning to master.

DOMAINE SERRES-MAZARD, TALAIRAN

Jean-Pierre Mazard is a cheerful middle-aged man who exudes enthusiasm about his appellation and his region. His tasting room has photographs of the region, of the Cathar castles and the abbeys of Lagrasse and Fontfroide. Visitors can watch a slide show about the local fauna and flora, which includes numerous varieties of wild orchids. May is the best month for orchids in the Aude, but even in June I saw beautiful pyramid orchids nestling in the grass by the side of the road. In Mazard's tasting cellar there are various old vinous artefacts, such as a *barral*, a teeny wooden barrel that the workers took into the vineyards, and from which they drank using a reed, just like a modern straw. Talairan is one of the seven villages in the *terroir* of Saint Victor. Its origins are Roman and in the Middle Ages the village was fortified, although there was never a château. Talairan was also known for its iron mines, but those disappeared after the Second World War. Now there is some local production of goat's cheese and truffles, but otherwise it is wine that dominates the local economy.

Mazard and his wife created the Domaine de Serres-Mazard when they took over their parents' vineyards in 1985, naming the estate after Mazard's two grandparents. His parents had sold their wine to the *négoce*, but Mazard wanted to do something more creative. From his fifty hectares, he makes three qualities of red wine, some for bulk sales to the Vignerons du Val d'Orbieu, a vat-aged wine under the name of Cellier St Damien and finally a barrel-aged wine, made for the first time in 1989, under the Château Serres-Mazard label. He has experimented with different oaks. Russian oak has what he calls a clean attack, but with a drying finish, while American oak does not begin well, but has a good middle and an even better finish. French oak is very linear, with a good beginning, middle and end. Mazard uses medium-toasted

Vosges and Allier, and looks for balance, with the flavour of the wine surrounding the tannins. He gives Château Serres-Mazard just six months ageing, including some in new wood. The 1995 is a blend of Syrah, Grenache Noir and Carignan with just a little Cinsaut, and when tasted in June 1998, it was rich and plummy with ripe fruit and hints of thyme and the other herbs of the *garrigue*.

Mazard's white wine, a blend of Marsanne, Grenache Blanc, Macabeu and Clairette, was rounded and perfumed, while his *rosé*, mainly from Cinsaut, was soft and ripe. The St Damien Corbières, predominantly from Carignan but with some Grenache Noir and a little Syrah and Cinsaut, was sturdier and less refined than the Château Serres-Mazard, but with good rounded fruit none the less.

Mazard is a fount of information about the region. He talked about the local *fête*, a day in June when all the producers open their cellars and there is not just wine but also cheese and honey. Visitors can also watch a medieval tournament – and no French *fête* is complete without a dinner, at which a special *cuvée* of wine produced by the host village is served. Next came a story about the naming of the village of Lagrasse. Local legend has it that the village was originally called Lamaigre – in other words, 'the slim' as opposed to 'the fat' – but when Charlemagne came here while he was fighting the Saracens, he is said to have eaten so well in the village that he changed its name to Lagrasse, which of course is what it remains today. And inevitably we discussed the tremendous development of the Midi, causing Mazard to observe that 1979, the very first year that I visited the vineyards of the south of France, was the Stone Age!

CHATEAU DU VIEUX PARC, CONILHAC

Château du Vieux Parc is in the village of Conilhac, within the *terroir* of Lézignan on the northern side of the appellation. The soil there is clay and limestone, with vineyards on gravel terraces above the Orbieu. You are at the utmost limit of any influence from the oceanic climate of the Atlantic, for it is noticeable that the rain brought in from the sea by the Marin wind stops at Lézignan in the east and the rain from the Cers stops at Moux, just to the west of

Conilhac, making the area very dry indeed. Louis Panis and his wife Claudine had been PE teachers, but took over this family property in 1987 when an older brother became ill. Altogether they have fifty-five hectares, of which thirty are in the appellation – including five for white wine, which they made for the first time in 1997. From the rest they produce *vin de pays*, from varieties such as Merlot and Cabernet Sauvignon as well as Syrah and Grenache Noir. They have been gradually replanting their vineyard. However, Panis's father first planted Syrah soon after he did his first bottling in 1976, and all their Corbières has been bottled since 1996. There are two hectares of twenty-five-year-old Mourvèdre, which ripens quite well here, although it is always the last variety to be picked. They find that it adds a little extra something to the blend.

We walked to the cellar through the old park. The dark foliage made it cool and shady, almost sinister. The cellar is partially underground, which keeps it cool, and there are concrete vats, with a separate barrel cellar elsewhere. With a stuffed woodcock looking down at us, the tasting room demonstrated Panis's love of hunting. The birds come here during the winter months, either from Scandinavia or eastern Europe.

Our tasting began with the white wine, which includes a small amount of Grenache Blanc fermented in barrel to give some extra weight and complexity. There is a little Rolle, which is planted on arid terraces, as well as some Roussanne and Marsanne, which require deeper soil. For the 1998 vintage Panis was planning two *cuvées* of white, one with oak and one without. I liked this 1997, which was rounded and perfumed with no trace of oak on the palate. The traditional Corbières, from Carignan with some Syrah, Grenache Noir and Cinsaut and just a little Mourvèdre, was supple and fruity with liquorice and spice. The Carignan undergoes a carbonic maceration, while the other varieties are destalked for a classic vinification. A destemmer was bought in 1994 and makes for softer tannins. A second red wine, made from the oldest vines with the smallest yields, including some eighty-year-old Carignan, is given ten to twelve months of oak ageing. For this, Panis buys reconditioned barrels of one wine, from Seguin Moreau, which represents a significant saving on new barrel: 1350 FF each as opposed to 3000 FF. The wine was rich and concentrated, with ripe fruit and some oaky vanilla notes; it would benefit from some bottle age.

DOMAINE DE L'HORTE, MONTBRUN

From Conilhac we took a scenic route over the hills to the village of Montbrun and the Domaine de l'Horte, a property bought by Jean-Pierre Briard in 1988. For the first couple of years he sent his grapes to the village co-operative, but now he has restored the house and built a new cellar, buying second-hand vats from Gaillac and installing a barrel-ageing facility. Once a large estate of 146 hectares, this was subsequently divided into three, but Briard is the only wine producer. He has the usual five red varieties, including some very old Carignan; he makes no white Corbières, but instead a Vin de Pays de l'Aude from Sauvignon and some Gewürztraminer, which officially is not allowed. The Sauvignon provides acidity and the Gewürztraminer fruit and aroma. It proved to be an appealing combination, with weight and flavour. Briard also admits to half a hectare of Pinot Gris, another variety that is not officially recognised. The Domaine du Jardin, as the Sauvignon and Gewürztraminer blend is called, provoked a discussion about the region, which combines the regulations of an appellation with the liberty of a *vin de pays*, but still not enough freedom. You have parallel lines and different parameters, such as methods of cultivation, vinification and *élevage*, as well as grape varieties, that may result in quite different wines from the same village.

Montbrun is on the edge of the *terroir* of Lézignan and surrounded by hills that are quite different from the terraces around Lezignan. The wines taste different. They are more rustic, with higher acidity giving structure and a longer life. The soil is clay and limestone, with some deep sand that the Mourvèdre likes. As for climate, it is neither Mediterranean nor oceanic, with the hills between Conilhac and Montbrun seeming to act as a barrier against the rain. However, Briard feels that the *terroirs* of the appellation need to be redefined so as to create less confusion.

His Cuvée Tradition is intended to provide easy drinking. Briard blends either during or immediately after the fermentation, for Grenache Noir and Mourvèdre ripen at about the same time. Carignan is kept separate and Syrah is often added to a vat mid-harvest. There are *remontages* and *délestages*, and the wine spends twelve months in vat, making for some ripe berry fruit with firm, spicy flavours and a certain rugged finish. A Réserve Spéciale is a selection of old vines, including ninety-year-old Carignan and fifty-year-old Grenache Noir, as well as some Syrah planted in 1982 and a little Mourvèdre. It is given twelve to fourteen months in the wood of one or two wines, bought from Château Beauregard in Pomerol. The 1995 was solid and structured, quite tannic but with good fruit. The 1990 Cuvée Tradition showed the ageing potential, with the warm, spicy fruit of the *garrigue*. Briard considers Corbières to be a wine of *moyen garde* or average ageing ability, but the consumer needs to be educated to understand this.

CHATEAU OLLIEUX LES ROMANIS, BOUTENAC

Château Ollieux les Romanis adjoins the estate of Château les Ollieux. They were one property until 1896, when two daughters split their inheritance. Madame Jacqueline Bories is a friendly, cheerful woman who took over the estate in 1984, when she began putting wine into bottle. Until then it had all been sold to the *négoce*. The vineyards of some sixty hectares are all around the house and the enormous cellar that dates back to the last century. Today the estate is very much a mixture of ancient and modern. There is a railway line constructed in 1896 to facilitate the moving of the wine. Concrete vats and *foudres* cohabit, as well as *barriques* and stainless steel vats, and there is a pneumatic press. From the cellar door there is a view of the nearby Château de Montséret. The tasting counter is in an old barn, where swallows winged in and out to their nests. There is a collection of old carriages, which Bories eventually plans to display, but for the moment they are shrouded in dust.

The *terroir* here is Boutenac and its typicity is Carignan. Bories has some hundred-year-old Carignan, and for her it is above all Carignan that forms the basis of Corbières, giving particularly good results if vinified by carbonic maceration. Mourvèdre also works well here. She tried out an *élevage* in barrique for the first time with the 1994 vintage – reluctantly, as she admitted, as it is not part of the tradition of the Midi. Now she makes three red wines: a Corbières Tradition, the identical wine unfiltered at the request of her British importer, and an oak-aged wine. The blend of the Tradition is about fifty per cent Carignan with more or less equal amounts of Grenache Noir, Mourvèdre and Syrah, which are given three or four years *élevage* in vat, not *foudres*. We compared the identical wine from the 1994 vintage filtered and unfiltered. The blend was the same and the wine was bottled on the same day, but there was a palpable difference. The filtered wine had more obvious tannins, with firm peppery fruit, while the unfiltered wine had a different structure, a certain ruggedness, with more subtle tannins. Bories believes that it will last long. As for the oak-aged wine, made from equal parts of Carignan, Grenache Noir, Mourvèdre and Syrah, it was more international in style. About ten to fifteen per cent of it is given six months in barrel and the effect is very apparent, with vanilla and tannin and firm fruit on the palate. Bories tried her first white vinification in *barrique* with the 1997 vintage, but sadly it was not available for tasting.

DOMAINE DE VILLEMAJOU, VILLEMAJOU

Georges Bertrand of Domaine de Villemajou was one of the earlier pioneers of Corbières, not only a passionate exponent of carbonic maceration, but also of *élevage* in barrel, which he began as early as 1979. It was a revolutionary step at the time. When I visited him in 1987, we were treated to a vertical tasting back to 1978. His son, Gérard Bertrand, not only continues his father's work on the family estate, but has also bought the Minervois property of Domaine Laville-Bertrou and has in addition developed a *négociant* business with a selection of Languedoc properties, as a means of extending sales into the supermarkets. Domaine de Villemajou, in the eponymous village, now totals 110 hectares, with an impressive cellar of more than fifteen hundred barrels. It is a rare sight in the Midi, and seems more in keeping with Bordeaux. This is where we tasted a range of different wines from the estate. The vineyards are within the *terroir* of Boutenac and the precise regulations for the proposed *cru* are still under consideration. They include restrictions on the percentages of grape varieties, with a maximum of fifty per cent Carignan and thirty per cent Grenache Noir, combined with a minimum twenty per cent of Syrah and /or Mourvèdre. A minimum ageing time of twelve to eighteen months is envisaged, as well as a second *labelle* tasting and a minimum price per bottle. The INAO has yet to give its official consent.

Le Blanc de Villemajou, from Grenache Blanc, Roussanne, Marsanne and Bourboulenc, is fermented in new barrels that are then used for the red wines. The 1997 vintage, when it was nearly a year old, was firm and structured and the influence of the oak was all too apparent, but there was acidity too, which is a characteristic of the *terroir*. The 1996 had benefited from the extra ageing, with more honeyed, leafy flavours, so that it was rounded and complete. The Rosé de Villemajou is also fermented in *barriques*, which is unusual for a *rosé*. It is a blend of seventy per cent Syrah with Grenache Noir and Gris. The oak was not at all obvious on the palate. There was just a little more structure than you usually find in a *rosé*, with some rounded fruit and a hint of spice.

Domaine Georges Bertrand Corbières, the supermarket label, is a blend of Syrah, Carignan, Grenache Noir and Mourvèdre, which are blended before spending eight months in wood. The 1994 vintage, when it was three years old, was rounded and smoky with structure and fruit. The 1995 Moulin St François, from a vineyard within the estate, is a similar blend, but more structured in taste, with some spicy, perfumed fruit and peppery tannins. The Carignan is vinified by carbonic maceration, while the other varieties are destemmed for a classic vinification. Domaine Villemajou comes from the best vineyards of the estate, with a selection of the best grapes, including some eighty-year-old Carignan, as well as Grenache Noir, some Syrah, a little Mourvèdre and a drop of Cinsaut. Each variety is fermented separately and spends six months in stainless steel vats before blending, after which the wine is given eight months of *barrique* ageing, including a percentage in new oak. This meant that the oak was much more marked on nose and palate, but there was fruit underneath, with plenty of potential for bottle ageing.

CHATEAU LASTOURS, PORTEL-DES-CORBIERES

Château Lastours is up a long track outside the village of Portel-des-Corbières. It is not only a wine estate but also home for some sixty mentally and physically handicapped people – what the French call a *centre d'aide de travail* – who derive a sense of purpose from their work in the cellars and vineyard. The director of the estate, Jean-Marie Lignères, is himself confined to a wheelchair as a result of a very bad car accident. He used to be a racing driver and there is a track over the estate that is used by people training for the Paris–Dakar rally. Unsuspecting visitors can have their nerves tested with a breathtaking tour of the estate, not only for the views over the coastal *étangs*, the city of Narbonne and the Montagne de la Clape, but also for the sheer drops and steep gradients of some of the route. On a clear day you can see the Pyrenees.

The property was bought by a bank, the Societé Marseillaise de Crédit, in 1970 and the first wine was made in 1975, but until about 1988 everything was sold to the *négoce*. Château Lastours is within the *terroir* of Durban, making structured, solid wines akin to those of nearby Fitou. Altogether there are some 155 hectares, with vineyards ranging between forty and three hundred metres in altitude, which entails a long vintage taking six weeks. The white grapes are not usually ripe until the beginning of September, some two weeks later than in the warmer parts of the appellation. The vines are on terraces, with limestone and clay soil and a very high percentage of pebbles. They are sheltered from both the north wind and the sea breezes.

The cellars are well equipped, with concrete vats for blending and smaller stainless steel vats, together with various refinements to make things easier for the physically handicapped people. Château Lastours gave up using carbonic maceration in 1985 and now everything is destalked, with careful temperature control for the fermentation in stainless steel vats. Two attractive barrel-ageing cellars are built into the hillside. Only the best wines, what they described as 'the cream', are bottled. A Gris de Gris is made from Grenache Gris, which has pink flesh and a grey skin when it is ripe, making for a light colour with fresh delicate fruit. The white, a blend of Grenache Blanc and Bourboulenc, is kept on the fine lees, making a wine that is both rich and elegant, with some leafy fruit. A second white, Le Dry, from equal parts of Grenache Blanc, Bourboulenc and Muscat, tastes predominantly of Muscat, with spicy orange fruit and a hint of sweetness on the finish. It has replaced the *vin doux naturel* they used to make. Châtellerie de Lastours is a pure Carignan, a basic Corbières with firm sturdy fruit. Arnaud de Berre is a blend of Carignan and Grenache Noir, fermented at 16° to 18°C, a low temperature for a red wine, and kept in vat for a couple of years. It is plummy and supple with some tannin and spice, and is best drunk slightly chilled. Simon Deschamps, from Carignan and Grenache Noir with a small amount of Syrah, spends two years in vats, resulting in a good concentration of flavour, with firm cherry fruit. The final red, Château de Lastours itself, is a blend of Carignan and Grenache Noir given two years in barrel, making for a solid mouthful of warm *garrigue* and chunky fruit. And last of all, a Vin de Liqueur from barrel-aged Grenache Noir was ripe and raisiny, sweet and concentrated.

DOMAINE DE L'ILLE, BAGES

Domaine de l'Ille is run by Pol Flandroy, a genial Belgian with a sense of humour, who first became involved with the estate when his father invested in it back in 1979 and then arrived here in 1983 to run the twelve hectares of vineyards. His father no longer has a share, and the estate is now owned by a group of private investors with forty-eight hectares of vines on the most beautiful part of the coast between the villages of Bages and Peyriac. Bages is a pretty hilltop village with narrow streets, houses with pale blue shutters and a sun-soaked square. On the edge of the *étang* there were fishing nets hanging up to dry. You take a winding dirt track past the lake and travel hopefully to arrive eventually at a small cellar on the water's edge. You should be able to see pink flamingos here and other migratory birds. I was unlucky, for there were only large, raucous seagulls. The vines are all around the lake, making for a more temperate climate than further inland, so that there is never a problem with frost. This is the *terroir* of Sigean, which adjoins the coastal part of the appellation of Fitou. There are not many producers here, with the Cave Rocbère, of which more on page 160, accounting for sixty per cent of the production of this particular *terroir*.

For Flandroy, the wines of Sigean are more rounded and have more body than other Corbières. He produces a white, a pink and three different red wines. First of all we tasted some 1998s, dipping into various vats and barrels. I asked him when he did his blending. 'Well, that depends on my mood' was the reply. He has a variety of different barrels, including some of American oak, but is tending to reduce the proportion of new oak. The cellar is neat and well run, with an attractive barrel cellar. Flandroy would like to enlarge it. but that is problematic, as the water table is so high and you also have to be very careful about pollution around the *étangs*, which form part of a nature reserve. With so much still water around, mosquitoes are also a problem. He has found pieces of amphora in the vineyards, as well as a very attractive little piece of pottery, a *vendangeur* with a bunch of grapes. Maybe there was a Roman villa here once. He does not know.

The 1998 generic red, mainly Carignan with some Syrah and Grenache Noir, was still in vat, and was rounded and fruity with a hint of liquorice. It will spend some time in wood before bottling. Cuvée Angélique, a blend of Syrah, Grenache Noir and a little Mourvèdre, is firm and peppery, with older vintages showing a potential for ageing, with some backbone and fruit. Cuvée Andréas, which is intended to be more structured, includes some oak-aged wine from the 1998 vintage. The 1996, from Carignan, Syrah and Grenache Noir without any oak, was firm and sturdy with some ripe fruit. The white is a blend of Bourboulenc, Grenache Blanc and Rolle, with some herbal fruit and a definite iodine note from the sea.

CHATEAU PRIEURE BORDE-ROUGE, LAGRASSE

You have to admire Alain Devillers. Despite being confined to a wheelchair as a result of childhood polio, he exudes the most enormous amount of energy. You sense that nothing is impossible for him, and in this he is supported by his wife Natasha. The purchase of Château Prieuré Borde-Rouge in 1994 represented a career change. He had worked in the Ministry of Finance and then took a sabbatical year in order to study oenology at l'Isle-sur-Sorgues. Afterwards he began looking for a property, initially in the southern Rhône and then spreading his horizons, considering some sixty estates altogether before finally arriving here outside the village of Lagrasse. The previous owner had sent all his production to the Vignerons du Val d'Orbieu. By contrast, Devillers now bottles all his wine, making a white, a *rosé* and two reds, including one aged in oak. He has twenty-three hectares: eighteen are in the appellation of Corbières, and there is some Merlot for *vin de pays* on more fertile land close to the river. Devillers does not see any uniformity in the soil of the *terroir* of Lagrasse. Some is pure lime-stone and some is mixed with clay. His vineyards are on a vein of red clay, which makes for pepper and spice in the wines. The white wine, a blend of Grenache Blanc and Macabeu with a drop of

Clairette, is fermented in oak and is full and nutty. For red wine there is Carignan, Grenache Noir and Syrah, but no Mourvèdre, as it is too cold here. The first red Le Jardin de Frédéric, named after their son, has some firm spice and fruit, while the Château Prieuré Borde-Rouge has oak on the nose, with a solid, cedary palate and some substance. It had spent several months in oak, in second-hand barrels from an impeccable address – Château Margaux.

DOMAINE DE ROQUENEGADE, LAGRASSE

From Château Prieuré Borde-Rouge we took the scenic route over the Montagne d'Alaric, past an old village of stone *capitelles*, some intact and some just piles of stones. There were clusters of pink orchids, and from the viewpoint near the top a breathtaking panorama of the Corbières vineyards and the village of Lagrasse. Our destination was Domaine Roquenégade, the property of Frédéric Juvet, an affable Swiss who has worked at Château Giscours and Château d'Yquem. His first vintage at Roquenégade was 1991. We walked through the vineyards in warm June sunshine, accompanied by both his cat and his dog. The property is surrounded by hills, with the remains of a castle in the rocks. The vineyards, lying at an altitude of some two hundred metres, face south. All together Juvet has twenty-seven hectares, including some Carignan planted in 1945, some Grenache Noir and Syrah and some Cabernet Sauvignon, Merlot and Tempranillo. Apparently Tempranillo enjoyed something of a fashion at the end of the 1960s. He is replacing some of the Carignan, as it ripens simply too late here, and is also planting some white varieties, Grenache Blanc and Roussanne. His white was lemony and fresh. A Merlot Vin de Pays de l'Aude was plummy with some stalky tannin, while the oak-aged Cabernet Sauvignon was more structured and rugged with cassis fruit, and the Domaine Roquenégade Corbières had firm fruit with dry tannins.

DOMAINE ST AURIOL, LAGRASSE

Domaine St Auriol is the property of Claude Vialade and her husband Jean-Paul Salvagnac, who bought it in a completely run-down condition in 1981. Vialade has had a long involvement with the development of the wines of this part of France. In the 1980s she was the export manager of the Vignerons du Val d'Orbieu, which she left in 1991 in order to become more involved with Domaine St Auriol. Since then she has also become very involved with the smaller growers' *syndicat* of the Corbières, the Union des Crus Signés, the members of which are all independent producers, with quite different aims from those of the co-operatives that dominate the larger *syndicat*. Vialade is also a vocal advocate of the creation of *crus*, within and ultimately outside the appellation of Corbières.

As for Domaine St Auriol, it is within the *terroir* of Lagrasse, which she sees as an intermediate region on the edge of the Mediterranean climatic influence. They never lack water, but they never have too much either, so Syrah performs well here. Domaine St Auriol were amongst the first to plant Roussanne and Marsanne in 1987, a year before they were allowed in the appellation. They ferment their white wine, which also includes Grenache Blanc, Macabeu and Bourboulenc, in barrel, which they believe enables the wine to last longer. There was no doubt that a 1989, drunk when it was ten years old, was opulently mature, with herbal notes, length and elegance. A red 1989 drunk on the same occasion showed a similar potential for longevity, with warm, mature fruit and an elegant, cedary palate, while a 1985, mainly from Carignan and aged in barrel, was quite firm and structured, but lacked the elegance of the 1989. A recent vintage of white was solid and nutty, while a recent red was supple and elegant.

Domaine St Auriol have seventy-two hectares of vines altogether, forty-five at St Auriol and the rest at Domaine de Montmija in the nearby village of Ribaute. There are extensive projects for new plantings, entailing the clearance of large expanses of *garrigue*. The soil here is a mixture of clay and limestone, and there is also some schist. The old cellar contains not only the usual stainless steel vats, but also some solid thick-walled stone vats. As well as French oak, they are experimenting with Russian and American oak.

LES VIGNERONS DE CAMPLONG, CAMPLONG

Co-operatives account for an important part of the production of Corbières, and there are several that work well for their appellation. Among these must be included the co-operative in the village of Camplong, on the southern side of the Montagne d'Alaric within the *terroir* of Lagrasse. Les Vignerons de Camplong is a small co-operative, founded in 1932, with some sixty-five members cultivating two hundred and fifty hectare of vines, all in the village of Camplong. However, six or seven people account for eighty per cent of the production, which means that there is a strong cohesion in the management. About ninety per cent of its production is appellation Corbières, which is unusually high, for co-operatives tend to make large quantities of *vin de pays*. A few of the vineyards, in a fertile area by the river, are classified as Vin de Pays de l'Aude, but most are on the terraces of the Montagne d'Alaric, on stony, clay and limestone soil, with the 620-metre high mountain providing protection from the Marin, the south and south easterly winds that usually bring rain. The co-operative has been run by the very competent and likeable Odile Dénat for the past twenty years. She is very much in favour of the concept of the *terroirs* for Corbières, for she considers that they enhance the reputation of the appellation and will improve its quality.

All the grapes are hand-picked, which is also unusual for a co-operative, but the vineyards are too small and the slopes too steep for large machines – and in any case all their Carignan is vinified by carbonic maceration, for which you need whole bunches. They produce three qualities of Corbières: Peyres Nobles (*peyres* means stones in Occitan); Château de Camplong, which is an eighty-hectare vineyard belonging to two members; and Fontbories, which is aged in oak.

First we tasted the white Peyres Nobles, a pure Grenache Blanc, with a light, lemony flavour. Les Vignerons de Camplong have had a pneumatic press since the mid-1990s and the fermentation temperature is controlled at 18°C. They are considering another grape variety for extra aroma, maybe Muscat, which is allowed up to ten per cent in the appellation, but as much as that would overwhelm the flavour. Just two or three per cent would give the added lift, but their Muscat will not be in production until 2002. Marsanne and Roussanne are other possibilities. The first vintage of white Fontbories was 1990. Again, it comes from Grenache Blanc – the oldest vines of which are over sixty years old – fermented in new oak and kept in barrels for five months. I found the flavour rather tarry and overwhelming. The pink Peyres Nobles is a blend of Grenache Blanc and Noir, Cinsaut and Syrah, all *saignée* after about six or eight hours, to make for some ripe raspberry fruit and fresh acidity.

The red Peyres Nobles is a blend of Carignan, Cinsaut and Syrah vinified by carbonic maceration, with some destemmed Grenache Noir. It was soft and fruity, with the suppleness coming from the carbonic maceration. Château Camplong is a blend of sixty per cent Carignan with small amounts of Grenache Noir, Syrah, Mourvèdre and Cinsaut. Mourvèdre is at its limit here. The wine was immensely drinkable, with ripe, plummy, rounded fruit. Fontbories, made for the first time in 1982, spends six months in barrel and includes some old Carignan, as well as Grenache Noir, Mourvèdre and Syrah that are given a three-week maceration. It was solid and substantial, a combination of perfumed fruit and structured oak, providing good ageing potential.

CAVE DU MONT TENAREL D'OCTAVIANA, ORNAISONS

The co-operative at Ornaisons goes by the name of Cave du Mont Tenarel d'Octaviana; the emperor Octavian passed through the area – there is a Roman villa near by – and Mont Tenarel dominates the skyline outside the village. This co-operative is somewhat larger than the one at Camplong, having 450 members cultivating 1320 hectares in Ornaisons and the surrounding villages. They touch three different *terroirs*, Lézignan, Boutenac and Fontfroide, and perceive quite pronounced differences between them. Fontfroide has sandier soil and the grapes ripen earlier; Boutenac is the latest to ripen, having a type of sandstone soil described as *grès pouding*; while Lézignan is pebbly clay and limestone, giving grapes that ripen neither early nor late. The members pay great attention to the differences, vinifying each *terroir* and grape variety separately, and in the case of Carignan keeping the older vines – forty-five years old or more – apart. Carbonic maceration plays an important part here too, for Grenache Noir, Syrah and Carignan, while the *vin de pays* from Merlot and Cabernet Sauvignon is destalked for a traditional vinification.

Altogether the co-operative puts some seven different qualities and styles of wine into bottle, with variations in blend and *élevage*. Their first oaked vintage was 1987, starting with just twenty-five barrels; now they have eight hundred and fifty, housed in a separate barrel cellar in the hamlet of Gasparets, an attractive hall with *barriques* and *foudres* underneath the Musée de la Faune, which features the regional wildlife. A brief glimpse at the museum revealed an excess of stuffed animals; I preferred the barrels below. Several of their wines are named after constellations, such as Eridan, a blend of Macabeu and Grenache Blanc with some firm fruit. Marsanne and Roussanne have also been planted to enhance the aroma, but were not yet in production. Château Hautrive-le-Haut, a separate estate, is made from Grenache Blanc, which is given some skin contact, fermented and then aged in wood for six or seven months, with a malolactic fermentation and a weekly *bâtonnage*. Their first vintage of this wine was 1989. I thought it well made, but with very opulent sweet oak on nose and palate.

Octobian, after another constellation, is a blend of Carignan and Grenache Noir given a couple of years of *élevage* in concrete vats. Le Morragon commemorates a local landowning family and is also a blend of Grenache Noir and Carignan, with some rugged, spicy character. Croix du Sud, or Southern Cross, is yet another Grenache Noir and Carignan blend, kept in *foudres* for fifteen months or so. It had the rugged flavour of the *garrigue*. The red Château Hautrive-le-Haut includes some Syrah as well as Grenache Noir and Carignan, which are aged in barrel for six months, then blended and given a year's *élevage* in vat. It was firm and structured with quite well-integrated oak. Finally their Cuvée Prestige, Sextant, made for the first time in 1993, is a blend of Syrah and old Carignan, all vinified by carbonic maceration and given six months *élevage* in new barrels. There are strict selection criteria. The Carignan is a minimum of sixty years old, although the Syrah is much younger, as the first vines were not planted until the mid-1980s. The flavour is rounded and oaky, with supple tannins. You feel that they are trying hard, but are perhaps hampered by their size and by the conservative attitude of some of their members. There is an insufficiently large volume of high-quality wines to create a better image for the appellation, and the wines are still much too cheap in the supermarkets.

CELLIER AVALON, MONTGAILLARD

The Cellier Avalon in the village of Montgaillard is not so much a co-operative as a group of people who work together, within a similar organisational structure to a commune or a kibbutz. One of the pressing problems of rural France is depopulation: young people leave the villages where their parents have lived all their lives, with the result that the population is ageing and agriculture is dying. In the nearby village of Massac the vineyards have all disappeared and the inhabitants consist of a handful of elderly people. The contrast with Montgaillard is marked. This is a lively little village, with enough children to justify a small school and with several families cultivating the vineyards, but this is a transformation that has taken place in the space of ten years or so. In 1988 there were just twenty-eight inhabitants, but by 1998 that number had increased to sixty-five, including twenty children. The village itself has bought fifteen houses, which have been made available for people coming to work and settle here from other parts of France. Every effort is made to attract the right kind of people – not necessarily those with money to invest, but people with the appropriate attitude, work ethic and approach to the project. Everyone is involved in the Cellier Avalon, working in the vineyards, in the cellar and at wine fairs. Only the oenologist draws a regular fixed salary.

Sylvie Larregola took me to see the ruins of the castle above the village. She described the area as 'the roof of the Corbières', as it has some of the highest vineyards of the appellation, at three hundred and fifty to four hundred metres. This is the *terroir* of Termenès, which is characterised by its cool nights, markedly different from those of vineyards at a lower altitude, and this makes for good white and *rosé* wines. The vintage is usually two to three weeks later than in the other parts of the Corbières, so that they are usually starting the harvest as the others finish and there is a little more rain. From the castle ruins there were magnificent views towards Mont Tauch, which dominates the skyline, and in June the ruins were a riot of summer flowers.

Michel Larregola took over the running of the Cellier Avalon in 1987, and has helped to encourage the planting of better grape varieties, at the rate of five to ten hectares a year. When he arrived here, there was virtually no Syrah, but now there are thirty-five hectares. The wine is made in a cellar dating from the 1930s, with the conventional cellar architecture and the indestructible concrete vats of the period. Cellier Avalon vinify the grapes from three villages, Dernacueillette, Maisons and Montgaillard. The soil at Montgaillard is stony clay and limestone, and in the other two villages it is schist. In 1998 seven families had 140 hectares, where there were only ninety hectares in production in 1988. Two hundred hectares will be the maximum. They aim to have half the vineyards planted with *cépages améliorateurs* by 2002, white as well as red, so in addition to Syrah, Grenache Noir and Mourvèdre, there is Roussanne, Marsanne, Rolle, Grenache Blanc and Muscat.

Cellier Avalon have a firm belief in what they are doing, and their enthusiasm for what they have achieved is infectious. The wines are convincing too. A white Domaine des Mitounes, from Grenache Blanc and Macabeu, was fresh and fruity with a pithy hint of grapefruit. A second white, Vertiges, from Grenache Blanc, Macabeu and eventually Roussanne when it comes into production, is fermented in oak, with a regular *bâtonnage* over five months. It was very oaky on the palate, reminding me of a white Rioja. Rosée d'Octobre, from pure Syrah, is a play on words, for the vintage may be as late as October when there is morning dew or *rosée* on the grapes.

They make three reds. Domaine des Mitounes is a blend of Carignan, Syrah and Grenache Noir, with some attractive peppery spice, for Syrah in this cooler area is especially peppery in character. Château Avalon, mainly from Syrah with some Grenache Noir, is firm and structured, while Vertiges, a pure Syrah, is given five or six months in barrels. Their first vintage of pure Syrah in wood was the 1995, redolent of ripe berries, rich and rounded and packed with peppery flavours. I much preferred it to the white Vertiges. A pure Syrah is possible, as the appellation regulations stipulate no maximum percentage. There is also a little Vin de Pays de Cucugnan, from Carignan and Merlot grown in vineyards around the village in the southern part of the Corbières.

Cellier Avalon have also tried a late harvest wine, picking some Grenache Blanc on a brilliantly sunny 6 January 1997. The bunches had been protected with plastic bags to keep off birds and inclement weather, and the grapes were quite shrivelled and raisiny. They are waiting to see how the wine will develop, for there is no tradition of late harvest wines in the Corbières. It is a very exciting project that will do much to enhance the region and which deserves to succeed.

CELLIER CHARLES CROS, FABREZAN

Fabrézan is a sleepy little village on the banks of the Orbieu. Its one claim to fame is that it is the birthplace of Charles Cros, a man of many parts, a poet who also invented the phonograph and refined the process of colour photography. There is a small museum in his memory attached to the town hall, but as it is only open during the rather limited office hours, I never saw it. Appropriately, the co-operative in Fabrézan is known as the Cellier Charles Cros. Three hundred members have fifteen hundred hectares. Nearly all the production is of red wine, with some Merlot Vin de Pays d'Oc and Vin de Pays d'Hautrive en Pays d'Aude as well as Corbières. This seems a well-run co-operative that is trying hard to improve its quality. The vineyards are mainly within the *terroirs* of Boutenac and Lagrasse, but they do not see any great climatic differences between the two. Nor are the geographical differences very evident; Boutenac perhaps has more terraces.

However, Cellier Charles Cros have been working on a selection of vineyard sites over the last fifteen years, establishing three quality levels using various criteria. They consider the soil, looking for clay and limestone on hillsides for Carignan. Schist is also acceptable, but not alluvial soil. The age of the vines is significant, as well as their health, or *état sanitaire*, and the type of pruning, which must be *gobelet* for Carignan. For Syrah, they want what they call *semi-coteaux*, slightly hilly vineyards that are not too arid, and the *guyot* system of pruning. Their first Syrah were planted about 1984. Different prices will be paid for different grape varieties. Despite all this effort, only about five per cent of the Cellier Charles Cros production is bottled, and they sell a significant proportion of their wine *en vrac* to the Vignerons du Val d'Orbieu. During the summer months, however, the members' wives run a stall in the village square, selling bottles to passing tourists.

There is an old phonograph in the tasting area – all that was needed was the dog to make the logo for His Master's Voice. The names of the wines continue the musical theme. A white Corbières

Arpège from Grenache Blanc with some Macabeu and Marsanne was fresh and lemony. They make four different red Corbières: Fabrézan, Arpège, Charles Cros and Délicatesse, usually with carbonic maceration for Syrah and Carignan, but not for Grenache Noir. Charles Cros, a blend of Carignan, Syrah and Grenache Noir, is given a long maceration and *élevage* partly in vat and partly in barrel. It was rounded and supple with hints of vanilla. Délicatesse, from Syrah with some Carignan, is their best red and an example of pure carbonic maceration, with fifteen months of oak ageing. It was a mouthful of smoky oak, vanilla and firm fruit. They have worked with barrels since the mid-1980s, trying out different coopers but always using French oak. Fabrézan is a blend of Carignan, Grenache Noir and Syrah with *élevage* in vat, making for a rugged, leaner wine, while Arpège, a blend of Carignan with Grenache Noir and Cinsaut, was more supple and easy. You felt that they were trying hard, but were slightly hampered by economic and market realities. The sharp spring frost of 1998 would slow the renovation work in the cellar, as they knew they would have less wine to sell and consequently less money to invest.

CAVE ROCBERE, PORTEL-DES-CORBIERES

The co-operative at Portel-des-Corbières, the Cave Rocbère, is a tourist attraction. This is a pretty little village, with houses in soft sandstone. Bright red and black flags, the colours of the local rugby team, were flying from the rooftops. The co-operative stands above the village, with a smart shop front offering panoramic views over the surrounding countryside. The hillside underneath is riddled with the galleries of gypsum mines that were in operation until the 1920s. Altogether there are thirty-five kilometres of tunnels, some eighty metres below ground, of which the co-operative uses just seven hundred metres, partly as a barrel store. They have also created a museum, opened in 1994, that contains a reconstruction of the old mine face as well as various Roman artefacts, both original and modern imitations – the Domitian Way ran close by and land here was given to Roman legionnaires who settled here as farmers. There are various vinous artefacts and old pieces of equipment, and a cooper's workshop is planned. As for the barrels, they have about a thousand *barriques*, with American oak from

Boutes, the cooper in Narbonne, and also Seguin Moreau and Vicard, as well as some *foudres*.

This is the largest co-operative of the Corbières, with some eight hundred members and 2400 hectares of vines producing 120–140,000 hectolitres annually, of which about 50–60,000 are Corbières; in other words, a tenth of the production of the appellation. About twenty thousand hectolitres are bottled, with the rest sold *en vrac*. Above ground, in a corner of the bustling shop, we tasted a range of wines. They have two brand names, Vent Marin for a more modern style of varietal wines and Rocbère for more traditional Corbières. Sauvignon was planted in the mid-1990s and makes a not very refined Vin de Pays d'Oc. Chardonnay, planted in about 1992, is lightly fruity, while the Corbières Blanc, from Rolle and Grenache Blanc, is more individual with some lightly grassy, floral fruit. Rolle was planted at the same time as Sauvignon.

As for red wines, a Rocbère Vieux from Carignan and Grenache Noir, given three or more years *élevage* in vat, was soft and supple. Rocbère Macération, including Syrah, which was first planted about 1980, was ripe and rounded. Château de Mattes, one individual estate, with old Carignan and Cinsaut vines, as well as a little Mourvèdre and Syrah, spends twelve months in vat. It seemed sturdier and more peppery. This is the *terroir* of Sigean, which has a lower altitude, limestone soil and a maritime climate, so that Mourvèdre works well as a result of the maritime humidity and is included in the Corbières Vent Marin, with its appealingly spicy flavour. Grand Opéra, named quite simply because the director, Henri Fourques, enjoys singing, is made by carbonic maceration from Syrah, old Carignan, Mourvèdre and some Grenache Noir. It spends eight months mainly in French oak. Fourques finds that American oak has a more obvious flavour, and I certainly detected vanilla on the nose and palate, with some ripe cherry fruit and supple tannins. Terra Vinae is their best red wine, with forty per cent Mourvèdre as well as Syrah, Grenache Noir and some very old Carignan. It spends twelve months in oak, resulting in an attractive spicy, oaky flavour, with good texture and body. We finished on a sweet note, a late harvest wine from Grenache Blanc, from grapes both *passerillés* and with botrytis. It was a delicious combination of biscuity, honeyed fruit with balancing acidity, providing a fitting finish before heading for Fitou.

OTHER ESTATES

With so many producers in the Corbières, there have been inevitable omissions. What follows is a brief selection of other producers whose wines I have enjoyed over the last few years. Domaine du Révérend and Domaine du Trillol, in the village of Cucugnan on the southern edge of the appellation, represent a Bordelais interest in the Midi. Peter Sichel of Maison Sichel first invested in the Corbières in 1989 and now his son Benjamin makes the wine in both properties. Another Englishman, Nick Bradford, bought his estate at Albas in the *terroir* of Saint Victor in 1989 and sells his wines under the name Domaine des Pensées Sauvages.

The Cave d'Embrès et Castelmaure, with its oak-aged Cuvée des Pompadours, has continued to work well for its members, under the guidance of an energetic director, M. Pueyo. Since their very first bottling in 1968, André and Suzette Lignères have consistently produced stylish wine at Château la Baronne outside the village of Fontcouvert on the slopes of the Montagne d'Alaric. Jean de Cibeins at the Château de Cabriac produces sturdy, structured wines from the foot of the Montagne d'Alaric. Dominique Gibert at Domaine Faillenc Sainte Marie, also on the Montagne d'Alaric, combines elegance with concentration, making wines with restraint and backbone, using old Bordelais barrels for his *élevage*. Anne de Voluntat at Château les Palais makes an intriguing Cuvée Randolin from very old Carignan blended with Syrah and Grenache Noir that is partly aged in new wood. Henri Leferrer was formerly a *régisseur* at Domaine de la Romanée Conti and in 1989 began a new venture in the Corbières with the creation of Domaine du Grand Crès at Lagrasse. His wines are elegant and structured. And there are many others that I have not been able to visit: Château Haute-Fontaine, Château Fontsainte, Château Mansenoble, Château Gléon-Montanié, Château Etang des Colombes, Château Pech-Latt, to name but a handful.

Key facts

VDQS 1951, AC 1985; fourth largest AC, with twenty thousand hectares in eighty-seven *communes*; fifty-four co-operatives and four hundred private estates.

Red, with five per cent each of white and pink wine.

Grape varieties:

RED: Carignan, reduced to fifty per cent maximum by 2003; Cinsaut, Grenache Noir, Syrah, Mourvèdre.

WHITE: Grenache Blanc, Bourboulenc, Macabeu, Marsanne, Roussanne, Rolle.

Eleven *terroirs* recognised, but not used on the label; most important are Sigean, Durban, Fontfroide and Lagrasse.

Soil is variations on limestone and clay.

Vintages

1999: Not an easy year, with an August heat wave and rain in September, but some good wines none the less.

1998: General enthusiasm for a year that produced ripe fruit and well structured wines. Some hail in August.

1997: A larger vintage, the result of some summer rain, making for lighter, more immediately fruity wines.

1996: Another vintage affected by cooler weather, making for less structured, more accessible wine.

1995: A good year with a warm summer, making for warm, ripe wines throughout the appellation.

Fitou

Fitou prides itself on being the oldest appellation for table wine in Languedoc, dating from 1948. Earlier appellations, such as Rivesaltes and Maury, were all for *vins doux naturels*, indicating what was considered at the time to be the true vocation of this part of the Midi. The nearby appellation of Côtes du Roussillon did not follow until 1977, and Corbières had to wait until 1985.

The creation of the appellation of Fitou was the result of an early push towards quality by a group of determined wine growers who wanted the best for their area, and who pursued their quest for an appellation with an energy that was not apparent elsewhere in the region in the post-war period. Today, however, the differences in quality between Fitou and Corbières or Côtes du Roussillon are more blurred, although Fitou is currently enjoying a commercial success, which gives its producers a price advantage over its neighbours. The very first harvest declaration in 1948 produced just two thousand hectolitres, while today by contrast the average annual production is about one hundred thousand hectolitres. The appellation has grown as people have preferred to make table wine rather than the Rivesaltes for which many of the vineyards in the area were first planted.

The appellation of Fitou divides into two distinct areas: Fitou-Maritime, with vineyards on the coastal plains around the village of Fitou itself and the Etang of Leucate; and Fitou de Hautes-Corbières, with vineyards on the rugged hillsides of the Corbières range, where they are interspersed with those of Corbières itself. Nine villages make up the appellation: in Fitou-Maritime they are Fitou, Leucate, La Palme, Caves et Treilles (two villages separated by the motorway) and Feuilla, while Fitou de Hautes-Corbières comprises Cascatel, Villeneuve-les-Corbières, Paziols and Tuchan.

Apparently the initial intention was to create two appellations, Fitou and Côtes de Tauch, but instead the INAO opted for a single appellation, which was in fact delayed by the outbreak of the Second World War. With a lack of foresight, the villages between the two zones did not wish to accept the constraints on grape varieties and yields and so refused the appellation. Now, of course, they regret it.

Fita in Occitan means a border or frontier, and the village of Fitou with its ruined hilltop castle did once form the part of the frontier between Catalonia and France, confronting the much better preserved fortifications of Salses in Roussillon. The origins of the vineyards of Fitou are Roman, for this was one of the many vineyards created by the Romans when they came to Narbonne. The Domitian Way ran through the region and Roman amphorae have been found locally. But from then on Fitou seems to have fallen into oblivion. According to Hubrecht Duyker in his *Grands Vins du Rhône et du Midi*, it was drunk at the courts of Louis XIII and XIV but otherwise received little recognition.

The nineteenth-century wine writers gave it scant mention. Jullien listed it among the wines of Narbonne with Leucate, Treilles and Portets, while Rendu mentioned it as one of the most esteemed *crus* of the Aude, along with La Palme, Sigean (now a Corbières village) and Leucate. However, the introduction of better transport into the area, notably the construction of the railway line to Narbonne through the villages of Tuchan and Villeneuve-les-Corbières, helped to develop the wine. Viticulture was encouraged in the Hautes-Corbières after the phylloxera crisis, replacing to some extent the cultivation of wheat and the breeding of sheep.

Unlike Corbières and Côtes du Roussillon, Fitou is for the moment firmly red, although there are moves afoot to develop a white wine in the appellation, and there is even talk of a *vin doux naturel*, in an effort to shed the tarnished reputation of Rivesaltes. The principal grape varieties of Fitou are Carignan and Grenache Noir, with either Syrah or Mourvèdre. You will find Syrah in the dry hills of the Hautes-Corbières, where it ripens early and is usually picked at the beginning of the harvest towards the end of August. By contrast, Mourvèdre ripens later and needs the maritime atmosphere of the coastal vineyards, enjoying the humidity of the early morning sea mists. For most producers it is Carignan that provides the typicity of the appellation, with a minimum of thirty per cent in the blend so that Syrah does not overwhelm the wine. Carignan, especially from old vines, gives the wine structure and backbone. Grenache Noir must also be a minimum of thirty per cent and rounds out the wine, providing body and alcohol, while Mourvèdre and Syrah, which have been allowed in the appellation since 1982, must not exceed thirty per cent. Fitou must consist of at least two grape varieties, but unlike the other red appellations of the Midi, Syrah and Mourvèdre are not obligatory *cépages améliorateurs* – at least, not yet. However, from 2008 one or other must represent ten per cent in the blend. The INAO also insists on a minimum alcohol of 12°, and the obligatory period of *élevage* was increased from nine to eleven months for the 2000 vintage. You might also find Lladoner Pelut, a very close relative of Grenache Noir, as well as Cinsaut and Terret Noir, and until recently a small amount of white grapes, up to ten per cent of Macabeu, could be included in Fitou, but no longer.

The INAO has in principle accepted the idea of an appellation for Fitou Blanc. The aim is to create a wine not dissimilar to a white Châteauneuf-du-Pape, with some *élevage* in oak, which would distinguish it from Corbières Blanc. The grape varieties under consideration are those traditional to the region, which were originally planted for Rivesaltes. Macabeu is likely to form the base, with some Grenache Blanc and just a hint of Muscat, both *à petits grains* and *à gros grains*. They have been working on this, in conjunction with SICAREX, since about 1991, with seven producers acting as guinea pigs. The ultimate aim is to produce a barrel-fermented wine that would be different from any neighbouring appellation or local *vin de pays*.

It is possible to discern a difference of style between the two main types of Fitou. In general, Fitou-Maritime tends to be suppler and lighter with less tannin, and is best drunk relatively young, while the wine of the Hautes-Corbières has a firmer structure and will age longer. That said, much depends upon the style of the individual producers. The appellation is largely dominated by the six village co-operatives, which account for eighty-seven per cent of the production, but there is also a growing number of independent producers.

I spent an afternoon in the Fitou Maritime, fortified first by lunch at La Cave d'Agnès, a friendly restaurant in the village of Fitou opposite a tiny eleventh-century chapel. In fact, Agnès is Joanna and English, and she provides a tempting array of regional *hors d'oeuvres* of infinite variety, after which carnivores can attack barbecued steaks of gargantuan proportions.

DOMAINE LEPAUMIER, FITOU

Our first visit was to Domaine Lepaumier, which has cellars right in the centre of the village of Fitou and a total of thirty-two hectares of vines. Fernand Lepaumier bottled his first wine in 1987, whereas his father had always sold to the *négoce en vrac*. Their Fitou is very typical, a blend of two-thirds Carignan to one-third Grenache Noir, made purely by carbonic maceration, which softens some of the rugged edges of the Carignan. The 1996 vintage had a solid, dense flavour with tannin and warmth, while the 1995 was a little more developed, with some spicy fruit, and was drinking beautifully in the summer of 1998. Domaine Lepaumier have planted Mourvèdre, but as the vines were still only six years old, the grapes were included in a *vin de pays*.

CHATEAU ABELANET, FITOU

Régis Abélanet also has his cellar in the village of Fitou. His family can trace the ownership of their vineyards back to 1697, for there is a deed in the archives of Carcassonne. His great-grandfather provided evidence for the INAO to prove the earlier reputation of Fitou, with gold medals from the Concours Régional de Montpellier in 1877 and 1885. In those days you received a medal made of real gold, not just a piece of paper. His father was the first person in the village to put his wine in bottle. It was as recently as 1960, and everyone thought he was mad. Then in the 1970s he was the first to plant Syrah in the area. Abélanet prefers Syrah to Mourvèdre, as Syrah provides the aroma that Carignan may lack. Nonetheless, he is very enthusiastic about Carignan, describing himself as *un fervent du Carignan* when it is grown on schist. With low yields, no more than 40 hl/ha, pure Carignan can be excellent, while the addition of Grenache Noir and Syrah makes for a more supple wine.

Régis Abélanet was all set to be a lawyer, a *notaire*, but was put off when his first client turned out to be someone who had come to make their will. The day we met, he had been up all night spraying his vines against oidium, for it is much better to spray at night when there is no wind. He considers that carbonic maceration flattens the wine and much prefers a traditional vinification, destalking the grapes, a long *cuvaison*, grape variety by grape variety, and a hot vinification of up to 32°C, otherwise Carignan can lack body and substance. His blend is roughly sixty per cent Carignan with Syrah and Grenache Noir. Usually his wine is aged in French oak, but in 1997 he experimented with some American oak, which gave quite a sweet, herbal flavour. I preferred the 1996 with its firm, sturdy flavour. He also makes a Cuvée Vieilles Vignes, mainly from Carignan but with a little Syrah and Grenache Noir, which is warm and rugged with a firm concentration of fruit and tannin.

CAVE COOPERATIVE DE FITOU

From there we went to the village co-operative, which was founded in 1933. Claude Raffanel, the director, explained how the improvement in cellar equipment – a destemmer, temperature control and a pneumatic press – has changed the profile of the appellation. Ten years ago the difficult vintage of 1997 would have been even more problematic, but now they are able to overcome complications caused by humidity and rain. The Cuvée Terre Natale is a classic blend for this part of the appellation, with equal parts of Grenache Noir and Carignan and just ten per cent of Mourvèdre, aged for twelve months in vat. The 1996 was firm and tannic, while the 1995 had developed some of the warmth of the *garrigue*, with a rugged finish. 1995 was quite a concentrated vintage, while 1996 was more supple. They also produce a Cuvée Prestige, aged in oak, mainly from old Carignan vines, with some Grenache Noir and a little Mourvèdre. Mourvèdre provides a useful antidote to the tendency of the Grenache Noir to oxidise. The wine tasted quite youthful, with warmth and perfume. The co-operative is also one of the cellars working on the proposed Fitou Blanc, but the sample I tasted had spent four months in oak and seemed to have completely lost its fruit.

LES VIGNERONS DU CAP LEUCATE, LEUCATE

From Fitou we drove over the plateau of Leucate, which lies between the *étang* and the sea. It seemed to consist of a maze of stone walls, most of which had long since crumbled into rubble, but which are now being rebuilt to form a jigsaw puzzle of tiny plots of vines. The broom was in flower, providing splashes of brilliant yellow; a local saying has it that when the broom flowers, you should take care of your vines – that is, during the months of May to July – and then in August you can go on holiday.

Leucate is a prosperous looking village and its co-operative boasts a smart tasting and sales area. The white wine was more impressive here, and the example I tasted benefited from some maturity. 1994 Terre Ardente had spent nine months in wood as well as time in vat, and had only recently been bottled. It had hints of herbal oak and perfumed honey, with a certain *moelleux* character.

As for red wines, there are various labels and estates. Fitou du Vigneron de Combe Neige, a blend of old Carignan, Mourvèdre and Grenache Noir, had firm rugged fruit. The *élevage* takes place in vat, but confusingly old Carignan vines can easily give the impression of a wine aged in wood. Domaine Cézelly, from more or less equal parts of Carignan, Mourvèdre and Grenache Noir, was firm and smoky. As opposed to the schist in the hills, the soil here is mainly clay and limestone, so they find Syrah to be much less powerful; it performs much better on schist, making richer, fatter wines. Their oldest Mourvèdre vines are only fifteen years old and for the moment the grapes are vinified by carbonic maceration, as you can extract more from the variety that way. 1993 was the first time they used small barrels, both French and Russian oak. I tasted the 1994 Le Maritime, as their oaked *cuvée* is called, a blend of more or less equal parts of Carignan, Mourvèdre and Grenache Noir, which was firm and tight, but a touch woody on the finish.

COOPERATIVE DES PRODUCTEURS DE MONT TAUCH, TUCHAN

From Leucate I headed inland to the wild hills of the Hautes-Corbières with their Cathar castles. Mont Tauch, at nine hundred metres, is the highest mountain of the Corbières and rises dramatically behind the village of Tuchan, home of the Co-operative des Producteurs de Mont Tauch, which, with an annual average of 42,000 hectolitres, is the largest producer of Fitou. They also make Corbières, *vin de pays* and Rivesaltes, but their reputation is based on Fitou. Most of the vineyards are on a plateau surrounded by mountains, which give the area a particular microclimate with late springs and very hot summers.

I saw some impressive installations covering a large area on the outskirts of the village, which prompted me to ask about financing. The co-operative does receive some subsidies, from both national and local government as well as from Brussels, but a large part of their investment is self-financed, with the inevitable loan from the Crédit Agricole. They have a brand-new vinification cellar and also a new *quai de réception*, which allows them to make a more detailed selection of grapes at vintage time. They recently amalgamated with the co-operative of the nearby village of Paziols and some rationalisation is taking place: Paziols has the barrels for *élevage*, but the wine is made at Tuchan.

Further changes will take place following a yet more recent merger with another two neighbouring co-operatives, Durban and Villeneuve, of which more on page 173–4. There have been developments in vinification in recent years, with a new method of *débourbage* and greater care being taken over oxidation for their white wines. As for reds, they do much more *égrappage* for Syrah and Grenache Noir. The technique of *délestage*, running the juice off the cap, is proving successful, and they are now experimenting with mechanical *pigeage* and rotary vats, all in the interests of better extraction of flavour.

However, some of the co-operative's most important innovations are taking place in the vineyard. They are working on methods of cultivation, replanting vineyards with better grape varieties and introducing more precise ripeness checks, so that they receive the grapes of similar maturity all together and thus avoiding extremes of quality. They are looking at the surface area of the leaf and the health of the grapes. Everything is carefully controlled, with measures to ensure that their growers are meeting the various criteria and can be remunerated accordingly.

Although Corbières is also produced in the village – in fact, in some instances Corbières is treated almost as a second wine – there should be a distinct difference between the two wines. Corbières is generally more supple, while Fitou, with its obligatory period of ageing, is more powerful and structured. This was certainly true of the co-operative's range, with some supple peppery Corbières contrasting with the more rugged Fitou. Of the Fitou, Château de Ségure is firm and plummy, while the Prestige de Paziols is youthful and oaky. Terroir de Tuchan impressed me the most, with its firm integrated oak, youthful structure and appealing smoky fruit.

DOMAINE ROLLAND, TUCHAN

In the centre of the village, in a town house on the square, I tracked down Louis Colomer of Domaine Rolland. What should be his front parlour is in fact his tasting room, and he has a small, simple cellar out the back, with concrete vats as well as four old stone ones. A great-great-grandmother, Mlle Rolland, married a M. Colomer, hence the name of the estate. He is the fifth generation wine grower here, and he remembers his grandfather selling his wine in *demi-muids*, sending it by train from the old station at Tuchan. Colomer has thirty hectares, mainly of Fitou, in fifteen different plots all around the village, including some eighty-year-old Carignan. For him there is no question about it: Carignan forms the base of Fitou. You need small yields to obtain the necessary concentration, which will allow the wine to age for seven to ten years. The rainfall is low and there is a lot of wind and sunshine, all of which keep the yields low.

Colomer makes two *cuvées* of Fitou, both by carbonic maceration, which he has practised for twenty-five years. He does not see the point of ageing his Fitou in wood, for it is already tannic enough. His 1995, a particularly good vintage, was impressive: powerful and elegant at the same time, with rounded fruit and a long finish. The 1996 was more aromatic, and I also tasted a Cuvée Spéciale, a selection of the best vines, which was more structured with plenty of body. Colomer has recently planted some Viognier, which is not allowed for either Corbières or the proposed Fitou Blanc, but it is a variety that he likes and he will probably try fermenting it in wood once the vines are in production.

CHATEAU NOUVELLES, TUCHAN

Château Nouvelles was one of the estates that helped to establish the early reputation of Fitou, for the Daurat family have been here since 1834 and first bottled their wines before the Second World War. The vineyards, outside the village of Tuchan, are dominated by the imposing ruins of the Château d'Aguilar. There are traces of a Roman villa and the remains of a medieval castle on the property, together with a hotchpotch of more recent buildings and an old-fashioned cellar with enormous hundred-year-old *foudres*, which are used for Rivesaltes, not Fitou. However, the twentieth century is encroaching, with stainless steel as well as concrete vats, and there are some new barrels for the experimental white Fitou. Jean Daurat would like to see the introduction of more aromatic varieties such as Marsanne and Roussanne, or even Gros or Petit Manseng, but he thinks that as it is they are just copying Corbières.

He has forty hectares of Fitou and a further thirty-five for Corbières and Rivesaltes, including some eighty-year-old Carignan and some much younger Syrah and Grenache Noir. He too is adamant that the typicity of Fitou comes from Carignan, and that people who use too much Syrah lose the originality of the appellation. Not only must the yields be low, but the grapes must be ripe, with 13° the absolute minimum or else the wine will be thin and mean.

His blend is usually half Carignan with fifteen per cent Syrah and thirty-five per cent Grenache Noir. Mourvèdre is not possible here. The soil is mainly schist, which is very good for both Carignan, giving a very good aroma, and for Syrah. Vinification entails some carbonic maceration for Grenache Noir and Carignan, but not for Syrah. However, the 'secret of the house' is the long ageing in *foudres*, usually for as much as five years. They do not add any tannin, but simply refine the wine, rounding out the tannins. The wine evolves very much for the first couple of years, but you must be meticulous about topping the *foudres* up every week, as they drink up the wine.

The 1993 Fitou, tasted in the spring of 1999, is very typical of the style of Château Nouvelles, with a dry, slightly meaty, spicy flavour. It compared favourably with the 1995, which exceptionally had only spent two years in *foudres* as it had to be bottled especially for the fiftieth anniversary of the appellation. It was dry and tarry, and did indeed taste as though it would benefit from more wood ageing. They also produce a magnificent range of Rivesaltes, all of which except the Vintage are given two years ageing in glass *bonbonnes* under the roof. The ten-year-old, with eight years in *foudres* as well as the two years in *bonbonnes*, had wonderful nutty flavours with hints of coffee, while the fifteen-year-old was drier and more intense. Jean Daurat explained that it is very easy to make. You just have to be patient and wait – and then he admitted that he really preferred to drink dry white as an aperitif.

DOMAINE DE ROUDENE, PAZIOLS

Domaine de Roudène is a small estate in the village of Paziols. On the other side of the valley you are in Roussillon. Mme Faixo explained how she and her husband settled here in 1974, taking over her mother-in-law's vines. Until 1986 they delivered their grapes to the village co-operative, but in that year they took the step of creating their own cellar. They now have twenty-two hectares in production of Fitou, as well as a little Corbières and Rivesaltes, made mainly from Carignan and Grenache Noir, with some Syrah which they planted ten years ago. Their Fitou vineyards are much steeper than those of Corbières.

We tasted in a neat little tasting cellar, with a phylloxera syringe hanging from the wall and an old wooden *érafleur*. With ripe berry fruit and liquorice overtones, the 1996 was much softer than the wine of Château Nouvelles, providing an intriguing contrast of style. It was aged in vat, although they are buying some barrels. Mme Faixo talked of the adventure of creating a wine estate. She comes from the adjoining department of the Ariège, which is rare for the south in having no wine of any note, just a departmental *vin de pays*.

CAVE PILOTE, VILLENEUVE-LES-CORBIERES

In 1948 the Cave Pilote of Villeneuve-les-Corbières was one of the experimental cellars for the then new vinification method of carbonic maceration. Professor Flanzy, the oenology professor at Narbonne University, developed the technique as a micro-vinification with INRA, and when he needed somewhere to try it out on a larger scale, the Cave Pilote obliged. The co-operative was also one of the first to put its wine in bottle, which was quite a revolutionary step in the early days of the appellation at the end of the 1940s. When the co-operative was formed in 1947, each member brought his own *foudres*. At that time Fitou was made almost exclusively from Carignan, as Grenache Noir was always used for Rivesaltes and Syrah was only introduced into the appellation in 1982. The director of the co-operative, Gérard Ploy, sees Syrah as the artistic touch, providing just a hint of make-up for the Carignan. Low-yielding Carignan gives wonderful wines with great concentration, while Grenache Noir provides alcohol but has less colour than Carignan; it is a late ripener, making for a longer harvest, but as it fades in wood, Ploy puts only Syrah and Carignan into oak.

The co-operative has a particularly impressive barrel cellar, which would not look out of place in a Bordeaux château. There is old and new oak of several different provenances, including Russia, Slovenia, America and France. Ploy prefers central European oak to American oak, which he finds too aromatic and smoky. The wine takes on the aroma very quickly and then stagnates, so that it needs a longer ageing period in American oak; but if the *élevage* is too short, the flavour of oak is overpowering. Central European oak gives some good results, but the production methods are not very meticulous. However, there is a significant price difference: you can buy a Slovenian barrel for FF 1600, whereas a French barrel will cost a further FF 1000.

Ploy believes carbonic maceration to be good for young wines. It produces an attractive flavour in Carignan, but will not last longer than three or four years. However, for Syrah he finds the flavour too short, while he prefers to vinify Grenache Noir traditionally, like Châteauneuf-du-Pape. The soil here is schist and Cave Pilote make a range of different Fitou from various estates, as well as an oak-aged wine, Marquis de Villecor, and a basic generic wine. The flavours were warm and rugged, just like the countryside.

There are other producers worth seeking out. I have enjoyed the wine from Domaine Lerys in the village of Villeneuve-les-Corbières, and from Jerôme Bertrand of Domaine Bertrand-Berger, a young estate in Paziols. Mme Colette Roustan-Fontanel makes some sturdy Fitou at Château les Fenals, where Voltaire's nephew was the *régisseur* and sent wine to Louis XIV.

The future for Fitou looks good. There have been difficult times, but for the moment the demand for Fitou is greater than the supply, resulting in a significant price difference between it and Corbières: the average bulk price for Fitou is FF 850–900 per hectolitre, as opposed to FF 500–550 for Corbières. There is also talk of a second-level Fitou, a village wine or a *cru*, which is a concept the INAO will not accept until the overall quality of the appellation has reached a good average. Jean Daurat would like a *cru* based on old vines and traditional varieties with a higher degree of alcohol; in other words, a wine that would be the very best of each vintage and would probably not be made each year. It would encapsulate all the flavours and warmth of the sun-soaked hills of Fitou.

Key facts

AC 1948; earliest table wine AC of Languedoc.

Two zones over nine villages, Fitou Maritime and Fitou de Hautes-Corbières; annual production 100,000 hectolitres; some vineyards can also produce Corbières and Rivesaltes, so precise area difficult to define.

Currently only red, with the base Carignan, a minimum of thirty per cent, plus Grenache Noir, Cinsaut, Lladoner Pelut, Terret Noir, Syrah and Mourvèdre, the last two being restricted to thirty per cent and not obligatory for the AC. Minimum of two varieties necessary; 12° and eleven months *élevage*.

Proposed Fitou Blanc: from Grenache Blanc, Macabeu, Muscat and others.

Vintages

1999: A wet spring with some hail; a warm but damp summer, followed by a warm, windy September.
1998: A dry spring, a hot, dry summer and a mild September made wines with good fruit and concentration.
1997: Cool wet early summer followed by a dry September; better than some parts of the Languedoc.

1996: Wet winter followed by a warm spring. Cool early July followed by a hot end of month. Some hail in August; warm and sunny September.

1995: Hot year with low rainfall, making for an early harvest, with well structured, sturdy wines.

Limoux

Limoux is a cheerful, bustling town. An attractive arcaded square provides the focal point, and the Café du Commerce is the local meeting place. Sit there long enough and you will see *tout* Limoux. The square serves as the market-place, and on 1 May there are flower ladies with the traditional bunches of lily of the valley. In the late winter the town comes alive with carnival festivities, with masked pirouettes in the streets. Crossed by the fourteenth-century Pont Neuf, the river Aude flows through the town and provides riverside views. I stayed in the rather incongruously named Hotel Moderne et du Pigeon, a rather elegant town house that had once been one of two separate hotels. There are no pigeons, but it had been extensively modernised since my previous visit ten years earlier.

Limoux lies south west of the city of Carcassonne and its imposing medieval citadel. The outskirts of the town proclaim its vinous activity, with loud signs advertising Blanquette and Crémant and offering cellar visits and tastings. The vineyards of the appellation cover a radius of some twenty kilometres around the town, between Carcassonne to the north and Quillan to the south. To the west they border the Côtes de la Malepère. In 1998 there were 3206 hectares of vines in production, planted mainly with Mauzac, the traditional variety of Limoux, but also with a substantial amount of Chardonnay, some Chenin Blanc and other varieties such as Cabernet Sauvignon, Merlot and Pinot Noir for *vins de pays*. Essentially there are four different appellations. First comes Blanquette de Limoux, which was created in 1938 and is based on Mauzac. The Méthode Ancestrale also dates from 1938 and involves a slightly different procedure from the traditional Champagne method used for the other two sparkling wines.

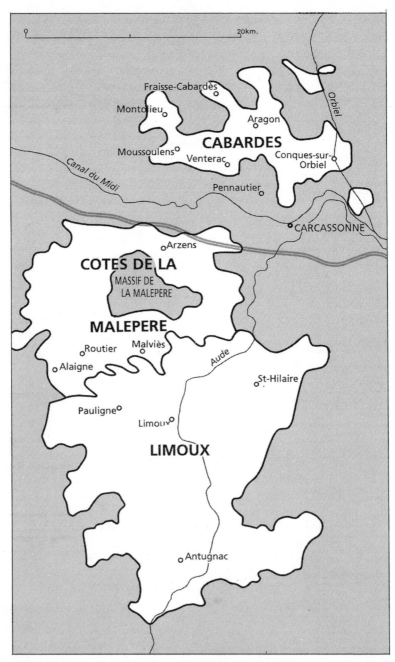

Limoux, Côtes de la Malepère and Cabardes

Crémant de Limoux, which includes a higher proportion of Chardonnay and Chenin Blanc, is a more recent creation, dating from 1990, while the still white wines of Limoux were given an appellation in 1993, with an obligatory period of *élevage* in oak until the beginning of the May following the vintage.

This is a wild, undulating region, with the valleys defined by the Aude and its various tributaries. The variety of microclimates and aspects has led to the definition of four different zones: Autan, Océanique, Méditerranéen and Haute Vallée. This is one of the coolest areas of the whole of the Midi. Autan is the area around Limoux itself, with vineyards at an altitude of two hundred and fifty metres protected by hills on both the east and west, making for a warm climate and early ripening grapes. The Haute Vallée is the highest and therefore coolest part of the appellation, with vineyards in the valley of the Aude in villages like Antugnac and Couiza. The Méditerranéen area lies to the east, with a warmer climate tempered by some maritime influence from the sea, while the Océanique zone, in the east, has a higher humidity than the other areas. Altogether the appellation covers some forty-one villages.

Limoux proudly claims to be the oldest sparkling wine of France, with an even longer history than Champagne. The monks of the Benedictine abbey of Saint Hilaire take credit for the discovery of the vinification process. Their twelfth-century abbey, a Romanesque church with peaceful Gothic cloisters, still stands in the sleepy village. It was fortified during the Hundred Years War and was very wealthy until its fortunes suffered because of the plague. You can also see the remains of the two refectories, one for travellers staying in the abbey and one for the monks, which are joined by a central pulpit to enable a monk to read to both guests and brothers. The chapel contains the tomb of Saint Sernin, the first bishop of Toulouse, with a twelfth-century sculpture depicting his martyrdom carved in marble from the Pyrenees. Saint Hilaire was the patron saint of the Counts of Carcassonne.

The first records of viticulture in the region date back to the tenth century, and during the Middle Ages various privileges regarding the sale of their wine were granted to the inhabitants of Limoux. In 1388 the chronicler Froissart referred to the *délectables beuveries de vin blanc Limouxin*. Authorities have set the date of the discovery of sparkling wine as early as 1531, although the ultimate source for this date is unknown. However, it predates Dom

Pérignon in Champagne by more than a century, for Dom Pérignon was cellar master at the abbey of Hautvillers from 1668 until his death in 1715. The discovery was presumably accidental, in that the monks found their wine began to ferment again in the spring after the winter cold, and managed to contain the carbon dioxide. Blanquette de Limoux was made by this method for several centuries until the Champagne method was adopted, but the tradition still lingers on in the small production of Méthode Ancestrale.

Sixteenth-century archives refer to the white wines of Limoux. In 1544 Blanquette was sent to the Sieur d'Arques and in 1578 to the Prévôt-Général of the king. In 1584 the Duc de Joyeuse celebrated the capture of Brugairolles with Blanquette. By the eighteenth century its reputation had spread further afield. In 1746 there was an order stipulating that thirty pots of Blanquette de Limoux should be sent to the students of the University of Paris, and in 1772 Paul-José Barthez, an eminent doctor of the University of Montpellier, recommended the use of Blanquette in the Paris hospitals.

In the nineteenth century it seems that Limoux was noted for its red as well as its white wines. Jullien said of the white wines that they had sweetness and elegance, sufficient alcohol and an attractive bouquet. A few years later Guyot compared the red wines with those of St Georges d'Orques, today part of the Coteaux du Languedoc, saying that they were lighter, but could rival a good Burgundy. They were made from Terret Noir, Picpoule, Carignan and Ribeyrenc. He mentioned Blanquette but emphasised that the area was important for its red wines. Rendu cited Limoux as one of the esteemed *crus* of the Languedoc and described Blanquette de Limoux as a white wine with a certain reputation; but he also said that the red wine from the hillsides was much better, though twice as expensive. He explained that Blanquette was bottled as soon as the tumultuous fermentation was finished and that ten thousand hectolitres of red wine were produced against three thousand of white. A few years later Mouillefert described Blanquette de Limoux as being very heady and having a good flavour. Red wine is made in Limoux today, but only as *vin de pays*, either de l'Aude or de la Haute Vallée de l'Aude, but more attention has been paid to it over recent years, with particular interest in Pinot Noir.

The essential difference between Blanquette and Crémant de Limoux is the preponderance of Mauzac, the characteristic grape of

Limoux. This variety provides the base of all the sparkling wines of Limoux. It is called Blanquette, which means white in Occitan, because of the white hairs on the underside of the leaves of the vines. Elsewhere it is only found in any significant quantity in the vineyards of Gaillac. It can be distinguished by a characteristic taste of quince, a bitterness on the finish and some firm acidity that makes it a highly suitable base for a sparkling wine. However, pure Mauzac can be short on intrinsic flavour, which encouraged people to experiment with Chardonnay and Chenin Blanc, the grape varieties that contribute respectively to Champagne and the sparking wines of the Loire Valley. The first plantings of these were made in the 1960s, and from 1975 a maximum of thirty per cent of Chardonnay and Chenin Blanc was allowed in Blanquette de Limoux. The precise proportions could vary within that total percentage, and then in 1978 Clairette, of which ten per cent had been allowed in the original appellation, was removed completely as it had always been found to oxidise and age badly. The final refinement came with the creation of Crémant de Limoux in 1990. The percentage of Chenin and Chardonnay in Blanquette was reduced to a total of ten per cent, so that Crémant de Limoux describes wine with a higher proportion of Chardonnay and Chenin, a minimum of thirty per cent with a maximum twenty per cent of either variety. The ageing period on the lees of the second fermentation is a minimum of twelve months, as opposed to nine months for Blanquette and fifteen for Champagne.

Chardonnay and Chenin Blanc have undoubtedly enhanced the quality of sparking Limoux. Chardonnay is popular as it is one of the grape varieties of Champagne and gives attractive aromas. It ripens early and is often picked at the end of August before it becomes overripe and loses its acidity. In contrast, Chenin Blanc is a late ripener with a very good acidity level and a honeyed bouquet when fully ripe. In 1984 there were 264 hectares of Chardonnay and 170 hectares of Chenin Blanc in production, but by 1999 they had grown considerably in importance, to 1,125 and 379 hectares respectively – although some of that Chardonnay is used for still wine. Every producer's best *cuvée* invariably contains the maximum proportion of each, and there are also producers who prefer to ignore Mauzac and the attendant regulations completely to concentrate on Chardonnay alone, or maybe with some Pinot Noir.

LES CAVES DE SIEUR D'ARQUES

The largest producer of Limoux is the Cave Coopérative de Limoux, which was founded in 1946 and now has 750 members who between them are responsible for about three-quarters of the appellation. In addition, there are about six other large producers, some of whom make wine only from their own grapes and others who buy in grapes and juice. Altogether twenty-eight producers bottle Limoux. The installations of the co-operative are pretty impressive, although small scale compared to some Champagne houses. There is the usual forest of stainless steel vats, new Bucher pneumatic presses all controlled by computer, a highly technical laboratory and nearly a kilometre of underground galleries quarried out of the hard sandstone to house the barrels for their still table wines.

Their range of sparkling wines consists of four different Crémant and five Blanquette de Limoux under various brand names, of which the most widely distributed is the Crémant de Limoux le Sieur d'Arques, from sixty per cent Mauzac and equal parts of Chardonnay and Chenin Blanc; this is given three years on the lees, resulting in some lemony, yeasty fruit. They also make a Méthode Ancestrale now that they have overcome the initial problems of instability.

However, the co-operative's most recent technological advances have been in the direction of table wines, concentrating particularly on still Limoux, defining the four distinct climatic zones within the appellation and working on the use of wood for fermentation. They have compared the results of skin contact with a traditional fermentation and examined different degrees of toasting and different origins of wood, Vosges, Allier, Nevers and Limousin, as well as American and Russian, or more precisely oak from the Ukraine. The French is best, predictably, but they also find that the fine grain of the Russian oak gives some interesting results, with fewer extracted tannins. The best plots of Chardonnay are chosen to produce just two barrels from each village, and since 1989 there has been an annual auction on Palm Sunday, the Toques et Clochers, with a three-rosette chef presiding over the occasion. The young wines tend to taste ostentatiously oaky, but none the less it was also possible to discern the climactic differences. The Méditerranéen, which has the warmest climate, was full and buttery after ten months on the fine lees, whereas the Autan from around Limoux was tighter, with firmer fruit, good acidity and less butter. The Océanique was quite rounded, but lighter and fresher, while the Haute Vallée, from vineyards at about four hundred and fifty metres, had a tight nose and an equally closed palate, with balanced oak, fruit and acidity. I was assured that they all had good ageing potential, but that the Méditerranéen and the Autan would develop earlier.

About fifteen years ago the co-operative bought the rundown Château de Flandry just outside Limoux, and they have restored the cellars, but not the house, and use the fourteen hectares of vineyards, planted with Mauzac, Chardonnay and Chenin Blanc, to experiment with cultivation techniques, such as leaf plucking and green harvesting. They have also experimented with an oak-aged Bordeaux blend of Cabernet Sauvignon, Merlot and Malbec.

ANTECH S.A.

Maison Antech is one of the larger producers, but remains very much a family concern. Françoise Antech, a member of the sixth generation, is gradually taking over commercial responsibilities from her father as he approaches retirement. Meanwhile, her uncle runs their vinification plant in Limoux and her sister and brother-in-law look after the family vineyards in Saint Hilaire. Originally the family produced still wine, but her father and uncle turned to sparkling wine some thirty years ago and now they make Crémant and Blanquette de Limoux, with just a tiny amount of still Chardonnay. As well as using the grapes from their own vineyards, they buy from thirty-five producers with whom they have long-term contracts and they work closely with them in the vineyards, advising on picking dates. The harvest usually starts at the beginning of September, although in 1997 it began exceptionally early, on 25 August, and lasted about a month, beginning with Chardonnay, then Chenin Blanc, and then a pause while the Mauzac ripened. The harvest should be over before the rains of the September equinox. The prices of the grapes are set each year by the *syndicat*. Chardonnay is inevitably the most expensive, at FF 6.70 per kilo, with Chenin Blanc at FF 5.40 and Mauzac at FF 5.15 for the 1999 vintage.

Production methods are absolutely classic. The grapes are delivered to the presses in three-hundred kilo containers. One hundred and fifty kilos provide a hundred litres of juice, which is categorised in a way similar to Champagne: the first sixty-five litres constitute the *tête de cuvée*, the next twenty-five litres the *premier taille* and the rest the *rebêche*, which goes to the distillery. The juice is left to fall clear overnight, and the fermentation temperature is carefully maintained at 18°C for twelve to fifteen days. Mauzac is particularly difficult to vinify, as it can oxidise easily and if the fermentation temperature rises too high, the flavour tends to go appley. The base wines undergo a malolactic fermentation and are blended in December, an *assemblage* of different climatic areas and grape varieties, with the aim of maintaining both the typicity of the appellation and the house style of the producer. Sugar and yeast are added to provoke the second fermentation, and the wine is left on the lees for a minimum of nine months for Blanquette and twelve months for Crémant, but it may well be longer, depending on producer preference. At Antech they use giropalettes, so that the *remuage* takes about four days, and at *dégorgement* they add a liqueur, 17–21 gms/l of sugar for the *brut* and 35 gms/l for *demi-sec*. It is also possible to find *demi-doux*, but that is rare. People tend to prefer their Limoux *brut*, although *demi-sec* has become more popular in the last few years.

Like Champagne, sparkling Limoux certainly seems to benefit from extra ageing and yeast autolysis. Antech's 1990 Crémant, tasted in the spring of 1998, was disgorged in 1997 and had an attractive nutty note on the nose, with honeyed, creamy toasted flavours on the palate. Their Crémant contains twenty per cent Chardonnay and the same of Chenin Blanc, but they would like to include more Chardonnay in the Crémant in order to create a greater distinction between it and Blanquette.

While there is no doubt that Limoux can provide excellent drinking value, its prices are affected by the price of Champagne. When Champagne prices fall too low, down to FF 45 per bottle rather than FF 55–60, Limoux has very much less room for manoeuvre, when Crémant is usually about FF 35–40 and Blanquette FF 30. If the differential is too small, people tend to favour cheap Champagne rather than a Crémant from elsewhere. However, the creation of the appellation Crémant de Limoux has undoubtedly enhanced the image of Limoux and brought it into line with the other Crémants of France.

DOMAINE LA BOTTEUSE, ANTUGNAC

It was Bernard Delmas in the village of Antugnac who explained the intricacies of the Méthode Ancestrale. The grapes are pressed and fermentation begins in the normal way, but is then stopped by filtration at a certain density, leaving half-fermented must which is left in vat over the winter and bottled in February or March. The second fermentation starts when the weather warms up and the remaining yeasts come to life, and then stops of its own accord when five or six atmospheres of pressure are reached, leaving about 80–100 gms/l of residual sugar and 5°–7° alcohol. The yeasts die of their own accord, but no one can quite explain how or why – possibly from the effects of the pressure within the bottle. Finally the wine is disgorged to remove the lees, but it is never star-bright. The whole process is all a little haphazard and the result is a lightly sweet, soft, fruity wine, with less weight than a Crémant or Blanquette as it is lower in alcohol. This is the tradition of Limoux that was in danger of disappearing, but it is now enjoying something of a gentle revival, and deservedly so.

Delmas has eighteen hectares in production, which he has converted to organic viticulture. The climate is enormously advantageous, so his main problem in the vineyard is the *cicadelle*, a small insect. In the cellar he avoids gelatine and uses very little sulphur. The typicity of the Haute Vallée is acidity, for it is cooler and fresher than the rest of the appellation. None the less, Delmas wants his grapes to be really ripe with plenty of flavour. He would also like to make Crémant with more Chardonnay than the regulations currently permit, while at the same time maintaining the individuality of Mauzac and Blanquette, which really represent the typicity of Limoux. Now that the name Languedoc has begun to acquire a certain cachet and recognition in the marketplace, there is some talk of an appellation Crémant du Languedoc, which would put Blanquette in a regional context, but for the moment it is nothing more than an idea.

Delmas's first vintage of still wine was in 1994 and he continues to experiment with oak and *élevage*, keeping the best vats for the appellation. Most of his still wine is sold as Vin de Pays de la Haute Vallée de l'Aude, as pure Mauzac or as blends of Chardonnay and Chenin Blanc or of Chardonnay and Mauzac. He wants to develop his Chardonnay, as he considers that its full potential has not yet been realised, and he would also like to try out some barrel-fermented Chenin Blanc. More could be done with Mauzac too, which must not be overlooked. Robert Plageoles, one of the leading exponents of Mauzac in Gaillac, has visited and encouraged, so Delmas has tried skin contact for Mauzac, which enhances the palate. He is also considering a longer ageing on the fine lees, again to extract more depth of flavour. Above all, Mauzac must not be buried under Chardonnay. Pinot Noir is another subject of tentative experimentation, with a first planting in 1997.

We talked about the development of the region and its wines. Wine is the main commercial activity in Limoux. There used to be some light industry, but the last shoe factory has just been taken over. Otherwise there is a little wheat, but no animal farming. Tourism could be developed, and there is also scope for increasing the vineyards. Things are better than they were ten years ago, when a lot of people were leaving the area; they are now returning and much greater attention is being paid to viticulture, with more interest from the younger generation. The growers' *syndicat* has worked hard to prevent vineyards in the appellation from being pulled up, by arranging *primes d'arrachage* for *vin de table* vineyards and subsidies for the purchase of appellation land. The price of a hectare of vines varies according to the grape variety. Mauzac is the cheapest at FF 60,000. Chenin Blanc costs FF 60–80,000, while Chardonnay is the most expensive, starting at FF 80,000 and going up to FF 100,000. Young people are being helped to set themselves up as *viticulteurs*, and villages that had been in danger of dying are coming to life again, so the future of the area looks better than it did a few years ago.

VIGNOBLES VERGNES, SAINT HILAIRE

One of the largest private estates, producing wines only from their own grapes, is Domaine des Martinolles, which belongs to the Vergnes family. Jean-Marc Vergnes' grandfather bought the original seven hectares, which have been gradually added to, most recently with the purchase of two neighbouring estates in the village of Saint Hilaire, Domaine Lamoure and Domaine du Plan Pujade, making a total of sixty-five hectares. The vineyards have been largely replanted over the last few years, with more Chardonnay, Chenin Blanc and Pinot Noir, and as well as the four Limoux appellations they make a range of *vin de pays*. Sparkling wine accounts for two-thirds of their production.

The cellars have been modernised, with automatic cooling equipment since 1990, and the immediate advantage for Jean-Marc Vergnes that he can now sleep through the night. Vignoble Vergnes make Méthode Ancestrale from the oldest vines and healthiest grapes grown on the best slopes. It is pure Mauzac and it was originally sold on the lees; now it is disgorged, but it is never absolutely bright and on the palate it tastes fresh and honeyed. Domaine des Martinolles is the first estate you reach when driving from Carcassonne, so that it comes within the Mediterranean zone, giving wines with good fruit and less acidity. The Blanquette, with ten per cent Chardonnay and five per cent Chenin, spending two years on the lees, is ripe and honeyed, while the Crémant, with twenty per cent each of Chardonnay and Chenin and three years on the lees, is more concentrated and firmer on the palate. Vignoble Vergnes also find sparkling wine difficult to sell, for the public simply sees Champagne and The Others and does not really appreciate the subtle differences between all the other sparkling wines. However, as the Languedoc acquires a more positive image, so the demand for Limoux is increasing.

Vignoble Vergnes are working on still wine, and they too believe in the potential of Mauzac with improvements in vinification, a cool fermentation and no skin contact. Their first attempt at an oaked Chardonnay was in 1993. Twelve months in Burgundian barrels with *bâtonnage* proved too much and they tried again in 1997. Meanwhile they have made some delicately fruity unoaked Chardonnay as a *vin de pays*. The 1997 unoaked Pinot Noir had some liquorice fruit and so in 1998 they intended to try putting it in wood. They admit to being very much on a learning curve with Pinot Noir. Meanwhile, there are moves to obtain an appellation for red wines, curiously enough not for Pinot Noir but for Cabernet Sauvignon, Merlot and Grenache Noir – in other words, grape varieties similar to those in the adjoining Côtes de la Malepère. The Commission of the INAO was due to visit in the spring of 2000.

DOMAINE DE L'AIGLE, ROQUETAILLADE

Not everyone conforms to the appellation. Jean-Louis Denois from Domaine de l'Aigle is an angry young man, articulate and committed, questioning the narrowness of the appellation regulations. He wants to show the potential of the *terroir*, but accuses the INAO of *apartheid viticole* by wanting everyone to cultivate its typicity with mediocre grape varieties. Therein lies the handicap of the Languedoc. Denois would describe Limoux as an island of freshness in the south, with its typicity a combination of ripeness and acidity, and he is convinced that Limoux is missing an opportunity with Pinot Noir and Chardonnay. These ideas do not come from the conventional background of a southern French wine maker. Denois is a *champenois* by birth and studied oenology at Beaune. In 1979 he went out to South Africa to work for Boschendal, helping to develop their sparkling wine, and subsequently joined another good sparkling wine producer from the Cape, Villera. On his return to France he started up a *négociant* business, producing the sparkling wine brand Charles Fère, which he subsequently sold to Boisset, the Burgundian *négociant*. He arrived in Limoux in 1988, with the purchase of some twenty-year-old Pinot Noir vines, and he now has twenty hectares of vines in a wild, windy spot outside the village of Roquetaillade. They are planted with Chardonnay, Pinot Noir, Chenin Blanc and just a little Mauzac. There is also a tiny plot of Riesling and Gewürztraminer, just a thousand plants of each, which has incurred the wrath of the INAO. Domaine de l'Aigle is the largest producer of still Limoux and makes a little Crémant de Limoux, but most of the sparkling wines do not conform to the appellation at all.

We were treated to a comprehensive tasting, providing Denois with a forum to expound his views. The Blanc de Noirs, Tradition, from seventy per cent Pinot Noir with Chardonnay, is elegant, with firm fruit. The Crémant de Limoux, from thirty-five per cent each of Chardonnay and Chenin Blanc with the balance made up of Mauzac, has in theory the wrong proportions for the appellation. Denois would like to see four grape varieties in Crémant, including Pinot Noir, without any constraints of minimum and maximum percentages. The wine has a delicate, youthful taste with an elegant finish. It has spent only twelve months on the lees, for Denois does not favour excessively mature flavours. Instead he picks his grapes as ripe as possible, maybe as much as three weeks later than growers closer to the town of Limoux, for the later harvest gives a greater intensity of flavour. This is a region of long autumns, and the altitude of his vineyards also makes a late harvest possible. In these cooler vineyards, Denois will have twice as much acidity in his Chardonnay, but the same degree of alcohol as a wine from the warm coastal plain.

Then we went on to still wines, some purely experimental and some for sale. There was a steely Chenin Blanc, made without oak, followed by the same wine fermented in a four-year-old barrel. The initial oakiness had faded to leave a rich buttery wine, balanced with firm acidity. The problem with Chenin Blanc is that the available clones tend to give large yields with high acidity. Next came an enigma. The wine was very perfumed, with steely acidity and hints of bitter orange. I wonder whether it might have been Viognier, but no, it was Riesling, planted as an experiment to demonstrate the climatic conditions of the area. There are two *cuvées* of Chardonnay: Classique, which is a blend of several vineyards, and an individual vineyard, Les Aigles. The 1996 was already delicious, with an immensely appealing toasted character and elegant fruit and flavour. A little new wood is used for Les Aigles and none at all for the Cuvée Classique. The old wood provides oxidation and a suitable environment for lees contact. Wood should not mean new oak, for oak is just a device and the fruit must be the dominant character. However, these wines age beautifully and become even more satisfying. The 1995 was less immediate than the 1996, with layers of flavour and potential. The 1992 was almost like Chablis on the nose, with some leafy but honeyed fruit and very good acidity, while the 1991 was more closed, with tight fruit. Intriguingly, the 1990, with its broad, nutty palate resulting from twelve months on lees reminded me of a New Zealand Chardonnay from Kumeu River. Finally Denois' first vintage, 1989, made from grapes he had bought, had the slightly mushroomy, *mousseron* notes of mature Chardonnay, with firm acidity.

The long autumns lend themselves to late harvest wines. A 1995 Chenin Blanc with botrytis was picked on 1 November and partially fermented in new oak. It had an intensely concentrated flavour, with the roasted characteristics of noble rot. A 1997 blend of Chenin

Blanc and Chardonnay, picked during November and December, was quite apricoty with an elegant honeyed finish.

For Denois, Pinot Noir is the only possible choice for red wine. Again he makes two wines, a Cuvée Classique from young vines and Terres Rouges from a single vineyard. The Cuvée Classique spends six months in old wood, while part of the Terres Rouges matures in new wood and is consequently more structured and tannic; both have good fruit. There is a lot to learn about Pinot Noir, especially in the vineyard, but Denois is convinced that *surmaturité* or over-ripeness is the secret. He is not alone in his enthusiasm for the variety, for the co-operative of Limoux also produces a very creditable Pinot Noir under the Anne de Joyeuse label, and there are now more than a hundred hectares in production. (Since my visit, Domaine de l'Aigle has been sold to the Burgundian *négociant* house of Antonin Rodet.)

DOMAINE COLLIN, TOURREILLES

Philippe Collin is another *champenois* who shares some of Jean-Louis Denois' frustration at the pigheadedness of the INAO. He settled in the village of Toureilles in Limoux in 1980 and has gradually created an eighteen-hectare estate from which he produces still wines and Blanquette de Limoux, but not Crémant. He hopes for an appellation Crémant de Languedoc in which it would be possible to include Pinot Noir, and meanwhile makes a Cuvée Prestige from eighty per cent Chardonnay and twenty per cent Pinot Noir that is delicate and creamy. He finds the climate highly suitable for Pinot Noir and Chardonnay. As for Mauzac, he describes it as a rustic variety and considers that it makes good Méthode Ancestrale with the required typicity, but that with the Champagne method its typicity disappears. A still Limoux, fermented in old Burgundian wood and given plenty of lees stirring, was full and toasted with good body and acidity, while his first vintage of Pinot Noir, the 1997, had some convincing fruit.

DOMAINE DE FOURN, PIEUSSE

An equally serious but more conventional estate is Domaine de Fourn, the property of the Robert family, with one hundred and twenty hectares in the Mediterranean zone of the appellation, making it the largest single estate. The family began producing their own wine in 1937. Before that they sold everything to the *négoce*. Their Carte Ivoire Blanquette, a pure Mauzac with twelve months ageing, is light and lemony, while a 1995 Blanquette, Carte Noire, including ten per cent Chenin Blanc with the Mauzac, spends eighteen months on lees and is creamy with a hint of honey. The 1994 Crémant de Limoux, with twenty per cent Chardonnay and ten per cent Chenin Blanc, was quite full and rounded. They would like to see less Mauzac in the Crémant and would also favour the inclusion of some Pinot Noir. Domaine de Fourn also make some Méthode Ancestrale from pure Mauzac, which is yeasty and honeyed.

DOMAINE DE LAMBERT, SAINT POLYCARPE

A new venture in Limoux is the purchase in 1998 by the Rothschilds of Mouton of Domaine de Lambert in the village of St Polycarpe. The vineyards are being extensively replanted with Chardonnay, as well as Syrah, Grenache Noir and the Bordelais varieties: Cabernet Sauvignon and Franc, Merlot and Malbec. The Chardonnay will produce appellation Limoux Blanc, while for the red varieties, they are pinning their hopes on the creation of a new appellation, Limoux Rouge. Whatever happens, Domaine de Lambert illustrates the new energy in Limoux and will be an estate to watch in the coming years.

Limoux has progressed enormously in ten years. Wine making methods are more refined, and the creation of the appellation Crémant de Limoux represents a significant step forward. However, there are unanswered questions. Are the percentages too restrictive, given that many producers flaunt them openly? If they can use Chardonnay, why not Pinot Noir too? Will the putative appellation of Crémant du Languedoc come to anything? Probably even more significant is the progress in still wines. The white wines are no longer thin and acidic – making you realise, as in Champagne, just why bubbles were favoured – but now have flavour and substance. There is a place too for Pinot Noir in the still appellation, maybe in preference to the Merlot and Grenache Noir of Limoux's neighbours. With a glass of Blanquette or Crémant offering an original alternative to Champagne, Limoux provides a fascinating island of sparkling wine, a cool haven in the warm south.

Key facts

Four appellations from forty-one villages around Limoux:

Blanquette de Limoux: AC 1938; mainly Mauzac, with some optional Chardonnay and Chenin Blanc; nine months on lees.

Méthode Ancestrale: AC 1938.

Crémant de Limoux: AC 1990; Mauzac, with a combined minimum of thirty per cent Chardonnay and Chenin Blanc and a maximum of twenty per cent of each; twelve months on lees.

Limoux: Still wine, with obligatory *élevage* in oak until May following vintage.

Four defined regions within the AC: Autan, Océanique, Méditerranéen, Haute-Vallée.

Claims an older history than Champagne.

Côtes de la Malepère

France divides broadly into three large viticultural regions, and the Côtes de la Malepère are where two of them meet, for they lie on the frontier between the Languedoc and Aquitaine. What the French call *le partage des eaux*, the watershed between the Atlantic and the Mediterranean, is at Castelnaudary, some twenty-five miles to the west.

The Massif de la Malepère lies just south west of the city of Carcassonne and north west of the small town of Limoux. It covers some thirty square kilometres, rising to 440 metres, and is an ancient geological formation, even older than the Pyrenees, forming a promontory between the Mediterranean and the plain of Aquitaine. The vineyards are on its lower slopes, at about two hundred and fifty metres, with pastures for grazing on the higher land. From a viewpoint near the summit you can see the Pyrenees to the south and Carcassonne and the Montagne Noire to the north. The lower slopes are peppered with little villages. Montréal, with its imposing church, was a Cathar village, while neighbouring Foujean was Catholic. The village of Alaigne was built in a circular shape to resist invasion during the Middle Ages.

These vineyards are a melting pot of grape varieties. Those of the Midi mingle with those of Bordeaux, giving the wines an almost unique originality, although this is of relatively recent creation. Viticulture is virtually the only form of agriculture here. In the first half of the twentieth century there were large estates owned by people from Narbonne, who planted Carignan and Cinsaut without realising that the growing conditions were quite different from those of the coastal plains. This meant that by the early 1960s the wines produced here were fit for little other than blending with heady brews from North Africa. With the independence of Algeria in 1963, that market was lost. The Carignan, Aramon and Alicante gave neither yield nor alcohol, and certainly not quality. Something needed to be done to save the region's agricultural economy. Various responsible organisations, notably the Chambre de l'Agriculture de l'Aude, therefore decided to create an experimental vineyard in order to determine which would be the most suitable grape varieties for the area.

It had already been realised that, although the Côtes de la Malepère are situated in the department of Aude and thus belong geographically to the Languedoc, climatically this is a transitional zone, with more affinity to the Atlantic climate of south western France. There are fewer hours of sunshine than on the coastal plain, and there is no lack of summer rain, so that the vines here do not have to withstand periods of drought. They are more likely to be affected by spring frosts. The natural vegetation of the area illustrates the climatic mix. There are the holm oaks and Alep pines of the Mediterranean, the *chêne pubescente* of the sub-Mediterranean, the common or pedunculate oak of the Atlantic and finally the beech of the mountains. The various oaks give an indication of which grape varieties grow best on which part of the Massif. As for the soil, it is very mixed; Malepère translates literally as 'bad stone'. As well as stony sandstone terraces of glacial origin, there are slopes of clay and limestone. The north and south faces of the Massif contain more gravel, as a result of the river Aude changing its course at some time.

A research station was set up in 1965 at Domaine de Cazes in the village of Alaigne, to study the behaviour of several grape varieties in the various microclimates and soil types. The feasibility of introducing Bordelais grape varieties was soon realised, and the present *encépagement* of the Côtes de la Malepère consists of three principal varieties: Merlot, Cot or Malbec, and Cinsaut – a maximum of sixty per cent of any is allowed. The secondary varieties, for which the maximum percentage is thirty, are Cabernet Franc, Cabernet Sauvignon, Grenache Noir, Lladoner Pelut and Syrah. The choice and permitted percentages allow plenty of room for manoeuvre, but whereas it is possible to make Côtes de la Malepère without any Midi grape varieties, it would be virtually impossible not to include any Bordelais varieties.

Cabernet Sauvignon, Cabernet Franc and Merlot were first planted outside the experimental vineyard at the beginning of the 1970s, and the Côtes de la Malepère were given VDQS status in 1976. However, bureaucracy then deemed that they should have been a *vin de pays* first, so they were temporarily relegated until 1983. Now they have aspirations for an appellation; indeed, the day before my visit in March 1998 they had received Jean-Claude Bousquet, the owner of Domaine du Pech-Redon in La Clape, and more significantly, the regional president of the INAO, in order to present their case – or as they put it, to 'demonstrate the reality of the appellation'. The visit went well and they are optimistic about the ultimate outcome, but it will probably not be before 2002 or 2003. Merlot will become the principal grape variety with a minimum of fifty per cent, with Cabernet Franc and Malbec as the main supporting varieties, a minimum of twenty per cent by 2006. For the moment the Côtes de la Malepère are red and pink, and any white wine is a *vin de pays*.

The area of the VDQS now covers thirty-one villages, with the greatest concentration of vineyards on the largest, southern side of the Massif de la Malepère. There are also quite extensive plantings on the northern side, but the much smaller eastern and western slopes are less important. Altogether 6300 hectares are classified, of which 3200 hectares are planted with vines, but of those only 1100 have the correct varieties for the VDQS – and even then in 1997 only 550 hectares actually produced Côtes de la Malepère. The simple fact is that it can be more remunerative to make Vin de Pays d'Oc, or even Vin de Pays de l'Aude. A co-operative member receives FF 4.90 per kilo for VDQS grapes, for which the maximum yield is 61 hl/ha, including the annual PLC, or classification ceiling, that allows an extra percentage on top of the annual yield. If on the other hand he produces grapes for a Vin de Pays d'Oc, he may only earn FF 4.20 per kilo, but the maximum yield is 90 hl/ha. Financially there is no contest; a much bigger differential is needed between VDQS and *vin de pays*.

The Côtes de la Malepère are the most westerly of all the vineyards of the Languedoc, so that the dominant climatic influence is really the Atlantic. Some would say that the vineyards are now eighty per cent Atlantic to twenty per cent Mediterranean. Merlot is the most widely planted of the principal varieties, with support from Cabernet Sauvignon and Malbec. However, producers would like the proportion of Cabernet Franc increased. Cinsaut is now merely tolerated, and they would like it relegated to a secondary variety. Its inclusion in such a high proportion goes back to the original creation of the VDQS, when it dominated the vineyards. At the time, there would have been no Côtes de la Malepère at all without Cinsaut. Nowadays it is more likely to be used for *rosé*. Of all the Midi grape varieties, Grenache Noir is the most successful, growing on the warmer northern and eastern slopes with a Mediterranean influence, while Lladoner Pelut gives very similar results, but in practice is rarely planted. Today, Syrah is debatable. The growers' *syndicat* considers it to be marginal, for it does not perform well in the climatic conditions of the Massif, and so far no one has planted it in any quantity. There are fears that, if people do plant it, it could change the typicity of the Côtes de la Malepère.

DOMAINE DE CAZES

Meanwhile, Camille Vilotte continues to run the experimental station at Domaine de Cazes with its twenty-six hectares of vineyards. He is working on different rootstocks, particularly for Cabernet Sauvignon and Chardonnay, and is considering different clones for Merlot and Cabernet Franc. There has also been some research on new crossings, and Marselan, a cross between Grenache Noir and Cabernet Sauvignon, shows some potential and is just beginning to be planted in commercial vineyards. Treatments in the vineyards and micro-vinifications in the cellar also come within the competence of the station.

UCCOAR

The Côtes de la Malepère are dominated by four co-operatives. They were partly responsible for setting up the research station, and are now linked in one of the largest producers' associations of the Midi, UCCOAR, which stands for the Union des Caves Coopératives de l'Ouest Audois et du Razès – the Razès is a small area on the south western slopes of the Massif de la Malepère. The UCCOAR may have originated in the area, but it has extended its activities far beyond and now concentrates primarily on *vins de pays*. The association arose from a need to promote the area, as well as to plan and control the investment necessary to finance the development of the vineyards. It is still responsible for marketing seventy per cent of the production of the Côtes de la Malepère, although that figure is gently decreasing as more individual producers come into play, for the development of the private estates is very recent. There are now ten such estates, of which five or six bottle their wine, whereas on my first visit in 1987 there were no more than two or three.

CAVE COOPERATIVE LA MALEPERE, ARZENS

Bruno Maillard is the young wine maker at the co-operative in Arzens. He has come fresh from oenology studies at Montpellier and is keen to make his mark. After a quick visit to the co-operative's vast installation with its forests of vats, we adjourned to the village café to taste and talk over lunch with Marie-Noëlle Grojean, the very competent and likeable secretary of the growers' *syndicat*. Like the other co-operatives in the area, that of Arzens makes not only Côtes de la Malepère, but also a range of *vin de pays* and some *vin de table*, as well as a little Cabardès, the adjoining appellation, of which more in the next chapter. Altogether they have 380 members cultivating 2600 hectares of vines. In fact, varietal Vin de Pays d'Oc is by far the most important part of their production, totalling some sixty-five thousand hectolitres compared to just five thousand of Côtes de la Malepère.

They are practising what they called a *politique d'encépagement*, to persuade their producers to plant the grape varieties of the VDQS. Merlot in particular is encouraged. Their vineyard charter considers the age of the vines, their yield, the type of pruning and the general treatment in the vineyard. A technician from the Chambre d'Agriculture in Carcassonne advises on sustained viticulture.

The co-operative's Côtes de la Malepère appears under the names of the estates of various members. Domaine de Foucauld, from about sixty per cent Merlot and forty per cent Cabernet Sauvignon with just a drop of Cabernet Franc, was soft and supple, with sufficient tannin but no astringency. The Château de

Festes reverses the percentages, with more Cabernet than Merlot. The wine was aged for a few months in vat and had a firm nose and palate, with more body than the previous wine. It went very well with a warming *cassoulet* on a cool spring day, when the only spot of colour came from the flowering cherry trees. At the time of my visit, Maillard had just put his first wine into wood.

His range of *vin de pays* included Vin de Pays d'Oc, not only from Merlot, Cabernet Sauvignon and Syrah but also from crossings such as red Portan and white Chasan, and a red Domaine de Chapitre from Grenache Noir and Ejiodola – which I was told is a crossing of Fer Servadou and Abouriou, grape varieties more commonly found in Marcillac and Côtes du Marmandais respectively, developed by a Basque member of the INRA, hence its unpronounceable name. Fruit was their aim and that was certainly achieved, with a supple, plummy wine that was eminently drinkable.

CAVE COOPERATIVE DU RAZES

The other key co-operative of the area is the Cave du Razès on the main road outside the village of Routier. Their five hundred members have between them 3300 hectares, and again, at 22,000 hls, the Côtes de la Malepère represents just a small part of their production compared with Vins de Pays d'Oc and Aude, at 80,000 hls and 100,000 hls respectively. In addition to their generic Côtes de la Malepère, they produce wine from six specific estates, three of which are bottled and three sold in bulk. They too are encouraging their members to improve their vineyards, which are classified according to the age of the vines, the yield, the *terroir*, aspect and *état sanitaire*. Wine making methods are straightforward, with some barrel ageing for one estate, Château Montlaur. They have been working with *barriques* since 1989 and we tasted the 1994 vintage, of which a third had spent twelve months in oak. Initially they used more oak but are now finding the right balance. There was a hint of vanilla on the nose and more on the palate, with some rounded, sturdy fruit, and the oak adding body. Domaine du Beauséjour, with a high proportion of Merlot and no oak, was quite rounded and supple, while Domaine de Fournery seemed rather rustic in comparison.

DOMAINE DE MATIBAT, ST MARTIN-DE-VILLEREGLAN

Jean-Claude Turetti of Domaine de Matibat outside the village of St Martin-de-Villereglan bought eighteen hectares of vines back in 1973. The former owner had taken his grapes, of varieties appropriate for *vin de table*, to the co-operative at Pauligne. Over the years Turetti has gradually replanted, starting with Chardonnay, Merlot and Cabernet in 1973, and has extended his vineyard holding to thirty-three hectares. His Chardonnay can be either Vin de Pays d'Oc or de la Haute Vallée de l'Aude, as can his Sauvignon, which came into production in 1998. The village of St Martin is on the edge of the appellation of Limoux, and when that appellation was created back in 1938 the village could have been included, but the wine growers of the time were not convinced of the future for sparkling wine, and consequently their children are now struggling to create an appellation for still wine. In fact Turetti does have some Mauzac, which he sends to the co-operative in Limoux.

We sampled his wines in a neat little tasting room adjoining the cellar and insulated barrel room. First we had a fresh, lightly buttery Chardonnay with the characteristics of a cool temperature fermentation. A pink Cabernet Franc with some lively raspberry fruit followed, and then two Côtes de la Malepère. The first, from a Bordeaux blend of Merlot, Cabernet Sauvignon, Cabernet Franc and Malbec, spent twelve months in vat and had some rounded, spicy fruit. The better grapes are kept for the oak-aged wine. They are given a longer fermentation, two weeks as opposed to one, and spend twelve months in wood, giving some tannin and backbone as well as fruit. It promised well.

CHATEAU DE COINTRES, ROULLENS

Next we saw François Gorostis at Château de Cointres in Roullens. The estate came through his wife's family, but although Gorostis is a doctor by profession, he too comes from a wine family: his uncle is André Lignères of Château la Baronne in the Corbières. Anne Gorostis' grandfather was a *négociant* in the 1920s, with some vineyards of Aramon Teinturier. Her father began the shift away from *vin de table* by planting his first Merlot in 1977, and his

199

daughter now has seventeen hectares in production, of which ten are for Côtes de la Malepère, consisting mainly of Merlot, Cabernet Sauvignon and Grenache Noir, with a little Syrah coming into production. They do not like Malbec, as it is too erratic, whereas Grenache Noir does well and they would like to plant more, as it gives body and weight to the wine. Their other vineyards, planted with Merlot and Grenache Gris, are on the plain and produce Vin de Pays des Côtes de Prouilhe, the local *vin de pays* which takes its name from a tributary of the Aude.

Marc Dubernet is their consultant oenologist, even though they are not part of the Vignerons du Val d'Orbieu. Gorostis explained how the investment in a new Vaslin press in 1997 had made an enormous difference to the quality of their wine, for he no longer has to pump the grapes to remove the traces of bitterness. Otherwise his vinification techniques are very straightforward. He would, albeit a little nervously, like to try *barriques*, but Dubernet has told him very firmly, 'You are not there yet', partly because he does not have the appropriate cellar conditions. We tasted with our every move observed by a shaggy Flanders sheepdog who answered to the name of Faust. A 1997 Grenache Gris was quite delicate and rounded, but with enough acidity to prevent the oxidation to which Grenache Gris is prone. A pink Côtes de la Malepère, from equal parts of both Cabernets, Grenache Noir and Cinsaut, was fresh and fruity. A vat sample of red 1997 Côtes de la Malepère, from fifty per cent Merlot, forty per cent Cabernet Sauvignon and Cabernet Franc and ten per cent Grenache Noir, had some firm berry fruit and promised well, while the 1996 had a slight earthiness. I particularly liked the 1993, which had rounded berry fruit and hints of cedar wood. We finished with a 1989 that was attractively mature, smoky on the nose with a dry finish.

DOMAINE LA LOUVIERE, MALVIES

Some of the most impressive investment in the appellation is to be seen at Domaine la Louvière outside the village of Malviès. The Château de Malviès is also an important producer of Côtes de la Malepère, but its owners live in Toulouse and the elegant château was firmly shuttered when we passed. Domaine la Louvière is the property of Herr Grohe, a German who apparently made his money producing bath taps. Although Grohe is another absentee landowner, his *régisseur* was there to show off the new installations. There are stainless steel vats and a separate insulated barrel room, with plans for an underground cellar, a rare facility in the south of France. The forty-one hectare estate is planted mainly with Merlot and Cabernet Franc, but no Cabernet Sauvignon as they find it too tannic, and there is also a substantial amount of Chardonnay, from which they are planning a barrel-fermented wine. For the moment it is fermented in stainless steel so that it is fresh and lemony with a creamy finish, and is sold as a Vin de Pays des Côtes de Prouilhe.

There are also three red *vins de pays* in their repertoire: a pure Cabernet Franc that is barrel-aged in a variety of oaks, American, French and Russian; a pure Merlot that has spent seven months in barrel; and a Syrah Merlot blend, part aged in wood and part in vat, with a spicy nose, ripe berry fruit and a hint of oak on the finish. They find that wine aged in French or Russian oak is slower to develop, while wine in American oak quickly takes on a vanilla character that in turn fades quite quickly.

As for their Côtes de la Malepère, there are two qualities, with and without oak. The 1994 unoaked wine, from sixty per cent Merlot, thirty per cent Cabernet Franc and ten per cent Cinsaut blended immediately after fermentation, was still quite solid and closed on both nose and palate. The 1993, made in the same proportions, with twelve months in old wood, had a closed nose and a firm, cedary palate. It clearly demonstrated just why this little-known appellation deserves a wider reputation.

DOMAINE LA FORT, MONTREAL

The only other producer to use oak barrels on any scale is Marc Pagès at Domaine la Fort outside the village of Montréal. His father had run the family estate, producing wine for *vin de table* and *vin de cépage* for local *négociants*, while Pagès had worked as a journalist, based in Reims. However, he had studied oenology at Toulouse, has a particular interest in wine economics and, as well as doing various *stages* in France, has worked on a wine estate in Oregon. Pagès has the broad horizons of someone who has travelled and seen things beyond his appellation, together with the questioning attitude of a successful journalist. He is bright and alert, searching for answers and very committed to his young appellation. He returned to France on his father's retirement in 1994 with the express purpose of developing the family vineyards.

This is an old *bastide*, a semi-fortified farm house with a medieval tower dating back to the twelfth century. From the courtyard there is a view of the tiny village of Montréal with its church tower. The barrels are kept in the old stables, which have doors painted a cheerful blue. Inside there are symbols on the walls, the sun on the eastern side indicating warmth and an arrow on the west representing the wind. You have to stand in a precise position to see both the full sun and the arrow. This was where we tasted, which proved somewhat chilly on a cool spring day.

Pagès has twenty hectares of vineyards around the village, planted with Merlot, Cabernet Sauvignon, a little Cinsaut, some Grenache Noir and also Chardonnay. As yet he has no Cabernet Franc and he would also like to plant some Syrah, and maybe some Malbec. He is curious too about Viognier and Pinot Noir. For the moment he makes four or five wines, two *cuvées* of Chardonnay and two Côtes de la Malepère, as well as an experimental *rosé*. The Chardonnay are Vins de Pays d'Oc, one kept in vat and the other fermented in barrel. For the first he seeks to emphasise the fruit by bottling it early, while the second is fermented in wood and spends six months on its lees. It is the subject of numerous experiments and the result is a combination of smoky oak on the nose and a ripe buttery palate, making it one of the more individual Chardonnay of the Midi. In contrast, the unoaked wine is lemony and fruity.

The experimental pink Côtes de la Malepère was vinified in oak and also spent six months on its lees, making a rounded, full-bodied wine with well-integrated oak, a *rosé* of some substance and surprisingly successful. Domaine la Tour du Fort is the lighter, unoaked Côtes de la Malepère, mainly from Merlot with some Cabernet and Grenache Noir, which undergo an eight-day fermentation and are blended in late winter for bottling in June. There was rounded fruit on the nose and palate, with a peppery backbone and an attractive supple character. In contrast, Domaine le Fort spent twelve or thirteen months in wood. Fermentation takes three weeks and each grape variety is aged separately. The 1996 had a rich vanilla nose and on the palate there was great potential, for it was still solidly oaky, with tannin and youthful cherry fruit. Pagès said it was a wine to keep for five or six years.

CHATEAU ROUTIER, ROUTIER

Michèle Lèzerat of Château Routier is a vivacious woman with a friendly smile who gave us a warming welcome of tea by an open log fire. Hers is one of the more established estates in the appellation. She took over the family vineyards in 1984, after studies in law and literature. She talked of the changes and problems since my last visit in 1987. There have been some difficult vintages, with frost and hail drastically reducing yields, particularly in 1996, when the leaves damaged by hail turned brown, resulting in a very small but concentrated crop the following year. The harvest can be quite prolonged, given the diversity of grape varieties and vineyard sites with their different aspects and microclimates.

Lèzerat now has forty-two hectares in production. She has planted some Chardonnay and some Sauvignon, and has also made improvements in the cellars, buying an *égrappoir* and beginning to work with oak. She bought her first barrels in 1994, and they are kept in the old cellars of the château, along with various pieces of defunct vineyard and cellar equipment. Her wines have certainly acquired more structure and substance since my first visit. A 1995 Côtes de la Malepère, from sixty per cent Merlot, thirty per cent Cabernet Sauvignon and ten per cent Grenache, that had spent fourteen months in vat was rounded and supple with some attractive cassis fruit. The 1995, which included Malbec rather than Grenache Noir, had more structure and tannin, with some elegant smoky fruit, while the oaked version, from seventy per cent Merlot and fifteen per cent each of Cabernet Franc and Malbec, underwent a four-week *cuvaison* and was solid and chunky with good fruit and ageing potential. Her best wine, Cuvée Jean Lèzerat, is named after her father and is made from sixty per cent Merlot, thirty per cent Cabernet Franc and ten per cent Cabernet Sauvignon; it is neither filtered nor fined and spends eighteen months in wood. The 1996 had a deep colour, with a smoky nose, firm fruit on the palate and layers of flavour. It was a good note on which to finish, amply illustrating the charm and potential of this little-known appellation sandwiched between Carcassonne and Limoux.

CHATEAU DE ROBERT, VILLESISCLE

Mention should also be made of Château de Robert, the other property, apart from Château de Malviès, to put wine in bottle. It is run by Hélène Artigoua, whose wines, tasted at a wine fair in Paris, had a certain rustic charm, but were less refined than those of some of her neighbours. She has twenty-two hectares on the western slopes of the Massif de la Malepère and makes two red Côtes de la Malepère, again with and without wood. Her Cuvée Tradition from fifty per cent Merlot, of which she has eight hectares, with twenty per cent Cabernet Sauvignon and fifteen per cent each of Malbec and Grenache Noir, is bottled early after a few months in vat. The 1997 had a rugged *bordelais* flavour, while the 1995 Cuvée Merlin, a blend of Merlot, Cabernet Sauvignon and Malbec that had spent twelve months in wood, had a tight vanilla flavour and was firm and structured. She also has some Grenache Noir that came into production in the 1996 vintage, and some Syrah that came a year later, which she is keeping for her oak-aged wine as the yields are so low. She finds that Malbec also provides body and is good for ageing.

Ten years ago the Côtes de la Malepère were without doubt one of the lost vineyards of France, often omitted from wine maps or surveys of French wines. As Marc Pagès explained, their marginal position in the Languedoc surprises people to whom the Côtes de la Malepère are unknown. It is a tiny appellation, as yet without any image or reputation. Yet it can offer some surprises, especially as a result of its transitional position, combining Cabernet and Merlot from the south west with Grenache Noir and Syrah from the Mediterranean. Over the last decade the individual producers have made great strides in the search for quality. More people are putting their wine in bottle and vinification methods have improved. There is a new confidence in the vineyard, as demonstrated by the request for appellation status. These may never be great wines, but they deserve more recognition, for they provide enjoyable drinking, combining the warmth of the Mediterranean with the structure of the south west in a way that is unique – apart from neighbouring Cabardès on the other side of the Aude valley.

Key facts

Aspiring AC, VDQS since 1983 for red and *rosé*, but not white; covers thirty-one villages around the Massif de la Malepère.

Eleven hundred hectares have the correct grape varieties, but only about 550 hectares produce the wine; the others prefer to make *vin de pays*.

The meeting of Bordeaux and the Midi in the vineyard: maximum sixty per cent each of Merlot, Cot and Cinsaut and a maximum thirty per cent each of Cabernet Franc, Cabernet Sauvignon, Grenache Noir, Lladoner Pelut and Syrah.

Vintages

1999: A wet summer followed by a dry September and early October, which ripened the grapes beautifully. Wines with good potential.

1998: Small production following the April frost. A fine summer, but one of the few parts of the Languedoc not to suffer from summer drought. Exceptional quality with good concentration and ripe tannins.

1997: A sunny September made for soft tannins and lower than average acidity levels. Fruity, accessible wines.

1996: Hail damage. Rounded, fruity wines.

1995: Powerful tannins, making wines with ageing potential.

Cabardès

Cabardès, on the north western side of the city of Carcassonne, is separated from the Minervois by the river Orbiel, but it has much more in common with the Côtes de la Malepère on the southern side of the Aude Valley, for here too both Midi and Bordeaux grape varieties coexist. Cabardès is almost like an island between two climates, in that it is hotter than Bordeaux but cooler and wetter than the Languedoc, making the diversity of grape varieties possible. On its western edge, vineyards give way to fields of wheat, as the lavender and thyme of the warm south disappear, and in the north there are the first foothills of the Massif Central. Although the grape varieties are a mixture of Bordeaux and the Midi, the emphasis is slightly different from that of the Côtes de la Malepère, with a higher proportion of southern varieties and in particular Syrah. There are also Cabernet Sauvignon, Malbec, Merlot and Grenache Noir, although Cinsaut has been virtually eliminated from the area. The disappearance of Carignan as well was recognised in the modification of the regulations when Cabardès became an appellation in 1998. Unusually, Fer Servadou, the grape variety of the Aveyron, also features in the appellation decree, but is only planted by one producer.

As in the Côtes de la Malepère, the climate is part Mediterranean and part Atlantic. But there are also differences: Cabardès tends to be warmer and drier than the Côtes de la Malepère, for it is a little further east, and it also has similarities with the Minervois. The vineyards are on the sunnier slopes of the foothills of the Montagne Noire, rising in terraces until you reach the *garrigue* where no vines will grow. In the spring you can see the snow-capped hills of the Montagne Noire in the distance. It is a very windy region, for both the Marin and the Cers can blow hard, although the Montagne

Noire, the last outpost of the Massif Central, protects the area from the winds of the north. The soil is varied too, mainly clay and limestone, with a higher proportion of limestone and more stones than in the Côtes de la Malepère, for the geological origins are different. The large chunks of limestone reflect the heat and light and retain the warmth.

Like so many of the wine regions of France, Cabardès fell into oblivion after the phylloxera crisis. *Le gros rouge* was its prime objective until people began to plant Cabernet Sauvignon and Merlot at the end of the 1960s, a move that saved the area from terminal decline. In 1973 Cabardès, or the Côtes du Cabardès et de l'Orbiel as it was once called, was recognised as a VDQS for red and pink wine, but not for white. As in the Côtes de la Malepère, any white wine is a *vin de pays*. Altogether fourteen villages were included in the VDQS, of which the most important are Aragon and Montolieu near the town of Conques-sur-Orbiel. Then in 1998 Cabardès was accorded appellation status and the long-winded name Côtes du Cabardès et de l'Orbiel was shortened to Cabardès *tout court*. The name originates from the local Lords of Cabaret who defended the nearby Château de Lastours against Simon de Montfort during the Cathar Crusade in the thirteenth century.

As the appellation stands at present, there must be a maximum of sixty per cent of the *bordelais* varieties as opposed to forty per cent of Mediterranean grapes. However, the INAO would like a minimum of forty per cent of each, for it fears a preponderance of Atlantic grapes and wants to uphold the position of the Mediterranean varieties. In practice, the percentages depend very much on the personal preferences of individual producers, and some estates could find that a minimum of forty per cent of each poses problems of adaptation.

THE CO-OPERATIVES

Co-operatives are much less important for Cabardès than for the Côtes de la Malepère, as here they have tended to concentrate their activities on *vin de pays*, either as varietal wines, with Vin de Pays d'Oc, or Vin de Pays l'Aude, or the local Coteaux de la Cité de Carcassonne. There are four co-operatives altogether. The one at Villegailhenc is tiny and insignificant. The co-operative at Arzens in the Côtes de la Malepère produces an infinitesimal amount of Cabardès, and that leaves Aragon and Conques, both of which produce wines that are representative of the appellation. Most of the production of Cabardès is in the hands of eighteen private producers, virtually all of whom put at least some of their wine in bottle, which may well explain why Cabardès has become an appellation while the Côtes de la Malepère remains a VDQS for the moment. The four hundred hectares of appellation land produce an annual average of twenty thousand hectolitres.

CHATEAU PENNAUTIER AND CHATEAU LA BASTIDE

A sunny spring day in Cabardès took me to several estates, each with different characteristics. Château Pennautier, in the eponymous village, is an elegant seventeenth-century building with an unadorned façade. It was subsequently enlarged by Le Vaux, architect of the château of Versailles, and the landscape designer Le Nôtre planned the grounds. The château has been in the hands of the same family for several generations, but the family name changed after the First World War when Paule de Pennautier married Christian de Lorgeril. The family archives indicate that an ancestor, Pierre-Louis Rech de Pennautier, sent wine from his property to the French armies fighting the war of the Spanish Succession in 1752, while an earlier Pierre-Louis de Pennautier helped Colbert to finance the building of the Canal du Midi. The present incumbent, Nicolas de Lorgeril, is president of the growers' *syndicat*. As well as Château Pennautier they own the nearby property of Château la Bastide, a fortified castle dating from the thirteenth century. The old keep is still standing, and the cellars, built at the end of the eighteenth century, have enormous stone vats, each holding two hundred and fifty hectolitres.

Each of the properties covers around a hundred hectares, but not all is Cabardès, for the vineyards on the plains produce *vin de pays* and Cabardès is firmly restricted to the hillsides. None the less, they are the largest producers of the appellation. Each property is run quite separately and the wine is made by Bertrand Seube, a young oenologist who trained at Toulouse and Bordeaux. He favours a long *cuvaison* of 30–35 days with plenty of *délestages* and *remontages* in order to extract the maximum from the grapes, with each grape variety vinified separately. Château Pennautier first began working with *barriques* in 1992 for their best wines, the Collection Privée of Château Pennautier and the Tête de Cuvée of Château la Bastide, each wine spending a year in barrel after blending. They have experimented with ageing each variety separately, but find that this reduces the typicity of the wine. The wines are well made, with good fruit and structure and well-integrated oak. It is tantalising trying to determine whether it is the Atlantic or the Mediterranean that dominates the flavour. As another producer observed, it is like parents and children. You find the qualities that you seek in your wine, so if you prefer the Mediterranean flavours, that is what you will taste.

CHATEAU DE VENTENAC

Alain Maurel of the Château de Ventenac has a strong commercial drive, backed by determination and common sense. He described how he had developed his estate. His father was a wine grower in another Cabardès village, Moussoulens. Alain himself studied economics, knowing that he wanted to stay in the region, and in 1973 bought vineyards that at the time were merely producing *vin de table*. He has spent the ensuing twenty-odd years replanting them with Merlot, Cabernet Sauvignon, Grenache Noir and Syrah, following the Bordelais pattern of 6200 plants to the hectare rather than the then more usual Languedoc density of 3500 plants. The rainfall here is an annual average of 700 mm, as opposed to 900 mm in Bordeaux and 450 mm in Narbonne, which means that the vines can cope with the extra density. At the beginning people said he was mad, but now they are copying him. He limits the yield to two kilograms per vine and is convinced that his quality comes from the limited production. He drew a comparison with peaches, contrasting the difference in taste between a large watery peach and a small concentrated one.

From 1980 he began renovating his cellars, installing temperature control and a pneumatic press; now he is planning a barrel cellar. He first began working with oak in 1990. The third stage of development is the commercial aspect. His first bottling was a hundred thousand bottles in 1986, and now all his production, which has increased sevenfold, is sold in bottle. He finds himself handicapped by his lack of English, so his wine is sold through a merchant in Montpellier and includes a healthy export business.

As for the wine itself, Maurel considers the best varieties to be Merlot, Cabernet Sauvignon and Syrah. Grenache Noir can prove quite difficult to ripen. His unoaked wine spends eighteen months in vat, after blending as early as possible, in December. Ideally it should be aged for longer, but you need money for that. The 1995 had some herbal, peppery fruit, while the 1996 Les Pujols, which has spent eight months in oak, also needed time to evolve, for it had a ripe vanilla nose with rounded, fruity body and soft tannins.

CHATEAU DE VILLERAZE, CONQUES-SUR-ORBIEL

Caroline Schwal of the Château de Villeraze has had quite a different experience. Her father was a *négociant* in Sète and her parents bought the property when they returned to France from Algeria in 1962. She admits that she was twenty-six before she ever drank wine, but was immediately captivated. She had wanted to work on the land since she was very small. For a while she lived in Switzerland, working for a French wine magazine, the *Journée Vinicole*, and then in 1994, when she was in her early thirties, her father sold his *négociant* business to Skalli and allowed her to take over responsibility for the vineyards at Château de Villeraze. As she herself said, 'You have to be completely mad'. But she is also quite single-minded in her objective to make the property work, despite her inexperience and lack of capital. She did a year's wine making course at Carcassonne, and her parents gave her a tractor and some cooling equipment for the cellar, but no other financial help.

Now she is sweeping a new broom through the property. The former *régisseur*, who had been there for thirty years, was accustomed to churning out *vin de table* for the *négoce*, or as Schwal put it, it was an *exploitation qui crachait du pinard*. The agricultural expert she asked to examine her vineyards deemed them a disaster and advised extensive replanting, but that is something she will have do slowly. There has been Merlot on the estate since 1973 and her father did plant some Malbec and Syrah in the early 1990s. Meanwhile, she has a new young *régisseur* who is as committed to renovating the property as she is, and also a new oenologist, Lucien Robert, chosen because he makes the other wines that she likes in the appellation, including those of her neighbours at Château de Salitis, who have encouraged her enormously.

So far Schwal bottles only a tiny proportion of her wine, as she needs to sell *en vrac* in order to finance her running costs. The 1997, made up of roughly sixty per cent Merlot with twenty per cent each of Malbec and Syrah and a drop of Cabernet Franc, was blended in March after four months *élevage*. It had charm, with some tannin, a hint of liquorice, berry fruit and a long finish. The 1996 from a similar blend – for she aims to maintain the same profile each year – had some solid berry fruit and soft tannins, and a Vin de Pays d'Oc, Cépage Malbec, had ripe berry fruit and hints of violets. There were also two dessert wines, one from Grenache Noir and a Muscat called Le Coucher du Soleil. During the 1930s, people were apparently encouraged to plant Muscat in the area and some vines remain on the property. Both wines are *vins doux naturels*, but are called *vin de liqueur* as they do not conform to any appellation regulations.

I left feeling an immense admiration for Schwal's tenacity and courage. Life for a single woman who goes against the norms of a region is tough, for rural France does not readily welcome outsiders or people who do not conform. She admitted that during the previous four years she had led what she described as *une vie de galère*, without, I suspect, very much support from her parents. From the quality of her first wines, she deserves to succeed. I sincerely hope she does.

CHATEAU DE SALITIS, CONQUES-SUR-ORBIEL

Anne Marondon and her husband gave me a friendly welcome at Château de Salitis, a short drive along a dirt track from Château Villeraze. They took over the family property from Anne's uncle ten years ago and now, as well as Cabardès, make a *vin de liqueur* from Muscat and several white Vins de Pays d'Oc. They explained that Château de Salitis had been known for its white wine early in the nineteenth century and that they have therefore replanted a large part of their vineyard with Chardonnay, Sauvignon, Grenache Blanc, Viognier, Rolle and Marsanne. When quizzed about white

Cabardès, they said 'not before 2020!' The soil is stony and the microclimate gives them cool nights. The 1997 Sauvignon was fresh and pithy. I thought the Viognier lacked varietal character, but liked the smoky character of the blend of Grenache Blanc and Rolle. Then we moved on to Cabardès.

They explained that their production of Cabardès has increased significantly. Ten years ago they produced only a hundred and fifty hectolitres, but now they make about a thousand hectolitres out of a total production of about four thousand. It all depends on market demand. The 1996 is a blend of forty-five per cent Syrah and Grenache Noir and fifty-five per cent Merlot and Cabernet Sauvignon. The *assemblage* takes place immediately after fermentation and the wine is bottled a few months before sale. They favour a long *élevage* and in the spring of 1998 were selling the 1993. They have tried oak ageing, but it is very expensive to do well and does not enhance their wine, so they prefer to keep it in vat. I was treated to a vertical tasting going back to their first vintage of 1988. This was lightly herbal with a long, warm finish. The 1990 had a warm, meaty nose and quite a solid, spicy palate, while the 1991 was more Atlantic in character with some firm tannin. Although there is more Syrah in the vineyard, the Grenache Noir has a greater impact as the wine ages and in the 1993 you certainly could taste the weight of the Grenache Noir, with some firm tannin and a warm, spicy finish.

DOMAINE LA VENTAILLOLE, VENTENAC-CABARDES

Marie-Claude and Robert Curbières at Domaine la Ventaillole have an example of a new estate that was once part of a co-operative. Curbières bought his land in 1974 and took his grapes to the co-operative at Aragon for twenty-five years before establishing his own cellar. At the very beginning he had ten hectares of vines such as Aramon and Carignan for *vin de table*, and he now has fourteen hectares (with more land to plant) of Grenache Noir, Syrah, Cabernet Sauvignon and a little Fer Servadou, which he described as *notre cépage d'amour*, as Marie-Claude comes from the Aveyron. There is also some Chardonnay, and some Cinsaut for *rosé*. He made his first red wine in 1992 and his first Chardonnay in 1996, which had a lightly herbal nose with hints of aniseed. The 1992

Cabardès, from forty per cent each of Grenache Noir and Syrah and twenty per cent of Fer Servadou, was quite cedary in taste, and I thought I recognised some of the peppery character of Marcillac, the one wine that is made from Fer Servadou alone.

Curbières bubbles with enthusiasm and ideas. In the vineyard he is working towards organic viticulture, while in the cellar he considers himself *comme un artiste du vin*. He has thick-walled stone vats and a deep well in his cellar, and has kept various pieces of old equipment. In the adjoining stable there was an exhibition of a friend's paintings and he organises other cultural events such as concerts, all in an attempt to encourage people to visit the property and discover the wines of Cabardès.

DOMAINE CAUNETTES-HAUTES, MOUSSOULENS

The vineyards of Domaine Caunettes-Hautes were created by Gilbert Rouquet's father in the 1970s. He began with eight hectares of vines as well as wheat and sheep, and gradually planted more vineyards so that the estate now totals sixty-five hectares of Merlot, Cabernet, Sauvignon, Syrah and Grenache Noir, though not all for Cabardès. In fact, Cabardès represents only about a quarter of their production for they make *vin de pays* too. The cellar is quite modern, with stainless steel vats, cooling equipment and a pneumatic press, and they also have an ageing cellar with seventy barrels.

We tasted with Hélène Rouquet. The blend of their generic Cabardès is thirty-five per cent each of Merlot and Cabernet Sauvignon and thirty per cent Syrah. As they are on the western side of the appellation, with more rain, they find that the Bordelais varieties fare better. The grapes are destalked, which removes some of the harsher tannins, but it is only recently that *égrappage* became the norm. The wines destined for oak ageing are given a three-week *cuvaison*, with a shorter period for the wines that spend twelve months in vat. The unoaked wine was soft and supple, while the wines with oak ageing had more structure and tannin.

They are also experimenting with a late harvest white wine, from Sauvignon grapes that are *passerillés*, or dried on the vines, for this is not an area of noble rot. The 1996 Cuvée Ste Catherine was their first vintage of this style. The grapes were picked in November and the wine was fermented in new wood. In the spring of 1998 it was deep golden in colour and tasted ripe and honeyed with smooth, unctuous apricot fruit and well integrated oak. The yields were tiny, just five hectolitres per hectare, making it very expensive to produce, not only for the yield, but also for the labour and the new barrels.

DOMAINE DE CABROL, ARAGON

The wines that impressed me most in Cabardès came from Domaine de Cabrol, on the northern edge of the appellation. The vineyards lie at an altitude of two hundred and fifty metres and from there the road leads north into the *garrigue*. The estate is run by two brothers, Michel and Claude Carayol, who took over their father's property ten years ago. As Claude, the wine maker, put it, he had made very traditional and very ordinary wine, adjectives that cannot be applied to today's production. They began by gradually replanting the vineyards, a hectare or two every year, with Syrah, Grenache Noir and Cabernet Sauvignon. Merlot, which is popular with other producers, is categorically decried here as 'the Carignan of the future' for giving nothing but quantity, and is firmly banished from the estate.

To describe their wines, the brothers evoke an image from the church at Conques-sur-Orbiel, where a pillar supporting the font depicts both the east and the west winds, thereby illustrating the transitional climate of the area. Accordingly they produce two Cabardès, Le Vent d'Est made from seventy per cent Syrah with some Cabernet Sauvignon and Grenache Noir, and Le Vent d'Ouest, in which Cabernet dominates the blend and is softened by some Grenache Noir. The grapes are given a long fermentation and *cuvaison*, followed by *élevage* in vat rather than barrel, demonstrating that oak is by no means essential. In any case, not everyone can afford to use oak barrels, whether they would like to or not. Syrah dominates the palate of the east wind, with peppery fruit, soft tannins and an elegant finish in the 1995, while the west wind is much firmer and more structured, with blackcurrant fruit. It was a fascinating contrast, showing how two quite different wines produced from the same vineyards can typify the intriguing diversity of Cabardès.

I left with the impression that Cabardès had progressed tremendously since my last visit eleven years earlier, with new producers who are greatly committed to their region and their wines. Sadly, one property that was working well in the mid-1980s, Château de Rayssac, has reverted to bulk wine production as the simplest solution for its absentee owner, and a second, Château Rivals, is currently for sale. There is a dynamic *syndicat* run by an Englishman, Adrian Mould, who has successfully managed the elevation of Cabardès to appellation status. The appellation's slogan, Vent d'Est, Vent d'Ouest, gives a succinct image of its wines.

Key facts

VDQS 1973, AC 1998 for red and *rosé*; four hundred hectares covering fourteen villages near Conques-sur-l'Orbiel.

An Atlantic and Mediterranean climate – *vent d'est, vent d'ouest* – allows Cabernet Sauvignon, Malbec, Merlot, Grenache Noir and Syrah, and also Fer Servadou. More Syrah and less Cinsaut than Côtes de la Malepère.

Average annual rainfall 700 mm.

Vintages

1999: Very good harvest conditions made for ripe, rounded wines.
1998: Severe spring frost in April made for low yields and exceptional quality.
1997: Rain affected some maturity levels at harvest time, making for lighter, fruity wines.
1996: A mild spring and hot summer led to an early harvest and well balanced wines.
1995: A hot summer made for tannic wines that lack softness.

Minervois

===

Minervois and Corbières go hand in hand as twin appellations. They are separated by the valley of the Aude and the Canal du Midi, with the vineyards of Minervois, lying on the foothills of the Massif Central between the medieval city of Carcassonne and the Roman city of Narbonne, facing those of the Corbières on the first slopes of the Pyrenees. Minervois is a slightly smaller appellation, with eighteen thousand hectares, but many of its preoccupations are the same. Since the creation of the appellation in 1985 Minervois has undergone a considerable transformation in quality, with the widespread planting of better grape varieties and the tentative beginnings of a system of *crus*. There is an underlying energy stemming from newcomers to the region or from a change of generation in existing properties.

The wine takes its name from the isolated village of Minerve that perches in what seems to be an unassailable position on steep cliffs above the confluence of the Cesse and the Briant. If you approach the village from the west you are rewarded with dramatic views of the Canyon de la Cesse, and the steep cliffs continue towards the village of La Caunette. In summer the rivers dry to the merest trickle – *fêtes* are even held on the riverbed – but with heavy winter rain they can turn overnight into gushing torrents. Minerve is Roman in origin and takes its name from Minerva, the goddess of wisdom. The surrounding countryside is wild, and on a grey day it can seem harsh and unforgiving. By contrast, one evening in late summer the village of Minerve, with its cluster of little houses, tiny church and the remains of medieval ramparts, looked soft and gentle bathed in the evening sunshine. Little grows but vines and olive trees on these arid, rocky hills, which are the first foothills of the Montagne Noire.

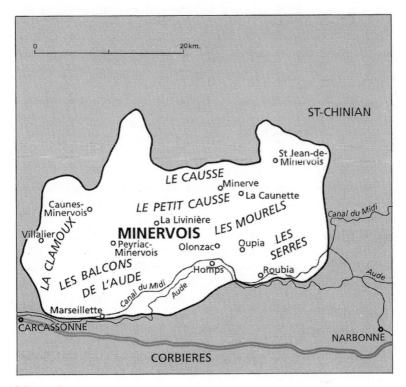

Minervois

The ramparts of Minerve were built in the twelfth century. The village played its part in the Albigensian Crusade as one of the last strongholds of the Cathar heresy, which had a strong following all over this part of France at the end of the twelfth century. The Cathars believed that all material things, including our own bodies, were the work of the devil. They regarded wealth and possessions as evil and were opposed to reproduction, marriage and family life. Pope Innocent III launched a crusade against them under the command of Simon de Montfort, father of the founder of the English parliament, and many Cathars died at Minerve after a successful siege by him in 1210.

The Roman legions that occupied Narbonne in the first century BC were responsible for introducing viticulture here. Cicero wrote of the vines of Minerve, which he called the Pagus Menerbensis, and Pliny the Younger preferred the wines of Minerve to those of Betoeres, the Béziers of today. After the desolation caused by the Albigensian Crusade, the region faded from historical significance. Minervois is said to have been drunk by Francois I, Henri IV and Louis XVI, and in the fourteenth century Jacques de la Jugie, Seigneur de la Livinière, which is today the leading village of the appellation, sent wine to the papal court of Avignon for his uncle Clement VI.

The nineteenth-century writers accorded the wines of the Minervois no more than a passing mention, and the region suffered from phylloxera and the economic problems of other parts of the Midi. The better-quality vineyards planted on the arid hillsides fell into disuse as viticulture shifted towards the coastal plains to concentrate on the industrial production of le gros rouge. It is only in the last couple of decades that the process has begun to be reversed, with a positive move towards smaller yields and better quality. Minervois was recognised as a VDQS in 1951 but it was not until 1985 that it became an appellation, along with Corbières and the Coteaux du Languedoc.

The appellation of Minervois covers a varied area, including some sixteen villages in the Hérault and forty-five in the Aude. The scenery is equally various: in some parts it is wild and rugged, but elsewhere there are swathes of vineyards, looking green and lush after warm spring rain, and little villages of variable charm and interest. Finding a café can sometimes present a challenge. The town of Olonzac forms the administrative centre, while the little village of Siran houses the *syndicat*'s offices, including a state-of-the-art tasting room, in the renovated château. Olonzac is usually rather sleepy, especially in the midday sunshine, but it really comes to life on market day, when stalls of tempting local produce, colourful vegetables and tasteless clothes sprawl through the streets to the accompanying smells of an enormous paella and roasting chickens. The main social attraction of Siran is *boules*, played in the square under large plane trees. If you are sipping tea outside the local café, it makes a surprisingly good spectator sport. Rieux-Minervois is worth a detour for its awe-inspiring Romanesque church, while Caunes-Minervois is known for its abbey and the Hotel d'Alibert, with its beautiful renaissance courtyard. Its marble quarries were once important, providing stone columns for the palace of Versailles.

Steps are being taken to organise Minervois into various geographical and geological zones. For the moment, the only one with any official recognition is that of La Livinière. Maurice Piccinini, formerly director of the village co-operative and then manager of the large estate of Ste Eulalie, has been one of the prime movers in the creation of the *cru* of La Livinière, which was finally achieved for the 1998 vintage and retrospectively for the 1997 vintage. Piccinini talked of the economic problems of the Minervois, explaining that it is a large geographical area. As a VDQS it covered thirty-six thousand hectares, which were reduced to eighteen thousand when it became an appellation in 1985. The reality is that, in 1995, the production of only four thousand hectares was declared as appellation Minervois. The other fourteen thousand had produced either *vin de pays* or, worse still, *vin de table*. And of that four thousand hectares, only half was sold well, at a sensible price with some recognition of quality. The problem is that, if you make *vin de pays* instead, you are allowed much more freedom of choice in both cellar and vineyard and you can produce twice as much as the appellation without having to sell your wine for a very much lower price. To prevent problems of excess or insufficient supply, the producers now have to declare three years in advance which vineyards they will harvest as Minervois and which as *vin de pays* – and then, of course, they have to conform to the appellation regulations regarding yields, vineyard and cellar work. This means that you cannot change a vineyard from one to the other overnight, which enables better regulation of the market.

The creation of the *cru* of La Livinière took more than ten years. Piccinini, together with other like-minded producers such as the village co-operative, Roger Piquet at Château de Gourgazaud and Jacques Maris of Domaine Maris, began working in that direction in 1987. At the time, people were not really proud of their wine; they needed motivation, and that is what the new *cru* has provided. It includes the adjoining villages of Azillanet, Siran, Cesseras, Félines-Minervois and Azille. The geology is based on the limestone and clay of the Petit Causse, the cliffs that run at an altitude of about 140 metres at the foot of the Montagne Noire between Caunes-en-Minervois and La Livinière. A precise delimitation of the vineyards has been carried out and no one will have lost their status as Minervois. However, not all Minervois in those villages is eligible to be La Livinière – only about 2600 hectares out of a possible 5200 hectares. The composition of the wine demands a greater emphasis on Syrah, with the so-called *cépages améliorateurs*, Syrah, Mourvèdre and Grenache Noir, accounting for sixty per cent of the blend – Syrah and Mourvèdre in particular must make up a minimum of forty per cent – as opposed to ten per cent in basic Minervois, while Carignan and Cinsaut are limited to a maximum of forty per cent. There is, in fact, nothing to prohibit a pure Syrah, but you are not allowed to say so on the label. The minimum alcohol level is a natural 12° without enrichment of any kind, and the maximum yield is 45 hl/ha. The tasting for the *agrément* takes place fifteen months after the vintage, and in the meantime *élevage* may be in vat or barrel, depending on the producer's preference. The wine must be bottled at the place of production, so it cannot be sent off to a *négociant* elsewhere in France, and there is an obligatory three months in cellar after bottling. A minimum bulk price has been fixed of FF 1000 per hectolitre, or FF 40 per bottle, tax included, to the consumer, compared with the usual average of FF 15–20 for basic Minervois in a supermarket. For the moment, the wine is labelled Minervois–La Livinière, but ultimately an appellation La Livinière is envisaged, with no mention at all of Minervois on the label.

The delimitation of other areas is under discussion, but as yet no actual applications have been submitted to the INAO. However, it is possible to see how the Minervois divides up into different zones, each with a similar cohesion and identity. The Balcons de l'Aude encompass the villages around the dried-up Etang de Marseillette, from Laure to Puicheric, with vineyards on alluvial soil and gravel from the Aude. Le Petit Causse in the north eastern part of the appellation includes the villages of Minerve and La Caunette, stretching toward St-Jean-de-Minervois. Here the soil is less homogeneous, although based on limestone and clay, and the altitude ranges from one hundred to two hundred and fifty metres, with vineyards facing in different directions. The climate is harsher here and more influenced by the mountains. Work needs to be done on the selection of the *terroir* and the area is about five or six years behind the Balcons de l'Aude. Mention has been made of La Clamoux in the west. This is the area adjoining the new appellation of Cabardès, where the climate is more humid than elsewhere in the appellation, but still hot. On the south eastern edge, where there is a more maritime influence on the climate, there are few producers of the appellation, with the odd exception such as Château Belvize, and *vin de pays* tends to dominate. However, there is some talk of Les Mourels, while Les Serres has been mentioned for the very southern edge of the appellation, though only tentatively for the moment.

Although white and pink wine are included in the appellation, most Minervois is firmly red. However, attempts are being made to improve the quality of the white wine by the introduction of more flavoursome grape varieties, namely Roussanne, Marsanne, Rolle and Muscat, in contrast to the original white varieties in the decree of 1985, which were Grenache Blanc, Macabeu, Picpoul, Bourboulenc, Clairette and Terret. Chardonnay and Sauvignon will remain firmly as *vin de pays*, as probably will Viognier. There is no doubt that it is a blend of several varieties that contributes to the individuality of the appellation, giving the wines complexity and length. Usually Grenache Blanc or perhaps Macabeu forms the base; Bourboulenc is tending to disappear from the vineyards because of virus problems, though it can contribute some interesting flavours. Roussanne, first introduced in the late 1970s, seems to provide more aroma and finesse than Marsanne, while Rolle, first planted in the mid-1980s, has as yet an uncertain future in the vineyards. Muscat is limited to just ten per cent, as any more would completely overwhelm the blend. Most of the original white varieties lacked flavour and freshness, defects that have been remedied by the improvement of vinification methods as well as the introduction of fruitier grape varieties.

In common with most of the appellations of the Midi, the true typicity of red Minervois comes from the blend of the usual five grape varieties, with variations reflecting each producer's preference. Carignan has always provided the backbone and Grenache Noir the body and alcohol. Cinsaut is favoured more for *rosé* than red wine, but as will be seen it does have its supporters. Syrah and Mourvèdre are the essential *cépages améliorateurs*, and usually Syrah in preference to Mourvèdre in view of the distance of the vineyards from the sea. You may encounter a pure Syrah, but there are doubts as to its success. The instigators of the *cru* of La Livinière promoted Syrah at the beginning, but now hesitate over its viability as a varietal wine. Although the appellation lays down minimum and maximum percentages, these relate to the composition of your vineyard, not to the blend of your wine. Each variety has its place in the appellation.

The other current topic of discussion is the putative appellation of Minervois Noble. This apparently existed within the decree of the VDQS, but was dropped when the appellation was created. Yves Castell, secretary of the *syndicat*, remembers that, when he arrived in the region in 1973, just four growers produced Minervois Noble, and by 1980 only one family was carrying on the tradition. It would have been sad for this wine to disappear completely, and therefore many of the more energetic and inquisitive producers are now trying their hand at a late harvest wine, often from Grenache Blanc, with varying degrees of success. However, there are legal and logistical problems that need clarification. The INAO seems reluctant to accept the existence of these wines, turning a blind eye to them as experiments, and so for the moment they can only be labelled *moût de raisin frais partiellement fermenté, issu de vendanges passerillés*, a term that lacks a certain marketing cachet and translates as 'partially fermented grape must produced from wind-dried grapes'.

CAVE LA LIVINIERE

As in most appellations of the Midi, the village co-operatives are an important force, and the Minervois is lucky in having some that are distinctly more dynamic than the average. The co-operative of La Livinière has worked well for its appellation over the last two decades. I was impressed when I first visited them back in 1987, and they have continued to maintain their attention to quality, more recently as one of the leaders in the creation of the *cru* of La Livinière. The co-operative's early moves towards quality focused on the use of carbonic maceration as a means of rendering the large quantities of Carignan then present in the vineyards more friendly and accessible. This was a decision taken when the cellar was built in 1978. There still is a lot of Carignan, but significantly less than ten years ago, and the co-operative would ultimately like a minimum of eighty per cent of *cépages améliorateurs* for the cru of La Livinière; in other words, they want to concentrate on Syrah with some Grenache Noir.

Today the co-operative has 185 members and is responsible for 650 hectares, mainly around the village. They produce the *cru*, Minervois and various *vins de pays* – d'Oc, Coteaux de Peyriac and Hérault – as well as *vin de table*. The director, Bernard Coutal, showed me round the cellars accompanied by his sleek grey tabby cat. The crop is hand-picked, as it has to be for carbonic maceration, and there is a careful selection of grapes on arrival at the cellar and an efficient mini-conveyor belt to feed the fermentation vats. They are convinced that carbonic maceration lasting anything from eight to twenty days is not only best for Carignan, but that it also gives good results for Syrah, which was first planted in the village in the 1980s. The flavours are more intense and fruitier, but the biggest difference comes in the quality of the tannins, which are softer and more supple. You need ripe tannins to begin with, so they meticulously monitor the ripening grapes in the vineyard.

The co-operative was also among the pioneers of *élevage* in *barriques* in the appellation and built its first barrel cellar at the beginning of the 1980s. Usually they buy refurbished second-hand barrels from their cooper, preferring them to brand-new barrels except for the *cru*, which can cope with new wood more successfully as it is so much more concentrated. A second barrel cellar is under the co-operative shop for passing customers to admire. Their next project is an insulated warehouse for bottles, something that so many cellars in the Midi lack, even though it can have a significant impact on ageing potential.

I tasted a small selection of their wines, mainly those in the Jacques de la Jugie range, named after a former lord of the region.

The white comes from Bourboulenc, vinified and aged in wood, with some rounded, herbal fruit and well-integrated oak. The pink is a pure Syrah, and the red, a blend of Syrah with some Grenache Noir and Carignan made partly by carbonic maceration and partly from destalked grapes, was ripe and rounded, with some spicy liquorice fruit. It spends a year in wood. The 1996 Cuvée des Meuliers, made entirely by carbonic maceration without any oak ageing, had dry, spicy tannins with a peppery finish, and the 1997 Grand Terroir, a blend of Syrah and Grenache Noir again vinified by carbonic maceration, with ten months in new wood, was firm and oaky with a long, sweet finish. It promised well for the new *cru*.

CAVE POUZOLS-MINERVOIS

Unusually it is Mourvèdre that is the speciality of the co-operative of Pouzols-Minervois. The director, Jean Escande, explained how there had originally been Mourvèdre in the village in the early 1900s, but that it had all been pulled up when the growers wanted quantity rather than quality. In the early 1980s they began looking at different grape varieties and realised that Mourvèdre would only ripen in a particular soil on the hill behind the village, a type of limestone they call *éclats calcaires*. They also have *galets*, like the large pebbles of Châteauneuf-du-Pape, from the bed of the Cesse, which are good for Syrah and Grenache Noir, and there are alluvial soils suitable for Sauvignon and Merlot for *vin de pays*. You sense that this is a co-operative working hard for its appellation and its members. An increasing number of the younger generation are wanting to take over their parents' land, in sharp contrast to ten or so years earlier. Today there are no vines for sale in Pouzols, and the vineyard is flourishing. In 1992 the co-operative planted what they call a vineyard *de collection*, with examples of forty-seven different grape varieties, including some once commonly found in the Minervois that disappeared with phylloxera. It is still too early to draw any conclusions from the experiment.

Their barrel cellar was built in 1989 and contains an attractive collection of amphorae, both old and new. They make five red Minervois, with variations according to the *terroir* and the blend, including two aged in oak. But first I tried the Sauvignon of the year, picked about three weeks earlier on 18 August. Although it had finished fermenting, it still looked like grapefruit juice and had as yet to develop some varietal character. The Minervois Ancien Comte de Pouzols, made by carbonic maceration from the maximum amount of Carignan with a small proportion of Grenache Noir and Syrah, is intended to be a summer red, with light fruit and spice. The Minervois St Phar, from the property of the Comte Albert de St Phar, who owns vineyards in the village although he lives in Geneva, is a blend of Grenache Noir and Syrah aged in wood, making for red berries and vanilla on the nose and the chunky spice of the *garrigue* on the palate. The Minervois Premier de Fontalières is pure Mourvèdre, which is possible without breaking appellation regulations, but you cannot say so on the label. It had spent seven or eight months in new wood, making for some meaty fruit and a structured palate; later that evening it went very well with a dinner based on a gutsy sausage from the local butcher.

The co-operative of Pouzols is involved with the revival of Minervois Noble, making a late harvest Grenache Blanc they call Grain de Douceur. The grapes are picked at the end of October rather than in early September and the wine is left to ferment in barrel until it stops of its own accord the following spring. It was honeyed and ripe with notes of quince and citrus fruit, and good acidity to prevent a cloying finish. Finally there was Carthagène, one of the traditions of the Minervois, produced by a method similar to the ratafia of Champagne and Chablis or Pineau de Charente. Theirs is based on Syrah and Grenache Noir with a little Macabeu and Bourboulenc, muted with *eau de vie* from the Languedoc and kept in wood for several months. It was light red in colour, with hints of liquorice and cherries, and the alcohol was well integrated and in balance. The grapes are picked before they are fully ripe, at 11° potential alcohol, for if they are too sweet, the taste will cloy.

CAVE DE PEYRIAC

The harvest was in full swing when I visited the Cave de Peyriac in early September, and the director Joël Venture looked rather tired and dishevelled. He has been at Peyriac since 1983 and recalls that, when he arrived, there were people in the village who did not know what a *barrique* was. The co-operative was one of the first to begin working with barrels, in 1981, and they now have a handsome cellar built in 1992. They were also the first co-operative to buy a destemmer, and as the *terroir* of Peyriac gives quite sturdy wines, they find that *éraflage* provides more supple tannins. They only carry out carbonic maceration when the grapes are in perfect condition.

The soil here is limestone and clay, and it is very stony. Indeed, Peire is the old name for stone in Occitan, so the derivation of the village name is obvious; it too has the *galets roulées* similar to those of Châteauneuf du Pape. However, Peyriac is known for its white wines, and they have planted some more aromatic varieties. Marsanne and Roussanne came in the mid-1980s, as did Sauvignon and Chardonnay, while Rolle followed a little later in the early 1990s. They also have a little Viognier, which they would like to see incorporated into the appellation. Their white brand, La Tour St Martin, named after a surviving tower of the village's old château, is a fragrant blend of Grenache Blanc, Macabeu, Marsanne and Roussanne, with just a hint of Viognier.

When Venture arrived here in 1983, not only were there no aromatic grape varieties, but no Syrah, Merlot or Cabernet Sauvignon either. Today their Minervois blends are based on Carignan, Syrah, Grenache Noir and Mourvèdre, while Cinsaut is mainly used for *vin de pays*, as are Merlot and Cabernet Sauvignon. Their red La Tour St Martin is the most representative of Peyriac, a blend of Syrah, Grenache Noir and Carignan with *élevage* in vat, giving a deep colour, a certain peppery character on the nose and some supple fruit and tannin on the palate. Their oaked *cuvée*, Château de Peyriac, which they have produced since 1985, is a blend of sixty per cent Syrah with forty per cent Mourvèdre, given twelve months oak ageing. I tasted the 1994 when it was three years old, but still found it very oaky. Mourvèdre ripens late here and is only really successful in five out of ten years, so maybe it is a mistake. They have also made a white Château de Peyriac, mainly from Marsanne, but again the oak tended to overwhelm the fruit so they discontinued that *cuvée*. The price difference for the consumer between an oaked and an unoaked wine is FF 15 per bottle, with La Tour St. Martin costing FF 20 as opposed to FF 35 for the Château de Peyriac. I had no doubt about where my own preference lay. Venture is not bothered by any potential *cru*. For him the most important thing is the appellation itself. Quite simply, Minervois suffers from a lack of reputation and that must be addressed.

CELLIER ARMAND DE BEZONS, VILLALIER

The co-operative in the little village of Villalier goes by the name of Cellier Armand de Bezons, after a local historical figure. You are very close to Cabardès here, so they see themselves as at the gateway to the Minervois. In some ways the climate is more like that of Cabardès: there is more rain than the average in the Minervois, and the soil is a mixture of gravel, clay and limestone. There is no talk of a *cru* here. In the words of the cellar manager, his cellar is 'archaic', with the classic concrete vats of the average French co-operative – but it is not so archaic that it does not have a pneumatic press and cooling equipment. They also have a separate barrel cellar and have worked with wood since 1989. They are part of the Pays Cathar organisation, which covers the various producers of the region, not just of wine, but of cheese, honey and other products, recognising not only the quality of their products but also the quality of their reception of visitors. And they certainly gave me a friendly welcome, with a comprehensive tasting of their Minervois.

Domaine de Cérons is a property belonging to two or three of the members. The white is a blend of Marsanne and Grenache Blanc, light and rounded. Marsanne was first planted in the village ten years ago. The red is mainly Syrah, made by carbonic maceration. It had a meaty, spicy flavour and was a touch raisiny on the finish. The *rosé*, a blend of Syrah and Grenache Noir, was redolent of ripe raspberry fruit. I liked the Minervois Tradition, again mainly from Syrah, made by carbonic maceration with an *élevage* in vat. It was ripe and peppery, with some appealing mineral fruit. Finally, Cristal de Grotte describes a pure Syrah aged for fourteen months in the caves at nearby Limousis. A blend of carbonic maceration and traditional vinification, it was ripe and rounded with some sweet fruit and soft tannins. The oak was well integrated, with an elegant finish. The co-operative also works with the Australian wine maker

Nerida Abbott. She chooses the vineyard plots she would like to use, which tend to be the same each year, and uses the co-operative's facilities for her vinifications in a partnership that works well, representing just one example of interest in the region from the New World.

CHATEAU DE PAULIGNAN, LA LIVINIERE

The very first person to plant what were regarded back in the early 1960s as the quite unorthodox grape varieties of Syrah and Mourvèdre was Jacques Tallavignes at the Château de Paulignan. He is considered by many to have been the father of the appellation. Sadly, after he died his sons proved not to have their father's talent and aptitude, and the property has been sold; the château itself now provides *chambres d'hôte*. One son, Jean-Antoine Tallavignes, has retained twenty hectares, while Michel Escande of Domaine Borie de Maurel has bought what he considers to be the best part of the estate, the northern part in the *garrigue*.

CHATEAU DE GOURGAZAUD, LA LIVINIERE

The pioneering spirit of the older generation of the Minervois is still represented by Roger Piquet at the Château de Gourgazaud. He is the former managing director of the large *négociant* company of Chantovent, but he admitted that he much preferred growing grapes and making wine to running a company, and that when he bought the Château de Gourgazaud from Chantovent on his retirement from the company in 1985, he fulfilled a lifetime's ambition. When Chantovent had acquired the property in 1973, there was nothing but Aramon and Carignan in the vineyards and Piquet began the move towards more noble grape varieties. The first Syrah was planted in 1974. We take it for granted today, but it seemed revolutionary at the time and Syrah is now an important part of the 108-hectare vineyard. There is also Mourvèdre, a little Grenache Noir and Carignan but no Cinsaut, large plantings of Cabernet Sauvignon, Chardonnay and Viognier, and some

Sauvignon and Marsanne, making an extensive range of *vin de pays* under the label Les P'tits Grains, as well as three red Minervois, but no white or pink ones.

Piquet has been involved with the development of the *cru* of La Livinière since its conception. He describes the soil as very stony clay and limestone with glacial debris and good drainage. He is forthright in his opinions and does not mince his words. Cinsaut is worthless. He is anti-Grenache, as it is alcoholic, has no flavour and oxidises after two or three years. As for old Carignan, 'Don't make me laugh. Of course the yields are low, as half the vines are missing.' And what about Minervois Noble? That he sees as something to keep the *syndicat* busy. 'You cannot create a market if you only produce 9 hl/ha, and there are so many other good sweet wines. It is folklore.'

Piquet showed me round the cellar accompanied by his two dogs, Kim and Black. There is a new cellar for white wines, with gleaming stainless steel vats and some barrels. The last of the Viognier was just being picked, for the harvest had begun a week earlier. We tasted the juice, which was sweet and perfumed. Piquet likes Viognier and is planting more. The Chardonnay of the previous vintage had some attractive peachy fruit, but without much weight. Chardonnay was first planted in the late 1980s. The best goes into oak for four months, and there is also a light, buttery unoaked wine.

There is an ageing cellar for the red wines. They bought their very first barrels from Château de Camensac in Bordeaux in 1974 and their first new barrels in 1990, which are used for the Minervois Réserve. This is a blend of eighty per cent Syrah with Mourvèdre, given twelve months *élevage*. It was solid and structured, needing time. Cuvée Mathilde, named after Piquet's granddaughter, born the year he bought the property, is the same blend, but kept for eighteen months in vat. This for me was classic Minervois, a sturdy mouthful of tannic, peppery fruit. The Classique is similar but with less ageing. Piquet likes Mourvèdre, provided that it ripens properly with a low yield. He does not use carbonic maceration as he has so little Carignan. I was left with a feeling of sadness that Piquet was beginning to run out of energy, but there should be continuity as his son works on the export side and Guy Bascou, in his role as consultant oenologist for the ICV, is now responsible for the wine making at Château de Gourgazaud.

DOMAINE PICCININI, LA LIVINIERE

As mentioned above, Maurice Piccinini has been involved with the wines of Minervois for some years, first as director of the co-operative of La Livinière and then as manager of the large estate of Ste Eulalie. It was only when his son Jean-Christophe showed signs of following his father's profession, by studying oenology at Montpellier, that he took the step of creating a family estate in 1991. They now have thirty hectares of vines and a small cellar in the village built up against the old ramparts. In fact, part of it is over what was once the village moat, and when they were installing new vats they discovered deep water under the stone floor. Their white Minervois is a blend of Grenache Blanc with some Muscat, Marsanne and Macabeu, fermented in wood, so it is oak that dominates the palate rather than any particular grape variety. Their *rosé* is half Syrah and half Grenache Noir, and for that too they may try a vinification in oak to make a wine with a longer life. There is a Merlot Vin de Pays d'Oc, with some plummy fruit. The basic Minervois is a blend of sixty per cent Syrah with equal parts of Grenache Noir and Carignan that is over fifty years old and given a twenty-five day maceration. It had good rounded fruit. Clos l'Angély comes from vines that are at least thirty years old, with twelve months *élevage* in *barriques*, giving some firm blackcurrant fruit. The Cuvée Line and Laetitia, named after Maurice Piccinini's daughter and daughter-in-law, comes from even older vines, harvested in the middle of October when the grapes are almost overripe and given a thirty-five-day maceration, with eighteen months *élevage* in wood. The oak was well integrated but still quite apparent on the young wine, with a firm backbone of tannin.

CHATEAU OUPIA, OUPIA

Château Oupia has been in the hands of the Iché family since 1860, but nothing remains of the original twelfth-century château. André Iché was in the middle of the harvest, the 1997 vintage, when I visited, and things were not going well. The *érafloir* had chosen that moment to break down. Nor, after heavy rain in August, were the grapes as healthy as they might have been. Nearby Olonzac had been flooded three times when the Espène river burst its banks, which was hard to imagine on a hot, still September afternoon. Marie-Pierre Iché explained how her father had taken over his parents' vineyards in 1969. They now have fifty-three hectares around the village of Oupia and further north at La Caunette, including some hundred-year-old vines. Until 1985 everything was sold *en vrac*, but now their whole production is bottled, with a very varied range of wines.

Their white Minervois is a blend of Marsanne and Roussanne fermented in stainless steel vats, resulting in a full, rounded, fruity wine with intriguing layers of flavours. The *rosé*, a blend of Syrah, Grenache Noir and Cinsaut, is redolent of ripe raspberries. Then there are several different red Minervois. The Minervois Tradition, made in the standard way without any wood or carbonic maceration, is a blend of Carignan, Syrah and Grenache Noir, with the rugged, almost rustic flavours of Carignan and scents and herbs of the *garrigue*, giving a spicy, tannic finish; it is a benchmark Minervois. In contrast, Cuvée des Barons, first made in 1985, is mostly aged in wood and also includes some carbonic maceration for the Carignan, which is blended with Syrah and Grenache Noir after the malolactic fermentation. It needs time, for the young wine is packed with ripe, oaky vanilla flavours, with a firm backbone of tannin. Cuvée Nobilis, best described as a selection of Cuvée des Barons, comes from Syrah with some Carignan and Grenache Noir, aged in wood for twelve months and left unfiltered. It is even more substantial on the nose and palate. Cuvée AR 26 is an oddity, made just once in 1995. It comes from a plot of Grenache Noir, a vineyard in the *lieu-dit* of Pomerol, but for obvious reasons they cannot put Pomerol on the label and so instead they label it by its number in the local land register. The wine is rich and raisiny on nose and palate, with liquorice and tannin. And the Ichés too are experimenting with Minervois Noble, made from Grenache Gris.

DOMAINE VILLERAMBERT-JULIEN, CAUNES-MINERVOIS

Domaine Villerambert-Julien adjoins Domaine Villerambert-Moureau, sharing the attractive sixteenth-century *bastide*. Once it was all the property of the family of the Marquis de Vernon, who owned it for six centuries until they sold part of it to the Julien family in 1858. After the First World War, the Julien family turned down the opportunity to buy the remaining part of the estate, as the land did not seem such a good investment at that time. The Moureau family therefore took over that part of the estate in 1926 and the two families now coexist side by side. Marcel Julien bottled his first wines in 1978, a revolutionary step at the time, and his son Michel began working with him in 1989. Michel's mother Lucette introduced me to their red wines in a neat, stone-floored outhouse with a small museum containing old cellar artefacts. They make a basic Minervois called l'Opéra from Carignan with some Grenache Noir and Syrah, aged in vat and with rounded, warm fruit. The average yield for this is 50–60 hl/ha, while for the oak-aged Cuvée Trianon, they only want about 35 hl/ha. They practice green harvesting, and Mme Julien laughingly explained how the old farmers used to say that *louis d'or* were falling from the sky when it rained in July, for that meant a large harvest and therefore plenty of cash. The Cuvée Trianon was both elegant and structured, quite perfumed, with the smoky notes of the *garrigue* and well-integrated oak; a wine to age. It promised well for the future of the estate.

CHATEAU BELVIZE, BIZE-MINERVOIS

Château Belvize is near the village of Bize-Minervois on the eastern edge of the appellation, closer to St Chinian, so the climate has a more maritime influence and the soil a heavy limestone base. There is talk of the potential *cru* of Les Mourels, but in fact they are quite isolated, without any other serious producers near by. The neighbouring property of Château de Cabezac has just changed hands, but you need the strength of numbers to fight battles with the INAO. Frédéric Corpel is a young man whose father-in-law, a *négociant*, bought the estate ten years ago. At the time it was a typical Midi estate, planted with a lot of Cinsaut and Carignan, a little Syrah and Grenache Noir and no white varieties at all. They have replanted some vineyards and grafted others, so that they now have Syrah, Grenache Noir and Mourvèdre for Minervois as well as Viognier and some other white varieties, Cabernet Sauvignon for Vin de Pays du Val de Cesse, and some Merlot for Vin de Pays d'Oc. There are twenty-five hectares all around the cellar and they would like to buy more, but people do not want to sell their land, even if they are not taking care of their vines. Corpel cited the example of an untidy vineyard across the valley. The owner neglects it, but keeps it so that he can retain his hunting rights. You do not have the freedom to hunt if you do not own some land of your own.

Money has been invested in the cellar. They have kept the concrete vats but not the *foudres*, and have added stainless steel vats and barrels as well as an insulated warehouse for storing bottles, essential in the summer heat of the Midi. They produce a variety of different wines. A white Vin de Pays d'Oc is a blend of Marsanne, Bourboulenc, Muscat and Viognier, blended after fermentation and bottled early, giving some intriguing fruit and a dry palate. The white Minervois is mainly Bourboulenc and Marsanne with just a drop of Muscat; it shows fresh fruit and crisp acidity. The pink Minervois, from Syrah, Grenache Noir, Carignan and Mourvèdre, had more body and weight than a *vin de pays*, which includes some Cabernet. A red *vin de pays* that has a little of everything – Cabernet Sauvignon, Carignan, Cinsaut, Syrah and Merlot – is given a fairly short maceration and some *élevage* in vat. It was quite firm and structured, with some tannin but not a lot of body.

They make three different red Minervois. Their aim with the Minervois Tradition, which has the same blend as the *rosé*, is fruit and they succeed, with firm, peppery fruit on the nose and palate, and a certain spiciness on the finish which comes, Corpel said, from the Mourvèdre. Mourvèdre ripens with difficulty, even though they carry out a green harvest and it is picked at least a week after the other grapes. The Cuvée Réserve, from equal parts of Syrah and Grenache Noir with twenty per cent Mourvèdre, is blended after six months ageing in wood. I found the 1997 full of vanilla on the nose and palate. In contrast, the Cuvée des Oliviers, made for the first time in 1994, is a blend of forty per cent each of Grenache Noir and Mourvèdre with twenty per cent Syrah, given twelve months of oak ageing. The 1996 is solidly oaky, with vanilla and tannin, needing time, while the 1995 was beginning to show the ageing potential, with less obvious oak and more elegant cedary fruit. The blend was different from the others, with more Syrah and less Mourvèdre, while the 1997, from fifty per cent Mourvèdre with some Grenache Noir and Syrah, still tasted very youthful, with ripe, solid fruit. The name refers to the revival of olive trees in the area: there is an olive oil co-operative outside the village of Bize-Minervois that is a good source of large containers of rich oil and a selection of Les Lucques olives flavoured with different herbs.

It seems that every estate worth its salt is experimenting with Minervois Noble, and Château Belvize is no exception – save that when they wanted to make some in 1998 someone stole the grapes that were still on the vines in mid-November. In previous years they have produced about six hundred bottles from raisined Bourboulenc grapes, fermented very slowly in barrel with some lees stirring. I found the 1994 rather ungainly; it had acidity and honey, but lacked balance and elegance. However, with Corpel's enthusiasm and energy this is an estate that deserves to do well.

CHATEAU PIQUE-PERLOU, ROUBIA

Château Pique-Perlou is another relatively new property that is also rather isolated from its neighbours, for it is on the very south eastern edge of the Minervois in the village of Roubia, close to the Canal du Midi. There is a strong maritime influence here, although the climate is hot and dry. Les Serres would be the potential *cru*, but like Les Maurels, it is nothing more than a topic for discussion at the moment. Serge and Véronique Serris are an enthusiastic young couple who used to send their grapes to the village co-operative, but in 1993 took the decision to 'fly with their own wings' because the co-operative simply did not have the same quality aims as they did. They are very much part of the new generation of young energetic producers who are 'advancing the region'. They have thirty hectares, part in *vin de pays* and part in Minervois, in the hills near Pouzols. In Occitan, *pique perlou* is an expression the old farmers used to describe going to work in vineyards far up in the hills. They have some very old Carignan and Grenache Noir vines, while their Mourvèdre and Syrah are much younger. It is the ninety-year-old Carignan, with its low yields, that makes the typicity of their red wines. They give it a long maceration, at least thirty-five days with *pigeages* and *délestages*.

I liked their wines. The 1996 white, a pure Grenache Blanc, has a firm, nettly character and a rounded palate, with notes of honey on the finish. They work on the fine lees during the winter with a regular weekly *bâtonnage*, and consider it a shame that the whites are not aged as they develop well with bottle age. The 1997 was still quite crisp, and you could taste the benefit of an extra year's ageing. Their *rosé* is a blend of Syrah and Grenache Noir, which are fermented together. The two varieties would not normally ripen together, but they juggle with the vintage dates by pruning the Grenache fifteen days earlier than usual, which makes for an earlier harvest. The wine has ripe fruit, with good body and fresh acidity. As for red wines, the Cuvée Tradition comes from equal proportions of Mourvèdre, Grenache Noir and Carignan, of which about a quarter is given some *élevage* in oak for ten to twelve months. Serris is adamant that he does not want the taste of wood, but does want the extra complexity it brings. The wine had firm, ripe cherry fruit and was young and stylish, needing time to develop in bottle. In 1998 they made their first *haute gamme*, fermenting it in an open-top wooden vat and then putting it into *barriques* for the malolactic fermentation. They looked for very ripe grapes, picking in mid-October rather than mid-September, which gave an extra concentration to the grapes. Yields were tiny after a severe prune and an unusually sharp spring frost. When the wine was nine months old, it had great concentration on the nose, and ripe and almost sweet oak and tannin on the palate. In 1998 they made three *barriques* and they may try ten in 1999.

Since 1996 the Serris too have been experimenting with late harvest wine, from fifty ares of Grenache Blanc that they pick in November when the grapes are raisined and some have noble rot. The juice is fermented in barrel, taking about three or four months, and then remains in wood until bottling about two years later. The 1996 was golden, with nutty, honeyed notes and a lemony acidity. In 1997 there was more noble rot, making a more harmonious wine, with notes of orange marmalade. That year they also picked in two *tris* fifteen days apart, which they felt improved the quality. In June 1999 the 1998 was still fermenting in barrel. If you put your ear to the bunghole you could hear a gentle murmur. There was a concentration of flavour in the mouth with a prickle of carbon dioxide. It is all a gamble, for you could lose the entire crop if there is a storm, though they usually have wonderful long autumns in the Minervois. Serge Serris has ambitions for the future and is very critical of his own work. 'You have to question yourself every morning in our profession.' He should go far.

CHATEAU COUPE-ROSES, LA CAUNETTE

Château Coupe-Roses is in the village of La Caunette, which is perched on the cliffs above the river Cesse in a similarly dramatic position to the nearby village of Minerve. The château of La Caunette was destroyed in the sixteenth century. Françoise de Calvez made her first wine in the dreadful year of 1987, when a metre of rain fell on the vineyards. When I met her in 1997, things were not looking too good either, as she had lost forty per cent of her crop to hail on 16 August, when 200 mm of rain had fallen in an hour, causing dreadful erosion. The family business formerly consisted of twenty hectares, with old cellars and sales *en vrac*; she has expanded to forty hectares and built a new cellar, and now sells most of her wine in bottle. She makes eight different wines and is very experimental in her approach, encouraged by her oenologist husband. She enthused about the potential *cru* of La Caunette – or will it be called Minerve, or perhaps le Petit Causse? – that will cover the vineyards on the stony plateau above the two villages and also include the villages of Aigne and Aigues-Vives. It is still a long way from reality.

I tasted a selection of her wines. Viognier was planted in 1991 and makes a Vin de Pays d'Oc. Given three months of *élevage* on the fine lees, this has some delicate varietal character on the palate, with hints of apricots and a rounded body. Her white Minervois is a blend of Roussanne and Grenache Blanc, given some skin contact. The *rosé*, made by *saignée*, with each variety added to the vat as it ripens – first Syrah, then Cinsaut and finally Grenache Noir – resulting in a two-month fermentation, has ripe, rounded raspberry fruit and some structure and body.

A pure Carignan, vinified by carbonic maceration, is called Bastide de Coupe-Roses. De Calvez explained that *coupe-roses* is in fact a soil formation, a type of clay that is pink in colour from the presence of manganese. It can be used for making bricks and tiles, and the original family cellar was in a building that had once housed the tile kilns. The wine had some attractive berry fruit and was spicy with a rugged finish. The 1994 Minervois Tradition, from Grenache Noir and Syrah with an *élevage* in vat, was quite light, but with warm berry fruit. The 1995, a better vintage, was richer and more powerful. De Calvez explained that she looked for power and structure, but not drying tannins. The Grenache Noir spends two months on the skins at fermentation and the Syrah just one month. The 1995 Minervois Prestige, a pure Grenache Noir with some berry fruit and a certain spicy quality, is given sixteen months ageing in 400-litre barrels. Most intriguing are the late harvest wines, both a dry and a sweet version. The Vin Blanc Sec carries this legend on the label, *Issu de Vendange Extrême et Vieilli Suivant la Tradition Occitane*, and spends eighteen months in wood. It was light amber in colour and the taste reminded me of Vin Santo, with that elegant, biscuity flavour of *biscotti di Prato*. In 1996 de Calvez tried for the first time to make a sweet version, from Roussanne and Grenache Blanc that spent twelve months in barrel. She stopped the fermentation leaving 40 gms/l residual sugar balanced with 14° alcohol. The wine tasted of sweet bitter oranges. De Calvez explained that her great-grandparents would have made a wine like this, for it was the custom fifty years ago and she is now trying to update that tradition. People did not buy aperitifs then. Instead they drank their own home-made aperitifs, perhaps a Carthagène or something like this. It would probably have come from Grenache Gris and Grenache Noir and be *rancio* in style, with the wine left outside in glass jars during the winter, as is still occasionally done for Rivesaltes and other *vins doux naturels*.

CHATEAU GIBALOUX-BONNET, TREBES

Château Gibaloux-Bonnet is in the middle of nowhere, or so it seemed when I got lost in the narrow lanes somewhere between the villages of Trèbes and Laure. Jean-Baptiste Bonnet showed me around the cellars. His father worked in the chemical industry and had bought the property in 1969, but they did not begin bottling their wine until 1981. Now they have sixty-six hectares of vines, which have gradually been replanted over the years. Forty hectares produce Minervois and the rest Vin de Pays d'Oc, a label they prefer to the less well-known Vin de Pays des Coteaux de Peyriac. When the system of *crus* becomes more established, they would be within the Balcons de l'Aude, with vineyards on terraces of schist. The cellars are well equipped, though not for carbonic maceration, all mechanised, streamlined and insulated. They make a range of different wines, which are a happy combination of the experimental and the commercially successful.

Their white Minervois, a blend of Marsanne, Grenache Blanc and Macabeu, is light, rounded and easy to drink. There is a barrel-fermented Chardonnay that is given regular *bâtonnage*. Chardonnay was planted in the late 1980s and initially they fermented it in vat, but quickly moved on to oak, making a ripe and buttery mouthful of flavour. Their Minervois Tradition, from Syrah, Grenache Noir and Carignan, was light and peppery, with soft, easy fruit. In contrast, the Cuvée Prieuré Gibaloux – recalling the fact that the land once belonged to the monks at Caunes – is from fifty per cent Syrah, thirty per cent Mourvèdre and twenty per cent Grenache Noir, spending twelve months in wood. Their first *élevage* in barrels was for the 1986 vintage and the experience shows, with well-integrated oak and some solid fruit. Pinot Noir was planted in the mid-1980s, but they have found it a temperamental and rather disappointing variety, so hitherto it has been sold off *en vrac*, though perhaps an *élevage* in wood will make a difference. Finally, since 1994 they have made a Minervois Noble, Cuvée de Jeanne, named after young Bonnet's grandmother, from the same grape varieties as their white Minervois. The grapes are left on the vines until mid-October, by which time they are nicely raisined or may have developed some botrytis. The wine ferments very slowly in barrel for five or six months and then they stop the fermentation, leaving about 80 gm/l residual sugar. It was intensely honeyed on both nose and palate.

CHATEAU LA GRAVE, BADENS

Even though they were in the middle of the vintage, Jean Pierre Orosquette and his wife Josiane gave me a friendly welcome at Château la Grave, which is outside the village of Badens in the south western part of the appellation. They too would be part of the future *cru* of Les Balcons de l'Aude. There have always been vines in the family. They bought this estate in 1978 and now have ninety hectares, planted with as many as fifteen different varieties. As well as Minervois, they make Vin de Pays des Hauts de Badens, preferring the local identity of the nearby village to the anonymous mass of Vin de Pays d'Oc, even though they are the only producers of any significance of this tiny *vin de pays*. Chardonnay is given about sixteen hours of skin contact, which makes for noticeably more flavour, followed by a fermentation in vat. It was ripe and buttery, with an attractive, textured mouth feel. The vineyard is by the dried-up Etang de Marseillette on a north-facing terrace with very gravelly soil, hence the name of the estate.

Their white Minervois Expression comes from old Macabeu vines with just a little Muscat. They pick early in the morning, as Macabeu has a tendency to oxidise, and then give some skin contact, making for a lemony, nutty flavoured wine with fresh acidity. Minervois Privilège, made for the first time in 1991 from the same varieties, is fermented in new oak, where it stays for six months with regular *bâtonnage*. It is a much more substantial wine and the price difference is significant too: FF 50 as opposed to FF 29 for the Minervois Expression – in other words, an extra FF 21 to cover the cost of the new *barriques* and the additional work they entail.

As for his reds, Orosquette wants wines with body but without aggressive tannins. Minervois Expression is a blend of Syrah with some Grenache Noir and a little Carignan, given quite a long maceration of about twenty days followed by eighteen months in vat, making for some easy, peppery fruit. Minervois Privilège, with slightly less Syrah, is given twelve months *élevage* in wood, making a wine with more body and substance. We finished with a quick taste of Carthagène, the traditional aperitif that is made throughout the south from Nîmes to Perpignan, but usually just for family consumption. Theirs comes from Merlot and Grenache Noir muted with *fine du* Languedoc, making a rather tasty flavour of dried fruit and figs. And then I sped to my next appointment.

CHATEAU BONHOMME, AIGUES-VIVES

Jean-Pierre Aimar of Château Bonhomme outside the village of Aigues-Vives is a newcomer to the Minervois and sees things with the objective manner of an outsider who is finding his way. He laughingly related how he arrived here on 14 September 1996 and began picking grapes the next day. However, his official beginning was 1 January 1997. He has had a varied career, first as a chartered accountant and then running a jersey manufacturing business in the Tarn. I could not help noticing that the jersey he was wearing had seen distinctly better days! He had wanted to make wine ever since he was twenty, but first he had to make some money. He is convinced of the enormous potential of the Languedoc. 'We are in a pioneering phase, where the Côtes du Rhône were fifteen years ago. The Midi has *un charme fou*, but there is one problem: the character of the men. They are all very macho, very sure of themselves, with *grandes gueules*, so that they are not afraid to shoot their mouths off. They don't know what uncertainty is.' He first began looking for an estate in 1995. The Rhône Valley was too expensive and Corbières was too big an appellation with too many internal quarrels, while Minervois is smaller, with a better image. He looked at fifteen estates before he found Château Bonhomme, which was owned by Americans who lived in Switzerland. The estate was more or less bankrupt, but the sixty hectares of vines, some for Minervois and some for *vin de pays*, were in relatively good condition. So, quickly putting his accounting experience to good use, Aimar set up a limited company for friends and fellow investors.

The estate had produced bulk wine for the previous fifteen years or so, and the cellar was equipped for that purpose, with enormous vats and a continuous press – 'but now we are condemned to produce quality wine.' Aimar is gradually renovating the facilities, investing in a Vaslin press, new pumps and a destemmer, and renewing the doors of the concrete vats. In 1997 he picked later than everyone else, as he was busy painting the cellar. During 1998 he has been working on his vineyard, analysing the different plots and redoing some of the palissage, converting the Syrah from *gobelet* to *cordon royat*.

Eventually he is planning two red wines, and he knows what he wants to make: wines that are elegant, rounded and above all harmonious. 'So often you get a Neapolitan slice – the first layer is structure from the grapes, then there is a layer of tannin and vanilla from the oak and the third layer is a bitter finish.' That is what he wants to avoid. All his grapes are destalked and he is working on long *cuvaisons*. I tasted his first white wine, a 1997 Grenache Gris that had spent six months in barrel. The oak was inevitably very apparent, but there was fruit underneath, a full flavour with acidity and length. Time will show how it will evolve. The 1997 red, from Carignan and Syrah with an *élevage* in vat, was perfumed and plummy with an attractive peppery character, with tannins and hints of liquorice. It promised very well for the future.

DOMAINE LA COMBE BLANCHE, LA LIVINIERE

Guy Vanlancker is an intense but friendly Belgian who arrived in the Languedoc in 1981. It was *le hazard de la vie* that brought him here. He was a schoolteacher but did not enjoy it, and his wife wanted a change. He bought some old vines above the village of La Livinière and took the grapes to the co-operative. Then in 1988 he began to make a little wine himself. Meanwhile he was working as the *régisseur* for Domaine Laville-Bertrou, which belongs to Gérard Bertrand, who also owns Domaine de Villemajou in the Corbières. Now he runs Domaine de Cantaussels, a property bought in 1995 by M. Bohler, a Luxembourgeois who has apparently constructed an impressive state-of-the-art cellar. Sadly, I did not have time to go and see it, but instead I enjoyed my encounter with Guy Vanlancker in his own cramped little cellar in a backstreet of La Livinière, where I was treated to a fascinating and generous tasting, interspersed with Vanlancker's thoughts about the region.

He has nine hectares altogether, from which he does about twelve or fifteen separate vinifications to make five or six wines. You sense that there is a perfectionist at work here, who demands the utmost from himself. His white wine is a Vin de Pays des Côtes de Brian, from Roussanne blended with Viognier, both fermented in barrels, some new and some one wine old. The grapes are picked very ripe, so there is a potential alcohol level of 14.5°, but the effect in the mouth is somehow absorbed by the oak. The 1998, recently blended when I tasted it in June 1999, was ripe, powerful and obviously oaky. The 1997 was quite perfumed, with apricots, oranges and spice, and the 1996, in which only the Roussanne went into wood, was firm, nuttier and more lemony, with less opulence and more elegance. The 1995, a pure Roussanne and Vanlancker's first *élevage* in oak, was quite *bordelais* in style, with a certain solid, nutty flavour. It was an intriguing demonstration of the evolution of a wine. Vanlancker has given up using the Vin de Pays d'Oc label, criticising it for its lack of individuality in making varietal wines that are too technological.

His Minervois Tradition is a blend of Syrah, Grenache Noir, Carignan and Cinsaut but no Mourvèdre, as he does not really like it and prefers Grenache Noir instead. Part of it is aged in vat and part in wood. The 1996 was appealingly perfumed and the 1995 was riper with more spice and structure. The 1994 had developed some very enticing cedary notes, with a dry, elegant finish. Another Minervois, la Chandelière, is a blend of sixty per cent Syrah with Carignan, Grenache Noir and Cinsaut. Vanlancker is adamant that he works by *assemblage*, not by precise proportions of grape varieties. You obtain more complexity and originality with several different vats or barrels, and there is a multiplicity of soil variations in the Minervois too. Above all, he wants harmony and substance. The proportion of wood in La Chandelière has developed from just ten per cent in 1996 to one hundred per cent in 1998, while in 1995 he had no wood and no destemmer either. Vanlancker reckons that the wine would have been better with both *éraflage* and wood ageing, for while 1995 was noticeably more powerful and tannic than the 1996, it was less elegant. The 1998 promised well, with sweet, ripe spicy fruit and some smoky oak, while the 1994 was very concentrated with firm, cedary flavours. Vanlancker used an attractive analogy, saying that if a wine has been in wood it has been coated, rather like the wrapping paper on a present. These are wines that demonstrate the importance of a slow evolution, for he is not looking for instant results.

As well as Minervois there is a Pinot Noir, Côtes de Brian, from a vineyard called L'Enfer. A barrel sample was a combination of sweet fruit and firm oak. There is Tempranillo too, planted in Les Dessous de l'Enfer in 1983. It is vinified in the same way as the Pinot Noir, with lots of *pigeage* and *élevage* in oak – both *barriques* and 500-litre barrels, which are rather more difficult to handle.

Vanlancker is involved with the development of the *cru* of La Livinière, but has certain reservations. The quality must be good and people must not be allowed to cash in on the novelty. The good producers are known for their quality, and the concept of the *cru* is paying a higher price for a smaller quantity. The aim is to find the best quality at a price the client will pay. Vanlancker is also very aware of the harsh financial realities of making wine. There is an enormous gulf between making wine and making money, and there is no doubt that he has problems of cash flow and is severely undercapitalised.

Our tasting finished with his only late harvest wine, made in 1996 from twenty ares of Grenache Gris picked in November, giving a yield of just six hectolitres. It spent two years in wood and was liquid orange marmalade on the nose and palate, rounded and harmonious, with length. There is no doubt that Guy Vanlancker deserves greater recognition, for his wines are stylish and individual.

DOMAINE BORIE DE MAUREL, FELINES-MINERVOIS

Michel Escande of Domaine Borie de Maurel is president of the new *cru* of La Livinière, having taken over the responsibility from Maurice Piccinini. He considers that the INAO has given a rubber stamp to something that already existed, for there was already a committed group of about twenty-five producers who were making wines with a more restricted choice of grape varieties and a stricter delimitation of vineyards. However, this is the first time that the INAO has created what he called a *sur-appellation* in the region.

Escande's parents came from the village of Félines-Minervois on the northern edge of the appellation, and he spent his youth sailing the Mediterranean until it was time to settle down with his pretty wife Sylvie. His father's eleven hectares provided the basis for an estate and he has bought more land, including the better vineyards from the Château de Paulignan in the *garrigue*, and now has a total of twenty-eight hectares, with cellars in Olonzac. We talked in his tasting *caveau* at home in Félines-en-Minervois. He is a difficult man to pin down, for his mind flits from one philosophical concept to the next and from one topic to another. He related how he had first made wine at the age of twelve, from *grapillons*, the second bunches that are often left on the vines because they are not fully ripe. He added sugar and the bottles exploded. Was this an auspicious omen?

For Escande, wine making is a combination of the whim of the year and the continuity of the estate. You combine the mood of the market with the vintage. 'We are here as catalysts to make the very best from what nature gives us. You need the sensitivity to observe nature. It is all a question of balance.' He is convinced that it is possible to make great wine in the region. The problem is the market, which has the wrong expectations from the Languedoc. The current methods of cultivation do not help either, but people are gaining greater expertise in the vineyard.

Escande makes six wines altogether, a white, a pink and four reds. Esprit d'Automne is mainly Carignan, with some Syrah. The Carignan provides structure, combining with the young peppery fruit of the Syrah, and there is a certain liquorice character on the finish. A pure Cabernet Sauvignon, Cuvée Léopold, named after his grandfather, is given some *élevage* in wood, making for ripe cassis fruit and soft tannins – what Escande called an iron hand in a velvet glove. A pure Mourvèdre, Cuvée Maxime, named after his second son, had smoky fruit with soft tannins and a certain cedary fruit on the finish. Cuvée Scylla, made for the first time in 1992, mainly from Syrah with just a drop of Grenache Noir, is rich and almost chocolatey with ripe fruit and tannins. For *élevage* Escande has stainless steel and concrete vats and *demi-muids*.

The white wine, from Marsanne and a little Roussanne, is intriguing, with a herbal character and some mineral notes. You could be forgiven for thinking that it had been fermented in wood, for it has structure, acidity and weight, but it has not been near a barrel. If you have ripe grapes, you obtain alcohol but risk losing the acidity, which provides structure. It is a difficult balance to achieve. The alcohol can provide length, while some skin contact and regular *bâtonnage* adds flavour and weight. Some of the juice has been clarified before fermentation and some is left on the lees, and the combination of the two makes a satisfying balance. Escande is fairly scathing about Minervois Noble, as he does not consider it to be an authentic part of the appellation. Instead he has made a *vin de paille* from Terret Blanc. This, for him, is much more traditional, as people used to hang bunches of Terret in their attics until Christmas.

CLOS CENTEILLES, SIRAN

When writing of Daniel Domergue at Clos Centeilles, I must confess to a bias, as he has been a good friend ever since we first met over an earlier book. For me, Domergue is one of the rare producers in the Minervois who has been making consistently fine wine for nearly twenty years. In the mid-1980s his wines stood out, having a finesse and concentration of flavour rarely found in the appellation at that time, and over the years his range has evolved into several distinctive red wines. There was no history of wine making in his family. Domergue has a degree in German, and with his first wife Hélène he ran a bookshop in Marseilles. Then, tired of the city rat race and expecting their first child, they came to the

Minervois and bought five hectares of vines, Carignan and Alicante, at Trausses that nobody wanted and which they immediately pulled up. At the same time they studied viticulture and oenology and planted Syrah, Cinsaut, Grenache Noir and Mourvèdre.

Domergue has never ceased to question the establishment. He sees himself as a twentieth-century Cathar, a voice crying in the wilderness against the restrictions of the INAO and the short-sighted attitudes of his fellow growers. 'We are a little anarchical here' was one of the first things he ever said to me, after inviting me to lunch with a spontaneous hospitality that is rare in *la France profonde*.

When I first met Domergue he was making wine in a small cellar rented from the Château de Paulignan and he acknowledges a huge debt to Jacques Tallavignes, who advised and encouraged him at the beginning. Life has moved on, and Daniel is now in the tiny hamlet of Centeilles, up a dirt track outside the village of Siran, with his second wife Patricia, while Hélène Domergue (née Serrano) has become a very successful wine maker in her own right at the Château de Violet. There is a tiny twelfth-century chapel at Centeilles, dedicated to *la Vierge grosse*, the pregnant virgin, that has the fragile remains of frescoes on the walls, delicate traces of yellow and red paint. Domergue is passionate about the diversity of vines that grew in the vineyards of the Midi before they were destroyed by phylloxera, and he has planted a small vineyard in a brave attempt to restore varieties such as Picpoul Noir, Oeillade, Riberenc and Terret Noir to their former importance. There were two families of varieties in the Midi: those such as Cinsaut, Picpoul and Oeillade, and the Spanish varieties such as Monastrell, as well as Grenache Noir, Mourvèdre, Macabeu and so on. Unlike most of his colleagues, who tend to dismiss Cinsaut as suitable only for *rosé*, he pleads the cause of the variety to the extent of making a wine, Capitelle de Centeilles, that is pure Cinsaut. And he proves his point. Cinsaut is an antioxidant, and if you give it a long *cuvaison*, as much as two months, in order to compensate for the loss of tannin from the stalks, with a low yield in the first place, you will obtain fine results. The grapes must be really ripe in the first place, and the actual fermentation takes about ten days, with regular *pigeages*. You must not put it in wood or else it will lose its fruit. Cinsaut also withstands drought conditions; indeed, 'it has the sobriety of a camel and will cross the desert without a drop of water!' Campagne de Centeilles is also based on Cinsaut, with about twenty per cent of Syrah, while the more substantial, partially oak-aged wine Clos de Centeilles comes from equal parts of Syrah, Grenache Noir and Mourvèdre. This is a wine that will age for several years, as a vertical tasting demonstrated at Vinisud, the biennial regional wine fair in Montpellier. From 1996 to 1990 there was not a disappointing wine, but a range that illustrated the vintage variations and epitomised the peppery flavours of the Minervois. And a 1985 Cuvée des Terrasses drunk when it was twelve years old was still lively, with the warm, herbal fruit of the *garrigue*.

Domergue is scathing about Carignan, describing it as the interloper that became established in the Midi after phylloxera. This does not stop him from making Carignanisme, a delicious pure Carignan, by carbonic maceration. But as he says, if you can make something good from Carignan, then you can make something so much better from the more interesting varieties. His Mourvèdre ripens successfully for it is trained on a double lyre, resulting in a much better exposure of leaf area and grapes. Domergue condemns green harvesting, for all it does is make the existing bunches bigger. You should prune tightly in the first place. Low yields concentrate the flavour in old vines. However, if the yield for Carignan is too low, it will concentrate the vulgarity and rusticity of the variety, whereas in a good variety you concentrate its finesse. Pinot Noir is Domergue's only defeat. Somehow, I do not know why, he has never quite managed that elusive combination of silky fruit and tannin.

On my last visit we tasted the 1998 wines. A Carignanisme was redolent of ripe cherries, with some peppery fruit. Campagne de Centeilles had some firm fruit, Capitelle de Centeilles was ripe, with soft tannins and length, and Clos de Centeilles had spicy fruit and structure, with that wonderful combination of concentration and elegance that is the hallmark of Domergue's wines. We finished with a delicious *vendange tardive*, L'Erme de Centeilles, made from forty-year-old Grenache Blanc vines, which was peachy and honeyed with a delicious balance of refreshing acidity.

OTHER PRODUCERS

There are so many other estates I could have mentioned in the Minervois. Robert Eden, the great-nephew of the earlier British prime minister, has bought the former Domaine Maris in La Livinière, as well as Domaine de Montahuc in St-Jean-de-Minervois, Domaine de Combebelle in St Chinian and Domaine la Bégude in Limoux, and is developing interests in Corbières and Fitou. Château Fabas was making its mark in the 1980s and has since been bought by a *champenois*, Roland Augustin. Jean-Louis Poudou at Domaine la Tour Boisée took over a family estate in 1982 and since his first bottling in 1988 has made a serious range of Minervois. Pierre-André Ournac may be the sixth generation at Château de Cesseras, but he only began bottling his wine in the last decade, producing some impressive Minervois la Livinière. Château de Violet, owned by the eccentric Madame Faussié, is a quirky hotel as well as a wine estate, where Hélène Serrano makes a range of satisfying wines. And there are many others.

Key facts

VDQS 1951, AC 1985; red, white and pink; covers sixteen villages in the Hérault and forty-five in the Aude, centred on Olonzac and named after village of Minerve.

Eighteen thousand hectares delimited; AC made from only about four thousand.

Grape varieties:

RED: Carignan, Cinsaut, Grenache Noir, Syrah, Mourvèdre.

WHITE: Grenache Blanc, Macabeu, Picpoul, Bourboulenc, Terret, Clairette, Marsanne, Roussanne and Rolle.

Minervois Noble is a potential dessert wine; new *cru* of La Livinière, with stricter requirements; other *crus* under discussion.

Vineyards on limestone and clay foothills of Massif Central.

Vintages

1999: Minervois was one of the successful regions of the Languedoc, with the more westerly vineyards avoiding rain at vintage time. Almost as good as 1998.

1998: Severe spring frosts on 13 April severely reduced the crop, making for structured wines with concentrated flavours.

1997: A cooler year; some problems with rain and rot, especially at the beginning of the harvest. Lighter, more accessible wines.

1996: Another cooler year, with some rain, making for a larger crop and softer wines.

1995: Well structured, tannic wines, with body and weight. One of the best vintages of the decade, along with 1990, 1998 and 1999.

St Jean-de-Minervois

St Jean-de-Minervois is a sleepy little village in the north eastern corner of the Minervois, close to vineyards of St Chinian. People first began planting a little Muscat here for their home consumption at the turn of the century and the vineyards developed between the two world wars, resulting in the creation of the appellation in 1950. As well as having its own appellation for Muscat de St Jean-de-Minervois, the village is also part of the appellation of Minervois, but look for a village café and a reviving cup of coffee and you will be sadly disappointed. At one end of the village there is an imposing new *mairie*, at the other end the co-operative, and in between a collection of narrow streets and shuttered houses. Barely a dog stirred when I was there, and the *depôts de vente* for the co-operative were firmly closed.

DOMAINE BARROUBIO

First I went to Domaine Barroubio in the eponymous hamlet just outside the village. Just fourteen people in three families live there. Roses were in bloom on a summer's afternoon and a pair of dogs basked in the sunshine. Jean Miquel and his mother Marie-Thérèse gave me a friendly welcome. They explained that only part of the *commune* is classified for Muscat de St Jean-de-Minervois and that there is a distinct difference between the soil for that and for Minervois itself. Once Jean Miquel took me to see the vineyards, this became all too apparent. The Muscat – that is, Muscat *à petits grains* (for no Muscat d'Alexandrie is allowed here) – is grown on a very stony limestone plateau that runs across the *commune*, covering 150–160 hectares of land and measuring five kilometres by one kilometre. The Muscat vineyards are all south facing, lying at an altitude of three hundred metres. There are huge blocks of limestone that have to be broken up, forming a bed of pebbles some fifteen to twenty centimetres deep. These perform two useful functions. They absorb the heat, reflecting it back on to the grapes and ensuring that they reach the necessary 15° and they retain moisture underneath, protecting the vines from drought in this seemingly arid terrain. The Minervois vineyards are quite different, less stony, with red clay as well as limestone.

The Muscat vines are pruned in what they call a *gobelet fermé*, that is, a vertical bush vine with its vegetation kept upright, but only about 40–45 centimetres high. One of their new vineyards has been planted with wires, which they find give a better leaf area than the *gobelet*, with better aeration, so that fewer treatments are required and the grapes ripen better. The leaves can also protect the grapes from sunburn, for sometimes it is so hot that you could almost fry an egg on the pebbles. The thin-skinned Muscat is fragile and susceptible to rot, so they need to take preventative measures against oidium. Yields are low; 28 hl/ha is the maximum allowed in the appellation, but that is rarely attained. Picking is all by hand. You know when the grapes are really ripe for that is when the bees and wasps swarm to the vineyards.

Jean Miquel's father was left two hectares of Muscat vines by a great-uncle in 1968 and was, as his son put it, the only member of the family mad enough to take on the challenge, even though he was busy building the resort of Cap d'Agde at the time. Thirty years later, the estate totals seventeen hectares of Muscat and eight of Minervois, and Jean Miquel is taking over from his mother. He plans to modernise the cellar. All the concrete vats have been relined and there is now a pneumatic press as well as efficient temperature control, which is absolutely essential for producing fresh Muscat. The juice is chilled after pressing for *débourbage* and the fermentation starts at a cool temperature of 14–16°C. The moment of decision is when you add the alcohol that will stop the fermentation. The regulations dictate a density of between 1058 and 1062, which should give you 15° and 125 gms/l of residual sugar in the final wine, with the added alcohol representing between six and ten per cent of the volume. The *mutage* is Mme Miquel's responsibility. She takes an empirical approach, using a glass, a mustimeter (to measure the sugar in the juice) and her palate. There is a certain amount of flexibility. They prefer to have riper grapes, which require less alcohol, thereby obtaining what they consider to be a better-balanced wine with more finesse. A longer fermentation of riper grapes gives the same alcohol and sugar balance, but requires less grape spirit. That way you avoid an alcoholic finish to the palate, but there are risks. A slower fermentation is better, for if the Muscat is fermenting too quickly with very ripe grapes, it is much more difficult to stop. Once the wine is finished, it should remain in vat for as short a time as possible, in order to retain all its natural freshness and aroma. 1998 Domaine Barroubio was already on sale before Christmas that year.

I tried it the following June, when it was deliciously grapey, redolent of the richness of Muscat, ripe and rounded, but not cloying or heavy. The alcohol was well integrated and it left a long, lingering finish in the mouth. Mme Miquel explained that Muscat de St Jean-de-Minervois used to be much heavier, and that when she and her husband began working on a younger, fresher style of wine, everyone in village said they were mad. Previously, the wine had been kept until the December of the year following the vintage before obtaining its *labelle* and then often for a further year in vat before it was ready for sale.

Happily, tastes have changed. Not only has the Muscat become fresher in flavour, but over the last five years or so the Miquels have developed a Vendange Tardive. The grapes for this are picked a month later, in mid-October, when they are *passerillés*, dried by the wind and quite dehydrated. The yield is even lower: just 10–12 hl/ha. The alcohol is added at a higher density and sugar level, resulting in a more concentrated but less obviously Muscat flavoured wine. The wine is denser, not exactly heavier, but there is more body and complexity on the palate.

CAVE DE ST JEAN-DE-MINERVOIS

The village co-operative is by far the largest producer of Muscat de St Jean-de-Minervois. It was founded in 1955, five years after the creation of the appellation, and now accounts for one hundred and fifty hectares of Muscat, some eighty per cent of the appellation. Its fifty members also produce Minervois and various *vins de pays*: d'Oc, Hérault and the local Côtes de Brian, named after a small stream. This co-operative works well for its appellation. You feel that they have kept abreast with the times, although I was told that they still produce a special *cuvée* that is amber in colour after four years of ageing especially for their more old-fashioned customers. I was not given the opportunity to taste it.

Fortunately, the vinification process for their more mainstream wines epitomises modern technology. Ascorbic acid helps to prevent oxidation and enzymes are added to help with the *débourbage*, so that they are fermenting clear juice with cultured yeast. They keep the fine lees apart, filtering them and fermenting them separately, to blend back into the wine, for the co-operative director, Alain Taillan, considers that they add an extra aroma. Skin contact would have too powerful an effect, really accentuating the aroma of the Muscat. The *état sanitaire* is also a significant factor in analysing the fermenting juice, as the presence of rot can increase the density and give a false reading when you are deciding on the moment of *mutage*. They have also experimented with *mutage* at different sugar levels and, like Domaine Baroubio, also produce a late harvest wine. However, the term Vendange Tardive is fiercely guarded by the appellations of Alsace, so theirs is called simply Vendange d'Automne and they make just two hundred hectolitres, of which forty are put into oak for three months. Again, it provides an intriguing contrast with the classic Muscat, which was honeyed with a bitter orange finish, while the late harvest wine was heavier, with quite solid apricot flavours. Their first late harvest was made in 1990, with just two barrels. They have also tried making a sweet wine without any *mutage*, but fell foul of French wine legislation, with the authorities pompously proclaiming that *ça n'existe pas*!

DOMAINE SIGE

I tracked down Michel Sigé in the centre of village. He took over his father-in-law's vineyards some thirty years ago and has ten hectares of Muscat and some Minervois, as well as thirty hectares of *vin de pays* on the plain near Narbonne. There is no doubt that Muscat is the most remunerative. It is selling well at the moment, enjoying a certain revival, while the small appellation of St Jean-de-Minervois has a cachet and a price advantage that larger Rivesaltes would envy. A bottle of Muscat de Rivesaltes costs the French consumer

35 FF at the cellar door, whereas for St Jean-de-Minervois he must pay 45 or 50 FF. There is also a significant difference in the returns on Minervois and Muscat. Compare the prices in bulk: Minervois fetches 5–600 FF per hectolitre, while St Jean-de-Minervois reaches 3000 FF, although allowance must be made for the cost and tax on the spirit. Put another way, a hectare of Muscat should earn the producer about 50,000 FF, as opposed to 30,000 FF for Minervois.

Sigé's methods do not vary significantly from those of his colleagues, except that he favours an older style of wine. He picks his grapes as ripe as possible, at 15° or 16° potential alcohol, or even 17°. However, unlike Domaine Baroubio, he does not bottle his wine for a year, but prefers to keep it in vat on the fine lees, which gives it more body. Certainly his wine tastes heavier and more solid than Domaine Baroubio, but that is how his customers like it. In addition, in more prolific years he makes a Muscat Sec, which is bottled in the spring after the harvest for earlier drinking. The 1998 vintage had a distinctive Muscat aroma the following June, with fresh, pithy flavours and an imperceptible touch of residual sugar, just 2–3 gm/l on the finish. Sigé explained that thirty years ago it was the fashion to drink Muscat as a dessert wine. It was a much heavier drink then, as there was no means of temperature control. Now it is possible to regulate the fermentation temperature by putting a *drapeau* or metal plate inside the concrete vats, which makes all the difference to the flavour of the wine.

There are just three other individual producers with vineyards in St Jean-de-Minervois, and they illustrate the close links that St Chinian also enjoys with St Jean-de-Minervois. The Simon family of Clos Bagatelle in St Chinian have had vineyards in the appellation for over twenty years. As outsiders, they have to maintain a separate cellar, for one of the criteria of the appellation is, quite rightly, that the wine should be vinified within the area of production. Their wine is quite heavy and honeyed, with a note of fennel on the finish. I also found a hint of aniseed on the nose of the wine made by the second St Chinian producer to have vineyards in St Jean-de-Minervois; namely Marc Cabaret of Domaine du Sacré Coeur, of whom more on page 288. He has just two hectares and explained how difficult it is to find land to buy in the village. At FF 300–350,000 per hectare, as opposed to FF 100,000 per hectare of St Chinian, it ranks as some of the most expensive vineyard land in the whole of the Languedoc. Finally there is Robert Eden, who is building a substantial landholding in the south of France, including the recent acquisition of Domaine de Montahuc, an old estate in St Jean-de-Minervois, from which he has yet to produce some wine.

Today the market for Muscat de St Jean-de-Minervois is buoyant with interest. It will only ever be a small enclave within the Minervois, but there is a slow development of the vineyards within the confines of the strictly delimited area. There has also been a considerable amount of replanting, with half the vines currently less than fifteen years old. That, however, is less of a handicap than it would be for red wine. Unlike the other Muscats of Languedoc and Roussillon, St Jean-de-Minervois is at some distance from the sea, which makes for wines with a higher level of acidity than in a Muscat de Lunel or Rivesaltes. In this it has more in common with Beaumes-de-Venise, with an appealingly fresh lemon and honey flavour that makes a delicious dessert wine, or in France an aperitif, on a balmy evening.

Key facts

A *vin doux naturel*, coming only from the village of St Jean-de-Minervois; part of AC Minervois and a separate AC for *vin doux* in 1950; about a hundred and fifty hectares.

Only Muscat *à petits grains;* 15° with 125 gm/l residual sugar.

Vineyards are south facing, lying at three hundred metres on a stony limestone plateau.

Coteaux du Languedoc

A large, somewhat amorphous appellation covering many of
the vineyards between Narbonne and Nîmes, the Coteaux du
Languedoc is currently in a state of flux. The original appellation of
1985 included twelve different *terroirs* together with three *crus*. To
those inexperienced in French viticultural and bureaucratic jargon,
the difference between a *cru* and a *terroir* is somewhat blurred.
Faugères and St Chinian were deemed to be *crus*, as they were
already appellations in their own right, and Clairette du Languedoc
is seen as the third *cru*, while remaining an independent white
appellation within the Coteaux du Languedoc. So travelling
roughly from west to east the *terroirs* are Quatourze, La Clape,
Picpoul de Pinet, Cabrières, St Saturnin, Montpeyroux, St Georges
d'Orques, Pic St Loup, Méjanelle, St Drézery, St Christol and
Vérargues, all of which were VDQS in their own right and thus
provided the base for the new appellation of Coteaux du
Languedoc. At first the appellation was only for red and *rosé* wine
– with the one exception of the white *terroir* of Picpoul de Pinet –
but it covered a much larger area than the original VDQS, for it
incorporated vineyards around the towns of Pézenas and Lodève
and further west around the village of Langlade. Then in 1988
white wine was added to the appellation.

Since then, much work has been carried out in analysing the
climatic and geological differences of the region, resulting in the
definition of several broad areas or *terroirs* within the appellation.
The Terrasses de Béziers, as the name implies, will cover the
vineyards around the town on the plateau of Vendres, including
the villages of Sauvignon, Sérignan and Vendres, but nothing in the
coastal area. There are very few producers of note here. Likewise,
Pézenas will include vineyards around the town in villages like

Roujan, Caux and Neffiès, as well as the original *terroir* of
Cabrières. The Terrasses du Larzac encompasses a large area in the
northern part of the appellation, including Montpeyroux and St
Saturnin and the vineyards around the Lac de Salagou and up in the
valley of the Hérault – the last vines of the Coteaux du Languedoc
before you reach the Massif Central. The Grès de Montpellier is
a large area behind the city of Montpellier, including the original
terroirs of St Georges d'Orques, Méjanelle, St Drézery, St Christol
and Vérargues. Finally, Terres de Sommières would encompass the
vineyards on the eastern side of the appellation around the town of
Sommières, including those of Langlade.

Ultimately, a three or four-tiered pyramid appellation is
envisaged, not unlike that of Bordeaux. Languedoc would be the
all-encompassing appellation for the whole of the Hérault and the
Aude, in the same way that Bordeaux covers the Gironde; it may
ultimately incorporate Corbières and Minervois as well. The
Coteaux du Languedoc may or may not continue to exist, and the
next layer of the pyramid would be the *terroirs* such as Grès de
Montpellier or Terrasses de Larzac, while the pinnacle of the
pyramid would consist of what are now called *crus*, some of the
original *terroirs* that have developed a more individual identity
within the Coteaux du Languedoc, such as Picpoul de Pinet, la
Clape and Pic St Loup. These three are recognised as *crus*, rather
than being lost in a larger *terroir*. The same goes for St Chinian and
Faugères, while St Saturnin and Montpeyroux are defending their
position to remain as individual *crus*, and less significant ones
like Vérargues and St Drézery may well be incorporated into the
appropriate *terroir*.

The *terroirs* will give some of the marginal areas of the Coteaux
du Languedoc a certain regional identity. Inevitably, local village
rivalries and differences come into play here, as everyone strives to
defend their own interests. The whole question is under discussion
and will be for a few years yet. The INAO is typical of French
bureaucracy, or of any bureaucracy for that matter, in not being
celebrated for the speed of its decision making. The experience
of Alain Reder of Domaine de Comberousse as a member of the
syndicat of the Grès de Montpellier did not bode well, for he not
only found the INAO commission unsympathetic, but felt that they
failed to appreciate the originality of the region and were confused
by the diversity of grape varieties. He explained how a *terroir*

such as the Grès de Montpellier would have stricter production conditions than a basic appellation Languedoc, with Syrah, Grenache Noir and Mourvèdre accounting for seventy per cent of a blend. The minimum alcohol level would be 12°; the vines would have to be at least six years old to contribute to the *terroir*, and there would be a year's obligatory *élevage* before the *labelle* tasting. The Grès de Montpellier is in some ways the key to the whole system, as it encompasses many of the previous *terroirs* and borders most of the others. Time will tell, and meanwhile the region continues to develop an infinite variety of characterful wines while ignoring the constraints of officialdom. A journey through the Coteaux du Languedoc logically begins in Quatourze, almost in the suburbs of the city of Narbonne.

Vintages

1999: Quality depends on when the rains fell and how the vineyards coped with the August heat wave. Areas that escaped rain at harvest, such as La Clape, made wine as good as 1998, whereas areas like Pic St Loup suffered badly from dilution.

1998: A wonderful vintage, with great substance and potential longevity, ripe fruit and concentration, coming from a small crop and a warm dry summer.

1997: Rain at the harvest caused problems for all but the most meticulous growers, so that the wines are lighter and fairly fruity, but with no great depth.

1996: Comparable to 1997, with similar problems of rain at the wrong time and a cooler summer.

1995: More akin to 1998; a very dry year making sturdy, structured wines with firm tannins.

Quatourze

Quatourze is the westernmost *terroir* of the Coteaux du Languedoc, with vineyards almost touching the suburbs of Narbonne. Despite the proximity of the motorway, it is a beautiful spot on a spring day with a clear blue sky, almond trees in flower and a view of the Canigou, the highest mountain of the Pyrenees, while in the other direction you can see the unfinished Romanesque cathedral of Narbonne. However, a clear view of the Canigou is not so desirable, for it is an indication that the wind is about to change – and sure enough, the Marin, the wind from the sea, brought rain the following day.

Quatourze is a compact area, limited by Narbonne in the west, the Etang de Bages to the south and on the eastern side protected from the sea by the Massif de la Clape. The vineyards are on a plateau that rises just seventeen metres above sea level. The soil is stony, with clay and *galets roulées* that, according to Marc Dubernet, are the same large pebbles that you find in Châteauneuf-du-Pape. This is one of the driest parts of the Coteaux du Languedoc, lying in a corridor between the Pyrenees and the Massif Central through which the Tramontane, the dry north wind, passes. Rainfall averages about 450 mm a year, which is significantly less than in Montpellier further round the coast. Winters are mild, and during the hot summer months the white quartz stones reflect heat on to the vines, as they do in Châteauneuf-du-Pape. However, sea breezes can alleviate some of the stress of the vines. The vintage tends to be early, as a result of the proximity to the sea. There is very little problem with rot, resulting in wonderfully healthy grapes most years.

There are two theories about the origin of the name Quatourze, both based on the fact that the word means fourteen in Occitan.

With such a low rainfall, the wine here can be strong and alcoholic, often reaching a natural 14°. During the Middle Ages most of the land – that is, all the estates with saints' names (the one exception being Château Tapie, which belonged to the Tapie family, who were related to the painter Toulouse-Lautrec and also had associations with La Clape) – belonged to the bishop of Narbonne and would normally have been taxed at a tenth of its revenue, but as the land was so poor and arid, the bishop only took a fourteenth.

CHATEAU NOTRE-DAME-DU-QUATOURZE

Today Quatourze consists of some hundred and fifty hectares of vines and really owes its existence to the energy of one family. Yves Ortola is a fourth-generation Algerian who bought the abandoned property of Château Notre-Dame-du-Quatourze in 1965. In Algeria he had grown clementines as well as wheat and grapes, and here he has planted an avenue of olive trees. He now works with his son Georges, an energetic man who has helped to extend their vineyards and develop their wines. They now own two other estates, Château Tapie and Château de Lunès, which makes them responsible for some seventy hectares. Château St Charles is the one other independent property, but otherwise about a quarter of the production of Quatourze is vinified by the co-operative of Narbonne.

Georges Ortola would like to see more producers of Quatourze, as he feels somewhat isolated; it is a huge responsibility to maintain the reputation of a wine virtually single-handedly. There is always the lingering fear of urban encroachment. Vineyards have been abandoned as the land is so much more valuable for building, and the Ortola family fights a battle every five years, when the *plan d'occupation du sol* is revised, to ensure that the area of Quatourze continues to be registered as an agricultural zone.

When Quatourze first became a VDQS in 1951, Carignan was the sole grape variety. Since then, an extensive replanting programme has taken place, introducing Mourvèdre and Syrah to the vineyards in the mid-1970s. They now have thirty hectares of Syrah, twenty of Grenache Noir, some fifty-year-old Carignan and a little Cinsaut. The *cépages améliorateurs*, Syrah, Mourvèdre and Grenache Noir, already account for eighty per cent of their vineyards and gradually the Carignan and Cinsaut will disappear.

There is never any problem in ripening Mourvèdre here. The Syrah and Mourvèdre are trained on wires to open up the foliage, while the Carignan and Grenache Noir are bush vines. Everything except the Carignan is picked by mechanical harvester. As for white wine, they have some very old Macabeu that provides body and substance, but introduced Rolle in about 1990 to add some notes of vivacity and freshness.

The wines are vinified in the functional cellars at Château de Lunès, while those at Notre-Dame-du-Quatourze are now used for ageing and storage. Everything works by gravity, and since the cellars are partly underground, they remain cool. Each plot and grape variety is vinified separately, making about forty different wines, which are then blended to make a white, a pink and two red wines, under the name of Château de Lunès or Notre-Dame-du-Quatourze. The white is a blend of Macabeu with some Rolle that is given some lees contact before fermentation, to extract some flavour from these potentially discreet varieties. The 1996, when it was eighteen months old, was delicate, quite full, with herbal notes and acidity on the finish, and some carbon dioxide retaining the freshness. The 1997, tasted from vat, had a rich herbal nose and almost a hint of Viognier on the palate. It demonstrated a startling improvement since my previous visit ten years earlier.

Georges Ortola enthused about his *rosé*. 'Rosé for us is a real wine and not an insipid drink.' He talked of a stricter selection of *rosé* in the region and of an association called Les Languedoc Rosés, with even tighter quality control than the basic appellation, that aimed to enhance the reputation of the pink wines of the region. His is a blend of Syrah, Grenache Noir and Cinsaut, made by *saignée* and fermented at a relatively low temperature of 16°. It had quite a deep colour, and was rounded and fresh.

In his red wines Ortola looks for aroma, silky tannins and body. He has learnt by experience, for his original training was in computer science, but he changed directions to join his father; 1983 was his first vintage. As he belongs to the Vignerons du Val d'Orbieu, he benefits from the advice of one of the Midi's most thoughtful oenologists, Marc Dubernet. His basic red wine is made from Carignan, vinified by carbonic maceration and blended with Syrah and Mourvèdre the following January or February. This is the moment when they decide which are the best vats, to be given some barrel ageing for about twelve months. The basic 1996 had some lovely peppery fruit, with supple tannins, spice and liquorice. It was a good year in the Quatourze, with much less rain than in other parts of the Languedoc. Ortola first began working with wood in 1992 and selects the best Mourvèdre and Syrah for barrel ageing, in new to four-year-old barrels. The oak gives more vanilla flavours and more body and sweetness. When the 1995 was three years old, it tasted very young, but the wood ageing should enhance its potential longevity. It promised well.

It was exciting to see how this estate had evolved in the past decade. When I met Yves Ortola in 1987, his enthusiasm for wine was all too apparent. He described himself as *un amoureux du vin* who certainly could not imagine life without it. His faith in this small area has won through and his son Georges is energetically continuing the family's quest to improve the vineyards and wines, with notable success. But they are not complacent: 'We are half-way there.' It will be interesting to see what the next ten years bring.

Key facts

VDQS 1951, AC 1985; westernmost *terroir* of the Coteaux du Languedoc; compact vineyards outside Narbonne, kept alive by one energetic family.

The usual five grape varieties – Carignan, Cinsaut, Grenache Noir, Syrah and Mourvèdre – for red and *rosé*, with Macabeu and Rolle for white.

Dry, stony area with average annual rainfall of 450 mm.

La Clape

The Massif de la Clape, the rocky outcrop to the north west of Narbonne, was once an island and only became part of the mainland in the Middle Ages when the river Aude silted up. Until that time Narbonne was an important port and a prosperous city. The unfinished cathedral of St Just demonstrates both its former aspirations and the dramatic effect of the loss of its sea trade. The Massif, described by one producer as a *montagne vallonnée*, a mountain with several valleys between the hills and rocks, reaches 214 metres at its highest point. It contrasts sharply with the surrounding plain and the gaudy seaside resort of Narbonne-Plage. The road round the mountain is spectacular, as the scenery changes sharply from mountain to sea, the blue water contrasting vividly with the rough, scrub-covered hillsides.

La Clape is one of the better known vineyards of the Coteaux du Languedoc. In France it benefits from the tourist trade of the Mediterranean, and in English-speaking countries its name has unfortunate associations that make it memorable even to those who have never drunk it. It was first recognised as a VDQS in 1959 and became part of the appellation of the Coteaux du Languedoc in 1985, but without any significant change in regulations. From the 1998 vintage more stringent requirements about grape varieties were introduced, denoted by the label La Clape–Coteaux du Languedoc. The vines must be five years old, rather than the usual three for an appellation, with a minimum alcohol level of 11.5°. Any wines that do not conform are declassified into Coteaux du Languedoc. Eventually they hope for a separate appellation of La Clape as part of the Languedoc, in the same way that Pauillac is part of Bordeaux.

New varieties, namely Marsanne, Roussanne and Rolle, are now allowed for white wine, although Bourboulenc, also known locally as Malvoisie, must form the backbone with a minimum of forty per cent, and the inclusion of Clairette, Grenache Blanc, Macabeu and Picpoul is possible. The white wines of La Clape had an originality of flavour at a time when those of the Coteaux du Languedoc were still dull and bland. Jean Ségura, the former owner of Domaine la Rivière-Haute, is given the credit for this, as he established a reputation for making white wines on his estate with wonderfully distinctive flavours. I well remember a 1986 that was rich and rounded, with the flavour of nuts and honey – and all this without the influence of oak. Sadly, the estate was sold after his death, and the new owners do not seem to share his commitment.

Pink La Clape must come from a minimum of sixty per cent Grenache Noir, Syrah and Mourvèdre, while Carignan and Cinsaut make up the balance. The percentages have been changed for the red wine. The combined minimum percentage of the *cépages améliorateurs*, Grenache Noir, Syrah and Mourvèdre, has been increased from forty to seventy per cent, and Grenache Noir, as before, must represent a minimum of twenty per cent. Again, Carignan and Cinsaut may make up the balance. Carignan is restricted to a maximum of thirty per cent, a reduction from forty per cent, and there is no minimum percentage, which means that La Clape may be made from a blend of Grenache Noir, Syrah or Mourvèdre, if the producer so desires. Syrah tends to be the base of the better wines, even though it has only been planted in the area in any quantity since about 1980.

CHATEAU MOUJAN, NARBONNE

My first visit was to Château Moujan. Michel de Braquilanges is the sixth generation of his family to run the estate, returning to the land after a career selling mechanical harvesters in the Midi and Corsica. A great-grandfather was the engineer responsible for levelling the plains in the area around Narbonne so that the vineyards could be flooded as a preventative measure against the phylloxera louse. The life cycle of the louse includes forty days below ground, so if the vineyards are flooded for that period, it will die. Some of the vineyards on the coastal plain are barely eighty centimetres above sea level, so that they are quite often flooded anyway. Deliberate flooding was also done in the Camargue and around Agde in the Hérault.

De Braquilanges is also president of the growers' *syndicat*, a position that has called for great diplomacy, for the situation is fraught with village rivalries. La Clape is a small, compact area including five *communes*, although curiously Gruissan, on the southern edge of the Massif, is considered part of the Corbières. There are forty producers with about one thousand hectares in all, half of whom put their wine in bottle. The rest send their grapes to the four co-operatives, Armissan and Fleury being the most important. De Braquilanges is well aware of the importance of communication in making La Clape better known. He would like an annual *fête du vin* that would move from village to village, but people would have to agree – and that is the hardest part. He is convinced that the geographical identity of the Massif should be exploited, for unlike the other *crus* or *terroirs* of the Coteaux du Languedoc, it does have a very precise geographical delimitation. There is also talk of a *route des vins*, but as the Massif de la la Clape is a *site classée*, the Commission des Sites has to vet any proposed signs.

We went for a drive through the vineyard, which illustrated the rocky terrain of the region, with its series of valleys. The soil at Château Moujan, a stony mixture of clay and white limestone, is considered the best. In other parts of the Massif it is sandy and there is also white marl, as well as limestone on red clay. Altogether Château Moujan consists of seventy-five hectares of vines, fifty-five of which are in the appellation while the others produce *vin de pays*. De Braquilanges's father planted the oldest vines, some Carignan, in 1950, and now they have Syrah, Grenache Noir and a little Cinsaut, as well as Grenache Blanc and Bourboulenc for white wine, with some recent planting of Rolle, Marsanne and Macabeu. Mourvèdre does not ripen well here, as the vineyards are on the inland side of the Massif. It does much better on the maritime side, for it needs the marine humidity to stop the skin from cracking and splitting and to prevent problems with rot. If Mourvèdre ripens too quickly, as it does inland, the skin becomes hard and brittle. Carignan works well here, and de Braquilanges's father sees it as the backbone of the wines. He has always favoured Carignan, maintaining that it produces much better wine here in the warm, sunny vineyards of La Clape than anywhere else. It is a mistake to group the vineyards around Narbonne with those of Montpellier, as the climatic conditions are quite different.

The cellar still contains the original giant *foudres* of 360 hectolitres or more, but they are no longer used, as their size is quite impractical. They also have large vats built of stone in the 1850s, rather than the reinforced concrete more usual in later decades. The doors are made from single stones. These vats are a reminder of the previous existence of the estate, when they had vineyards on the plains, planted with Aramon and yielding a heady 200 hl/ha rather than the more modest 35 hl/ha of today. The largest *foudres* have been replaced by stainless steel vats, and instead of the old continuous press there is now a gentle pneumatic press.

For the moment their white wine is a blend of Bourboulenc and Grenache Blanc, with the former providing the fruit and the latter the body. On the palate it was quite appley and full, rounded with a dry finish. A vat sample of the difficult vintage of 1997, from Syrah and Grenache Noir, both given a long *cuvaison*, and Carignan vinified by carbonic maceration, was soft and fruity, with easy appeal. The 1995 had more warmth, with the herbs of the *garrigue* and a long dry finish, and the 1992, which de Braquilanges considered *très Clape*, had a certain dusty warmth and elegance.

CHATEAU PECH-REDON, NARBONNE

Château Pech-Redon is at the highest point of La Clape. The etymology of the name is interesting, for in Occitan a *pech* is a hill or mountain and *redon* means rounded, which accurately describes the Massif de la Clape. You take a narrow road that twists its way up the hillside, offering far-reaching views over the countryside. There are the remains of a Roman villa on the property; indeed, many of the estates of La Clape are of Roman origin and supplied wine to Rome, whereas the wine from the vineyards on the surrounding plains was consumed locally. Until his death in 1988, Château Pech-Redon was the property of Jean Demolombe, who has been described as one of the great visionaries of the Languedoc. He was ahead of his time in planting the first Mourvèdre and Viognier here in the 1970s. The estate is now owned by Christophe

Bousquet and his father Jean-Claude, who is president of the *syndicat* of the Coteaux du Languedoc. He was originally a member of the co-operative of St Saturnin, from which the only escape was to sell your vineyards – which he did, encouraged by his son, who was keen to do his own thing after oenology studies at Montpellier.

They have forty-two hectares planted with the usual five red grape varieties, with Bourboulenc and Grenache Blanc for white wine, some Chardonnay and Cabernet Sauvignon for *vin de pays* and Alicante which they bottle as *vin de table*. There are several different plots of vines, some around the plateau of Pech-Redon, some right at the summit of La Clape and others lower down the hillside. The highest vines are much later to ripen, for the conditions are cooler and windier, with fresher nights in summer. The wind also brings drought, as a solid chunk of rock called the Coffre du Pech-Redon, which does indeed look like a treasure chest, seems to protect the vines from rain. La Clape is one of the driest parts of France, with less than 500 mm rainfall a year. In 1995 they went from April to November without a drop of rain, but fortunately there is always some humidity from the sea breezes. Also, the vines go deep into the rock, tapping the underground water supplies in the Massif. The rosemary bushes flower early here, at the beginning of spring, making it a highly desirable spot for apiculturists to keep their hives.

Christophe Bousquet is a young, thoughtful and discursive producer, questioning in his attitudes. We talked and tasted in a neat little tasting room that had once been the old forge, with the date 1901 over the furnace. He is convinced of the enormous potential of La Clape, but considers it largely untapped. Many of his fellow producers are half asleep and certainly not exploiting all the possibilities of their appellation. It is the newcomers who are bringing money into the area and waking people up.

Bousquet's white wine is a very traditional blend of Grenache Blanc and Bourboulenc. He fears that if Bourboulenc is replaced by more aromatic varieties such as Marsanne and Roussanne, the typicity of the appellation will disappear. He wants his Bourboulenc grapes to be almost overripe, which gives body and weight to the wine. In 1997 they were picked right at the end of October, two months after the Syrah. The yield was small, just 25 hl/ha, and the wine is rich, with rounded, herbal flavours and a good body, mouth feel and length, making it a powerful advocate for the typicity of the Mediterranean. Vinification methods are classic, with not too cold a fermentation temperature and some *élevage* on the fine lees for six months, which also adds weight to the wine. Bousquet looks to the example set by Jean Ségura for white wines – which sadly many of his fellow growers have not followed – but unlike Ségura he does not do a malolactic fermentation as he considers it would make the wines lose their freshness.

Bousquet's red wines also portray all the scents and herbs of the *garrigue* of the Mediterranean. The Cuvée Réserve, intended for early drinking, is a blend of sixty per cent Syrah and ten per cent Carignan, both vinified by carbonic maceration, with Grenache Noir made in the traditional way. It has some appealing berry fruit on the nose, with the pepperiness that is typical of the higher vineyards of La Clape. If you give the grapes a longer maceration you obtain more tarry, cedary, resinous flavours, as in the Cuvée Sélection, which spends at least twelve months in vat. The wine is racked each season, during a waning moon and a north wind. Apparently the sea wind, the Marin, can cause reduction in wine. There is no filtering or fining, and the flavour of the 1995 vintage when it was three years old was redolent of the *garrigue*, with mineral overtones, fruit and tannin. It still needed time.

It is with *élevage* in wood that the real potential for longevity can be exploited. Jean Demolombe had started working with *barriques* in 1980 and Bousquet followed his example for the 1988 vintage. For the moment their barrel cellar is in an old stable with very thick walls, so that the temperature does not change significantly, but they have a project for an underground cellar and would also like to do some *élevage* in bottle. Bousquet is convinced of the ageing potential of the Coteaux du Languedoc, and of La Clape in particular. We do not really know the potential yet, but with such fine tannins it should be possible. For him, elegance is the typicity of La Clape. The Narbonnais compare Corbières and La Clape as the British might compare Bordeaux and Burgundy. Corbières is more structured and masculine, while La Clape is more elegant and feminine. Bousquet's barrel-aged 1995, from fifty per cent Grenache Noir, thirty per cent Syrah and twenty per cent Carignan, had the vanilla overtones of oak, with firm tannin, fruit and the herbs of the *garrigue* on the palate.

CHATEAU ROUQUETTE-SUR-MER, NARBONNE-PLAGE

Château Rouquette-sur-Mer, just outside Narbonne-Plage, is as the name implies on the seaward side of La Clape. The estate belongs to Jacques Boscary, who took over the family property about thirty years ago. First of all he took me for a drive through the vineyards. He has fifty-five hectares in production in a four hundred-hectare estate, which means numerous small plots of vines nestling in the *garrigue*. The original fourteenth-century château was abandoned after phylloxera, when it was noticed that vines survived in the sandier soil nearer the sea and the vineyards were therefore shifted towards to coast. The château was badly damaged during the Second World War and is now a picturesque ruin lost in the *garrigue;* the remains of German defences nearby are a reminder of the vulnerability of this coastline.

Today Boscary is clearing new sites for vineyards away from the coast. He has the usual five red grape varieties and has recently planted a lot of Mourvèdre in a vineyard with wonderful views of the sea. For white wine he has Bourboulenc and some Roussanne, and he has just planted Viognier (which may eventually be allowed in the appellation) as well as some Muscat *à petits grains* on an experimental basis, as it will certainly never be included in La Clape. The vineyards on the flatter land at the entrance to the property are planted with Merlot, Cabernet Sauvignon and Alicante for *vin de table* or *vin de pays*.

Boscary makes two qualities of each colour, with differing degrees of oak. The Cuvée Classique is lightly oaked and the Cuvée Henri Lapierre, named after Boscary's grandfather, who first bought the estate, spends more time in wood. The 1996 white Cuvée Classique included just ten per cent of oaked wine, but this was so delicate as to be imperceptible. It was a blend of Bourboulenc, some of which was given some skin contact, with just twenty per cent of Roussanne, making for some attractive leafy fruit and freshness. The 1996 Henri Lapierre was a similar blend but mostly fermented in new wood, and it still tasted quite oaky when it was two years old. However, it had length and body and could be expected to age. So far Boscary has limited experience of the effects of oak, although the 1994 had certainly developed more flavours of the *garrigue*, with herbal, tarry notes.

I thought the Henri Lapierre *rosé* was more successful than the white, even though Boscary said that *on s'amuse* in making an oaked *rosé*. It had spent six months in wood and had developed a certain smoky, tarry character, with more substance than some *rosés*. The percentage of the red Cuvée Classique to be aged in wood depends on the vintage; in 1996 it was eighty per cent, with about a third in new barrels from Seguin Moreau. The oak was well integrated, adding length and body, with rounded fruit, while the 1994 had developed more intriguing animal notes, with some appealing dusty, herbal fruit, conveying the scents of the *garrigue*, balanced with silky tannins. The 1995 Cuvée Henri Lapierre, from a selection of Carignan, Syrah and Mourvèdre, had all been kept in wood for at least twelve months. It was firm and tannic, with the underlying herbs of the *garrigue*. Boscary is experimenting with *microbullage*, which allows for the oxygenation of the wine without increasing the wood effect. He is currently enlarging his cellar to include an insulated barrel cellar, something that so many estates in the Midi lack.

CHATEAU MIRE L'ETANG, FLEURY D'AUDE

From Narbonne-Plage I drove along the seafront through St Pierre-sur-Mer and past the evocatively named Etang des Pissevaches to Château Mire l'Etang, which was bought by the Chaymayrac family in 1972. There were already vines here, but all the bad varieties, so Syrah was first planted in 1976. The vineyards are very close to the sea and the mouth of the Aude, so the vines feel the influence of the Golfe du Lion. Altogether they have fifty hectares, around the house and on the pebbly plateau. A quarter of their production is white wine, from Bourboulenc and Grenache Blanc as well as Roussanne, which has only recently come into production. The 1997, with a high proportion of Roussanne, was perfumed and rounded, with good acidity.

As for red, they have since 1989 made a barrel-aged wine, Cuvée des Ducs de Fleury, for which they choose the best Syrah and Grenache Noir for a longer-lasting wine. They tried Mourvèdre in oak for the first time in 1997, but it was not so successful. The vines were only ten years old and 1997 was a problematic vintage as it rained three times in August. That, combined with the humidity from the sea and the heat from the stony vineyard, resulted in an attack of mildew. The simple 1995 red had some attractive perfumed fruit with peppery overtones, while the Cuvée des Ducs de Fleury, which had spent ten months in oak, was more substantial, a solid mouthful of spice and wood.

Pierre Chaymayrac is also very enthusiastic about Carthagène, the Midi's answer to the *ratafia* of Champagne, made from unfermented grape juice, with the fermentation stopped by the previous year's *marc*. He has planted some Muscat, again not for the appellation but for Carthagène, for which it is one of the traditional varieties. He would also like to try making a late harvest wine. Like Christophe Bousquet, he is critical of the lack of ambition among some of his fellow growers and sadly pessimistic for the future of La Clape.

CHATEAU FERRI-ARNAUD, FLEURY D'AUDE

The cellar of Château Ferri-Arnaud is in the village of Fleury. Joseph Ferri is a friendly older man with a enthusiasm for life, bubbling with opinions: 'You should make wine, love and cook, all with passion.' He has a much more positive attitude than Chaymayrac, and certainly more faith in the future of La Clape. Over the years he has gradually created his own estate of thirty hectares in twelve different plots, with variations of *terroir*. His white wine is mainly Rolle, because it is more aromatic, with some Grenache Blanc, for he does not like Bourboulenc. I found it full, biscuity and quite old-fashioned in style. He also makes a Chardonnay *vin de pays* and firmly refuses to put it in wood. He tried it once and did not like it. Just bottled, the 1997 tasted quite supple and subtle.

Ferri does like oak for red wine, and has made an oaked *cuvée* since he bought his first two barrels in 1993. He now has fifty and has experimented with American oak, but found it much too strong. His 1996, from eighty per cent Syrah and twenty per cent Grenache Noir, was quite closed. There was less obvious *garrigue* fruit than in some wines, but also less apparent oak, with some silky tannins and an elegant palate. The 1995 was more tannic, with peppery fruit and a dry, meaty nose. I liked the unoaked wine too, from Carignan, Grenache Noir and Syrah, all vinified by carbonic maceration, with peppery fruit and a structured backbone.

CHATEAU PECH-CELEYRAN

At Château Pech-Céleyran I was given a friendly welcome by Nectar, a rather intimidating guard dog who fortunately was not taking his responsibilities too seriously that sunny spring afternoon. The property is separated from the main mountain of La Clape and stands on a small, isolated hill of its own. It has belonged to the Saint-Exupéry family, who have cousins at Château Tiregand in Pecharmant near Bergerac, for three generations. The estate also has associations with Toulouse-Lautrec. In 1850, when it was divided between two sisters, the elder – Adèle Tapie de Céleyran, mother of Toulouse-Lautrec – took what was then considered to be the better, more profitable half, with vineyards on the plain, while her younger sister took this half, with vineyards on the hill opposite, where of course today the better wine is made. In the Toulouse-Lautrec museum in Albi there are some charming water-colours painted at Château Céleyran.

As well as forty hectares of La Clape, Jacques de Saint-Exupéry also cultivates over fifty hectares of *vin de pays* for the local Côtes de Pérignan or broader d'Oc. The nearby village of Fleury d'Aude was originally called Pérignan, but when Cardinal de Fleury, the finance minister of Louis XV, visited the village, its name was changed in his honour. For de Saint-Exupéry, his hectares of *vin de pays* provide a outlet for his desire for experimentation, guided by his oenologist, who 'puts him back on the right track when he goes too far'. He makes two Chardonnay, one with wood and one without, which I preferred. He planted Viognier around 1990, and the 1997 had some convincing varietal character. There is also some Petit Manseng, which may be for a *vendange tardive* from raisined grapes, but that is still very much at an experimental stage. Marsanne and Roussanne were planted at the same time as Viognier and are included in his white La Clape with Grenache Blanc and Macabeu. It is given some *élevage* on the fine lees, which enhances the body of the wine, and it had a full, almondy palate.

As for red wine, Pinot Noir is his main grape variety for *vin de pays*, of which his first vintage was 1981. I tasted the 1995, which I found quite herbal, with some sturdy tannins. It is labelled simply Pinot de Pech. There are also Malbec, Cabernet Sauvignon and Merlot, all planted over twenty years ago. De Saint-Exupéry is convinced that the Vin de Pays d'Oc has greatly enhanced the reputation of the Languedoc, to the benefit of the regional appellations. He makes two red La Clape. One is a supple, easy-drinking wine with a large proportion of Grenache Noir, some Syrah, Carignan and a little Mourvèdre from a long carbonic maceration. The 1997 was redolent of the perfumes and spices of the *garrigue*, with some delicious fruit and supple tannins. The second wine, from the same composition of grape varieties, spends from twelve to eighteen months in barrel. It was sturdier, with more liquorice and tannin. De Saint-Exupéry first experimented with *barriques* in 1987 and finally abandoned the enormous *foudres* in 1997. However, they are kept for their visual impact in his large cellar, which once accommodated thousands of hectolitres. It was built in 1850 with several solid stone vats one metre thick, which have been lined with epoxy resin. Now there are stainless steel vats, as well as a pneumatic press.

OTHER ESTATES

The wines of Château les Capitouls also deserve a mention. The estate belongs to Charles and Sophie Mock, who arrived here in 1982 and replanted the vineyards, which at the time consisted entirely of Carignan. Particularly intriguing is their late harvest Viognier, which was honeyed and ripe after eighteen months *élevage* in wood. As for La Clape, their Grand Terroir is structured, but elegant and very satisfying. The wines of Domaine Laquirou also have a good reputation, but no one was at home when I tried to visit. Nor can you drive over the Massif de la Clape without noticing the impressive Domaine de l'Hospitalet, with its sixty hectares of vines outside Narbonne-Plage. It is the property of the Ribourel family and a vivid example of the new investment taking place all over the Midi.

As for the future of La Clape, Jacques de Saint-Exupéry takes an optimistic view of the things; 'We are very lucky. We are in a corner of paradise, with a magnificent terroir, but we need to work together.' Progress has been made, or as Michel de Braquilanges put it at the tenth anniversary of the Coteaux du Languedoc, 'We are not yet adults, but we are reaching the age of reason.'

Key facts

VQDS 1959; *terroir* and now *cru* of Coteaux du Languedoc; five communes around the Massif de la Clape; about a thousand hectares.

Grape varieties:

REDS: the usual five, with Grenache Noir a minimum of twenty per cent and Syrah, Grenache Noir and Mourvèdre a combined minimum of seventy per cent; Carignan a maximum of thirty per cent.

WHITES: Marsanne, Roussanne, Rolle, Bourboulenc, Macabeu, Clairette, Grenache Blanc, Picpoul.

11.5° minimum; at least five-year-old vines.

St Chinian

St Chinian became an appellation in its own right in 1982, three years before it was incorporated into the Coteaux du Languedoc as a *cru* alongside Faugères. It is a large area covering some twenty *communes*, with 2,700 hectares of delimited vineyards stretching from the Minervois in the west to Faugères in the east. Before the creation of the appellation the area was a VDQS, named de l'Orb et du Vernazobre after the two rivers that cross the vineyards, covering more or less the same area. There was a slight extension of the delimited vineyards in 1982, to include amongst others the village of Murviel. St Chinian itself is the size of a small country town, while most of the other *communes* are mere hamlets. There is a large square lined with plane trees, providing welcome shade in the midday sun, and in one corner you will find the Maison du Vin, which provides an attractive shop front to the appellation. Here you can taste and buy wines from all the producers of the appellation, or if you are looking for wines from further afield, the Espace Vin close by offers plenty of temptation.

The very earliest records of viticulture in St Chinian go back to 826, when a monk named Aniane, who was to become St Aniane and thus gave his name to St Chinian, planted vines. During the Middle Ages viticulture was a subject of dispute between lay landlords and the church, which tried to maintain a monopoly over the sale of wine. The town of St Chinian was destroyed during the Wars of Religion in the sixteenth century and in 1590 it was recorded that the Duc de Montmorency ordered the villages of St Chinian, Berlou and Pierrerue to provide him each week with eighteen sheep and three *charges* of wine.

Viticulture has played a vital part in the economy of the area throughout its history. Little else will grow on the rugged foothills

St Chinian

of the Cévennes that form the greater part of the appellation, which is split in two by the river Vernazobre, with quite different soils on either bank. To the north and west, the soil is based on schist and includes St Chinian itself as well as the villages of Roquebrun, Berlou and Murviel, while the southern part of the appellation is a mixture of limestone and clay. Consequently you can find two quite different styles of St Chinian. The wine produced from schist is light, eminently fruity and supple, with flavours of the *garrigue*, ripe fruit and liquorice, and is destined for relatively early drinking, perhaps after a couple of years, while that from clay and limestone is more solid and substantial, with more marked tannins, and benefits from longer ageing.

In common with so many other parts of the Midi, St Chinian is moving slowly towards the development of a hierarchy within the appellation, singling out the two villages of Berlou and Roquebrun. Both are based on schist, but are in different valleys with climatic variations, and there is also a difference of emphasis in their grape varieties. Roquebrun concentrates on Syrah, whereas Berlou still retains some old Carignan. Co-operatives are an important force and it is perhaps no coincidence that both villages have co-operatives that could be considered leaders in the appellation.

LES COTEAUX DU RIEU BERLOU

Fifteen years ago, if you had asked any reputable producer in the region who else they rated in the Languedoc, the name of the co-operative of Berlou was bound to feature in the list. It was at the forefront of experimentation with carbonic maceration, and since the late 1970s, under the guidance of a former president, Georges Dardé, the co-operative has encouraged its members to plant the *cépages améliorateurs*, Grenache Noir, Syrah and Mourvèdre. At the end of the nineteenth century the Hérault directory recorded that the village of Berlou produced excellent wine which rivalled that of Roussillon. The village was called Berlou in the Middle Ages and its name is thought to have come from the Latin *ver luporum*, meaning 'spring of wolves'. Maybe there were once wolves in the nearby Forêt des Albières. Today you will find the co-operative's wine under the brand names of Berlou Prestige and Schisteil, a fusion of schist and soleil, the two principal elements that contribute to the wine. Sadly, however, the co-operative of Berlou has lost its momentum in the last few years and has been overtaken by other producers. Recent tastings showed wines that seemed to lack structure and definition, and the general consensus is that the quality is no longer as exciting as ten years ago, even though they have good vineyards. Undoubtedly Berlou has been superseded by the Cave de Roquebrun.

LA CAVE DE ROQUEBRUN

Roquebrun is an attractive little village perched above the river Orb, with a ruined castle dominating the skyline. Les Mimosas, an attractive town house in the main street, provides welcoming *chambres d'hôte* and tasty meals. The co-operative, on the edge of the village, is one of the newest of the Midi, for it was founded as recently as 1967, just two years after that of Berlou. The impulse came from a group of independent producers who decided to group together to sell their wine, with the additional incentive that co-operatives receive subsidies that are impossible for an individual producer to obtain. Carbonic maceration was already a consideration, and so the cellar was constructed specifically to work by gravity, thus eliminating the need to pump the wine. Virtually all the red wine grapes are fermented by that method. There are now 114 members cultivating a hundred hectares all around the village. Their first vintage using *barriques* was 1992 and four years later they built a new cellar for them.

This is a co-operative that is working well for its members, with a dynamic sales programme, not linked to any of the *groupements de producteurs*, combined with a rigorous approach to quality. The vines are divided into three categories according to their age, system of pruning, yield and *état sanitaire*. The final decision as to what goes where is made at the vintage, with each grape variety vinified separately. They have two pneumatic presses, which are useful for providing skin contact for the white and *rosé* wines.

White St Chinian is under discussion. The INAO has agreed in principle after the visit of one commission, but a firm decree has as yet to be passed – perhaps in time for the 2000 vintage, or perhaps not. Until then, any white wine is simple Coteaux du Languedoc, from grape varieties such as Roussanne, Marsanne and Grenache Blanc, which they began planting at Roquebrun in about 1988. Some people also favour Viognier, but it is too marked in character and so may feature with a maximum ten per cent. Rolle and Muscat are other possibilities. For their Roquebrun Clos de l'Orb, a blend of eighty-five per cent Grenache Blanc with just a little Roussanne is given twelve hours skin contact, with great care taken to prevent oxidation. It is very perfumed, almost Muscat-like, while the Château Roquebrun, from seventy per cent Roussanne with Grenache Blanc, is fermented in wood. Here they lose what they call the *accent du terroir*, as the oak dominates the young wine.

There are numerous *cuvées* of red wine. Domaine des Olivettes, a Coteaux du Languedoc because it comes from more fertile vineyards on the bank of the Orb that are not allowed in St Chinian, is a blend of Syrah, Grenache Noir, Mourvèdre and Carignan, with some attractive peppery fruit. The length of maceration for the vintage depends not only on the grape variety but also on the condition of the grapes. Ideally a *cuvaison* for healthy Syrah would last about twenty to twenty-five days at around 30°C, reaching as high as 35°C. Domaine de Laurel is composed of plots of older wines, with spicy, peppery fruit and an underlying suppleness. Roquebrun Prestige includes the oldest Mourvèdre, about twenty years old, with good structure and ripe berry fruit, while Le Sir de Roc Brun is the same wine but aged in barrel for twelve months. They are adamant that the wood must not deform the wine. However, the vanilla notes of oak were quite obvious in the young wine. The problem is the financial impossibility of ageing wines. For the moment they simply do not have the means to finance stocks of wine and their customers must understand the need to do this themselves. Le Baron d'Aupenac is another oak-aged *cuvée*, this time in new oak for eighteen to twenty-four months, with a high percentage of Syrah and just ten per cent each of Grenache Noir and Mourvèdre. The oak was well integrated, with good concentration. Best of all I liked the Cuvée Roches Noires in which Syrah is the dominant variety. There is no oak and the flavours are everything good Syrah from the Midi should be, with peppery fruit and firm tannins.

Our tasting finished with a discussion about the preferences of the wild boar. They love sweet Muscat and also ripe Cinsaut, but they no longer have any natural predators. Once there were wolves, but now there is only man, and foolishly the boar have been allowed to breed with the wild pigs. The result is two litters a year rather than one, with six or seven piglets instead of one or two. In some areas they can present a significant threat to the ripe grapes.

There are other co-operatives. That of St Chinian works reasonably well for its members. Puisserguier is considered to be quite technologically advanced, making good white and *rosé*, while Cébazan is more old-fashioned, concentrating more on volume than quality. It is the independent producers who contribute much more in interest and variety, even though they only account for a third of the production.

CHATEAU COUJAN, MURVIEL-LES-BEZIERS

François Guy at Château Coujan near Murviel-lès-Béziers did much for the early reputation of St Chinian. These days he tends to let his daughter Florence assume responsibility for the wine making and takes life a little more slowly. However, the wit and humour, as well as the questioning attitude, are happily still very apparent when you visit. Château Coujan is Roman in origin with a long history, and has been in the hands of the Guy family since 1868. Before that it belonged to the Marquise Gabriella de Spinola, from one of the great families of the Languedoc, whose descendants included Jean d'Ormesson, an academician and novelist. The existing château, with its air of shabby elegance, dates from 1868. Currently Guy has about ninety-five hectares in production. The vineyards are based on fossilised coral, which looks rather like pieces of honeycomb. You find it when you dig deep into the soil and it provides excellent drainage.

I spent a friendly hour tasting in a rather chaotic cellar, lined with old *foudres*, where a boisterous Pyrenean sheepdog called Sky kept getting underfoot. Florence opened bottles and her father provided an entertaining commentary, showing his healthy disrespect for officialdom and a questioning attitude towards the development of the Midi. They still use their *foudres*, even though the oenologists hate them. You have to wash them properly and they provide limited oxidation in a contained atmosphere. They produce both *vin de pays* and appellation St Chinian, depending on demand. Rolle was first planted ten years ago and makes a Vin de Pays des Coteaux de Murviel as well as accounting for half of their white Coteaux du Languedoc. Rolle blends well with Grenache Blanc, making what Guy called a 'happy marriage', with some perfumed, nutty fruit. The *rosé* contains a little of everything except Carignan, of which they still have quite a lot. 'That is our typicity, a mortal sin!' It tends to be used for *vin de pays*, with the more interesting wines coming from the *cépages améliorateurs*, of which Guy was a pioneer; in 1966 he was one of the very first to plant Cabernet Sauvignon and Merlot in the Midi.

The Cuvée Gabriella de Spignola is a blend of Mourvèdre, Grenache Noir and Cinsaut that spends twelve months in *foudres*, and it has some dry, spicy fruit. The Cuvée Bois Joli, as the name implies, is aged in barrel for one or two winters, depending on the evolution of the wine, and includes the best Syrah and Mourvèdre. Various vintages of humble Vin de Pays des Coteaux de Murviel, from blends of Cabernet Sauvignon and Merlot, showed just how well these wines can age. The 1990 was still very youthful when it was seven years old, the 1981 had elegant notes of cedar wood and the 1977 was beautifully elegant and mature, with soft tannins and again dry cedar wood. Cabernet Sauvignon and Merlot do better here than in Bordeaux, Guy observed provocatively, for they are easier to grow here and we can get our grapes really ripe – with the inference that they cannot in the Gironde.

Pinot Noir was not allowed to be planted until 1992. The 1996 was light, with raspberry fruit, but without much real varietal character. Much more intriguing and successful was the Vendange Tardive from Petit Manseng. In 1995 the grapes were picked on 10 November, with a little noble rot, and fermented very slowly until the end of June, while the 1996 was still fermenting in April 1997. The wine is honeyed, with fresh acidity and notes of poire William and quince. As they are not allowed to use the term Vendange Tardive, they call it *dernière cueillette*, or last picking. The vineyards are changing all the time, with plantings of more Syrah, Rolle, Roussanne and Sauvignon. Guy first planted a little Viognier in the 1980s, but now he cannot be bothered with it 'as everyone else is doing it'.

DOMAINE DES JOUGLA, PRADES-SUR-VERNAZOBRE

Domaine des Jougla in the little village of Prades-sur-Vernazobre is another long-standing family estate. Alain Jougla is a thoughtful, bearded man with an engaging smile, while his wife Joceline is lively and vivacious. He took over from his father some twenty-five years ago, and their daughter, who had just returned from a *stage* in Chile, will eventually follow in her father's footsteps. However, they can trace the family back to at least 1595 in the same village. They have forty hectares of vines, mainly for St Chinian, but also a little Cabernet Sauvignon and Merlot planted ten years ago for *vin de pays*. Some of their vineyards are on schist and some on limestone and clay. Jougla considers that there is now a good standard of vinification and cellar work in the appellation. What is needed now is an effort in the vineyard. Their first Syrah was planted at the end of the 1970s, and he has some Grenache Noir from the 1950s. They are also planting more white varieties, in particular Viognier. As for Mourvèdre, it all depends upon the yield. Thirty hectolitres per hectare is the absolute maximum or else it is too dilute. It is important to balance the crop, with the correct ratio of leaf area to grapes. Green harvesting is useful, but must not be done too early or else the remaining grapes become too big, especially if it rains. *Véraison* is the best moment for a green harvest.

We tasted in an attractive little *caveau* in the village. A white Coteaux du Languedoc is made from Grenache Blanc and Bourboulenc. The grapes are picked early in the morning and the juice given a couple of hours of skin contact before fermentation. The flavour was delicate and grassy, slightly herbal. A Viognier *vin de pays* is made in the same way, with a green harvest to limit the yield to about 18 hl/ha. It had a peachy flavour and some weight, with a slight bitterness on the finish.

They make three qualities of red wine. The Cuvée Classique comes from equal parts of the five Midi varieties. Those that ripen together are fermented together, with a final blend before bottling. They used to do some carbonic maceration, but now prefer to destalk everything for a traditional vinification and the *élevage* is in *foudres* and vats. The Cuvée Tradition contains Mourvèdre, Grenache Noir and Syrah, and is firmer and more structured than the Cuvée Classique, with its appealing perfume of the *garrigue* and soft tannins. Jougla first used *barriques* in 1986, for the Cuvée Signée, which consists of Syrah and Grenache Noir with just fifteen per cent of Carignan. He has tried several French coopers and likes Vicard best but he does not like American oak at all, as the taste is much too obvious. Ideally he would love to have an underground cellar for his barrels, but that is an expensive project and one that few private producers in the Midi are able to contemplate.

Jougla's cellars are an insulated building on the outskirts of the village, with some wonderful century-old *foudres* that are lovingly maintained alongside the stainless steel vats. Usually his wine goes into the *foudres* after the alcoholic fermentation and stays there until the following May, with some *élevage* in vat before bottling. Jougla favours *délestage*, which he described as a percolation like making coffee, and also has a system of *remontages* involving the injection of nitrogen into the vat, which pushes up the juice to submerge the cap. He has had a pneumatic press since 1990.

Before I left, Jougla asked if I would like to try a glass of Grenache. This was obviously something rather special, so of course I accepted. He led me up a steep ladder to the attic, where there was a row of tiny sixty-litre barrels. This is a tradition of the Midi that could be seen as a local variation on Banyuls or Rivesaltes; however, the wine is not fortified, but fermented in wood and then aged in small barrels on the lees, exposed to the extremes of seasonal temperature changes under the roof in a combination of oxidation and maderisation. The taste was rich and chocolatey, with a dry alcoholic finish and a long lingering aftertaste, not unlike a rather fierce oloroso sherry.

CHATEAU LA CROIX STE EULALIE, COMBEJEAN

Michel Gleizes at Château la Croix Ste Eulalie in the hamlet of Combejean also makes what he calls 'my father-in-law's folly' from Roussanne. This year's must is added to last year's lees, not unlike a Vin Santo, and the wine is kept in small barrels, again somewhere where it is subjected to the extremes of temperature, particularly the summer heat. It tasted quite sweet and indeed the aroma was not unlike Vin Santo.

Gleizes is one of the new producers of St Chinian, for his first vintage was in 1997. However, his involvement goes back much longer. His father put the family vines into the St Chinian co-operative in 1956 and he was president of it from 1988 to 1996. However, when his twenty-five year contract came to an end, he took the opportunity to leave, motivated by a desire to pass something on to his children. It was an opportune moment, for there is quite a substantial sum to pay if you withdraw your vines before the contract expires. The morning we met, he had been up all night treating his vines, as the weather forecast had threatened rain in the afternoon. It never came, but Gleizes was promising himself a siesta. People are much more thoughtful about treatments now, no longer systematically spraying their vines every two weeks whether they need it or not.

He talked about his work as the president of the co-operative. 'You are the one who has to set an example if you want your members to do something.' Consequently much of his vineyard has been replanted or grafted over in the last fifteen years, and he now has a lot of Syrah as well as Mourvèdre, Grenache Noir and some Carignan. He does not really like Cinsaut and has very little, just for *rosé*. The co-operative is also working towards quality, but with a different approach from an independent producer. He wanted to do more, which is why he left. 'You have to call yourself into question every morning. The Languedoc is in the process of writing a large page in its history and you have to be there.'

The traditional white grapes of St Chinian were Clairette, Terret Blanc, Carignan Blanc and Grenache Blanc, but no Ugni Blanc. Since about 1985 people have been planting Roussanne, Marsanne and Rolle, which have been allowed in the appellation Coteaux du Languedoc since 1990 and will be in the future white appellation of St Chinian. Viognier is still under consideration. Gleizes makes an intriguing blend of equal parts of Roussanne and Grenache Blanc, with twenty per cent Viognier. Roussanne provides a little point of acidity, Grenache Blanc the body and Viognier the perfume, giving a blend that is rounded and ripe with some acidity and a lemony finish. He has also tried the same blend in 225-litre barrels, each variety fermented separately, with regular *bâtonnage* and a final *assemblage* in May. One-year-old oak adds an extra dimension, while the same wine in 600-litre new barrels was much more obviously oaky, although Gleizes feels that these larger barrels may provide a better balance of oak to volume of wine.

In 1997 Gleizes made two red wines. The one with an *élevage* in vat was made partly by carbonic maceration and partly with a classic fermentation from Syrah with one third Mourvèdre. It was spicy and perfumed, with notes of cinnamon. The oak-aged wine, including some new barrels, is also a blend of Syrah and Mourvèdre, all destalked and given a long maceration, over three weeks for Syrah and nearly four for the Mourvèdre, with regular *délestages*. The flavour was ripe and solid, with rounded berry fruit and well integrated oak. It promised well.

CLOS BAGATELLE, ST CHINIAN

Clos Bagatelle has been in the hands of the Simon family since 1623, but usually passing from mother to daughter. As Christine Simone joked, her brother Luc is the exception. Brother and sister spark off each other in a friendly, teasing way. They have a total of fifty-four hectares, on schist in the hamlet of Donnadieu and on limestone and clay in St Chinian. There is a difference between the two. Syrah performs very well on the schist, with low yields of around 32–35 hl/ha, and there is also some eighty-year-old Carignan. The soil is very dry and not very deep. By contrast, in St Chinian the soil is deeper and they get very good Mourvèdre, as it likes the clay and limestone. They do not make any white wine, believing that it is too hot in St Chinian, and prefer to concentrate on red, but they do have eight hectares of Muscat in St Jean-de-Minervois.

There are some wonderful old *foudres*, in which the red wine undergoes the malolactic fermentation. They favour carbonic maceration and would like to vinify all their Syrah and Carignan that way, but have a problem of space. They began working with barrels in 1982, and in 1996 built a separate underground barrel cellar, a rare sight in the Midi. They make two oak-aged *cuvées*, the Cuvée Sélection, from equal parts of Carignan, Syrah, Grenache Noir and Mourvèdre that are blended before *élevage*, and La Gloire de Mon Père, of which the first vintage was 1995. Here the final *assemblage* is done after *élevage* and the percentages vary considerably from year to year, depending on the characteristics of the vintage. In contrast, Donnadieu Cuvée Camille is kept in *foudres* rather than *fûts*, and has some soft, ripe fruit. The 1995 Gloire de Mon Père was dry and cedary, while the 1991 Cuvée

Spéciale, drunk when it was eight years old, showed the ageing potential of St Chinian, with elegant fruit and harmonious tannins combined with the warmth of the Midi.

CHATEAU LA DOURNIE, ST CHINIAN

Véronique Etienne is the seventh generation of her family at Château la Dournie since it was bought in 1850. The property is on the edge of St Chinian, next to Clos Bagatelle, and has a château dating from 1850 and an attractive park with an infinite variety of mature trees of great stature. Etienne is a friendly, efficient young woman who explained how her father had inherited the property in a run-down condition from his great-aunts and how much her parents had invested in it since 1960. It was her mother who made the wine. 'Now it is our mission to enhance the reputation of the estate, especially as France is finally beginning to recognise that the Languedoc is a valid viticultural region.' Etienne has ninety hectares in production around the château, from which she makes two red St Chinian, a *rosé* and some varietal *vin de pays*, Chardonnay, Merlot and Cabernet Sauvignon, for only half her land is in the appellation.

We tasted in what was once the cowshed, now attractively whitewashed but retaining the old stalls. The *rosé* was fresh and fruity. The Cuvée Tradition, from Syrah, Grenache Noir and Carignan, spends twelve months in vat, resulting in some spicy fruit, while the Cuvée Bois is given nine months of *élevage* in barrel. The blend is the same as for the Cuvée Tradition – sixty per cent Syrah, twenty-five per cent Grenache Noir and fifteen per cent Carignan in 1996 – but a choice of the best vats. There was a successful combination of fruit, spice and oak.

CHATEAU VIRANEL, CESSENON

Gérard Bergasse of Château Viranel at Cessenon is a cheerful, articulate man full of enthusiasm and ideas, so that we were inevitably late for the following appointment. First we were given the history of the estate. The origins were Gallo-Roman; then it belonged to the church, then to a lawyer, and was bought by his family in 1550. His great-grandfather Fabien Bergasse developed the vineyards at the end of the nineteenth century. Before that, poly-culture was the order of the day, with two mills, one for wheat and one for oil, and the estate producing a bit of everything. The present château was built at the beginning of the twentieth century, and has a splendid bacchic frieze with bunches of grapes galore. We went to a viewpoint above the vineyards, where his great-grandfather had erected a cross and buried two bottles of wine, one of white and one of red Grenache. We looked over the river Vernazobre towards the village of Cessenon. The soil here is very red, a mixture of clay and limestone very rich in iron. Bergasse has about forty hectares, half in the appellation and half in *vin de pays*. His cellar is functional and very typical of the spacious cellars of the Midi.

We talked and tasted. *Rosé* is a speciality here. 'Each time you buy my *rosé*, the red will be even better', for the juice of Grenache Noir and Syrah is run off, making for a more concentrated red wine, and some Cinsaut added afterwards. It was ripe, with fresh fruit and a long finish, especially for a *rosé*. A Grenache Blanc was rounded, leafy and lightly honeyed, with a dry finish. There are two qualities of red wine: Viranel Tradition which does include some oak-aged wine, though quite how much 'depends on my mood', and the Cuvée Fût, which he has made since 1992, all of which spends several months in oak. For Bergasse, the characteristic of Viranel is a certain supple silkiness, and that you certainly find in the 1997 Viranel Tradition with its smooth fruit. The 1993, a good year, had an elegant flavour of the herbs of the *garrigue*, while the 1989, which would have been made with a higher proportion of Carignan using a continuous press, and would have been kept in *foudres*, had a light, cedary palate and dry warmth, demonstrating the ageing potential of the wine. For Bergasse, Grenache Noir forms an important part of the typicity of St Chinian, providing suppleness, warmth and generosity.

We finished with the Cuvée Gabriel, named after a grandfather. It is pure Alicante Bouschet, a Vin de Pays de Cessenon, an intriguing combination of animal notes and *garrigue*, with some cinnamon and a solid, sweetish finish. Last of all came a pure Grenache Noir, from grapes picked on 7 November 1998 at a potential 23°. Bergasse obtained just eight hectolitres from one hectare. The leaves were removed so that the wind dried the grapes, and a group of

friends helped to pick them. As for vinifying them, *'Quel bordel!'*
They tried to press them in a small basket press but there was
virtually no juice. What there was Bergasse fermented for six weeks.
He was worried about volatile acidity, but it turned out all right in
the end, a combination of sweet fruit and tannin, not unlike a ruby
port – another of the many examples of the unexpected with which
the Midi abounds.

BORIE LA VITARELE, CAUSSES-ET-VEYRAN

As well as the long-established family properties, there are several
new estates in St Chinian. Some have been created by outsiders from
other regions, while others like Michel Gleizes were already in
existence but took their vines to a local co-operative. Cathy Planes
and Jean-François Izarn at Borie la Vitarèle made their first wine in
1990. His father was a chef and he loves cooking too, ruefully
admitting that wine making is much more demanding. Currently
Izarn has seven hectares of vines in a valley lost in the middle of
nowhere near the village of Causses-et-Veyran, but he ultimately
envisages about ten or twelve hectares. The valley bottom is
classified in Vin de Pays des Coteaux de Murviel, while his St
Chinian vineyards are on the slopes, dominated by red cliffs. He
only makes reds, aiming for wines with an intense concentration,
not unlike the man himself. Each grape variety is vinified separately,
destalked and given a thirty or forty-day *cuvaison*, with regular
pigeages, fifteen minutes every morning, and a five-minute
remontage every evening, followed by a twelve month *élevage*
in wood on the fine lees. Izarn has tried several different coopers
and has now settled on second-hand barrels from Saury in Brive.
He does not want new wood as it masks the character of the
wine.

We tasted our way around the cellar, with various barrel samples
from the rich 1998 vintage. Izarn picks his grapes as ripe as
possible, for he is seeking what he calls the *côté chaleureuse*, the
warmth, as well as the body of the Midi, with a combination of
concentration and finesse. Trévallon in the Coteaux des Baux and
Rayas in Châteauneuf-du-Pape are his inspiration. There is a St
Chinian based on Syrah, a Coteaux du Languedoc with more
Grenache Noir than Syrah, and two *vins de pays*, a pure Merlot that

is not barrel-aged and a blend of Cabernet with some Merlot and Syrah.

1997 is a lighter, fruitier vintage than 1998. The 1997 Coteaux du Languedoc had some supple cherry fruit with a warm finish, while the Coteaux de Murviel, la Combe, was quite solid, with ripe blackcurrant fruit, soft tannins and a warm finish. Finally, the 1997 St Chinian, registering a hefty 14.5° even in this lighter year, was an intense mouthful of spice and liquorice. Over dinner, while Izarn demonstrated his culinary skills, we drank some older vintages. A 1994 St Chinian was solid and concentrated, and a 1991 St Chinian from almost pure Syrah was firm and structured, while the 1995 la Combe showed youthful cassis fruit and a 1993 Coteaux du Languedoc some warm, peppery characteristics. The flavours were intense, but for my taste buds the high alcohol levels masked some of the finesse of the wine. The sky turned a deep azure colour, the outline of the hills provided a dramatic silhouette and our conversation was almost drowned by the raucous frogs in the nearby river.

DOMAINE DU SACRE COEUR, ASSIGNAN

Marc Cabaret from Domaine du Sacré Coeur came to wine after a mid-life career change. He explained how he had owned super-markets in Bordeaux and then in the Hautes-Alpes. At the age of forty-five he decided that he had had enough, so he sold his business and looked for a vineyard. It took him four months of exploring the Midi. He arrived in St Chinian at sunset one evening and was enchanted by the scenery. With the help of SAFER he came across two elderly men who were selling their vines because neither had an heir. One had been a co-operative member and the other had had a small cellar. Both said that they would help the newcomer, but in fact one married for the first time at the age of sixty and went off to enjoy urban life in Béziers, and sadly the other missed his vines so much that he committed suicide. So Cabaret was left to his own devices. But God was with him, for he found an oenologist, Jean Natolie, an associate of Marc Dubernet of whom many people speak highly. Cabaret laughs about his inexperience. He had bought thirty hectares of vines, made up of seventy-eight different plots. He only had the cadastral plan to tell him which were his vines, and on two occasions he picked his neighbours' grapes. His great stroke of luck was winning a gold medal with his first vintage.

Rural France tends to view outsiders with suspicion and Cabaret admits that it was difficult at the beginning. He was even accused of buying his medal. However, once they see you working in your vineyard in inclement weather, they begin to realise that you are one of them. They made him president of the appellation a year or so ago, so he is now fully accepted. He still admits to being an apprentice *vigneron*, but he does not regret it for a moment. It is fabulous, so much better than selling tins of peas. And you sense that he really cares about his appellation. He is a stocky, forthright man with a good sense of humour and sound ideas, and he is desperately keen to improve the reputation of St Chinian so that people can earn a decent living from their vines. He feels that some of the wine growers, in their commercial inexperience, expect too much from the local *négociants*, but that nevertheless the wine is worth much more than the current bulk price of 600 FF per hectolitre.

And his wines are good. The light 1997 is a blend of one-third each of Grenache Noir, Syrah and Carignan, making an easy-drinking mouthful of soft berry fruit. More serious is Cuvée Kevin, named after his youngest son, who was born in 1993. It is the same blend, half of which is aged in barrel and half in vat, with some firm, smoky fruit and a certain concentration, with well-integrated oak. Cabaret is a fervent defender of Carignan. 'We are not here to make pure Syrah. It is Carignan that provides our typicity.' His 1998 includes as much as forty per cent Carignan in the Cuvée Tradition. He has recently added two hectares of St Jean-de-Minervois to his estate.

MAS CHAMPART, BRAMEFAN

Matthieu and Isabelle Champart are also outsiders. He was a farmer in the Aube and she is Parisian. They came to St Chinian on holiday in 1976 and simply stayed, creating the sixteen-hectare estate of Mas Champart. First we went for a drive through the vineyards, with dramatic views of red cliffs and grey rocks contrasting with the dark green shrubs of the *garrigue*. Amid the bushes there was a *capitelle*, or stone hut, that provided shelter for shepherds taking their flocks from the plain up into the hills of the Cévennes for the summer months. They also have olive trees and some fields for wheat. Their vineyards are planted with the usual five red varieties of the Midi, including some fifty-year-old Carignan vines. As for white varieties, they have Viognier, Grenache Blanc, Roussanne and Bourboulenc. They found it difficult to define the typicity of St Chinian, as there is such a multitude of different *terroirs*. Limestone is the main characteristic of their vineyards, making for firm tannins, quite high acidity and a certain freshness of flavour. Indeed, St Chinian is not a homogeneous area in that there can be as much as three weeks difference in ripening times between Berlou in the north and Assignan in the west.

Their first vintage for white wine was 1996. In 1998 Viognier made up about half the blend and half of the wine was fermented in new *demi-muids*. Roussanne and Viognier ripen together and so are fermented together, as are Grenache Blanc and Bourboulenc. The wine undergoes a malolactic fermentation and on the palate it is Viognier that dominates. The *rosé* is delicate and fresh, a blend of Cinsaut, Syrah and Mourvèdre. They make two red wines, the Tradition aged in vat and the Cuvée Causse du Bousquet aged in wood. The 1997 Tradition, from Syrah, Grenache Noir and Carignan, had some lovely ripe fruit, with a certain backbone. For the 1997 vintage a proportion of Causse du Bousquet spent seven months in barrel and another part fourteen months in *demi-muids*. This was more structured, with more obvious oak, but well integrated in a harmonious palate. The Mourvèdre gives what they described as *la petite côté austere*. In 1996 they had less new wood but the wine seemed more tannic, with a firm palate. In 1995 they used only old barrels and the wine developed beautifully in the glass, with substance combined with elegance. Isabelle and Marc Champart are a friendly, modest couple, a little self-effacing but with hidden depths, rather like their wines.

DOMAINE CANET-VALETTE, CESSENON

Marc Valette at Domaine Canet-Valette provides a sharp contrast of character and style. He is an opinionated, intense man in his late thirties who has just spent a considerable sum building a state of the art cellar, quite unlike anything else you will find in St Chinian. It is well conceived, with stainless steel galore, including broad vats for *pigeage* that are emptied by gravity into cement vats below, and with the barrel cellar below ground. His first vintage was as recently as 1992. His grandfather had been a wine grower in the Minervois, and he himself discovered wine in the 1980s, to the extent of becoming passionate, if not obsessed, about it. He now has eighteen hectares in one block outside the village of Cessenon. At the very beginning he took his grapes to the co-operative. He bought his first barrels in 1995 and he now has 600, 400 and 300-litre barrels, mostly second-hand, as well as some conical fifty-hectolitre wooden vats. You find variations in the wine originating from the different sizes and also from the barrels themselves. He particularly likes *demi-muids* as they respect the product. 'We get ripe grapes here, so we do not need new wood.' Valette has also tried *microbullage*, but did not like it, considering that it masked the fruit and dried out the wine.

We tasted wines from vat. Essentially he makes two different *cuvées*: the Tradition, from Mourvèdre, Carignan, Cinsaut and a little Grenache Noir, and the Cuvée Maghani, which apparently recalls a festival from the *Rubáiyát of Omar Khayyám* and is a blend of more or less equal parts of Syrah and Grenache Noir. The 1997 was ready for bottling. It had been blended the previous week and was neither fined nor racked. It had an intense, concentrated nose, with solid berry fruit, very ripe with firm tannins. Unlike most growers, Valette considers 1997 to be a better vintage than 1998. His vines are in a particularly drought-prone site and in 1998 it was too dry, so that he had problems in obtaining ripe grapes. For this reason he does not like Mourvèdre much and finds that it does not express itself well. He wants wines that will age with a lot of body and concentration. For him, the typicity of St Chinian is its warmth and power, but it is hard to define, as there are so many different *terroirs* as well as blends of different grape varieties. He picks his grapes when they are almost overripe, so that his 1998s had great concentration, to the extent of being almost port-like. A Syrah Grenache Noir blend, given a one hundred-day *cuvaison* and extensive *pigeages*, was rich, with acidity and tannin. A proportion of his Syrah and Grenache Noir goes into wood immediately after fermentation and he usually gives his wines eighteen months of *élevage*.

DOMAINE MOULINIER, ST CHINIAN

Pascal Moulinier is another young enthusiast. His grandparents were agricultural labourers in St Chinian. One grandfather had a hectare and a half and the other had seven hectares, but you cannot live off that. His father worked in the civil service in Paris for fifteen years and returned to the south in the early 1980s, since when the family vineyards have been developed to cover twenty-one hectares. Most of it is virgin vineyard land, limestone, schist and sandstone, from which they have cleared all the trees and shrubs. Now they are building a brand-new cellar in the middle of the vines. We saw the building site, in a sea of brilliant red soil. Syrah comprises half their vineyards and they are planting more, looking at less productive Syrah clones. Mourvèdre is interesting too in cooler vintages like 1996 and 1997.

From 1980 to 1988 the family took their grapes to the co-operative. Then for four years their wine was made at another estate. 1992 was their first vintage in their own small cellar, and for the first couple of years they made wine for early drinking. In 1994 they tried out *élevage* in barrel for one vat and this led them to buy more barrels, cooling equipment and a destemmer. Moulinier feels that it is too early to say what is typical of St Chinian. Things have been turned completely upside down. You cannot say that Syrah is typical, for it has only been here for fifteen years, and the same could be said of Carignan – there was none here a hundred years ago. We compared a couple of barrel samples of Syrah grown in different *terroirs*. On schist the perfume is immediately appealing, with supple, ripe fruit, while on limestone there is more acidity, which initially masks the tannins. The wine from limestone seems to absorb more wood than that from schist.

They make various different *cuvées* of red wine. The Tradition, mainly from Syrah with Grenache Noir and Mourvèdre, grown on schist as well as limestone, is perfumed with some immediately appealing fruit, ripe berries and tannin. Cuvée des Sigillaires, usually a blend of Syrah and Grenache Noir, although in 1997 they included Mourvèdre, is more structured from a longer maceration and *élevage* in wood. It was smoky, with ripe fruit and soft tannins. The 1996, with no oak ageing, was less harmonious, while the first vintage of this *cuvée*, the 1995, had rounded berry fruit from the ripe Grenache Noir. Finally, there is Les Terrasses Grillées, a pure

Syrah, which may be blended with a little Mourvèdre in a cooler vintage, such as 1996. It is given a six-week *cuvaison* and then barrel aged for twelve to fourteen months, including a malolactic fermentation in barrel, with *bâtonnage* of the fine lees. 1994 was the first vintage of this *cuvée*, a blend of schist and limestone, that Moulinier referred to as *le big bang*, for it was their first long *cuvaison* and first *élevage* in wood. It was ripe and solid, densely packed with flavour and having length but not elegance.

CHATEAU MILHAU-LACUGUE, PUISSERGUIER

We tracked down Jean Lacugue up a dirt track in what seemed to be the middle of nowhere near the village of Puisserguier. You drive over the plateau of Casedarnes, near the ruined abbey of Fontcaude. The clay soil is bright red. Red poppies, with scented honeysuckle and yellow broom, lined the road and a hare ran across our path. Jean Lacugue's father bought Château Milhau-Lacugue some thirty years ago. There had been a Roman villa here, and in the Middle Ages the property had associations with the Knights of St John of Jerusalem and also with the nearby abbey of Fontcaude. It was on the Malcarèse road, one of the routes used by pilgrims going to Santiago de Compostela. A family from Béziers bought the property after the Revolution. Their main activity was distillation and the large cellars are dated 1875. Lacugue's parents believed in quality and realised that they needed vineyards in the hills, not on the plains. Lacugue studied oenology at Montpellier and now makes the wine.

We were treated to a comprehensive tasting. His white Coteaux du Languedoc is an unusual blend of Grenache Blanc and Chenin Blanc, planted in 1980 for experimental purposes. It provides a note of vivacity, but is quite neutral in a young wine, developing more flavour as it ages. He also makes a pure Chenin Blanc as a Vin de Pays des Coteaux de Fontcaude, which covers the six *communes* around the abbey; in other words, the southern clay and limestone part of St Chinian. The wine is fermented in barrels, both new and old, and given regular *bâtonnage*. The flavour was quite intriguing, with hints of honey and apricots as the Chenin Blanc begins to develop. There is also a red *vin de pays* from Cabernet Franc and Merlot, and he is experimenting with Pinot Noir. The 1996 Pinot

Noir spent two years in wood and had some sweet fruit on the palate, but the wood still dominated the flavour. How would it age, I wondered?

Lacugue's St Chinian *rosé* is a blend of Grenache Noir, Syrah and Cinsaut, with full-bodied, ripe fruit. There are three red St Chinian. The Cuvée Tradition, which he calls the Cuvée des Chevaliers, is made from Syrah and Grenache Noir, with eighteen months in vat and *foudres*. It had the wonderful spicy notes of the *garrigue*. The Réserve du Commandeur comes from Syrah and Grenache Noir, with twelve months barrel ageing giving some firm fruit and a background of well-integrated oak. Lacugue wants wines that will age twenty years from now. Finally, La Truffière, also from Syrah and Grenache Noir, and given three years *élevage*, including two in barrel, was firm and structured as a barrel sample. The 1994, the first vintage of La Truffière, which is only made in the best years, showed ageing potential, a wine with broad shoulders that was warm and smoky. We finished our tasting with the 1990 Réserve du Commandeur, with its rich, warm, spicy aroma. It was still very youthful when it was nine years old, with the scent of the *garrigue*. Lacugue observed that Paris was not built in a day. 'We have everything to learn, beginning with the vineyards. In ten years' time we will have mature vines.' With wine growers like this, who have a firm sense of commitment, the future for St Chinian looks good.

Key facts

AC in its own right 1982, then a *cru* of the Coteaux du Languedoc; red and pink, with white to come; 2700 hectares in twenty *communes* around the town of St Chinian.

The usual grape varieties of the Languedoc.

12° minimum.

Schist to the north and west of the Vernazobre river, clay and limestone to the south.

Vintages

1999: Irregular climatic conditions, but the best growers have done well, with fine Syrah.

1998: Drought and low yields have made for very concentrated wines for ageing.

1997: Rain in August and a dry sunny September gave good results.

1996: Storms in August; low yields for Syrah and Grenache Noir, giving some aromatic, fruity wines.

1995: Frosts in April and a dry summer made for some concentrated wines.

Faugères

The appellation of Faugères was created in 1982, three years before that of the Coteaux du Languedoc, and was subsequently incorporated into that appellation. It is now seen as one of the *crus* of the appellation, covering seven villages that lie between the valley of the river Orb and the plain of Béziers, in the foothills of the mountains of the Espinouse, an outpost of the Massif Central. The small, sleepy village of Faugères gives its name to the appellation. There is little here to divert the traveller. More spectacular is the countryside. Narrow lanes wind from hamlet to hamlet. There is a viewpoint that provides a breathtaking panorama over the vineyards by the ruined remains of three towers. Their origins are Roman and in the sixteenth century they were turned into wind-mills. Today they are in the process of restoration and provide an emblem for the appellation.

Apart from vines, little will grow here on the poor soil, which is schist. There is a growing number of olive trees, demonstrating a revival of interest in a crop that was virtually destroyed after the hard winter of 1956, and there are a few grazing animals; the village name of Cabrerolles indicates the former importance of goats in the region. For the moment, though, vines remain the sole agricultural activity of any importance. and there is no doubt that Faugères is a flourishing appellation.

There are thirty-five producers altogether, including the three co-operatives of Faugères, Laurens and Autignac, four producers who do not bottle any wine at all and three estates, namely Alquier, Vidal and Ollier-Taillefer, that have been putting wine in bottle for over twenty-five years. A third of the producers are under the age of thirty-five, which is significant, as the Languedoc has tended to suffer from the stagnation of old age and the consequent reluctance

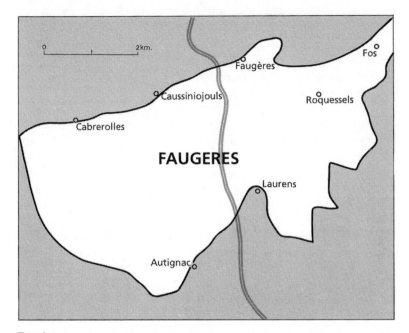

Faugères

to innovate. Currently there are about two thousand hectares in production, with a much larger area, 5500 hectares, delimited, but most of that land is covered with *garrigue*. Probably three thousand hectares would be the maximum feasible area. The advantage of such a compact appellation is that everyone knows everyone else and there is a lively exchange of ideas.

The soil of the vineyard of Faugères is the same schist as in the adjoining vineyards of St Chinian, with vineyards at an altitude of between one hundred and fifty and four hundred metres. The grape varieties are those found throughout the Languedoc, with the *cépages améliorateurs* representing fifty per cent of the appellation. Carignan has declined in importance, but still accounts for about a third of the vineyards. For the moment Faugères is firmly red, with a little *rosé*, but there are moves afoot to create a white wine, with plantings of Marsanne, Roussanne, Grenache Blanc and Rolle. Marsanne is proving particularly successful, and Viognier and Muscat are also possible contenders for inclusion in the appellation – but for the time being, any white wine remains a Coteaux du Languedoc or a *vin de pays*. As always, the INAO is taking its time to make a decision, but as Françoise Ollier, the cheerful secretary of the *syndicat*, optimistically put it, 'We remain very hopeful.'

The development of *lutte raisonée*, or sustained viticulture, is one of the current preoccupations of the growers' *syndicat*. There are three weather stations in the appellation, at Faugères, Lenthéric and outside Laurens, that advise the growers, helping them to eliminate some unnecessary treatments. There are no actual organic growers in the appellation, but a general commitment to use natural products in the vineyards. One or two people, although agreeing with the principles of sustained viticulture, nonetheless consider its promotion to be a marketing ploy.

DOMAINE ALQUIER, FAUGERES

The family that has done most to create the name of Faugères, and which has also contributed significantly to the growing reputation of the whole of the Languedoc, is the Alquiers. In the mid-1980s the estate was run by Gilbert Alquier, who died in 1989, and now it is his two sons, Jean-Michel and Frédéric, who continue to follow their father's ideals. I found Jean-Michel Alquier at his cellars behind an ivy-covered facade on the outskirts of the village of Faugères. The date 1874 on the house marks the beginning of the estate. Just after the war Gilbert's father was the first to plant Grenache in the area, and he himself pioneered Syrah in the 1960s.

The two brothers each own thirteen hectares of vines, and Jean-Michel Alquier makes the wine for both of them. First he took me to see the vineyards. There was an intoxicating scent of thyme and other herbs in the spring sunshine, and you could see just how stony the soil is. There is some hundred-year-old Carignan, some fifty-year-old Grenache Noir and some Mourvèdre that was planted in the 1970s. Most of the vines are trained on wires in the *cordon royat* method, although *gobelet* is better for the Grenache Noir. The topsoil is shallow and the roots of the vines find their way through the cracks in the friable schist. As for white vines, Viognier was planted in 1988 and Jean-Michel also has some Marsanne and Grenache Blanc, while his brother has Roussanne as well as Marsanne. The vineyards are separated by dry stone walls, and patches of woodland protect the vines from the wind. In one vineyard an old *capitelle* still remains intact.

We talked as we tasted around the attractive barrel cellar. Jean-Michel has learned from his father, without any formal studies. He is a friendly man, with his father's understated charm. For him, wine making is a question of following your nose, *un travail de pif*. He does not want to produce the super-structured wines that are currently the fashion of the Midi. Faugères can be quite hard at the beginning, and if you macerate your wine for some time, you need something to give elegance and roundedness. Barrels are the answer. Jean-Michel's father was one of the first to introduce *barriques* to the appellation in the early 1980s, and he is now considering six hundred-litre *demi-muids*. His aim is a *vin de garde*, for that is how you judge an appellation, by its keeping potential.

His first real vintage for white wine was 1995. Alquier admits to being inspired by white Hermitage. Viognier, Marsanne and Grenache Blanc are fermented in barrel and kept in wood for twelve months. The result is wonderfully complex, with layers of flavour, length and a richness in the mouth. As for red wines, there are three different qualities: a basic wine, if any wine from Alquier can be considered basic; Maison Jaune, evoking the sunshine of the south, for wines that are barrel aged, including fifteen per cent new wood; and finally Les Bastides, from one particular five-hectare vineyard, which is also aged in oak, with thirty-five per cent new wood. I tasted the 1996s in the spring of 1998. The basic Faugères is a blend of Syrah, Grenache Noir, Carignan and Mourvèdre, with young, spicy fruit, hints of black cherries and a firm structure on the palate. Maison Jaune, from Grenache Noir, Syrah and a little Mourvèdre, each vinified separately and aged in wood for twelve months, also had notes of black cherries, with ripe fruit. This was not an easy vintage, as it rained in the middle of September, although fortunately the Mistral dried the grapes, adding extra concentration. The same wine in new wood was tighter and tougher, with more vanilla. The two will be blended before bottling. The 1996 Les Bastides had more concentration, while the 1992, from an unusually wet vintage that required what Jean-Michel called *extra cuisine dans la cave* – in other words, a very strict selection and a long *cuvaison* to extract the maximum flavour and body – was rounded and complete, with a harmonious elegance and length, but not much weight.

We finished with a sweet wine, a 1995 from ninety per cent Viognier and ten per cent Marsanne. The grapes were picked at the end of November, when they were fully botrytised, and the wine was fermented and kept in barrel for two years, resulting in a splendid concentration of honey and oak. That year the autumn was a perfect combination of humidity and sunshine, whereas for his first attempt in 1994 the grapes had insufficient botrytis, and in 1996 they were *passerillés* but not botrytised – that, for Jean-Michel, is not so good, as it means that the wine will not age, as it does not have the roasted character of noble rot.

CHATEAU LA LIQUIERE, LA LIQUIERE

Château la Liquière was another of the original pace-setters in Faugères. On this visit I met Sophie Vidal, whose grandparents created the estate. The château itself no longer exists, but they built their house over its old cellars. Their son Bernard was the first to vinify Faugères by carbonic maceration back in 1967, guided by Jean-Henri Dubernet, one of the people responsible for the development of this technique in the Midi. They now have a total of sixty hectares of vineyards, lying at an altitude of about three hundred metres. The red schist is packed with iron, and there is also a grey-blue schist that is not so stony. Some of the oldest vines are trained *en eschalas*, like a *gobelet* but with a supporting post, and a newer vineyard is planted along the hillside in small terraces, instead of in rows following the downhill slopes. They have practised sustained viticulture for the last five or so years, using only organic products.

The Vidal family are pioneering white Faugères and have planted Roussanne, Viognier, Muscat, Grenache Blanc and Terret Blanc, not all of which are yet in production. Their 1997 Coteaux du Languedoc, Cuvée Schistes, from Grenache Blanc, was vinified in wood and aged for about five months. The oak was well integrated, with some weight and body in the mouth. The label shows a profile of the soil in a photograph by Bernard Vidal. He remains responsible for the vineyard, while his daughter, a qualified oenologist, is now the wine maker. They make three different reds. Cuvée les Amandiers, from equal parts of Grenache Noir, Carignan, Mourvèdre and Syrah, is soft and smoky, with some attractive spiciness. The Grenache Noir and Carignan are fermented by carbonic maceration, necessitating not only hand picking but also a sorting table to eliminate any unsuitable grapes. The Cuvée Vieilles Vignes, with a high proportion of Grenache Noir and Carignan and just a little Syrah and Mourvèdre, is rounded and warm with some tannin, fulfilling their aim of a wine that is both elegant and easy to drink. Cuvée Cistus is barrel aged. Their first *élevage* in wood was for the 1988 vintage, while the first vintage of Cuvée Cistus was 1992. The base is Syrah, with some Carignan, Grenache Noir and Mourvèdre, which are given twelve months of oak ageing. They do not want a single variety to dominate the palate, which was rich and concentrated, with oaky undertones. They too are trying late harvest wines with the 1997 Bouquet d'Automne, which has a photograph of a fennel head in the sunset on the label. It is a blend of Grenache Blanc with a little Muscat, fermented to leave 40 gm/l residual sugar, so that it is not too heavy, with a herbal nose and some delicate honey. For the future they see more barrel ageing, more white wine and more vinification of separate vineyard plots. It all promises well.

DOMAINE OLLIER-TAILLEFER, FOS

Alain Ollier of Domaine Ollier-Taillefer is a friendly older man with a small cellar in the pretty illage of Fos, which has a restored château and just eighty-five inhabitants. He is the fifth generation here. He remembered that, when the vineyards of Faugères were first delimited in 1948, they were planted mainly with Carignan and just a little Cinsaut. The VDQS came in 1955, and now he has Grenache Noir, first planted in 1968, Syrah planted two years later and some Mourvèdre added in the 1980s. His remaining Carignan is at least fifty years old. He began working on white wine about ten years ago, planting Rolle, Roussanne, Grenache Blanc and Viognier, and has gradually increased the family property from ten hectares in the 1960s to a total of twenty-five hectares today. He worked with horses until the first tractors arrived in the 1960s, and until a couple of years ago he still had his hundred-year-old *foudres*. In the neat little *caveau* where we tasted, there were old photographs of earlier vintages. His grandfather used to take a barrel of wine to Béziers, thirty-five kilometres away, every Friday morning for the weekly market. Ollier did his first bottling in 1975 and now sells nearly all his production in bottle.

His white wine, a Coteaux du Languedoc called Cuvée Allegro, with forty per cent Rolle, twenty-five per cent Roussanne to provide aroma, thirty per cent Grenache Noir for body and just a drop of Viognier, had delicate fresh fruit. For the moment it is unoaked.

There are three red wines. A Cuvée Tradition, from forty per cent Carignan vinified by carbonic maceration and forty per cent Grenache Noir and some Syrah that undergo a traditional vinification, spends eight months in vat, making for some light smoky fruit. The Cuvée Réserve, with equal parts of Mourvèdre and Syrah, twenty per cent Grenache Noir and just ten per cent Carignan, has a long *cuvaison* and spends three years in vat. Ollier finds that the Mourvèdre ripens well, provided it is grown in deep soil, in *schistes profondes*, and is pruned tightly for a maximum of 25–30 hl/ha. The wine has the dry *garrigue* fruit that is typical of Faugères, what Ollier described as an aftertaste of gun flint, or *pierre à fusil*, with good ageing potential. In the 1980s Ollier only made the Cuvée Tradition, but then began working on longer *cuvaisons*, for more tannic and longer-lasting wines. He first used *barriques* in 1994 and now produces an oaked Cuvée Castel

Fossibus, which spends twelve months in wood. In an old vaulted cellar he has also tried *demi-muids*, which he likes, as the wine ages more slowly. The blend is the same as for the Cuvée Réserve, with the oak rounding out the tannins. It was well made, but less individual in style. Asked about the typicity of Faugères, Ollier replied: 'Each grower makes his own little soup!'

CLOS FANTINE, AUTIGNAC

The number of independent producers in Faugères has grown in the last few years, sometimes the result of a change of generation leading to the withdrawal of vineyards from the co-operative. Oliver Andrieu at Clos Fantine is one such example. His grandfather joined the co-operative in Autignac when it was founded in 1938, but Andrieu, fresh from his oenology studies, felt frustrated. There was really no opportunity to participate, so he found a cellar to rent, an old sheepfold carved out of the schist, and bought a press and some vats. His first vintage in 1996 was sold mainly to the *négoce*, but in 1997 he bottled two different wines. The first was a blend of forty per cent Mourvèdre, thirty per cent Carignan and some Grenache Noir and Syrah, given some *élevage* in concrete vats. He would like to try *barriques* when he has more space. Mourvèdre is difficult, but you must not get too worked up about it, and you should certainly not overfeed it. The wine was ripe and rounded, with good structure and some smoky fruit. His *haute de gamme*, called Courtiol after the vineyard, which is planted mainly with Syrah and some Grenache Noir, had warm red fruit and some liquorice notes, with understated hints of the *garrigue*. It was impressive for a maiden vintage.

DOMAINE ST ANTOINE, LA LIQUIERE

Frédéric Albaret at Domaine St Antoine is a complete newcomer. His parents were townsfolk, but he studied agriculture and oenology, and came to Faugères because you could still find vineyards for sale there in the early 1990s. His first vintage was 1995. He is a youngish man with forthright opinions. He has the usual five red varieties in his vineyards, and wants to make a good red first before he moves on to white. His tiny fermentation cellar in the village of la Liquière is very compact, with stainless vats and some concrete ones under our feet. He has a separate barrel cellar, for he is very interested in the problems of *élevage* and began by buying lots of new wood. He is searching to find the right combination of wood and fruit, as well as the balance between new and old wood. Syrah is good in *barriques*, whereas Mourvèdre does better in larger wood, such as the *demi-muids* of Bandol.

The Cuvée Magnoux, named after the *lieu-dit*, is a blend of Mourvèdre and Syrah with just ten per cent of Carignan, and spends twelve months in wood. The flavour was still dominated by vanilla, but that will diminish with some bottle age. It is all a question of balance, and people must be encouraged to age the wine. The Cuvée Tradition, from fifty per cent Grenache Noir with Cinsaut, Carignan and a little Syrah, is destalked and given about a month's *cuvaison*. Albaret does not like carbonic maceration, as it has a reductive effect and gives you only primary flavours. This wine was firm and peppery, with a good balance of tannin and a long finish. It is intended to be a more accessible wine than the Cuvée Magnoux. For Albaret, the typicity of Faugères is its finesse and fruit, with a certain originality coming from the schist. He likes wines that are blends of grape varieties, for a single variety is limiting. A good wine grower is always questioning his own achievements, with a constant search for the best.

CHATEAU LIGNIERES, FAUGERES

Elke Kreutzfeldt at Château Lignières is a welcoming German who came to Faugères because her daughter married a wine grower's son from Béziers. This represented a career change, as she had previously worked in insurance and property in Paris. She and her husband spent two years searching before finally buying this run-down property from the SAFER in 1993. They have fifteen hectares with more to plant, and plans for renovating the cellar to allow space for *élevage* in wood, for after making their first oaked wine in 1997, she sees *barriques* as the future. Her 1997 spent eight months in wood and for the 1998 she was planning fourteen months. Her Faugères Classique, given a thirty-five days' post-fermentation maceration, was firm and structured, with a dry, tarry nose and palate. The Cuvée Romy, after her granddaughter, is a blend of sixty per cent Syrah with equal parts Grenache Noir and Mourvèdre. The oak was well integrated, and I detected thyme on the nose, with more herbs of the *garrigue* on the palate.

DOMAINE BARRAL, LENTHERIC

Didier Barral is another young grower who withdrew the family vines from the co-operative; in this case the one at Laurens that his father had joined thirty years previously. The co-operative was very understanding, but his father thought he was making a big mistake He is an intense young man, very opinionated, with an engaging smile when he does smile. You are aware of a great sense of commitment; this is someone who questions everything he does. He is very critical of *lutte raisonnée* or sustained viticulture, seeing it as a way of giving the wine a commercial tag. 'It is like saying that you drive a car reasonably. Of course you should think about what you are putting on your vines.' He wants to recreate his grand-father's vineyard as it was before the arrival of chemicals, so he uses natural fertiliser, adding as an aside that Napoleon apparently forbade the use of chicken manure in vineyards as it was too rich.

Barral has a large, functional cellar with an old-fashioned basket press, which does a great job but is difficult to clean and cannot be moved. He criticises modern technology for masking the authenticity of the terroir. Syrah is easy and fashionable. You use cultured yeast and some lightly toasted oak and you have what he calls 'academic wines'. He favours a very simple vinification. Everything is hand picked and carefully sorted. *Triage* is the moment that determines your work for the whole year, for it can make or break the wine. You can do a long maceration with confidence if you know that there are no bad flavours in your grapes. If the grapes are really ripe he might leave the stalks, as they will be ripe too, while in other years he may destalk a proportion of the crop. He avoids cultured yeast and favours a long *cuvaison*, with *pigeages* and *remontages*. He dislikes carbonic maceration, as it explodes the fruit and there is nothing behind it. Carignan can be very good in Faugères without carbonic maceration, for if you treat all the different varieties properly in the vineyard, there is no reason why you should not get something good from each of them in the cellar.

We tasted our way around barrels and vats. Barral makes a *rosé* and two reds, giving both two years of ageing in vat or barrel. Cuvée Jadis always spends two years in wood and sometimes longer, for barrels provide the best expression of the wine, making for more complex flavours. If Mourvèdre is particularly good, as in 1993, 1994, 1996 and 1998, Barral will make a separate *cuvée*, called Valinère after a stream below the village, blending it with a little Syrah. The barrel samples of the 1998 vintage were particularly convincing, with well-integrated oak that did not mask the fruit, combining elegance with body. For Didier Barral, there is no doubt that the future lies in more *barriques*.

CHATEAU DES ADOUZES, ROQUESSELS

The village of Roquessels is dominated by the remains of a medieval castle. Here Jean-Claude Estève at Château des Adouzes began gradually removing his parents' vines from the co-operative in the mid-1980s, so that his first vintage was 1986. He was lucky that he had his grandfather's original cellar, but people criticised him as though he were committing treason. Such are the machinations of village politics. He now has forty hectares of vines, but as yet no white varieties, only the usual five reds. He makes two *rosés*, Domaine Estève from Cinsaut and Grenache Noir, and Château des Adouzes from Syrah and Grenache Noir. Then there are various red wines. Domaine Estève, mainly from Syrah and Carignan, is given a traditional *élevage* in vat and had perfumed fruit and soft tannins. Château des Adouzes Tradition, from Syrah and old Carignan vines, was rounded, with hints of the *garrigue*. Estève first began planting Syrah twenty years ago and Mourvèdre in 1990. In 1998, when he had a very small crop and consequently more vat space, he tried out some long macerations of thirty to thirty-five days. Château des Adouzes *vieilli en fut* is the same blend as the Tradition and is given twelve months barrel ageing. Since 1996 Estève has carried out the malolactic fermentation in wood, which he finds gives more harmonious results, and he is also experimenting with American oak, but without any positive conclusions as yet. The 1995 oak-aged Château des Adouzes was elegant, with a smoky flavour and unobtrusive oak, while the 1996 Cuvée de l'An 2000, with a higher proportion of Syrah and more new oak, was a touch more international in flavour.

CHATEAU DES PEYREGRANDES, ROQUESSELS

Marie-Geneviève Boudal is a pretty, *petite* blonde and Jean-Claude Estève's cousin. Her father, Pierre Benazech, died in 1995, but she wanted to keep the family vineyards, even though her husband is an architect in the Tarn and she had been working as an interior designer. Benazech had been the founding president of the co-operative of Faugères, but left in order to begin bottling his own wine while Faugères was still a VDQS. In recent years the estate has been a little neglected, but now Boudal wants to make her mark.

Unlike her father, she uses carbonic maceration for Carignan, destalks the other varieties and has introduced *élevage* in wood. She has also changed the name of the property to the Château des Peyregrandes. Her first vintage was 1996. The Cuvée Prestige is a blend of Syrah and Carignan, both aged in wood, with quite marked vanilla characteristics. I preferred the second *cuvée*, which had much less oak and was elegant and spicy, fulfilling Boudal's quest for suppleness and fruit.

DOMAINE DU METEORE, CABREROLLES

Domaine du Météore does indeed take its name from a meteor crater outside Cabrerolles, a village dominated by its ruined castle. The crater is a gaping hole in the earth's surface some sixty metres deep and two hundred metres in circumference, with seventy ares of vines at the bottom. The tasting room at Domaine du Météore also houses a mini-museum devoted to meteors, which are apparently more common than I had naïvely realised. Geneviève Libes-Costes and her husband are the third generation of the family to run the vineyard. Her husband's grandfather was an electrician with some vines, and the next generation developed the vineyards so that there are now twenty hectares from which they make a varied range of wines.

They have recently planted white varieties, Roussanne, Marsanne and Viognier, and also, like everyone else, more Syrah. Their first vintage of white Coteaux du Languedoc was 1995. First they had made a *vin de pays* from traditional varieties such as Terret Blanc, Carignan Blanc and Grenache Blanc, but then they discovered the white wines of the Rhône valley. It is too dry for Chardonnay here and they like the idea of a blend. I liked the wine, which was half Marsanne, half Roussanne, partly vinified in wood and partly in vat. It had intriguing nutty flavours, with good body and some solid fruit. They tried *bâtonnage* on the Roussanne but felt it gave too strong an aroma. Mme Libes-Costes said, 'We are novices,' but the wine was far from amateur. They also produce Viognier as a *vin de pays*, but hope that a small percentage of Viognier will eventually be included in the appellation. Part is fermented in barrel and the wine had the perfume of Viognier, but for the moment it lacked weight as the vines are too young.

They make two qualities of red wine. The Tradition, from equal parts of Grenache Noir, Syrah Mourvèdre and Carignan, is given a classic vinification with a ten to fifteen-day maceration and a short *élevage* in vat. The 1995 had some attractive peppery fruit, while the 1994 was spicier, with more animal notes. They first began using barrels for the 1993 vintage, trying out six or seven coopers with different degrees of toasting, and they are considering *demi-muids*. 'We are open to everything. We are looking.' You really feel that this is an estate searching for the best. The barrel-aged Réserve is a blend of Mourvèdre and Syrah. The 1994 was in the spring of 1997 solid and meaty, a substantial mouthful of flavour with tannin and oak in the background. Mourvèdre does well, especially now that the vines are a little older. This is a wine that needs bottle age, which prompted a discussion of the financial difficulties of keeping wine, and also the problems involved in building up a stock of older vintages. In 1993 a considerable part of the vineyards of Faugères suffered from hail, resulting in a crop of thirty thousand hectolitres rather than the usual seventy thousand and consequently a lack of wine to meet demand.

CHATEAU CHENAIE, CASSINIOJOULS

There have been Chaberts in the little village of Cassiniojouls for three hundred years. Eric Chabert at Château Chenaie is an intense young man who is utterly committed to the family vineyards. His father André made wine until he took the comfortable option of joining the co-operative. It was not difficult to withdraw, which Eric did for the 1994 vintage. He has had no formal training, but was eager to see the results from his own vineyards, rather than losing his grapes in a communal vat. He was reticent when I asked him about his vinification methods: '*C'est ma cuisine, ça*; I do what I like, I don't copy anyone.' And the inference was that he did not want anyone copying him. The work in the vineyard is all-important. 'You grow good grapes and you can make good wine. You need a lot of little extras to get away from the run of the mill.' His grapes are given lots of care and attention. 'We cosset them.' There is a strict green harvest in the middle of August. He picks by hand and is meticulous in sorting the grapes.

For the moment he has three different cellars scattered around the village. We tasted in the old cellar of the château, with its vaulted ceiling and archaic press. First there was a white wine, a pure Roussanne fermented in oak and given plenty of *bâtonnage*, resulting in layers of flavour and fruit. Chabert makes three red wines. The Cuvée Tradition is from Grenache Noir, Carignan and Syrah, with a drop of Mourvèdre and Cinsaut. There is no wood, just some wonderful ripe fruit and the herbs of the *garrigue* coming out in the Carignan. Cuvée les Douves – a *douve* being the stave of a barrel – is essentially Syrah, with Grenache Noir and Mourvèdre and just a hint of Carignan, of which a proportion is aged in wood. It was quite solid, with a certain presence of oak. However, the charm of the schist of Faugères is that it makes for wines that both age well and drink well when they are young. Finally there is a Cuvée Mourvèdre; that is to say, about ninety per cent of Mourvèdre with just a little Syrah, all aged in barrel. I tasted the 1996, which had ripe vanilla and supple tannins. Mourvèdre is difficult in both cellar and vineyard, for it is fragile and capricious, but with plenty of care gives fine results. This is an estate to follow.

CHATEAU DE GREZAN, LAURENS

The Château de Grézan is an extraordinary building. At first glance you might be forgiven for believing it to be a medieval château with its crenellated battlements, but then you look more closely. It was in fact built towards the end of the nineteenth century, during the wealthy period of the Languedoc when fortunes were made from agriculture, not just wine but also wheat and olives. The *nouveaux-riches* of Béziers built houses like this to show their material success, often choosing the Bordeaux architect Garosse, whose firm still exists. Essentially you picked your château from a book of architectural designs.

There was originally a Roman villa on the site, and in the Middle Ages a commandery of the Knights Templar that depended upon the nearby Château de Laurens. The current owners, the Lubac family, have been here for twenty-odd years, and since 1989 have been in association with other partners. Altogether they have a hundred and twenty hectares of vines, eighty within the appellation of Faugères while the rest produce Vin de Pays des Coteaux de Laurens, with Pinot Noir, Gamay, Chardonnay, Cabernet Sauvignon, Syrah and Merlot, and intriguingly some Pinot Meunier also.

As for Faugères, they make three quite distinctive wines. A basic wine mainly from Grenache Noir, with Syrah and Cinsaut, was quite solid, but just a touch jammy. They practise a technique called *vinomacération*, which entails heating the grapes with some of last year's wine in a closed vat to a temperature of about 35–40°C for about an hour. This has the effect of heating the grape skins to extract colour, richness and structure. The Cuvée Arnaud Lubac is a blend of Grenache Noir, Syrah and Mourvèdre from vines that are twenty to thirty years old, and is given a year's *élevage* in barrel. This is a wine that will age, with the oak that dominated the palate in its youth fading after five or six years. Finally there is the Cuvée Vieilles Vignes, made from Syrah and Mourvèdre that are at least thirty years old and Grenache Noir that is over forty-five years old, and given two years of *élevage*. The 1992 vintage was very solid and concentrated, with vanilla oak and underlying fruit. I also tasted a buttery Chardonnay with some convincing flavours and well-integrated oak, and the light, raspberry flavoured Pinot Meunier. The elegant restaurant attached to the château offers an opportunity to drink these and other Faugères.

DOMAINE DES ESTANILLES, LENTHERIC

Michel Louison is an entertaining, extrovert character with a mop of silver hair, a beguiling smile, a lively mind and a fountain of ideas. When I visited him in the village of Lenthéric, I found him in the middle of a building site, the future Château des Estanilles. We went to look at the vineyards accompanied by two energetic fox terriers, Margaux and her son Pétrus. There is one particularly steep vineyard, Le Clos du Fou, which overlooks the village. 'The madman, that's me, for that is what people called me when I planted vines here.' In the bank at the top you can see the different-coloured schists. Brown is better than grey, and there are numerous fossils, for originally the sea was here. Louison has four different Syrah clones, with six thousand vines to the hectare, in two main plots, Estagnolles and Fontanilles – from which comes Estanilles, the name of the estate. Altogether there are thirty-four hectares, seven of which belong to his daughter Sophie, who is fresh from her oenology studies.

Louison arrived here in the mid-1970s. He comes originally from Touraine and had been an electrician. He still retains the questioning attitude of an outsider. The INAO in particular is the subject of his scathing tongue. 'They prevent us from making progress. There is an enormous potential for white wine here and yet they will not allow Viognier in the appellation.' He would also have liked Petit Manseng, for it provides some useful acidity, but it was deemed to be unacceptable as it comes from outside the region. Chenin Blanc has also been tried, but the summer heat makes for flavours that are too heavy. Not so long ago Louison had said that in 2000 the best Faugères would be white, but now he has given up the struggle and is content to make a very enjoyable Coteaux du Languedoc, from mainly Marsanne and Roussanne, with some barrel ageing and *élevage* on the lees.

Louison is also very enthusiastic about Syrah, but again does not conform to appellation regulations, for the INAO insists on some Grenache Noir too in the blend. He makes three different reds. A Cuvée Tradition is the most classic, with Mourvèdre, Syrah and Grenache Noir and just a little Cinsaut and Carignan. It had a dry, spicy nose, with some firm, smoky fruit. There is no carbonic maceration here, but a twenty-day *cuvaison*. The Cuvée Prestige has more Syrah but no Cinsaut, and half of it is kept in wood for a year. The 1997 had some well-integrated oak, with firm fruit and a good backbone. For the 1998 he was going to include some barrel-aged Cinsaut from old vines, which was beautifully perfumed and spicy. Finally there is a Cuvée Syrah, with a theoretical drop of Grenache Noir. I tasted the 1996, of which one-third had been in new wood.

In the spring of 1999 it was still quite oaky and structured, and rather leathery in flavour. Louison said it was not tasting well, adding as an aside that Syrah can be temperamental, like women. Our tasting finished with an intriguing Mourvèdre *rosé*, again with a theoretical drop of Grenache Noir, that had been fermented and then aged in wood for twelve months, in fact treated just like a white wine, with *élevage* on the lees and regular *bâtonnage*. Mourvèdre does not oxidise, so the flavour was rich without being oaky and quite intriguing. Louison first made this in 1988. He recounted how the American critic Robert Parker gave it ninety out of a hundred and the fax machine was violently sick.

CAVE COOPERATIVE DE FAUGERES

The co-operative of Faugères is working hard for its appellation, even if members are leaving it to set up on their own. It was created in 1970, and that is when the cellars were built. They are working on *sélection parcellaire*, examining the condition of the vines and grapes of each plot. As recently as ten years ago there was very little Syrah or Mourvèdre, but the planting of Syrah has been encouraged, with this shift in emphasis dramatically reducing the amount of Carignan. Nevertheless, for reasons of *encépagement* – they may not have the varieties in their vineyards – only half of their hundred and fifty members produce Faugères, so they also make *vins de pays*, both Coteaux de Laurens and Hérault. White wine is the subject of some experimentation, with plantings of Roussanne, Marsanne, and a little Viognier, Grenache Blanc and Bourboulenc.

There are six levels of red wine, with a Cuvée Spéciale from a selection of better vineyards as well as various individual properties, such as Mas Olivier, Château Caussiniojouls and Domaine Coudougno. *Barriques* were first used in about 1992, and they also have some *demi-muids*, but no longer any traditional *foudres*. The wines I tasted seemed quite oaky in style, but showed a definite improvement on those of some ten years earlier. The winemaker, Luc Salvestre, is a serious young man who studied at Montpellier. This is his first position and there is time for him to make his mark.

CAVE COOPERATIVE DE LAURENS

The co-operative of Laurens has an eye-catching shop on the main road that does good business, while the cellar is in the village itself. Frédéric Galibert, the youngish director, is an enthusiastic exponent of his appellation, which he explained over an extensive tasting. For him the individuality of his co-operative comes from the use of carbonic maceration for about a third of the wines, but never for Grenache Noir as the skins are too thin and split too easily. Asked about typicity, his answer was the schist. It is very poor soil with a high acidity level, which limits the yields and makes for supple tannins. However, if the wine is too acid, the tannins are accentuated.

Like many other co-operatives, that of Laurens is now working to much stricter quality criteria. There can be as much as FF 150 per hectolitre difference in price for good and bad grapes, and the worst are declassified into *vin de table*. Laurens is apparently the strictest of the three co-operatives in the appellation, and it is not unknown for grapes refused there to be accepted elsewhere. They would also like to improve the hand picking. This is a big battle, as it is essential for carbonic maceration.

They also have a sizeable barrel-ageing facility and altogether make about thirty different *cuvées*, usually depending upon individual properties. The Cuvée Trois Tours, after the three windmills outside the village of Faugères, is a successful expression of the *terroir*, from sixty per cent Syrah and equal parts Mourvèdre and Carignan, with solid, ripe fruit and soft tannins. Château St Roch de Laurens includes some wine that has been aged in barrel for twelve months and is much more international in style, with vanilla and oak. The basic Cuvée Tradition, with fifty per cent Carignan and some Syrah and Grenache Noir, had firm liquorice fruit. Château du Fouzilhon is a Coteaux du Languedoc from an adjoining village, but not part of Faugères, as its mayor did not support the creation of the appellation of Faugères. The price difference between the two appellations is at least FF 100 per hectolitre, FF 600 for Faugères and FF 500 for Coteaux du Languedoc. They tried American oak in Domaine de Moncèze and found that the wine absorbs the oak very quickly and that the vanilla flavour was very obvious. And from there I left the hillsides of *garrigue* behind and headed for Picpoul de Pinet on the coast.

Key facts

AC in its own right 1982, then a *cru* of Coteaux du Languedoc; red and a little pink, with white to come shortly; two thousand hectares in seven villages; thirty-five producers, including three co-operatives.

Grape varieties:

RED AND PINK: the usual five.

WHITE: this is currently Coteaux du Languedoc, but Marsanne, Roussanne, Grenache Blanc and Rolle are the main contenders for the white wine AC when it comes.

Vineyards on schist, lying at 150–400 metres.

Vintages

1999: No stress from drought; some rain in August and September resulted in a little rot, but the wines are rounded, fruity and attractive. Comparable to 1997.

1998: A dry year with summer drought and high temperatures. Very concentrated wines.

1997: Fruity, elegant wines with quite high yields, the result of quite a rainy year, but with a warm, dry September.

1996: Accessible, fruity wines, not for keeping.

1995: Concentrated and balanced wines coming from a small yield.

Picpoul de Pinet

Quite the best introduction to Picpoul de Pinet is to be found at the restaurant La Côte Bleue outside Bouzigues, on the Bassin de Thau. Bouzigues is known for its oysters, and from the restaurant dining room you can look out over a broad expanse of oyster beds, eating molluscs that were in the water an hour or two earlier and sipping delicate Picpoul de Pinet, and all seems right with the world. It is a perfect combination, the refreshing acidity of the wine simply complementing an oyster like a squeeze of lemon.

The *cru* of Picpoul de Pinet forms a rather surprising oasis of white wine in a sea of predominantly red Coteaux du Languedoc. Its official position is in a state of transition. It became a VDQS in 1954 and was subsequently incorporated in the appellation of the Coteaux du Languedoc, as the one white *terroir* of the appellation. Now it wants to stand alone as an independent appellation, without the mention of Coteaux du Languedoc on the label. The relevant dossier has been lodged with INAO and in the spring of 1999 the optimists were hoping that things would be in place for the following vintage – but bureaucracy could not move that fast and at the time of writing they are still awaiting a response.

Picpoul is the grape variety and it is grown in a small area centred on the village of Pinet. Five other villages are included in the appellation, namely Florensac, Pomérols, Castelnau-de-Guers, Mèze and Montagnac, all lying between the attractive town of Pézenas and the Bassin de Thau. The *terroir* explains the reason for this oasis of white wine. Quite simply the soil is too generous for red wine. It is mainly limestone, which suits white wine, with some clay, some sand and, appropriately, a scattering of fossilised oysters, and the vineyards are on what the French call *costières*, which are neither plains or hills, lying at an altitude of about fifty metres. They once formed the old seashore. The climate is very much influenced by the sea, so that the nights are cooler during the hot summer months and the vines benefit from the maritime breezes.

This was an area that produced flabby white wines for the vermouth trade, but that market has long since disappeared, bringing instead a much-needed improvement in the quality of the wines. However, the region had a certain historical reputation. A seventeenth-century agronomist cited it as one of the best *crus* of the Languedoc, and under Louis XVI the wine growers had their own distinctive mark for branding their barrels. In the middle of the nineteenth century the Duc de Morny, Napoleon III's minister of the interior, is reputed to have said of Picpoul de Pinet that this was the wine that reconciled him to the republicans of the Hérault.

Although about two thousand hectares are delimited for the appellation, only 830 hectares are currently planted with Picpoul, but this is steadily increasing as demand for the wine grows. When it was a VDQS, other varieties apart from Picpoul could be used, but the creation of the appellation Coteaux du Languedoc in 1985 demanded Picpoul alone. Now the other white varieties, such as the traditional Terret Bouret, or Terret Blanc, and Grenache Blanc, as well as more recent introductions such as Chardonnay and Sauvignon, Marsanne and Roussanne, are destined either for *vin de pays* – Oc or Côtes de Thau – or for white Coteaux du Languedoc. Within the appellation area the tendency is to plant Picpoul, while any red varieties produce *vin de pays* rather than Coteaux du Languedoc.

CAVE DE PINET

Each village has its co-operative, and there are also about sixteen independent producers. My first visit was to the Cave de Pinet. It was founded in 1923, making it one of the oldest co-operatives of the Hérault. At that time all the production went to Noilly Prat in Marseillan, who appreciated the oxidised colour of the wine. You have a very good view of the topography of the appellation from the co-operative roof, looking towards the sea and the Mont Ste Claire outside Sète. The appellation is in two parts, with plains towards the Bassin de Thau and tiny hills and little valleys running down towards the sea. The motorway crosses the vineyards, following the route of the old Roman road.

The co-operative in Pinet has undergone an extensive investment programme, equipping it with everything necessary for efficient white wine production, including facilities for skin contact to give extra flavour. They make two principal cuvées: Carte Noire, which is fresh and delicate, with good acidity to complement the local seafood, and Duc de Morny, which is a selection of the best wine of the vintage, but not necessarily from the same vineyard each year. Since 1994 they have worked with *barriques*, initially for Picpoul de Pinet, but now for a Coteaux du Languedoc, Domaine de la Rose, made from fifty per cent Picpoul, with forty per cent Grenache Blanc and ten per cent Roussanne. The wine spends five or six months in wood, one third of which is new, with regular *bâtonnage*. It was difficult to find the right balance of old and new wood, and to my taste buds the oak still overwhelmed the wine. However, it is not meant for ageing, as Picpoul can oxidise and evolves quickly, while the other varieties add structure and body.

Two local curiosities are Fine de Picpoul de Pinet, a grape spirit matured in 500-litre barrels, and Carthagène, made from the juice of Picpoul grapes blended with the Fine de Picpoul and aged for twelve months in old Cognac barrels. With some bottle age, it was full and biscuity, harmonious and long.

CAVE DE POMEROLS

There is a friendly rivalry between the co-operative in Pinet and the one in the village of Pomérols. They too have espoused all the latest vinification methods. They machine-pick in the early morning, starting at four a.m. and stopping before the heat of the day has set in, around ten a.m., taking great care to avoid oxidation. The Picpoul grapes are divided into three categories; the best go into a special *cuvée* and the worst are rejected. They have a pneumatic press and practise skin contact for some of their Picpoul de Pinet in order to extract extra flavour from this somewhat delicate grape variety. One of the problems of Picpoul is its lack of staying power. It is not a wine to age, and at one time would hardly survive the heat of the summer. One solution is to keep the wine on the fine lees with a regular *bâtonnage*, which helps add concentration and body.

The normal *cuvée* is delicate and flinty, with an underlying mineral character, while the best *cuvée*, under the Hugues de Beauvignac label, a purely fictional character who is supposed to be a Cathar knight, spends ten months in *barriques*, one-third of which are new. They have been working with wood since the 1989 vintage and seem quite proficient, in that the oak in the 1997 vintage did not unduly mask the flavour of the wine. It was present, but not in an aggressive way, and the wine retained some lemony acidity, but with more body than the unoaked wine.

They also produce *vins de pays*, for which they prefer to use the more specific regional identity of Côtes de Thau rather than the all-embracing Vin de Pays d'Oc. Chardonnay and Sauvignon form a substantial part of their production, and there are Merlot and Cabernet Sauvignon too. The Sauvignon was the most convincing, with understated varietal fruit. As we tasted, the director, M. Foucret, talked of the commercial difficulties attached to Picpoul de Pinet. Three or four years ago there was a problem of over-production, and the wine was hardly known outside the region. It is difficult for them to communicate their precise origins, as the very much better known Pomerol, although quite a different wine, apparently cramps their style. Promotional activity has helped a little to remedy that, but essentially Picpoul is known in the region, but not in France.

There have been problems with *négociants* selling the wine too cheaply. The *syndicat* attempts to fix the price each year at around FF 700 per hectolitre, and the cost per bottle should be around FF 15–20. Problems arise with *négociants* dropping the bottle price to FF 10. There is also some Picpoul planted in villages adjoining the appellation that is sold more cheaply, without the consumer realising that there is any difference, and so they would like to revert to the old spelling of Piquepoul in order to emphasise their precise origins.

DOMAINE DE LA GRANGETTE, CASTELNAU-DE-GUERS

Robert Mur's family came originally from Rioja, but they emigrated to France in 1916 after their vineyards were destroyed by phylloxera. In 1930 his father bought a share in Domaine de la

Grangette and in 1965 he was able to buy the rest of the property and settle here. Originally it was planted with nothing but Aramon. His father added Grenache Noir, Cinsaut and Picpoul, and he has continued the replanting, not just of Picpoul, but also more red varieties, Syrah, Merlot and Cabernet Sauvignon. The property has never been anything but organic. Mur simply refused to have anything to do with chemical treatments when they first appeared, and he is adamant that he wants to pass on healthy, living land to his children.

The buildings are grouped around an attractive courtyard, with a small barrel cellar as well as the original stone vats dating back to the eighteenth century. The tasting room is in the old stables, where Mur remembered feeding horses not so long ago. He talked of the history of the area. This is an old estate that once produced wheat and turned to monoculture at the beginning of the twentieth century. In the Middle Ages it was part of the Baronnie de Guers and it lay on three main routes. The old Roman road linking Spain and Italy ran close by; then there was the salt road, the Chemin du Sel, running from Marseillan into the Massif Central, for salt was sent inland for the curing of hams; and finally there was the fish road, the Chemin de la Poisonnerie, for the transport of fish from the port of Marseillan inland to Pézenas and the northern part of the Hérault.

There are now fifty hectares of vineyards, as well as another fifteen of woodland that help to protect the vines from pollution by the neighbours' use of non-organic treatments. Mur makes two styles of Picpoul de Pinet, an oaked and a non-oaked wine, and also a variety of *vin de pays*, which he prefers to call Oc rather than Côtes de Thau as it has a stronger identity on the export market. However, he would prefer the Vin de Pays d'Oc to place less emphasis on the grape variety and concentrate on the *terroir*. As for Picpoul de Pinet, he gives it eight to twelve hours of skin contact so that the acidity in the juice attacks the skins and liberates the aroma. The grapes are destalked to avoid any bitter herbaceous flavours from the stalks. The wine was delicate and subtle, with more body and less acidity than some Picpoul, and floral hints. Mur suggested hawthorn. The oaked *cuvée* was just that, and I remained unconvinced by the combination of Picpoul and wood. The charm of Picpoul de Pinet lies in its delicate mineral, lemony flavours that make it so compatible with an oyster.

DOMAINE DE ST MARTIN-DE-LA-GARRIGUE, MONTAGNAC

I first visited Domaine de St Martin-de-la-Garrigue, outside the village of Montagnac, when it was run for his family by François Henry, who produced a range of flavoursome *vins de pays*, either Vin de Pays de l'Hérault or Vin de Pays des Coteaux de Bessilles. The property is Roman in origin; St Martin was the name commonly used when a Roman site was converted to Christianity. There is a tiny chapel that was built in the ninth century, and archives refer to the priory of St Martin-de-la-Garrigue in 847. In the Middle Ages there was a fortified *bastide* and in the eighteenth century two wings were added to the central façade. François Henry's father had bought it in 1975, when the vineyards were planted with Carignan, Aramon and some Grenache Noir, as well as hybrid varieties that he described as worse than deplorable. Henry systematically replanted the vineyards, choosing Cabernet Sauvignon and Merlot as well as Syrah and Mourvèdre, and also Chardonnay. Then in 1990 family matters intervened and St Martin was sold, first briefly to a Parisian and then, in 1992, to the present owner Umberto Guida, the retired managing director of the supermarket group Promodès. François Henry departed to pastures new in St Georges d'Orques.

The estate is now run by the bright and competent Jean-Claude Zabalia, whose previous career includes similar positions in Corbières at Château Caraguilhes and Château Etang des Colombes. His first vintage here was 1993. There are now sixty hectares of vines. Zabalia explained that originally only twenty hectares were classified in the appellation and purely for Picpoul de Pinet, which had been of no interest to Henry. However, the INAO has been examining the parameters of the Coteaux du Languedoc, including the position of the village of Montagnac, and this provided the opportunity for the presentation of a very complete dossier asking for the extension of the appellation to include the vineyards of St Martin-de-la-Garrigue. The request was successful, and as a consequence from 1997 ninety per cent of the vineyards of the estate are classified within the appellation of the Coteaux du Languedoc. The vineyards include two main soil types, one a mixture of gravel and sandstone, the other limestone, which is suitable for Picpoul de Pinet. Meanwhile, there has been a considerable investment in both vineyard and cellar, with replanting and grafting of different varieties in the vineyard and an extension of the cellars with the installation of new stainless steel vats. It is a dramatic example of what can be achieved when money is no object. A barrel cellar is a project for the future, and a mobile bottling machine was hard at work in the courtyard.

They now produce nine different wines, both *vin de pays* and appellation, with various blends and *cuvées*. We tasted extensively both from vat and bottle. Zabalia is refreshingly frank about his wines. He wants to make wines that will age but does not like aggressive tannins, so he uses *barriques*, not for the wood effect, but for rounding out the wines, which must be ready to drink, although with ageing potential, when they are bottled. In a nutshell, he makes the sort of wines that he enjoys drinking himself: wines with fruit, body and ripeness, but not overripeness. The Blanc Tradition, from Terret Blanc, Grenache Blanc and Marsanne, is rather lemony and earthy, a rounded, slightly herbal, old-fashioned style of wine. Picpoul de Pinet is much more fragrant, with good acidity and honeyed notes. They have to do a lot of work in the vineyard, including two green harvests, as Picpoul is a very productive grape and they reduce the yield to 25–30 hl/ha. The grapes are picked when they are very ripe, almost *passerillés*. The Coteaux du Languedoc Blanc, Cuvée St Martin, is a blend of six grape varieties, Marsanne, Grenache Blanc, Picpoul, Terret Blanc, Roussanne and a drop of Viognier. Here the Picpoul provides the freshness, Marsanne and Roussanne the flavour and the low acidity, and Grenache Blanc the body. The Viognier and Roussanne are fermented in barrel and stay in wood on their lees for three or four months to give structure. The result is some elegantly perfumed fruit. Chardonnay is made in a very Burgundian way, with fermentation partly in new wood, some malolactic fermentation and lees stirring. The flavour is long and buttery.

The best red wine is the Cuvée Bronzinelle, a blend of Syrah and Carignan made by carbonic maceration with Mourvèdre and Grenache Noir vinified in the traditional way; it had ripe, spicy flavours and a firm backbone of tannin. Much less successful was the Cuvée Reserve, a Merlot/Cabernet blend, and Zalablia admitted that he would not have chosen to plant those two varieties, nor Chardonnay. The Cuvée Tradition, from Carignan and Syrah, was soft and supple, with some Midi spice. Most serious of all is a new addition to the repertoire, the Cuvée St Martin, from two parts Syrah to one part Mourvèdre, which are aged for several months in *barrique* after *assemblage*. The 1996 had an excellent concentration of flavour, with smoky blackberry and cherry fruit.

DOMAINE FELINES-JOURDAN, MEZE

Domaine Félines-Jourdan is on a dirt track outside the village of Mèze, with fine views of the Bassin de Thau. Claude Jourdan explained how their vineyards are in two parts, some by the *bassin* and the rest on hillier land near Montagnac, next to Domaine St Martin-de-la-Garrigue, where the soil is red and stony. The Picpoul does better there, whereas the land near the *bassin* is mainly clay and limestone and better for red wine. Her father's family were wine growers in Montagnac and her parents bought this property in 1983. Now her father does something quite different, while she makes the wine and her uncle takes care of the vineyards.

They too pick in the very early morning, between three and eight o'clock. Jourdan explained how they do not intentionally give the juice any skin contact, as but their cellar is an hour's drive away from their vineyards, they cannot avoid it altogether. They do favour some *élevage* on the lees, usually until February, and do everything possible to retain the aroma of these delicate grapes. The result is a fresh, lemony flavour, with a certain body and weight coming, so Jourdan said, from the *terroir*. I also enjoyed her Vin de Pays d'Oc, a blend of Syrah and Grenache, with a nose reminiscent of the scents of the *garrigue* and a full, spicy palate, making a much more original wine than a plain varietal Vin de Pays d'Oc. Even more intriguing was a late harvest Muscat, picked at a potential 16°, which was fermented and aged in wood for nine or ten months. It had an intriguing bitter orange taste, with firm finish. However, there is no doubt that the real vocation of the area is the delicate, smoky white wine that complements the shellfish from the neighbouring waters.

Key facts

VDQS 1954; now the sole white *cru* of the Coteaux du Languedoc, with aspirations to independence; six villages, including Pinet, around the Bassin de Thau; 830 hectares in production.

Picpoul is the sole grape variety, planted on limestone at fifty metres.

Pézenas and Cabrières

Cabrières is one of the original *terroirs* of the Coteaux du Languedoc. It first became a VDQS in 1954, was subsequently incorporated into the larger appellation in 1985 and now looks set to become part of the larger *terroir* of Pézenas. However, there is a strong feeling that Cabrières is quite individual and separate from the neighbouring villages. The village is surrounded by hills, giving it a very precise delimitation, and the vineyards are dominated by the Pic de Vissou, which rises to 480 metres.

The name Cabrières is associated with goats, deriving originally from the Latin *caper*. At the beginning of the twentieth century there were as many as three or four thousand sheep and goats in the village, which had about seven hundred inhabitants. Today the goats have all gone, for the last goatherd died in 1984, and there are about three hundred and fifty inhabitants. They have a school and a *mairie*, but no café, and viticulture is the main occupation. The co-operative of Cabrières accounts for eighty-five per cent of the production, and has ninety-three members cultivating about four hundred hectares. Of those, about thirty-five make their living from their vines alone, and there is also one private estate, Domaine du Temple.

The geology of the village is intriguing. There were copper mines here in the third millennium BC, which makes them the oldest in France, and the mining continued until the middle of the nineteenth century when it became too unproductive. The vineyards lie on the band of schist that runs from Berlou to Cabrières, including the whole of Faugères and the northern part of St Chinian. These are very old soils containing a host of marine fossils. The schist gives suppleness no matter how long a maceration you give the wine, making for soft, well-integrated tannins, with the aromatic character of red fruit and the Mediterranean scents of the *garrigue*. Sometimes the acidity can be a little low, but this is not usually a problem with Cabrières.

Cabrières has a historical reputation for its pink wine, going back to a reference of 1357 in the archives of Montpellier to the *vin vermeil* of Cabrières. The co-operative was founded in 1937 and until about 1950 they produced virtually nothing but *rosé* based on Cinsaut; today they are still allowed a higher proportion of Cinsaut than is usual in the Coteaux du Languedoc. The president of the co-operative, M. Trinquier, remembers *rosé* being sent in barrel to England in the early 1950s, and in the tasting room there is a bottle of Vin Vermeil from 1950. *Vermeil*, or vermilion, implies a deeper colour than light *rosé*, and indeed they have always obtained deep-coloured *rosés* here, making the perfect *vin de café*, which was the main vocation of the village.

In the last few years the emphasis has changed to producing a much higher proportion of red wine, sixty-five per cent as opposed to thirty-five per cent for *rosé*, with a little Clairette du Languedoc as well. All the vineyards of the village are classified as Coteaux or Clairette du Languedoc, so provided a producer has the appropriate grape varieties there is no reason why he or she cannot produce appellation wine.

CAVE DE CABRIERES

Facilities at the co-operative have improved enormously since my first visit in 1987. In fact, it has been given a complete face-lift. They first began using barrels for *élevage* in 1991 and now have an elegant barrel cellar visible from the smart tasting area. Usually there is a small exhibition – on one occasion consisting of some wonderful old photographs of the area – and there is also a small display about the copper mines with various fossils. In 1998 they bought two pneumatic presses and have found that these made an enormous difference in the quality of their white and *rosé* wines. They are working on their vineyards, encouraging their members to plant more Syrah and Clairette. There is very little Mourvèdre here, as Cabrières is a little too far from the sea and the soil is too dry.

You will find the co-operative's wines under two main brands. There is the more basic L'Estabel, named after a hot spring that appears every fifty years or so in a nearby hillside, the last occasion being as recently as 1996. Then there is the better Cuvée Fulcrand Cabanon, after the village priest who is said to have introduced the wine of Cabrières to Louis XIV. He was jokingly referred to as 'our first salesman' and Cabrières was apparently known at that period for its medicinal qualities – the 'French paradox' of the time, mused the president. Fulcrand Cabanon *rosé*, mainly from Cinsaut with some Syrah, is light and fresh, with ripe strawberry fruit, while the red is mainly Syrah with some Grenache Noir, redolent of the scents of the *garrigue* with some smoky fruit. A Cuvée Prestige without wood, from Grenache Noir and Syrah with some Mourvèdre, was soft and smoky, while oak ageing gave the same blend more structure and some peppery notes. Prieuré St Martin-des-Crozes, named after a tiny tenth-century Romanesque chapel in a nearby hamlet, spends time in old wood, while Château Cabrières is kept in new wood for a few months, with some structured vanilla fruit. The château itself was destroyed during the Wars of Religion.

DOMAINE DU TEMPLE

From the village I took a winding road into the hills to Domaine du Temple. The name recalls the estate's original associations with the Knights Templar in the thirteenth century and the red cross of the Templars appears on its labels. The previous owner withdrew his vines from the village co-operative in 1965 and planted Syrah and Mourvèdre, but did not make a great success of managing his property, with the result that it changed hands in 1990 and was bought by a group of four associates. I met Guy Mathieu, a young man who is responsible for the vinification, and M. Bilhac, who had worked on the estate for the previous owner. They have eighteen hectares, including the usual five red varieties of the south, and in 1997 planted some Viognier. The original cellar has been renovated and enlarged, and they have invested in barrels and cooling equipment.

We tasted in what had been the vaulted stable for the goats. I liked their wines. There was a simple, fruity *rosé*, Cuvée Tiveret, named after the ruined chapel of Ste Marie-de-Tiveret, while the red, from young vines, both Syrah and Mourvèdre, had the attractive smoky scents of the *garrigue*, with some rugged tannins, reminding you of the surrounding countryside. The Cuvée Jacques de Molay is named after the last grand master of the Templars, burnt at the stake by Philip the Handsome when the order was abolished in 1314. The *rosé* had an appealing herbal character, while the red was tannic and structured, again with some perfumed fruit. It comes from older vines, mainly Syrah with twenty per cent Mourvèdre. Château Tiveret is the same blend, but spends eight months in wood. Their oenologist Guy Bascou has encouraged them to work with oak, beginning with just six barrels. The Cuvée Baron de Nages, which recalls the last nobleman to own the property before the French Revolution, is mainly Grenache Noir with a little Cinsaut and Syrah. It had some ripe smoky fruit, with good structure.

They told me how difficult it had all been, for you need money and sweat to create what they have achieved and now they are beginning to see the light at the end of the tunnel. They have certainly come a long way in ten years.

CAVE DE NEFFIES

The village of Neffiès lies in the hills behind Cabrières. It is not part of Cabrières, but would be included in the *terroir* of Pézenas if and when that denomination is accepted. The co-operative is the main producer of the village and provides a good example of an organisation that is working well for its members. There has been viticulture here since Roman times, substantiated by various archaeological remains, including a head of Bacchus. The co-operative was founded in 1937, and now has 230 members with five hundred hectares over nine villages. There are a large number of retired members for whom their vines are a hobby; with the time to lavish lots of loving care, they have some wonderful old Carignan. About thirty of the members make a living from their vines, which it is possible to do with about fifteen hectares. The average age of these people is forty, which is relatively young for a co-operative membership.

Although eighty per cent of the vineyards come within the

appellation of Coteaux du Languedoc, not everyone has the right percentages and varieties, so out of an average production of thirty thousand hectolitres, the appellation accounts for only seven thousand hectolitres. Vin de Pays d'Oc, from varieties like Merlot, Cabernet Sauvignon and Chardonnay, makes up six or seven thousand hectolitres, and the rest is Vin de Pays de l'Hérault or basic *vin de table*. They feel that the potential of their vineyards is not fully exploited, and that they need to improve their viticulture through more work on plot and grape selection, all of which would enhance the reputation of the area. At the moment it seems that it is foreigners who appreciate the wines of the Languedoc, not the French. But things are improving and prices are becoming more realistic too, with an average price of FF 12.50 for a bottle of Languedoc in a supermarket. Previously the wines of the Languedoc 'were conspicuous by their absence'.

In the cellar they are well equipped for carbonic maceration and they make a serious range of wines. It was October, so we tasted the recently released *primeur*, which was still a little shell-shocked from bottling. Château Vailhan, Cuvée Castel Biel, mainly from Syrah grown on schist, was lightly perfumed. The Cuvée Prestige, Catherine de St Juéry, recalling the wife of the Seigneur of Neffiès in the seventeenth century, is pure Syrah, which in theory is not allowed. It was ripe and perfumed, redolent of blackcurrant gums, with good tannins. The Cuvée Arnaud de Neffiez, of which the first oak-aged vintage was 1995, spends twelve months in *barriques* and comes mainly from Syrah, with ten per cent Grenache Noir. The oak is ripe and sweet, but well integrated, with spicy fruit, cinnamon and cloves underneath. They are optimistic for the future.

DOMAINE DE FONTARECHE, NEFFIES

Domaine de Fontarèche, outside the village of Neffiès, was created by Bernard Belhasen. He has just five hectares of vines and has practised biodynamic viticulture for the last twenty years. He is an intriguing example of a change of direction, as he originally studied history of art, with the ambition of becoming a sculptor. Now he sculpts the land instead, savouring the pleasure of working with something that is living and influencing the countryside. For the last seventeen years he has worked with a horse rather than a tractor, and has a magnificent white mare whose name is Cassiopé, after the constellation. He described the immense satisfaction he obtains from working with a horse, for he dislikes noise and anything mechanical, and with biodynamics you are giving life back to the countryside and restoring the soil.

Belhasen produces just two wines. There is an intriguing white wine made from Terret Bourret; this was one of the traditional white wines of the south, although originally produced in vast quantity, with a careless vinification, for the vermouth trade. He obtains about 18 hl/ha from his infertile land, aiming for almost overripe grapes that have begun to turn to raisins, with a potential alcohol of 14°. The wine is fermented in barrels of three or four wines, with natural yeast of course, and given a regular *bâtonnage* over ten months. The colour is quite deep, with solid herbal fruit and a long, rich, subtle flavour. Unusually for a southern white, it does undergo a malolactic fermentation, and its substantial 14.2° is not apparent in the mouth. The red is a classic combination of Syrah, Grenache Noir and Carignan, part of which is aged in barrel for ten months and part in vat, before blending. The oak was well integrated, with fruit and body and an underlying elegance, making a harmonious whole. Belhasen deserves to do well. He is wholeheartedly committed to his principles, providing a lone voice in support of biodynamic viticulture in the Hérault.

PRIEURE DE ST JEAN-DE-BEBIAN

The Prieuré de St Jean-de-Bébian is an estate outside Pézenas that was originally a twelfth-century priory; sadly, the church is now in ruins, though not beyond hope of restoration. The reputation of the property was first established by Alain Roux, one of the more maverick and individual wine makers of the Midi. He arrived there in the mid-1970s with no experience of wine making, although his father was a *négociant*, and planted all thirteen varieties of Châteauneuf-du-Pape, as he was convinced that the soil was identical, having the same large stones as the southern Rhône. The fact that in the mixture of Grenache Noir, Mourvèdre, Syrah, Muscardin, Terret Noir, Vaccarèse, Counoise, Cinsaut, Clairette, Bourboulenc, Picpoul, Picardan and Roussanne there were several varieties that are not eligible for the appellation, was deemed to be of no importance. Who could tell, if the wine tasted good – and it did. I remember the 1985, which had a solid concentration of fruit and flavour that at the time was virtually unique to the Languedoc. Then Roux began to lose interest in his estate and 1991 was his last good vintage.

Meanwhile, Chantal Lecouty, who has had a varied career as a wine writer and editor of the *Révue du Vin de France*, was looking to buy a property in the Midi. St Jean-de-Bébian was her ideal, but at the time it was not for sale. She spent a year looking and eventually found an estate. The owner was an elderly gentleman. They shook hands on the sale, but with fateful timing, a week later, before any papers had been signed, he died. She then heard that St Jean-de-Bébian was on the market and she rang Roux. As she put it, he was at home, sober and even remembered who she was. She viewed the property at 11 a.m. and by 3 p.m. they were at the lawyers, with everything signed and sealed. She arrived at St Jean-de-Bébian in June 1994 with no practical experience of the physical process of wine making, only an enormous amount of theoretical knowledge from her journalistic career. Roux stayed to help her with her first vintage, and on the afternoon the last vat finished fermenting, he told her that her wine was a great success and that he was flying to Caracas that evening! He is now running the long-term car park at Los Angeles airport while planning to plant a vineyard in Oregon, and meanwhile he remains in regular contact.

Chantal Lecouty is bubbly and enthusiastic, self opinionated and confident. She cares passionately about her estate and has invested enormous energy and money in its renovation. The house has been completely transformed and is now charming in its cheerful southern colours, with a yellow ochre façade contrasting with pale blue shutters the colour of *bouille bordelaise*. The old sundial, with its motto Nihil Sine Sole, has been restored, and the courtyard has pots of flowers, as well as a mischievous puppy called Syrah who was found in the vineyard during the last vintage. Lecouty remembers Roux saying to her that the secret of good wine making is low yields and very ripe grapes and the rest is a load of rubbish. He had no oak barrels and, indeed, the wine making at St Jean-de-Bébian was very simple. Lecouty has introduced some changes, which have undoubtedly made the wine more refined. She destalks between a half and a quarter of her grapes, but not all, for it depends on how ripe the stalks are. Quite simply, if they taste good they will taste good in the wine. She also takes enormous care at the vintage, using small containers that will not crush the grapes and allowing only an hour to elapse between the fruit leaving the vine and arriving in the vat. She was also one of the first people in the Midi to buy *une table de tri*, or sorting table, for the visual elimination of any rotten or sub-standard grapes.

The most significant change she has made in the wine making is the introduction of oak barrels. She has two barrel *chais* in an attractive old barn and has experimented with woods of various origins. She has found Tronçais too violent, whereas Bertranges is better, and she prefers light toasting. Syrah needs *barriques* and new wood, while Grenache Noir is better with old wood and *demi-muids*. Mourvèdre needs longer ageing, while Grenache Noir is ready earlier. Where Roux fermented everything together, she treats each variety separately, so that the red wine consists of forty per cent of Grenache Noir, with twenty-five per cent each of Syrah and Mourvèdre, while the other ten varieties make up ten per cent. Lecouty has also planted some Grenache Blanc and Clairette to blend with Roussanne for the white wine, which is made in a Burgundian style with light *bâtonnage* and oak ageing.

The red wines are not filtered. The 1996 St Jean-de-Bébian was firm and tannic, with the menthol of the *garrigue*. It had some youthful fruitiness, but will close up for two or three years before beginning to develop the aroma of a mature wine. The 1995 was redolent of ripe blackberries, very concentrated, showing an intense combination of power and elegance, and quite like a Châteauneuf-du-Pape in character. Over lunch in the local brasserie we drank the 1996 Chapelle de St Jean, made from some younger vines, as well as Carignan and Cinsaut. It had some appealing rounded fruitiness, balanced by tannin, but not a trace of wood. Certainly this is an estate whose progress will be fascinating to observe.

DOMAINE DES AURELLES, CAUX

The first vintage of Domaine des Aurelles was as recent as 1995, and the two young partners, Karl Mauguin and Basile St Germain, are well on the way to establishing a serious reputation for their wines. They are also striking examples of outsiders coming to the area with fresh ideas. They met in Bordeaux while they were working for Latour and Haut-Brion. Mauguin trained at Talence and St Germain worked in Cognac, but they had the idea of doing something together. The most difficult thing was to find a suitable cellar, and for the moment the wine is made in a tiny cellar in the pretty village of Caux, but as most of their vineyards are in the nearby village of Nizas, they are hoping to build a new cellar there eventually. They have about fifteen hectares in five different plots on quaternary *villefranchien* terraces, with gravel and sand, and basaltic deposits of lava from the Massif Central. It is potentially fertile, but limited by the very dry conditions.

Mauguin explained that they had bought some vines in production that were planted in the traditional spacing of the Midi, at three to four thousand plants per hectare, but that they are now planting new vineyards at a density of six thousand plants. This means that each vine produces fewer grapes, making for better concentration and extract in the wine. The roots go down deeper instead of spreading nearer the surface of the soil and consequently are much better able to resist drought. With fewer vines in a vineyard, seventy per cent of the roots of the plant are likely to be in the top fifty centimetres of soil, which dries out in the summer; if there is no rain, the vine suffers from drought and the grapes stop ripening.

They make two different red wines, as opposed to their original idea of a first and second wine, in the manner of so many Bordeaux châteaux. Aurel is a blend of Grenache Noir, Syrah, Mourvèdre and a hint of Carignan, and is intended as a *vin de garde*, while Solen comes from Grenache Noir and Carignan with a little Syrah and is destined for earlier drinking. Vinification methods are meticulous. The grapes are picked into small boxes and they use an *égrappoir* but not a *fouloir*, so that whole berries go into the fermentation vats, which are broad rather than tall, and less *marc* is submerged in less juice, which makes *pigeage* easier. The maceration is relatively short, usually about fifteen days, but care is taken to extract everything from the berries; they add the *vin de presse* for volume and body. Usually there are about ten different batches, depending on aspect and climate, such as a Grenache Noir that ripened two weeks later than another.

Solen, named after the sunshine of the Midi, is dominated by fifty-year-old Carignan vines. The 1997 is refined and elegant, with subtle tannins and a certain cedary character, almost reminiscent of the south west. In contrast, the 1997 Aurel is more Mediterranean in character, with the spicy flavours of the south and the underlying elegance that is the hallmark of the estate. The wines are kept in vat rather than barrel before bottling. They did try an *élevage* in oak for their first vintage, using a couple of *barriques* from Domaine de Chevalier, but did not like it, particularly the idea of the Mediterranean varieties impregnated with the taste of Bordeaux. Nor do they want new wood. They also make a tiny, anecdotal quantity of white wine, Aurel Blanc, from one-third Clairette and two-thirds Roussanne, which in 1998 was fermented in new wood. It did not have the elegance of the red wines. And a Solen Blanc is planned, from Clairette, Terret Blanc and Ugni Blanc.

The attraction of the Midi is that it is a rare, if not unique, region where you can buy land at a reasonable price and expect a good return on your investment. The average price of a hectare of vines here, depending on their condition, is FF 70,000, compared to say FF 600,000 in Châteauneuf-du-Pape. It is a significant factor in encouraging newcomers to the region. I left with the impression that this was an estate to watch. Karl Mauguin is serious and thoughtful, utterly committed to his work and his wines are understated and elegant.

Key facts

Pézenas covers vineyards around the town, mainly on the hills to the north, with red, white and pink wines made from the usual grape varieties of the Coteaux du Languedoc.

Cabrières, a VDQS and one of the original *terroirs* of the Coteaux du Languedoc, is now likely to be incorporated into the *terroir* of Pézenas, but it has aspirations to maintain its own identity.

The original reputation of Cabrières rests on its *rosé*, which has a higher percentage of Cinsaut.

Production is dominated by the village co-operative.

The soil is schist.

Clairette du Languedoc

Clairette du Languedoc was one of the earliest appellations of the Languedoc, for it was created in 1948, but from then on it seems that the wine lost its direction and reputation. As Jean Renaud, the dynamic young director of the Cave d'Adissan, put it, the appellation decree was in fact the testament of the appellation. But things are now changing, particularly at Adissan. The appellation regulations stipulated that Clairette would be the sole grape variety, but failed to define the method of vinification, thereby allowing for enormous variations of style; the wine could be young and dry, old and maderised, sweet and even fortified.

CAVE D'ADISSAN

Jean Renaud is determined and energetic, and most important of all, he has a cause – to revive the tarnished reputation of his co-operative along with the faded fortunes of Clairette du Languedoc. His grandfather was the managing director of Les Salins du Midi at the time of creation of the brand Listel, and although his parents did not own any vineyards, he was brought up in a wine culture and studied oenology at Toulouse University. After military service he had a job lined up with Domaines Listel when this opportunity at Adissan presented itself. This was a challenge, for the co-operative was on the edge of the precipice of bankruptcy. He has succeeded in motivating his members, improving quality, eliminating the inferior wines, renovating the cellar and is now reviving the appellation of Clairette du Languedoc, experimenting with several different styles, sweet wine in barrel and an oxidised *rancio* as well as the classic dry white wine. 'There is nothing written about Clairette. You have to create everything yourself – but the problem is, which way do you go when you are in the middle of the desert? You are looking to revive the lost traditions, so you try something out and then ask the old people in the village to come and taste and tell you if you are on the right track or not.'

The co-operative at Adissan was founded in 1928, mainly to produce Clairette, which grew well here on the very poor, shallow, marl soil. They also had some Cinsaut and Terret Bourret, which are other drought-resistant varieties. Then, after the Second World War, at around the time of the creation of the appellation, most of the vineyards of Clairette were replaced by high-yielding Carignan. Now they are motivated by quality once again. Great efforts are being made to plant the right grape variety in the right place, with an analysis of the soil as well as assistance with loans to finance the replanting. The 180 members have six hundred hectares between them, of which 120 are Clairette. Not all is declared in the appellation, for Clairette, with its low acidity, can fulfil a useful blending role, lowering the acidity in other wines. It is also a question of market demand. In 1991 they bottled just 2,700 bottles of Clairette du Languedoc, but by 1998 that figure had risen to sixty-five thousand.

Renaud explained that the quality of Clairette depends on gentle handling, as it is not an easy variety to vinify well. They needed a very gentle *égrappoir*, which removes the stalks leaving both them and the grapes intact, and the harsh continuous press has been replaced by a pneumatic press. Skin contact is bad for Clairette, as it contains too many of the polyphenols that make for bitter flavours. The 1997 was quite golden in colour, with a full, honeyed nose and some soft, biscuity fruit on the palate and low acidity. The *moelleux*, from grapes picked three weeks later, was lightly honeyed and quite delicate and fresh, with some sweet fruit and 40 gm/l of residual sugar. At 12–45 gm/l a wine is classified as *moelleux* and even sweeter is *doux* or even *liquoreux*. Their first *moelleux* in 1992 was the first example of this style of wine for forty years.

Rancio wines also form part of the tradition of Clairette, so in 1991 they tried a *rancio sec*, which was bottled in the spring of 1998 after being kept in a half-empty vat rather than in barrel. The nose reminded me of the Vin Jaune of the Jura, which has a similarly firm, nutty, almost salty taste. *Rancio* is included in the appellation decree but must not be sold before it is three years old

– a necessary provision, for when *rancio* wine is young, it is quite disgusting. With age, however, the light amber colour deepens and the flavours become more supple as the acidity drops. The alcohol level must be at least 14°. Then in 1992 they experimented with a *rancio moelleux* by filling a barrel three-quarters full and leaving the wine to age gently. The wood seems to make the wine sweeter, with notes of *pain d'épice* and honey, as well as providing some structure. And in 1998 they tried out their first *moelleux* in barrel, which had just finished fermenting at the time of our visit in the spring of 1999. Renaud confessed his aim to make his co-operative one of the best producers of *moelleux* in the Midi within the next few years. I suspect he will succeed.

There is no doubt that Renaud is intensely ambitious for his co-operative and his appellation and he deserves to do well. You really sense that this is a co-operative that is going places. All the members of the *confrérie*, or wine brotherhood, of the appellation, are young, with an average age of thirty, which is rare for any appellation in the south. The emblem of the *confrérie* is the semi-circular copper tray traditionally placed at the foot of the vine to collect the very ripe berries for a *moelleux* wine. They hope to use them again for an even later harvest.

CAVE DE CABRIERES

The co-operative of Cabrières is also developing its vineyards of Clairette du Languedoc. As well as the dry wine, they have made a *vin de liqueur*, which is like a *vin doux naturel* in that some grape spirit is added so that about 40 gms/l of sugar remain and the wine is then kept in vat for two years. There was a hint of orange peel, with some rich, nutty fruit. They too have tried a Clairette *moelleux*, just a small amount for the local market. The grapes must be picked with a minimum potential alcohol of 13.5° so that you obtain 12°, with 1.5° remaining as sugar. Theirs was 12° plus 2° – in other words, a wine with about 40 gms/l sugar – but it was not as elegant as the wine from Adissan. A *moelleux* is not easy to do well, for Clairette is such a fragile variety that it is easily affected by rain, so that oxidation can set in.

Two other co-operatives in the villages of Aspiran and Paulhan also produce Clairette du Languedoc, but otherwise it is three independent producers who contribute to the quality of Clairette. Altogether the vineyards cover some three hundred hectares in ten villages between Pézenas and Clermont-Hérault, namely Le Bosc, Ceyrac, Fontès, Nizas, Pérat and St André-de-Sangonis, as well as the four co-operative villages.

DOMAINE DE CLOVALLON, BEDARIEUX

Catherine Roque of Domaine de Clovallon at Bédarieux has a small vineyard of Clairette du Languedoc, which exceptionally she is allowed to vinify outside the appellation. She explained that, of the various permutations of the appellation, *sec*, *moelleux*, *liquoreux* and *rancio*, it was *rancio* that tempted her. She tried it with two barrels, keeping them closed for the statutory three years without any topping up, and at the end one was quite dry while the other had 200 gms/l of residual sugar, so she blended the two together. The wine was the colour of amontillado sherry, with a nose of honeyed marmalade; it was wonderfully rich and unctuous on the palate, again with marmalade notes and a firm backbone. Her Clairette du Languedoc *sec*, given some *élevage* in wood, had some rounded fruit and a hint of bitter oranges, which, for Roque, is one of the characteristics of the grape variety.

DOMAINE CONDAMINE-BERTRAND, LEZIGNAN-LA-CEBE

The Jany family at Domaine Condamine-Bertrand outside the village of Lézignan-la-Cèbe have played their part in the fortunes of the young appellation. We sat and tasted at a heavy oak table in the salon, with its charming painted ceiling. Bertrand Jany talked of his grandfather's efforts for the appellation and of how his great-aunt had been secretary of the growers' *syndicat*. Originally Clairette had been used for vermouth, particularly Noilly Prat. When he took over the family property in 1980 he was the only independent producer of Clairette du Languedoc and the wine made by the co-operatives at the time was worse than indifferent.

His dry Clairette du Languedoc is given a simple vinification, chilled for *débourbage* and then fermented at a cool temperature.

The nose was delicate and the palate lightly honeyed, with a certain spicy character and, I thought, almost a hint of Muscat fruit, while Jany suggested that aniseed is one of the characteristics of Clairette. He too has tried a Clairette *moelleux*, for the first time in 1993, and he fermented it in wood for the first time in 1996. It spent a total of eight months in wood and had some ripe honeyed fruit, with hints of orange and oak, and quite an alcoholic finish. In 1998 the grapes for the *moelleux* were picked on 16 October and went partly into new oak, partly into one-year-old oak. Yields are tiny, about 22 hl/ha for the late harvested grapes, while the oldest Clairette vines only produce about 15 hl/ha, with a heady 16°–17°.

You cannot make a living from Clairette alone, so they make a variety of other wines as well. They have some Chenin Blanc, which was first planted when they believed that it might be included in the appellation Coteaux du Languedoc. Now they have Viognier as well. There is also Petit Verdot, which is usually blended with Cabernet Sauvignon for a Vin de Pays d'Oc. Although the Bordelais suggested that it would not ripen properly, Jany tried it and on the contrary finds that it does ripen well, providing good colour as well as softening and fleshing out the tannins of the Cabernet. Mourvèdre is particularly difficult, for the weather is either too dry or too wet, and therefore is simply not worth the trouble. His Coteaux du Languedoc is an appealing blend of Grenache Noir and Syrah, with some spicy fruit and a tannic backbone. The tasting area in the cellar has an intriguing collection of old machines and pieces of equipment, including an *échaudeuse* that produced steam for cleaning barrels.

CHATEAU ST ANDRE, PEZENAS

Jean-Louis Randon at Château St André outside Pézenas took us for a tour of his vineyards. You could see the Pic de Vissou in the distance, the extinct volcano of Céréssou and the valley of Hérault. He has about twelve different plots of Clairette making up about six hectares, mainly on the limestone soil that Clairette appreciates. Clay can be too heavy, making the vines too productive. Clairette is also quite an alcoholic variety and can ripen very quickly, gaining as much as half a degree in a day if the weather is very hot. Compared to other white varieties in the region, it is a late ripener and is not usually picked until the end of September. Some very old vines were planted in narrow rows, and there are young vines too, all bush vines, requiring hand picking.

As Clairette is very sensitive to oxidation, the vinification must be meticulous, involving a cool fermentation, no skin contact and no oak. The malolactic fermentation depends on the vintage. Sometimes all the wine may undergo a malolactic fermentation, and sometimes only half, and then it is left on the lees until bottling in the spring. Randon explained that he perceives two styles of Clairette. You can pick it very ripe, in which case the wine will age well, or you can pick it earlier, making a lighter wine that will be fresh and fruity for one summer and then fade. He favours the fuller style. His 1997 had a leafy, lemony nose and a certain honeyed character, some concentration and body, and a dry finish. The 1998 is a very rich year, making 15° from thick-skinned grapes, which we tasted as a vat sample when it had barely finished fermenting. It had some intriguing flavours and promised well.

For the moment Clairette du Languedoc may be of only local interest, but if Jean Renaud has his way, we shall be hearing more of it. It certainly deserves a wider reputation, if only as one of the many vinous curiosities with which France abounds.

Key facts

AC 1948 for white wine only; covers ten villages near Pézenas.

Clairette is the sole grape variety, grown on limestone soil. A variety of different styles from dry to very sweet, even fortified, as well as *rancio*. Overripens easily and difficult to vinify well.

Of local interest only.

St Saturnin

Most of the time St Saturnin is a sleepy little village. There is a cheerful restaurant and a small, comfortable hotel, but no shop. The peace is broken by the hourly chimes of the church clock but otherwise little disturbs the somnolent atmosphere – except on the middle Sunday of October, when the village suddenly bursts into noisy animation to celebrate the Fête du Vin Nouveau. The small square in the centre is filled with stalls selling local cheese, olives and colourful Provençal textiles. There are pony rides for the children and the village co-operative mans a stand offering the wine of the year. Most diverting of all are the sheepdog trials, using not sheep but obstreperous geese and ducks with minds of their own. And a good time is had by all.

The surrounding countryside is wild and rugged, especially from the viewpoint at the Rocher des Vierges behind the village. Little grows here apart from vines and a few olive and almond trees. The village is Roman in origin and was originally called St Saturnin-de-Lucian, after a Roman notable who settled here. Later, the bishop of nearby Lodève used it as a summer residence. Nowadays, viticulture is virtually the sole activity and is concentrated in the hands of the village co-operative.

The co-operative has 190 members with 780 hectares of vines, not only in St Saturnin but also in the neighbouring villages of Jonquières, St Guiraud and Arboras. It produces *vin de pays* as well as Coteaux du Languedoc, for not all the producers have the appropriate grape varieties for the appellation. However, with the correct varieties they reckon that you can earn a decent living from ten hectares of vines. There is just one estate outside the co-operative, Domaine Poujol, run by two elderly brothers, with twenty-four hectares mainly of Carignan but with apparently just three thousand vines of Syrah, from which they make rough, tannic wine that they sell *en vrac* to people who bottle their own wine.

Meanwhile, the co-operative has conducted an energetic policy of encouraging people to plant better varieties, and various subsidies are available for replanting. The co-operative pays FF 30,000 per hectare, which will cover the cost of disinfecting the land as well as the cost of the posts and wires for training the vines. Vineyard land needs to lie fallow for seven years before planting, or alternatively you can replant after three years if the ground has been disinfected. There is also a *prime de groupement* of FF 18,000 per hectare, which comes in the form of government aid. First they encouraged Grenache Noir, but now there is an emphasis on Syrah. There is some Mourvèdre too, which needs a green harvest in August to reduce the yield to 35–40 hl/ha. To compensate for the small yield, however, the producers are paid as though the crop were higher. The very old Carignan vines have been retained and although traditionally this is not a region for white wine, they are now experimenting with white varieties. They have a small vineyard of Chenin Blanc, which was originally considered as a possibility for inclusion in the appellation, and in 1998 they made a late harvest wine from it for the first time.

They are very proud of their new *cave d'élevage*, built into the hillside behind the cellar buildings so that the temperature remains a constant 14°C. Their first vinification in wood for both red and white wine was 1994, and now their Cuvée Seigneur des Deux Vierges, named after the hill outside the village, is a regular part of their repertoire. The white is a blend of Grenache Blanc and Bourboulenc with some experimental Chenin Blanc, fermented in new oak in barrels of varying sizes, mainly 300 litres but also some 400 and 500 litres, and given regular *bâtonnage*. The oak was well integrated in the 1996, with a toasty nose and quite a full, alcoholic palate. The red 1995, a blend of Syrah with some Grenache Noir and Mourvèdre, had spent about six months in wood. The oak was more marked on the palate than on the nose, but nonetheless quite harmonious, with vanilla and some smoky, rounded fruit.

St Saturnin has a reputation for its *vin de primeur*, thus providing the excuse for the village *fête*. *Vin de primeur* was made for the first time in 1982 from a blend of equal parts of Cinsaut, Grenache Noir and Syrah, and since then the proportion of Syrah has been gradually increased as more has become available. In

1998, however, they decided to revert to the original recipe, which proved more satisfactory, with a traditional vinification as they are not equipped for carbonic maceration here. The wine is full of spicy, smoky fruit and is eminently easy to drink, with more body than most *vin de primeur*. The Vin d'Une Nuit, a light red wine, is another popular line. It was made in error when a cellar hand ran the juice off a fermenting vat after just one night. The wine tasted good and has remained in the co-operative's repertoire ever since. Made from Carignan, Cinsaut and Grenache Noir with a touch of Syrah, it is a light, fruity wine without any great depth of flavour, but perfect for undemanding drinking in the village café,

A couple of estates are vinified separately. Domaine St Jean, a blend of Syrah and Grenache Noir, has some rugged, firm fruit, while Château d'Arboras, from Grenache Noir, Syrah and a little Cinsaut, is rounded and lightly spicy. Most characteristic of the terroir of St Saturnin is Le Lucian, with firm, chunky fruit and a smoky nose. Its warm, rugged flavour is evocative of the surrounding countryside.

Key facts

Originally the VDQS of St Saturnin, then incorporated into the appellation and now likely to become part of the proposed *terroir* of the Terrasses de Larzac.

Production is dominated by the village co-operative.

Montpeyroux

Montpeyroux has the advantage over its neighbour St Saturnin of having not only a competent co-operative but also several independent producers, a couple of whom would rate in any list of top twenty Languedoc producers. Progress here in the last fifteen years has been dramatic. When I first visited Montpeyroux in 1987, the village co-operative was the only producer of any note. Eight years later I met a small group of five private producers, all of whom, in addition to the village co-operative, were working hard to develop their quality and reputation. By 1998, at least two of the ten *caves particulières*, including people whose first vintage was in 1997 or 1998, were beginning to establish an international reputation. There is a good feeling of cohesion amongst the producers, for together they organise the annual wine fair in June and have a much more independent approach than St Saturnin, which is dominated by its co-operative.

Montpeyroux is the last wine village before the Massif Central, with some of the most northerly vineyards of the Coteaux du Languedoc. The skyline is dominated by mountains: Mont St Baudile, which gives its name to the local *vin de pays*, rises to 847 metres, and in the distance you can see the Pic de Vissou. The wines of Montpeyroux have always enjoyed a certain reputation, for the village could never produce the enormous quantities that the vineyards of the plain did. It became a VDQS in 1958, at a time when Carignan dominated the wines, and then, with the creation of the Coteaux du Languedoc in 1985, became one of the *terroirs* of that appellation.

Today Montpeyroux comes within the putative *terroir* of the Terrasses de Larzac, but the producers firmly defend their independence and aim to raise it to *cru* status, like Pic St Loup and la Clape, with stricter criteria than for Coteaux du Languedoc. Since 1994 yields for Montpeyroux have been restricted to 50 hl/ha, as opposed to 60 hl/ha for Coteaux du Languedoc. The soil is a mixture of clay and limestone, with supplies of underground water from the foothills of the Massif Central protecting the vines from drought.

DOMAINE AUPILHAC

Sylvain Fadat of Domaine Aupilhac is the leading light of Montpeyroux. Young, friendly and articulate, he is full of ideas, which he happily expounds over a tasting in his cellar in the centre of the village, behind one of those enormous rounded doorways in a sombre stone building. Both his grandfather and father had vines, and his first vintage was in 1989, from just seven hectares mostly planted with Carignan. He now has twenty-two hectares in production, but is planning further planting on land where there were vineyards at the end of the nineteenth century, but which first needs to be cleared of scrub.

First we tried a Vin de Pays du Mont Baudile, from equal parts of Ugni Blanc, Grenache Blanc and Chardonnay. A tiny part had been fermented in new oak and the rest in older wood, with regular *bâtonnage* and a malolactic fermentation. The taste was smokily perfumed and rounded. Fadat has some Roussanne, Marsanne and Rolle coming into production. Next came another *vin de pays* called Lou Maset, from Grenache Noir and Cinsaut, with a small amount of Cabernet Sauvignon, Cabernet Franc and Merlot from a vineyard at Aniane, with some ripe berry fruit, perfume and soft tannins. The Grenache Noir is grown at three hundred metres and tends to be too overtly fruity for inclusion in the appellation wine. It was very refreshing, filling a necessary role, for you cannot drink wine with a concentrated flavour all the time.

We continued with more substantial red wines, Fadat meanwhile discussing the pros and cons of *pigeage* and *délestage*. His red grapes are destalked and fermented in open-top vats, with quite a long *cuvaison*, including a pre-fermentation maceration. He likes *pigeage*, for it crushes the skins and diffuses the juice well, giving more fruit and body without adding tannins. *Délestage* is very practical, but he criticises it for adding tannin. He also does some

344

remontages, but with plenty of aeration or you obtain reductive tastes.

1997 was a difficult year, as there was rain in August. The spring came early, with flowering as early as 13 May. Then there was a cold snap that blocked everything, so at the harvest the ripeness levels were very irregular, with both green and ripe grapes on the same vine. With Grenache Noir they had to do two pickings. Fortunately, the warm September helped to ripen the crop. 1998 was a much better year. Syrah was picked on 31 August and run off on 6 October. However, very dry years can make for tannic, unbalanced wines as the plant takes something back from the grapes in order to survive the drought.

The 1997 pure Carignan, which spent fifteen months in *foudres*, was ripe and appealing, with soft tannins. The 1997 Coteaux du Languedoc has also worked out well. Each variety was matured separately until August and then blended and returned to wood; the wine was spicy, with liquorice and cherries. A 1997 Coteaux du Languedoc from new wood and with a different blend was firmer and drier. However, Fadat admitted that he is not really in favour of new wood. His Mourvèdre came into production in 1993. It is in a south-facing vineyard in good deep soil that does not become too dry and it ripens late. A 1996 Coteaux du Languedoc was quite sturdy, while the 1993 Coteaux du Languedoc had some rich, rugged fruit. We finished with a pure Carignan from the 1991 vintage, which had all the herbal flavours of the *garrigue*. Fadat's wines have greatly improved over the years and he promises to go still further.

DOMAINE DE FONT CAUDE

Alain Chabanon at Domaine de Font Caude is another name to watch. His first vintage was in 1990, but he had a varied career before settling in Montpeyroux. He studied in both Montpellier and Bordeaux and worked in Madiran with Alain Brumont, at Domaine de Peraldi in Corsica, and at the co-operative of Sommières on the eastern edge of the Coteaux du Languedoc. Then in 1987 he saw an advertisement in the *Midi Paysan* for fourteen hectares of vines for sale in the village of St Guiraud. He now has twenty-one hectares in production, seven of which are vinified in a small cellar in the hamlet just outside Montpeyroux and fourteen that are committed to the co-operatives of St Saturnin and Gignac. When the co-operative of St Saturnin was founded in 1951, it insisted that its members committed their land to its production for the ensuing fifty years, making it impossible to withdraw land until 2001, even for a new owner or an heir to a vineyard. Font Caude is a warm spring between the villages of St Etienne and Lagamas where Chabanon eventually hopes to have his cellar.

Currently Chabanon makes a white Chenin Blanc – as a *vin de table*, not even as a *vin de pays* – as well as a *rosé* and two red wines. Yields for the Chenin Blanc are tiny, just 12 hl/ha in 1995 as a result of damage by winds that reached 136 kilometres per hour. 1996 produced rather more, with 30 hl/ha; he also made a *liquoreux* for which the grapes were picked on 9 November when they were all black and rotten, yielding just ten hl/ha but with a potential of 31° alcohol. The dry wines are delicate and honeyed, but with the firm acidity characteristic of Chenin Blanc.

The vinification process for the red wine is very straightforward, with *égrappage* and then *pigeages* and *remontages* during a long maceration. Grenache Noir takes two to three weeks to extract fruit and body, while Syrah needs five weeks. He uses the *vin de presse* and keeps the Syrah in wood and the Grenache Noir in vat. The difference between the two wines, Domaine de Font Caude and Esprit de Font Caude, comes principally from the *élevage*, for both are a blend of Syrah and Grenache Noir. In the *domaine* wine, made from equal parts of Syrah and Grenache Noir, the Syrah is aged in wood for twelve months, while for the Esprit, which is Syrah with just ten per cent of Grenache Noir, the Syrah spends two years in wood. The 1995 had good tannin and concentration, while the Esprit, which is unfiltered, was very concentrated and ripe. Chabanon does not consider his wines to be typical of either the Midi or Montpeyroux. Montpeyroux can sometimes be a touch rustic, while his wines are finer, with more elegant tannins. He also makes a fruity *rosé*, although 'for me, *rosé* is not a wine, it is a drink'.

CAVE COOPERATIVE DE MONTPEYROUX

For Gérard Pelat, director of the co-operative of Montpeyroux, the typicity of Montpeyroux comes from its structure – what the French call *charpente* – combined with alcohol, depth of colour and what he described as the *côté garrigue*, the herbs and scents of the shrubs on the hillsides. He considers his wines to be more Mediterranean in style, whereas those of neighbouring St Saturnin are lighter – partly, he suggested, because the oenologist there comes from Gaillac.

The co-operative was founded in 1950 and now has two hundred and fifty members, who own about six hundred and fifty hectares. Their average age is sixty, and there are many retired *viticulteurs*, but there has also been an influx of younger people, so that forty or fifty families do make a living from their vines. There had been noticeable improvements here since my last visit in 1987. They have been offering financial incentives to encourage the planting of Syrah; Mourvèdre has been proving more problematic and Grenache Noir is working well. Much stricter controls on ripeness levels are carried out in the vineyard before the vintage, and the reception of the grapes is now computer controlled, with a careful selection of different qualities. They first began using *barriques* in 1992 and bought a pneumatic press in 1997.

We tasted a range of wines. There was a sturdy 1995 Coteaux du Languedoc, while the 1995 Cuvée Spéciale had more peppery flavours. Domaine de Peyrou is a blend of Syrah and Grenache Noir, from a single property belonging to two members. Château de Roquefeuil takes its name from a fourteenth-century château, destroyed at the French Revolution when the Roquefeuil family left Montpeyroux. All that is left is the remains of the tower and an icehouse. The wine is a blend of Carignan, vinified partly by carbonic maceration, with some Syrah and Grenache Noir, making for some rounded, peppery fruit in the 1996, while the 1994 showed some ageing potential, with a more vegetal, smoky character. Domaine de Goutal, the *cuvée bois* in that a third was given some *élevage* in *fût*, was a little on the clumsy side, while a completely oak-aged 1997, as yet nameless, was more structured, with well integrated oak.

DOMAINE AIGUELIERE

Aimé Commeyras was president of the Montpeyroux co-operative for ten years between 1974 and 1984, but became disillusioned with his members' reluctance to accept the pursuit of quality. At the co-operative they might have noticed that one vat tasted better than another, without really knowing the reason why. He wanted to find out why and this led him to create Domaine l'Aiguelière, in association with Claude Villar and an oenologist, Pierre-Louis Teissèdre. The estate now consists of twenty-five hectares, mainly planted with Syrah, some Grenache Noir and a little Cabernet Sauvignon. Each grape variety is vinified separately, with regard to its particular *terroir*, and the *élevage* usually takes place in barrels. Wood accentuates the differences between the various *terroirs* and complements the wine.

Commeyras is an elderly, ponderous man with a slow and measured manner of speech and he took us through various vat and barrel samples. Côte Dorée is mostly Syrah, aged in Tronçais and Allier oak. The vineyards are on gravel, which makes for a finer, more elegant wine than Côte Rousse, which is the same blend aged in Nevers oak, but from vines on clay and limestone. Both spend eight months in new wood and the difference was certainly apparent on the palate. The 1998 Côte Rousse was intensely concentrated and rich after three weeks' *cuvaison*, numerous *remontages* and no *égrappage*. Commeyras began working with barrels in 1991, buying just two, and in 1992 he bought a further ten. Now he has 120 and continues to buy new barrels each year. There is a second label Tradition made from fifty to sixty per cent Syrah with thirty or forty per cent Grenache Noir and just a drop of Cabernet, with two *cuvées*, one oaked and the other kept in stainless steel. Finally he makes a wine for earlier drinking called Grenat, from eighty-five per cent Grenache Noir with a little Syrah to add body and colour. Commeyras said categorically that he made the kind of wine he liked to drink, and it seems that Robert Parker likes them too, for all the bottles were sold out. I was left wondering just how these wines would age, for like so many of the new wines in the Languedoc they have to establish a track record.

DOMAINE ST ANDRIEU

Charles Giner of Domaine St Andrieu described himself as having reached *un age canonique*. We tracked him down in the centre of the village, for his tiny cellar is under his house, a series of small rooms with *barriques* and an elderly basket press. He gave us a warm welcome. This is an old family property that Giner took over in 1992. The grapes went to the Montpeyroux co-operative, which suited him at the time as he was gainfully employed by IBM in Paris. Then redundancy hit and he seized the opportunity to make his own wine, withdrawing four and a half of the twenty-five hectares from the co-operative, which is much more flexible about such matters than neighbouring St Saturnin. Giner's first vintage was in 1993 and his first bottling in 1995, but he dates his first real vintage from 1996, for that was the first year that he was able to destalk his grapes and do a long vinification.

The composition of his vineyards has changed considerably since 1982. Originally it was mainly Carignan, but he has planted Grenache Noir and Syrah, a little Cinsaut and Mourvèdre and also some white varieties, Rolle and Marsanne, so that 1999 was his first white vintage.

As for red wines, he vinifies each plot separately, separating the *vin de presse* from the free-run juice. He favours a long maceration of up to thirty days and makes four wines altogether. The first is Vallongue, which he called his *cuvée de convivialité*. It is based on Carignan, with some Grenache Noir and Syrah and just a little Mourvèdre, and is the lightest and fruitiest of the range, with herbal notes; it is eminently drinkable. Next comes La Séranne, with some very old Carignan – he does not actually know how old – as well as Mourvèdre, Grenache Noir and a little Syrah. He is less enthusiastic about Syrah than some of his colleagues, as he feels that it can eliminate individuality. The 1996 has some deliciously perfumed fruit, redolent of all the scents of the *garrigue*. Les Marnes Bleues, a blend of Grenache Noir and some barrel-aged Mourvèdre, was more structured and powerful. Giner finds no problem in ripening Mourvèdre here and wants to retain its individuality. Finally there is L'Yeuse Noire, a blend of La Séranne and Les Marnes Bleues, that has spent twelve months in wood. 'I am sacrificing myself to fashion,' he said, 'in using oak.' The name recalls the first time he came to Montpeyroux, when he was struck by the dramatic contrast of the white rocks and the black silhouettes of the holm oaks, or *yeuses*. The 1996 tasted smoky, with obvious oak on the palate. I agreed that he was indeed sacrificing himself to fashion.

THE OTHERS

These are all people who firmly believe in the future of their area –
in Montpeyroux in particular and in the future of the Terrasses de
Larzac and the Languedoc in the broader scheme of things. People
are coming back to the village and to the vineyards. There are
newcomers too, setting up their own vineyards and cellars. Laurent
Marcillaud, the author of *Grands Vins du Languedoc*, has a cellar
in Montpeyroux. Domaine l'Estagnols was set up by a former
president of the co-operative. Domaine des Thérons began about
twenty years ago, with a first bottling in 1991 and Château
Mondagot as the best label; while Domaine du Plô is very much
in the old school, for M. Langeon has been making wine since
1946.

Key facts for Montpeyroux

One of the most northerly villages of the Coteaux du
Languedoc, Montpeyroux was formerly a VDQS, then a *terroir*
in the appellation, and is now hoping for *cru* status rather than
incorporation into the Terrasses de Larzac.

Smaller yields than Coteaux du Languedoc, with 50 hl/ha rather
than 60 hl/hl. Limestone and clay soil.

Enormous potential, with a competent co-operative and several
keen independent producers.

MAS JULLIEN, JONQUIERES

The village of Jonquières is a short drive from Montpeyroux, and
there on the outskirts we tracked down Olivier Jullien of Mas Jullien.
He is one of the most original wine growers of the Languedoc, a
young man who has established a well-deserved reputation since his
first vintage in 1985. His grandfather was a *viticulteur* who took
his grapes to the co-operative and his father did likewise until 1995,
when he decided to follow his son's example and began to make his
own wine under the Cal Demoura label.
  Olivier Jullien is a friendly man, with a relaxed attitude to life in
general and to wine making in particular that belies a creative

talent and a questioning mind. He does not hesitate to challenge established perceptions, especially those relating to wine regulations and grape varieties. He is adamant that the administration does not correspond to reality. First we went for a walk in the vineyards, enjoying the autumn sunshine and encountering hunters who were waiting for the doves migrating north from Africa. Jullien has some fifty different plots of vines, scattered over thirty-five kilometres from St Jean de Foz to Cabrières, but most are concentrated between Jonquièrcs and Montpeyroux, around the Ravine de Lagamas. As well as the more traditional varieties, he has a row each of Petit Manseng and Chenin Blanc.

Then it was back to the neat little cellar, with its stainless steel and concrete vats, pneumatic press and *cave d'élevage* with barrels and small *foudres*. We tasted three white wines. Les Vignes Oubliées does indeed include some varieties that have fallen out of fashion, such as Carignan Blanc and Terret Blanc, as well as Grenache Blanc, which are fermented and then kept in wood for twelve to eighteen months, giving a certain nuttiness and layers of flavour and texture in the mouth. La Méjanne is a blend of Chenin Blanc, Viognier and Grenache Blanc. It had a more lemony, leafy flavour, with the peachy character of the Viognier on the palate. Clairette Beudelle comes from superbly ripe Clairette. There is no botrytis, but the grapes are brown in colour with a potential alcohol of 20°. They are fermented in wood and the wine stays in barrel for about three years while it is allowed to oxidise very slightly. Jullien is convinced that *les anciens* picked Clairette when it was really ripe, but as it was usually sold to the vermouth producers, there are no records of what was done to it. In any case it is a marvellous variety; the wine had an amber colour, with notes of rich orange marmalade. And as the method does not conform to any legislation, it has the usual ungainly expression on the label: *moût de raisins partiellement fermentés, issu de raisins passerillés.*

Next came three red wines. Les Etats d'Ame, with a poem on the label, was fruity and accessible, with soft tannins. Les Cailloutis, from equal proportions of Carignan, Syrah, Grenache Noir and Mourvèdre, is usually blended just after the malolactic fermentation. Part of it goes into two ten-hectolitre *foudres* and the other ninety per cent spends two years in vat before bottling. It was delicious, with smoky cherries on the nose, ripe fruit and long, silky tannins on the palate. Les Depierres is a blend of *terroirs* and grape varieties, namely Syrah and Grenache Noir grown on schist and Mourvèdre and Grenache Noir grown on limestone. The 1995 was redolent of southern warmth, with some chunky berry fruit and a long finish. In the more difficult vintage of 1997 Jullien blended the two wines together to make Cailloutis Depierres, a wine with less concentration. Usually these are wines that need some bottle age.

CHATEAU DE JONQUIERES, JONQUIERES

The Château de Jonquières is a gracious building just outside the village of Jonquières. A dog was asleep in the courtyard, oblivious to its elegant surroundings. The origins of the château are eleventh century, and a Renaissance staircase, balcony and towers were added in the seventeenth century. It has in an indirect way always been in the same family; the present incumbent is François de Cabissole, who met his wife Isabelle when she came to help with the grape picking. Originally the grapes went to the co-operative at St Saturnin, but in 1992 de Cabissole somehow managed to extricate his vineyards from its grasp. Since then he has developed a range of wines, of which the whites are more satisfying than the reds.

There was a Risée de Blanc made from forty-year-old Clairette vines picked when they are very ripe and left to ferment very slowly. *Risée* is the term for a small wind on the sea before a storm. The nose was reminiscent of quinces, with a certain biscuity character on the palate. The 1995 Comte de Lansade, named after the uncle from whom he inherited the property, is half Grenache Blanc and half Chenin Blanc, which was planted originally as an experiment and has since been deemed unsuitable for the appellation, so that this is a *vin de table*. A further legislative complication means that you cannot use the word *château* for a *vin de table*, even if you have the most superb *bona fide* château like Jonquières! Two-thirds of the blend is fermented in barrel and kept there for six months, which gives it some leafy, honeyed fruit on the nose and palate.

There are two red wines. Château de Jonquières is a blend of Grenache Noir with some Syrah and Mourvèdre that I found a little jammy and soft. Although it had good fruit, it lacked structure. The Cuvée la Baronne is aged in oak, with sixty per cent Syrah, some Mourvèdre and just a drop of Grenache Noir, with the oak providing some backbone.

MAS DES CHIMERES, OCTON

Mas des Chimères, in the village of Octon near the Lac du Salagou, has been a family estate for several generations, but the concentration on viticulture is much more recent. Guilhem Dardé is a friendly young *vigneron* with a bushy moustache worthy of an RAF pilot. He explained that sheep farming had been important in Octon, with numerous flocks grazing on the plateau of Larzac above the village, providing milk for Roquefort cheese. Until transport improved in the 1960s, the cheese was made in the village, but today the milk from the one remaining flock is collected daily. Dardé's grandfather had had sheep, but his father began to concentrate on vines in the 1960s. Guilhem took over from him in 1984 and a few years later decided to leave the village co-operative and make his own wine. His first vintage was 1993. As a co-operative member he had seventeen hectares producing twelve hundred hectolitres, an average of 70 hl/ha, and as an independent producer he cultivates thirteen hectares from which he obtains about six hundred hectolitres – in other words, a dramatically lower average yield of about 45 hl/ha. This is a vivid illustration of the kind of trans-formation brought about by a new generation that is keen to pursue quality.

Dardé explained how this area would become part of the proposed Terrasses de Larzac, an area that will stretch from Gignac to Octon. The criteria for selection are stricter than for basic Coteaux du Languedoc. There is a climatic homogeneity and also some very specific *terroir*, an iron-rich red sandstone called *ruffe* that retains the heat. It is 250 million years old. There is also basalt, which is younger. Later I drove past the Lac du Salagou – which gives its name to the local *vin de pays*, Coteaux du Salagou – and in the spring sunshine its dramatic red cliffs made a sharp contrast with the blue water.

Dardé talked about the different attitudes to viticulture amongst the co-operative members. He admits to irrigating occasionally, perhaps once a year in July. In theory it is not allowed, but the sandy, volcanic soil retains no water and if he did not irrigate, the vines might become so stressed as to lose their leaves. The nights are longer in August, so that there is less of a problem. Some of the co-operative members add fertiliser, but he has not used any since he left the co-operative. He sows grass between the vines to provide some organic matter and to prevent erosion.

We tasted in his simple cellar. There are four old vats left from the time of his father, who had stopped making wine when the village co-operative opened in 1945. Dardé has invested in a new concrete tank, as he finds that concrete maintains a more consistent temperature in a uninsulated cellar. He also has some four or five-year-old barrels, bought second-hand as he does not want a marked taste of wood. If you are going to buy second-hand barrels, you must taste the wine that has been in them. He makes a variety of different wines, illustrative of the enormous richness of the Languedoc. For white wines he has Terret Bourret, which used to be a base for vermouth and now makes a soft, biscuity, slightly herbal wine. There is Chasan, a cross of Listan and Chardonnay, which is lightly leafy, indeed not unlike a young Chardonnay. A 1996 Viognier was very convincing, with fruit and flavour and the textured mouth feel of the variety.

As for red wine, there is a pure Cinsaut, made as a light wine for summer drinking and labelled Oeillade. There has been some ampelographical confusion between Cinsaut and Oeillade. Before phylloxera they were recognised as two separate but very closely related varieties, but because Cinsaut responded better to grafting, Oeillade was gradually abandoned. The wine is lightly peppery with a little backbone, serving as an example of how the bad reputation of a grape variety can be redeemed. It depends on how you make it. Most people make Cinsaut as a *rosé*, but as this and Daniel Domergue's Capitelle de Centeilles in the Minervois demonstrate, the variety can also make exemplary red wine. A pure Carignan, named Cuvée Marie et Joseph after his parents, from very old vines, some of which were planted in the 1920s, also vindicates the reputation of that variety. Seventy per cent is vinified by carbonic maceration, with the rest given a traditional vinification to add more body. It was warm, dry and spicy, with a firm backbone. Dardé's Coteaux du Languedoc is a blend of Syrah, Grenache Noir and Carignan, with the proportions varying according to the vintage. For the 1993 vintage he tried a little wood ageing, putting some Syrah in two-year-old wood for seven months. The Syrah in the 1994 spent a year in wood, and all the 1995 was put in wood. It now depends very much on the character of the wine and the vintage. The *assemblage* of grape varieties is all-important, giving more complexity to the wine, while the Carignan and Cinsaut are to prove people wrong and upset their preconceived ideas.

Asked about the name of the estate – which means chimera in English – Guilhem Dardé talked of a wild dream, a quest in wine and life. I left with an impression of a dedicated small producer, thoughtful and searching.

MAS BRUNET, CAUSSE-DE-LA-SELLE

Mas Brunet, outside the village of Causse-de-la-Selle, is another isolated estate in what may become the *terroir* of the Terrasses de Larzac. Marc Coulet explained the development of the family business. He is a rather reticent young man, shy and thoughtful, with a good analytical mind. Unusually for the Midi, he studied oenology at Reims. At the turn of the last century, this was an estate of self-sufficient polyculture, with fruit trees, vegetables, sheep and goats as well as vines. His grandfather, who was born in 1906, was more interested in vines. He developed the vineyard to six hectares (alongside the sheep), built a cellar and sold his wine to the *négoce*. Marc's uncle and father took over in the 1950s and extended the six hectares to sixteen, but not before the severe frosts of 1963 had reduced their vineyards to just two hectares. Coulet spoke of his father with affection, describing how he had a vision that was quite different from what was usual in the south. He had not studied, but he had a great love of nature and an enormous belief in the potential of the vineyard. So in the 1970s, after their first bottling in 1973, they began to sell at the cellar door in bottle and bulk, as well as to local restaurants. Indeed, today they are open from eight in the morning until eight-thirty in the evening every day. Marc joined the business in 1988 and his cousin Serge followed a year later; they now have twenty-one hectares.

There is Syrah, first planted in 1973, Grenache Noir and some Cabernet Sauvignon planted in 1980. Then in 1991 they introduced white varieties, Roussanne, Rolle and Viognier. Marc's parents took a courageous step, for back in 1973 this area was not even recognised as a VDQS and the *vins de pays* were only just being developed. They were not included in the first delimitation of the Coteaux du Languedoc and finally became an appellation with the redefinition of the vineyard in 1990. Their nearest neighbour is the co-operative of St Jean-de-Buezge in the valley of the Buezge, some six kilometres away. Here they are very much on the northern edge of viticulture in the Hérault and a long way from the Mediterranean. The *terroir* is very diverse with a variety of different soils, including clay, limestone and some sand. It is poor but deep. For the moment the Terrasses de Larzac are ill defined, but they could stretch from Ganges to Lodève, including the vineyards of St Felix-de-Lodez and Aniane. Montpeyroux and St Saturnin could also be included, but they would like to retain their individuality as *crus* and remain separate from the broad mass, as they feel that the future of the Coteaux du Languedoc lies not in the large appellation but in the smaller *crus*.

We spent a happy hour tasting our way around barrels and vats from the 1998 vintage. Coulet's father initially used small *foudres*, but since 1992 they have been buying *barriques* and now have 130, of which a fifth are renewed each year. Some are larger 320 or 400-litre barrels, and Vicard in Cognac is their preferred cooper. Their white wine is a blend of Roussanne and Rolle with just ten per cent of Viognier. Part of it is fermented in wood with *bâtonnage*, and the oak is well integrated, with a rich, structured flavour. Altogether there are four reds: Mas Brunet, a Coteaux du Languedoc from Syrah and Grenache Noir; Cuvée du Mazet, a *vin de pays* from Syrah, Grenache Noir and Cinsaut; a Vin d'Une Nuit from Cabernet Sauvignon and Merlot, which are, as the name implies, given a very short maceration of three or four days, after which the wine is aged in wood for six months, resulting in some fresh cherry fruit with sufficient acidity and tannin; finally there is Bruneroc, a much more substantial blend of Cabernet Sauvignon and Merlot, given at least a three-week maceration. At an altitude of two hundred and fifty metres they find that Cabernet Sauvignon ripens better than Carignan, but Cabernet and Merlot are not so good in very dry years and perform better on clay and limestone. The skins from the Vin d'Une Nuit are added to the vat of Bruneroc to achieve extra concentration, and the wine is given twelve months wood ageing. They favour a daily *remontage*, as well as the occasional *délestage*, which they believe gives softer tannins and more rounded flavours.

An estate with twenty-five years' experience of selling wine in bottle is fairly rare in the Midi. Coulet talked of the evolution even in the ten years or so that he has been in the business. When he and his cousin first started work, they thought their cellar was well equipped, but in fact they have replaced just about everything. They now have a pneumatic press rather than a Vaslin, an *égrappoir*, a more efficient pump and a centralised cooling system. Various vats have been renewed and the cellar has been insulated. All that remains is the original bottling line. There are countless projects. They are planning better varieties in the vineyards, more Syrah and white varieties. They are working on better grape exposure, pruning short with a *cordon royat* rather than *guyot*, and are considering increasing the density from three thousand plants per hectare to four thousand five hundred, which will noticeably improve quality. They also do a green harvest and have picked by mechanical harvester since 1984, replacing their first machine with a more refined model in 1995. Coulet described it as *une evolution en douceur*.

CHATEAU DE GRANOUPIAC, ST ANDRE-DE-SANGONIS

Claude Flavard has his cellars at Château de Granoupiac on the outskirts of the village of St André-de-Sangonis. First we talked in the sitting room, in front of a log fire that was welcome on a chilly March afternoon. A sleek black cat called Réglisse, which means liquorice, purred loudly. Flavard explained that when the property changed hands fifteen years previously, the former owner had kept the house but sold the cellars and vineyards. Formerly he had vineyards scattered in four different villages, taking his grapes to different co-operatives, but he realised that progress within the co-operative would be impossible and that the solution was a cellar of his own and a more homogeneous vineyard. The château dates from the 1850s, the period when the Languedoc was moving toward monoculture, concentrating on wine and acquiring its wealth. There is also an eleventh-century chapel dedicated to St Pierre de Granoupiac. However, the area has Gallo-Roman origins. They have found pottery in the vineyards and the salt road to the Massif Central passed nearby.

Flavard talked of the changes to the vineyards, which are on the gravelly alluvial terraces of the Hérault. This was land that originally produced 140–150 hl/ha. It took five years to change, suppressing irrigation and fertilisers and modifying the pruning. No weed-killer is used, as that causes even more damage to the soil than fertiliser. Nineteen of his twenty-five hectares are in Coteaux du Languedoc and he also produces some *vins de pays*, both d'Oc and de l'Hérault. The local *vin de pays* is Côtes de Céréssou, but any reputation it might have had has been spoilt by an incompetent co-operative. As well as the usual five red varieties of the south, he has some Merlot for Vin de Pays d'Oc as well Grenache Blanc, Rolle and Roussanne, which were planted in the mid-1980s.

Flavard described the cellar as a financial abyss that requires endless expenditure. He still has some wonderful large *foudres*, one of which dates from the creation of the original cellar in 1830, while the others are rather newer, dating from the 1930s and 1940s. They provide enormous storage capacity. Since 1998 he has replaced some with *barriques*. It hurt to get rid of the *foudres*, or more graphically it gave him *mal aux tripes*. Smaller *foudres*, with say a six-hectolitre capacity, may be the answer. The purchase of an *égrappoir* allowed for a longer maceration, twenty-five or thirty days rather than a couple of weeks.

As for the wines, there was a fresh, fruity *rosé* from Cinsaut, Syrah and Cabernet Sauvignon, a ripe plummy Merlot that had spent twelve months in *foudres* and an attractively perfumed Coteaux du Languedoc. The 1997 had hints of nutmeg and liquorice, while the 1998 from Grenache Noir, Syrah and Mourvèdre had some lovely spicy berry fruit, with youthful tannins. I was left with the impression of a modest, reflective man who is quietly working to achieve the best from his vineyards.

Key facts for Terrasses de Larzac

One of the proposed new *terroirs* of the Coteaux du Languedoc, covering some of the most northerly vineyards of the appellation.

Area as yet ill defined, but perhaps stretching from Lodève to Ganges in the north and from Octon to Gignac in the south.

Includes the existing *terroirs* of St Saturnin and Montpeyroux, as well as scattered estates conforming to the appellation requirements of the Coteaux du Languedoc.

Pic St Loup

The profile of Pic St Loup has changed dramatically in the last twenty years. In the mid-1980s the co-operative of St Mathieu-de-Tréviers dominated the production of the region, but since then there has been an incredible surge of new producers, as newcomers have arrived in the area and land has changed hands or been withdrawn from the co-operative. Now, at the beginning of the twenty-first century, Pic St Loup is one of the most energetic *crus* of the Coteaux du Languedoc and in the process of establishing its own independent appellation.

This is dramatic countryside. The Pic St Loup is a pointed mountain, rising to 638 metres, that dominates the skyline some thirty kilometres north of Montpellier. You would not think you were so close to a bustling metropolis, although there is an underlying current of opinion that some land is more valuable for construction than for vineyards. Climb, as we did, to the top of the Pic St Loup on the first sunny Sunday afternoon of spring and you will have *tout* Montpellier keeping you company, not just the young and fit, but their dogs and children as well. The view at the top is well worth the effort, for you look across to the valley to the Montagne de l'Hortus. There is also a small chapel dedicated to St Loup. Local legend has it that in the early Middle Ages a man called Loup from the village of St Martin-de-Londres near the foot of the mountain fell in love, but he had two rivals. The three men decided to go on the Crusades to prove their valour, but when they returned a few years later, the object of their affections had disappeared. Disillusioned, they each took the vows of a hermit and Loup settled on the nearby mountain.

Along with many of the other early *terroirs* of the Coteaux du Languedoc, Pic St Loup became a VDQS in 1955. Thirty years

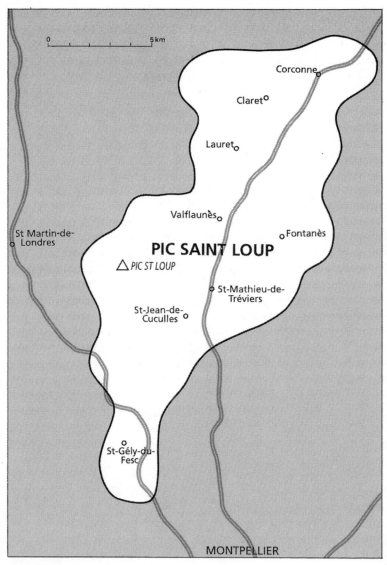

Pic St Loup

later it was incorporated into the appellation of the Coteaux du Languedoc, and now its *syndicat* is working for a separate, independent appellation that would be quite distinct from the various putative *terroirs* of the Coteaux du Languedoc. In 1994 it achieved the status of a *cru*, with subtle differences in the regulations compared with basic Coteaux du Languedoc. The emphasis is now very much on the *cépages améliorateurs*, Syrah, Grenache Noir and Mourvèdre, which must account of ninety per cent of a blend. The yield is restricted to 50 hl/ha without any PLC, and the minimum alcohol level is fixed at 11.5° as opposed to 11° for the Coteaux du Languedoc. The vines must be a minimum of six years old or, as the French say, have reached their *sixième feuille*, or sixth leaf. Usually for an appellation, three leaves are sufficient.

The grapes of younger vines may be used for *rosé* or for Coteaux du Languedoc. A precise delimitation of the vineyards has been carried out, and in the thirteen villages of the appellation, eighty-five per cent of the potential vineyard land, totalling five thousand hectares, is classified as Pic St Loup. However, only about one-fifth is planted with the appropriate grape varieties. There is still far too much Carignan and Cinsaut, which can be used for Coteaux du Languedoc or for the local Vin de Pays du Val de Montferrand, and much of the delimited land remains virgin *garrigue*.

The ruined Château de Montferrand sits on the top of another hill outside the small town St Mathieu-de-Tréviers, which is the centre of the appellation, and the Romanesque church of St Martin-de-Londres is well worth a visit for the simplicity of its architecture. This is an area of little villages and tiny hamlets. Another Romanesque church, Notre-Dame-d'Aleyrac, nestles in the vineyards and in spring is surrounded by cherry trees resplendent with delicate pink blossom.

So what distinguishes the Pic St Loup from the other *crus* of the Coteaux du Languedoc? The wine growers say that its typicity comes from having a more northerly climate than the others. Average temperatures are cooler and the rainfall a little higher. The vineyards are dominated by a chain of cliffs, with large areas of rocks giving deep but poor soil, with good drainage. Breezes and wind improve the *état sanitaire* of the grapes, helping to protect them against the twin problems of rot and frost.

This compact area some eighteen kilometres long and three kilometres wide on the east side of the Pic St Loup includes thirteen villages, from Corconne in the north, just inside the neighbouring department of Gard, down to St Gély-du-Fesc, close to the suburbs of Montpellier. At the last count there were twenty-two independent producers, as well as four co-operatives that account for forty per cent of the production. The co-operative of St Mathieu-de-Tréviers is still the most important and that of Corconne is also working well for its appellation, while those of Claret and St Gély-du-Fesc are relatively unimportant.

CAVE COOPERATIVE DE ST MATHIEU

The co-operative of St Mathieu already had a keen ethos of quality in the mid-1980s, encouraging its members to plant the better grape varieties and improving its installations. Fifteen years later, it has a state-of-the-art bottling line that it allows the independent producers to use, to the extent that it apparently bottles at least three-quarters of the total production of Pic St Loup. Unlike some more narrow-minded co-operatives, it has encouraged the pioneering new cellars to go it alone, rather than imposing penalties and restraints. There are some independent producers who still send a significant part of their crop to the co-operative, which helps their cash flow by providing a ready outlet for their wine.

The co-operative members planted their first Syrah in 1975 and it performs very much better here than Mourvèdre, which has problems in ripening because of the distance from the sea. Subsidies are available to encourage replanting, and as they also prefer to vinify Syrah by carbonic maceration, they pay a bonus for hand-picked grapes to compensate for the additional labour costs. A decision is taken prior to the harvest as to which vineyards will be picked this way. The cellars are efficient and streamlined, and as for the wines, bottled under the Coteaux du Pic label, they are convincing examples of their appellation. A quarter bottle that I drank on the British Airways flight home from Montpellier provided a spectacular demonstration of the improvement in the wines of the Languedoc. Ten years ago I would have hesitated; today it was delicious.

DOMAINE L'HORTUS, VALFLAUNES

Jean Orliac at Domaine de l'Hortus was amongst the first of the new wave of producers in the Pic St Loup, helping to focus attention on the untapped potential of the area. His vineyards are dramatically situated in the valley between the Pic St Loup and the Montagne de l'Hortus. The wind was blowing hard on a spring morning and there was the scent of thyme in the air. Orliac first came here as a student from Montpellier and saw his future vineyards while rock climbing. He had trained as an agricultural engineer, but was uncertain about exactly what direction to take. His grandfather had been a *vigneron* and he wanted an active life in the open air, creating something aesthetic. Pic St Loup provided him with the opportunity to help establish the reputation of an appellation, and a friend's father rented him five hectares back in 1978. In 1980 he took the plunge and bought thirty hectares of land, but did not put his first wine in bottle until 1990. The soil is a mass of limestone rocks from the cliffs above, and underneath there is clay that provides good water reserves for the deep-rooted vines. Orliac explained the microclimate of his vineyards. There is more rain here than on the coast. On one side of the valley it is much hotter, and that is where he has planted Mourvèdre, on the south-facing slopes. There is mastic here, but not on the cooler side of the valley. That is how you identify each microclimate, by looking at the natural vegetation. And where there is mastic there is no box, because that likes cooler conditions – as does Syrah, which he has planted opposite, on the north-facing slope. There is Grenache Noir in the middle, on the valley floor. There was also a riot of pretty blue flowers, *aphillantes de Montpellier*.

Orliac's cellar, a large wooden shed, was built for the 1995 vintage. As the valley is a listed site, any building project has to be carefully vetted. Orliac makes an intriguing white wine, which he calls his Blanc Classique, from equal parts of Sauvignon and Chardonnay with twenty per cent of Viognier. He is planning to plant Marsanne and Roussanne too. The nose of the 1996 was dominated by Sauvignon, while there was some buttery Chardonnay on the palate. The Viognier was quite masked, but added a discreet extra dimension. A Grande Cuvée is fermented in wood. For the moment Pic St Loup is only red and pink, with any white wine a Coteaux du Languedoc, as there was such a limited experience of white varieties in the area when the request for a separate appellation was made in 1994.

As for red wines, the Cuvée Classique is approximately fifty per cent Syrah, thirty per cent Grenache Noir and twenty per cent Mourvèdre, aged for a few months in older barrels, while the Grande Cuvée, with a higher percentage of Mourvèdre and less Grenache Noir, uses some new wood. A tasting from vat illustrated the characteristics of the different grape varieties. The Grenache Noir was ripe and warm, the Mourvèdre tight, peppery and structured, and two different Syrah showed the effect of micro-climate: that from the coolest vineyard was firm and peppery, more complex than the wine from the warmer vineyard, with its riper, more obvious blackcurrant gum fruit. In bottle, the 1995 Cuvée Classique was rounded and supple, with soft tannins, while the Grande Cuvée from the same vintage was more structured, with a balance of fruit and oak. What Orliac wants above all is elegance in his wine and, if the vintage gives it, some power. These are wines to age, as time will show.

CHATEAU DE LASCAUX, VACQUIERES

Jean-Benoît Cavalier at Château de Lascaux in the village of Vacquières is an articulate exponent of his appellation, and his enthusiasm is infectious. He explained how the soil changes throughout Pic St Loup. Although it is all based on clay and limestone, there are variations; indeed, Lascaux, the name of the hill outside the village where most of his vines are planted, means chalky stone in Occitan – and it is. 'We know so little about the potential of our area, but it is enormous. We need to know our *terroir* better and work out which grape variety is most suitable where. We need a better control of our vinification methods. With different experiments each year, we will gain in originality and complexity, as we master the vinification and *élevage*.' The Pic St Loup was formed by a repercussion of the creation of the Pyrenees. There is more *garrigue* than vineyards here and there used to be flocks of sheep, which were taken up into the Cévennes for the summer months. Silkworms too were important at the end of the nineteenth century, not only for Lyon, but also for nearby Ganges, an important centre for silk. At one time polyculture was the norm, but then the emphasis shifted to viticulture, with a few olive trees. 'However, we lost the tradition of quality as we sought to emulate the wines of the plain. People thought they could achieve the same enormous yields here, without realising that the conditions are quite different. The quality vineyards were stifled by the mass of *vin de table* and that is what we are now rediscovering, the wonderful diversity and originality of the Languedoc.'

Cavalier took over the family estate from his grandfather in 1984. Originally the vineyards were part of the co-operative, but in 1990 he put the old cellar back into working order. There is an attractive *chai d'élevage* with heavy rafters that was once the sheepfold. We tasted in an attractive vaulted *caveau*, dating back to the twelfth century, in the centre of the village next to the church. There was a notice on the door saying *chat lunatique*, but I did not have the opportunity to meet the mad feline. For Cavalier, the climate of Pic St Loup is Mediterranean but with a strong continental influence, as this is the most northern *cru* of the Coteaux du Languedoc. There is more rain here and in August, when the days are hot, the nights are much cooler than on the coast. Mourvèdre does not ripen here unless you choose a very good site, so Cavalier has mainly Syrah and Grenache Noir, as well as white varieties, Marsanne, Rolle, Viognier, and a more recent planting of Roussanne.

Cavalier makes two white wines. Cuvée Classique is from equal parts of Marsanne and Rolle, with twenty per cent of Viognier. There are ten days between the harvest for each variety, as the Viognier is ready at the beginning of September and the Rolle does not ripen until the end of the month. They undergo a classic vinification and the wine is left in vat on the fine lees until it is bottled the following spring. It was rounded and delicate. Pierres d'Argent, with different proportion of the same varieties, namely fifty per cent Viognier and twenty-five per cent each of Rolle and Marsanne, is fermented in wood and given some *bâtonnage*. It should develop well in bottle, with fruit and a firm, oaky backbone.

Some of Cavalier's vineyards are outside the delimited area of Pic St Loup, so he also makes a Coteaux du Languedoc from seventy per cent Syrah and thirty per cent Grenache Noir, which spend twelve months in vat. It has some attractive peppery fruit and soft tannins. His Pic St Loup Cuvée Nobles Pierres, from ninety per cent Syrah and ten per cent Grenache Noir, is given eighteen months of *élevage*, including a year in *barriques*, which he first began using in 1990. In the young wine the notes of vanilla were quite obvious, but there was a good concentration of flavour as well as ripe fruit in the fine 1995 vintage. Cavalier aims to work on the elegance of the tannins, while retaining concentration and body in the wine. You find different characteristics in Pic St Loup. Sometimes there are ripe, red fruits, sometimes spice and sometimes the scents of the *garrigue*, bay in particular.

CHATEAU LA ROQUE, FONTANES

The soft stone Château la Roque near the village of Fontanès was once part of the Benedictine abbey of Maguelone, and the monks grew grapes here. Then from 1259 until the last member of the family was killed in the Franco-Prussian war in 1870, it belonged to the la Roque family. Jack Boutin arrived there in 1985. This represented a dramatic career change, for he had been a civil servant – although his grandfather had had a vineyard at Sommières in the Gard. Boutin took over property belonging to his grandfather while he searched for his own property in Pic St Loup, taking the grapes to the co-operative for basic *vin de table*, which he described as the Pepsi Cola of France. He found Château la Roque, with its abandoned cellars and vines that nobody else had wanted to buy, and set about learning how to make wine and put everything back into working order.

Boutin makes two qualities of both red and white as well as a fresh, fruity *rosé*. His Blanc Classique comes from equal proportions of Rolle, Marsanne, Grenache Blanc and Viognier, which are all fermented together. They do not all ripen together, but are incorporated into the vat over four or six weeks. I detected Viognier on the nose, while the palate was more representative of Rolle. The white Clos des Bénédictins is the same blend, vinified and aged in wood for eight months. The red Cuvée Classique is made from twenty-five per cent Syrah, forty-five per cent Grenache Noir and thirty-five per cent Mourvèdre, which are blended after an *élevage* in vat the September after the vintage and bottled the following January or February. Thyme, laurel and the herbs of the *garrigue* were the dominant flavours, with some ripe, rugged fruit. Boutin's oaked *cuvée* is called Cupa Numismae after a coin that was found in the wall of the château – a gold coin apparently minted to pay the ransom of John the Good, the king of France, after the Black Prince took him prisoner at the battle of Poitiers in 1356. The label depicting a knight on horseback recalls the coin. As for the wine, it comes from Syrah and Mourvèdre, the oldest vines with the lowest yields, and spends about fourteen months in oak, making for a solid, meaty palate with tannin and texture.

MAS DE LAVABRE, CLARET

Olivier Bridel comes from Normandy and had worked in the pharmaceutical industry in Bordeaux. He related how he left Castillon-la-Bataille, on the eastern edge of the Gironde, and explored the south west, looking for a vineyard. He finally arrived here by a circuitous route in April 1995 and found the abandoned vineyards of Mas de Lavabre, which had belonged to the Bonfils family in Sète. The origins of the property are Roman, and in the Middle Ages there was a forge, which was abandoned in the twelfth century as a result of the plague. Vines became important at the end of the eighteenth century, which was when the château was built. With the objective viewpoint of an outside and a relative newcomer to wine, Bridel is a thoughtful wine maker. The cellar is simple and efficient. Some stone vats with walls eighty centimetres thick remain, and there is a small barrel cellar.

Much of his wine is vinified by carbonic maceration, and he makes three qualities of red wine: Château Lavabre, with some *élevage* in oak; Domaine du Pontjoli, with less oak ageing; and a Coteaux du Languedoc, Domaine de Lavabre. The proportions of the grape varieties vary, with more Carignan in the Coteaux du Languedoc and only a tiny amount in the Pic St Loup. Domaine de Lavabre has ripe, accessible fruit with soft tannins, while Château Lavabre is more oaky and international in style. However, as the wine ages, the oak diminishes and the fruit takes over. Domaine du Pontjoli bridges the two. Bridel has also planted some Chardonnay and Viognier, and has experimented with Grenache Blanc in *barriques*. As for the future, he envisages more work in the vineyard, for he has land to plant. 'We must keep our sense of the vineyards. That is what will save the Languedoc, not the oenologists.'

CLOS MARIE, LAURET

Christophe Peyrus left the French navy to take charge of his wife's family property. Her grandfather had been an independent wine grower, but her father joined the co-operative of St Mathieu in the 1950s. First of all we met her grandmother, after whom the estate is named; she was a wizened old lady of ninety with a sprightly voice, who insisted on telling us her age and that her own mother had reached a hundred and three. She was evidently aiming to do the same. Peyrus arrived from the vines and took us to the cellar. Wine is nothing new to him, for his family were *vignerons* in Cahors. He has ten hectares in production and is gradually replanting, concentrating on Syrah, Grenache Noir and Mourvèdre. He has also grafted some Roussanne and has some old Maccabeu and Clairette. In 1998 he made just six barrels of white, laughingly describing it as his *danseuse* for he lavished so much care and attention on it.

We wandered around the cellar, glass in hand, tasting vat and barrel samples. Peyrus ferments each variety separately, as well as each small vineyard, all in an attempt to understand his *terroir*. He has three different soils: the white clay and silt; red clay and limestone; and at the bottom of some slopes, more silty soil with fewer stones. Usually he makes four different red wines, blended according to the age of his vines and the *terroir*: Quatre Saisons has an emphasis on fruit, with a short *élevage*; L'Olivette is given fourteen months *élevage* in vat and barrel; Cuvée Simon, named after his son, goes into barrel; and in the best years he makes Les Glorieuses, which is given twenty months of *élevage*.

Peyrus exudes enthusiasm, talking about the differences in his wines. 'Nothing is fixed yet in the Midi, so I can do what I like.' He is not sure about new wood, but buys four or five barrels a year and now has about forty altogether. The tannins must be in balance. What he really wants is fruit and elegance, and that is certainly what he achieves. He talked about the different *terroirs*. The white soil makes for more elegant wines, while Syrah on clay and limestone is more structured and tannic. Mourvèdre is difficult. The results are interesting, but it is too far from the sea here. And does he miss the sea? He says he has adapted well. The future for Pic St Loup is promising, with so many young producers wanting to improve quality.

CHATEAU DE VALFLAUNES, VALFLAUNES

We tracked down Fabien Réboul in the little village of Valflaunès. He is such a new arrival that he did not yet have a sign up to mark his cellar, for 1998 was his very first vintage. He has travelled the world before returning to his roots in the Pic St Loup. We enthused about Dry River at Martinborough in New Zealand, where he had worked with Neil McCallum, and compared the difference of attitude in Oregon, where he had also spent some time. Réboul said that they were good wine makers, but there was no team spirit; New Zealand was much better. He has some land from his grandmother and his father, and has started his cellar from scratch, buying vats, cooling equipment and second-hand barrels from Château Ausone. He has yet to put wine into bottle, but envisages two *cuvées*, one predominately Syrah with some Grenache Noir and the other vice versa. We tasted vat and barrel samples, which inspired confidence. Réboul also believes in old Carignan, because it can give colour and structure. Grenache Noir can be problematic, because Pic St Loup is a late ripening area and even if the grapes are ripe enough to reach a potential 14°, you do not always obtain enough body and extract in the wine. Syrah does much better, while Mourvèdre is a challenge. He is a thoughtful wine maker, but is adamant that wine is made in the vineyard. All you have to do in the cellar is to work hygienically. The typicity of Pic St Loup is its finesse. It is much more elegant than the other *crus* of the Coteaux du Languedoc, and he certainly does not want hard wines with too much extract. It all promises much for the future and Réboul deserves to do well.

MAS DE MORTIES, ST JEAN-DE-CUCULLE

Rémy Duchemin arrived in Pic St Loup in the summer of 1993. This was a change of life style, for he used to produce video films in Paris, and his brother-in-law Michel Jorcin was a farmer near Grenoble, rearing goats to make cheese. Duchemin already knew the area, which he had explored when a university student at Montpellier. They took two years to find what they wanted, looking initially in Provence and then widening their horizons, eventually to arrive at Mas de Mortiès. It is a wonderful spot, wild and isolated, surrounded by vines, but not too far from the village of St Jean-de-Cuculle. We were given a very noisy welcome by a vociferous pug, Mimoulette, while Lulu, the elegant Scottish greyhound, greeted us more calmly as we waited for Duchemin to return from his vines. The property had been part of the dowry for a member of what Duchemin called the *haute bourgeoisie* of Montpellier but had become very run-down and they were able to buy it on her death.

For their first vintage in 1993 they hired an oenologist, borrowed a press and bought two vats. Since then the cellar has gradually been extended and modernised, with stainless steel vats. Now Duchemin admits that he would prefer concrete vats. There is a neat barrel cellar in what was once the stables. Duchemin did a year's wine-making course and finds the advice of an oenologist enormously helpful in difficult years, for they stop you from making serious mistakes and have a good overall view of each particular vintage. How many wines does he make? Well, that depends on the vintage, but usually a white, *rosé* and two or four reds. He has grafted some Viognier and also has some Roussanne. In 1997 they were fermented in oak and given nine months on the lees with regular *bâtonnage*. In the spring of 1999 the oak still masked the fruit, but there was a satisfying mouth feel, with some body. As yet there are no definite regional characteristics, for people have very little experience of white wine. In 1998 he also fermented some Roussanne in vat, which he will probably blend with that fermented in oak. Unoaked, it was full but fragrant, and the oak will probably add an extra layer of flavour.

Red wines may include a simple Coteaux du Languedoc based on Grenache Noir, a Pic St Loup based on Syrah, which may or may not be oak aged, and a *tête de cuvée*, which is likely to be a single varietal. In 1995 he made a pure Carignan and in 1998 a pure Syrah. The 1996 Pic St Loup Cuvée Classique was a blend of Syrah and Grenache Noir with some Carignan. He uses carbonic maceration for the Syrah and Carignan with quite a long *cuvaison*, so that it turns into a traditional vinification as the grape skins break down. He wants wines that will age. The tannins in the Pic St Loup are very elegant and not aggressive, so that you can drink the wine early, but they do also allow for ageing. The 1996 Cuvée Bois, from a similar base but with a different *élevage*, including twelve months in wood for half the wine, was an elegant combination of structured tannins and the smoky fruit of the *garrigue*. Duchemin is trying out various different coopers; he likes the discreet wood of Dagaud & Jaegle, whereas barrels from François Frères make more of an impact.

Rich is the word to describe the 1998 vintage. A vat sample of the Cuvée Classique was rounded and ripe, with firm tannins and spicy fruit, while the Grande Cuvée was more structured and included some Mourvèdre. There was no problem with ripening Mourvèdre in 1998, while 1997 proved more problematic. We finished with the 1998 pure Syrah, with the intense varietal character of pepper and violets. It was denser and less elegant than the other red wines. Duchemin is cheerfully confident of the future of Pic St Loup.

ERMITAGE DU PIC ST LOUP, ST JEAN-DE-CUCULLE

Duchemin's nearest neighbours are the Ravaillé brothers at Ermitage du Pic St Loup. They are literally at the foot of the Pic St Loup, with their winery close to the beginning of one of the paths up to the summit. This is an estate that the Ravaillé family has owned since the Revolution. Originally there were sheep, as well as olive trees and vineyards. We were shown around by Jean-Marc Ravaillé. A mischievous thought went through my mind that his stance and rotund figure reminded me of Tweedledum – or was it Tweedledee? His grandfather had his own wine cellar and then joined the co-operative of St Mathieu in 1951. Then in 1992 the three brothers made the decision to bottle their own wine, and they are now busy restoring the old cellars, parts of which date back to 1250 and the origins of the estate. They now have forty-five hectares in various different parts of the *cru* and some of their grapes do still go to the co-operative. Grenache Noir was planted after the 1956 frost, Syrah at the end of the 1970s and Mourvèdre ten years later. Their oldest white vines are some forty-year-old Clairette and there is some young Roussanne. Some Viognier has been grafted on to Carignan and they have also retained a small vineyard of very old Carignan. Essentially, they make a white, a *rosé* and two or three red wines.

We tasted vat and barrel samples of some wonderfully ripe 1998s. There is a Cuvée Classique, aiming for an easy-to-drink style of wine, while the Cuvée Ste Agnès, a barrel-aged blend of eighty per cent Syrah and twenty per cent Grenache Noir, is more substantial.

Each vineyard is vinified separately; the malolactic fermentation takes place in wood, a small part of which is new, and the wine is racked regularly. They too are trying out different barrels and different coopers – Damy, Saury and François Frères among others – and are tending to favour Allier wood and medium toast. They feel that they have a lot to learn about barrels and are conducting numerous experiments, trying out different sizes, varying the ratio of wood to wine. They also favour a long *élevage* in wood, with 1997s still in barrel in the spring of 1999. For Ravaillé, the typicity of the Pic St Loup comes from a combination of *terroir*, linked to man and the wine itself. The rocky slopes give notes of *garrigue*, bay, eucalyptus, tapenade and red fruit. Certainly their wines were rich, and in some instances curiously sweet, with notes of ripe cassis and even orange peel.

LA GRAVETTE, CORCONNE

Corconne is the most northerly village of Pic St Loup, perched under a dramatic backdrop of cliffs. The village co-operative, called la Gravette, was founded in 1939 and now has ninety-five members with five hundred and fifteen hectares in Corconne and the surrounding villages. Its original vocation was *vin de table* and then it produced the VDQS of Pic St Loup. It now makes a small amount of Coteaux du Languedoc and Pic St. Loup and some Vin de Pays d'Oc, while a considerable part of its output remains simple Vin de Pays de l'Hérault or even *vin de table*. Ninety-five per cent of the vineyards of the village of Corconne are classified in Pic St Loup, but not everyone has the appropriate varieties, for there is still a large proportion of Carignan and Cinsaut. This is the coolest and wettest part of the Pic St Loup, and although some people planted Mourvèdre here twelve years ago, it has yet to ripen properly.

As for white wine, they have some Marsanne and Roussanne, with the young vines making a *vin de pays* that is clean and fresh with some delicate floral fruit. The white Coteaux du Languedoc, from Marsanne, Roussanne, Rolle and Grenache Blanc, including a proportion fermented in *barrique*, was solidly oaky on the palate. In 1997 half the wine was put in wood and the oak effect was overpowering, but for 1998 the amount was reduced to a more discreet twenty per cent. A Sauvignon Vin de Pays d'Oc was quite pungent. As for red wines, a Coteaux du Languedoc, from Grenache Noir with twenty per cent of Syrah, was warm and spicy with some tannin. They have two individual estates for Pic St Loup, Domaine de Tourtourel, where the soil is very stony, and Domaine des Vignes Hautes, from equal parts of Grenache Noir and Syrah, grown in poor soil under the cliffs. The first is kept in vat, making for firm cherry fruit, while the second spends twelve months in wood, giving some oaky, tannic flavours. The barrels are kept inside an enormous renovated concrete vat.

The director, Jean-Luc Laurent, is young and keen. He talked about the change in people's attitudes, giving a simple illustration of how proud they have become of their wine: when he first arrived, the members brought pastis to the management meetings, but now they bring their own wine. Prices have increased too. In 1991 FF 12.50 was the retail price of their most expensive bottle, while by 1999 they could ask FF 40 for a bottle of Pic St Loup. The wines showed a consistent quality. They have projects for the future, including improving their pressing equipment and the reception area for the grapes. These will be mainly self-financed, although they can obtain some subsidies as this is deemed to be a *zone défavorisée*. Once they obtained as much as fifty per cent, but now that has dropped to nineteen per cent, with the money coming from Brussels and the regional government.

CHATEAU DE LANCYRE, LANCYRE

Lancyre is a tiny hamlet near the village of Valflaunès where Bernard Durand and other members of his family run the Château de Lancyre. His great-grandfather came here in 1870. There were sheep as well as vines, but in the 1970s they gave up the sheep and developed the vineyards. Durand is a jolly farmer, sporting a check beret the afternoon that we met. He took us to see the site of a new vineyard, where sheep had once grazed. They found a large ammonite when they cleared the *garrigue*, showing that this area had once been covered by the sea, some 150 million years ago. The ground was unbelievably stony, with large white boulders that had been removed by a bulldozer lying at the side of the field. The soil, such as it is, has to be well prepared before the vines are planted. Altogether they have seventy-five hectares of vineyard in production, around the hamlet and by the pretty Romanesque chapel of Notre-Dame-d'Aleyrac.

Durand talked about the development of the property. At the beginning all the grapes went to the co-operative. After the big frost of 1956, which destroyed so many of the vines, they replanted Carignan and Cinsaut, while Grenache Noir followed in 1965. It has always been in the vineyards here, but had been underrated. Their first Syrah was planted in 1987, with some Mourvèdre, and Viognier followed in 1992, with some Roussanne T-budded on to Carignan. 1984 was the vintage of their first bottling. Before that they sold in bulk to the *négoce*. This is now very much a family concern, employing nine members, one of who is studying oenology.

There are two white wines, both from Roussanne with some Viognier. The unoaked wine was delicate and fragrant, with hints of quince, but by contrast the oaked wine, given the full Burgundian treatment, was much more solid and nutty, with a firm structure and some ageing potential. A Coteaux du Languedoc, from Syrah and Grenache Noir with just ten per cent of Carignan and Cinsaut, was peppery and rustic, while a Pic St Loup from old Syrah and Grenache Noir – that is to say, twenty-five or thirty years old – was solid and sturdy, what the French would call *costaud*, rather like our host, and *sauvage*, or wild, like the countryside. The Grand Cuvée, from Syrah, Grenache Noir and just ten per cent of Mourvèdre, spends twelve months in barrels, of which one-third are new. There was structure and vanilla on the palate. They first used *barriques* in 1991, trying a variety of different coopers, and now favour medium-toasted Allier oak. Where the barrels are now were once Durand's grandfather's old *foudres*, and in the corner was a museum piece, a very early tractor from the 1920s.

MAS BRUGUIERE, VALFLAUNES

Guilhem Bruguière runs the family estate of Mas Bruguière in the tiny hamlet of la Plaine near Domaine de l'Hortus. He took over his father's vines in 1973 and until 1986 continued to send the grapes to the co-operative. Then in 1986 he made just five thousand bottles, using an old basket press, and has gradually continued to extend his production. He is a short, stocky man in his forties, with a firm sense of commitment to his appellation. His family has been here since the Revolution, gradually building the small hamlet. He and his son are the only ones to work here, although his three sisters and brother each have holiday homes around an attractive courtyard.

Bruguière explained that, as the climate here is cooler and fresher than in other parts of the Languedoc, both Carignan and Cinsaut tend to overproduce, so that if it rains in August, the grapes are more like small plums. Syrah does much better, for the climate is not dissimilar to that of Hermitage in the northern Rhône, and the characteristic elegance of Pic St Loup comes from the more northerly climate. Bruguière has Syrah, Grenache Noir and a little Mourvèdre for his red wines, but no longer any Cinsaut or Carignan, and has planted Marsanne and Roussanne for white wines, making a total of nine hectares, but with more land available.

There are some wonderful examples of ammonites in his tasting room, which we admired before exercising our taste buds. Bruguière produces three red wines. The simplest is Vinam de Cadiz, made from Grenache Noir and forty per cent Syrah, half of which is vinified by carbonic maceration. It was appealingly fruity. The name recalls a vineyard that was part of the village of Valflaunès and belonged to the bishop of Maguelone in the twelfth century. Next came Mas Bruguière Classique, called l'Arbouse after the *arbousier* or strawberry trees that abound in the *garrigue*. It is a blend of Syrah and Grenache Noir, and the 1997 had some attractive sweet, spicy fruit and was eminently drinkable, what the French call *gouleyant*. The Cuvée Barrique, which includes Mourvèdre as well as Grenache Noir and Syrah, spends about eleven months in oak. In the 1997 the wood was well integrated, adding structure but certainly not overwhelming the fruit.

The white wine, Les Mûriers made from Roussanne, was delicate with floral flavours, for it was fermented in vat rather than barrel. Oak would be tempting, but the quantity is currently so tiny. The name is a reminder of the importance of mulberry trees in the region. Most of the farms here used to breed silkworms, but that tradition died out forty or fifty years ago with the development of synthetic fibre. As well as vines, olive trees and silkworms, there were pigs, cereals and fruit trees. The monoculture of the vine really came with the recovery from the phylloxera crisis.

CHATEAU CAZENEUVE, LAURET

André Leenhardt, the current president of the growers' *syndicat*, is a relative newcomer to the region, having arrived at Château Cazeneuve in 1988. He worked for the Chamber of Agriculture in Montpellier for ten years, but not in viticulture. He was involved in a programme to diversify the various crops in the region and in experiments with aromatic plants for both medical and industrial purposes, looking for alternatives to the vineyards that had been pulled up in the 1980s. The idea of being a farmer had always been there at the back of his mind, though not necessarily a *vigneron*, but he has caught what he called the *virus de la vigne*. His immediate family had nothing to do with wine, although an uncle was a *pinardier*, selling cheap wines to cafés. Cazeneuve came up for sale in 1987 and although the SAFER said it was in a bad condition, he bought it none the less, doing a year's wine making course and also keeping his salaried job for two or three years. There were table grapes such as Muscat and Clairette in the vineyards, as well as wine varieties. He is gradually replanting and will eventually have twenty-five hectares in production. His first vintage was 1991 and 1998 was the first year when he did not send any grapes to the co-operative. Leenhardt has modernised the very old cellar that had not been used for years, and has turned the former sheepfold into an attractive barrel cellar.

Roussanne is likely to be the basis of the white wine, with Marsanne, Rolle, Grenache Blanc and a little Viognier. Muscat might also be a possibility, but certainly not Chardonnay or Sauvignon. 'In an appellation the expression of the *terroir* is as important as the expression of the grape variety.' Roussanne seems to work well here, so Leenhardt's 1997 white is a blend of eighty per cent Roussanne with fifteen per cent Grenache Blanc and just five per cent Viognier, with some oak influence. He intends to reduce the percentage of new barrels, while older vines will give the wine more body and substance. Les Terres Rouges is made from young vines, mainly Grenache Noir with thirty per cent Syrah and twenty per cent Mourvèdre, that are given a fifteen-day maceration; the wine is bottled in May for relatively early drinking. Les Calcaires has much more Syrah, with a little Carignan and some Mourvèdre, and is given a longer *cuvaison*. It spends a year in vat, demonstrating that you can make wines to age without putting them in wood. La

Grande Cuvée is mainly Syrah with a little Grenache Noir and Mourvèdre, which spend about thirteen months in barrels, of which one-third is new. The flavour is firm and structured, with good fruit, promising ageing potential.

We talked about the future of the appellation as we enjoyed a picnic lunch by a magnificent flowering mimosa tree. There are old people who think that the vineyards will not exist in ten years time, as some of the land, with its proximity to the urban sprawl of Montpellier, is so much more valuable for building. The going rate for building land in the spring of 1999 was FF 1,500 per square metre, while in comparison vineyard land cost FF 200–250,000 per hectare. Interest in the area from outside continues. Jean-Marc Boillot from Pommard has bought ten hectares, and a Swiss has just purchased Mas de Foulaquier, a neglected property next to Mas de Lavabre. The choice of grape variety depends on the vineyard. Grenache Noir and Syrah generally do best, and of course as the vines gain in age, they hope that the wine will improve in quality. With its new status as an aspiring appellation, the future for Pic St Loup looks rosy.

Key facts

VDQS 1955, incorporated into the appellation in 1985 and now a *cru* within the Coteaux du Languedoc having stricter requirements: thirteen villages around the rocky outcrop of Pic St Loup; 50 hl/ha maximum.

Syrah, Mourvèdre and Grenache Noir a minimum of ninety per cent; minimum of 11.5°.

Cooler climate than most of the Coteaux du Languedoc.

Enjoying spectacular development, with new producers and a competent co-operative.

Vintages

1999: Rain in September diluted the crop; much depends on individual producers.
1998: A great vintage, as elsewhere in the Languedoc, with ripe fruit giving structured wines with ageing potential.

1997: Some rain in August caused rot and made for a vintage that needs selection.

1996: Another problematic year caused by rain at the wrong time, but again careful producers have done well.

1995: A good vintage, with ripe fruit making appealing, rounded wines.

Grès de Montpellier

The proposed *terroir* of Grès de Montpellier will cover a large area of the hinterland of Montpellier, taking in the existing *terroirs* of St Georges d'Orques, Méjanelle, St Christol, St Drézery and Vérargues, as well as numerous estates that are currently just plain Coteaux du Languedoc. Vérargues has virtually disappeared from usage, whereas the producers of St Georges d'Orques and Méjanelle still maintain their particular identity.

St Georges-d'Orques

St Georges-d'Orques has long enjoyed a reputation for its wines. In the seventeenth century they were exported as far afield as Russia, Switzerland and the Netherlands, as well as to England; there is a record of a purchase of St Georges-d'Orques by the Earl of Bristol in 1715. Thomas Jefferson appreciated the wines when he was ambassador of the newly independent United States in Paris and encouraged their importation across the Atlantic. In the early nineteenth century the English interned in Montpellier during the Napoleonic Wars acquired a taste for them, and according to Morton Shand in *A Book of French Wines*, decanter labels bearing the name St Georges referred not to the better known village of Nuits St Georges in the Côte d'Or, but to St Georges-d'Orques. In fact, there are about one hundred *communes* in France that include St Georges in their name. There are various possibilities as to the meaning of the word *orque*. It might be another term for what the French call a *jarre*, an enormous earthenware container like the *orci* in which Tuscans keep olive oil. Another suggestion is that it was a mythical dragon, while the dictionary definition of *orque* is killer whale.

The village was mentioned by the nineteenth-century authorities. Jullien, writing in 1816, listed it with Vérargues, St Drézery and St Christol, saying that the wines had an agreeable taste with body and alcohol, and after five years' ageing made distinguished bottles that could compare with those from Burgundy. Rendu wrote that there were five hundred hectares of vines, of which Terret Noir and Prian formed the base, with Oeillade and Clairette, while Carignan, Morastel and even Aramon had been introduced. The wines were distinguished by their honest taste. They were heady wines that developed after three years into something better than average.

Mostly they were drunk in Paris. Vizetelly, at the end of the nineteenth century, said that St George was the only wine of real character in the Hérault.

The village of St Georges-d'Orques lies close to the western suburbs of Montpellier. At first glance the terrain does not appear as propitious for the production of good wines as that of villages like Montpeyroux and Faugères in the hilly countryside to the north. Here the land is more gently undulating. François Henry, from the recently created Domaine Henry, took me to a viewpoint over the vineyards. It was a spring afternoon with cistus coming into flower, and you could see the high-rises of Montpellier on the skyline. About five or six hundred hectares are delimited, but only about half are in production, in the *commune*s of St Georges-d'Orques and also Murviel-lès-Montpellier, Laversune, Pignan and Juvignac. The highest vineyards lie at about one hundred and sixty metres, which is considerably lower than those of Pic St Loup or Faugères to the north. There are two types of soil: terraces of pebbles to the south towards Murviel, and to the north and west jurassic limestone with a strong presence of iron, so that the soil is noticeably red in colour. There is even a vineyard called Costa Raste, or *côte rôtie* in French. For Henry it is this soil, with a deep subsoil, that gives St Georges-d'Orques its legendary finesse and a good balance of acidity, as well as tannin, with ripe fruit.

CAVE COOPERATIVE DE ST GEORGES-D'ORQUES

Until recently, the production of St Georges was dominated by the village co-operative and by the smaller co-operatives at Pignan and at Montarnaud and Murviel-lès-Montpellier combined. The co-operative at St Georges-d'Orques was founded in 1948 and now has two hundred and fifty members, with six hundred and fifty hectares in St Georges and the surrounding villages. Only a third of their average annual production of thirty thousand hectolitres is St Georges-d'Orques or Coteaux du Languedoc. In addition, they make a wide range of *vin de pays* as well as bulk *vin de table*. There are various different *cuvées* of St Georges-d'Orques. The Cuvée Tradition, a blend of Syrah, Grenache Noir and Carignan, was rugged and lightly spicy, with no great depth of flavour. A Sélection Terroir is made from older vines, with a high proportion of Syrah.

They have been working with *barriques* since 1985 and age the identical blend in wood for eight or ten months, giving it a touch of vanilla. I preferred the spicy, supple fruit of the unoaked wine. The Cuvée Thomas Jefferson is a blend of two or three vintages, from two parts Syrah to one part Grenache Noir, with some firm vanilla fruit after a period of barrel ageing. It was well made but quite international in flavour.

In common with many of the co-operatives of the south, they are encouraging their members to work for quality, paying them according to the final destination of their grapes and considering vineyard selection, with numerous small vinification vats. Twelve or fifteen days is the minimum *cuvaison* for a red wine, as they are trying to achieve more body and weight in their wines. As for white wines, Viognier is a particular enthusiasm – one grower called it their *dada*, or hobby – and its planting is encouraged by a subsidy of FF 30,000 per hectare. We tasted the 1998, which had been given some skin contact and was quite smoky and fragrant on the palate, but just a touch confected. They are also working on a barrel-fermented late harvest Viognier and there are some Chardonnay and Sauvignon too.

DOMAINE HENRY, ST GEORGES-D'ORQUES

Much more interesting are the independent producers of St Georges-d'Orques, most of whom did not exist ten years ago. When François Henry arrived here in 1992, there were just two, the Château de l'Engarran and Domaine Fourques, and ninety per cent of the production was in the hands of the co-operatives. Now there are at least eight individual growers.

Henry came to St Georges d'Orques after the sale in 1990 of his family's estate of St Martin-de-la-Garrigue. He wanted the opportunity to create something that was really his own, and St Georges appealed because it already had a certain reputation, but with the potential for creative growth. He now controls eleven hectares of vines, from which he makes an imaginative range of wines.

Les Paradines Rosé, the name of a *climat*, is a blend of equal parts of Grenache Noir, Cinsaut and Carignan; it is ripe and fruity, redolent of strawberries, with fresh acidity. A pure Cinsaut *rosé* from vines that are between twenty and forty-five years old is packed with ripe cherry fruit. There are two *cuvées* of red St Georges-d'Orques, the best grapes going into Le St Georges and everything else into Les Paradines, which is usually a blend of Grenache Noir, Syrah and Cinsaut, with some appealing fruit. Le St Georges, which also includes Mourvèdre, is much more serious in stature, with firm, structured fruit. Henry criticises the people who place too much confidence in Syrah, for he considers that it should not dominate the blend. He is looking for finesse, not power, and that is what he has achieved. There is an attractive medallion on the label depicting the old iron mark that was stamped on barrels of St Georges during the first half of the eighteenth century.

Henry is a source of historical knowledge about his area. Apparently there were very strict regulations about production in force in the eighteenth century, more severe than today's appellation regulations. You were obliged to observe the *ban de vendange* and the municipality paid for guards to ensure that the ban was observed. If anyone did break it, their grapes were automatically declassified and they were fined. In 1753 the *ban de vendange* was 10 October, which seems very late by today's standards, when the vintage is usually in September.

Henry's final wine is a late harvest red wine, a selection of over-ripe *grains nobles* that have been dried in the autumn sunshine. The grapes, the traditional varieties of the region – he declined to say which – are picked in three *tris* ten days apart and the fermentation stopped by chilling, leaving about 80 gms/l sugar with 12° alcohol, after which the wine goes into barrel for about five months. The flavour was long and gently sweet, an intriguing combination of chocolate and raspberries.

CHATEAU DE L'ENGARRAN

The Château de l'Engarran was built in the seventeenth century as a rich man's folly and as a home for his mistress away from the prying eyes of Montpellier. The soft stone came from the quarry at the nearby village of Pignan. There is a chapel, now bare except for the tomb of a former owner, Laurent Quetton de St Georges, and the facade of the château bears a frieze depicting the three ages of woman: a young girl, a mother who looks to the future and an old woman surveying her past. The gardens *à la française* were designed by a pupil of Le Nôtre, with elegant pathways. The château was at its most splendid on a February evening during Vinisud, when Françoise Grill and her two daughters, Constance Rérolle and Diane

Losfelt, hosted a dinner. The gardens were floodlit and we dined in the old vaulted cellars.

The property has been in the family for five generations, since 1924. It was Mme Grill who took what in 1978 was the dramatic step of starting to put her wine in bottle, after a regular order in bulk to Monoprix came to an untimely end. She was vindicated when the wine won a medal at the Concours de Paris, and twenty years later it still retained a warm, rustic flavour. They now produce 100,000 bottles a year, half in appellation St Georges-d'Orques and half in Vin de Pays des Collines de La Moure. Diane Losfelt has been the wine maker since 1983, after training in Montpellier, while Constance Rérolle is responsible for sales. Today the two sisters make a powerful team, exuding enthusiasm for their property. The cellars are well organised and inspire confidence, with a range of wines that is well conceived. There was a delicate, refreshing *rosé*; a Sauvignon Vin de Pays d'Oc with good varietal fruit, showing an almost New Zealand richness; a cheerful Vin de Pays des Collines de la Moure, made mainly from old Carignan, which Rérolle described as 'our Gamay'; and a slightly more substantial Garrigue de l'Engarran from young vines.

As for St Georges-d'Orques itself, there are various qualities. Cuvée Ste Cecile is a blend of Grenache Noir, Carignan and Cinsaut that spends a year in *foudre*. The light oxygenation tones down the acidity that is typical of the soil of the area. It was quite light and rugged in flavour. More serious is the Cuvée Classique from fifty per cent Syrah, thirty per cent Grenache Noir and twenty per cent Carignan, with the exact blend varying from vintage to vintage. It too spends time in *foudres*, but was more tannic and substantial, with rounded, spicy fruit. Finally the Cuvée Quetton St Georges is a blend of eighty per cent Syrah and twenty per cent Grenache Noir. A quarter of the wine spends six months in *barriques*, while the rest is aged in *foudres*. The first vintage was the 1995, which in the spring of 1997 had well-integrated oak with some vanilla and ripe fruit. The first time she tasted it, Françoise Grill is supposed to have exclaimed, 'I never would have believed that we could make a wine like this at l'Engarran.' It illustrates the progress that has been made in the Midi in twenty years.

CHATEAU DE FOURQUES

Lise Fons-Vincent is a friendly woman, a cousin of her neighbours at the Château de l'Engarran. While l'Engarran is an elegant unity, the Château de Fourques is a much older hotchpotch of architectural styles. There is no elegant façade here, just some slightly incongruous palm trees in the courtyard. The origins of the château are eleventh century, but most of it was built in instalments between the fifteenth and eighteenth centuries. We walked in the vineyards, while Mme Vincent explained how she had taken over the property from her grandfather. He had sold to the *négoce*, but with the expertise of a marketing degree, she wanted to sell her own wine in bottle. The vineyards were in good condition, with twenty-five hectares planted all in one block on the *galets roulées* of St Georges, including a lower vineyard that is Vin de Pays des Collines de la Moure, even though the difference in altitude is only three or four metres. However, it is all a question of soil, and in particular its fertility; the lower vineyard is simply too rich for an appellation wine, while the soil of the St Georges-d'Orques vineyards is red in colour and full of stones.

In the distance we could see the nearby village of Juvignac, the pointed Pic St Loup and the hills of La Moure. The almond blossom was in flower and the urban sprawl of Montpellier seemed very remote. An old man was busy pruning vines. He can manage five hundred plants a day at a princely 70 centimes per vine. Mme Vincent's oldest Syrah was planted in 1984 and she also has some Chardonnay and Merlot, but no Mourvèdre as she finds it too problematic. She is planning to plant Grenache Blanc and Rolle for white wine, but in the meanwhile makes a refreshingly unoaked Chardonnay.

Unusually, because it is so decried, she still has some Aramon, vines that her grandfather planted in 1962 and which produce just 30 hl/ha. Aramon is not unlike Cinsaut in flavour and behaviour but with larger grapes, from which she makes an attractive *rosé*. There is a restaurant outside Perpignan called L'Aramon and when its owner advertised in the *Midi Paysan* for examples of Aramon for his wine list, he just received three replies, which illustrates to what extent this notorious variety has disappeared from the vineyards of the Midi. There is also a more conventional *rosé* from Syrah and Cinsaut, with more layers of fruit and flavour, demonstrating by comparison the shortcomings of the Aramon. Merlot, planted in 1991, makes a smoky, plummy *vin de pays* and there are two *cuvées* of St Georges-d'Orques. The first is from equal parts of Carignan, Grenache Noir and Syrah, which spend two years in vat, developing some meaty, rustic fruit, while the *haut de gamme*, a blend of eight per cent Syrah and twenty per cent Grenache Noir, is altogether more elegant and serious.

DOMAINE DE LA PROSE

Domaine de la Prose is a much more recent creation, for Alexandre and Patricia de Mortillet bought the property in 1990. There were already some vines and a shed for storing equipment, but that was all. They have built an attractive house and a streamlined cellar, which you approach along a dirt track lined with holm oaks and olive trees that takes you up into the hills, to about a hundred metres in altitude. There are views towards the isolated church of Maguelone, and you can also see the sea and feel the influence of the maritime breezes. There is no problem here with drought or frost, and the good aeration means that very little treatment is needed in the vineyards. Indeed, for them the typicity of St Georges is the freshness that comes from the climate. Theirs are not heavy wines.

The son of the family, young Bertrand de Mortillet, makes the wine, after training at Blanquefort in the Gironde. His first vintage was 1995. For the first couple of years he fermented in stainless steel vats, but in 1998 he tried out some conical wooden vats and the results were fantastic. To quote his more extrovert mother, 'Now the quality is exploding', giving much more concentration. The temperature also remains more stable in wood than in stainless steel, staying hotter for longer. They are also experimenting with different barrels and find that Burgundian *pièces* seem to suit their wine best. The range of la Prose has developed into three reds, as well as a white and a *rosé*.

The white is a blend of Rolle and Grenache Blanc, with a certain herbal quality and hints of aniseed. In 1998 they tried fermenting

Rolle in wood, which seemed to adapt better than Grenache Blanc. The *rosé* is a blend of Syrah, Grenache Noir and Cinsaut, with rounded, raspberry fruit. As for reds, the basic wine is a blend of equal parts of Grenache Noir and Syrah with some ripe berry fruit. The Cuvée Prestige, from eighty per cent Syrah and twenty per cent Grenache Noir, had the ripe, spicy fruit of the *garrigue* and was particularly appealing, while the *fût de chêne*, from the same blend, was more solid and tannic, with less charm. Finally there was a late harvest Grenache Noir, from grapes picked at the end of November. One and half hectares yielded just one hundred and fifty litres of wine, from grapes that were fully *passerillés*, with even a little noble rot. The fermentation stopped at 17°. There were hints of prunes and bitter chocolate, with a sweet, concentrated flavour.

DOMAINE DES BELLES PIERRES

Damien Coste at Domaine des Belles Pierres is an enthusiastic young man who is busy creating his own estate. He said he had a *coup de tête*, or brainstorm, in 1994 and withdrew his vines from the village co-operative of Murviel-lès-Montpellier when it decided to link up with the co-operative of the village of Montarnaud, which is not even within the area of St Georges-d'Orques. It was his grandfather who had joined the co-operative in the first place. For his first vintage, he was able to borrow facilities at Château de Fourques, and he has gradually equipped a small cellar, helped by advantageous loans as a 'young wine grower'. With his new associate Régis Sudre he has seventeen hectares of vines. There is Sauvignon, some Petit Manseng planted in 1991, more recent plantings of Merlot, Cabernet Sauvignon and Viognier, and for the appellation, some Roussanne, Marsanne, Rolle, a little Muscat *à petits grains* and some Grenache Blanc, with the usual five grape varieties for red wine. Altogether Coste makes about eight different wines, and has acquired a particular reputation for white wines. That is what he really enjoys. Reds are more problematic, as he was not able to carry out the long *cuvaison* that he wanted until he bought his *égrappoir* in 1998.

We spent a happy hour tasting our way round the cellar, enjoying a diversity of different flavours and ideas, some single varieties from vat or barrel and some finished blends. A pure Sauvignon was an enjoyable drink, but not very typical of the variety. This is a question of *terroir*, according to Coste. The vineyards at Murviel-lès-Montpellier are on gentle slopes, a very stony mixture of lime-stone and clay. Generally he does not want to make varietal wines for there is too much competition and in any case the results are less interesting. His red Vin de Pays d'Oc called Mosaic (a blend of Merlot and Grenache Noir with a little Cabernet Sauvignon) was quite tannic, with hints of liquorice. He first used oak for his red wines in 1998 with some Syrah, which he was planning to blend with some Mourvèdre, which had reached 14° and was almost port-like in concentration. The wine will be called Le Chant des Ames, while the unoaked St Georges-d'Orques is called Les Bimarelles, meaning little rows. For Coste, the typicity of St Georges-d'Orques is the spiciness of the *garrigue*, for which you must have very ripe grapes.

Coste first used barrels for his white wine in 1994 and here you feel that he is in his element. His white Cuvée Bimarelles is based on Roussanne and Viognier that were fermented in barrels of two wines. The oak was well integrated and the flavour rich and perfumed, with the Viognier particularly apparent on the palate. He had also tried fermenting Rolle in wood, but was not quite sure what he was going to do with it. It was very rich on the palate, full, biscuity and textured. A blend of Marsanne and Roussanne was rich and sweet, while still fermenting gently in late October. If a little sugar remains, it might not pass the *labelle* tasting, in which case it will be classified into *vin de table*, not even *vin de pays*, and labelled Ineptie, or ineptitude. This man has a sense of humour. A blend of Muscat with just twenty per cent Roussanne was redolent of ripe Muscat fruit.

We finished with some intriguing examples of late harvest Petit Manseng and Grenache Blanc. Coste had first made a pure Petit Manseng, but he wanted to retain the typicity of the Mediterranean so he has subsequently blended it with Grenache Blanc. He is also planning to plant some Servant, an old table grape variety, which apparently resembles Petit Manseng, with thick skins that make it eminently suitable for *passerillage*. In theory, Petit Manseng is not allowed here, but the *syndicat* of the Vin de Pays d'Oc has submitted a dossier to the appropriate authorities. In 1998 the Grenache Blanc was picked at the end of October and the Petit Manseng in three separate *tris* between the middle of October and early December, while the last picking for the 1996 vintage was on 5 January 1997. There is no climatic difficulty in obtaining wind-dried grapes; the main hazard is presented by the wild boars, who have a penchant for sweet grapes. Yields are tiny, with eight to twelve hectolitres per hectare, and the wine was rich and peachy, with roasted notes on the finish. A pure Petit Manseng was even more apricoty, with the characteristic firm acidity on the finish. Damien Coste deserves to go far.

DOMAINE DE LA MARFEE

Thierry Hazard also has vines in the village of Murviel-lès-Montpellier and he made his very first wines in 1997 at Château de Fourques. We visited him at home in a tree-lined street near the centre of Montpellier, where his wife, with immense tolerance for her husband's obsession, has allowed him to turn the ground floor of their house into a minute barrel cellar. Hazard describes himself as *un passioné du vin*, although by profession he is a qualified chartered accountant. He is quite young and very serious, an intense man but with some humour. He related how he had looked long and hard for suitable vineyards, particularly in Pic St Loup, and had been on the point of signing a contract when he found more suitable land in Murviel – what he described as 'the *terroir* that was my destiny'.

He now has seven hectares in twelve or thirteen different plots, but only two hectares actually in production at the moment, for he is replanting the others. Domaine de la Marfée is called after a wood near where he grew up in the Ardennes that evokes childhood memories. In his maiden vintage he made two *cuvées*, Les Vignes qu'on Abat, meaning 'the vines that people are pulling up', mainly very old Carignan vines that produce just 15–20 hls/ha. Hazard believes that Carignan can be a good variety. Les Champs Murmurés, or whispered fields, includes everything else, some old Grenache Noir, Mourvèdre, Syrah, Cabernet Sauvignon and also a little Carignan. Murmurés is a play on words, including a reference to the numerous stone walls or *murs* surrounding the vineyards of Murviel, where a large plot is forty ares.

First we tasted barrel samples of the 1998 vintage: Syrah from different plots, some Carignan and a blend of Cabernet Sauvignon and Mourvèdre. Each variety is fermented separately and given a long *cuvaison* of at least four or five weeks, with the exception of the Grenache Noir, which needs only fifteen days. Hazard is very meticulous. He has chosen Dagaud & Jaegle for his coopers, asking them to season his wood for a year longer than usual. Then we adjourned upstairs to the sitting room for the 1997 Les Vignes qu'on Abat. Given it blind, you would never believe that this was almost pure Carignan, with just a drop of Grenache Noir and Syrah. It had spent fourteen months in wood, with no racking, and had a deep colour, a closed nose and some rich berry fruit. There was good structure, well-integrated oak and an attractive long fruitiness. The *régisseur* at Château de Fourques guided him for the 1997 vintage, but in 1998 he felt confident enough to go it alone. This man is a thinker. 'I am a beginner' – *un bleu à cent pour cent* as the French would say – and his aim is not to make money, but to produce the kind of wine that he likes to drink. His personal cellar next to the barrels certainly showed good taste, and his progress will be fascinating to follow. His English importers have already proclaimed him the new superstar of the Languedoc, but only time will tell.

DOMAINE TERRE-MEGERE, COURNONSEC

Domaine Terre-Megère is in the village of Cournonsec which, although it is close to St Georges-d'Orques, is not included in the original *cru*, but is part of the larger *terroir* of the Grès de Monpellier. Michel Moreau made his first wine in 1986. Before that, he reared donkeys for trekking, but decided that he had had enough of dealing with stubborn mules. However, he does retain a donkey on his label. He now has twenty-three hectares of vines, including ten hectares up in the *garrigue* behind the village on limestone and red clay. Then there are lower vineyards on more fertile alluvial soil, where he has Merlot and also grows asparagus. As for grape varieties, there is a real hotchpotch: Viognier, Grenache Blanc, Marsanne, Clairette, Muscat, Chardonnay, Grenache Noir, Mourvèdre, Syrah and Cinsaut, but no Carignan, as well as Merlot and Cabernet Sauvignon for *vins de pays*. Altogether he makes three Vin de Pays d'Oc from Merlot, Cabernet Sauvignon and Viognier, as well as three qualities of Coteaux du Languedoc, the classic *cuvée*, an *haut de gamme* called Les Dolomies – the name of the vineyard in the *garrigue* – and La Galopine, which is a blend of several varieties.

Originally Moureau took his grapes to the co-operative, but there were problems. Merlot is an early ripener, and one year it was ripe and ready to pick when the co-operative was still on holiday, so he found a cellar, with an earth floor and a single vat, and has developed from there. His vines in the *garrigue* gave yields that were too low for the co-operative, at 30 hl/ha, and he made the very first declaration of an appellation wine from his village. Initially he wanted the co-operative to introduce a fine wine category, but realised that it was simply not motivated by quality.

We talked and tasted in the simple cellar. Moureau is a thoughtful man with a friendly smile. He talked about the potential *terroir* of Grès de Montpellier. There are at least twenty producers in the area who are doing well, and he sees a good potential for it. However, it is not a very homogeneous area compared with la Clape or Pic St Loup, stretching as it does from Villeveyrac and the Abbaye de Valmagne to the west of Montpellier, round to St Christol in the east. Moureau believes that the concept should help to develop the reputation of the region. Yields will be reduced to 50 hl/ha, with no extra PLC allowed, and the permitted percentage of Carignan and Cinsaut will drop from fifty to thirty per cent, with a minimum degree of 12° rather than 11°. Also, there will be a twelve-month delay before the wines may be sold, with the objective of encouraging the production of more structured wines with some potential for bottle ageing.

Moureau has produced Viognier since 1990. His original cuttings came from Condrieu, and he has since passed on cuttings to producers in Pic St Loup. He finds that Viognier adds length and longevity to Chardonnay, the two complementing each other perfectly. Viognier must be picked at 14°. Lower than 13° is a crime, according to Marcel Guigal in Côte Rôtie. In La Galopine there is at least fifty per cent Viognier, with fifteen per cent each of Chardonnay and Grenache Blanc and the balance made up of Clairette and Marsanne, and part of the wine is barrel fermented. The 1997 vintage was ripe and perfumed, with some smoky fruit. Moureau said that he would have liked more intensity, but I found layers of flavour, making an intriguing comparison with the pure Viognier, which was lighter and more delicate.

Moureau likes what he calls *surmaturité* for his red grapes,

grapes that are convincingly ripe and rich in sugar and flavour. He favours long macerations, uses a proportion of pressed wine and works with micro-oxygenation for *élevage* in vat. He finds that the Bordeaux system of regular racking does not work in the extremes of temperature of the Midi, but admits that 'really we are still learning'. He would like to build an insulated cellar for barrel storage so that he can use more wood, but for that you need money. He is enthusiastic about barrels and seems to manage them well, finding them a pleasure, but is insistent that you must keep them in the right environment. The classic Coteaux du Languedoc, from Grenache Noir, Syrah and Mourvèdre, blended after the malolactic fermentation, had a dry, spicy palate, with the pepperiness of the *garrigue*. Les Dolomies, mainly from Syrah with some Grenache Noir and Mourvèdre, was more substantial, leathery on the nose with perfumed fruit and length. Moureau admits that he never obtains really concentrated Mourvèdre here. Les Galopines is a blend of the best and oldest vines, with rich, spicy fruit and layers of flavour.

DOMAINE POUJOL, VAILHAUQUES

Robert and Kim Cripps are an Anglo-American couple who settled in the Midi in 1994. They are welcoming hosts and have the objective view of outsiders to a region, coming to it without preconceptions but enormous enthusiasm. They have both had varied careers in the wine trade in England, France and California, and dreamt of making their own wine somewhere with sunshine. Provence and the southern Rhône were too expensive, and the Languedoc seemed the most interesting for its freedom and flexibility. They would rather have an interesting piece of land in an unknown appellation than a bad plot in a good appellation. It took six months to find Domaine Poujol, outside the village of Vailhauquès, which is not too far from the suburbs of Montpellier and just three kilometres away from the vineyards of Pic St Loup as the crow flies. Ultimately they will become part of the Grès de Montpellier, even though their vineyards are cooler than the rest of the *terroir* and have more in common with Pic St Loup.

There is a splendid view from the highest point of their vineyards, looking over the valley. Although you can see the high-rises of Montpellier in the far distance, you do not feel close to a large conurbation. The Cripps are firmly against the use of insecticides and take great care over what they use to treat their vines. They would rather lose a few grapes and keep the wild flowers, which are prolific in spring. They favour dense plantings, as many as six thousand five hundred vines per hectares. The vines for the varietal *vins de pays* are planted in wide rows with a large leafy area, whereas true *vin de terroir* comes from vines that give a small crop of concentrated fruit. Not enough attention is paid to the choice of rootstock, which should be decided by soil analysis. Cripps favours 3309 and is very damning of the popular 140, as it can produce too much foliage.

Their cellar is functional, with the traditional cement vats. There were some *foudres*, but they were so rotten that they had to be removed stave by stave and now the Cripps are trying out some 600-litre barrels. Their vineyard of twenty-one hectares includes oddities like forty-year-old Carignan Blanc as well as more conventional Midi varieties, and Merlot and Cabernet Sauvignon. Carignan Blanc is not allowed in Vin de Pays d'Oc, but can be included in Vin de Pays de l'Hérault. They pick it in two *tris*, the first quite early during the harvest to make a crisp wine with herbal notes, and a second when the grapes are very ripe, at a potential 15°, so that after vinification in oak the wine is rich and buttery, with a nutty palate. Their red Vin de Pays de l'Hérault comes from fifty per cent Merlot blended with forty per cent Cinsaut and ten per cent Carignan, making an eminently friendly wine, with ripe, rounded fruit and soft tannins. In 1998 part of their *rosé* was fermented in oak with intriguing results, giving a ripe, balanced wine with a firm finish. There is also a Carignan and Cabernet Sauvignon blend, giving a combination of blackcurrant fruit and warm rusticity. Robert quipped, 'Maybe we shall call it *la bête noire*, or perhaps we should blend it with something else.' The more traditional Coteaux du Languedoc is a blend of Syrah, Grenache Noir, Carignan and Cinsaut, with ripe, perfumed fruit and instant accessibility. You sense that nothing will stand still here.

DOMAINE LA PEYRE ROSE, ST PARGOIRE

Then there are new estates created out of almost nothing. Marlène Soria was working as an estate agent selling holiday apartments at

la Grande Motte on the coast when she and her husband bought a
tumbledown property as a holiday home in 1973. Domaine la Peyre
Rose is in the middle of nowhere, near the village of St Pargoire.
You travel hopefully along a bumpy dirt track through the vines,
wondering indeed if this is the right track, for some jealous
neighbours – such are the petty rivalries in *la France profonde* –
have removed the large stone with a splash of pink paint indicating
the entrance to the property. It is wonderfully isolated, with a small
house and vineyards surrounded by *garrigue*. When the Sorias first
arrived here, there was neither water nor electricity. They planted
their first vines in 1983 and made their first wine in 1988, which is
when Marlène Soria gave up estate agency. They dug a 160-metre
well to find water and have installed an electric generator. Now they
are planning a solar panel and a cellar has been built, operational
just in time for the 1998 vintage.

Madame Soria talked of how she had a *coup de coeur* for the
place. She took us for a walk through the vineyards and I could
quite see why. It is a wild, windy spot, with the vegetation of the
garrigue, the pink cistus and heather and the pink stones giving the
name of the estate. Her husband was working in the vineyard,
accompanied by their donkey. She is shut in when the grapes are
ripe, as one year she escaped, and returned looking like Dracula
after a feast of juicy red grapes. Rabbits and wild boar can also pose
a problem. Soria initially planted vines as an antidote to her work
as an estate agent, and thought she could take her grapes to the local
co-operative. However, they expect you to sign up for thirty years,
so she thought again and bought some second-hand vats, an old
wooden press and a pump.

She has two different *terroirs*, from which she makes two wines,
Cuvée des Cistes, with large stones, originating from old volcanoes,
giving more acidity in the wine, and Cuvée Léone, on a band of
limestone and clay that retains water, making for riper wines. Cistes
is predominantly Syrah with fifteen per cent Grenache Noir, and
Léone, named after the woman who sold them the property, is
Syrah with ten per cent Mourvèdre. Léone is the more immediately
appealing wine, while Cistes takes longer to evolve, even though
both vineyards are picked at the same degree of ripeness. In the
cellar Soria works as simply as possible – as she put it, letting the
grapes do want they want to do. She destems and conducts a long
fermentation, but there is no barrel ageing for she does not yet have

the appropriate cellar conditions. She would like to try out small thirty-hectolitre *foudres*.

We compared a couple of vintages of Cistes and Léone. The 1995 Cistes had a deep colour, some red fruit on the nose, firm, tight tannins and fruit underneath, with the flavours of the *garrigue* and a long finish. Léone was more open and accessible, with a peppery nose, rugged fruit and a long rich finish. In 1994 Cistes was more redolent of black fruit, with chunky tannins and good concentration, while Léone was smoky and meaty, and more structured. There was no great climatic difference between the two years. It is always very dry, with a strong north wind preventing any problems with rot. The white wine, mainly from Rolle and Roussanne, with some old vines of Ugni Blanc and Terret Blanc and a hint of Viognier, was quite herbal in character, with good acidity and ripe fruit. Soria has Muscat and Grenache Blanc too, but they have yet to come into production.

ABBAYE DE VALMAGNE, VILLEVEYRAC

The green Michelin guide gives the Abbaye de Valmagne a single star, but for me it merits more than a detour for its enchanting cloisters and chapter house, with the former chapel housing large oak *foudres* between the columns. The abbey was founded in 1138 by Raymond Trencavel, Viscount of Béziers, and between the twelfth and fourteenth centuries was one of the richest Cistercian abbeys of the south of France. After the French Revolution it passed to the Count of Turenne, who turned it into a thriving viticultural estate, and since 1838 it has belonged to the d'Allaines family. Mme Diane d'Allaines and her son Alain are welcoming hosts. We sat in an elegant salon and Alain d'Allaines talked about the history of the property and the enormous development of the past few years. There was a period in the last century when the Languedoc was more prosperous than Bordeaux and wine was referred to as *l'or rouge* or red gold. In 1868 the property won an award for its Picpoul, but today there is none, as it does not come within the zone of Picpoul de Pinet. It also produced silkworms until the beginning of the nineteenth century. Before the phylloxera crisis the vineyards were planted extensively with Monastrel, also known as Morastel, which has now virtually disappeared from the Midi, although apparently ANTAV, the organisation responsible for much viticultural experimentation, does have a hectare planted with six different clones.

D'Allaines first began planting Syrah and Mourvèdre in 1982, and white varieties, Roussanne, Marsanne, Bourboulenc and Grenache Blanc followed later in the decade. He now has thirty hectares of Coteaux du Languedoc and a further forty-five hectares for Vin de Pays des Collines de la Moure, and also Vin de Pays d'Oc, made from Merlot and Cabernet Sauvignon as well as the traditional varieties. There have been great changes in the cellars in last few years. Quite simply they have become more hygienic, which in turn allows for greater risks in the wine making, such as much longer vinifications. Twenty-five years ago the cellar manager simply poured in the sulphur dioxide and hoped for the best. The estate bottled its first wines in 1975 and now the problem is to convince people that these are bottles that merit some ageing, for this is not part of the traditional culture of the Midi.

I particularly like the white Coteaux du Languedoc, which we sipped as we talked. It is a blend of Marsanne and Roussanne with just ten per cent Viognier, which still has only experimental status within the appellation. The wine is delicate but rich at the same time, with a good concentration of flavour. As for red wines, since 1994 they have made two qualities of Coteaux du Languedoc, both with a high proportion of Syrah – at least sixty per cent – and anything between twenty-five and forty per cent Mourvèdre, with a bit of Grenache Noir. The Cuvée de Turenne, named after an earlier owner, is given a few months of *élevage* in wood. The unoaked wine is supple and fruity, the Cuveé de Turenne more substantial and a 1988, drunk when it was nine years old, was warm and raisiny with a certain rusticity, demonstrating that flavours have become more refined in recent vintages.

DOMAINE DE COMBEROUSSE, COURNONTERRAL

I enjoyed my visit to Alain Reder outside the village of Cournontérral. But first the challenge was to find him. The instructions said follow the telephone wires, so I did, not entirely confident that they were the right telephone wires. The track wiggled and bumped through the *garrigue*, past huge bushes of cistus that were about to come into flower. Finally I arrived at a large shed adjoining a small house. Reder is an older man with a dry sense of humour, who, it proved, does not hesitate to speak his mind, especially on the subject of vinous bureaucracy. For the moment his wines are *vins de pays*, or maybe plain Coteaux du Languedoc, but there is talk of including Cournontérral and other villages in the Grès de Montpellier. The commission had visited the previous week and had apparently been confused by the diversity of different grape varieties. 'They didn't understand anything; they were afraid.' Reder was scathing about small brains inside big heads. So it looks unlikely for the moment, which is a great shame, as the Grès de Montpellier would link the various other *terroirs* that adjoin it and give some focus to an area without much identity.

Reder also condemned oenologists. They have braked the development of white wine in the area. 'They said the grapes should not be riper than 11.5° and the fermentation should not be hotter than 16°C. Well, I pick at 14° and ferment at 22°C. They said the juice must be clean. Well, sometimes I hardly *débourbe* at all. Oenologists are a guarantee. They provide you with a no-risk policy, but you will never produce a great wine if you never take a risk. Where would the originality come from?'

Reder's background is unusual. He was brought up in Algeria, where his parents had vineyards. The family originally come from Lorraine, but left, like many others, after the Franco-Prussian War in 1870 and settled in Algeria. He worked in Africa, particularly in Nigeria and Rwanda, then came back to France in 1972 and bought twenty-five hectares of scrubland. There was no water, no electricity, nothing. He kept sheep on the land and then in 1986 planted just two hectares of vines, some Chardonnay and some Chasan, and the following year planted more, as well as some Grenache Blanc. To make white Coteaux du Languedoc then, you needed Grenache Blanc plus another variety like Clairette, Picpoul or Bourboulenc. There was really no white wine in the appellation, just Picpoul de Pinet and la Clape, but the mid-1980s saw *le boom du blanc*. Chardonnay was fetching FF 1200 per hectolitre then, but now it barely obtains FF 800. Then in 1990 Roussanne, Rolle and Marsanne were allowed in the appellation, so he planted Roussanne and Rolle and now has twelve hectares in the *garrigue*. The vineyards are dominated by the imposing cliffs of the Montagne de la Moure, and the soil is limestone, with a marine influence tempering the night time temperatures.

The first wine was a Chasan, a Vin de Pays d'Oc called Cupidone. 'I always christen my wines.' Chasan can be described as a poor man's Chardonnay, for it has a little weight and body, with some delicate fruit. Next came la Sauvagine, from some powerful Grenache Blanc at 14° or more, tempered by some Rolle at 11.5° to provide vivacity, balancing the very ripe with the barely ripe. It had an intriguing flavour, a certain spiciness and some herbal fruit. Roucaillet is a blend of equal amounts of Rolle and Roussanne with twenty per cent of Grenache Blanc. There were hints of aniseed, with some herbal fruit and perfume. Reder uses small fermentation vats of ten or fifteen hectolitres – 'what I pick in a day' – and separates the free-run juice, the first and last pressings, giving both the Roussanne and Rolle a few hours of skin contact. He is fervently anti-wood. We finished with Djebel, *vendemias de paserillas*, that is, a wine from dried grapes. Djebel in Arabic describes a dry mountain, in other words the countryside at our feet. The wine is made from Rolle, with a regular *tri* every ten days or so. The grapes had little noble rot and the wine was golden in colour, with a flavour of Madeira cake soaked in sherry for a trifle base. Reder starts the fermentation and adds the grapes at each picking. There is no control. In 1996 the wine reached 17° with natural yeast, leaving 35 gm/l of residual sugar. 'It was an experiment which worked. I just let it take its course.' The quantity is tiny, fermented in large blue plastic containers, which Reder jokingly described as *mes futs de cinq vins*.

Méjanelle

The vineyards of Méjanelle lie south east of Montpellier. In some places they are almost part of the suburbs of the city and adjoin the city airport, while in others they seem curiously isolated along deserted country lanes, within the *communes* of Mauguio, St Aunès and Montpellier itself.

In the Middle Ages the bishops of Montpellier had vineyards here and the wines were said to be strong and full-bodied, with plenty of spirit and substance. In 1596 Thomas Platters described his peregrinations around Montpellier and the tasting that he enjoyed at the Château de Grammont. At that time the wine of Méjanelle was called *vin de grès*, a reference to the soil of the vineyards, with their large stones called *galets* or *grès*, which today account for some of the typicity of Méjanelle. The name was taken up in the proposed classification of Grès de Montpellier, of which Méjanelle will be part. In 1626 a certain Abraham Goelnitz wrote that the wines of the Coteaux de la Méjanelle were the most alcoholic of the whole of France. I am not sure that the same would be true today.

CHATEAU DE FLAUGERGUES

Château de Flaugergues is the oldest estate. First there was a Roman villa on the site and then the monks of Grammont cultivated vines here from the eleventh century, until the property was bought by Etienne de Flaugergues in 1690. The present incumbent is his descendant, Count Henri de Colbert. He is also a descendant of Louis XIV's minister Jean-Baptiste Colbert, who did so much for the economy of France in the seventeenth century. The château dates back to the end of that century, making it one of the oldest of the several follies around Montpellier. Today it is open to visitors and although the Michelin guide does not give it a star, I would certainly consider it worth at least a detour. The facade is Italianate and the interior contains a magnificent staircase, hung with Brussels tapestries depicting the life of Moses. There are various family collections in the salons and a wonderful old kitchen with an enormous fireplace and copper pans. The elegant gardens leading to the vineyards are planted with an enormous variety of different trees and provided my first taste of a fejoia, a fruit more commonly found in New Zealand than France.

The typicity of Méjanelle comes from the soil, the large *galets* resembling those of Châteauneuf-du-Pape, which can be as much as three metres deep, with a mixture of clay and limestone soil. As in Châteauneuf du Pape, they reflect the sunshine during the day, making for wines that are high in alcohol, preferably at least 13.5°. Any lower and the wines are too light, with unripe tannins and a pale colour, while in the wonderful vintage of 1998, some wine even reached a natural 16°. The other determining factor is the proximity to the sea, with the marine influence giving cool night-time temperatures.

Henri de Colbert is one of the enthusiasts of the world of wine. He talked discursively of the shared pleasure of making wine and cultivating the vines, of enjoying what Nature has given us, allowing us to make wine that gives pleasure to people. The wealth of this area came from viticulture. He now has thirty hectares in production, virtually all Syrah, Grenache Noir and Mourvèdre, with Carignan almost entirely eliminated from the vineyards, while for white wine there is Marsanne, Roussanne, Grenache Blanc and Rolle. De Colbert enthused about the 1998 vintage, with its combination of good weather and low yields, no more than 40 hl/ha. They were able to begin blending the different grape varieties at vinification, something he prefers to do, believing that 'an early marriage is a better one', and thus achieved a better control of the fermentation temperatures. The wines also benefited from some micro-oxygenation.

They make four red wines, one white and one pink. White wines have progressed enormously in the last few years, with the introduction of more aromatic grape varieties. The 1997 has a rich, smoky nose, with good acidity and concentration from the very ripe grapes. The Rolle provides acidity, the Grenache Blanc body and the

Marsanne and Roussanne fruit. The red Cuvée Tradition is mainly Grenache Noir, with Syrah and Mourvèdre, from younger vines, giving some cherry fruit. The Cuvée Sélection, with a traditional vinification, had a more concentrated flavour and the spicy notes of the south, while the Cuvée Sommelière, vinified by a carbonic maceration lasting as much as five or six weeks, was more solid and raisiny. Finally, the Cuvée Fûts de Chêne is aged in oak for about twelve months, and when the 1996 vintage was only two years old, the oaky vanilla notes were still very obvious on nose and palate. The wine was ripe and rounded, but needed time.

Asked about the future, de Colbert boasted of his ambition that Flaugergues should become the Haut-Brion of the Languedoc. He is very insistent that making wine depends upon teamwork, both in vineyard and cellar. He wants to respect the traditions of the Midi, while maintaining the typicity of Méjanelle and the diversity of the Languedoc.

MAS CALAGE

For Pierre Clavel at Mas Calage there is no typicity in the wines of Méjanelle. It is true that the *terroir* is characterised by the particular stony soil, but then each estate has its own originality. Two other estates bottle their wines: Domaine Trinquier, a new property that did a first bottling of Méjanelle in 1996, and Mas du Ministre. Unexpectedly, there is no co-operative for Méjanelle, but many of the wine growers with vineyards close to the airport sell their wine *en vrac* to *négociants*. This makes Mas Calage the one other significant name in the area.

Pierre Clavel's father Jean is well known in the Languedoc as a former director of the Syndicat des Coteaux du Languedoc and one of the originators of the concept of an all-embracing appellation of Languedoc. He is also the author of two books on the region, but as there were no vineyards in the family, Pierre Clavel worked at other things before coming to Méjanelle for his first vintage in 1986, at the age of twenty-six. He is a friendly man with an infectious giggle. Like Henri de Colbert, he is thrilled – euphoric was the word he used – with the 1998 vintage, but admitted that it had been difficult too. You had to struggle to get it right. They began picking on 28 August and the last grapes were gathered on 4 October, making a six-week harvest rather than the usual three weeks. We went for a walk through the vineyards in autumn sunshine. You can just see the Pic St Loup and the outline of the Cévennes in the distance, and in the other direction there is the sea. The vines seem to be planted in a sea of stones, but underneath there is clay, which makes any problems with drought rare. The average age of the vines is thirty years, but there are some young vines and some as old as seventy.

Clavel makes a variety of different wines, both *vin de pays* and appellation. There is a Chardonnay, a Vin de Pays de la Bénovie, from a small area around St Christol named after a small river. Quite surprisingly, the vines are sixty years old, for they were planted by a previous owner with cuttings from Champagne. Clavel first began using oak for white wines in 1989, and as well as Chardonnay, the Roussanne is fermented in new oak. He buys his barrels from Francois Frères and the Tonnellerie de Mercurey, preferring a mixture of staves from different sources, with a variety of degrees of toasting. The objective is a gentle oxygenation, not a heavy wood influence. He makes two white Coteaux du Languedoc, one predominantly Roussanne and the other mainly Grenache Blanc.

There are four or five different red wines, depending on the vintage, including an oak-aged *vin de pays* made from Merlot and a Cuvée Réserve, La Copa Santa, made for the first time in 1990, that is given nine to twelve months of *élevage* in oak. The appellation wines are all blends of Syrah, Grenache Noir and Mourvèdre and sometimes a little Carignan. Mas de Clavel is simple, with an emphasis on fruit, while Mas Calage Méjanelle should have structure and body. We tasted the 1996, with its solid tannins and hints of pencil shavings, while the 1995, in contrast, was quite chunky and meaty, with a smoky nose and a substantial palate. The Copa Santa, with its oak ageing, is a wine to keep for seven to ten years.

Clavel insists upon the conviviality of wine, and he expects his customers to visit the estate once a year, not just for a hurried appointment, but to spend some time over a meal, enjoying the wines. Together with Henri de Colbert, he is an excellent ambassador for Méjanelle, preventing it from disappearing without trace into the suburbs of Montpellier.

St Drézery

The sleepy village of St Drézery has little to recommend it to the passing visitor. It received a passing mention from the nineteenth-century authorities Jullien and Guyot, which provided some basis for its recognition first as a VDQS in 1951 and subsequently as a *terroir* in the appellation of the Coteaux du Languedoc in 1985. With the proposed changes to that appellation, it will become part of the Grès de Montpellier alongside the neighbouring *crus* of St Christol and Vérargues. Apart from the village co-operative there are a couple of independent producers. In the mid-1980s, Louis Spitaleri at Domaine du Mas de Carrat was attempting with some success to bring his wines above the ordinary, planting Syrah, Mourvèdre, and Merlot long before any of his neighbours. Although he still owns the property, he plays a much less active role in the area than ten years ago.

CHATEAU PUECH-HAUT

Now the reputation of St Drézery rests with a more recently created estate, Château Puech-Haut, the property of Gérard Bru. You approach the estate down an attractive avenue of olive trees and neatly pruned rosemary bushes. Bru is very much a self-made man, an industrialist who boasts of his origins in the Minervois. He happily described himself as a bulldozer, which, to the Anglo-Saxon ear, sounds more poetic in French than English. Certainly you sense that he would let little stand in his way. The vineyards were planted some twenty years ago on land that was cleared of *garrigue*, and until 1993 all the grapes went to the village co-operative.

First we sat in an impressive salon, furnished with heavy, overpowering furniture, and talked while Bru smoked a cigar. The fireplace had come from an antique dealer in Paris, and the house itself was the former préfecture of Montpellier that had been due for demolition. He had simply transported it. No expense has been spared in the cellars. You are greeted by a fresco depicting a religious scene and the walls are painted in yellow ochre. There is a forest of stainless steel vats and a hall of large conical oak vats, each supported by a pair of stone ram's heads. A barrel *chai* contains some two hundred new barrels, from several different coopers.

From the tasting room there is a view over the vineyards, fifty hectares in one large plot, and in March the almond trees were in flower at the bottom of the valley. A glass-topped table showed the *galets roulées* found in liberal quantities in the vineyard, which so efficiently reflect the heat back on to the grapes. Puech is Occitan for a hill, though that hardly describes the terrain, which is gently undulating. All the wines are aged in wood, on the advice of Michel Rolland, the roving Bordelais oenologist and owner of Château Le Bon Pasteur in Pomerol, who has acted as a consultant since 1997. The white wine is mainly Roussanne, with some Marsanne and a drop of Viognier, for Bru is inspired by the white wines of the Rhône Valley. It is fermented in wood, where it stays for eight months before blending. The oak was still very overpowering when the wine was only eighteen months old, and time will tell how it will age. A blend of Syrah and Grenache Noir, the Cuvée Prestige, spends twelve months in wood, after a month-long *cuvasion* and regular *pigeage*. Even though this was the 1996 vintage and therefore made before Rolland's involvement, it nonetheless tasted very *bordelais*, with smoky oak. A blend of Syrah and old Carignan vines, a Tête de Cuvée not made every year, also spends twelve months in oak, making for a very international style of wine. In a way it all seemed very divorced from the Midi.

St Christol

St Christol is a small village to the east of Montpellier, not far from the departmental boundary with the Gard. It was one of the original *crus* of the Coteaux du Languedoc, and will ultimately be incorporated into the *terroir* of Grès de Montpellier, thereby losing its specific identity. The village co-operative dominates the *cru*, but there are also two independent producers who are working well for their area. In addition, a new estate, Domaine de l'Ocelle, has recently been created by a Monsieur Warnery and there is the longer-established Domaine Guinand.

CHATEAU DES HOSPITALIERS

Our first stop was at Château des Hospitaliers, which Serge Martin-Pierrat's parents, who were teachers not *vignerons*, bought some twenty years ago as a run-down château, with about four hectares of vines and a small cellar. The Hospitaliers is a reference to the Knights of the Order of Malta; the property, which lies close to the old Roman road, was one of their first possessions in France. They planted vines here in the tenth century and wine has been made in St Christol ever since. Subsequently the land belonged to the Convent of the Ursulines in nearby Sommières, and the present château dates back to the seventeenth century.

The cellars and house are built around a pretty courtyard, with numerous varieties of sage in flower in October. Serge Martin-Pierrat and his wife Sylviane gave us a friendly welcome. Lively and vivacious, she works as an oenologist, consulting for estates between the Ardèche and the Aude. He has a mop of curly hair and

405

a broad smile, and they are both enthusiastic and well informed about their area. They explained that there is an enormous diversity of soils in St Christol, which allows for several different grape varieties. Some of the soil is very deep and rich, with large amounts of clay and gravel. There is no water stress here, as they have more rain than other parts of the Coteaux du Languedoc, and on occasions even snow. Hail can be a problem too.

In the vineyard they follow the principles of *culture raisonnée*, or sustained viticulture, run by FARRE, the *Forum de l'Agriculture Raisonnée Respecteuse de l'Environment*. This is not as restrictive as organic viticulture and they consider it more effective, pointing out for example that in organic viticulture the only remedy for mildew is copper, which can sterilise the soil. Their older vineyards are planted at a density of four thousand plants to the hectare, while for the new plantings they have increased the density to five thousand five hundred. The wires are higher for Syrah and lower for Grenache Noir, taking into account the respective vigour of the two varieties.

We talked as we tasted a comprehensive range of their wines. First came a white Coteaux du Languedoc, made from Grenache Blanc blended with a little Roussanne. They explained how Roussanne had almost disappeared. Twenty years ago the INRA had encouraged its planting, but usually mixed up in the same vineyard as Marsanne, as single-variety vineyards were not the norm at that time. Until 1997 Roussanne was considered a secondary variety in the appellation, but now, with a change in the regulations, it has become one of the main varieties, along with Marsanne, Rolle, Picpoul, Bourboulenc and Macabeu. Ugni Blanc is now firmly deemed *accessoire* and restricted to a maximum of thirty per cent, as are Terret Blanc and Carignan Blanc. There must always be a minimum of two grape varieties. A second white Coteaux du Languedoc had some oak-aged, low yielding Roussanne as its base, with an attractive smoky nose and rich, buttery flavours. They also have some old Chardonnay vines, over fifty years, giving an average yield of 20 hl/ha, which is very low for Chardonnay, especially in the Midi. The wine is fermented in oak, for Martin-Pierrat feels that otherwise it lacks interest. It had a tight, toasted character, with more elegance than many a Midi Chardonnay.

They make a range of red wines based on the usual grape

varieties, but predominantly Syrah and Grenache Noir. The Cuvée Tradition had light peppery flavours, and the Cuvée Spéciale, from Grenache Noir with a little Cinsaut, was supple, with some smoky fruit. The Cuvée Prestige was much more complex, with a firm, spicy nose, good tannin and fruit, while the Cuvée Réserve is aged in oak for about fourteen months, with 1991 being the first vintage in wood. The 1996 had well-integrated oak, with firm tannins and smoky fruit. It was not an easy vintage, for the spring was cool and wet, while further rain in the summer created problems with the *état sanitaire*. The 1995 Cuvée Réserve had a similar smoky character, but with firmer tannin and more structured fruit. That year there was rain in the spring, but the hot summer made for more solid wines. The 1994 was quite chunky and concentrated, and the 1993 had some vegetal notes, balanced with tannin.

We finished with a late harvest Roussanne made for the first time in 1997. It was picked at the end of September with a potential of 21–22°, but the fermentation stopped naturally at 15°. It was fermented in oak and had a rich, concentrated flavour, with notes of botrytis and a wonderfully balanced combination of honey and acidity.

DOMAINE DE LA COSTE

Luc and Elisabeth Moynier bought Domaine de la Coste in 1975. An example of how attitudes have changed in the last twenty years came from our guide for the day, Jean-Philippe Granier, who works at the Mas de Saporta. He vividly remembered his father, who worked for the SAFER, the organisation that facilitates sales of land in rural France, coming home saying 'some mad guy', namely Moynier, 'has bought a vineyard outside St Christol, where he will die of starvation as the land is so poor'. M. Granier senior simply did not believe in the region in 1975, but he does now.

Moynier took over the story. He is a larger than life character with a bushy moustache and a relaxed, welcoming manner. He had just got married and was working with his father, but really wanted to do his own thing. He had looked everywhere for some land, around Nîmes, Lattes and Fréjorgues, before finding this almost abandoned estate. Nine out of twenty-five hectares were in production and everything was sold *en vrac*, but people were no longer buying *vin de table*. St Christol had just been given its VDQS in 1975, and there was everything to do. The soil was frightening, for the vineyards were covered in enormous stones. They borrowed money from the Crédit Agricole to plant vines, but they could not have a loan for Syrah. They had to plant Carignan and Cinsaut; it was 1979 before they were allowed to plant Syrah and Mourvèdre. The first years were difficult, for they suffered from hail in 1975 and again in 1976, so did not make their first wines until 1977. Moynier saw himself as having the necessary will and idealism; he was young and never became discouraged. They had twelve hectares of tomatoes to help with the cash flow and they survived. They now have thirty-one hectares of vines, divided roughly equally between Syrah, Mourvèdre, Grenache Noir, Cinsaut and Carignan, with six or so hectares of each. The vineyards, just outside the village of St Christol, are low lying, at just sixty metres. The stones absorb the heat, making for some wonderfully ripe grapes, with Grenache Noir performing particularly well here.

At first they made their wine in Moynier's father-in-law's cellar in the next village of Beaulieu, but in 1983 they built their own cellar. In the beginning they had three fermentation vats outside. In 1987 they added the roof, in 1989 the walls and in 1990 a tasting room, which was full of people coming and going the afternoon of my visit, with Luc Moynier ensuring that they all had what they wanted to taste and drink. Their first bottling was in 1981, just five per cent of their production, and now they bottle seventy per cent of their wine.

Moynier now makes five different red wines with various blends, as well as a Vin de Pays d'Oc from Merlot, grown on sandier soil. There is a pure Mourvèdre, Cuvée Merlette. The 1995 lacked body, but he tried micro-oxygenation for the 1998, which made it more supple, with softer tannins. He does not have any barrels, not because he is against wood but because he has no suitable place to keep them. That may be a project for the future. He also tried carbonic maceration for the first time in 1998 and he would like an *égrappoir fouloir*, but you cannot do everything at once. I liked his Cuvée Sélection best, an attractively perfumed, peppery blend of Syrah and Grenache Noir. The future of Domaine de la Coste looks good, as the next generation are interested in following their parents' footsteps.

Key facts for Grès de Montpellier

Proposed *terroir* that covers the vineyards in the hinterland of Montpellier, incorporating the existing *terroirs* of St Georges d'Orques, Méjanelle, St Drézery, St Christol and Vérargues.

With the exception of St Georges d'Orques, there are very few producers in each area.

The grape varieties and appellation regulations conform to those of the Coteaux du Languedoc.

Terres de Sommières

Despite the traffic jam, Sommières tempted me to stop, but I was late. Instead I enjoyed a quick glimpse of the imposing château as I negotiated the narrow streets and the Roman bridge over the river Vidourle. Terres de Sommières is the easternmost of the proposed *terroirs* of the Coteaux du Languedoc, destined to include the vineyards to the west of the Roman city of Nîmes.

MAS MONTEL, ASPERES

I was heading for Mas Montel outside the villages of Aspères, which has been in the hands of the Granier family since 1945. Marc and Marcel bought a virtually abandoned estate, paying what seemed like an enormous sum at the time – FF 3.5 million – especially when you consider how little wine fetched then. Today, the next generation, Jean-Philippe and his brother Dominique, are running the property, while Marcel still retains an active interest and acts as a welcoming host. I found him explaining the history of the estate to a group of French teachers from Germany. He reminded me of an absent-minded professor, both in appearance and stance.

We settled down to a comprehensive tasting in a room with numerous old vinous artefacts. He explained that they have fifty hectares planted with a hotchpotch of different grape varieties, the usual Midi red varieties as well as Cabernet Sauvignon, Chardonnay, Viognier and Grenache Blanc, with a project to plant some Roussanne. The first Cabernet Sauvignon was planted in 1962 and the first Syrah in 1975; their first bottling was in 1978. As well as vineyards, they have fifty hectares of cereals.

Les Marnes is a blend of Grenache Blanc and Viognier, for which the first crop was 1997. The Viognier character was apparent, with quite rich, honeyed flavours. An unoaked Chardonnay was light and refreshing, and there is also an oaked Chardonnay. Cuvée Psalmodi, so called after a chapel in the village that was attached to the abbey of Psalmodi in Aigues-Mortes, is a blend of Merlot, Grenache Noir and Syrah, kept in vat. Granier believes firmly in what he called the *mariage de cépages à la cuve*, considering that a blend is much better integrated if the grape varieties can ferment together, but that of course depends upon ripening times. Jericho, a blend of Syrah vinified by carbonic maceration, with a little Grenache, was warm and spicy.

They still have the traditional Midi cellar of old *foudres* made from Russian oak, some of which are over a hundred years old. A warm, winey, raisiny smell pervades the cellar, and later I peered inside one of the barrels that had just been emptied. There was a mass of wet red tartrate crystals glistening on the sides. All their red wine spends time in *foudres*. For the Granier family they are quite simply *un merveil* for they allow for very gentle oxygenation, but they need attention and careful maintenance and you cannot afford to neglect them.

Their two Coteaux du Languedoc also spend time in *barriques*. Mas Granier is a blend of Syrah, Grenache and Mourvèdre, with some spicy fruit on nose and palate, while Mas Granier les Grès, from a similar blend, spends between eighteen and twenty-four months in *barriques* and has more vanilla characters on the palate.

I asked Granier if he could define the character of Terres de Sommières. He thought it was really too early, for the area is such a recent concept. The soil is a mixture of limestone and clay, with lots of flints, which can be so sharp as to puncture the tyres of the tractor. Now they use a caterpillar tractor instead. As their wines demonstrate, they obtain some wonderful expressions of the *garrigue*, rather than red fruit, and he considered them more tannic than Pic St Loup, with good ageing potential. I admit that I would beg to differ here, finding them charmingly fruity rather than tannic.

LANGLADE

The other village within the Terres de Sommières that has a long-standing reputation is Langlade, whose wines were singled out for mention at the end of the seventeenth century. The leader of the Camisard revolt, Jean Cavalier, is said to have over-indulged in the wines of Langlade, with the disastrous consequence that he lost the subsequent battle of Nage against the troops of Louis XIV. However, it was in the nineteenth century that the wines received the most praise. In his *Ampelographie Française* Rendu observes that the vineyard of Langlade is planted with Terret Noir, Espar (a synonym for Mourvèdre) and Grenache. He particularly praises the quality of the Espar, which gives light wines that are rich in colour and particularly pleasant as they do not have the violence of the alcoholic wines of Midi. In 1893 B. Chauzit and J.B. Chapelle, in their *Traité d'Agriculture à l'usage du Midi de la France*, cited Langlade and Tavel as the two most important *crus* of the department of the Gard. Viticulture was almost the sole agricultural activity of the village, and the wines were recorded as obtaining higher prices than those of many neighbouring villages and as being exported to Holland. Phylloxera struck a severe blow to the viticulture of Langlade and although vines were replanted at the end of the nineteenth century and the wines won prizes in London and Brussels before the First World War, it never again acquired quite the same importance.

DOMAINE ARNAL

In the mid-1980s Henri Arnal was the leading light of the village, an energetic man who had come to wine making after selling his business manufacturing steel girders. He had planted vineyards of Grenache Noir, Syrah and Mourvèdre in the mid-1970s in order to make a Coteaux du Languedoc, without any of the Carignan that was ubiquitous at that time. There were Chenin Blanc and Chardonnay too. He was already nursing an ambition of *cru* status for Langlade, but that was not to be. It will be incorporated into the Terres de Sommières, but will be recognised as having a particular aptitude for Mourvèdre.

Sadly, it seems that Arnal's sons do not have their father's talent.

A recent tasting of their wines showed them to be sound, with various different blends of Coteaux du Languedoc, including an almost pure Mourvèdre, but lacking the excitement of ten years earlier.

CHATEAU LANGLADE, LANGLADE

Michel Cadène is a friendly wine grower who is responsible for Château Langlade. I have only tasted his wines at a couple of wine fairs and never visited his cellars. The wines leave an impression of rustic fruit, so for the moment Langlade is not fulfilling its earlier reputation.

OTHERS

And that was the end of my peregrinations through the Coteaux du Languedoc. But each vintage brings its new producers. At the 1999 annual spring tasting of the Coteaux du Languedoc, at the Mas Saporta outside Montpellier, there was Xavier Peyraud, a grandson of Lucien of Bandol fame, who is following in the family footsteps with some elegant *rosé* produced from his father-in-law's vines at Mas des Brousses at Puechabon near Gignac. His red Coteaux du Languedoc, from an elegant blend of Syrah and Grenache Noir, was finely crafted too. Mme Ellner at Domaine des Conquètes near Aniane is a *champenois* who has sought warmer climes; 1996 was her first vintage. Catherine Dô of Domaine de Campaucels at Montagnac made her first wine in 1997, and her 1998 Clos Ste Camelle from Grenache Noir and Syrah promised well, with the ripe, rounded fruit of the vintage. Isabelle Venture at Mas de la Séranne at Aniane also began well, with her first vintage in 1998 making a ripe, liquorice-flavour Coteaux du Languedoc. She has come to wine from industrial food production, or more precisely a cake factory. Alex Mir at Château de Belles Eaux at Caux made his first wines in 1995 and his 1998s had some appealing fruit.

The region will continue to evolve. These are vineyards that have made enormous progress in the last ten years and they will go on developing at the same pace, thanks to the influx of keen, enquiring and talented producers. Quality here depends firmly on the man or woman behind the estate. It helps if they have money and if their vines are in a more favourable *terroir*, but the human factor counts enormously, achieving results that would have been unheard of twenty or even ten years ago. There may be unanswered questions about the legal definition of the Coteaux du Languedoc in the broad scheme of the Midi, but frankly they are irrelevant to the quality of the wine.

Muscat de Frontignan

Frontignan is a fairly unprepossessing little town lying on the Etang d'Ingril. The skyline is dominated by an oil refinery, and the main road from Montpellier, which skirts the edge of the town, is lined with gaudy notices advertising Muscat in bottle or in *cubitainer*, luring the unsuspecting tourist with promises of tasting. What they fail to say is that most of this Muscat does not come from the vineyards of Frontignan at all, but from further afield. Ten years ago Greece, and in particular the island of Samos, was the source, but today it is more likely to be Rivesaltes. It looks rather like a fairground and quite belies the real quality of Muscat de Frontignan. Small wonder, therefore, that the serious producers of Frontignan seek to encourage sales in bottle.

Frontignan boasts a long-standing reputation. Pliny the Younger described the Muscat wine of Frontignan in his letters and called it *viae apianae*, the paths of bees. Arnaud de Villeneuve, the doctor who discovered the effect of adding alcohol to fermenting grape juice, wrote in the early fourteenth century that, on the advice of the king of Aragon, who was lord of Frontignan, he had been drinking two glasses of Muscat de Frontignan every day for several weeks and already felt ten years younger. He proposed to continue treating himself with this wonderful wine until he was only twenty years old.

In later centuries Muscat de Frontignan travelled to Paris, where in 1704 the *limonadiers* of the capital included it amongst the wines they were allowed to sell *en gros*. Frontiniac was drunk in England in the seventeenth and eighteenth centuries; John Locke, the political philosopher, sang its praises in 1676. Voltaire too ordered wine from Frontignan, writing to his supplier in 1774: 'Keep me alive by sending me a small quarter of the best wine of Frontignan.'

Perhaps its most famous consumer was Thomas Jefferson, who visited Frontignan in 1789 while he was American ambassador in Paris. His correspondence with a Dr Lambert, who was mayor of Frontignan and a producer of Muscat, has been preserved in various archives in the United States. In 1790 he asked for wine to be sent across the Atlantic: 'Although I am far away from you at the moment, Sir, I would still like to receive your excellent wines. Please therefore have the kindness to send ten dozen bottles to our President, General George Washington, and five dozen for me, of both white and red, but more of the latter.' Evidently Frontignan produced red as well as white wine at the time. Certainly, a century or so later Rendu mentioned both red and white Muscat and compared the red with the *vin de Constance*, referring to Constantia from South Africa.

Of the nineteenth-century authorities, Jullien was the most appreciative of the quality of Muscat de Frontignan. He rated it as the best in the kingdom after Muscat de Rivesaltes, writing that it was distinguished by its sweetness, a lot of body, a very pronounced taste of fruit and a very smooth perfume. It benefited from ageing, would keep a long time and could withstand a journey by land or by sea. It certainly sounds like a rather more robust wine than that of today which, although it will travel, is generally intended for early consumption.

Like the other Muscats of the Hérault, but not Muscat de Rivesaltes, Muscat de Frontignan comes purely from Muscat *à petits grains*. Confusingly, Muscat de Frontignan may also be a synonym for that grape variety in France, while other names for it, such as Muscat Frontignan, have been used in California, and even white Frontignan and Frontignac in Australia. It grows mainly on the white, chalky soil known as Calcaire de Frontignan that is peculiar to this small area. Apparently the chalk acts like a sponge, soaking up the water during the wetter spring months and then gradually releasing it, so that the vines never suffer from stress. There is also some harder limestone, mixed with red clay and stony deposits from the hills of nearby La Gardiole, as well as some Jurassic limestone on a rocky plateau, where there are in fact very few vines. The chalk is best of all. Most of the vineyards are on the eastern side of the Etang de Thau which, combined with their proximity to the sea, ensures a suitably warm microclimate. The area of the appellation has been delimited to 2100 hectares, but only about eight hundred and fifty are in production, and about six hundred of those are cultivated by members of the Frontignan co-operative, which was created in 1909. In addition, there are half a dozen private producers, of whom the best known are Château de la Peyrade and Château de Stony.

CHATEAU DE LA PEYRADE

The Pastourel family came to Frontignan in 1977. They were already wine growers around Pézenas, but were attracted by the reputation and the challenge of Frontignan. They bought the Château de la Peyrade and have developed their vineyards to cover some forty hectares, all planted with Muscat à *petits grains*. The château, built in the 1830s, is an elegant building standing back from a busy roundabout on the edge of the industrial complex of Sète. There have been various additions to the original design, including a veranda that would not be out of place on an American plantation house, but looks slightly incongruous on classical French architecture. A grove of olive trees in the grounds and a small vineyard provide a welcome oasis in the midst of tarmac and concrete. The original proprietor was the Vicomte de la Peyrade, a mayor of Sète who helped the Duke of Angoulême to escape to Spain when Napoleon returned to France after his escape from Elba. Louis XVIII gave him the title in recognition of his services.

Initially, Yves Pastourel produced a simple, fresh Muscat made in the traditional manner, with *mutage* at the appropriate moment, and played his part in improving the quality of Muscat de Frontignan, transforming it from a heavy, syrupy, oxidised wine into something fresh and elegant, fine-tuning vinification methods to avoid oxidation, controlling fermentation temperatures and doing everything possible to retain the perfume and aroma of the grapes. It can be difficult ascertaining the right moment to add the alcohol so that you obtain the perfect balance, although now they have computer readings to help. As with the other *vins doux naturels*, 15° is the minimum alcohol level, with 125 gm/l of sugar. There is an argument for reducing the sugar level to produce a lighter, more elegant wine, but with such a small number of producers it is often difficult to effect a change in the appellation regulations.

However, this has not prevented Yves Pastourel and his son Bruno from experimenting, so that they now make six different wines, all based on Muscat. Some people think that Muscat is monotonous, but that is not at all the case. We tasted in the rather smart tasting area, which has a tempting shop selling wine from other estates as well as local products, olives and lavender. First there was a Muscat Sec, Cuvée de Lilas, picked when the grapes were fully ripe. It was fresh and fruity, though not overtly Muscat-like. Next came the Cuvée des Abeilles, a *moelleux*, for which the fermentation is stopped by chilling at 14° when 40 gms/l of sugar remain. It was fresh and flavoursome, lightly honeyed, with orange hints. Both these wines fall outside the parameters of the appellation and are Vin de Pays d'Oc. What they call the Cuvée Classique is bottled as it is needed during the year, in order to retain the essential freshness of the grapes. It has a lemony, citrus nose, what the French call *agrumes*, with quite a solid, honeyed palate. More elegant is the *haut de gamme*, which they have developed over the last eight years or so from a selection of the best vineyards. For this, only the first part of the free-run juice is used, and it is bottled in the December following the vintage, so that it is enticingly elegant and floral in flavour.

Pastourel began experimenting with barrels a few years ago, and the Cuvée Barriques Oubliées, made from late harvested grapes with a potential 22°, spends four years in wood, demonstrating just how the wood absorbs the sweetness of the wine and enables it to age. It is much more golden in colour, with a concentrated orange marmalade flavour. Another late harvest wine, Les Feuilles Mortes, made from *passerillés* grapes, spends two years in old barrels. The 1995 was redolent of concentrated marmalade, with a certain dryness on the finish, but still sweet and balanced. A 1998 late harvest, picked on 15–20 October rather than at the end of August, and tasted from vat, was the essence of fresh grape juice, while another, from heavily raisined grapes, was fermented in new oak. The oak had masked the flavour of Muscat, so that it tasted more like a young Sauternes, with perfumed vanilla and hints of apricots. Even more powerful was a wine that had been given a long period of skin contact followed by fermentation and *élevage* in oak, so that it was firmly apricoty in flavour, but with more tannin, both from the oak and the grapes themselves. They were as yet uncertain whether the various late harvest wines would all be blended together, as they were in 1995, or whether several different wines would be bottled, as 1998 was such an exceptional year.

The producers of Frontignan can use a distinctive twisted bottle. The story goes that when Hercules returned from his labours, he was gasping with thirst as he passed through Frontignan and asked for water. They could only give him wine, which he enjoyed so much that he twisted the bottle in order to obtain the very last drop, and that is indeed what the Frontignan bottle looks like. I was also told that Frontignan had the first cylindrical bottle in France, with the silhouette of a Bordeaux bottle, and to this day glass producers describe a claret bottle as *un Frontignan*.

CHATEAU DE STONY

At Château de Stony, I met Frédéric Nodet, who is young, enthusiastic and very well informed about his appellation. He talked at length about the history of the area, explaining how a great-great-grandfather had been a *négociant* in Sète, dealing in wine for the vermouth trade. This was between 1840 and 1870, the prosperous period for the town, when the port was developed by the *négociant* families, who were mainly of foreign origin, Dutch, Swiss and German. At that time there was very little Muscat and they dealt mainly in red wine, which was transported in barrels, often *barriques perdues*, meaning that they were not returned. This necessitated a lot of coopers, who were mainly of Italian origin. To this day there is a strong Italian influence in the cuisine of Sète; the term *sétois* is used to describe a tomato sauce with herbs and spices to accompany the various fish of the Mediterranean. Sète was virtually an island until the middle of the nineteenth century, when the road linking it to the mainland at La Peyrade was built. The name La Peyrade refers to the stony path through what was a marsh, and the name Stony may indeed have originated from a current fashion for English usage. There was little contact between the foreigners of Sète and the people of the hinterland around Frontignan, but gradually, once the road was built, the town's notables began to move out, escaping the unhealthy conditions of the port. The Château de Stony was built in the middle of the nineteenth century, reaching completion in 1866.

Frédéric Nodet's parents took over their property from his maternal grandmother; the story goes that her brothers enjoyed gambling, and the estate is said to have changed hands twice in the same night. At that time, the grapes went to the Frontignan co-operative. His parents replanted the vineyards, so that they now have seventeen hectares. Frédéric is the wine maker, his brother Henri runs the vineyards, while a third brother, Benoît, is responsible for sales. Nodet made his first wine, just twenty-five hectolitres, in 1983. It was criticised for being atypical, too light in style, but Yves Pastourel encouraged him, and Nodet recognises that Pastourel really gave the appellation a new impetus as an outsider.

Now Nodet makes about twelve different *cuvées*, each from a different vineyard, depending its *terroir*, which will eventually be blended into three different wines. Distinct differences originating from the soil are quite discernible. The wine from the chalk is finer, while wine from the red clay soil is heavier. He filters the fine lees, which are then added to the Tête de Cuvée as they provide greater concentration. He explained how he had initially been reluctant to *débourbe* as he was afraid of losing something, but in fact it makes for a more delicate wine, but without any loss of originality. He too is working on a late harvest style, picking the grapes in mid October and considering the length of barrel ageing in new wood; this might be more like Sauternes. It all illustrates an enquiring mind, eager to do the best for the family estate.

Nodet also insists upon the importance of work in the vineyard. Good wine does not come from expensive equipment in the cellar, but from attention to the vines. The main viticultural problem is rot. Research shows that the fungus enters the vines as early as the flowering period, but that it will only develop if climatic conditions are appropriate. If the summer is warm, it does not develop, but if there is a wet summer, it does, so if you treat the vines at flowering, you can avoid the problem and reduce the number of treatments later in the season. This also means that it would be possible to pick later, towards the end of September or even in mid-October. The grapes are tasted twice a week from mid-August until the vintage. Muscat oxidises easily, so they only pick early in the morning when the grapes are cooler, about 17–18°C as opposed to 25–28°C in the mid-afternoon. Warm juice can be problematic, as it is harder to stabilise. However, Nodet does not like his fermentation temperature too low, as he fears that it would produce a wine that is too *technologique*. For him, the typicity of Frontignan comes from the soil and the mild Mediterranean climate.

His Muscat Sec is fresh and grapey, with a slight bitter orange finish. It is given a long *élevage* on the fine lees, which adds structure, allowing for some ageing, and must be a minimum of 13° or else it will be dull and flat. The 1997 Classique Cuvée was past its best by the spring of 1999, for it had turned a little heavy and honeyed and was 'not representative of what I am doing'. Very much better was the 1998 Sélection, which was delicate and yet concentrated at the same time, with rich, fresh Muscat fruit and a good taste on which to leave for the nearby appellation of Muscat de Mireval.

Key facts

AC 1936; 850 hectares of Muscat *à petits grains* in production on the eastern side of Etang de Thau.

A mixture of soils, of which chalk, or *calcaire de Frontignan*, is considered the best. 15° plus 125 gm/l residual sugar.

Muscat de Mireval

Muscat de Mireval is very similar to its neighbour Muscat de Frontignan, for it comes from the same grape variety, Muscat *à petits grains*, made in very much the same way, with minimal differences in *terroir* and climate. Indeed, you could be forgiven for wondering why Mireval is not part of the appellation of Frontignan, but apparently the latter did not want to be associated with Mireval when the appellation was created in 1936. So Mireval had to wait until 1959 for its own appellation. It is all to do with what the French call *une histoire de clochers*, or church bells; in other words, village politics and local jealousies. Later there was talk of linking up the two appellations, but that came to nothing, so they each continue to guard their independence and originality.

The vineyards for Muscat de Mireval cover two villages, Mireval itself and Vic-la-Gardiole, on stony limestone soil. Vic-la-Gardiole has one of the few fortified churches of the Languedoc, dating back to the twelfth century. Unfortunately it was firmly locked the afternoon I was there, but Gilles Sénéjac, the president of the growers' *syndicat* and the owner of Mas Pigeonnier, lives in the house attached to the church, the oldest part of which dates back to the ninth century. We talked in the vaulted drawing room with its large stone fireplace, while a sturdy tabby cat glared at us from the window sill. Sénéjac explained that Muscat had originally been allowed to oxidise and age, but that now there has been a change in style, as in Frontignan; people want something fresh and fruitier, lighter and more elegant, which they would be more likely to drink as an aperitif than a dessert wine. The regulations are the same as for Muscat de Frontignan, 15° with 125 gm/l of residual sugar, but there is talk, as in the other Muscat appellations, of changing the legislation to allow for wines with a lower amount of sugar, though as yet no dossier has been presented to the INAO.

The production of Muscat de Mireval has developed over the last thirty years from two thousand hectolitres a year to eight or nine thousand. Sénéjac explained that his grandfather had bought his property after the Second World War with the original intention of making red wine, but the emphasis shifted to Muscat during the 1960s. There are now 266 hectares in production, and the two largest producers are Jeanjean, who are newcomers to the appellation, and the village co-operative. Rabelais praised Muscat de Mireval in *Pantagruel* – *Puis vint à Montpellier où il trouva fort bon vin de Mirevalux et joyeuse compagnie* – and so the co-operative is named the Cave de Rabelais. François I is also said to have drunk Muscat de Mireval, but the nineteenth-century authorities are remarkably silent about it.

DOMAINE DE MAS NEUF

The arrival of Jeanjean has given the appellation a much-needed injection of energy, including a sales agreement with the co-operative. The two Jeanjean brothers, Hugues and Bernard, each own an estate, Mas Rouge and Mas Neuf respectively. I went to Domaine de Mas Neuf, an eighty-hectare property with vines on the edge of the Etang d'Ingril. These large estates originally belonged to families from Montpellier, who were doctors in the city and absentee landowners. Pruning scissors are said to have been conceived at Mas Rouge, for the owner was inspired by his friend, the ampelographer Doctor Guyot who wrote a survey of French vineyards at the end of the nineteenth century. We walked through the vineyards in the autumn sunshine while Benoît Blancheton, who manages the estate, explained that the vineyards had been neglected by the previous owner and they were changing the system of pruning from bush vines to *cordon royat*, with the branches trained on wires. The existing cellar has been considerably renovated. They aim for the grapes to reach the cellar as quickly as possible, thereby avoiding any oxidation, and they use a pneumatic press with a closed cage for a slow, gentle pressing. However, a pneumatic press can be too gentle, as it makes no impact at all on raisined grapes. Indeed, snails and snakes have survived a cycle in a pneumatic press.

The ideal would be the basket press that they use in Sauternes, but failing that, they finish the pressing with a standard Vaslin press. They make two qualities of Muscat de Mireval, one sold under the Domaine du Mas Neuf label and presented in an eye-catching blue bottle, and the other a generic wine under the unlikely name of Domaine de Gibraltar, which is apparently a *lieu-dit* on the estate.

Bernard Jeanjean, who plays the part of the affable French peasant, with a thick Midi accent belying a shrewd brain, talked about their work. He explained how an advertisement for Domaine du Mas Neuf in an airline magazine struck a chord, as several of his customers had been asking for Muscat, and led them to purchase the property in 1994. They make several different selections from various parts of the vineyard, and in the cellar they work as much as possible by physical means. They are experimenting with lees stirring and skin contact and are also considering alternatives to *vin doux naturel*. They are trying out a *moelleux* fermented in barrel, what Jeanjean called a modern Sauternes method, not a *vendange tardive*. You do obtain botrytis here, thanks to the humidity resulting from the proximity to the lake, and they stop the fermentation at 13° plus 2.5°. They are working with Seguin Moreau, and also with the cooper at the co-operative at Buzet, who provides them with Tronçais wood that they have seasoned for two years. As well as French oak, for which they ask for a Sauternes *chauffe* or toasting, they have American and Russian oak. Jeanjean explained that as they have no reference points – the notion of a harmony between wine and wood is not part of the culture of the Languedoc – they are trying all kinds of different things in an attempt to understand how *barriques* work. The first vintage of the oaked wine, in 1997, was christened L'Incompris, as no one really understands it! I tasted a couple of barrel samples of the 1998 and found honey and oak. Indeed, it was not unlike a Sauternes in texture, as the oak had masked the flavour of Muscat.

DOMAINE LA CAPELLE

The best of the independent family estates is undoubtedly Domaine la Capelle, which has made great strides in the last ten years or so. Jean-Pierre Maraval is a friendly man in his early thirties, who has done much to develop his parents' vineyard, extending the range of wines far beyond a simple Muscat de Mireval. He runs a neat, functional cellar, with vats of various shapes and sizes – allowing for several different batches of wine and blending possibilities – as well as some experimental small *foudres* for red wine. Ten years ago he had no means of chilling the juice, but is now well equipped; he also has a pneumatic press, which helps to prevent oxidation. However, he is not sure that the wine does not taste as good from a Vaslin press. He has also tried skin contact, but finds that it makes the wine too heavy, as people want something light and delicate these days.

Domaine la Capelle consists of thirty-seven hectares, of which twenty-five are planted with Muscat *à petits grains*, and there is also just half an are of Muscat d'Alexandrie or Muscat *à gros grains*. This is better for making table wine, a Muscat Sec, of which the 1998 was a blend of sixty per cent *gros grains* and forty per cent *petits grains*, which tasted dry and grapey with fresh sappy fruit. It is not an easy wine to make, as it can be bitter on the finish. It is all a question of balance, with the grapes picked a week earlier for the table wine.

In 1997 Maraval made his first non-muted wine, a late harvest wine from grapes picked at a potential 19°, with the fermentation stopped at barely 15°, leaving 55 gm/l residual sugar. It is evocatively called Gelée d'Automne. He is preoccupied with the idea of lowering the sugar level in the *vin doux naturel* and this is an experimental alternative. However, it is only possible in drier autumns, when one hectare – the vineyard with the best drainage that suffers least if it does rain – is left after the main harvest. The flavour was concentrated and honeyed, but also fresh and elegant. As for the traditional Muscat de Mireval, Maraval makes two qualities, in contrasting styles. There is a younger, lighter wine, with a certain elegance and a floral character not always associated with a *vin doux;* for this, Maraval selects the grapes with a higher acidity level for an early bottling. It is essential to have the correct balance of sugar and acidity. The second, for a later bottling, has what he described as a more *confit* character, like crystallised or candied fruit. It was deeper in colour, rich and harmonious, with more concentration and well-integrated alcohol. Our tasting finished with his red wine, a Vin de Pays des Collines de la Moure, from the *garrigue* behind the village. It is an unusual blend of Cabernet Franc and Grenache Noir. Everyone has Cabernet Sauvignon, so he preferred to plant Cabernet Franc about ten years ago. The wine had spent twelve months in small *foudres* and had a rugged, muscular character, providing a good antidote to sweet Muscat.

Key facts

Virtually indistinguishable from Muscat de Frontignan.

AC 1959; 266 hectares in two villages; vineyards on stony limestone soil.

Muscat de Lunel

Lunel is a bustling little town that is particularly animated on Sunday mornings, which is market day. It proudly proclaims itself to be La Cité de Muscat. Muscat was produced around Lunel in the sixteenth century, for Félix Platter, a student from Basle, wrote in 1552: 'On leaving Nîmes, the road crossed a plain planted with olive trees as far as Lunel, where I drank my first Muscat wine.' Jean-Jacques Rousseau wrote of enjoying the Muscat of Lunel at the Auberge du Pont du Vidourle towards 1750, and Laurence Sterne in 1760 described Muscat de Lunel as the best Muscat wine of the whole of France, at a time when Muscat was more widely planted than in the handful of appellations that remain today. Another source found Lunel more delicate, while Frontignan travelled better by sea. Thomas Jefferson came to Lunel at the end of the 1780s and described the vinification method in some detail. He mentioned the impossibility of obtaining older wine, for demand is such that the harvest is sold the first year. Some years later, Pauline Borghese sent Muscat de Lunel to her brother Napoleon Bonaparte when he was in exile on the island of St Helena.

The production of Muscat fell from favour because the yields were so small – Guyot mentions eight or twelve hectolitres per hectare. Production suffered still more from oidium and the ravages of phylloxera. The appellation of Muscat de Lunel dates from 1943 and covers about 260 hectares over just four *communes*, Lunel, Lunel-Viel, Saturargues and Vérargues. The vineyards are relatively low lying, at sixty metres just a little higher than the coastal plain. The soil is a mixture of sandstone and red clay, originating from the alpine deposits of glaciers from the Rhône, with a layer of *galets* that provide additional warmth, while the sea breezes bring humidity.

Production is inevitably dominated by the co-operative of Lunel, which was founded in 1956 and which, through its association with the Vignerons du Val d'Orbieu, successfully maintains the quality of the appellation; it accounts for ninety per cent of the production. There are just five independent producers, of whom I saw two.

DOMAINE DE BELLEVUE

Domaine de Bellevue has developed its reputation over the last ten years. Francis Lacoste's parents came back from Algeria and later, in 1981, bought this estate. Until 1987 the grapes went to the co-operative. At that time it was easy to extricate your land, but now they have created a contract that makes it much more complicated. Lacoste had to start from scratch, for there was no cellar; the previous owner, a doctor from Montpellier, had been a founder member of the co-operative, with a *régisseur* managing his property. However, when the Lacoste family came to restore the house, they found old vats in what had been the *régisseur's* flat.

It is an attractive spot. Although you are very close to the motorway, you take a dirt track and lose yourself in the *garrigue* to emerge with views of the sea in the distance, with the medieval town of Aigues-Mortes and the modern monstrosity of La Grande Motte on the skyline. The vineyards are in front of a low-lying house, with spring flowers in terracotta pots. Francis Lacoste is a thoughtful, modest man who really cares about his wines and his appellation.

I asked him about his vinification methods. 'Oh, I don't have any secrets,' he says, but admits that he has been greatly encouraged by his oenologist, Marc Auclair from the ICV, to extend his repertoire far beyond a simple Muscat de Lunel. He pays meticulous attention to every step. The grapes, only Muscat *à petits grains*, are picked by hand, for mechanical harvesting is not allowed in the appellation; in any case it is quite impractical, as the skins of the grapes are too fragile when they are even very slightly overripe. The bunches are gently pressed, carefully avoiding any oxidation. The moment of mutage is precisely calculated. Lacoste wants the lowest possible alcohol level, 15°, combined with the minimal amount of residual sugar, 125 gms/l, so that the wine is as light as possible with a good concentration of fruit. It all depends upon the relationship between the alcohol and sugar. It is possible to accelerate or delay the moment of mutage by changing the fermentation temperature, 'but I am not worried about mutage at five o'clock in the morning'. After talking to other Muscat producers, it does seem that one of the hazards is spending nights in your cellar waiting for the right moment to act, in a way that you never have to do with red wines.

It would, in fact, be equally possible to plant red grapes on the same land for Coteaux du Languedoc, either as part of the original *terroir* of Vérargues or now as part of the proposed Grès de Montpellier. However, the financial rewards are quite different. The appellation restricts the yield for Muscat de Lunel to 28 hl/ha, which with the PLC makes a total of 30 hl/ha. However, Lacoste admits that even 28 hl/ha is rare for him. The bulk price for Muscat is currently FF 1800 per hectolitre, compared to FF 600 for Coteaux du Languedoc, so despite the lower yield, it is much more remunerative.

Lacoste makes two *cuvées* of Muscat de Lunel. His Cuveé Traditionnelle has the filtered fine lees blended back into the wine, which makes for a wine that is quite heavy, ripe and honeyed, rounded with well-integrated alcohol. The Clos Bellevue, a Cuvée Vieilles Vignes from forty-year-old vines, his oldest, does not include the fine lees and is more elegant in flavour. You are hardly aware of the alcohol at all and the palate is wonderfully honeyed, with fresh acidity and a long elegant finish.

In some years Lacoste makes a late harvest wine, but only when his vineyard of old vines has a sufficient crop to make it feasible to leave some grapes to ripen for an extra month. Usually these grapes are picked in early October, but in 1998 the main crop was ripe by 24 August and the late harvest was left until 10 November. Some of the grapes had botrytis and some were *passerillés*. When I visited in March 1999, the wine was still gently fermenting, in one small barrel covered with blankets to protect it from any chill. The late harvest is not muted. Instead the fermentation stops of its own accord and the wine remains in wood for a total of twelve months. The first vintage, the 1992, was made by accident. It rained in the middle of the vintage, so they stopped picking, leaving the grapes on just one hectare of vines. It took time to get the pickers back and meanwhile the grapes had developed botrytis, so they kept them separate with the idea of producing a Muscat *à l'ancienne*, replicating the kind of wine made before the development of mutage. The 1992 was lees-stirred every month and after twelve months transferred into a stainless steel vat and finally bottled in the spring of 1994. Lacoste sent a bottle to Michel Bettane, a leading French wine journalist, who gave it a *coup de coeur*, the equivalent of a 99/100 score from Robert Parker, and turned it into an overnight success.

Bureaucracy, however, has difficulty in accepting this wine. As it is not muted, it does not conform to appellation regulations, but you cannot have a late harvest wine as a mere *vin de table*. Instead it is grudgingly described as *autre vin*. The label carries the mention *élevé en fûts de chêne* and that mouthful of a phrase found on late harvest wines all over the south of France, *moût de raisins partiellement fermentés, issu de vendange passerillé*. Maybe it will eventually be incorporated into the proposed late harvest category of Vin de Pays d'Oc. Since 1992 Lacoste has produced about 1800 bottles a year, in 1995, 1996 and 1998; with a high level of acidity, these are wines to age. The 1995 was redolent of orange marmalade, with oak in evidence, but very well-integrated oak, and a lovely long, concentrated finish. The yield was just six hl/ha. The 1996 was similar in style, but less harmonious as it needed some bottle age.

Lacoste has also tried making dry Muscat, but he does not like the taste. Instead he prefers to produce a little Sauvignon Vin de Pays de la Bénovie, so that 'he has something to drink with seafood'.

CHATEAU DU GRES ST PAUL

Jean-Philippe Servière's family has owned vineyards at Château du Grès St Paul near Lunel since 1840, and at the beginning of the last century his great-grandfather built an Italianate château. He was a successful *négociant*, but his successors were not interested in the estate and it was abandoned to tranquil decay. Bourgeois families did not tend their own vines, but employed someone else to do it for them – that is, until Jean-Philippe Servière, with his degree in political science and a doctorate in law, decided in the mid-1970s that he had had enough of the Parisian rat race. The rest of his family thought he was quite mad and were certainly not prepared to make any financial contribution to the estate. The property is a little further inland than Domaine Bellevue, with twenty-six hectares of vines but only eight of Muscat; the soil is similar, though, with *galets rouges* that stretch as far as they do in Châteauneuf-du-Pape.

Servière is really much more interested in his red wine. He likes Syrah a lot and also has some Grenache Noir, Mourvèdre and Merlot, with a bit of Carignan. He makes a delicious Coteaux du Languedoc, Cuvée Prestige, mainly from Syrah, with some Grenache Noir and Mourvèdre, but ignores the *terroir* name of Vérargues. In 1997 he began experimenting with new wood. Since 1994 he has also produced a Muscat Sec, Vin de Pays d'Oc, with some ripe orange fruit. As for sweet Muscat, the grapes are ripe at the end of August; the juice is given a light skin contact and *mutage* takes place in the normal way. When the grape spirit arrives at the cellars, the authorities demand that it be immediately contaminated with some Muscat juice, 'so that we don't turn it into pastis'. The resulting wine is sweet, ripe and honeyed, making a delicious dessert wine or aperitif, depending on whether you are in England or France.

Key facts

AC 1943; Muscat *à petits grains* grown in Lunel and three other *communes*, totalling 260 hectares; 28 hl/ha.

Soil is sandstone and red clay.

15° plus 125 gm/l sugar.

Vins de Pays d'Oc and others

The category of *vin de pays* was born of the urgent need to give hundreds of thousands of hectolitres of anonymous wine some kind of identity and at the same time to encourage a move towards quality. Something had to be done to solve the pressing viticultural crisis of the south, epitomised by the much talked-of European 'wine lake', which happily today is a thing of the past. However, as recently as ten years ago it dominated the wine industry of southern Europe – not just in France, but also in Italy and to a lesser extent Spain.

The first tentative steps towards the creation of the *vins de pays* were taken in 1973 when Jacques Chirac was minister of agriculture, and six years later they were defined by an official government decree. Essentially, *vins de pays* are superior *vins de table*. They are not, in the parlance of Brussels, deemed to be quality wines from a specified region, as are appellation and VDQS wines, but *vins de table* with some distinguishing individual character. The criteria of production are much stricter than for a basic *vin de table*, but also much more flexible than for an appellation or VDQS.

For *vins de pays* throughout France, yields are restricted to 90 hl/ha, which represents a dramatic reduction from the high yields of the 1970s, when 200 hl/ha was not unknown. Alcohol is another criterion. For *vin de table* a natural degree of 8.5° is necessary, whereas for *vin de pays* the minimum is 10°; by comparison, most appellations must be at least 11°, if not 11.5° or 12°, without the help of *chaptalisation*, which is permitted in the Midi for *vins de pays*, but not for appellation wines. In addition, the *vins de pays* are subject to strict analytical and organoleptic controls.

Vins de pays are demarcated by political and administrative geography rather than by geology. The single exception to this is the

Vin de Pays des Sables du Golfe du Lion, where the sand dunes are the decisive factor. Otherwise, there are *vins de pays* that cover a department, such as Vin de Pays de l'Hérault or de l'Aude, and those that cover a zone within a department, such as Coteaux du Fontcaude or Vallée du Paradis, which may have slightly more restrictive regulations, such as a lower yield of 80 hl/h and a higher alcohol level. The largest group of all are the regional *vins de pays*, of which there are four in France; only one concerns us here, namely Vin de Pays d'Oc, which covers the whole of Languedoc-Roussillon, the four departments of the Pyrenées-Oriéntales, Hérault, Aude and Gard. The regional name allows for blending between smaller *vins de pays*, and many producers now prefer to use the much better known name, with its significant marketing clout, rather than one that nobody has ever heard of. Others, on the contrary, feel overwhelmed by the massive anonymity of the Vin de Pays d'Oc.

In the years following the creation of *vin de pays* on the statute book, they proliferated and are now to be found all over France, although there is the greatest concentration in the Midi, which has no area without a *vin de pays*, even if it may lack an appellation. Usually the *vin de pays* and the appellation cohabit, allowing growers to make two wines; depending on their approach, the *vin de pays* can be very much better or infinitely worse than the appellation wine. Many of these *vins de pays* will remain unknown, for they have often been created to satisfy one or two growers who have known how to pull strings in high places. Some have acquired a reputation, fuelled by dynamic producers, such as Côtes de Thongue and Domaines Listel with their Vin de Pays des Sables du Golfe du Lion. Others will never progress beyond the official decree that created them and will remain shrouded in obscurity until they ultimately disappear.

The *vins de pays* allow for an imaginative flexibility as to which grape varieties may or may not be planted, and allow an outlet for varietal wines, which are rarely part of the French appellation system, and certainly not in the Midi. Vin de Pays d'Oc was recognised in 1987, with the intention of providing a marketing tool for the plethora of varietal wines produced in the south of France, using them to confront the challenge of the New World. The category now covers some thirty-one possible grape varieties, including twenty-five that can be used as a varietal wine. The most popular are inevitably Cabernet Sauvignon, Merlot, Syrah, Grenache Noir, and Chardonnay, Sauvignon and Viognier. If a grape variety is mentioned on the label, as is increasingly the case with the Vins de Pays d'Oc, the wine must come from that variety alone. For the 1996 vintage *bis-cépages* were introduced, allowing for two varieties on the label; now there is even talk of permitting three. The Vin de Pays d'Oc demand strict quality criteria, and in 1999 the category Grand d'Oc was launched, with even more demanding requirements concerning what they call traceability, meaning that the provenance of a wine can be followed from vine to bottle, with a consistent concern for quality. Finally, the price has to be in keeping with a wine that has aspirations to quality.

The Vins de Pays d'Oc include *vins de primeur*, which have the advantage over Beaujolais Nouveau in that they are released earlier, on the third Thursday in October, and are more often than not made from fully ripe grapes, which is not always the case further north. The *syndicat* is also working on a category to cover the many late harvest wines of the Midi, but for the moment only on an experimental basis since the 1999 vintage.

The flexibility over grape varieties has allowed some adventurous growers to plant unusual varieties under the guise of experimentation, with exciting results. However, you can encounter problems if you are planting on appellation land, where the INAO has the authority to determine what shall or shall not be planted. Domaines Listel had *bordelais* varieties in their vineyards soon after the Second World War, but it was only in 1973 that they could openly make a wine from Sauvignon Blanc and Cabernet Sauvignon.

Riesling and Gewürztraminer, to name but two, are conspicuous by their absence from the list of authorised varieties. As a result, Jean-Louis Denois of Domaine de l'Aigle in Limoux has fallen foul of the authorities for grafting a thousand vines of Riesling and Gewürztraminer without, they say, giving sufficient notification; he has been fined FF 10,000 and ordered to pull up the offending vines. Acquiescence, however, is not Denois's strong suit and so he is at the time of writing contesting the legal decision, convinced that he is fighting the cause of freedom to experiment on behalf of the many like-minded vignerons of the Midi. At Domaine de Bachellery they too have some Gewürztraminer, again planted on an experimental basis, but as yet they have not been asked to pull it up.

The most exciting *vins de pays* tend to be produced in areas where there are no competing appellations or VDQS. The regulations, although strict, allow scope for experimentation in a way that is not possible with the appellations, which must follow the *usages locaux, loyaux et constants* of the region. Grape varieties that are not part of a region's tradition can be grown under the broader umbrella of the *vin de pays*. In areas where there are also appellations, the *vins de pays* are usually very much the second string to the wine maker's bow. He may indeed use them for established Cabernet Sauvignon or more fashionable or innovative Viognier or Petit Manseng, but he may equally well use them for the Carignan or Aramon that he has not yet replanted. Also, the wine from young vines, not yet in full production for an appellation, may be *vin de pays*, as will any vats of wine not quite up to scratch. As such, the *vins de pays* provide a useful outlet for the second best.

In parts of the Midi, notably on the lower-lying land around Pézenas and Béziers, where there are no appellations, the *vins de pays* are treated with as strong a concern for quality as if they were an appellation. The Côtes de Thongue, of which more in the next chapter, is the leading example of a group of talented wine makers producing exciting wines under the designation of *vin de pays*. On paper, these wines may have a lower status than wines with an appellation, but in the glass the differences are very much less clear. There are some *vins de pays* that rival the best appellations, and there are some appellation wines that are no better than the average *vin de pays*. As always, what matters is who made the wine, and whose name is on the label.

FORTANT DE FRANCE, SÈTE

Much of the international success of the Languedoc originates from the varietal Vins de Pays d'Oc, which have given the French wine makers the opportunity to confront the New World on its own terms. Robert Skalli was one of the first to recognise the region's untapped potential and one of the instigators of the Vin de Pays d'Oc. He had observed the marketing clout of the varietal in California and realised that the same marketing techniques could be applied in France with *vins de pays*, which unlike most appellation wines allow the mention of a grape variety on the label. Early in the 1980s Skalli began looking at varieties that would produce a wine that was above all accessible, without any of the mystique that can surround appellation wines, but, as he put it, eliminating the misery attached to *vin ordinaire*. First he worked on Chardonnay, then Cabernet Sauvignon and Merlot, and next Syrah, persuading the more innovative growers to plant or graft these varieties. The outcome was the successful Fortant range, which has been extended to three categories, with Fortant de France and more recently Fortant de France Réserve, comprising around fifteen varietals, all Vin de Pays d'Oc. The extensive provenance of these wines, considering all the infinite variations within the enormous zone of the Vin de Pays d'Oc, allows for the blending and maintenance of consistent style and quality, with the aim of providing consumers with the flavours they want. This is a different concept from that of an appellation wine, which reflects the peculiarities of its *terroir*, irrespective of consumer preference.

Skalli's viticultural origins lie in Algeria. The family first settled in Corsica in 1962, setting up Les Coteaux de Diane, and then came to Sète two years later, where they developed a traditional *sétois négociant* business, dealing in bulk wine. Then in 1982 they opened a winery in California's Napa Valley, St Supery. In Sète, down by the port, they now have a state-of-the-art cellar for *élevage*, both in barrel and vat, and two streamlined bottling lines that reach top speed of six thousand bottles per hour.

Philippe Tolleret, the production manager, talked about the development of the brand and how things have changed. Initially they concentrated on the cellar, investing in modern technology, and then from about 1992 they turned their attention to the vineyard, considering factors such as pruning and training. From 1996 onwards they have paid more attention to the choices of *terroir* within the large area at their disposal, classifying the different vineyards from which the best grapes of Chardonnay, Cabernet Sauvignon and Merlot are destined for Fortant de France Réserve. Chardonnay tends to come from the Hérault and the Aude, whereas the Gard is better for Sauvignon, especially the cooler area towards the Cévennes. There are differences too with Syrah. From the Gard it is fresher and fruitier, with richer wines coming from warmer, less fertile areas. It is really like an artist's palette, with numerous blending possibilities, and Michel Rolland, the roving Bordelais consultant, advises on the *assemblage* of the red wines and comes regularly to Sète for tastings.

FLYING WINE MAKERS

Skalli began as an outsider in the Languedoc and there is no doubt that many other outsiders have made the region, and more especially the Vin de Pays d'Oc, what it is today. There is much talk of the influence of wine makers from the New World, which led to the coining of the expression 'flying wine maker', conveying an impression of a wine maker who jets round the world taking in vintages in both the northern and southern hemispheres, spending just a few days in each area. The concept originated with Tony Laithwaite of the Bordeaux Direct and the *Sunday Times* Wine Club. In 1987 he introduced Martin Shaw, now half of the successful Australian winery Smith & Shaw, to Domaine de Coussergues, a large estate outside Béziers within the Côtes de Thongue, where Arnould de Bertier had realised that his wines would benefit greatly from an injection of outside expertise. A good exchange of ideas ensued, and de Bertier continues to employ a flying wine maker, usually an Australian, for the vintage.

DOMAINE DE LA BAUME, SERVIAN

Around the same time, BRL Hardy, one of the giant Australian producers, was looking at unexploited areas with quality potential in Italy, Spain and France. With the advent of the single European market, the company believed that there would be an advantage to having a foothold in Europe. Naturally they wanted an area with a reliable climate, which meant the Mediterranean, and they preferred to work with familiar grape varieties, such as the Chardonnay and Cabernet Sauvignon of France, rather than the Sangiovese of Italy or the Tempranillo of Spain. This led them to the run-down estate of Domaine de la Baume, outside Béziers, in 1990. All that remains of the original cellar buildings are the outside walls. What looks like an old barn in fact houses a forest of gleaming stainless steel vats and a cellar of new barrels. They have their own vineyards of Chardonnay, Viognier and Syrah and buy grapes from some thirty different growers.

The manager, a lanky, amiable Australian called Ashley Huntingdon, is adamant that they are making French, not Australian wine here. The wine maker, Pierre Dubrion, is a Burgundian and it is true that the Chardonnay is elegantly under-oaked. Too much new wood would kill the fruit, so part of the wine is kept in vat to emphasise the fruit. They find that Languedoc Chardonnay is interesting for its aromas. In 1998 they made a Chardonnay Tête de Cuvée for the first time, from the very best fruit, which was all barrel fermented with some *bâtonnage*, and when tasted as a barrel sample in the spring of 1999 it certainly needed time. The white estate wine is an intriguing combination of Chardonnay and Viognier, with the precise blend varying from year to year. In 1997 Chardonnay was the dominant variety and in 1998 Viognier. The wine reflects the best from the estate in that particular vintage. Huntingdon explained how Chardonnay can sometimes lack fullness in the middle palate and how Viognier fills that hole.

The Sauvignon is very successful too. For Nigel Sneyd, the previous wine maker at Domaine de la Baume, Sauvignon is the grape variety that expresses most clearly what Australians do differently. He kept everything very simple, paying meticulous attention to detail, insisting on cool temperatures and avoiding any oxidation by protective handling of the juice. It is a delicate variety that needs careful treatment from vineyard to cellar. As for red wines, they make Merlot, Cabernet Sauvignon and Syrah, as well as a Tête de Cuvée from pure Syrah that spends some fifteen months in oak, including some American, though they are moving towards the greater elegance of French oak. The red estate wine is a blend of a quarter Cabernet Sauvignon to three-quarters Merlot, with some chunky ripe berry fruit and tannin.

JAMES HERRICK, NARBONNE

One of the success stories of the Midi is James Herrick Chardonnay. You cannot deny that Chardonnay is a great drink, and being an undemanding grape variety it adapts readily to the conditions of the Midi, allowing infinite permutations of wine making and blending. Herrick sold his vineyards to the other giant Australian producer,

Southcorp, in 1999, but not before he had created a highly successful enterprise; at the time of writing he is retained as a consultant. He is a genial mixture of Irish and New Zealander, with a relaxed attitude that belies an alert mind. He learned most of his wine making in Australia. Then, as he put it, he had a major rush of blood to the head, asking himself why France was not responding to the challenge of well-made, clean varietal wine when the Languedoc-Roussillon is a great place to grow grapes. He concentrated on the vineyards first, buying land or old vineyards in three different sites. There is La Motte, a cool site on alluvial silt near the sea; Les Garrigue de Truilhas, which is further north and quite the opposite, for the soil consists of big rocks over clay, making much weightier wines; and finally la Boulandière, which is on poor sandy soil near Lézignan in the Corbières and between the other two in style. It took about a year of searching in the cooler parts of the Midi between Nîmes and Carcassonne to find these three vineyards.

In his Chardonnay Herrick looks above all for fruit complexity, which now means no oak. His first vintage was 1992, and 1996 was the last vintage for which he used any oak on the Chardonnay. Now that the vines are older, he detects even more significant vineyard variations, so that the logical corollary is to take the best of each vineyard and make three separate wines, as well as the basic blend. The differences were very apparent in the 1998 vintage. Herrick favours lees stirring and some malolactic fermentation with oxidative handling. He never has very clean juice. Truilhas, which he describes as the rocky, hot vineyard, was rounded, ripe and buttery; La Boulandière was more delicate and minerally, with hints of fennel; while La Motte had good acidity and some yeasty, leesy flavours. Herrick has also produced some red wine since 1995, namely Cuvée Simone, a blend of Syrah, Grenache Noir and a little Carignan. He is developing more red wines, with some varietal Merlot, Syrah and Cabernet Sauvignon, as well as a Cabernet/Syrah blend, sold under names that recall the Roman past of the city of Narbonne.

The key to buying grapes is to determine when to pick. The average co-operative member is anxious to harvest before the equinoctial rains and the start of the hunting season. Nor is it economic to let your grapes ripen fully and thereby run the risk of climatic adversity, for the co-operatives are able to obtain a grant to

pay for concentrated must, which they think solves the problem
of unripe grapes. However, if the grapes are fully ripe and perhaps
lacking a little acidity, they have to pay for the tartaric acid to
rectify that themselves. Herrick combats this by purchasing the crop
three weeks before the vintage, then 'if we get it wrong, it is our
problem'. In 1997 he was able to pick two weeks later everyone
else, obtaining a smaller crop, but a higher degree of alcohol and
riper fruit.

DOMAINES VIRGINIE, BEZIERS

Domaines Virginie also benefits from Australian input. Pierre
Degroote is a Belgian *négociant* who went into business with
another producer, Bernard Montariol, and Virginie is the name of
Degroote's daughter, but she is a chartered accountant and not at all
interested in wine. The company is now owned by the enormous
négociants Castel Frères, but continues to operate relatively
independently, with over two hundred hectares of vines. In addition
they buy grapes, and everything is vinified in their cellars outside
Béziers, with its *chai* of four thousand *barriques*, by their Australian
wine maker Richard Osborne. Osborne is an outspoken Australian
with an imperfect command of French, who considers that he
combines French methods and Australian techniques. 'The French
are more *laissez-faire* than the Australians, but of course you make
wine according to where you are; you cannot change that. You do
not find the same diversity within an area in Australia that you do
here, with pockets of different microclimates.' Ask Degroote what
he has learned from Australia and the reply is night picking. Cool
the grapes and give them a longer *débourbage*, for three or four
days rather than a few hours. The French do not have the same
discipline and rigour as the Australians.

Degroote admits that Domaines Virginie would not exist without
the export market. They produce a wide range of some seventeen
different varietals suitable for sale in Britain, Japan and the USA.
There are the old faithfuls, three different styles of Chardonnay
with varying degrees of oak, as well as Sauvignon, and for reds,
Merlot, Syrah and Cabernet Sauvignon. All the time they are
exploring other options, so that Roussanne, Viognier, Rolle or
Vermentino and Pinot Noir have been added to the range. There are

also various estate wines, too numerous to list. They are now one of the largest producers of the Midi, claiming to produce a quarter of all the Chardonnay grown in the Languedoc-Roussillon.

DOMAINE LA CHEVALIERE, BEZIERS

Another key producer of Chardonnay is Michel Laroche at Domaine la Chevalière near Béziers. The Laroche family have owned vineyards in Chablis since 1850, and today Domaine Laroche is one of the largest producers of this small but well-known appellation. You sense that Michel Laroche has sometimes found the valley of the Serein a little too confining for comfort, and so in 1995 he bought a property on the outskirts of Béziers with a small eighteenth-century château and sufficient land to allow the construction of streamlined cellars with twenty thousand hectolitres of *cuverie* and around a thousand barrels. The purchase of some vineyard land near St Chinian has followed, but essentially wine is bought all over the Languedoc, from some fifty different growers from Nîmes to Carcassonne. I arrived at the end of the afternoon to find a line of some forty or more samples awaiting my attention. It was a daunting prospect, but I soon forgot the possibility of palate fatigue as I listened, fascinated, to Laroche and his oenologist discussing the varying characteristics of different areas and what would be the final *assemblage* of different varieties. We compared Syrah from Quissac in the Gard, north of Nîmes, with some from Neffiès in the Hérault, Chardonnay from Carcassonne with Chardonnay from Bédarieux, and Grenache Noir from Gignac and from the coastal plain near Beziers. The key concept of DLC, as they call Domaine la Chevalière, is not varietal wines but, on the contrary, *assemblage*. There are some varietal wines, Chardonnay, Viognier, Syrah and Merlot, as well as Terret Blanc Vieilles Vignes and Grenache Noir Vieilles Vignes, but the best are blends. The white Chevalière Cuvée Spéciale consists of Chardonnay, Sauvignon and Marsanne, while the red and *rosé* come from Merlot, Syrah and Grenache Noir.

For Laroche it all starts in the vineyards, which they follow closely, persuading their growers to allow their grapes to ripen fully. As a Chablisien from the northern climes of France, Laroche has plenty of experience of dealing with rot and prefers a later, riper vintage that might have a little rot, whereas most Midi growers are still very alarmed by rot and need to learn how to master it. Like Herrick, Laroche pays his growers by the hectare rather than by the hectolitre, so that they, not the growers, take the risks.

DOMAINE ST PAUL, LÉSPIGNAN

There is another Burgundian estate in the Languedoc. The Côte d'Or producers Moillard have planted just six hectares of Pinot Noir at Domaine St Paul at Léspigan, south west of Béziers. For the moment the vines are very young and little wine has been made.

ROBERT MONDAVI-VICHON MEDITERRANEE, MONTPELLIER

An outsider whose every move is being watched with great interest is Robert Mondavi. I went to see Mondavi's man in Montpellier, the genial Californian David Pearson. As usual, I got lost in the outskirts of the city near the airport, but fortunately, in the two years he has been in the Midi, Pearson has developed the relaxed local attitude towards punctuality. He explained how the decision was taken to turn Vichon into a French wine. Vichon was a Napa Valley winery set up in 1980 by three Californian restaurateurs and sold to Mondavi in 1985, who extended the source of the wine to cover the whole of California. There were considerable grape supply problems in California in the early 1990s, culminating in the decision to move Vichon to France. Market research apparently showed that many American consumers were already under the impression that Vichon, a name created from two letters of each of the names of the three original founders, was in fact French. However, Pearson is keen to emphasis that the move forms part of Mondavi's global strategy, alongside projects such as Opus One, Luce with Frescobaldi and the association with Errázuriz in Chile, with Caliterra and Seña. 1995 was the last vintage of Vichon California and the first of Vichon Méditerranée. The move alleviated the problems of grape supply, but with Vichon Méditerranée they are working on a two-tier approach, in that they not only wish to create an affordable brand, but also to produce the best possible expression of the region, an appellation wine that will come from their own vineyards. Where those would be had yet to be determined at the time of my visit, but since then a decision has been made to develop fifty hectares of land in the Massif de l'Arboussas near Aniane, in a project that will be called La Vallée de la Valcrose. Syrah will be the base, with other Midi varieties, and although the land is not within the appellation of the Coteaux du Languedoc, it is intended that the wine will conform to its criteria. The first vines will not be planted until the spring of 2002, so it will be some time before we see the first wine.

Currently Vichon has about ten sources of grapes scattered over the region, and a Bordeaux-trained wine maker, Thomas Duroux, whose responsibility it is to select the wines for blending and *élevage*. They rent the space for a barrel-ageing facility of 1000 barrels *chez* Jeanjean. For the moment their range consists of six varietals: Viognier, Sauvignon and Chardonnay for whites, and Syrah, Merlot and Cabernet Sauvignon for reds. Simplicity and accessibility is the key here. Sauvignon comes from Limoux and the Minervois. It is more difficult to cultivate than Chardonnay, for it is more sensitive to heat and needs a long ripening period in a cool site. They avoid skin contact for Sauvignon, as that can make it too heavy and cause it to lose finesse. In Viognier, which is a blend of the wines from the northern Gard, they are looking for finesse and this they have achieved, with some subtle fruit. Chardonnay is given just a little oak, ten or fifteen per cent, and comes from cooler areas, mainly Limoux, but also the Minervois and the northern part of the Hérault, beyond Bédarieux.

Sources can vary from year to year. In 1997 their Merlot came from Limoux and Rieux-Minervois, while in 1998 vineyards near Aniane were the main source. There is a similar diversity of source for Cabernet Sauvignon, including Minervois, the northern Gard, Limoux and St Félix-de-Lodez. The grapes from the southern Hérault are noticeably riper. In contrast, the Syrah comes from just one estate in the Minervois, whose owner makes the wine, which they buy after fermentation and age a small proportion in barrel. It was fresh and peppery. With Pearson's guidance, it seems that Mondavi have a firm commitment to the Languedoc. For the moment they are leading the American interest, although John Goelet, the owner of Clos du Val in the Napa Valley, has recently acquired Château Nizas in the Coteaux du Languedoc. Rumour has it that the largest of all Californian producers, Gallo, are also looking for vineyards in the Midi.

DELTA DOMAINES, VIAS

Delta Domaines are a group of six estates, du Bosc, Grange-Rouge, Pourthié, Terres-Noires, Cante-Cigale and Pioch, each with its own cellar, owned by two families, Besinet and Pourthié, all around the Bassin de Thau, between Cap d'Agde and Sète. Delta Domaines were already making an impact in the mid-1980s with their energetic marketing expertise. The leading estate, the flagship of the group, is Domaine du Bosc at Vias. Pierre Besinet is a chemical engineer by training, and so when he took over the estate from his father in 1978, he approached the situation with the outsider's imagination and broader vision. His father had already planted some Cabernet Sauvignon and Syrah, a revolutionary step at the time, but also still had the hybrids that produced wine for an aperitif company in Sète. The volcanic soil around Vias is particularly suitable for white wines, and the reputation of Delta Domaines rests on its whites, as a comprehensive tasting illustrated. The wine is made by Jean-Etienne Cros, a member of the Gaillac wine family, and Pierre Besinet's son-in-law Alban. They achieve a successful balancing act, continuing to experiment while at the same time producing a satisfying range of good value and enjoyable wines. The key is the *contrôle de maturité*, for they follow the ripening grapes very closely, determining the precise moment for the harvest. In 1996, for instance, they began picking Chardonnay on 14 August. The vintage date is also significant for Sauvignon if you are to retain its varietal character. Grenache Blanc and Sauvignon are both given some skin contact, with a classic fermentation, and since 1993 they have practised *bâtonnage*, trying it out first on Marsanne and now using it on other varieties to add more body. They have planted Roussanne, which will be blended with Marsanne, and at Domaine Pourthié they make some appealing Terret Blanc, the traditional variety favoured by the vermouth makers, notably Noilly Prat. Whereas 200 hl/ha was the norm for vermouth and the niceties of vinification were irrelevant, now with lower yields, early picking and a cool fermentation, Terret Blanc makes an appealingly fragrant glass of wine. Viognier from

Domaine du Bosc has some attractive peachy fruit, while Muscat Sec Perlé, recalling Cros's Gaillac traditions, retains a little carbon dioxide and just a hint of a prickle with some grapey fruit. There is Petit Manseng too, and also Altesse from Savoie, but neither is in production yet.

Reds include Cabernet Sauvignon, Merlot and Syrah, which are well made but less original than the whites. Their current priority is the renewal and improvement of their vineyards, with denser plantings, vines trained on wires to improve the leaf area, and integrated viticulture without any weed-killer. For *vins de pays* and *vins de table* you are allowed to irrigate until 31 July, though not for appellation wines, and this they do, for the volcanic soil has no water retention at all. This was an organisation that was performing well in 1986 and continues to do so more than ten years later.

CHATEAU DE RAISSAC, BEZIERS

I enjoyed my encounter with the Viennet family of the Château de Raissac. Jean Viennet is friendly and extrovert, with an impish sense of humour and a very clear idea of the market for Vin de Pays d'Oc. The family has four estates between Béziers and Pézenas. The elegant Château de Raissac has been in the family since 1823, and there is also Domaine des Lions, close to the sea, Seigneurie de Peyrat outside Pézenas, run by his brother Luc, and the cellars at Domaine de Puech Cocut, or Cuckoo Hill – hence the unlikely label that you see on supermarket shelves. They produce Vin de Pays d'Oc and Coteaux du Libron in a wide variety of different grape varieties. They pulled up the traditional vines, Aramon and Alicante, Ugni Blanc and Carignan Blanc, in the 1970s and planted Merlot and numerous other varieties. The Australian wine maker Nick Butler has been helping them for a month over the vintage since 1994, and Viennet says that they have learned a lot from him, especially about white wine vinification, working on temperatures and yeast enzymes. It is all what he called *une cuisine très particulière*, resulting in *des vins très clean*. Now there is a move towards less acidification and less wood. In the future they will need to develop something more original, concentrating the image of the estate and its wine. For the moment most of their wines are made to a price, to be competitive on the supermarket shelf, whereas the future lies with a higher quality second label.

We tasted a variety of different wines, a fresh Sauvignon, a delicate blend of Chardonnay and Vermentino, a peachy Chardonnay and Viognier, a pure Viognier with some apricot fruit, and an intriguing blend of Viognier, Chardonnay and Muscat, vinified in wood and still quite oaky on the palate. A Merlot was soft and easy. Since 1992 they have been trying hard with the challenging variety of Pinot Noir, but it is questionable whether it is suitable for the hotter vineyards around Pézenas. Maybe a more temperate site closer to the sea would be better. The 1997 spent eighteen months in old wood, but there was not quite enough fruit for the oak.

They were one of the first to plant Viognier ten or twelve years ago, without knowing quite what it would do, and their first vintage of Muscat *à petits grains* was 1998, which was added to the Chardonnay/Viognier blend. As Viennet observed, the art of *assemblage* is a bit like that of a *perfumier*. Then we went to see his wife Christine's *faience* museum, a stunning collection of French and English porcelain, and also her own work, stylish *trompe l'oeil* plates of food, tempting oysters and asparagus. One table setting included a bottle of Norwegian wine, for she is from Norway and there is just one four-hectare vineyard in the country. After a congenial lunch in the garden of the château, during which Jean Viennet demonstrated his talent as a chef, I was late for yet another appointment.

DOMAINE DE BACHELLERY, BEZIERS

Bernard Julien at Domaine de Bachellery is a relaxed character, discursive in his approach and a fount of information and ideas. He talked about the history of the property. The origins are Roman, for it is close to the Domitian Way, and in the sixteenth century it belonged to Jacques de Bachelier, president of the court of justice in Béziers. His daughter Jacquette de Bachelier joined a religious order and gave the land to the church, so that it belonged to the nearby Priory of Cassan until the Revolution, when a Béziers family, the Azais, bought it. They were friends of the poet Frédéric Mistral, who often stayed at Bachellery and wrote of the wine he called Tokay that it was *un beau et fringant jeune homme*. Château de

Bachellery, along with the adjoining estate, Domaine de Cabrials, finally came to the Julien family in 1983, with a third estate, Domaine de Bicarie, on the other side of the river Orb.

The vineyards have been completely replanted with an eclectic mixture of some nineteen different varieties. As well as the usual Midi and Bordelais varieties, you will find Gewürztraminer, Tempranillo, Aubun and Ejiodola, which is a crossing of Fer Servadou and Abouriou developed by INRA for some supple fruit. Tempranillo was planted in 1981, and Julien would like to try Touriga Nacional. The Gewürztraminer has caused him problems. He bought the vines in Alsace and made a declaration of planting, but it is not included in the list of prescribed varieties of the Midi, although it is allowed under European Union law. He observed that the people from Alsace are politicians, like the Corsicans, and that they are very forceful in the corridors of power in Paris. He calls his wine poetically Balade en Straminer. The vinification cellars are at Bachellery and the ageing cellars, with enormous *foudres* as well as barrels, are at Cabrials.

Julien produces a sound range of wines, some quite commercial and others more individual and original. There are two Chardonnays, one more obviously oaked than the other. They began working with *barriques* in 1994. A *rosé* called Perles de Rose, from Syrah and Grenache Noir, was quite solid and substantial, compared with a lighter *rosé* made from Pinot Noir. A Grenache Noir, from vines planted in 1951, was solid and peppery, with quite attractive rustic flavours. The Tempranillo had notes of spice and ginger, and the best red was Tenue de Soirée, a blend of whatever they consider most suitable. As they want the freedom to blend as they wish, there is no indication of grape varieties on the label. I tasted the 1997, which included Cabernet Sauvignon, Merlot and Syrah, with tannin, structure and some Midi spice. The wine had spent twelve months in wood and the oak was well integrated on the palate. We finished with the slightly sweet Gewürztraminer, which was soft, spicy and not too blowsy. In the 1980s they asked to be included in the zone of the Coteaux du Languedoc but did not succeed, as they are rather isolated from other vineyards, and you need the collective energy of a village to succeed with French bureaucratic organisations like the INAO. They have created a reputation through the varietal wines, but now they would like to give them a more regional flavour.

There are any number of smaller, more individual producers making *vins de pays*, either Vin de Pays d'Oc, if they prefer the better known label, or alternatively the smaller departmental or regional name to which they may also be entitled. What follows is a selection of those that I visited. They illustrate some of the wonderful originality of the Languedoc, with its eclectic diversity of people and wines.

MAS DE DAUMAS GASSAC, ANIANE

The most famous example of a *vin de pays* that has acquired a reputation and a price to compete, not with neighbouring appellations, but with appellations from the more classic regions of France, is Mas de Daumas Gassac, which according to the label is a humble Vin de Pays de l'Hérault. The wine, however, is far from humble. It has often been described as the Lafite of the Languedoc, and it represents an exciting example of just what can be done in the Midi with ability and talent, as well as money. Not to put too mercenary a point on it, money is essential if you are to change a vineyard in the dramatic way that Aimé Guibert has done. Luck and imagination have helped too. Aimé Guibert and his wife Véronique bought Mas de Daumas Gassac, which lies in the Gassac valley between the small towns of Aniane and Gignac, about thirty kilometres north west of Montpellier in the heart of the Hérault, in 1970. They wanted a holiday home in the country, not a vineyard. Guibert is a lawyer, and his family comes from Millau in the Aveyron, where they have a tanning business. Véronique Guibert is equally removed from wine, for she is an ethnologist, specialising in Celtic traditions.

The story of how they discovered that they were sitting on a viticultural gold-mine has often been told. Henri Enjalbert, who was not only the leading geologist at Bordeaux University but also an enthusiastic archaeologist and a great friend of the Guiberts, came visit them at Mas de Daumas Gassac, as there are Iron Age remains in the area. While he was there, he noticed the unique soil of the property, a red glacial powder half a million years old that for some reason had settled there but nowhere else in the region. The lack of round stones in the soil suggests that it was created by wind rather than by water. It is very fine and was usually blown into rivers to disappear into the sea, but at Mas de Daumas Gassac, for reasons that remain unexplained, it has formed a hill. Here, Enjalbert convinced Guibert, 'You have the potential to make great wine.'

Guibert planted his first vines in 1974 and made his first wine in 1978, with the help of the eminent roving Bordelais oenologist Emile Peynaud. Guibert is the first to give credit where it is due, stating quite categorically that without Enjalbert there would have been no Mas de Daumas Gassac, and adding that without Peynaud there would have been no *grand cru* – for rightly or wrongly, that is how he perceives his wine. The wine is made very much in the Bordeaux manner, with Cabernet Sauvignon as the principal red variety. Peynaud closely supervised the first few vintages, but now his involvement is far less, for he gave Guibert the confidence to make his own decisions. Twenty years on, the vinification methods very much follow the techniques determined by Peynaud for that first vintage, and indeed resemble those of any good Bordeaux château. The length of *cuvaison* can vary quite considerably, from just fifteen days in 1986 to six weeks in 1982 and 1985. Peynaud's firm principle is to taste the fermenting juice twice a day while it is in contact with the grape skins. The moment that the tannins in the pips begin to be extracted is the moment to run the juice off the skins.

Guibert now has thirty hectares in production. When the vineyards of Mas de Daumas Gassac were first planted, Cabernet Sauvignon seemed an obvious choice. In the early 1970s the traditional grape varieties of the Midi were much despised and Cabernet Sauvignon was seen as a remedy to the mass of mediocrity in the Languedoc. In any case, Guibert himself likes the structured taste of Cabernet Sauvignon and insists that Syrah does not perform well in the Gassac valley. So Cabernet Sauvignon is blended with tiny amounts of other varieties, such as Merlot, Cabernet Franc, Tannat and Pinot Noir. Guibert enjoys experimenting with different varieties; where else in the Midi would you find Italian varieties such as Nebbiolo, Dolcetto and Barbera?

The blend of the white wine is similarly eclectic, with equal proportions of Chardonnay, Petit Manseng and Viognier, and the remaining ten per cent a mixture of some fourteen different grape varieties as diverse as Marsanne, Roussanne, Sercial, Petite Arvine and Chenin Blanc. For each hectare of vines, there are two of *garrigue*. There are other herbs too – pungent thyme and lavender.

In the warm spring sunshine the scents are almost overpowering, and they can reappear in the wines. Viticultural treatments are kept to a minimum and the weeds and spring flowers in the vineyards are accepted as part of the natural balance of things. Compared to his neighbour, the South African-owned and very streamlined Domaine du Capion, Guibert observed, 'I look like the Middle Ages.'

They welcome visitors at Mas de Daumas Gassac, where you will see cellars that would not look out of place in Bordeaux and can taste the current vintages in what was once the winter quarters of the sheep, using their manger as a spittoon. Be prepared for solid mouthfuls of tannins, for these are wines that take time to develop, like any good Bordeaux. The white is ripe, perfumed and rounded and there is also a very lightly sparkling *rosé*. A newcomer to the range with the 1997 vintage is Le Vin de Laurence, a blend of late harvest Muscat *à petits grains* and Sercial.

Guibert is an articulate and confident exponent of his wines, the consummate self-publicist who has come to an area with new eyes and has seen the possibilities on offer. More importantly, he has known how to take advantage of them, and even more significantly, he has had the financial means to do so. He has broken barriers and contributed enormously to the dramatic change in the image of the Midi. Twenty years ago it would have been inconceivable to think of cellaring a wine from the Languedoc. Today, if you talk to any of the growing number of talented producers in the region, that is the thing to which they aspire. Guibert has also set a new level of expectation concerning price, especially for what on the label is a simple *vin de pays*. The category is irrelevant. Mas de Daumas Gassac has been able to command consistently higher prices than any other Languedoc estate and has set an example for others to follow. When we are prepared to pay a sensible price for a wine, which means one that is not only not too expensive, but not too cheap either, we are giving its producers the possibility of investing some money in better cellar facilities and new vineyards.

Not content with creating a pace-setting wine from his own estate, Guibert has turned his energies to the local co-operative in the village of Villeveyrac, encouraging them to diversify their range of wines while retaining some of the traditional grape varieties. His first venture, Figaro, won the top prize for a red wine in Britain's *Wine Magazine*'s International Wine Challenge, which means that the village now sports a sign saying *Figaro, le meilleur vin en*

Angleterre en 1993. Subsequently he has brought out a range of different blends under the Terrasses label, as well as a range of varietals under the Moulin de Gassac label – not the obvious newcomers to the Midi but some of the forgotten varieties, including Aramon and Terret, grown in poor, rocky soils and not on the fertile coastal plains. Even past the age of seventy, Guibert is a restless, driven man, in search of the next challenge and caring passionately about his region.

DOMAINE LA GRANGE DES PERES, ANIANE

Guibert has two close neighbours, both quite different in style. Laurent Vailhé is an intense young man with a redeeming streak of humour, who has made a name for himself at Domaine La Grange des Pères. His parents were members of the Aniane co-operative but encouraged their children to do something else. Vailhé was a physiotherapist, but came back to wine and studied oenology at Montpellier. He chose his *stages* or apprenticeships carefully, Trévallon in Provence, Chave in Hermitage and finally Coche-Dury in the Côte d'Or, which has given him an enthusiasm for Pinot Noir, as well as Syrah. He admits that you have to be mad to create an estate. It is an enormous financial and personal investment. He did not want to plant Syrah just anywhere, so he has bought land in the middle of the *garrigue* near Aniane. Apparently there were vines there a hundred and fifty years ago. Now he has eleven hectares of Syrah, Mourvèdre and Cabernet Sauvignon, from which he makes a single red wine, and for white he has Roussanne, as well as a little Marsanne and Chardonnay. The white varieties are on east-facing limestone slopes, while the Syrah and Cabernet Sauvignon are also on limestone, but facing north at three hundred metres, and the Mourvèdre is on *pierres roulées*, facing due south. Valhé has no problem in ripening his Mourvèdre. The soil may be richer at Bandol, but it is really all a question of yield; even one bunch too many and the grapes will not ripen. In 1996 he had achieved 16° by 13 September. You need to know how to treat Mourvèdre properly and watch the hydric stress.

Vailhé said that his wine making is very simple. It is a question of hundreds of little details. Syrah and Mourvèdre he gives a very long *cuvaison*, four or five weeks, while Cabernet Sauvignon has only a week to ten days, if that. It has very ripe skins and a longer *cuvaison* could make the wine too tough. The grapes are destalked, and he lets the fermentation take its course in stainless steel vats, with regular *pigeages* but no *remontages*. *Pigeage* gives a softer extraction than *remontage* and what he wants to achieve is powerful wine with a velvet hand. He tastes every vat every day to decide when to run off the juice, which goes straight into *barriques* for twenty-four to twenty-eight months. There are few people in the Midi who give their wines quite such a long *élevage* in barrels, of which one third are new. Vailhé works with François Frères, Seguin Moreau, Damy and Saury, using different levels of toasting depending on the vintage. He is adamant that you must have confidence in your cooper.

We tasted our way through numerous barrel samples. In his choice of Roussanne and Marsanne, he was influenced by Chave and finds Roussanne does better here than Marsanne, giving more body and weight. He wants his whites to age and they spend about two years in wood. However, there are no fixed rules – the vintage dictates. The barrel samples had a rich concentration of flavour, while the bottled 1995 had enormous complexity, with notes of acacia and peaches, creamy fruit and great length. In the red wine the Cabernet Sauvignon provides freshness and acidity, while Syrah gives elegantly peppery fruit with firm tannins. Vailhé is particularly pleased with his 1996, for his grapes were ripe with good acidity and he considers that in ten years' time it will be a great wine. The 1995 was rich and concentrated, with smoky, peppery fruit and firm tannins as well as enormous ageing potential. A tasting in London illustrated the ageing potential of these wines, with his first vintage, the 1992, beginning to evolve in a spicy, mature glass of wine.

DOMAINE DE CAPION, ANIANE

Domaine de Capion is on quite a different scale. I first visited Philippe Salesc in 1987. He had taken over his father's vineyards some ten years earlier and, encouraged by Aimé Guibert – who at the time he acknowledged as his spiritual father – he pulled up the old Aramon and Carignan from which his father had made mediocre wine and planted *bordelais* varieties, as well as Grenache Noir, Syrah, Chardonnay and Sauvignon. He promised to go far, but sadly the harsh economic realities of life led to financial problems and in 1996 the estate was sold to a South African winery, Saxenburg. When I visited in April 1998 Salesc was still there, as the commercial director, but one wondered for how long; indeed, he has since moved on, to work in the Gard. In 1998 he was an angry young man, resenting bitterly, I suspect, the new owners of his family property and expounding his thoughts about French wine bureaucracy with vehemence.

First his cousin showed me round the vineyards. They have forty-five hectares of neat vines, with a considerable diversity of grape varieties. Chardonnay and Sauvignon are still the most important whites, but there are now also Marsanne, Roussanne, Viognier and Muscat, while for reds they have Carignan, Grenache Noir, Cinsaut, Syrah, Merlot, Cabernet Sauvignon and Cabernet Franc. The cousin had just returned from a visit to South Africa, where he had found no specific differences, but that everything was just that much more technological, and he had no doubt that the South Africans would bring a more professional attitude to the property.

We tasted as Salesc expounded his ideas. He talked of the antagonism between the *vins de pays* and the appellations in the region. 'You do not need appellation regulations to make good wine. It is the market that sanctions your ambition. You are part of a three hundred thousand hectare vineyard and the good producers do not want to get lost in the crowd.' Salesc does not believe in the appellations any more, for they are dominated by large producers or *négociants*, who see the small producers not as *artisans du vin*, or craftsmen, but as wine makers. Most of his wines are labelled Vin de Pays d'Oc or even Vin de Pays de l'Hérault. He is critical of the cost of the administration of the appellation and also of the low prices that bulk Coteaux du Languedoc fetches. His only interest is quality, but good producers have problems in getting their wines *labelisé* if they do not conform to the norm. 'The Languedoc is lucky to have some freedom for research, so leave us to our folly. We do not want to be restricted. The more you give people a framework, the less successful the result.' In April 1998 Domaine de Capion was producing twelve wines, some varietals and some blends, of Marsanne and Roussanne, and another of Merlot and Cabernet as well as a typical blend of the Languedoc. The wines were well made and it will be interesting to observe the effects of the first South African investment in the Midi.

LA GRANGE DES QUATRE SOUS, ASSIGNAN

Hildegaard Horat is a slightly shy, thoughtful Swiss woman who owns La Grange des Quatre Sous outside Assignan in the appellation of St Chinian. However, she prefers to make Vin de Pays d'Oc. The morning of my visit her barrel cellar was being covered with earth for further insulation, and we were occasionally deafened by a loud thud as soil was dumped above our heads. There was a reassuring supporting pole in the middle of the cellar. Horat bought the property in 1975 and made her first wine from Carignan in 1983. Since then she has replanted the vineyards, using the lyre system. This is the main reason why her wine is not St Chinian, for with a density of only 3200 vines per hectare she is offending the appellation regulations, which demand four thousand vines. She prefers the large leaf area that the lyre gives you, with its much better exposure to sunlight, and has no difficulty in ripening Mourvèdre despite the distance from the sea. However, her yields are tiny, an average of 20 hl/ha.

Horat produces two white wines, a Marsanne/Viognier blend and a Chardonnay, both fermented in barrel with a malolactic fermentation and *élevage* on the lees. The Chardonnay was beautifully elegant and understated, with more finesse than many a Midi Chardonnay, while the Marsanne/Viognier blend was richer and fuller in the mouth. As for reds, there are three: Les Serrottes, Lo Molin and an unoaked wine, a blend of Mourvèdre, Grenache Noir and a little Syrah, which as yet is nameless. It was firm and peppery, with some cherry fruit. The Mourvèdre balances the tendency of the Grenache Noir to oxidation. Les Serrottes, from two-thirds Syrah to one-third Malbec blended after fermentation, is aged in a small *foudre*. As the wine matures, the peppery character of the Syrah is lightened by the Malbec. The 1996 had some firm, smoky fruit and the 1994, which was given about eighteen months *élevage* in *barriques* rather than *foudres*, was beginning to develop some attractive cedarwood notes. Lo Molin is a blend of equal parts of Cabernet Sauvignon and Cabernet Franc, which were planted in 1989. It makes for a more structured and tannic wine than Les Serrottes, and after eighteen months *élevage* filtration is unnecessary.

And then I spotted a barrel marked in chalk PT A. 'What's that?' I asked. The answer of course was Petite Arvine, in recognition of her Swiss origins. Horat has T-budded half a hectare and is making both dry and late harvest Petit Arvine, with the late harvest following the example of Chappaz in the Valais. We tasted the 1998, of which Horat had made just 110 litres. There were hints of honeyed apricots and rose petals, an intriguing layer of flavours. The dry wine was quietly undergoing its malolactic fermentation in barrel. I enjoyed Horat's wines enormously, but she was critical, observing that wines do not taste so well when the vines are in flower, as they were in early June.

DOMAINE LA COLOMBETTE, BEZIERS

François Puygibet is a friendly, bearded man with vineyards on the outskirts of Béziers and ideas that contradict the mainstream. He prefers to use the local Coteaux du Libron, after a tiny river, as he considers that Vin de Pays d'Oc has been taken over by the big producers for the supermarket trade. His principal white varieties are Chardonnay, Sauvignon and Muscat, but he also has experimental Gewürztraminer and Riesling, which causes offence in high places. Not content with unconventional grape varieties, he has planted his vines at a minimum of five thousand vines and more usually six thousand vines per hectare, and now he is experimenting with eight thousand vines. With such a density, the vine produces smaller leaves and grapes, giving greater concentration to the wine and a different structure.

As for reds, there are Grenache Noir, Lladoner Pelut – which is related to Grenache Noir, but according to Puygibet is better – as well as Syrah, Pinot Noir, Cabernet Sauvignon, Cabernet Franc and Merlot. He has also tried some Gamay, but it was not successful. For Puygibet, the wonderful thing about the Languedoc is that 'everything is possible and we are just at the beginning of discovering what we can do'. He took over the family land, just twelve hectares, in 1966 from his father, who had apparently wanted him to be a mathematics teacher. How fortunate for us that he did not take his parents' advice. He has learned his wine making *sur le champ*, or by experience, developing from sales *en vrac* to a serious and varied range of different wines, with a particular reputation for Chardonnay. In 1993 he shocked the wine establishment by winning the second prize in the Chardonnay du Monde competition, behind a Pouilly Fuissé, Domaine de la Valette. He makes two Chardonnay, an oaked and an unoaked wine. What he calls his classic Chardonnay is all fermented in *demi-muids*, with an appealing nutty, toasted character. The barrels are given a *chauffe totale*, that is to say, the top and bottom of the barrels as well as the sides are toasted. His first fermentation in oak was in 1992 and the following year he tried out six hundred-litre *demi-muids*.

We talked about the need to irrigate. The average annual rainfall here is about 600 mm. 1996 was the wettest year of the century, with 2400 mm, whereas in sharp contrast in April 1999 the Midi was seriously short of water, having had just 300 mm of rain since September 1997. Puygibet has a drip system of irrigation that he does not hesitate to use, commenting that the Australians are so much more intelligent about irrigation than the French. He has also tried out a different orientation of the vines, observing the differences between rows going north to south as opposed to those going from east to west. They have done work on this in New Zealand, he said, demonstrating that his horizons are distinctly wider than those of the average wine grower in the Midi. He also admitted to an enthusiasm for Henschke, a leading Australian producer of fine Shiraz. As for vinification, the key factor is the temperature, as in the kitchen.

The Sauvignon was delicate, with some convincing varietal character, and the Muscat was appealingly grapey. As for reds, the Lladoner Pelut spends two years in wood after a long *cuvaison* and had some young, ripe fruit and a certain structure, while the Grenache Noir, with only one year's *élevage*, seemed softer and a little jammier. Puech d'Hortes, meaning hill of the garden, is a blend of Grenache Noir, Syrah and Cabernet, with some light fruit, while the 1995 pure Cabernet Sauvignon, given a year's wood ageing, had developed some attractive cedary fruit.

DOMAINE DE CLOVALLON, BÉDARIEUX

One of the pace-setters in the Vin de Pays d'Oc is Catherine Roque at Domaine de Clovallon just outside Bédarieux in the northern part of the Hérault. She explained how Bédarieux had once had a viticultural tradition, which has since been lost. In 1339 a charter was issued protecting the wines of Bédarieux, stating that they were not to be mixed with wines from anywhere else. There are now plans to restore the old terraces and they have found traces of old vines. The town was also known for its cloth industry; there was no shortage of the necessary water here, as it had a water mill and three springs.

Roque originally trained as an architect, but then her husband inherited four hectares of vines. It was like a secret garden, but it required work and the enthusiasm took hold. She bought another six hectares and did a agriculture diploma, but has really learned from practical experience. 'I write down everything I do, including the *bêtises*, the stupid mistakes. I don't allow myself to make the same mistake twice.' She is a bright, energetic woman, good fun but with an underlying seriousness and full of ideas and information.

Bédarieux is separated from Faugères by some dramatic cliffs – including the Pic Tantajo, which rises to 618 metres – forming a sharp contrast in soil and climate. Bédarieux is limestone while Faugères is schist, and Bédarieux is much cooler than Faugères. Roque has just bought a further seven hectares in Faugères: 'I am now discovering schist.' She has kept the very old Carignan and some Syrah and Grenache Noir, but has pulled up four hectares to leave the land fallow and to allow it to recover from a diet of weed-killer and fertiliser. A neighbour will graze cows on it. She wants to try planting at ten thousand vines per hectare and was planning her vintage of Faugères for 1999.

At the very beginning, in 1986, she grafted a hectare of Chardonnay. The vineyard was treated rather like a garden, and it was not until the early 1990s that she began to take it seriously; then in 1993 she gave up architecture. Meanwhile, she had planted Viognier in 1988, Pinot Noir in 1989 and Syrah in 1991 'for my husband'. Viognier may be fashionable in the Midi now, but ten years ago no one knew anything about it. As for Pinot Noir, people said that it is no good in the Languedoc because it is too hot, but with a mountain range to the north Bédarieux is much cooler, particularly at night, giving the heat exchange that Pinot Noir enjoys.

Roque also has Petit Manseng, which is the subject of numerous experiments. She allows the grapes to dry on the vines, as they do in Jurançon, and in 1996 she even made a *vin de glâce*. The grapes were picked on 28 December when the temperature had fallen to −13°C. It took an hour before any juice appeared from the press and 'finally we had something that looked like honey'. There is Petite Arvine too, and also Riesling, which presents a problem, for Alsace constitutes a powerful part of the INAO and is intensely protective of its interests. And finally there is a small vineyard of Clairette at Cabrières. Exceptionally, she has been allowed to vinify her grapes here at Bédarieux, and as explained on page 124 has made a dry wine and a *rancio*.

So how many different wines does she make? It varies from year to year. She works on individual grape varieties, usually labelled Vin de Pays d'Oc rather than Haute Vallée de l'Orb, with the name of a *cuvée*. The Viognier had some convincing varietal character, hints of apricots and a certain unctuosity. Les Aurièges is a blend of Viognier, Chardonnay and the experimental varieties, with several layers of flavour. Blending white wine is difficult. If you work on the nose, you obtain primary aromas that do not last, so you must concentrate on the mouth, considering the acidity, body and length.

Roque makes two qualities of Pinot Noir, determined by the age of the vines. Pomarèdes comes from the older vines and spends a year in wood, with some sweet varietal fruit. The *cuvaison* lasts three weeks, with regular *pigeage*. She tastes the berries to decide when to run off the juice. Roque is very self-critical in admitting that she did not like either her 1994 or 1995 Syrah. I thought the 1995 had good fruit, but lacked elegance, while she is really pleased with her 1996 Pelagret, with its attractive spicy fruit, elegant tannins and a long finish. She has proved that Pinot Noir and Viognier can work in the Languedoc, and now of course others are following her example.

DOMAINE DE BARUEL, DURFORT

Domaine de Baruel is another estate far from any neighbours of note. I drove north out of Nîmes toward Anduze over the *garrigue* of the northern Gard. Next came a plain of vines outside the village of Tounac, doubtless destined for the village co-operative, and then I went on through the medieval village of Durfort. It had narrow streets and pretty houses, but no café. Finally I took a discreet turning down a dirt track that led me into the enchanting, isolated and verdant valley where Rainer Pfefferkorn bought an abandoned property some ten years ago. He comes from southern Germany and had worked in computer science, but after working on farms as a child had always dreamed of being a farmer. When he and his wife first came to view the property, they did not even realise that there were vines there. The grapes went to the co-operative and the cellar needed renovation. The surprise was the vineyard, planted with Cabernet Sauvignon and Syrah, just what Pfefferkorn would have chosen himself. Better still, the vines were young and in relatively good condition.

Pfefferkorn is a genial character, tall and lanky with a bushy moustache. He is self-taught from books and admits to working *avec l'estomac*, in other words following his gut reactions and instincts. You can appreciate his love of fine wine from the rows of empty bottles that line one wall of the tasting area of his cellar, with evidence of the great names from all over the world. He admits to being inspired by Trévallon, which is evident in his choice of grape varieties, from which he makes two wines, a pure Syrah from a two-hectare plot called Fontanille, and a blend of sixty per cent Syrah with forty per cent Cabernet Sauvignon.

This area is Vin de Pays des Cévennes, which was recognised in 1992. Before that it was plain Vin de Pays du Gard, but now there is talk of incorporating it into Terres de Sommières in the Coteaux du Languedoc. The soil is based on schist, and is poor and friable. There is more rain here in winter than in the Costières de Nîmes and the summers are very hot. Disease is not a problem, and so Pfefferkorn has begun to follow the principles of biodynamic viticulture.

1989 was his first experience of wine making, with a small batch of grapes that he did not send to the co-operative. The following year, having withdrawn the vines from the co-operative, he tried an *élevage* in small thirty-hectolitre *foudres*. He likes the gentle oxygenation that they provide and his wines usually stay in wood for a couple of years. He uses open-top wooden fermenters and at the beginning did the *pigeage* himself, every vat for half an hour twice a day. Now he has a mechanical *plongeur*, which is more regular and preferable to *remontage*, as it makes for more concentration. The *cuvaison* lasts two to three weeks and the Cabernet Sauvignon and Syrah are blended after *élevage*.

These are very appealing wines. The 1997 was a combination of peppery fruit and Cabernet structure. The 1995 had more concentration, with more cassis fruit balancing the peppery

Syrah, while the 1990 showed the ageing potential of these wines when it was nine years old. It was almost pure Syrah, with a mature, leathery nose and great concentration on the palate. The grapes were not destalked then, but they are now. The pure Syrah has elegant, peppery violet fruit and in 1997 was supple and long. White wine is a new project, with a recent grafting of a little Rolle and Roussanne, for which 1999 was the first vintage.

DOMAINE DE RAVANES, THEZAN-LES-BEZIERS

One of the more innovative estates is Domaine de Ravanès outside the village of Thézan-les-Béziers. I was given a noisy welcome by a neurotic dog, while Marc Benin and his father Guy proved much more friendly – in fact, so welcoming that I was seriously late for my next appointment. Marc explained how his grandfather had been a *négociant* and broker in Oran in Algeria, dealing annually in a million hectolitres of the so-called *vin de médicin*. He had bought Domaine de Ravanès in 1955, sending his son Guy over to manage it, while he had stayed in Algeria until 1965. In 1956 most of the vineyards were destroyed by the huge frost and not knowing any better, Guy Benin replanted with Carignan, Cinsaut, Alicante and Aramon. None the less, the *pieds noirs* were responsible for many of the innovations in the Midi at that time, 'for it was the Middle Ages here'. They brought new ideas about the cultivation of the vineyards and they had experience of vinification in a hot climate, resulting in improved technology. Originally Domaine de Ravanès was an estate of polyculture with an absentee owner. Marc Benin related how his father spent ten years arguing with the *régisseur*, who was also the president of the local co-operative. Initially there were twelve horses on the estate and ten labourers, and the average annual production was eight thousand hectolitres from sixty hectares of vines. In other words, they obtained an average yield of some 130 hl/ha, as was common in the Midi at that time. Now they make 2500–3000 hectolitres a year, with a much more modest 40–50 hl/ha.

Guy Benin loves good claret and that is what led him to plant his first Merlot in 1972, on gravelly land on the banks of the river Orb. They still have some of their *vignoble de masse*, but their individuality as wine makers comes from their *bordelais* grape varieties. They have tried Syrah and Grenache Noir, but with very limited success and prefer to concentrate on Cabernet, Merlot and Petit Verdot. Their Petit Verdot is called Le Prime Verd, for this is a grape variety that is neither on the recommended or authorised list of grape varieties, but is not actually forbidden. The 1995 vintage had a firm, structured character, with some convincing Merlot and Cabernet Sauvignon, aged in vat. A delicious 1994 Merlot had elegant cedarwood flavours. What they described as *une petite folie* was a 1980 Merlot, kept in vat for fifteen years. If it had spent that time in bottle, they thought it would probably have been dead. Instead it was firm and dry, with cedary fruit and quite intriguing. And their very first bottling, an almost pure Merlot from the 1979 vintage, was still very much alive. It also represented their very first experiment with barrels, and twenty years on had a mature, smoky nose with hints of black olives, while the palate was rounded and complete. The 1988 pure Cabernet Sauvignon was given twenty-seven months in wood, representing their first lengthy barrel *élevage*. There was a firm, structured cassis flavour, prompting Guy Benin to observe, '*C'est le Médoc ici.*' I could not disagree, for in a blind tasting I would not have thought otherwise.

Cuvée Diogène is also deceptive. The 1994 is three parts Merlot to one part Cabernet Sauvignon, vinified separately and blended a year before bottling. The wine spends eighteen months in wood, but not in new barrels, and had an appealing smoky flavour with elegance and length when it was five years old. The 1996, which included Petit Verdot, thirty-five per cent to fifty-five per cent Merlot and just ten per cent Cabernet Sauvignon, was given sixteen months in new wood. They are very enthusiastic about Petit Verdot, for it has acidity, even when picked at 14°, which makes for excellent structure. Indeed, the wine was both supple and structured, with considerable length and great appeal.

As for white wine, unusually Marc Benin works with Ugni Blanc, making two wines: a *moelleux* called Le Chapitre, and L'Ille made from botrytised grapes. Ugni Blanc is a late ripener and is usually picked towards the beginning of November. In 1989 he tried a dry late harvest wine and since 1992 has made *moelleux*. However, he has had problems with the Répression des Fraudes for using the term 'Vendange Tardive' on the label. The Alsace producers, even though they have only used this term with legal weight since 1983, guard it jealously. The case, brought by an Alsace grower, came to court, and Benin escaped lightly with a fine. His wine was judged to be 'unfit for human consumption', simply because it contained a tad too much combined SO_2, but no free SO_2, and a little too much volatile acidity. Benin continues to make the wine, but no longer labels it Vendange Tardive. Meanwhile, the Syndicat du Vin de Pays d'Oc may solve the problem for the many growers wanting to produce late harvest wines. As for its taste, the 1992 Chapitre was peachy with good acidity, with botrytis flavours and a touch of unobtrusive volatile acidity, while the 1996 L'Ille, a selection of *grains nobles* given twelve months in new wood, was still quite oaky, with honey and balancing acidity. In 1998 Benin finished picking the grapes for it on 28 December, making for a harvest that lasted over six weeks, with a yield of about three and a half hectolitres per hectare.

I enjoyed Benin's refreshingly forthright attitude. He was vocal in his criticism of the Vins de Pays d'Oc and much prefers the regional identity of Coteaux de Murviel, which covers thirteen or fourteen *communes* adjoining the Côtes de Thongue and is limited by two rivers, the Orb and the Libron. Domaine de Ravanès and Château Coujan in St Chinian are the two main producers of the Coteaux de Murviel, and the co-operative of Murviel-lès-Béziers also works well, while that at Thézan just produces *vin de table*. Benin is adamant that he does not want to be part of the standardisation of Vins de Pays d'Oc. To his mind, the *syndicat* has orientated itself towards what he calls technological wines. The tastings for the *agrément* do not allow for any individuality, as they take place between 15 November and the 15 May following the vintage, which is much too early for his wines. At least half the wines are presented by *négociants*, who are imposing their taste on the majority. As the Coteaux de Murviel is not very well known, his reputation rests in his own hands.

DOMAINES LISTEL, AIGUES-MORTES

The one *vin de pays de zone* that does have a geological and climatic unity is the Vin de Pays des Sables du Golfe de Lion. Domaines Listel dominate the production. There are numerous small growers who sell their grapes to Domaines Listel and a handful of independent producers, such as Domaine du Petit Chaumont. However, essentially the wine of the sands means Listel. Until 1995 they were part of Les Salins du Midi, who are large landowners for salt on the coast and are owned in turn by the Banque Indo-Suez. The Salins du Midi were founded in 1856, seven years before phylloxera was discovered in the Gard, and by 1875 it was noticed that the vineyards that they owned on the coastal sand dunes, to provide wine for their workers, remained unaffected by the blight. Quite simply the phylloxera louse cannot survive in very sandy soil. By 1900 they had developed seven hundred hectares of vines, and in 1999 they had 1850 in total, fourteen hundred hectares in the sand dunes at Château de Jarras, Domaine de Villeroy and Domaine du Bosquet, with three hundred in Provence, including Château la Gordonne in the Côtes de Provence and the Abbaie Ste Hilaire in the Coteaux Varois, and a hundred hectares in the Côtes du Rhône with Château Malijay, purchased in 1989. Les Salins du Midi are now part of an American company, and Domaines Listel, as they are now called, are part of the Vignerons du Val d'Orbieu. They are very much left to operate independently, and the Vignerons du Val d'Orbieu are considered to be a distinct improvement on the bank that was the previous owner of Les Salins du Midi, which simply did not understand viticultural investment. 'With the Vignerons du Val d'Orbieu, we speak the same language.'

Charles Pacaud, the amiable export director of Domaines Listel, stated firmly: 'Our tradition is innovation.' Certainly you feel that this is not a company to stand still, and they have remained at the forefront of viticultural developments in the Midi since the end of the Second World War. They still retain the magnificent cellar of enormous *foudres* that dates back to 1884, but it has not been used since the mid-1980s. It is now called the Cave Pierre Julien, after the man who led the renovation of the coastal vineyards after the devastation of the war. They were heavily mined and the first task was to remove the remaining ammunition. In sharp contrast to the old *foudres* are the state-of-the-art pneumatic presses and the *flottateur*, which is the latest technique in *débourbage* and infinitely more efficient than a centrifuge.

They are shareholders of the SICAREX estate at nearby l'Espiguette, where they are studying Aubun, a Rhône grape variety that performs well in the sand, and where Caladoc, a variety developed by INRA by crossing Grenache Noir and Malbec, has been planted as an experiment. They used to have Riesling but pulled it up as they have never obtained the necessary authorisation for it. If a grape variety is on the proscribed list, the most you can plant is fifty ares for personal consumption, and there is no question of your being able to sell it, even as *vin de table*. So there will never be Sangiovese or Savagnin from the Midi. We climbed the seventy-five steps to the top of the huge stainless steel vats to view the vast lakes of the Camargue and the extensive vineyards. There are huge white mountains of salt and the attractive outline of the fortified city of Aigues-Mortes. This is the port created by Saint Louis for the Eighth Crusade, but it is now some distance from the sea, as sand dunes and silt have taken their toll. Over three-quarters of Domaine Listel's vineyards are mechanically harvested, between the hours of eight p.m. and noon, but nothing in the heat of the afternoon. They conduct experimental work with Braud, the market leaders in mechanical harvesters, to keep abreast of the latest technology. In the vineyard they practise integrated viticulture and grass is sown between the vines to retain the soil, while fertiliser is provided by flocks of willing sheep.

The name Listel is inspired by the name of the Ile de Stel, one of the sandbanks of the Rhône delta, where vines have been grown since the fifth century BC. In Occitan the name means quite simply island of sand and they have found amphorae containing grape pips. In the early fifteenth century Charles VI praised the wines of Uzès and Aigues-Mortes, describing them as *vins des sables*.

Today, Domaines Listel are best known for their Gris de Gris, from Grenache Gris as well as Grenache Noir, Carignan and Cinsaut. Usually the term *gris* describes a vinification of red grapes *en blanc*, such as Gris de Toul, and usually these grapes do not become fully red in their vineyards in the sand dunes. This Gris de Gris is a pale orange-pink, with ripe fruit, fresh and rounded on the palate. Sauvignon and Grenache Blanc provide an unusual blend. Pacaud explained that they wanted the fruit of the Sauvignon and the body of the Grenache Blanc, but as the two grape varieties have to be *labelisé* separately if the names are to appear on the label, they have to be blended well after the vinification. Iles de Stel is a blend of Merlot and Cabernet Sauvignon, some from the sand dunes and some from vineyards further north, which is given some *élevage* in oak for six months. Domaine du Bosquet is a *bordelais* blend of Cabernet and Merlot, aged in *barriques*, which later successfully accompanied an *entrecôte de taureau*. The free-range bulls of the Camargue now enjoy their own appellation, this apparently being one of the indirect consequences of mad cow disease. And our tasting finished with a non-alcoholic product, Pétillant de Listel, a sweet grapey drink made from Muscat, Ugni Blanc and Clairette, that was deliciously refreshing. The range was competent. It is probably fair to say that you may never be excited by their wines, but you are unlikely to be disappointed either. This is in part a reflection of the scale on which they vinify their *vins de cépages*; more character comes from individual estates.

There are so many other producers of *vin de pays* from the Midi who deserve a mention, which sadly can be no more than passing, for the usual reasons of time and space. In the Haute-Vallée de l'Aude Jean-Luc Tessier makes an intriguing Mauzac/Chardonnay blend near the village of Autignac. Domaine de la Provenquière at Capestang near Béziers produces an unusual Sémillon, while at Domaine Lalaurie in the Coteaux de Narbonne they concentrate on red *bordelais* grape varieties. Domaine de la Caunette in the Coteaux de Libron makes some attractive varietal wines from the obvious Chardonnay, Merlot and Syrah, and at Domaine de Monpézat outside Pézenas they produce a convincing Cabernet Sauvignon Merlot blend from vines that are now twenty years old.

Today, the Syndicat des Producteurs de Vin de Pays d'Oc has over a thousand members, but it by no means represents all the producers of fine *vins de pays* in the Midi. The choice is infinite and depends above all on the producer's name on the label. There is, however, one area that stands out for its concentration of quality and interest and that is the Côtes de Thongue, whose producers maintain a fierce independence.

Key facts

Vin de Pays d'Oc, created 1987, covers four departments: Pyrénées-Orientales, Aude, Hérault and Gard. Thirty-one grape varieties allowed, of which twenty-five may be used as single varietals and mentioned on the label, representing France's answer to the challenge of the New World.

10° alcohol; chaptalisation allowed, unlike appellations in the Midi.

Bis cépages allowed since 1996.

Grand d'Oc is a new category, with an even stricter selection; also allows *vin de primeur*; *syndicat* working on late harvest wines.

Vin de Pays des Côtes de Thongue

There is one *vin de pays* in the Hérault that has a firm sense of unity, with a strong group of talented and committed producers, and that is the Côtes de Thongue.

The Thongue is a tiny river that flows into the Hérault near Pézenas. It is not much more than a stream at the end of summer, but has potential for serious flooding in winter. Some eleven villages make up the area, which is about thirty kilometres in length, stretching from St Thibéry and Nézignan l'Evêque in the south to Puissalicon and Magalas in the north. It adjoins the appellations of Faugères and the Coteaux du Languedoc, with vineyards planted on a mixture of clay and limestone soil. There are now about twenty producers, mainly private estates; the fact that the village co-operatives play only a small part in the region accounts for its strength and dynamism. This group of independent, searching and like-minded wine growers is successfully creating an identity for the Côtes de Thongue. They are virtually unique for a *vin de pays* in the Midi; you may find two or three producers elsewhere with their clout and energy, but certainly not as many as twenty. Such is the success of the region that other nearby estates would also like to be included, even though they are theoretically outside the Côtes de Thongue. All the producers could equally well label their wines Vin de Pays d'Oc, but now strongly feel that Côtes de Thongue has much more of a cachet and an identity. In some instances both are used, with Oc describing a varietal wine and Côtes de Thongue a more interesting blend.

Until the development of the *vins de pays*, this was an area that produced what was called *appellation d'origine simple* or, more basically, *vin de consommation courante*. For a couple of years when the *vins de pays* were first created, the area was included in

467

the Coteaux du Libron and then became Côtes de Thongue in the mid-1970s. Back in the 1950s, when the VDQS of the Midi were first talked of, the wine growers here had seen no point in any move towards quality, when they were successfully producing and selling enormous quantities of wine, with yields of 150–200 hl/ha commonplace in the fertile soil. The new president of the growers' *syndicat*, Jacques Boyer of Domaine la Croix-Belle, talked about his family. His great-grandparents had had vineyards planted with Mourvèdre, Syrah and Grenache, but that all changed with phylloxera, and his grandparents, who saw the price of wine multiply tenfold, planted high-yielding varieties like Aramon, Carignan, Alicante Bouschet and Ugni Blanc. At that time, nine out of ten people in the area lived from their vineyards. Then, when the viticultural crisis came, instead of confronting it and transforming their vineyards, the wine growers demonstrated and protested, but took no corrective steps.

DOMAINE LA CROIX-BELLE, PUISSALICON

Jacques Boyer took over the family property in 1977, ignoring his father's wish that he should go into a bank rather than become a *vigneron*, and made the decision to replant the vineyards with grape varieties like Syrah, Mourvèdre, Cabernet Sauvignon, Merlot, Chardonnay, Sauvignon and others. Boyer admits to fierce arguments with his father, who simply could not accept that quality would pay. He is an energetic man, with a firm sense of purpose and a strong commitment to his region, who is now president of the recently revived growers' *syndicat*. His friendly wife Françoise is also involved in the estate. He first bottled some wine in 1984 and has increased his sales in bottle steadily each year so that all his production is sold now in bottle, illustrating a development that you find in other estates, with a new generation or new owners bringing a change of direction.

Domaine de la Croix-Belle is in the village of Puissalicon, with seventy hectares of vines and functional cellars containing concrete vats and barrels, both large and small. The medieval château, which has been in the same family since the eleventh century, towers over the village. It has vineyards, but sadly the owners take no interest in the viticultural potential of their region. Boyer talked of the measures he has taken to improve his vineyards. Not only has he replanted with better grape varieties, but has also increased the density of planting from four thousand to five thousand vines per hectare. He prunes much shorter and also carries out a green harvest, so that yields average about 45–60 hl/ha, depending on the particular grape variety. The new varieties are in any case much less productive than the Carignan, Ugni Blanc and Aramon of his parents.

Champs de Lys is an intriguing blend of Grenache Blanc, with ten per cent each of Viognier, Chardonnay and Sauvignon. The Grenache Blanc provides the body, while there were hints of Viognier on the nose, with acidity and citrus notes from the Sauvignon. It was, for a blend of very individual varieties, surprisingly well knitted together. There are two Chardonnays: one, vinified in vat without a malolactic fermentation, was light and elegant, while the other, fermented in barrel with *bâtonnage* and a malolactic fermentation, was ripe and buttery. A *rosé* fermented in *foudre* and then racked into a vat was redolent of ripe strawberries, with good acidity and considerable appeal. Le Champs du Coq, a blend of Merlot, Cabernet Sauvignon, Syrah and Mourvèdre, had firm fruit and tannins, while Les Calades, from the same blend but aged in wood for twelve months after *assemblage*, was tighter and denser, showing plenty of potential but demanding bottle age. Boyer aged his first red wine in wood in 1985 and conducted his first barrel fermentation of white wine in 1988. The latest addition to his repertoire is No 7, which he sees as a blend of Bordeaux and the Mediterranean, a selection of the best plots and vats of Petit Verdot, Grenache Noir and five other varieties, which spends nine months in wood. The first vintage, the 1996, with tightly knit fruit, needed time but promised well. We finished our tasting with his first attempt at a late harvest Muscat, which was ripe and unctuous.

PRIEURE D'AMILHAC

Max Cazottes is an older man who has played his part in the development of the region over the last thirty years. He bought his property, the Prieuré d'Amilhac, with his brother Régis back in 1970 and they bottled their first wine, at that time a humble *appellation d'origine simple*, the following year. The same year he planted the first Merlot and Syrah in the area, with Cabernet Sauvignon, Cabernet Franc and Petit Verdot following the next year. In 1973 he tried Gamay and Pinot Noir, and then in 1975 some Chardonnay. By that time there was already a little Chardonnay in the vineyards of Limoux, and his enthusiasm for Meursault was another deciding factor. At first the different varieties were blended all together, with no mention of them on the label; varietal labelling only came with the development of the American market in the 1980s, when they followed the lead of Robert Skalli to concentrate on *vins de cépage*. Cazottes observed how much more open the Anglo-Saxon market of North America and Britain is to new ideas and concepts than the French.

He talked with enthusiasm and knowledgeable authority about the history of his estate. There was a Roman villa here in the first century BC and you still find remains of pottery in the vineyard. The villa survived until the fifth century AD and then the land passed to the church as part of the property of the bishop of Béziers. At the beginning of the seventeenth century it became the home of nuns, Les Dames de la Saint Esprit, until the Revolution. There is a simple Romanesque chapel adjoining the cellars, with an exhibition of paintings by local artists and a one thousand-year-old altarpiece. At the entrance to the cellars a small wine museum includes a splendid penny-farthing bicycle, various old carriages and a magnificent wine press that dates back to 1609. The cellars are a well-organised mixture of vats and barrels, both large and small, and there is a high powered bottling line to cater for the production of some two hundred and fifty hectares, here and on adjoining properties.

By the tasting counter there is a saying from Jean de Bousi, bishop of Béziers in 1605: *Je dis ma messe avec le bon vin d'Amilhac car je ne veux pas faire la grimace au Seigneur quand je communie* (I say mass with the good wine of Amilhac as I do not want to grimace to the Lord when I take communion.) We tasted a range of different wines. There was a Chardonnay partly fermented in oak, Hungarian and American as well as French. It was firm and smoky, with a buttery finish. A 1995 Merlot, aged in wood for twelve months, was particularly appealing, with attractive pencil-shaving notes and plummy fruit. A 1991 Cabernet Sauvignon with a firm, cedary palate could happily have held its own in a range of *petits châteaux* from Bordeaux, while the 1991 Pinot Noir, although demonstrating the difficulties of the grape variety, was not without appeal. We finished with a late harvested Sauvignon, which had fermented very gently in wood until the June following the harvest, picked with a potential alcohol of 24°, of which 6° remained as sugar. Ripe apricots were the dominant flavour.

Cazottes believes passionately in the quality of the region, but with a firmly pragmatic realism. He admitted that when he first studied oenology thirty years ago, he would never have thought that it would take so long to establish a reputation for his region, while fully realising that it will never have the standing of Bordeaux or Burgundy. The image is that of a good *rapport qualité prix*, or quality to price ratio, rather like a Japanese car. Nor can you establish the reputation of a region without making wines that will age, and there is no doubt that his do.

DOMAINE DE L'ARJOLLE, POUZOLLES

Louis-Marie Tesserenc at Domaine de l'Arjolle in the village of Pouzolles was another early pioneer. He is a cheerful, bearded man who is obviously passionate about what he is doing, for his wines demonstrate his enthusiasm for the rich eclectic variety of the Côtes de Thongue. 'That is the advantage of our region, that there is everything to discover.' The strength of a *vin de pays* is the liberty it gives you, whereas appellation laws only provide a framework for what already exists. Tesserenc first planted Sauvignon in 1981, inspired by a friend from oenology studies in Montpellier who settled in Sancerre, and 1998 was his first vintage of Zinfandel, or Primitivo, with plants bought from Italy. Ask him how many wines he makes, and *Ooh la la!* is the response. He admits to about ten, even though it is not economically viable to produce so many, but it is a way of giving yourself pleasure. He adores diversity. 'At vintage time everything is singing together' – a reference to the gentle noise of a fermenting vat – 'and you don't sleep much.' Tesserenc much prefers blends to a *monocépage*, as they are much more interesting, even if the varietal wines are an important marketing tool.

First we went to look at the vineyards, of which, together with five associates, he has a total of seventy-eight hectares, fifty in the village of Pouzolles and twenty-eight in nearby Morgon. Those at Morgon are dominated by the imposing château built by the architect Viollet-le-Duc, who is known particularly for his restoration work on the medieval city of Carcassonne. There were still grapes on the vines towards the end of October, as Tesserenc was hoping to make a red late harvest from Merlot for the first time, encouraged by his success with Muscat. He practises integrated viticulture, taking great care over vineyard treatments.

In the cellar, *barriques* are very much part of his method. 1988 was the first year that he experimented with *barriques* and he has gradually replaced the large *foudres* that were common throughout the Midi. We tasted a diverse selection of his wines. First came barrel samples of the recent 1998 vintage, wines that had barely finished fermenting. However, the 1998 vintage is so successful in the Midi that everyone was keen to show off its quality, and it seemed churlish to plead lack of expertise when confronted with wines that had a closer visual resemblance to grapefruit juice. To a palate unused to detecting the nuances in wines that were only just wine, these had weight, texture and richness. And we spat happily on the floor, for that is 'for our ancestors' in French country tradition. Then we went on to bottled wines. Equinoxe 1997 is an intriguing blend of Sauvignon, Muscat and Viognier, of which two-thirds are fermented in wood. When I first tasted it, the green pea fruit of the Sauvignon dominated the flavour, but with bottle age the palate had become more rounded and satisfying.

What Tesserenc calls his Chardonnay Top is a selection of his best grapes left on the vine until mid-September, which is three weeks later than his other Chardonnay; the wine stays in barrel until June, undergoing regular *bâtonnage*. Tesserenc works mainly with two coopers, Radoux and the Tonnellerie de Mercurey. It is a question of finding which are the most compatible with your wines, rather like a marriage. The first vintage of Chardonnay Top, the 1997, was quite firm and oaky, with good structure and several layers of flavour.

Méridionne 1997 was an intriguing and very successful example of an oak fermented *rosé*, made from Syrah with a small amount of Cabernet Sauvignon and Cabernet Franc, that is bottled in April or May. Although he does not use new barrels, the oak has the effect of giving the wine more body and substance, with good fruit and a long finish. The name is charming, meaning a little siesta in Occitan – perhaps when you have succumbed to an extra glass at lunchtime.

Tesserenc's red wines include a Cabernet Sauvignon/Merlot blend that spends eight months in old wood; it has a firm, plummy nose, soft tannins and attractive fruit on the palate. It is not a wine of great depth but offers immediate drinking pleasure. A Cabernet Sauvignon with a small amount of Cabernet Franc had more stature and elegance, with the classic notes of cedary pencil-shavings and layers of flavour. A more recent addition to the range is a blend of Syrah, Cabernet Sauvignon and Merlot, which, tasted from barrel, promised well, with smoky fruit, firm tannins and an underlying elegance. Tesserenc cheerfully said that he wasn't worried if it didn't sell because they would drink it all themselves, but somehow I suspect that customers will be forthcoming.

We finished with the 1997 Muscat *à petits grains* Vendange Tardive. Whether the wine can be given the label *vendange tardive* in the Midi remains a matter of uncertainty, with the Alsaciens energetically defending their claim to a monopoly on its use. The vines are trained in the lyre form, giving the wine its name, Lyre 1997. The grapes are mainly *passerillés* rather than botrytised, making for a sweet, concentrated palate, with an intense flavour of apricots and a good backbone of acidity. The first vintage was 1993 and just five thousand bottles were made in 1997.

LES CHEMINS DE BASSAC, PUIMISSON

Rémi and Isabelle Ducellier at Les Chemins de Bassac are an example of newcomers to the region. He was a history professor who inherited sixty hectares of vines in 1987. He kept the best fifteen hectares, which have been replanted with more appropriate grape varieties, and sold the other forty-five to obtain the financial means to create a cellar. An old cellar was found in the village of Puimisson, a vast, functional shed that has been renovated, insulated and furnished with vats, *foudres* and *barriques*. The tasting area is on a gallery above the vats so that you look down over the barrels. It is equipped with an attractive old barber's counter with three porcelain basins, now used for spitting. The name of the estate describes a pretty path through the vineyards, leading to a tumble-down old house.

Their white wine is a blend of sixty per cent Roussanne and forty per cent Viognier. Although it is fermented in tank, it is kept on the fine lees until June and regularly injected with nitrogen and carbon dioxide, so that the pressure of the gas gives a similar effect to *bâtonnage*, but on a larger scale. In the 1997 the Viognier dominated the flavour, with perfume and acidity. The *rosé* is a blend of Syrah, Cabernet Sauvignon, Mourvèdre and Grenache Noir, giving fresh raspberry flavours and good acidity. There are three red wines. The first is a blend of Syrah, Cabernet Sauvignon and Pinot Noir that is aged in forty-hectolitre *foudres*, with some perfumed and smoky fruit. Cap de l'Homme, a blend of mainly Grenache Noir with some Mourvèdre, had some solidly chunky berry fruit; and Pierre Elie, based on Syrah and Grenache Noir, was ripe and solid, with layers of flavour. Their vines are still young and there is potential to be realised.

DOMAINE DE COUSSERGUES, MONTBLANC

Arnould de Bertier at Domaine de Coussergues outside the village of Montblanc on the southern edge of the Côtes de Thongue, close to the coastal plain and the sea, is the southernmost estate of the area, while his brother Philippe has the adjoining Domaine de Montmarin. There are two hundred hectares at Coussergues and a hundred at Montmarin. Originally four estates made up the Seigneurie de Coussergues; the two remaining estates have been in the family for five centuries, apart from a brief interruption during the French Revolution when the family took refuge in Italy. It had always been a *domaine viticole*, but with other crops – wheat, fruit and vegetables – as well as sheep and wood for bakers' ovens.

Domaine de Coussergues was, in 1989, one of the first estates to receive a so-called flying wine maker, one of the itinerant Australians who brought their expertise and their different approach to hygiene and temperature control. The idea came from de Bertier's British importer, Tony Laithwaite of the *Sunday Times* Wine Club, and since then there has been a visiting Australian or two at each vintage. De Bertier's present wine maker, Natalie Arnaud, trained at Montpellier and then spent three years in Australia, in particular at St Halletts in the Barossa Valley. She admitted that she found more similarities between the Languedoc and Australia than between the Languedoc and Burgundy, and was impressed by the Australian way of bringing out the best of the vintage, not to mention the refreshing lack of restrictive legislation.

De Bertier is a smooth talker, discussing the balance between commercial demands and quality requirements. In a large estate like this, you need to produce hectolitres to meet your commercial demands. There are grape varieties like Marsanne, Vermentino or Rolle and Cabernet Franc that he produces in relatively large quantities to sell at lower prices, and other varieties, produced in smaller quantities and fermented or aged in barrel, that provide the top of the range, the *haut de gamme*. No hierarchy of *terroir* is possible in the Côtes de Thongue. That must come from the bottle, from the selection of wines for the best labels, and that depends upon the producer's decision. He makes a wide range of different wines, some labelled as Côtes de Thongue and some as Vin de Pays d'Oc, but the difference is one of marketing, not of yields or *terroir*. One of the most successful grape varieties is Syrah, while Pinot Noir is promising and Merlot not so good. You must have low yields – that is, about 50 hl/ha – to obtain good results with reds here. Chardonnay grows well, benefiting from the maritime influence at night.

Quality seemed variable, with highs and lows. Rolle, which is seen as a replacement for Ugni Blanc, provides a volume base as well as aroma, and had some lemony fruit and acidity. The first vintage of Viognier produced some ripe, peachy fruit, while the Chardonnay was sound but unexciting. Of the reds, a Syrah from twenty-year-old vines was the most appealing, with some attractive peppery fruit. De Bertier has a project for a red *haut de gamme*, from Syrah, with a little Cabernet Sauvignon and some Merlot, aged in wood. For the 1997 vintage, he experimented with both French and American oak, with different coopers and barrels of different ages. The wine spent twelve months in barrel and demonstrated the peppery character of Syrah, with some firm tannin and weight in the mouth.

DOMAINE DE BASSAC, PUISSALICON

Also in the village of Puissalicon is the one firmly organic producer of the Côtes de Thongue, Domaine de Bassac, an estate run by the three brothers Pierre, Louis and Henri Delhon. We met Louis, who is the wine maker and also president of the regional association of the Interprofession des Vins Biologiques. There are about seventy organic wine growers in the Languedoc, with some fifteen hundred hectares of land, representing a mere drop in the total vineyard area of around three hundred thousand. This is another family estate that has undergone a transformation because of a change of generation, for Delhon *père* was also a doctor and made table wine for the local *négoce* from Carignan, Aramon, Cinsaut and Grenache Noir. Yields were 100 hl/ha or more, and the wine was often distilled. Now they have Syrah, Merlot and Cabernet Sauvignon, and also some Sauvignon and Muscat, all vinified in rather old-fashioned cellars in the centre of the village.

Sauvignon was planted in preference to Chardonnay for reasons of personal taste. It had an attractively discreet flavour and just ten per cent was fermented in wood, which filled out the wine without giving any oaky flavours. Varietal Syrah, Merlot and Cabernet Sauvignon, vinified in vat, showed simple varietal flavours, providing pleasant drinking but no great depth of flavour. However, in the very good vintage of 1995 they wanted to show that they could make wines with more structure, concentration and ageing potential. The result was the Cuvée Jacques Delhon, named after their father, from Cabernet Sauvignon and Syrah fermented together and aged for eighteen months in wood. For my taste the oak was still too aggressive, but that will be tempered with time, and in any case represents the desire to experiment. The Muscat *moelleux*, with hints of orange peel on the nose and fresh, pithy fruit, was light and appealing, not unlike a *vin doux naturel* but without the addition of alcohol. It retained a delicate, honeyed fruit and acidity, with an alcohol level of 11.5° and 40 gms of residual sugar.

DOMAINE DE LA CONDAMINE L'EVEQUE, NEZIGNAN-L'EVEQUE

Guy Bascou bought Domaine de la Condamine l'Evêque, in the village of Nézignan-l'Evêque on the flattish land just below Pézenas, in 1980. His father had been a member of the Pomérols co-operative, growing grapes for Picpoul de Pinet, but did not have enough land to make a proper living. Bascou had specialised in oenology and began working for the ICV in the Aude, an experience that has given him a magnificent overview of the development of the region. Twenty years ago his own vineyards were full of all that was deemed the worst in the Midi: Aramon, Alicante, Terret Bourret and Carignan. Over the years they have gradually 'restructured' and now they have Merlot, Cabernet Sauvignon, Mourvèdre, Syrah, Viognier, Petit Manseng and Sauvignon Blanc, as well as a little Petit Verdot that is not yet in production. It represents a complete transformation, and from that diversity of vines they make thirteen different wines, mostly Côtes de Thongue. They do also make a little Vin de Pays d'Oc, with the disadvantage that you are obliged to contribute to the administrative costs of the large *syndicat*. Such is the cachet of Côtes de Thongue that there is no bulk market for it. All the independent producers bottle their wine, while the co-operatives might sell some of their production in bulk as Vin de Pays d'Oc.

Guy Bascou's son Guilhem now works with him. He has the basic wine-making diploma, but then decided that, instead of continuing his studies, it would be more rewarding to travel the world, so he worked for Roederer in California and the large co-operative of Robertson in South Africa. He showed me around the cellars. They have a series of concrete vats, sporting a mural in vivid colours painted by his sister, including a head of Bacchus and bubbles galore. The old *foudres* have all gone, for they began working with *barriques* about ten years ago and in 1998 installed their own bottling line. The quality of the wines is exciting. An oak-fermented Sauvignon was rich and spicy. A Viognier is fermented in oak, in old five hundred-litre *demi-muids*, and although the oak dominates the flavour of the young wine, it should also enable it to age. However, 1997 was only their third vintage, so it is still quite experimental. A young Merlot, *élevé* in vat, was ripe and plummy with some tannin, and a young Syrah had some appealing peppery fruit. Their Prestige Rouge, a blend of Cabernet Sauvignon and Merlot, was warm and structured after twelve months in wood. Bascou would now like to try a blend of Mourvèdre and Syrah in *barrique*. And in the corner of the tasting area was an evocative sculpture of a female torso. Bascou *père* explained that he had asked a friend to portray *la dégustation*, or wine tasting, and this was the result.

DOMAINE DESHENRYS, ALIGNAN-DU-VENT

Domaine Deshenrys is an old family estate. Henri-Ferdinand Bouchard studied law, his father was a *négociant* and his uncle ran the estate; his grandfather won a medal for his wine in 1911. And then Bouchard returned to the land in 1978 to concentrate on *vins de pays de bonne qualité*. He also has land in Faugères, and in 1998 built a cellar within the *cru* so that he can sell his wine as Faugères rather than Coteaux du Languedoc. However, his innovative spirit is firmly focused on the Côtes de Thongue. On the whole, Bouchard prefers the art of *assemblage* to the simple varietal. There is an oak-fermented Chardonnay, a ripe, plummy Merlot and a more structured Cabernet Sauvignon. His Cuvée Alliance, an intriguing blend of five different varieties, Sauvignon, Roussanne, Viognier, Petit Manseng and Muscat, was perfumed and pithy, with the Viognier the dominant variety on the palate. The Cuvée Tradition, including both *bordelais* as well as Midi varieties, Cabernet Sauvignon and Merlot as well as Syrah and Grenache Noir, had some attractive ripe, spicy fruit. The future Faugères, mainly from Syrah with some Grenache Noir, and in 1998 a little Mourvèdre, spends eight months in *barriques*. It was solid and chunky, but will soften with bottle age.

Bouchard has also experimented with sweet wines. Le Douceur de l'Automne is made from Muscat *à petits grains* picked in the middle of August at 14° and treated by cryo-extraction, a technique expounded by the Bordelais professor Dubordieu: the grapes are frozen down to −23°C and then pressed, so that you only obtain the sugar, which defrosts before the water. The wine was intensely perfumed, with concentrated honey, grapey Muscat flavours and a bitter finish. He has also tried a late harvest Petit Manseng, picked a month later than usual at the end of October and fermented very slowly over ten months in new wood. The taste was an appealing blend of honey and apricots, balanced with the characteristic acidity of the variety.

THE OTHERS

In my experience of French wine regions, it is rare for wine growers to meet together for social events rather than *syndicat* meetings, but our wander through the region finished at the co-operative in Alignan for a tasting and buffet. The tasting included several producers whose estates we had not been able to visit, and as far as I could see it provided an opportunity for assessment of the competition and discussion of the wines. It was a rare demonstration of a unity of purpose amongst a small coterie of wine growers who are justifiably proud of what they are doing. Judging from the tasting, I had probably already visited the best, but the others were trying hard. There was an elegant Sauvignon from Domaine la Reynardière, and another from Domaine Bellevue, which also produced a Chardonnay given two months in oak, making for some body but, refreshingly, no overt taste of wood. The co-operative at Abeillan was working hard on its Chardonnay. A Cabernet Sauvignon from the co-operative of Pouzolles had some firm cassis fruit, and a Cuvée Excellence, a blend of Merlot and Syrah from Domaine George d'Ibury, had blackcurrant notes with a hint of pepper.

Lunch was fun and included my introduction to *petits pâtés de* Pézenas. Apparently this regional speciality, a tiny pie made from mutton cooked with brown sugar and spices, giving a savoury-sweet flavour, has associations with Clive of India, who spent the winter of 1766 at the nearby Château de Larzac. During his stay, Clive's cook continued to prepare dishes that reminded his master of India, and this one has become part of the local culinary tradition, so that you will find the *petits pâtés* in any reputable *charcuterie* in the area. We finished with another tradition, roasted chestnuts washed down by the new wine of the year, released the previous week. Enthusiasm for the 1998 vintage was in the air and suddenly it was time to leave for the airport.

Key facts

Compact, quality-driven *vin de pays* named after the river Thongue and covering eleven villages near Pézenas; on clay and limestone soil.

Grape varieties and regulations are the same as for Vin de Pays d'Oc, which the producers could also make.

Often they make Côtes de Thongue as a blend and use the Vin de Pays d'Oc for their varietal wines.

Costières de Nîmes

The Costières de Nîmes are where the Rhône valley meets the Languedoc. Administratively, the appellation lies within the valley of the Rhône, but culturally it has much more in common with the Languedoc. It is quite a large appellation, covering a plateau to the south of the city of Nîmes, and is limited by the Rhône in east. On a clear day you can see the bauxite outcrop of Les Baux de Provence from the easternmost estates. The marshy flats of the Camargue lie to the south, while the motorway, La Languedocienne, runs along the northern edge; in the west the appellation adjoins the vineyards of the Coteaux du Languedoc.

The viticultural origins of the Costières de Nîmes are firmly Roman, for the nearby city of Nîmes, with its magnificent arena and the Maison Carrée, was an important Roman centre. However, the viticultural history of the region has been unremarkable. In the seventeenth century, wines from the villages of Bellegarde, Vauvert and St Gilles were sent to Paris and in the nineteenth century the same wines were sent from Sète and Aigues-Mortes to northern Europe. Guyot wrote favourably of the Vins des Costières, mentioning in particular those made from Mourvèdre, which was also called the Plante de St Gilles after the small town on the edge of the Camargue. Mourvèdre disappeared from the area with the phylloxera crisis, but is now enjoying a limited revival of interest.

The area was recognised as a VDQS in 1951, with the name Costières du Gard, and was elevated to appellation status in 1986. Then, in order to avoid any potential confusion with Vin de Pays du Gard, the name was changed with the 1989 vintage to Costières de Nîmes. The area of the appellation has been carefully delimited so that it covers some twenty-five thousand hectares in twenty-four

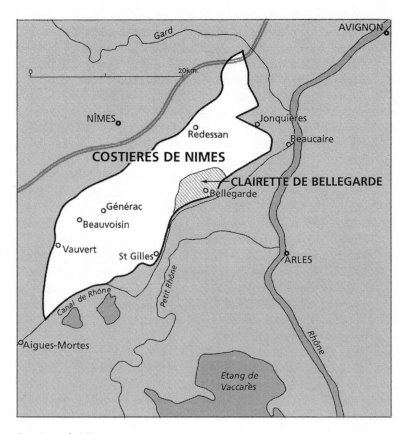

Costières de Nîmes

villages. However, only about twelve thousand are actually planted with vines, and of those only about three thousand five hundred actually produce the appellation. Quite simply, there is no demand for more. The rest are sold more cheaply as *vins de pays*, maybe as Vin de Pays des Coteaux Flaviens, after the Roman imperial dynasty, or more commonly as Vin de Pays du Gard, or if a single variety, Vin de Pays d'Oc. As elsewhere in the Midi, the *vins de pays* provide an outlet for experimental grape varieties not allowed in the appellation, and also for the excess production of Carignan.

The vineyard area is broadly determined by a very specific type of soil, namely *grès*, an especially stony soil of gravel and large pebbles, or *galets roulées*, that were brought down from the Alps by the Rhône. Apparently they are unique to the Costières de Nîmes, appearing neither in the Rhône valley nor in the Coteaux du Languedoc, although to my inexperienced eye they did not seem dissimilar to the *galets* of Châteauneuf-du-Pape. They tend to be a distinctive orange-red colour because of the high iron content in the soil, with some individual pebbles weighing as much as half a kilogram. Then two or three metres deeper there is a layer of clay that provides a necessary reserve of water, for it retains moisture, protecting the vines from drought during the dry summer months. The best way to understand the soil structure of the Costières de Nîmes is to visit the co-operative of Beauvoisin, for their tasting room contains a display of the soil profile, showing the layers of *galets*, *grès* and red clay, finishing with a layer of marine sand. The proximity to the sea also has a tempering effect, bringing a certain amount of humidity. At the same time, the large stones in the vineyard absorb the daytime heat and reflect it back on to the vines at night, thereby ensuring that the grapes are fully ripe. A detailed soil study has defined about ten different soils, including three large veins of variations of *galets roulées*. The altitude of the vineyards is insignificant, between twenty and a hundred metres, on very gentle undulating slopes, what the French indeed call *costières*.

The grape varieties of red Costières de Nîmes have more in common with those of the neighbouring Coteaux du Languedoc than with the Côtes du Rhône, while there is a greater variation in the white wine. The regulations currently demand the following minimum percentages in the vineyards: twenty-five per cent Grenache Noir, twenty per cent Syrah and forty per cent Carignan. In practice, however, there is now much less Carignan among the better producers, for recent years have seen a dramatic increase in Syrah and a sharp fall in Carignan, which it is generally recognised does not perform well in the area. Mourvèdre also features in the appellation, but can be problematic. Those who dismiss it claim that it ripens too late and that the *terroir* is too dry, but there are those who favour it. Cinsaut too is allowed, without any minimum or maximum percentage, but in fact there is very little.

As for white wine, Grenache Blanc is the base, and the appellation includes the more traditional Clairette, Macabeu and Ugni Blanc, as well as the more aromatic Marsanne, Roussanne and Rolle, of which Roussanne is proving particularly successful. There are also some plantings of Viognier in the hope that it will eventually be included in the appellation, but for the moment it has only experimental status or is used for *vin de pays*. The colour break-down of the Costières de Nîmes is approximately one-third pink to two-thirds red, with white wine accounting for just four per cent.

In contrast with so many appellations of the Midi, the village co-operatives are much less important within this appellation. It really is the private producers who are the driving force, and several of them are working well and establishing a convincing reputation. In the twelve years since my previous visit to the Costières de Nîmes, there have been changes. Among the estates that seemed to have much to offer, some have retained their reputation while others have disappeared from the limelight and new names have taken their place. As elsewhere in the Midi, nothing stands still. The stars of today are not those of a decade ago, and they may well have been superseded by others in ten years' time. There are about a hundred producers in all, including twelve co-operatives that account for about fifty per cent of the production. Of the private producers, it could be said that twenty are working well, creating a reputation for themselves and their appellation, with a further thirty making some progress in the right direction, while about fifty still continue to sell bulk wine to the *négociants*. However, the potential of the area has attracted outside investors, from elsewhere in France and also Switzerland.

CHATEAU DE MAS NEUF AND CHATEAU DE PIERREFEU, GALLICIAN

Olivier Gibelin is the president of the growers' *syndicat* and the owner of two properties, Château de Mas Neuf and Château de Pierrefeu. He is an ebullient, energetic and opinionated man who used to be a lawyer in the village of Vauvert, until he discovered what he called a *vocation tardive* at the age of forty and bought the Château de Pierrefeu in 1981. 'If your clients come and see you as a lawyer, it is for a *malheur* [misfortune], but if they come to you as a wine grower, it is for a *bonheur* [happy circumstances].' There were vines in the family, for his grandparents and parents had produced *bibine*, or plonk, on the plain, with the usual yields of the time, 150 hl/ha or more, of which the best apparently found its way to Beaujolais. In sharp contrast, he is concentrating on quality and applying his energy to his two estates and his appellation.

From the Château de Mas Neuf, with its attractive courtyard, you can see the *étangs* of the Camargue and in the distance the salt banks of the Salins du Midi, with the Tour de Constance at Aigues-Mortes just visible in the haze. Mas Neuf, with sixty hectares of vines as well as olive trees and orchards, adjoins the twenty hectares of Pierrefeu. The wines are vinified separately, but in the same cellar at Mas Neuf. For Gibelin, the charm of the Costières de Nîmes is its fruit. You must keep the fruit in the wine, even if you age it in wood. He sees the region as a pivot between the Rhône and the Languedoc, providing a frontier between the two regions, and laughingly cites himself as an example, in that his mother was a Protestant from the Languedoc with political views on the left, while his father was a Catholic from Provence who favoured the right. He pointed out that the soil of the Costières de Nîmes originated from the Rhône and the Durance, which makes the appellation part of the Rhône Valley, but nonetheless they want to retain its separate identity.

We tasted some young wines, including some whites that had barely finished fermenting. The white Mas Neuf is mainly Grenache Blanc with some Roussanne and Macabeo, while Pierrefeu has more Marsanne, which gives it elegance. A red Mas Neuf, a blend of Syrah and Grenache Noir vinified together if they are ripe at the same time, so that they have *une vie commune*, was appealingly fruity. When Gibelin bought Pierrefeu in 1981, there was just five per cent of Syrah in the vineyard. Now there is forty-five per cent, with fifteen per cent of Mourvèdre, and the balance is Grenache Noir, apart from a tiny amount of Cinsaut and Carignan. Originally both estates were planted almost entirely with Carignan. Opinion has it that Costières de Nîmes does not age, but Gibelin was prepared to prove this wrong by opening first a 1988 white, from Grenache Blanc, Macabeu and Roussanne, which had some lovely nutty fruit with good acidity, and was still very much alive at ten years old. Even more of a surprise was a 1982 Pierrefeu red, his first wine, made from Grenache Noir and Syrah. True, it tasted mature, but it was wonderfully warm and meaty.

CHATEAU DE CAMPUGET, MANDUEL

Château de Campuget was one of the pioneers of the appellation. It has belonged to the Dalle family since 1942 and today Jean-Lin Dalle is the wine maker. This is the largest estate of the appellation, for it comprises one hundred and twenty hectares of vines, as well a further thirty-two hectares bought from the Domaine de l'Amarine in 1988. Most of their production is red, from Syrah and Grenache Noir with a little Carignan, while the white Costières de Nîmes is made from Grenache Blanc, Roussanne and a little Marsanne. In addition, there is a range of varietal *vins de pays*: Chardonnay, some recently planted Viognier, Merlot and Cabernet Sauvignon. The two wines from the two estates are kept apart and sold under their separate labels.

The most surprising feature of their tasting room is a large stuffed crocodile, which Dalle's uncle brought back from Kenya. It leers down at customers and tasters, perhaps waiting to pounce if you do not like the wine. However, it has its place, for a crocodile under a palm tree is the emblem of the town of Nîmes, and that is the embossed logo used on the bottles of the appellation. Many of the Romans who settled in Nîmes were veterans from the campaigns in Egypt and they were allowed to mint their own money, with the head of Caesar on one side and the crocodile and palm tree on the other as a souvenir of Egypt. In the sixteenth century Francois I allowed it to become the coat of arms of the city. However, it was not until the 1850s, when someone returned from hunting in Africa with one, that a crocodile was actually seen in the area. The one at Campuget is a more recent arrival.

For each property there is a basic wine and an *haut de gamme*, aged in *barrique*. Campuget Blanc, from Grenache Blanc with some Marsanne and Roussanne, was fresh and delicate, while Amarine Blanc, with less Roussanne but including some older vines, was more rounded. Both *rosés* were light and fresh. The basic red Campuget had the easy charm of the appellation, with ripe berry fruit. The Cuvée Bernis, named after an old Nîmois family, from Amarine, was too oaky for my taste, with fourteen months in wood. More impressive was the pure Syrah, made for the first time in 1997 and aged in *demi-muids* as the quality was so good, had spicy fruit, with firm tannin and structure, fulfilling their ambition to make *un petit Hermitage*.

CHATEAU DE NAGES, CAISSARGUES

Château de Nages is a sizeable property outside the village of Caissargues, with a large modern cellar adjoining a seventeenth-century farmhouse that was undergoing renovation. Roger Gassier explained that his grandfather had had the foresight to buy the estate in 1941, while he was still living in Algeria. This meant that the family had a ready-made home, as well as something to do, when they returned to France in 1962. At first they produced basic *vin de table*, but since the early 1980s they have effected considerable changes in both vineyard and cellar. Their sixty hectares of appellation vineyards are planted with Syrah, Grenache Noir, a little Mourvèdre and now fewer than six hectares of Carignan, with Grenache Blanc and Roussanne for white wine. They have another thirty hectares, in different soil, for *vins de cépages*, namely Merlot, Cabernet Sauvignon and Viognier. The functional new cellar was built in 1992 and is well equipped with a pneumatic press, double vats for *délestage* and *barriques*. They have aged their red wines in wood since 1994 and began fermenting white wines in wood in 1998.

A sixty per cent Sauvignon to forty per cent Viognier blend was intriguing. At first taste the Viognier seemed to dominate, and then the Sauvignon took over, with a combination of Viognier fruit and Sauvignon pungency. The red Réserve du Château, from Syrah with one-third Grenache Noir, was perfumed and spicy, with body and fruit, combining suppleness and tannin. The 1995 Réserve Joseph Torres, after the grandfather who purchased the estate, was much more solid and structured, and to my taste buds lacked charm after twelve months of ageing in wood. I left with an impression of a dynamic estate that is going places. Roger Gassier trained in Montpellier and his son Michel has spent ten years in the United States, which gives him broader commercial horizons than many a wine maker in the Midi.

CHATEAU GUIOT, ST-GILLES

Several of the estates in the Costières de Nîmes that are now producing good wine have only come into existence during the last few years. Château Guiot, outside the town of St-Gilles, is one such example. The house and cellars are built around a large courtyard, with chickens and noisy peacocks picking over the heap of *marc* by the cellar door. Sylvie Cornut explained that her parents-in-law, who originally had a property in Uzès, further north in the Gard, bought their estate in the Costières de Nîmes in 1976 and for the first six years followed the example of the previous owners by sending their grapes to the co-operative at Générac. The vineyard has gradually been replanted, mainly with Syrah, and they already have some fifty-year-old Syrah, which is very rare in the area. There is also some Grenache Noir, a little Cinsaut and some Cabernet Sauvignon, while some Carignan remains, and for the moment there is no Mourvèdre or white varieties.

Three wines are bottled: a *vin de pays* called Mas de Guiot, made for the first time in 1996, from a blend of Syrah and Cabernet Sauvignon, aged in *barriques* for eight months; a red Costières de Nîmes, from Grenache Noir and Syrah; and a *rosé* from the same varieties, made by *saigné* in order to give the red wine a greater concentration. In any case, Cornut does not like *rosé* made by *pressurage*, as she believes that even with a gentle pneumatic press you obtain undesirable vegetal notes. Syrah dominates the palate of the red Costières de Nîmes, giving a firm, peppery flavour, a tannic backbone and an elegant finish. They have practised a warm post-fermentation maceration for the last four or five years, which they find gives more body and harmony. The Mas Guiot, from approximately two-thirds Cabernet to one-third Syrah, was warm and spicy, a combination of cassis and southern flavours, with a firm structure and considerable ageing potential.

DOMAINE SAINT ANTOINE, ST-GILLES

Jean-Louis Emmanuel at Domaine Saint Antoine bottled his first wine in 1995. His grandfather had bought the property in 1919, when there was Aramon, Carignan and Cinsaut. The first Grenache Noir was planted in the mid-1960s and now the red wine is made from Grenache Noir and Syrah; he also has apricots and asparagus, for this area is rich in market gardening. The estate was originally part of the duchy of Uzès and has associations with the Order of St Anthony, whose symbol appears on the label. Above the cellar door is the date 1821 and outside is a grove of wonderfully gnarled old olive trees that survived the devastating frost of 1956. Each year Emmanuel has gradually increased the proportion of wine he bottles, but still sells mostly *en vrac* to a local *négociant*. However, he is symptomatic of the new confidence in the appellation, and his wines have the characteristic flavour of the Costières, with spice and fruit, allowing, as he put it, 'the tourists to drink the sunshine'.

CHATEAU VESSIERE, ST-GILLES

Philippe Teulon at Château Vessière is the seventh generation at the family property that he has run since 1975, after studying oenology at Montpellier. He has a new cellar, built after the old cellar, a listed building dating from 1807 with old *foudres*, collapsed one evening in December 1994. The cause was a Belgian military aircraft, which missed the cellar by metres, but the shock waves of its swift avoiding action proved too much for the old building. The new cellar has a poignant reminder of what was obviously a terrible shock for the family, a jagged wall of stone contrasting with the adjoining smoothly plastered pink facade. The new cellar is well equipped with stainless steel and concrete vats, a pneumatic press and cooling equipment. As well as Costières de Nîmes, Teulon makes a range of varietal Vin de Pays d'Oc, Merlot and Cabernet, Chardonnay and Viognier, grown in the lower-lying vineyards, while Syrah, Grenache Noir, Roussanne and Grenache Blanc are used for the appellation wines.

Teulon exudes enthusiasm and he sees a rosy future, 'for we have a confidence that we did not have five years ago. Previously we had a complex about our wines, but now we are proud of them and beginning to reap the results of twenty years of hard work.' He is particularly lyrical about the 1998 vintage, which was still fermenting, comparing a vintage to the birth of a child. 1997 is a larger vintage than the 1998 but not as good, as there was rain at the end of the harvest. However, the red that I tasted was wonderfully fruity and spicy, with an immediate silky appeal combined with a firm, peppery flavour.

DOMAINE GRANDE CASSAGNE, ST-GILLES

Domaine Grande Cassagne, along a winding dirt track outside St-Gilles, is one of four neighbouring estates with the name Cassagnes, which may be a reference to the sweet chestnut trees common in the area. It was bought by the Dardé family in 1987 and the property is now run by two young half-brothers, Laurent Rouvin-Dardé, who is responsible for the vineyard, and Benoît Dardé, who makes the wine. You sense that they make a strong team, sharing a common philosophy. The vineyard was mostly Carignan, Aramon and Cinsaut when they arrived, but has been largely replanted since 1991, mainly with Syrah and Grenache Noir.

Now they are working on the cellar, with its traditional cement vats. They have invested in heating and cooling equipment, a pneumatic press and some experimental barrels. I liked their wines, which promise well for the future, even though their vines are mostly still very young. The reds are particularly impressive. They are working with *microbullage*, which they find helps to fill out the wines and soften the tannins, while avoiding *remontages* for aeration. They described it as being like an *élevage* in wood, but in vat instead, with an infinitesimal amount of oxygen going into a vat, just two litres per month per vat. Like Sylvie Cornut, they consider that a post-fermentation maceration softens the wine and makes for more supple fruit and tannin. None the less, their wines had more structure and concentration than those of their neighbours.

CHATEAU MOURGUES-DU-GRES, BEAUCAIRE

The first bottling at Château Mourgues-du-Grès was as recent as the 1990 vintage, with just two thousand bottles, but now three-quarters of their production from thirty hectares of vineyards is sold in bottle. This is a family estate, run by François Collard and his wife Anne, who are young and keen. His father sold wine *en vrac*, but also planted the first Syrah on the property, as well as some Grenache Noir, even though back in 1963 Syrah was deemed to be too fickle a variety and was not encouraged. François Collard realised that it was possible to do more. He studied agricultural engineering, rather than oenology, at Montpellier and worked as a journalist on *La Vigne* for five years. 'Here we have a vineyard where we can experiment, which is rare in France.' He has planted white varieties, which are not yet in production, and is also working on Mourvèdre. It has a difficult reputation. You need to develop the correct cultivation techniques. 1998 gave his first crop of Mourvèdre and it certainly was a challenge. It may not bring great weight, but might add an element of complexity. No one really knows yet.

Château Mourgues-du-Grès is on the eastern edge of the appellation near Beaucaire, which is known for its stone quarries. This is where you cross the Rhône into Provence. You can see the dramatic outline of Mont Ventoux in the haze and the Alpilles of Les Baux are only fifteen miles away. Mourgues means a nun, referring to an Ursuline convent at Beaucaire that once owned the estate. There is an attractive courtyard, with a sundial on the wall bearing the customary motto *sine sole nihil*. The house dates from the seventeenth century and we tasted and talked in the drawing room, with its simple vaulted ceiling and elegant lines. First came the *rosé*, amongst the best of the appellation, with its attractively smoky fruit and satisfying weight in the mouth. There are three red wines. Galets Rouges, named after the stones in the vineyard, is a blend of Syrah and Grenache Noir kept in vat, giving some young peppery fruit. The 1997 has lower acidity, making it a more open vintage than the 1996, but none the less with very appealing spice and fruit. Next came Terre d'Argence, or land of silver. This is a play on words, for the land belonged to the bishopric of Arles in the eleventh century and there are numerous alder trees with distinctive silvery leaves. It includes the older plots of low-yielding Syrah and

Grenache Noir and showed great promise, with firm tannins, berry fruit and layers of flavour, as well as a certain wild character. The 1996 was even more impressive, with body and length, softer tannins and some intriguing spicy flavours and fruit. Collard believes that with an *élevage* in vat, you bring out the identity of the *terroir*, whereas an *élevage* in wood means that you work on the tannins in the wine. For that he makes a Réserve du Château, Les Capitelles. The *capitelles* are the small shelters dating back to the time of the Roman road that crosses the property. Their first experiment in wood was in 1993, when they made just three thousand bottles. Usually the wine spends ten to twelve months in wood, in *demi-muids* rather than *barriques*, but when I tasted the 1996, when it was two years old, the oak was still very dominant.

Collard spoke of how he wants both strength and elegance in his wines. He waits for very ripe grapes, which will give him wines with depth, fruit and flavour. His vineyards are on south-facing terraces, on steeper slopes than some parts of the Costières. Really the heart of it all is the vineyard and the care you give your vines. They have come a long way since their first bottling.

CHATEAU DES TOURELLES, BEAUCAIRE

The neighbouring Château des Tourelles must feature as one of the tourist attractions of the appellation, for this is where you go back to the Roman origins: part of their wine production seeks to replicate what was made two thousand years ago. Young Hervé Durand explained that his father is an enthusiastic amateur archaeologist. They were continually finding pieces of amphora in the vineyard, and eventually discovered that amphorae had indeed been produced there – as many as three thousand a day in four or five large ovens. Then in 1990 they decided to try to reproduce the wine that would have been transported in such amphorae. The help of two professors was enlisted and texts such as Pliny and Columella were consulted.

They planted Muscat, as that grape variety was known to have existed two thousand years ago, and the vines were trained on pergolas, as they would have been in Roman times. In the cellar there is a reproduction of a Roman press and a large stone vat for treading the grapes. Various concoctions are used in the vinification process, and in the cellar there was a wonderful smell of grape juice cooking with quinces, to make a concentrated syrup that would be added to the wine. They date their wines from the foundation of Rome, so that the modern vintage of 1997 becomes 2750.

Turriculae follows a recipe from Columella that includes concentrated seawater, fenugreek, fruit syrup and dried iris rhizomes. They use Villard Blanc for the wine base, but that is probably not significant as the taste is dominated by the other additives, leaving a wine that tasted not unlike a coarse fino sherry, with a definite salty flavour. The 1993 version had developed nuttier flavours with more body, while still retaining the salty character. Mulsum, made from a Grenache Noir base flavoured with honey, pepper, cinnamon and other spices, might make a sweet aperitif, but with a dry tannic finish, while Carenum, made from Muscat, flavoured with the grape and quince syrup, as well as fenugreek and rhizomes, was nutty with a sweet marmalade flavour.

Visitors are encouraged at this attractive sixteenth-century *mas*, not just for the Roman wines, but also for more conventional Costières de Nîmes and Vin de Pays d'Oc. However, I must admit to a preference for the quirky originality of the Roman wines rather than the more prosaic Costières de Nîmes. Hervé Durand's father also planted in 1982 one of the first vineyards in Quebec, Le Vignoble de l'Orpailleur, or goldpanner, and there are now a surprising thirty-two vineyards in this part of Canada.

MAS DES BRESSADES, MANDUEL

Another leading estate that you feel is really helping to create the reputation of the appellation is Mas des Bressades. First of all I met the elderly Roger Marès, who explained how he had bought the property in 1965 and later bought Château Puy-Castéra in the Médoc. The family came from Montpellier and an ancestor was Henri Marès, a friend of Pasteur, who realised that sulphur was the appropriate treatment for oidium. Roger Marès studied oenology at Angers and his son Cyril, who now makes the wine, went to Montpellier and later worked at Chalone in California and with Bruno Prats in Chile before returning to Mas des Bressades. Although Roger Marès has owned the land since 1965, it was not until 1977 that he planted vines. Originally they had fruit and almond trees for market gardening, but now they have twenty-two hectares of vines. Two hectares of Cabernet Sauvignon were planted at the beginning, with Syrah, Grenache Noir, a little Cinsaut and some Carignan because 'they said you could not make wine without Carignan'. Later, in 1990, Marès added Grenache Blanc and Roussanne for white Costières de Nîmes, and also Viognier, which he hoped to include in his appellation wine. Marès had realised that it was simply not worth making what he called 'ordinary' wine, so he began working with *barriques* straightaway, making what he described as his first quality wine in 1986. It was a pure Syrah, given an *élevage* in oak.

A partially underground barrel cellar was built in 1998, with room to house a hundred and fifty *barriques*. I tasted various barrel samples, including a pure Viognier fermented in wood, and a Roussanne that would be blended with unoaked Grenache Blanc. The 1997 vintage promised well. The red range included an unoaked Cuvée Tradition from Syrah and Grenache Noir, with firm, peppery fruit; an oaked Cuvée Excellence, mainly from Syrah with a little Grenache Noir, that was both structured and elegant; and finally a *vin de pays*, a blend of two-thirds Cabernet Sauvignon to one-third Syrah, with a firm cassis flavour. A barrel sample of pure Cabernet had some appealing fruit, as did a pure Syrah with pepper and violets.

MAS CARLOT, BELLEGARDE

Young Cyril Marès is married to Natalie Blanc, whose father owns the neighbouring estate of Mas Carlot, one of the few producers continuing to make the tiny appellation of Clairette de Bellegarde. Natalie Blanc explained that she was all set to be a vet. When her father bought the estate, she was simply not interested, but later she came down at vintage time, had a *coup de foudre* and studied oenology at Montpellier instead. Now you sense that she has become a very committed and meticulous wine maker. As well as Clairette de Bellegarde, she makes some very successful Vin de Pays d'Oc from equal parts of Roussanne and Marsanne. You would need a third, traditional variety, Clairette or Grenache Blanc, for it to be an appellation wine. The wine is given some skin contact and some *élevage* on lees in vat. She wants aroma and body in the mouth, but not too much acidity, and that is what she has achieved, some smoky, aromatic flavours and a rounded, satisfying palate. A Costières de Nîmes vinified in wood is a blend of seventy per cent Roussanne with some Marsanne and Grenache Blanc, including a small amount of unoaked wine. The oak was very apparent in the young wine, but quite attractively so, with ginger notes on the palate; the wine should age well.

As for red wine, a Costières de Nîmes from Syrah, Mourvèdre and Grenache Noir, including some thirty-five-year-old vines, was rich and smoky, with ripe, plummy fruit. Blanc looks for aroma, finding that you obtain fruit from Syrah and spice and structure from Mourvèdre. She is less enthusiastic about Grenache Noir, as it lacks concentration, but you have to have it in the appellation. She pushes the maturity in the vineyards to the maximum in order to obtain concentration in the wine, at the risk of lower yields and rot from the equinoctial rains. In the best years she make the Cuvée Paul Blanc from Syrah and Grenache Noir, which is given twelve months *élevage* in wood. The 1996 had some attractive spicy flavours, with firm tannins.

This is an estate that has benefited from the change of ownership, for Natalie's father, Paul Blanc, is a Parisian hotelier with the means to invest in his estate; there is evidence of this in the cellar, with its *barriques*, stainless steel vats and pneumatic press. From the catwalk across the top of the vats outside there is an aerial view of the vineyards, a block of some seventy-five hectares all around the cellars. From a distance, the soil looks quite sandy, but the stones are very near the surface.

DOMAINE DU VIEUX RELAIS, REDESSAN

Pierre Bardin of the Domaine du Vieux Relais at Redessan is the only wine grower in the appellation to make a predominantly Mourvèdre blend – that is, one with as much as eighty per cent, plus twenty per cent of Grenache Noir. He is very committed to Mourvèdre, explaining that it was planted quite extensively in the Costières de Nîmes thirty or forty years ago, but disappeared because it taxed people's viticultural skills and proved simply too problematic in the vineyard. Mourvèdre does not like too dry a soil, and the layer of clay underneath the very stony topsoil ensures that there is no problem with drought. Bardin planted his two hectares twelve years ago. He finds that it adapts badly to mechanisation and must have the correct pruning, a low *gobelet*, giving a low yield, an absolute maximum of 40 hl/ha. Before the vines were fully established, he practised a green harvest. The grapes must be really ripe, with an alcohol potential of 14°. He admits that he does not achieve this every year and so his Cuvée Sélection is made only in the best years. The 1995 has some solid, dry, spicy fruit with body and tannin, making it a wine to age. It is kept in vat, for Bardin considers that wood removes the intrinsic flavour of the grape that he likes so much. And our conversation concluded with our sharing a mutual enthusiasm for good Bandol, his favourites being Tempier, Pibarnon and Pradeaux.

The property takes its name from its original function as a coaching inn on the Domitian Way. Bardin's father sold his wine to the *négociants* and it was only in 1987 that he began to bottle his wine, making two qualités, the Cuvée Sélection in the best years and the Cuvée Tradition from equal parts of Syrah and Grenache Noir. It was classic Costières, warm and spicy, and with more body and structure than some.

CHATEAU DE BELLE-COSTE, CAISSARGUES

Château de Belle-Coste has belonged to the Du Tremblay family for three generations. Bertrand du Tremblay explained that his grandfather, a doctor in Nîmes, had invested in the estate but only as an absentee landowner, and that he himself is the first member of the family actually to earn his living from it, concentrating on the vineyards. Previously there were orchards and sheep as well. At the beginning of the twentieth century fifty families lived here, but with the arrival of tractors after the Second World War the demand for labour dropped sharply and many people left. Even in the 1960s there were still six families, whereas today he employs just five people.

The farm buildings cluster around a courtyard, where chickens and bantams roamed between the tractors and farm equipment, watched by a noisy cockerel. There is a shop with tempting local produce – lavender is a popular theme – as well as a display of old farming tools and a charming nineteenth-century chapel in need of restoration. Altogether du Tremblay has sixty hectares, for both Costières de Nîmes and *vin de pays*, with Merlot and Viognier as varietal wines. The possible inclusion of Viognier in the appellation is still under discussion.

Sustained viticulture, rather than pure organic, is favoured, for there are times when chemicals may solve a problem. Rain at the equinox can be a hazard. Usually the Syrah and Merlot ripen beforehand and the Carignan and Mourvèdre afterwards, but Grenache Noir is often ripe around the equinox and can therefore be very susceptible to rot. Ideally they would like a wet spring and a hot summer, with a storm around 15 August to provide a little water, followed by a dry September. Frost is rare, but it did occur in 1998, as in many other parts of the Midi, as late as Easter Monday, 13 April, reducing the size of the crop quite dramatically.

The Viognier has some delicate varietal character. Just two per cent spends about eight months in wood, giving an imperceptible hint of some extra weight. The white Costières de Nîmes comes mainly from Roussanne with less than ten per cent of Grenache Blanc. Again, just a tiny drop spends a little time in wood. Du Tremblay prefers Roussanne to Marsanne, suggesting that Marsanne simply replaces Ugni Blanc, for its yields are large, unlike Roussanne which seems to naturally limit itself to 50 hl/ha; nor does Marsanne have as much flavour as Roussanne. The wine was an intriguing combination of smoky, herbal and nutty notes, in several layers, with just the merest hint of oak. The red Costières de Nîmes, Cuvée Ste Marie, from equal parts of Grenache Noir, Syrah and Mourvèdre, blended after the malolactic fermentation, had a firm, peppery character. The Mourvèdre provides structure, developing a meaty, *viandé* character after *élevage*, while the Grenache Noir gives body, what the French call *gras*, and the Syrah flavour and aroma. Like Pierre Bardin, Bertrand du Tremblay firmly believes in Mourvèdre. It is simply not true that there is a climatic limitation. The limitation comes from the soil, as Mourvèdre needs deep soil, and it must not be allowed to overproduce. It is just that Grenache Noir and Syrah are that much easier, whereas a blend of three grape varieties is much more interesting.

Du Tremblay is optimistic for the future of the appellation. Carignan is disappearing from the vineyards and there have been considerable developments in the cellar, implemented by more qualified wine makers. As a consequence, the Costières de Nîmes is becoming much better known.

COSTIERES ET SOLEIL, GENERAC

Some of the co-operatives are working well for the appellation, developing beyond being mere *viticulteurs* and processors of grapes into serious *vignerons*. Costières et Soleil, the co-operative in the village of Générac, is the largest producer of the appellation, as it groups seven small co-operatives with a total of four hundred and fifty members. It has an annual production of twenty-five thousand hectolitres of Costières de Nîmes, but *vins de pays*, both Gard et d'Oc, far exceed the appellation wines. As with the private producers, there has been considerable replanting of the vineyards, above all to replace Carignan with Syrah, but they have also planted Merlot and Cabernet Sauvignon for *vins de pays* and Marsanne and Roussanne for the appellation, as well as Viognier for *vin de pays*. A *vin de primeur* from Viognier, made for the first time in 1998, was fresh and pithy, but with little varietal character.

Considerable investment has been made in the cellar, particularly in new presses and systems of temperature control, for which a figure of 10 million FF was mentioned, part self-financed and part from government and European Union subsidies. They bought their first *barriques* in 1997 and are planning more, but for the moment their Costières de Nîmes is not a wine to age.

CAVE COOPERATIVE DE BEAUVOISIN, BEAUVOISIN

I first visited the co-operative of the pretty little village of Beauvoisin in 1987 and the changes there have been quite considerable. René Rouvin is still the director, a cheerful man with a thick mop of greying hair and a rich, fruity meridional accent. He explained that since 1996 they have worked *au parcellaire*: each individual vineyard with slightly different soil or a different grape variety has been noted, so that the computer follows each plot, recording the details of the vintage and where each batch of grapes ultimately goes. They have a total of one hundred and ten members with six hundred hectares of vines. However, many of them have only a few ares, let alone hectares, and seventeen or eighteen members account for two-thirds of their production. As at Générac, Costières de Nîmes accounts for only a quarter of the co-operative's production. Another quarter is *vin de pays* and the rest *vin de table*, which is decreasing as the *vin de pays* progresses.

The cellars have undergone considerable modernisation. Not only do they have a new computer, but also new tanks and reception lines. They make a range of different qualities of Costières de Nîmes. Their best wine, called Moulin d'Eole after the old windmill above the village, is made from equal parts of Grenache Blanc and Roussanne, picked at night and given fourteen or fifteen hours of skin contact. Only the free-run juice is used, and the resulting wine is rounded and biscuity with a dry, nutty finish. Domaine du Petit Chêne, as the name might imply, is aged in wood, in both 225 and 400-litre barrels. It is a blend of Syrah and Grenache Noir. I much preferred the wines that had been kept in vat, for they had fruit and spice, with attractive peppery flavours, while the Domaine du Petit Chêne, although not overtly oaky, lacked charm.

CAVE COOPERATIVE DE JONQUIERES-ST-VINCENT, JONQUIERES-ST-VINCENT

The village of Jonquières-St-Vincent is at the eastern edge of the appellation, where the Costières de Nîmes meet the Côtes du Rhône. The two are delimited by administrative geography, not by *terroir*, for you find the same *galets* in both appellations. Alphonse Daudet's story *Les Deux Auberges* is said to have taken place at the two inns in Jonquières. The co-operative is run by the young and friendly Christian Gourjon. He arrived here after his studies in Montpellier in 1993 and is keen to do well for his ninety-five members, who have four hundred hectares. They produce a small amount of Côtes du Rhône as well as Costières de Nîmes, and two *vins de pays*, d'Oc and Gard.

Gourjon has introduced a very demanding *cahier des charges*, or schedule of conditions, which the growers have to follow, with a selection according to *terroir* and payment according to quality. He is encouraging the planting of Syrah by giving higher remuneration; thirty hectares were replanted in 1998, mainly with Syrah. They produce a generic red Costières de Nîmes, but no white or pink, as well as four separate estates. Their Costières de Nîmes Tradition, from equal parts of Syrah and Grenache Noir, has light, fruity spice. It could be the Beaujolais du Midi. The 1995 vintage saw their first vinification with *barriques*; the wine from Domaine de la Boissière, mainly Syrah with Grenache Noir and a little old Carignan, spends twelve months in wood. I preferred Domaine des Trois Pierres, from older Syrah and Grenache Noir, which had some firm, spicy fruit and good structure, after a thirty-day maceration period and no wood.

Clément Arnaud, the president of the co-operative, described himself as having been born amongst the pebbles. He has twenty hectares of vines. His father was a member of the co-operative too, and he remembered that when he first became president in 1978, most of the vineyards were planted with Carignan, Aramon and Cinsaut. They were just beginning to plant Grenache Noir, while the oldest Syrah in the village is only fifteen years old. There were still a lot of hybrids in the mid-1970s that effortlessly produced 120–130 hl/ha of very indifferent wine for the local *négociants*. It is the vineyards that hold the key to the future. They must continue to plant the appropriate grape varieties, and Syrah above all.

CAVE COOPERATIVE DE PAZAC, PAZAC

The small co-operative of Pazac was established in 1958 by a group of *pieds noirs* returning to France from Algeria. You need a minimum of seven growers to form a co-operative, and they were eight. Their president is Nicolas Seydoux, chairman of Gaumont cinemas, who lives in a nearby village. Since 1988 the co-operative has been run by Jean-Louis Boyer, who has successfully managed the transition from *vin de table* to appellation. In 1989 he produced five thousand hectolitres of Costières de Nîmes, of which he only managed to sell a hundred and fifty, as they had no market; he was forced to declassify the wine. Now they produce six or seven thousand hectolitres of appellation, and nearly as much *vin de pays*, including Chardonnay and Sauvignon.

The cellar was originally a farmhouse, and has the date 1765 marked on one of its beams. The Cuvée du Pigeonnier, named after the charming dovecot in one of its towers, is made as both red and pink. Both are blends of Syrah, Grenache Noir, Cinsaut and

Carignan, for Boyer believes, especially with *rosé*, that the more grape varieties you have, the more complexity you gain. I found the *rosé* a little heavy, but the red was very appealing, with warm, peppery fruit and soft tannins. Next came the Cuvée Fontaine Miraculeuse, which recalls a story about Charles Martel passing through the nearby village of Meynes with wounded soldiers. They stopped to drink at the village spring and are said to have been cured of their injuries. The 1997 vintage, with eighty per cent Grenache Noir and some Syrah, was warm and quite alcoholic, while the 1996, with more Syrah and some wood ageing, was firmer and more structured. 1995 was their first vinification with wood and they have just had twenty *barriques* housed *chez le Président*, mainly for his own wine Château Clausonne. The 1996 was a pure Syrah, with firm oak on both nose and palate and sweet fruit behind the oak. Boyer reflected on the added value given by the oak, explaining that they had sold the 1995 Château Clausonne for what had seemed an astronomical FF 40 a bottle, when hitherto their most expensive wine had been just FF 20.

Boyer also firmly refutes the idea that Costières de Nîmes does not age. He finished our tasting with a 1995 Fontaine Miraculeuse, from Grenache Noir and Syrah that had undergone a month's *cuvaison*. The wine was still very youthful, with solid berry fruit, body and length. For him, the future of the Costières de Nîmes lies very much with red wine, especially with low-yielding Syrah, which will make a *vin de garde*.

Sandwiched as it is between the Coteaux du Languedoc and the Côtes du Rhône, with the vineyards of Les Baux-en-Provence just a few kilometres away, the Costières de Nîmes may run the risk of being dwarfed by some larger and more powerful neighbours. Les Baux-en-Provence has prestige, while the Côtes du Rhône have marketing clout and command significantly higher prices for their wines: FF 1000 per hectolitre, as opposed to FF 570 for Costières de Nîmes. Although the Costières de Nîmes have more in common with the Coteaux du Languedoc, they have an originality of their own and have undergone an enormous development in the last ten or twenty years. There has been a major transformation of the vineyards, with the steady replacement of Carignan by Syrah. Here lies one of the big differences from the Côtes du Rhône. While there may be similarities of soil, with *galets* originating from the alluvial deposits, the base of the Côtes du Rhône is very much Grenache Noir, whereas in the Costières de Nîmes it is now firmly Syrah.

Among the group of producers who are working hard for their appellation there is a unity of spirit: they are determined to create a reputation for their wines, and have a firm optimism about the future. The Costières de Nîmes can produce appealingly supple, soft and fruity reds – the Beaujolais of the Midi – that with longer maturations, more Syrah and the judicious use of oak become *vins de garde* that can only enhance the reputation of the appellation.

Key facts

Bridges the Rhône and the Languedoc. VDQS 1951 (as Costières du Gard), AC 1986 and in 1989 name changed to Costières de Nîmes; two-thirds red wine to one-third pink, with just four per cent white; 3500 hectares produce AC; twenty-five thousand hectares delimited and twelve thousand planted, but also for *vin de pays*.

Grape varieties:

RED: Grenache Noir, minimum twenty-five per cent; Syrah, minimum twenty per cent; Carignan, minimum forty per cent; Cinsaut; Mourvèdre.

WHITE: Grenache Blanc, Clairette, Macabeo, Ugni Blanc, Marsanne, Roussanne, Rolle.

Soil is gravelly pebbles; vineyards lie at between twenty and one hundred metres.

Vintages

Tend to follow the rest of the Languedoc.

1999: Heavy rain at the harvest diluted the wines.

1998: A small crop, with ripe grapes making rounded, rich wines with structure and alcohol.

1997: Summer rain caused problems, giving a large crop. The best wines were made by those who were patient.

1996: Similar conditions to 1996, making for a broad quality range.

1995: A warm summer and a dry harvest gave good results.

Clairette de Bellegarde

The unprepossessing village of Bellegarde is the centre of Clairette de Bellegarde, a small white appellation within the Costières de Nîmes. It was Philippe Lamour, former owner of the fine old estate of St Louis-la-Perdrix, who was the driving force behind the creation of this now rather insignificant appellation. He was a great friend of Baron Philippe le Roy, who laid the foundations for the system of *appellation contrôlée* from his estate of Château Fortia in Châteauneuf-du-Pape. Lamour's objective was the creation of a white appellation of comparable stature to Châteauneuf-du-Pape. He also wanted the red wines of his area to form part of the Côtes-du-Rhône, but people were not prepared to accept the constraints of the appellation and preferred the short-term option of selling high yields in bulk. In the early 1950s the price of Côtes du Rhône was not that much of an incentive, whereas today there is a much more marked difference. The appellation came in 1949, but the reputation has never followed, and Clairette de Bellegarde remains very much a local curiosity, difficult to find even on a restaurant wine list in nearby Nîmes.

Clairette, a variety that has been grown quite widely in the Midi and also features in another appellation, Clairette du Languedoc, is the sole grape variety and the area of production is limited to the *commune* of Bellegarde. Today the main producer is the village co-operative, which also vinifies the grapes from the Domaine de St Louis-la-Perdrix, and there are two individual producers, Château de Campuget and Mas Carlot. Most of the vineyards could equally well produce Costières de Nîmes and currently about a hundred hectares are planted with Clairette, on soil that is similar to that of Costières de Nîmes, namely the red *galets roulées* that characterise the vineyards.

CAVE COOPERATIVE DE BELLEGARDE

The problem with Clairette is that it lacks acidity and can oxidise easily, which makes vinification difficult. At the co-operative of Bellegarde they give it anything between four and twelve hours of skin contact in an attempt to extract the maximum amount of flavour, but they never use wood, as that would completely mask any fruit. Their best vat, bottled separately for an annual competition, was quite golden in colour, with a hint of honey on the nose and a certain herbal, nutty flavour in the palate; it had weight and body, but little acidity. There was a rather old-fashioned feel to the wine, as though modern wine-making philosophies had somehow passed it by.

CHATEAU DE CAMPUGET

The owners of Château de Campuget bought the old estate of Domaine de l'Amarine from the Godebski family and have absorbed the vineyards into their production. The Clairette now often forms part of the blend of their Costières de Nîmes, rather than a separate wine.

DOMAINE DE ST LOUIS-DE-PERDIX

The recent history of St Louis-de-Perdrix is also rather sad, as it has been taken over by the Crédit Agricole following the family's financial problems in the early 1990s. Philippe Lamour's widow still lives on the estate, but her children mismanaged the property and are no longer interested in it. The cellars are around an attractive courtyard, for this was once a hunting lodge belonging to the Duchess of Uzès – hence the association with partridges. The estate is now run by a young manager, Christophe Barraud, who is left very much to his own devices. He has been replanting the vineyards, replacing the Carignan with Syrah, and grafting Roussanne on to Cinsaut. A new vinification cellar has been built, allowing for vinification by carbonic maceration for all the remaining Carignan. He is the only one to do this in the Costières de Nîmes and he would like to try out some barrels. The wines are sound but not inspiring.

MAS CARLOT

The most exciting Clairette comes from Mas Carlot, where Natalie Blanc has some fifty-year-old vines. She explained how problematic she finds Clairette. If it is picked too late, it loses acidity and obtains high sugar levels, but if you pick too early, you lose any aroma. She tends to harvest it last of all the whites, at the end of September, after the Syrah, at about 13.5° and compensates for the loss of acidity by adding some tartaric acid to the fermenting must. She takes great care with the *débourbage*, chilling the juice at 5°C for twenty-four hours so that she obtains very clear must. She leaves the wine on its lees in vat, occasionally pumping gas into the vat to stir up the lees for *bâtonnage*. I liked her wine. It was full-bodied, with delicate flavours and a successful balance of acidity and alcohol. None the less, Clairette de Bellegarde will never have more than a local reputation.

Key facts

AC 1949; only Clairette and only from the village of Bellegarde.

Of strictly local interest, with production dominated by the co-operative.

PROVENCE

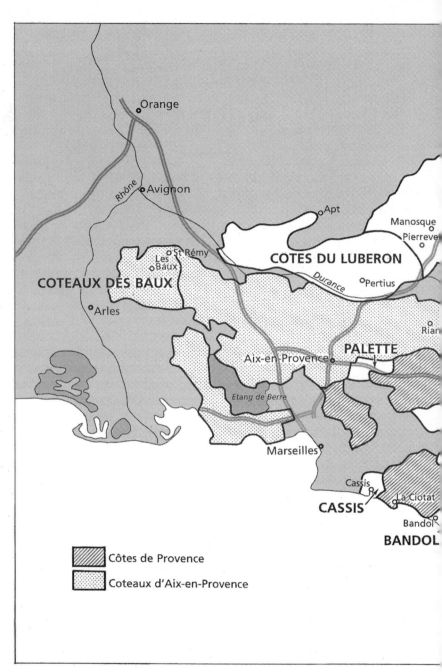

Orange

Rhône

Avignon

Apt

Manosque

Pierreve

COTES DU LUBERON

St Rémy

Les Baux

COTEAUX DES BAUX

Durance

Pertius

Arles

Rian

Aix-en-Provence

PALETTE

Etang de Berre

Marseilles

Cassis

La Ciotat

CASSIS

Bandol

BANDOL

Côtes de Provence

Coteaux d'Aix-en-Provence

Provence

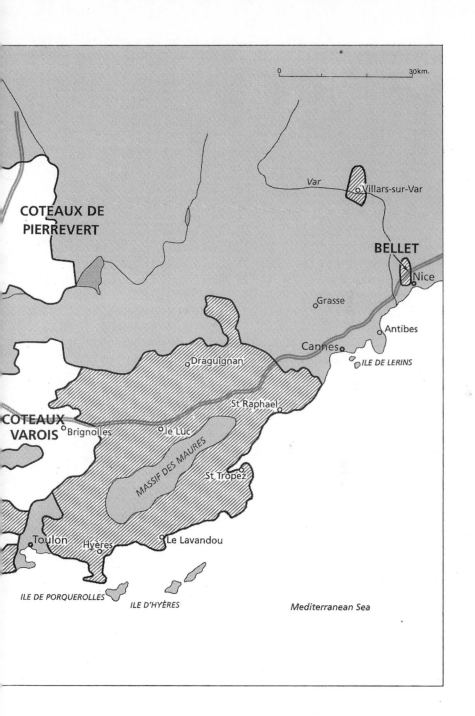

COTEAUX DE PIERREVERT

Var

Villars-sur-Var

BELLET

Nice

Grasse

Antibes

Cannes

ILE DE LERINS

Draguignan

St Raphael

COTEAUX VAROIS

Brignolles

le Luc

MASSIF DES MAURES

St Tropez

Toulon

Hyères

Le Lavandou

ILE DE PORQUEROLLES

ILE D'HYÈRES

Mediterranean Sea

0   30km.

There is a moment as you drive south from Lyon, somewhere around Orange, when the atmosphere subtly changes and you know that you have reached the warm south and arrived in Provence. True, a motorway sign bearing the symbols of a blazing sun and a parasol pine tells you *Vous êtes en Provence*, but it is more than that. The sun is stronger, the light is brighter and there are the warm scents of lavender, thyme and pine trees; it is quite different from the wilder atmosphere of the rugged hills of the hinterland of the Languedoc. Just before Aix-en Provence the Mont Ste Victoire looms into view, conjuring up the bold colours of Cézanne's paintings. If you have ever holidayed on the Côte d'Azur, sat at a café in St Tropez, eaten *bouillabaisse* on the port in Marseille and sipped the local wine, the chances are that you drank a pink Côtes de Provence from a funny amphora-shaped bottle. But the wines of Provence are so much more than pretty pink wines for holidays and picnics. The marketing gimmick of the amphora bottle does them a grave disservice, for there is a growing number of serious red and whites offering myriad tastes and flavours.

The largest appellation of the region is Côtes de Provence, with fine red and white wine as well as frivolous *rosé*. Around the town of Aix-en-Provence are the vineyards of the Coteaux d'Aix-en-Provence, and near by is the newly independent appellation of Les Baux-de-Provence with vineyards on the foothills of the Alpilles. The Côtes du Lubéron are where the Rhône valley meets Provence, with vineyards on the foothills of the Montagne du Lubéron. It adjoins the new but little known appellation of the Coteaux de Pierrevert. Between the Coteaux d'Aix-en-Provence and the Côtes de Provence comes the recent appellation of the Coteaux Varois, and within these larger areas are four smaller, more prestigious appellations. Cassis has a reputation for white wine, while Bandol is known above all for substantial red wines based on the Mourvèdre grape. Palette is a tiny appellation outside Aix-en-Provence, the oldest in Provence, with just one estate of consequence, while the vineyards of Bellet are hidden in the suburbs of Nice.

Coteaux d'Aix-en-Provence

The attractive town of Aix-en-Provence lies at the heart of the appellation to which it gives its name. Once these vineyards were called the Coteaux du Roy René, after the last Count of Provence to hold his court at Aix, who on his death in 1480 ceded his lands to the French king Louis XI. Aix-en-Provence is a delight to visit. The tree-lined Cours Mirabelle, with its fine fountains, has elegant town houses and lively cafés, with tables spilling out over the wide pavements in summer, under much-needed shade provided by the large plane trees. On Saturday mornings, the town buzzes with one of the best markets in the south, with stalls of tempting local produce, herbs and olives, fat *saucissons* and luscious vegetables. Another square hosts a colourful and scented flower market. There is an annual arts festival and you can visit Cézanne's studio.

Vines have grown on the hillsides around Aix for centuries, for they were first planted by the Greeks after they settled around Marseille. Even so, in the early nineteenth century Jullien wrote that there was no vineyard that merited the attention of gourmets, and later writers ignored the area completely. By 1956, the vineyards of the Coteaux d'Aix-en-Provence were sufficiently distinguished from the surrounding mass of *vin ordinaire* to be recognised as a VDQS, and there was disappointment in 1977 when they were not given an appellation to match that of the nearby Côtes de Provence. However, this prompted a renewal of efforts towards quality, with the result that the Coteaux d'Aix-en-Provence became an appellation in 1985, including the adjoining Coteaux des Baux-de-Provence. Les Baux-de-Provence is now a separate appellation for red and pink, but not for white wine. It is very compact, in contrast to the vineyards of the Coteaux d'Aix-en-Provence, which spread over forty-nine *communes*, two in the department of the Var and the majority in the Bouches-du-Rhône. In theory, the appellation extends all around the Etang de Berre to the outskirts of Marseille, but in practice, apart from Château Calissanne, industry has taken over here and the vineyards are concentrated on the foothills of the Chaine de la Trévaresse, around the villages of Le Puy-Ste-Réparade, Rognes and St-Cannat. They also spread as far as Rians in the east, touching the north western corner of the cooler appellation of the Coteaux Varois. The Chaine de la Trévaresse separates the northern part of the appellation from the sea and the Mont Ste Victoire forms the boundary with the adjoining Côtes de Provence. The soil throughout the appellation tends to be fairly uniform, clay and limestone, with sandier soil nearer the coast.

As an extended appellation without a natural centre, the Coteaux d'Aix-en-Provence seems to lack a really homogeneous identity, compared to its neighbours, les Baux-de-Provence and the Coteaux Varois. There are enormous variations in style and quality, with some seventy producers, ranging from large *négociants* with extensive vineyards to small *vignerons* with just a few hectares, as well as village co-operatives of indifferent quality. Nor is the identity helped by the existence of two growers' *syndicats*, one that includes all the big producers and the other, Aix en Vignes, being a splinter group of smaller growers who felt overwhelmed by the size of some of their colleagues.

Although the reasons for the creation of Aix en Vignes stem from local politics, the ten estates in the group are worth noting for their strong motivation towards quality. Pieter Fischer of Château Revelette explained their criteria and aims: organic viticulture, small yields, two wines, a lighter one and a prestige *cuvée*, requiring *élevage* in barrel. They work together to present their wines, and judging by my encounter with the group around the dinner table at Château de Beaupré, with Christian and Marie-Jeanne Double, they certainly share a great enthusiasm and a sense of common purpose that you do not always find amongst the very individualistic French growers. Dinner was preceded by a tasting, for everyone had brought their wines. Inevitably, some were better than others, but the overall quality was very convincing, and the group should serve as a good vehicle to establish a better reputation for the Coteaux d'Aix-en-Provence.

While Côtes de Provence is known more for its pink wine, the Coteaux d'Aix-en-Provence has acquired a reputation for its reds, even if it has produced more pink than red wine during the last three or four years. Pink wine is tempting, as it offers immediate cashflow and does not demand the time investment of a red wine. A wide mixture of grape varieties is allowed in the appellation, more than in the Côtes de Provence. As one grower said, '*C'est toute une salade.*' For white wine you may have Clairette, which is common to most of the white appellations of Provence as well as being the same variety as for Clairette du Languedoc and Clairette du Bellegarde. In addition there is Bourboulenc, Grenache Blanc, Sauvignon, Sémillon, Ugni Blanc and Rolle, while for red and pink the regulations allow for Cabernet Sauvignon, Carignan, Cinsaut, Counoise, Grenache Noir, Mourvèdre and Syrah. Permitted percentages – and these are percentages in the vineyard, not in the wine – have changed, with a significant decrease in the amount of Carignan, which now stands at a maximum of thirty per cent. Cabernet Sauvignon is also limited to thirty per cent, while the other varieties must not exceed forty per cent. A typical red blend is likely to consist of equal parts of Syrah, Cabernet Sauvignon and Grenache Noir. As for white wines, Ugni Blanc has dropped to thirty per cent; Sémillon and Sauvignon are also restricted to thirty per cent, and none of the other varieties may exceed seventy per cent, so that a typical blend is likely to be equal parts of Rolle, Clairette and Grenache Blanc, with the Bordelais varieties playing only a very minor part. Essentially, the character of the individual wines comes from the subtleties of the blend. Then there are the growers who plant varieties that do not feature in the appellation, such as Chardonnay at Château de Revelette, which is sold as a Vin de Pays des Bouches-du-Rhône.

CHATEAU VIGNELAURE, RIANS

The estate which really gave the Coteaux d'Aix-en-Provence its reputation outside the region is Château Vignelaure, and the man responsible was Georges Brunet, who bought a dilapidated château and run-down vineyard in 1964. He had already restored Château La Lagune in the Médoc to its former glory, and took up a new challenge in the beautiful, arid hills outside Aix-en Provence. When Dr Guyot wrote his survey of the vineyards of France in 1865, he said that you could make a great wine in this region by mixing

Syrah and Cabernet Sauvignon. He considered that Syrah gave structure to the Cabernet Sauvignon, for this was the period of Lafite *hermitagé*, when the wines of the northern Rhône were not infrequently sent to Bordeaux to boost less substantial claret. Cabernet Sauvignon was grown here in the nineteenth century and Guyot wrote that the wines made from it had a velvet flavour, while wines from Syrah were rich and full of flavour, like those of Hermitage.

Just over a century later Georges Brunet was guided by Dr Guyot's advice – though he also included a more traditional grape variety of the region, Grenache Noir – when he brought the vineyards back into production, making some very successful wines during the 1970s. He is considered a real innovator, for he was one of the very first to use stainless steel vats and new oak barrels, which had not been seen in the region before. Brunet then sold Vignelaure in 1986. For a few years it had a somewhat chequered history, belonging first to the chairman of Holiday Inns and then to the owners of Château du Galoupet in the Côtes de Provence, the Indian Shivdasani family, who sold it in 1994 to a partnership headed by a genial Irishman, David O'Brien, with the involvement of Hugh Ryman, making for a combination of Old and New World ideas. Since then, Ryman's company Rystone have sold their share of the estate to O'Brien.

Vignelaure has some of the highest vineyards of the appellation, at an altitude of three hundred and fifty metres, which O'Brien considers too high for the Provençal varieties. Mourvèdre ripens only one year in four. Syrah is good provided it does not rain in September, for the vintage is late here, lasting until mid-October in 1997. Cabernet Sauvignon, and also Merlot, which can only be grown as a *vin de pays*, really do much better. They have also planted a small amount of white varieties, Rolle, Sauvignon and Sémillon, which are only just coming in production. They now have sixty hectares of vines, with an extensive replanting programme to replace the old vines. There have been changes in the cellars too. The Shivdasani family installed stainless steel vats and any remaining *foudres* have disappeared, so that there are barrels, of American as well as French oak, from a variety of different coopers. Michel Rolland advises on blending, with the final *assemblage* taking place eighteen months after the vintage.

O'Brien's first vintage was 1995, which proved quite a difficult year; there was no rain from May until early August, so the vines suffered from stress. The wine is structured, with soft tannins and some blackcurrant fruit. A barrel sample of 1996 also promised well. It was a more concentrated vintage, and although the oak was still dominant, there was good fruit, making a rounded, elegantly harmonious wine. Once again, this has become an estate to watch.

CHATEAU REVELETTE, JOUQUES

Château Revelette is a nearby estate outside the village of Jouques, owned by a German, Peter Fischer, who bears a certain resemblance to the French actor Gérard Depardieu. He explained how he came to settle in Provence. He spent a year working with Emmanuel Gaujal, the leading oenologist in the Coteaux Varois, which gave him a very good introduction to the region, and then he succeeded in persuading his family that the time was right for him to set up on his own. It took a year to find Revelette, after he had looked at more than thirty properties. He had set certain conditions: he wanted to be in a tourist area, with good vineyard land that was suitable for white as well as red wine, and with an existing cellar. At Revelette he found everything he wanted, except the tourists.

We sat in the garden on a warm October afternoon. The peacocks were mercifully silent and the Alsatian dog Tango basked in the sunshine. However, the temperature had been at freezing point early that morning, illustrating the extremes of temperature on the northern edge of the appellation. Cool air comes down the Durance valley from the north, while the Mont Ste Victoire stops the Mediterranean influence, so that they are the last to finish the vintage in Provence. However, for Fischer, Château Revelette has proved that you can make great wine in this area. He began with twelve hectares in 1985 and now has twenty-five. His oldest Grenache Noir is forty years old and his oldest Syrah was planted in 1975. He finds Syrah the best grape, followed by his own plantings of Cabernet Sauvignon. The cellar is furnished with traditional cement vats, painted with an attractive Provençal skyline in the vivid colours of the region.

Fischer talks about his wines with enthusiasm. He has a friendly, relaxed approach to life, but you also sense the underlying commitment to his estate, combined with the broader horizons of someone who has experience from outside the confines of the hills of Aix. Altogether Fischer makes five wines, a château wine in each colour and what he calls a Grand Blanc and a Grand Rouge, which are fermented or aged in oak. The white château wine is a blend of Ugni Blanc, Sauvignon Blanc – which he really likes – and Rolle, with a drop of Clairette. It is fresh and lemony, with a nutty finish. In contrast, the Grand Blanc de Revelette is a *vin de pays*, a pure Chardonnay, of which one-third is fermented in new wood and kept on the fine lees for seven months. The 1994 reminded me of an Hermitage Blanc, with some rich, almost honeyed flavours and a firm backbone. Fischer did admit that some people thought it was Roussanne and Marsanne. The *rosé* had fresh, peppery fruit, with a little spice and some length.

The basic red is half Syrah with equal parts of Grenache Noir and Cabernet Sauvignon, with dry, peppery flavours, while the Grand Rouge de Revelette is half Syrah and half Cabernet Sauvignon. This is acceptable to the INAO, as Fischer, unlike Eloi Dürrbach at Trévallon – of whom more on page 536 – does have Grenache Noir in his vineyard. The wine spends twelve months in wood, in barrels that were first used for Chardonnay. When it is young, it is Cabernet that dominates the flavour, as in the 1995, while the peppery character of the Syrah had started to emerge in a very satisfying way in the 1993. A new project is some late harvest Chardonnay; Fischer is leaving grapes to dry on the vines, just to see what will happen.

DOMAINE DE LA REALTIERE, RIANS

Another neighbour, and a newcomer to the appellation, is Jean-Louis Michelland at Domaine de la Realtière. This is a lovely spot on the slopes of the Montagne de Vautubière, with views across the valley to the vineyards of Vignelaure. Michelland had a varied career developing rural agriculture in the Pacific, in Polynesia and New Caledonia, and then came to the moment to leave. He had studied oenology in the 1960s and had always dreamed of having his own vineyard, so, as he put it, he exchanged coconuts for oil and wine. It took two years to find La Realtière. The house dates from 1880, but the cellar had been abandoned and the grapes were being delivered to the co-operative at Rians. His first three vintages were made in the cellars at Vignelaure, until he had organised the cellar here for the 1997 harvest.

Michelland has that enquiring enthusiasm that comes from being an outsider. He described himself as *un jeune vieux* in the vineyard, and he is determined to produce the very best grapes. He is adamantly opposed to mechanical harvesters for a variety of reasons. Temperature can be a problem, as the grapes warm up in the sunshine, nor are the machines selective, so you get rotten grapes and leaves, and you also need to protect the grapes with sulphur. It may be four times more expensive to pick by hand, but he wants his grapes to arrive at the cellar as unblemished as table grapes.

There were nine hectares of abandoned vines when Michelland bought the property in 1994. Two have been pulled up and replanted with Syrah and Cabernet Sauvignon, while the others have been put back in order, replacing the missing vines. They include some very old Syrah, producing very thick-skinned grapes, and some low-yielding Grenache Noir, but no white varieties. There is also some old Carignan that he nearly pulled up, but now vinifies by carbonic maceration to make a red summer wine, Cuvée des Moissons, Vin de Pays des Coteaux du Verdon. It was vibrant with cherry fruit and a hint of cinnamon spice. His *rosé* was fresh, with some body, but not heavy, and his red, Cuvée Léa, a blend of Syrah and Cabernet Sauvignon, spends twelve months in wood. The 1996 vintage was deep coloured, long and elegant, with firm tannins on the palate. The 1997 also promised well when it was a year old, with young berry fruit and some puckering tannins.

DOMAINE DES BEATES, LAMBESC

Another relative newcomer to the appellation is Chapoutier, the highly respected producer of the northern Rhône. The majority of their vineyards and their cellars are based on Tain l'Hermitage, with a *négociant* activity extending all over the Rhône Valley, and they are particularly known for their interest in organic and especially biodynamic viticulture. In recent years they have expanded outside the Rhône Valley; they went into Banyuls in 1995 and in 1996 they bought Domaine des Béates, outside the village of Lambesc on the northern edge of the Coteaux d'Aix-en-Provence. The estate had thirty hectares of vines that had already been organic for ten years. The manager and wine maker Gilles Trouillet explained how he had arrived on 23 September, when the grapes were ready to pick. He tasted them, as that gives you a very clear idea of the wine you will obtain, and decided on three different *cuvées*; that essentially is what they have continued to make. There is Les Matines for early drinking, Les Béates and, in the best vintages, a red barrel-aged Terra d'Or.

The vineyards are planted with the appropriate varieties, Grenache Blanc, Rolle and Sauvignon for whites, and Grenache Noir, Cabernet Sauvignon and Syrah for reds. There is also a little Mourvèdre, but it is really only suitable for *rosé*, as is the Cinsaut. The existing cellar was already well equipped with stainless steel vats, but they have modernised it, introducing barrels, insulating the building and adding an elegant tasting area that offers an extensive view of the vineyards.

As well as working with the monks on the island of Lérins in the Côtes de Provence, Trouillet's previous experience was in Châteauneuf-du-Pape. The *terroir* is quite different here, for the soil has much more limestone and fewer *galets*, making for harder wines with more muscle in their youth, and there is, of course, much less Grenache Noir. The vineyards have gradually been converted from organic to even more demanding biodynamic practices. It takes about three years to see the difference in the vines; they become more resistant to disease, producing smaller but riper grapes, with a better natural balance and more flavour. They carry out a very strict selection at the vintage.

In a relatively short time they have established a sound range of wines. Les Matines white, from Grenache Blanc and Rolle, is soft and rounded, while Les Matines *rosé*, from Cinsaut, Grenache Noir and a little Mourvèdre, is fresh and simple. The red Les Matines, a blend of Syrah and Grenache Noir with twenty per cent Cabernet Sauvignon, given a short *cuvaison*, had some peppery fruit and was refreshingly unassuming. Les Béates is more serious in stature. The white, made for the first time in 1998, is a blend of Sauvignon, Grenache Blanc and Rolle, part of which is fermented in wood. That was just what it was doing at the time of my visit, so a tasting was impractical. Les Béates *rosé* is mainly Grenache Noir, run off the skins after three days, to produce a rounded, rather heavy wine with a deep ink colour. Les Béates red, from equal parts of

Cabernet Sauvignon and Syrah with twenty per cent Grenache Noir, is given a two to three week *cuvaison* and about fifteen or twenty per cent of it is aged in wood for twelve months. The 1997 promised well, with ripe fruit and tannin, making a rounded, meaty mouthful of flavour. Made for the first time in 1997, Terra d'Or is from Cabernet Sauvignon and Syrah, all aged in oak, some new, with the malolactic fermentation taking place in wood; at a year old it was ripe and concentrated, a rich mouthful of fruit and oak with considerable potential.

CHATEAU CALISSANNE, LANCON-DE-PROVENCE

On the western side of the appellation, quite isolated from the other estates and close to the Etang de Berre, is Château Calissanne, which has ninety-three hectares of vines, mostly on the hillsides behind the château, as well as fifty hectares of olive trees. From the top of the vineyards there were wonderful views of the Mont Ste Victoire, with the Mont Ste Baume further in the distance, and in the other direction the Montagne du Lubéron, with the Etang de Berre glistening in the spring sunlight at our feet. The air was filled with the fresh scents of Provençal herbs, rosemary and thyme, and there was a riot of cistus flowers. Some *garrigue* have been cleared to plant a new vineyard of Mourvèdre, with electric wires to protect the young vines against the ravages of wild boar and rabbits. Gradually they are shifting their vineyards from the plain, which is not necessarily appellation land, to a better position on the hillsides.

Calissanne has had a long history. There are the vestiges of a Roman fort dating from the beginning of the first millennium, which was inhabited until the Middle Ages. In the sixteenth century the property was connected with the Knights of the Order of Malta, and in the middle of the nineteenth century it belonged a wealthy Marseillais industrialist who, in return for allowing the railway to be built across his land, negotiated his own railway station at Calissanne. The name of the estate comes from the *calisson*, the typical almond biscuit of Aix, for originally there were orchards of almond trees here. The wealthy Marseillais eventually went bankrupt and today, after various changes of ownership, the estate is part of the English Compass Group and is run by the amiable director Jean Bonnet. He arrived here twenty years ago as cellar master and now, as director, is left very much to his own devices. He is still responsible for the wine making, with the help of the consultant oenologist Jean-Luc Colombo.

The château was built in the sixteenth century and today has an air of dilapidated charm, with its crumbling façade that has a dovecot at each end. You approach it along an alley of plane trees. The spacious cellars were built between the two world wars, but not underground, as the water table is too high. Bonnet prefers cement vats for fermenting his red wines, as they maintain a more regular temperature than stainless steel, and they have used small barrels since 1980. Each grape variety and plot of vines is fermented separately, so that they need about forty vats. Usually they make three qualities of each colour, the Cuvée du Château, the Cuvée Prestige and the Cuvée Clos Victoire, with red wine accounting for half their production and white just ten per cent. There are variations in the blend and method for each *cuvée*, demonstrating an ability to capitalise on the diversity provided by a large estate.

Of the white wines, the Cuvée du Château is a blend of Sémillon and Sauvignon, combining the weight of the Sémillon and the acidity of the Sauvignon. The Cuvée Prestige consists of Sémillon and Clairette, with a small part fermented in new wood and given four months *élevage*, while the Clos Victoire comes from very old Clairette, picked when the grapes are overripe. The wine is fermented in new wood and again is given four months *élevage*, so that is rich and full-bodied, with quite harmonious oak. No wood is used for the *rosé*, but the blends vary between Grenache Noir, Syrah and Cabernet Sauvignon, with the best coming from a pure Syrah, which was elegantly fruity.

As for their red wines, the Cuvée du Château, from Grenache Noir, Syrah and some Cabernet, had the peppery fruit of the *garrigue*. The Cuvée Prestige, from equal parts of Syrah and Cabernet Sauvignon, spends a year in *barriques*, but not new ones, and had structure and spice, with some berry fruit. The Clos Victoire, made for the first time in 1990, is a blend of sixty per cent Syrah and forty per cent Cabernet Sauvignon given a year in new wood, and tasted of sweet vanilla, with some ripe fruit. Bonnet considers that *élevage* in oak gives the wine more ageing potential, and when the Mourvèdre comes into production he plans to add it to the Clos Victoire. I was left with an impression of a serious estate that knows where it is going.

CHATEAU FONSCOLOMBE, LE PUY-STE-REPARADE

Some of the larger estates of the appellation lie on the busy main roads leading into Aix-en-Provence. When it was under the management of Yannic de Taisne, the son-in-law of its owner the Marquis de Saporta, Château Fonscolombe contributed considerably to the reputation of the appellation. Today it is run by James de Roany, who had a varied career in the wine industry before coming to Fonscolombe in 1995. He had also bought his own vineyards at the nearby Château des Gavelles in 1993. Somehow the wines at Fonscolombe seem to have stood still. Where it was a leader twenty years ago, introducing new techniques and grape varieties, today it merely continues to produce consistent wines, while others have taken on the innovative role in the appellation.

CHATEAU DES GAVELLES, PUYRICARD

More interesting were de Roany's own wines. Château des Gavelles is at Puyricard, almost in the suburbs of Aix-en-Provence. The property was originally called the Château Baron de Fabry after the previous owner, so with a change of ownership came a change of name. Gavelles is de Roany's second name and it is also the term for a faggot of vine cuttings that were put in a vat to separate the juice from the skins. De Roany is very committed to his appellation and because of his position as secretary of the main growers' *syndicat*, is very concerned to promote its reputation. A white wine, from mainly Rolle with some Ugni Blanc and Clairette, was delicate and fresh, while a *rosé* from Grenache Noir and Syrah, with a little Cinsaut, had some light strawberry fruit. The two red wines were the most satisfying, for these are intended for ageing rather than immediate drinking, as at Fonscolombe. The first is a blend of Grenache Noir and Syrah, part of which spends a year in second-hand *barriques* from Château Carbonnieux to provide some slow oxidation, but not the overt taste of new wood. The wine was structured, with peppery, spicy flavours, reminiscent of the scents of the *garrigue* of Provence. Cuvée Lou Gaveou, from Syrah with a little Grenache Noir, is made only in the best vintages, with most of the wine spending twelve months in wood. When I tasted the 1993 in 1998, it was still quite youthful, with hints of vanilla and some firm, spicy fruit, promising well for the future.

DOMAINE LES BASTIDES, LE PUY-STE-REPARADE

Domaine les Bastides is a close neighbour to Château Fonscolombe, but is on quite a different scale. The estate was created twenty-five years ago by Jean Salen, then a farmer with a few vines who delivered his grapes to the village co-operative. His original intention had been to make *vin cuit*, the traditional Provençal drink that accompanies the thirteen desserts of Christmas. His daughter Carole, who is now the wine maker after studying oenology at Beaune and Bordeaux, likened the process to making jam, for the quantity of juice is decreased by half by heating and may then be flavoured with orange peel and nutmeg. Their *vin cuit* is based on Grenache Blanc and they make just five thousand bottles a year. It does indeed go deliciously with Christmas flavours, not Christmas pudding or mince pies, but certainly a *galette des rois* or a Tuscan panforte, with a delicate flavour of orange and refreshing bite on the finish.

Jean Salen quickly realised that he could not survive on *vin cuit* alone, so he planted more vines, making all three colours of wine for the first time in 1977. Now they have thirty hectares, from which they produce two reds as well as a white and a *rosé* and the *vin cuit*. The white is a blend of Sauvignon, Ugni Blanc and Rolle, all fermented together, while the *rosé*, from Grenache Noir and Cinsaut, is rounded, with fresh acidity. They have no Syrah, which is unusual, and the red Cuvée Tradition is mainly Grenache Noir with a little Carignan and Cinsaut. It spends twelve months in vat, followed by eighteen months in *foudres* and tasted warm and smoky. The Cuvée Valéria, named after a Roman lady who lived in the nearby village of St Canadet and whose sculptured portrait is in the village church, is made from almost equal amounts of Cabernet Sauvignon and Grenache Noir, with a little Mourvèdre, and spends two years in *foudres* after a year in vat. Salen admitted that Mourvèdre was at its limit here. The wine had the cedary notes of Cabernet Sauvignon, with some rounded, warm fruit.

CHATEAU LA COSTE, LE PUY-STE-REPARADE

Another large property, Château la Coste has a hundred and sixty hectares of vines outside the village of Le Puy-Ste-Réparade. This is a family estate that since 1959 has belonged to the Bordonado family, who also own the sparkling wine company Auran. Jean Bordonado and his two sheepdogs Athos and Hélène gave me a friendly welcome. He explained that they have made an enormous effort to change the composition of the vineyards over the last ten years, replacing the Cinsaut, Carignan and Ugni Blanc with Syrah, Cabernet Sauvignon, Merlot and Chardonnay, and at the same time increasing their red production to sixty per cent of the total, whereas previously *rosé* had accounted for eighty per cent. We wandered round the cellars, tasting glass in hand, sampling some of the young wines that had barely finished fermenting. The cellars are well equipped with the latest modern technology. Bordonado explained that they favour physical rather than chemical treatments and give their red wines a very long maceration, up to six or even eight weeks, as this softens the tannins but at the same time makes for longer-lasting wines. In the vineyards they are almost organic, using natural fertilisers and a minimum amount of sulphur. They make *vins de pays*, which allow you the liberty to experiment, and several qualities of appellation wines, with different *cuvées*, some of which are aged in *barriques* and named after various children. They first began using *barriques* about 1990, but only for red wines in order to soften the tannins. Cuvée Cécile, from Syrah, Grenache Noir and Cabernet Sauvignon, with eight months *élevage* in oak, had a firm nose and some supple fruit balanced with harmonious tannins.

CHATEAU BEAULIEU, ROGNES

With two hundred and sixty hectares in production, Château Beaulieu is the largest estate of the appellation and has belonged to the Touzet family for four generations. I met Christophe, who is the wine maker, and his cousin Robert, who deal with sales, but first an aunt showed me round the château. There was first a Roman villa on the site and then the twelfth-century château, which was substantially enlarged at the beginning of the nineteenth century.

There is a small chapel where three generations of the Touzet family have been christened. An elegant staircase takes you to the salon, which is decorated in the colours of the Revolution, red, white and blue. From the windows you can admire manicured gardens with a backdrop of vines. Fifty years ago there were just thirty hectares of vines and polyculture was the order of the day, with wheat, olive groves and cattle.

They make two or three styles of appellation wine: the Gamme Tradition in the traditional elongated Provençal bottle; the Gamme Grande Cuvée, with a hint of oak, for the export market; and the Cuvée Exceptionnelle for red wine only, which is aged in wood for eight or twelve months. Then in 1997 they launched a range of varietal Vin de Pays des Bouches-du-Rhône for Cabernet Sauvignon, Syrah, Chardonnay, Sauvignon, with Cinsaut for *rosé*. They see a real explosion in the demand for varietal wines, in contrast to the appellation, which can be difficult to sell. They feel that it suffers from its proximity to the Côtes de Provence and from the fact that Provence is associated with pink wine, whereas the more interesting wines, as well as the reputation, of the Coteaux d'Aix-en-Provence are red.

Sémillon, Sauvignon and Ugni Blanc are the main grape varieties for their white appellation wines, which are fresh but without great depth of flavour. The pink wines contain a high percentage of Grenache Noir, as well as some Syrah in the Grande Cuvée and Cinsaut in the traditional *cuvée*. The red Tradition was light and peppery, while the Grande Cuvée was more characterful, with Syrah, Cabernet Sauvignon and a little Grenache Noir, given just three months *élevage* in oak. The grapes are grown in a vineyard planted on the site of an extinct volcano, with the *terroir* providing backbone and a firm, peppery character. The Cuvée Exceptionnelle comes from the same varieties but older vines, with a firm, peppery fruit and a structured flavour.

COMMANDERIE DE LA BARGEMONE, ST CANNAT

The Commanderie de la Bargemone, at St Cannat on the frighteningly fast N7, is managed for its owner Jean-Pierre Rozan by an Italian, M. Marriottini, who arrived here from Arezzo in

1973 when the first vines were being planted. The first vintage of the current ownership was 1977 and the vineyards have grown from just five hectares to fifty-seven. Eventually they are aiming for sixty-five. They make two *cuvées* of red and white wine, with the better wine called Cuvée Tournebride, but nonetheless pink wine accounts for two-thirds of the production, for the simple commercial reason that it sells more easily. The basic white, from Sauvignon, Grenache Blanc and Ugni Blanc, was fresh and lemony, while the Cuvée Tournebride, made for the first time in 1978, was dominated by slightly overripe Grenache Blanc, making it full and nutty on the palate. The red Cuvée Tournebride, with stirrups on the label to illustrate the equestrian connotations of the name, is made from the best grapes, thirty per cent of Syrah, twenty per cent of Grenache Noir and fifty per cent of Cabernet Sauvignon, with a longer *cuvaison* to give it more body. They are considering *élevage* in *barriques*, as their *foudres* are becoming too old. The 1993 had some good cassis fruit and soft tannins, making for undemanding, easy drinking.

CHATEAU DU SEUIL, PUYRICARD

The Château du Seuil is an imposing fourteenth-century building that has been gradually extended over the centuries, with an attractive courtyard that overlooks the listed garden, which is unusual in having an enclosed garden. There is a charming dovecot, with the traditional slippery tiles to keep marauding rats at bay. Janine Carreau-Gaschereau has lived there for twenty-five years, producing her first wine in 1974 – before which the grapes were delivered to the local co-operative. Now it is her daughter France Villez who makes the wine. They have fifty hectares of vineyards planted on the Chaine de la Trévaresse, lying at 380–480 metres and facing south west, with the white varieties at the top of the slope where it is cooler.

Mme Carreau-Gaschereau described the Coteaux d'Aix-en-Provence as a very old region but a very young appellation. 'It is difficult to say whether something is typical or not, as we are only just creating our appellation.' They have been using *barriques* since 1990, beginning with just ten barrels for a tiny quantity of both red and white wine, their Cuvée Grand Seuil. The white Grand Seuil is mainly Sauvignon with a small amount of Grenache Blanc, fermented in new oak, with a weekly *bâtonnage* for four or five months and then bottled at the beginning of summer. I found the oak very obvious, but underneath there was a ripe, honeyed flavour and some Sauvignon fruit. In contrast, the white Château de Seuil is a blend of Sauvignon, Grenache Blanc and Ugni Blanc. They have some very old Ugni Blanc, which gives good results and adds acidity to the blend, while Sauvignon ripens early and is usually picked at the end of August. Their best red is a blend of Cabernet Sauvignon and Syrah with just a drop of Grenache Noir, aged for twelve months in wood, of which a third is new, giving a good concentration of flavour and quite a tannic structure. The basic red, from one-third each of Cabernet Sauvignon, Syrah and Grenache Noir, and given twelve months of *élevage* in vat, was more accessible, with attractive peppery flavours and what the French call *fruits rouges*.

DOMAINE DU CHATEAU BAS, VERNEGUES

The Domaine du Château Bas lies just outside the village of Vernègues. You look across the valley to the hilltop village, which had a *château haut* that was struck by an earthquake in 1909. It is now deserted, although the cellars survived intact, and is listed as an historic monument, while the villagers rebuilt their homes lower down the valley. In the other direction is the scandalous eyesore of the TGV line, built on stilts and completely destroying the atmosphere of this historic property and its surroundings. Château Bas probably dates back to the first century BC, as the vestiges of a Roman temple remain. In the Middle Ages the property belonged to the Seigneurs of Vernègues. There is a twelfth-century chapel, while the cellars, which have vaulted ceilings from the same period, are said to haunted by the ghost of a woman who was beheaded in the courtyard.

The estate, which has eighty-six hectares of vines, belongs to a German company and is managed for the absentee owners by Philippe Pouchin and his wife Marilyne. The cellars consist of three galleries that survived the 1909 earthquake, and are well equipped with *foudres* and *barriques*, with both stainless steel and cement vats. They make three different qualities of wine in each colour.

There is a basic Cuvée Alvernègues, a more substantial Pierres du Sud and, since 1996, a Cuvée du Temple fermented or aged in *barriques*. The comparison of the three whites shows the difference of style. The Cuvée Alvernègues, from Rolle, Grenache Blanc and Ugni Blanc given some skin contact and kept on the fine lees for a few months, was fresh and pithy. Pierres du Sud, mainly from Rolle and Grenache Blanc, underwent a similar vinification, but was more rounded and smoky in flavour, with understated fruit and body, while the Cuvée du Temple, from forty per cent Sauvignon Blanc, thirty per cent Rolle and twenty per cent Grenache Blanc, had an attractive toasty character with the honeyed flavour of very ripe Sauvignon. The wine spends four months in wood, with regular *bâtonnage*. The red Cuvée du Temple is two-thirds Cabernet Sauvignon to one-third Syrah with eighteen months *élevage*, making for a firm concentration of blackcurrant and peppery fruit, with plenty of ageing potential. It was a good note on which to leave the Coteaux d'Aix-en-Provence.

The problem with the Coteaux d'Aix-en-Provence is that it has no obvious heart or centre. There are large producers and co-operatives that dominate the appellation by their size and smaller growers who feel rather overwhelmed in their midst. There is an enormous variation in what you can and cannot plant and blend, and great differences – for example between Calissanne and Vignelaure – in how those grape varieties perform in different parts of the appellation, so there is really no cohesion. It is little wonder that the Coteaux des Baux, with its very homogeneous vineyard area, wanted a separate appellation. Ultimately the choice of a Coteaux d'Aix-en-Provence depends upon the producer's name on the label. That is what matters.

Key facts

VDQS 1956; AC 1985, for red, white and pink.

Reputation based on red (at least thirty per cent of production) but currently produces more pink; white only about five per cent and includes white from Les Baux.

Forty-nine *communes* in the Bouches-du-Rhône and Var, mainly north of Aix-en-Provence.

Grape varieties:

WHITE: Clairette, Bourboulenc, Grenache Blanc and Rolle, maximum seventy per cent; Ugni Blanc, Sauvignon and Sémillon, maximum thirty per cent; typical blend is one-third each of Rolle, Clairette and Grenache Blanc, with perhaps a drop of Sauvignon or Sémillon.

RED: Cabernet Sauvignon and Carignan, maximum thirty per cent; Cinsaut, Counoise, Mourvèdre and Syrah, maximum forty per cent; typical blend is one-third each of Syrah, Cabernet Sauvignon and Grenache Noir.

On clay and limestone soil.

Wide variations in climate and altitude resulting from the extent of the appellation.

Vintages

1999: A warm summer with a little rain at harvest, but insufficient to cause any problems.
1998: The same fine vintage as in the Languedoc.
1997: Much more successful, with riper grapes and less rain than in the Languedoc.
1996: Well balanced wines, despite some summer rain.
1995: A lack of rain between May and August caused stress in the vineyards; some sturdy, structured wines.

Les Baux-de-Provence

The vineyards of Les Baux-de-Provence share a recent history with those of the Coteaux d'Aix-en-Provence. Originally the two areas formed two separate VDQS, but were then amalgamated as one appellation in 1985. However, the feeling always lingered amongst the producers of Les Baux that theirs was a homogeneous area in its own right, quite distinct from the much more amorphous Coteaux d'Aix-en-Provence. The region of Les Baux is very precisely defined, with its vineyards lying on the northern and southern slopes of the dramatic bauxite outcrop of the Alpilles, where the stark, deep grey rock of volcanic origin makes a lunar landscape devoid of vegetation. Seen from the air on the approach to Marseille, it seems to rise out of the plain that forms the delta of the Rhône valley. The little village of Les Baux is one of the popular tourist destinations of the south, packed with shops selling local crafts. I firmly prefer it out of season. In 1995 the differences between the appellations were finally recognised and the separate appellation of Les Baux-de-Provence was created for red and *rosé*, but not for white wine. For the moment that remains Coteaux d'Aix-en-Provence, for it is not deemed to have sufficient consistency to merit its own appellation. Time will tell.

There is no doubt that Les Baux has quite a different microclimate from the Coteaux d'Aix-en-Provence. It is warmer, windier and drier, so that the grapes tend to be healthier. As in Coteaux d'Aix, it is the diversity of grape varieties that determines the typicity of the wine. However, even within a small appellation of about 340 hectares, which includes twelve producers who are members of the growers' *syndicat* and one nonconformist whose wines have been relegated to mere *vin de pays*, there is still a distinct difference between the vineyards on the northern and southern slopes of the Alpilles. The soil on the northern slopes is sandier, making for wines with more tannin and acidity, whereas the southern slopes have more clay and limestone. Consequently different grape varieties prevail, with the north concentrating on Cabernet Sauvignon and Syrah, while the warmer south favours the more Mediterranean varieties of Cinsaut, Carignan and in particular Grenache Noir, which should always be the *cépage de base*. The climate here is warmer and the grapes ripen as many as fifteen days earlier, making for a more rustic style, while the wines of the north are possibly more refined. The appellation insists on three principal varieties, Syrah, Grenache Noir and Cabernet Sauvignon, but also allows for Mourvèdre, Cinsaut, Counoise and Carignan. Grenache Noir, Mourvèdre and Syrah must account for at least sixty per cent and Cabernet Sauvignon must not exceed twenty per cent – in the vineyard, that is. It is for this reason that Domaine de Trévallon, where there is Syrah and Cabernet Sauvignon but no Grenache Noir, has been declassified to Vin de Pays des Bouches-du-Rhône. The reputation of Trévallon is such that a demotion on the label is insignificant. As for white wine, the grape varieties are of course those of the Coteaux d'Aix-en-Provence.

DOMAINE DES TERRES BLANCHES, ST-REMY-DE-PROVENCE

The longest-established estate on the north side of the Alpilles is Domaine des Terres Blanches, which is the property of Noël Michelin. He used to produce coffee in the Cameroons, and when he returned to France in 1968 he settled here and built a cellar. Michelin's son-in-law Guillaume Rérolle has run the estate since 1990, after an earlier career as a town planner. The vineyards once included many hybrid varieties that have gradually been replaced, so that there are now thirty-two hectares in production. In this part of France, where the Mistral blows away any humidity, organic viticulture is an attractive and feasible option, and work in the cellar is kept very simple, with no fining or filtration for the red wines after a fairly lengthy period in tank or *foudre*. The 1994s were being bottled in the spring of 1998. The best red, named after one of Michelin's daughters, is the Cuvée Aurélia, from Cabernet Sauvignon with some Syrah and a little Grenache Noir, grown in the best vineyard sites. It had some firm, peppery fruit, but generally the other wines seemed quite light and lacking in substance.

DOMAINE HAUVETTE, ST REMY-DE-PROVENCE

Dominique Hauvette is a newcomer to the region. Tired of winters in the mountains of Savoy, she longed for sunshine – and here, as she put it, she has found paradise. In Savoy she had been a lawyer, but changed direction completely by studying oenology. Hauvette first came to Les Baux in 1982. Initially she had just two hectares, which have now been expanded to six, planted with Grenache Noir, Syrah, Cabernet Sauvignon, Clairette and Ugni Blanc. Ideally she would like ten hectares , but although she would have no difficulty in obtaining planting rights, as her vineyard is so small, the problem is to find available land. This is a region with a strong demand for building land, so people with land prefer to keep it for a future building, even if they leave it uncultivated. The difference in land values is enormous. If you could find a hectare of vines to buy, it would cost FF 200,000, while unplanted vineyard land costs FF 80–100,000. In contrast, land with planning permission is an astronomical FF 350–500,000 per hectare, depending on its exact position.

I was given a noisy welcome by Hauvette's six dogs, while the two horses and the cat kept their distance. First we tasted cask samples in a tiny cellar. A pure Clairette aged in barrel had some rounded, buttery fruit, while a blend of Cabernet Sauvignon and Syrah was peppery, with soft tannins. Some Grenache Noir that was being aged in *foudre* will be added to it latter. Usually Hauvette makes just one red and one white wine and no *rosé*. I liked her wines. The 1996 red, consisting of forty per cent Grenache Noir and equal parts of Syrah and Cabernet Sauvignon, had some warm berry fruit on the nose, with some attractive spicy flavours and soft tannins. The aroma of the *garrigue* that should typify Les Baux will develop with age.

CHATEAU ROMANIN, ST REMY-DE-PROVENCE

Château Romanin is a joint venture between M. Peyraud, a Parisian financier, and Jean-André Charial, chef and manager of Oustau de

Baumaniere, Les Baux's most famous restaurant, and now president of the appellation. The wine maker, Jean-Louis Andrieux, worked for Veuve Clicquot before coming south. This is an estate on quite a different scale from the others in Les Baux. You follow a long, winding dirt track from the main road through the vineyards, with the occasional sign to reassure you that you are still on the right road. Once there, you realise that no expense has been spared in the cellar design; the main part, housing several large *foudres*, looks not unlike a vaulted chapel carved out of the rocks. They follow the biodynamic precepts of Rudolf Steiner, with inspiring images of the sun in the active, vinification part of the cellar, while the moon features in the peaceful ageing cellar.

Altogether there are fifty hectares of vines, including twenty hectares of old vines and thirty that were planted between 1989 and 1994. For each colour they make two qualities of wine, La Chapelle de Romanin for earlier consumption and the longer-lasting Château Romanin, from the older vines as well as the best of the younger vines. Cabernet Sauvignon and Syrah are the main varieties for the red wine, with small amounts of Grenache Noir, Mourvèdre, Counoise, Carignan and Cinsaut. The wine making seems careful and the wines are well made and sound, but somehow the flavours did not really inspire enthusiasm. They favour a cool pre-fermentation maceration of the Syrah to obtain fruit but not tannin, followed by a traditional vinification with destemmed grapes. The 1993 Château Romanin was warm, cedary and nicely developed, while the Chapelle de Romanin seemed hard and stalky. The white Chapelle de Romanin, mainly from Ugni Blanc and Bourboulenc fermented in stainless steel, was soft and grassy, while the château wine, from Rolle, Clairette and Sauvignon, included some barrel fermentation so that it was quite solid and buttery.

MAS DE GOURGONNIER, MOURIES

Mas de Gourgonnier was my first destination on the southern slopes of the Alpilles. Although it was a rather grey spring morning, Luc Cartier took me for a drive through the vineyards. The rosemary was in flower, providing a splash of colour against the very red soil of the vineyards. Gourgonnier is a family estate going back five generations and now run by two brothers, Luc and

Frédéric. Their grandfather first planted vines here and they also have olive trees, but no longer any apricot or almond trees. Their forty-six hectares of vines includes a substantial quantity of Grenache Noir, as well as Syrah, Cabernet Sauvignon, Mourvèdre, Carignan and Cinsaut for red wine and Grenache Blanc, Sauvignon, Rolle and Ugni Blanc for white wine.

The cellar is functional, with some *foudres* and a few barrels for white wine. They did their first bottling in 1975. The basic white is lightly herbal, while Réserve du Mas, made since 1992, is fermented and aged in barrel, and is solid and nutty. I preferred the unoaked wine. As for red wines, a traditional red was soft and peppery, while the Réserve wine, from equal parts of Grenache Noir, Syrah and Cabernet Sauvignon, including the oldest vines, spends twelve months in *foudres*. It did not have the easy fruit of the Cuvée Tradition, though the 1990 vintage had developed the meaty flavours of the *garrigue*.

MAS STE BERTHE, LES BAUX-DE-PROVENCE

Mas Ste Berthe nestles at the foot of the Alpilles. The first vines were planted here in 1960 by Louis David. Today the current owner is his stepson Philippe Tarrou, while the wine maker is a Burgundian, Christian Nieff. However, he has been at Mas Ste Berthe for fifteen years and has, as he put it, evolved with the property. Originally polyculture was the order of the day, with table grapes and apricots, but now they concentrate on thirty-seven hectares of vines and four of olive trees. The composition of the vineyards has changed too. Where once there was Grenache Noir and Carignan, there is now Syrah and Cabernet Sauvignon as well as a little Mourvèdre, while the white varieties, such as Grenache Blanc, Sauvignon, Rolle and Ugni Blanc, were planted only in 1984 and the first white wine made in 1987.

In the vineyards they favour *lutte raisonnée*, or integrated farming with organic fertiliser, and they work the soil, but in difficult years they want the flexibility to use stronger treatments against rot. The cellar operates by gravity, with the fermentation taking place in stainless steel vats with facilities for temperature control. Nieff makes three red wines, of which only two are bottled. The best is the Cuvée Louis David, from one-third each of Grenache Noir,

Syrah and Cabernet Sauvignon, of which a part is kept in wood for nine months and given further *élevage* in vat. They have worked with barrels since 1986 and the wine had structure and tannin, while the Cuvée Tradition, mainly from Grenache Noir with smaller amounts of Syrah and Cabernet Sauvignon, was more immediately appealing, with ripe red fruit and the warmth of the *garrigue*. Finally, anything left over is sold off in *cubitainers* to local customers. The *rosé*, based on Grenache Noir for body and warmth and on Syrah and Cabernet Sauvignon for colour and structure, as well as Mourvèdre and Cinsaut, is ripe and rounded.

Grenache Blanc provides the base of the white wine, which has some delicate fruit. The Sauvignon and Rolle are given skin contact for extra flavour, while Ugni Blanc is useful for providing acidity. As yet, the vines are not really old enough to produce wine with sufficient structure to allow for oak ageing. They would like to develop their white wines and are considering Marsanne and Roussanne, which are not yet allowed in the appellation, although there are some experimental vineyards of them run by the Chambre d'Agriculture in Aix-en-Provence. Grenache Blanc and Rolle also fit more comfortably into the image of the south than Sauvignon or Sémillon, and as for Viognier, 'Well, you see it everywhere these days.' There is an attractive sales area to encourage visitors, and also what they called a *parcours pédagogique*, or educational walk, through the vineyards, which I declined to follow because there was a torrential downpour.

MAS DE LA DAME, LES BAUX-DE-PROVENCE

Mas de la Dame is another of the original wine estates of the area, bought by a Burgundian at the beginning of the twentieth century. His son, Robert Faye, renovated the property in the 1930s and did much for the region in the post-war years, for he was the first to replace his hybrid vines with noble varieties and he began bottling his own wine as early as 1949. The property then passed to his son-in-law M. Chatin, who died in 1988, and it now belongs to his three daughters, two of whom are actively involved, Anne Poniatowski and Caroline Missoffe. The origins of Mas de la Dame are fifteenth century and there have always been vineyards and olive trees here, as well as apricot and almond trees for the *calisson*, the traditional biscuit of Aix-en-Provence. In 1889 the house, with its magnificent backdrop of the Alpilles, was painted by Van Gogh, a picture that sadly was stolen from its owner in the 1960s and has never been recovered. Marc Ceysson has managed the estate since 1974 and the roving oenologist, Jean-Luc Colombo of Cornas fame, has brought a fresh eye to things since 1993.

The fifty-seven hectares are planted with Grenache Noir, Syrah, Cabernet Sauvignon, Cinsaut and Mourvèdre for the red wine and Clairette, Sémillon and Rolle for white wine. Sémillon provides body, while Clairette gives finesse and Rolle fruit. Usually they make two qualities of white, with a slight variation in the blend. The Blanc des Roches contains all three varieties, while the Cuvée Gourmande comes from equal parts of Clairette and Sémillon. Rosé du Mas is made from Grenache Noir, Cabernet Sauvignon and Syrah and has a hint of strawberry fruit. For the red wine there are three different qualities. The basic Cuvée Gourmande is from Grenache Noir with some Carignan and Cinsaut, the Réserve du Mas is from Grenache Noir, Cabernet Sauvignon and Carignan, and the Cuvée de la Stèle is from older vines, fifty-five-year-old Grenache Noir, forty-two-year-old Cabernet and forty-one-year-old Syrah, which are given twelve months *élevage* in barrel. They have worked with small barrels for ten years now and no longer have any large *foudres*. The Cuvée Gourmande was light and peppery, while the Réserve du Mas had ripe fruit. In contrast, the Cuvée de la Stèle seemed rather firm and austere. After lunch in a cheerful restaurant in the nearby village of Maussanne, Ceysson took me to see the village oil mill, which operates for twelve hundred members in the valley, producing one of the most highly rated oils in Provence, with its own appellation of Les Baux since 1997. The appellation for the oil of Nyons predates it by just three years.

CHATEAU D'ESTOUBLON, FONTVIEILLE

When I visited Les Baux in the spring of 1988, Jean-Pierre Lombrage was still the owner of Château d'Estoublon and president of the grower's *syndicat*. This is a château in the real sense of the word, built in the fourteenth century as a *maison de retraite* for the monks of the nearby abbey of Montmajour. The cellar, with a magnificent vaulted ceiling, dates back to the eighteenth century.

They have ten hectares of vine and thirty-five hectares of olive trees, which provide the same turnover despite the considerable difference in area. Jean-Pierre Lombrage is the fifth generation here. He explained that in his great-grandfather's time it had been a two thousand-hectare estate, but problems of inheritance reduced it to three hundred and fifty hectares of olives, some ten to twelve thousand trees, necessitating a considerable amount of labour and as many as three hundred people at the harvest. Each workman required a daily ration of two litres of wine, so in those days they kept vines to provide *la bibine*. His grandfather made the first moves towards planting noble vines for the VDQS, concentrating on just ten hectares.

Lombrage makes just one wine of each colour. The white, from Ugni Blanc and Grenache Blanc, was fresh and delicate; the *rosé*, mainly from Grenache Noir, Cinsaut and a little Syrah and Carignan, was ripe and rounded; the red from the same varieties was rather chunky and rustic, with some rugged tannins. Over a friendly dinner we discussed the aims of the *syndicat* and how they run a *Maison du Vin* in the village of Les Baux in an attempt to make the appellation better known. Their closest neighbours are the Côtes du Rhône, but compare the two promotional budgets: they have 70,000 FF a year, in sharp contrast to the Côtes du Rhône's 10 million. Like all good *vignerons*, they want to improve their quality, preserve their authenticity and avoid the 'Parkerisation' of the appellation, referring to the influence of the American critic. Since my visit, the estate has been sold to the Swiss Schneider family and doubtless things will change.

DOMAINE DE TREVALLON, ST ETIENNE-DU-GRES

For better or for worse, by far the best producer of the Alpilles is no longer a member of the appellation. As already mentioned, Eloi Dürrbach at Domaine de Trévallon has Syrah and Cabernet Sauvignon, without a single vine of Grenache Noir, so his wine has been condemned to humble *vin de pays* status since the 1994 vintage. But that is irrelevant in any assessment of quality. Dürrbach is an example of an outsider coming to a region without any preconceived ideas, but with an energetic approach and a determination to make the best wine possible. The property was bought by his parents in 1960, when his father, a painter, tired of the crowds of St Tropez. Dürrbach arrived here from Paris after studies in mathematics and architecture, and in 1974 planted his first vines, Cabernet Sauvignon and Syrah. Trévallon is outside the village of St Etienne-du-Grès, at the north western corner of the Alpilles, and the address, once Vieux Chemin Romain after the old Roman road, has been changed to Rue du Notre-Dame-du-Château. I was noisily greeted by a small, fluffy grey dog, answering appropriately to the name of Marsanne.

Dürrbach now has twenty hectares in production, having planted Marsanne in 1987 and Roussanne in 1990. He also admits to having a little Chardonnay, just for fun, but has rejected Viognier, having realised that he did not really like the taste. The inspiration for the white wine is the Hermitage Blanc of Gérard Chave, and also the white wine of Château de Beaucastel in Châteauneuf-du-Pape, while for red wine he also looks to Châteauneuf-du-Pape. Since 1990 the proportions of Cabernet Sauvignon and Syrah have been more or less equal in the red wine, whereas earlier vintages had a higher proportion of Cabernet Sauvignon. His wines have never been destalked, initially because he could not afford a destemmer but now he because does not want to change anything. He uses an open-top wooden vat for *pigeage* and complained that Cabernet Sauvignon stalks can be very scratchy. All Dürrbach's red wine is aged in small *foudres* for at least eighteen months, if not two years, and they have a concentration and a finesse that are not found anywhere else in Les Baux. He criticises the *syndicat* for its weakness in face of the INAO and for asking for too low a percentage of Cabernet Sauvignon, for fear that it would not be granted an appellation at all. The regulations insist on a maximum of twenty per cent of Cabernet Sauvignon in the vineyard, not in the wine, compared to thirty per cent in the nearby Coteaux d'Aix-en-Provence. Dürrbach believes that there should not be any limiting percentages and firmly considers the new appellation to be a monument to hypocrisy, for it includes wines made like his, from Syrah and Cabernet Sauvignon, even though the producers also have the prerequisite Grenache Noir in the vineyard.

Dürrbach's white wine is fermented in barrel but is not given any *bâtonnage*, for it already has enough body, prompting him to observe that a lot of people stir their lees without really knowing why. The taste was rich and intriguing, with nuances of flavour. As for the reds, they have a depth of complexity and ageing potential that is unparalleled by any of the other wines of the area. The 1990 when it was seven years old was warm and smoky, with supple tannins and some meaty flavours, while the 1985 had developed some cedary notes, with an elegant finish. The 1981, tasted on the same occasion, was a wonderful example of the ageing potential of Trévallon, with warm, elegant fruit and soft, balanced tannins.

Dürrbach also has a hectare of olive trees and nurses an ambition to have his own oil mill. As for the future, if given the opportunity he would also like to try his hand at making Châteauneuf-du-Pape, but apparently everyone wants to buy vines in that appellation at the moment. He rises above the petty local politics with his perceptive observations and wry sense of humour.

I headed back for the airport inspired by the example of Trévallon and wondering just why the other producers, with the possible exception of Dominique Hauvette, do not seem capable of producing wines of the same stature and depth of concentration. In comparison to Trévallon, the appellation wines of Les Baux have fruit and charm, but given the climatic and geological paradise of the region, I would have expected much more. I could not help feeling that life is quite easy for the producers of Les Baux. They do not have any commercial problems, for the tourists who visit the village provide a captive market, and perhaps this has made them complacent.

Key facts

AC 1985 with Coteaux d'Aix-en-Provence; separate AC 1995 for red and pink wine; 340 hectares of vines around the Alpilles – north side cooler, with wines based on Syrah and Cabernet Sauvignon, and south side warmer, with emphasis on Grenache Noir.

Grape varieties: Syrah, Grenache Noir and Mourvèdre, maximum sixty per cent; Cabernet Sauvignon, maximum twenty per cent; also Carignan, Cinsaut and Counoise.

Vintages

Very similar to those of the Coteaux d'Aix-en-Provence, with successful wines made especially in 1995, 1997, 1998.

Palette

Few people who leave Aix-en-Provence by motorway in the direction of Marseille notice a small vineyard up on a hillside outside the town, dominated by the elegant sixteenth-century Château Simone. Despite the proximity of the motorway, it is a tranquil spot, with an attractive terrace looking over the vines and horse chestnut trees turning yellow in the autumnal sunshine. There are views across the valley towards the Mont Ste Victoire, which dominates the skyline of this part of Provence. This is the appellation of Palette, one of the smallest in France, with just twenty-three hectares in production, and to all intents and purposes Château Simone *is* Palette, for it accounts for seventeen hectares. Another property, Château la Crémade, has not made any wine recently owing to family problems, and many of its vineyards have been sold for building. Co-operatives in the nearby villages of Fuvaux and Rousset make a little Palette, and finally a Monsieur Reynaud in the village of Meyreuil has planted two hectares of vines, which are not yet in production.

The name Palette comes from a hamlet outside the elegant city of Aix-en-Provence and the appellation lies within the adjoining *commune* of Meyreuil. In the sixteenth century the estate belonged to the Carmelite sisters of Aix-en-Provence. It was they who planted the first vines and excavated the magnificent cellars, still in use today, that are built into the hillside to provide natural insulation. They also had an oil mill here. A subsequent owner of the property was a Mademoiselle Simone, and for over two centuries since the reign of Louis XVI, Château Simone has been in the hands of the Rougier family. René and his son Jean-François are the seventh and eighth generation.

The first time I met René Rougier, he talked of his father's and grandfather's contributions to the reputation of Château Simone.

His grandfather had lived to the age of a hundred and three and had known both Cézanne and Winston Churchill, who painted the Mont Ste Victoire by the humpback bridge, the Pont des Trois Sautets, near the entrance to the property. Churchill sent him a telegram on his hundredth birthday. René Rougier's father was one of the pioneers of selling wine in bottle in Provence, for he first bottled Château Simone back in 1921, following the example of Châteauneuf-du-Pape, and the label still retains the same stylish, but elegantly old fashioned art deco design.

Palette was one of the early post-war appellations, recognised in 1948 by M. Chappaz, the vice-president of the INAO, who was responsible for the creation of many of the early appellations, notably that of Bandol. He appreciated the geological originality of Palette and Château Simone. At that time, the surrounding appellation of Coteaux d'Aix-en-Provence was not even dreamt of, and Château Simone was a small estate in the middle of a sea of *vin ordinaire*. But it is at the centre of a geological formation called the Cercle de Palette, with soil consisting of limestone debris called *calcaire de Langesse* from the Mont Ste Victoire. It is thin and poor and accounts for the typicity of Palette.

The Rougier family would have liked the appellation of Palette to consist of their vineyards alone, following the example of Château Grillet in the Rhône valley. However, the Cercle de Palette extends over a larger area of about three hundred hectares and so the neighbouring land had to be included. Most of it is pine forest that is very unlikely to be cut down, especially as it contributes to the microclimate of the vineyards. The tiny river Arc crosses the appellation in the valley below the vineyards, and provides an element of humidity, with autumnal morning mists and even occasionally some noble rot. The vines are north facing, which is a distinct advantage in this warm climate, giving the wines the character of a more northerly vineyard – according to Jean-François Rougier, this accounts for the *saveurs animaux* in the wine. The vineyards are protected from strong winds by an amphitheatre of hills, including the Mont Ste Victoire and the Mont de la Sainte Baume, but are open to the Mediterranean and the maritime influence. Consequently the grapes ripen well, but are not usually picked until October.

Phylloxera destroyed the vineyard in 1875, but the Rougier family replanted their land with the traditional grape varieties of

Provence. Another determining characteristic of Château Simone is the age of the vines, for the average is sixty years, and some are as much as a hundred years old. We walked through the vineyards where there were gnarled vines with thick, solid trunks that looked timeless and indestructible. They replace single vines as they die, rather than carrying out any systematic replanting. The work in the vineyard is very traditional; they leave the grass between the rows, as it helps prevent erosion, and the natural fertiliser is provided by the local riding clubs.

Today the red wine is made from about forty per cent Grenache Noir, twenty per cent Mourvèdre and as many as ten or fifteen secondary varieties, some of which are all mixed up together in the vineyard, while others are planted in more systematic plots. Syrah has always been grown here and there is Cinsaut, a little Carignan, some Picpoul Noir, Tibouren, Muscat Noir, some unknown Provençal varieties such as Castet and Manosquin (which means the *cépage de* Manosque, a town on the edge of the Coteaux de Pierrevert) and even varieties that they have been unable to identify. As for white wine, Clairette is the main variety, with a little Grenache Blanc, Ugni Blanc and Muscat Blanc.

Methods in the cellar are very traditional too. Although Jean-François Rougier has more or less taken over responsibility for the wine making from his father, this has not meant any change of style. Château Simone has its own typicity and there is no reason to change it. The first time I met René Rougier he proclaimed very solemnly, 'This is the house where the most respected word is tradition. That is what gives our wines strength. We try to adapt the techniques of modern science, while respecting the practices of the old days that made the reputation of Château Simone.' And over the years other reputations have come and gone, while Château Simone has continued to produce wines with an intrinsic originality and quality.

The harvest here often begins as late as 10 October, and with the cool nights they do not have to worry about the juice heating up. They always use indigenous natural yeast, which makes for a slower fermentation, as cultured yeast tend to work faster, producing higher fermentation temperatures. There are two white wines, a small amount that is bottled in the spring, which has fruit as its main characteristic, while their principal white wine is aged for eighteen months in *barriques*. These are never new barrels, but second-hand ones from reputable addresses such as d'Yquem, Carbonnieux and Fieuzal. They do not use new wood as it marks the wine too much. The wood must melt into the wine. But first the juice is fermented in small *foudres* and then the wine is given six months *élevage* in large *foudres*, going into *barriques*.

We tasted first the 1995 and then the 1989, which provided a fascinating comparison, for Jean-François Rougier said that you must either drink white Château Simone when it is young or else keep it for eight or nine years. In the autumn of 1997 the 1995 was ripe and rounded, very vinous with body, length and light peachy fruit. The wood was present but not at all intrusive. Rougier suggested that the weight, the *gras* of the white wines, came from the long, slow pressing in a basket press. The 1989 had developed a bouquet of *brioche*, with smells reminiscent of a bakery, with a certain nutty weight, not unlike a fine white Graves. It was elegant and subtle with a long finish and, according to Rougier, who should know, had not yet reached the plateau of its development.

The *rosé* is quite unlike most other Provençal *rosés*. This is not a summer quaffing wine, but more serious, powerful and substantial. It is fermented in small *foudres*, then racked into *barriques* and left on the lees until the following spring. Neither the white nor the *rosé* undergo a malolactic fermentation, for the very cool cellars prevent it from occurring of its own accord, but the wines are filtered before bottling as a precaution. The colour of the *rosé* was quite deep, with a rich bouquet of herbs and raspberries; on the palate it was mouth-filling but with firm acidity.

The red wine is fermented in either cement or stainless steel vats, then goes into large *foudres*, and after blending it spends two years in *barriques*. Vinification methods have not changed over the years. The fermentation temperature reaches about 30°C, resulting in good colour, extract and aroma. The grapes are mostly, but not all, destalked, depending on the desired ratio of solids to liquid. Great care is taken to use *barriques* that are not too marked, for the *élevage* is for oxygenation, not for a taste of oak. The malolactic fermentation usually takes place in the spring. The wine is then fined with real egg whites and bottled two or three years after the vintage.

We tasted the 1993, which had been bottled in January 1997. There was no development in the colour and the nose was firm and meaty, slightly smoky with a hint of oak, while the palate was quite spicy, with subtle tannins. It was both powerful and elegant. The tannins were present but not aggressive. The wine needed at least eight or ten years to reach its plateau, and then would easily last a further ten years or more. Other great vintages of Château Simone have included 1975, 1971, 1969, 1964 and 1947, and the more recent 1997 also promises to be exceptional.

Key facts

AC 1948 for red, white and rosé; twenty-three hectares in the *commune* of Meyreuil, on a distinct geological formation, the Cercle de Palette. Dominated by one estate, Château Simone.

A hotchpotch of grape varieties.

Very traditional.

Cassis

Cassis is a cheerful, bustling port with a perfect natural harbour protected by high cliffs. Sadly, the fishermen have almost disappeared – just two remain from the forty or so who operated in the immediate post-war years – and the port is now filled with the expensive yachts of the sailors who ply the Mediterranean for pleasure. The harbour is lined with cheerful restaurants and cafés, offering copious plates of *bouillabaisse, fruits de mer* and the Cassis speciality of sea anemones, washed down with the local white wine. An old fortress on the port, which used to provide protection against pirates and Saracens, has recently been restored by a member of the Michelin tyre family. The poet Frédéric Mistral wrote of Cassis: 'He who has seen Paris but has not seen Cassis, has seen nothing.'

You can escape from the bustle of the town and walk up on the cliffs above the *calanques*, the narrow inlets. The colours are vivid, making a brilliant contrast between the green parasol pines, the blue sea and sky and the white limestone of the cliffs. To the east of the town is Cap Canaille, at 416 metres the highest cliffs of France, and the Couronne de Charlemagne, a large rock with traces of old fortifications, dominates the skyline behind the town. They each offer a striking view of the turquoise Mediterranean and the town of Cassis. And yet how quickly the atmosphere changes with the weather! I have also seen Cassis in the autumnal wind of a late October evening, and on another occasion in a dramatic thunderstorm that cut off the electricity, accompanied by a torrential downpour that turned the streets into a gushing river. That evening we waded across the road to dinner, but the next morning we awoke to a brilliant blue sky and dry streets.

The Greeks of Phocaea on the west coast of Asia Minor brought vines to Cassis around 600 BC, at about the same time as they settled near Marseille. The Romans continued to plant vines here, usually on coastal land, but during the Middle Ages, because of the fear of attack from the sea by marauding Saracens, the vineyards gradually shifted to more suitable sites inland. The first reference to a specific vineyard in Cassis dates from 1199. There are subsequent occasional mentions in the local archives, and in 1530 it was recorded that the Albizzi family, who came from Florence, planted vines to the north of the town; their descendants are still at Clos d'Albizzi. The principal activity of Cassis was always maritime, but by the nineteenth century agriculture had also become important. Vines, olive trees and fruit trees were planted together on the hillsides outside the town and wheat was grown on the lower-lying, flatter land. Cassis was also important for its quarries, but now only one remains in operation.

Today the reputation of Cassis rests on its white wine. In earlier centuries, however, it was known for its sweet Muscat and also for fine red wines. René of Anjou did much to establish the reputation of the wines of Provence in the fifteenth century, and is said to have brought the Muscat grape to Provence from Italy. Muscat remained important in Cassis until phylloxera devastated the vineyards. In 1672 the governor of Burgundy asked for two small barrels of white Cassis wine to be sent to him for the visit of Louis XIV. In the nineteenth century Rendu described Cassis as the best white wine of Provence and classed the red wine in the first rank of fine wines of the department. The white wine was sweet, alcoholic and very powerful, to be enjoyed by those who like very strong wine. A Muscat wine was also made, from two-thirds Muscat and one-third Mourvèdre, that was not without merit.

The vineyards of Cassis were completely destroyed by phylloxera, and although they were replanted, they never regained their former importance. In the mid-nineteenth century, before phylloxera, there were 498 hectares of vines, but only 290 were recorded after the crisis. The vineyards continued to shrink until about twenty years ago, since when there has been a very slow increase. They reached 180 hectares in 1999, with just fourteen producers and no co-operative. The vineyards are limited to Cassis itself and do not include any of the surrounding villages, so they cannot really grow in size – indeed, they fight a steady battle against the encroachment of tarmac and concrete. Sadly, the land is now more valuable for holiday villas and there is a strong temptation to sell to building contractors as the town sprawls into the hinterland. The difference in value between land with and without planning permission is significant: FF 400 per square metre as opposed to FF 40 per square metre for agricultural land. This means that you could sell a hectare of land for building for FF 4 million, whereas one hectare of vines would cost FF 400,000. Despite the urban menace, however, the vineyard area has remained relatively stable, with a small increase in the production of appellation caused by a shift from *vin de pays* or *vin de table*. At the time of my visit, the 1988 *plan d'occupation du sol* was under review, with the INAO planning a *délimitation parcellaire* to check that all the vineyards were indeed suitable for inclusion within the appellation. At the moment you are able to plant vines for the appellation anywhere within the *commune* of Cassis, provided of course you have the planting rights; just two hectares are granted for the appellation each year.

Cassis prides itself on being one of the three earliest appellations, dating from 1936 along with Arbois in the Jura and Châteauneuf-du-Pape. The four estates that achieved the appellation in 1936 are all still in existence: Ferme Blanche, Clos d'Albizzi, Fontcreuse and Fontblanche. The appellation allows for red, pink and white wine, but not everyone makes red wine. The reputation of Cassis today is based on a dry white wine with a typicity originating from its climate and proximity to the sea, rather than the specific *terroir*. The permitted grape varieties for the white wine are Ugni Blanc, Clairette, Marsanne, Doucillon (the local name for Bourboulenc) and Sauvignon. Red and pink can come from Grenache Noir, Cinsaut, Carignan and Mourvèdre; more people are planting Mourvèdre, which should do well as a result of the proximity to the sea. Carignan can be good if the vines are old and the yields low, but usually a red Cassis is based on Mourvèdre and Grenache Noir and a *rosé* on Cinsaut and Grenache Noir. Unusually for a Midi appellation, there is no Syrah.

Ugni Blanc used to be the basis of Cassis, but now constitutes only about twenty per cent of the vineyards. It provides a dry white wine with some welcome acidity but little character; its chief virtue is that it produces good yields with unfailing reliability, so that it is useful *pour faire la quantité*. Along with Doucillon it has been firmly relegated to the position of a secondary variety. In a desire for more refined flavours, there has been a shift of emphasis and indeed a change in the appellation regulations, so that from 2000 Marsanne and Clairette together must constitute a minimum of forty per cent of the blend, a proportion that by 2005 must have increased to sixty per cent, with a minimum of thirty per cent of Marsanne. Marsanne, which has been grown in Cassis for as long as people can remember, provides fruit, fragrance and character, compensating for the deficiencies of Ugni Blanc. Clairette has the disadvantage of suffering from *coulure* but complements Marsanne well. I was told that Sauvignon has alway been grown here and that most, but not all, producers have a little, as it adds character and bouquet to the wine. However, it too has the disadvantages of susceptibility to *coulure* and also ripens much earlier than the other varieties, so that its flavours can be burnt by the sunshine. A grape called Pascal Blanc was included in the original appellation decree, but that has virtually disappeared from the vineyards, as has Terret Blanc, which is restricted to just five per cent.

The Mistral can blow hard in Cassis, but the vineyards are protected from the more extreme winds by their relatively sheltered position. Most of the vines are pruned in the *gobelet* system, without wires and with wooden posts providing support. Some of the more recent plantings are on wires, however, making the vineyards much easier to cultivate, though the stems often break in the wind. The great advantage of the Mistral, and this applies throughout Provence, is the way it deters rot, for the drying winds keep the vines healthy and disease free. Cassis also enjoys some cooling sea breezes, which can temper any extremes of temperature and make for a longer ripening season than further inland. Sunshine is usually abundant, with an annual average of 3000 hours, and the rain, averaging 600 mm a year, usually comes in spring and early autumn. However, summer cloudbursts can be torrential. In 1997, 140 mm of rain fell in four or five hours on one day in the middle of August. The wine growers were worried that the damp might provoke rot, as the grapes were nearly ripe, so the vintage started a couple of weeks later.

The soil is poor and stony, a mixture of limestone and clay. Yields are low, limited to 40 hl/ha, with a minimum density of four thousand vines per hectare. The summer drought provides a limiting factor on excessive yields, as the grapes simply will not ripen, and a green harvest is sometimes carried out. Many of the vineyards are on terraces, most dramatically on the lower slopes of Cap

Canaille, where the vines look as though they are about to cascade into the sea. The terraces prevent the erosion that can be caused by the heavy rains.

DOMAINE CAILLOL

Production rests in the hands of several private producers, all of whom are firmly committed to their appellation and have played their part in the significant improvement in the quality of Cassis over the last decade or so. I asked François Caillol about changes in vinification methods. He is a jolly, ruddy-faced man with a rich Midi accent. '*Ooh la la, ça a changé énormément*' – progress has been enormous. Now each estate has an oenologist who follows their wines. Before, they had to do everything themselves and there was no way to cool the vats, so the wine lost its flavour. For other producers, pneumatic presses have also had a dramatic impact on quality. Caillol also remembered working with horses, before the advent of tractors in about 1953. He used to earn FF 25 a day going out to work with his horse, while his father tended the family vines. The horse was sold in 1954. He took over the estate in 1959 and put their first wine into bottle.

Caillol now has twelve hectares of Cassis, as well as three hectares for Vin de Pays des Bouches-du-Rhône, which are outside the appellation. His vineyard is planted with forty per cent Ugni Blanc, one-third Marsanne and some Clairette, but he makes two qualities of white wine, one with fifty per cent Marsanne, which was delicately flavoured, with hints of iodine and salt, and had firm acidity and a nutty, almondy, salty finish. His basic white, from equal parts of Clairette and Ugni Blanc, was leafy and slightly herbal; Caillol said that it was more typical of the Cassis *d'autrefois*. I liked them both in their different ways.

CLOS STE MAGDELEINE

The vineyards of Clos Ste Magdeleine nestle under the imposing Cap Canaille and the views from the courtyard are quite dramatic, even on a rather grey day. We were accompanied on our walk through the vineyard by Igloo, a friendly black Labrador, and

Salomé, a shrill and very vocal Siamese cat with a patchwork coat. The vineyards are so close to the sea that seals have been known to come out of the water and eat the grapes. François Sack has nine hectares altogether, from which he makes white and a little pink, but no red wine. The property comes from his wife's family, for her grandfather bought the land in 1920 and Sack arrived here in 1976.

His white wine consists of fifty per cent Marsanne, thirty per cent of both Clairette and Ugni Blanc and just a drop of Sauvignon, while his *rosé* is a blend of Grenache Noir, Cinsaut and Mourvèdre. The grapes ripen at different times, the Marsanne well before Ugni Blanc and Clairette, so a homogenous blend is made after the fermentations are finished. You can taste the influence of the sea in the wine, with hints of iodine and a certain saltiness, for the vineyards are sometimes shrouded in a gentle, salty sea mist; this accounts for the typicity of Cassis.

CLOS D'ALBIZZI

François Dumon's family at Clos d'Albizzi first arrived in Cassis in 1523. The Albizzis were Florentine bankers who fell from favour with the Medici rulers of the city and left, first for Marseille and then Cassis. The estate now consists of thirteen hectares of vines, mainly for white wine, planted with equal proportions of Clairette, Ugni Blanc and Marsanne. A little *rosé* is made from Cinsaut and Mourvèdre, and with the recent planting of some Grenache Noir a red wine is planned. For the last fifty years the estate has produced nothing but wine, but before that there was a bit of everything, olive trees and other fruit trees as well as vines.

Dumon explained his methods of vinification. Everything is hand picked, as a mechanical harvest would be impossible on such terrain. He uses a pneumatic press, which has made a great difference to quality as it gives much finer juice that is easier to clarify, and he does not destem first, as he aims to do as little as possible to the grapes. He fills the press by gravity and does not use a pump, to avoid crushing the stalks. He avoids skin contact, as that can be problematic with Marsanne, which is susceptible to rot because of its fragility. The juice is allowed to fall clear over night before racking, and fermentation starts with natural yeast. Cultured yeast is useless, according to Dumon. He ensures that the temperature is not too low, about 25°C, to achieve a fuller, more rounded wine; with too low a temperature, the wine can lack substance. The fermentation takes about three weeks. He keeps the top of the vat cool, as that helps to concentrate or recondense any escaping flavour. He also encourages the malolactic fermentation, and the wine spends a month on the fine lees after fermentation. The various vats are blended and the wine is lightly filtered and bottled as and when it is needed. And the results were delicious. Cassis should either be drunk when it is young and fresh or left for seven or eight years. This was demonstrated by the 1996, which had delicate, salty fruit, while the 1990 had developed rounded, rich, honeyed flavours and a suggestion of quince. The cooler maritime climate of Cassis accounts for the finer flavours, making wines that are usually much longer-lasting than many a white Côtes de Provence, which by contrast tend to fade or maderise.

DOMAINE PATERNEL

Another wonderful demonstration of the ageing potential of Cassis came from Jean-Pierre Santini at Domaine Paternel, where our tasting finished with the 1987, which I had first tasted as *bourrut*, or partially fermented juice, on my previous visit in October 1987. As mature wine, it had a delicate golden colour, with elegant herbal, nutty fruit. Santini is a chubby, friendly man with a smiling face and a bushy beard. He is Corsican by birth and his aunt first planted the vineyards here. 1951 was the first vintage, and since then the property has gradually expanded as his two sons, Jean-Christophe and Olivier, have joined him, so that they will soon have twenty-seven hectares in production. For white wine he has Marsanne, Clairette and Ugni Blanc as well as some Doucillon, but no longer any Sauvignon, as it needed supporting wires and ripened so much earlier that it caused logistical problems in the cellar. As well as white, he makes a little *rosé*, from Grenache Noir, Cinsaut, old Carignan and a drop of Mourvèdre.

The wine making methods are very straightforward . The 1996 had delicate, fragrant fruit, while the 1995 had a fuller, nuttier palate. Santini has experimented with different percentages of Marsanne, and in 1993 tried a pure Marsanne, which he liked a lot, so now he makes just two thousand bottles each year, sold from the cellar door and named Cuvée Victor et Hugo after his two grandsons who were both born that year. The 1993 Marsanne had a honeyed, leafy nose, a firm structure and quince and honey on the palate. It seemed flatter than the blend of four varieties, while the 1995 Marsanne was dry with firm fruit and quite closed. A *monocépage* is allowed in the appellation, as the regulations do not dictate a maximum percentage for Marsanne, but for the purists Cassis should be a blend.

MAS BOUDARD

One of the more unsophisticated estates is Mas Boudard, run by Pierre Marchand. His grandfather first planted vines in 1926, at a time when he also kept a herd of cows in stalls in the centre of the town. Marchand learnt about wine making from his father, for he trained as an accountant but started working here in 1987. He has six hectares in three different plots, from which he makes all three colours of wine in a simple cellar that is really no more than a couple of sheds. Marsanne is the main grape variety for his white wine, which also includes ten per cent Sauvignon and twenty-five per cent each of Clairette and Ugni Blanc. His red and pink wines are made from fifty per cent Mourvèdre, thirty per cent Grenache, a little Cinsaut and a drop of Carignan. The white was flat and nutty, and Marchand suggested that it lacked fruit; this was the first time that he had not stopped the malolactic fermentation and the flavour had suffered. The red was immediately appealing, ripe, fruity and *gouleyant*. Across the courtyard there is a small modern building housing a producer of goats' cheese, who keeps a herd of goats in the hills behind Cassis. The cheese complemented the white wine of Cassis perfectly.

DOMAINE LA FERME BLANCHE

Domaine la Ferme Blanche is a large estate of thirty-two hectares right at the entrance to the town, owned and run by the Paret family with their oenologist Philippe Garnier. We met François Paret and his daughter Jéromine. Part of their cellars date back to the end of the seventeenth century and there are still some enormous cement vats, each holding nearly four hundred hectolitres of wine. Since 1991 they have been gradually replacing the large *foudres* for red wine with *barriques*, for they find that about three to six months of oak ageing for the Mourvèdre softens its tannins. There is no obligatory *élevage* for red Cassis, nor any tradition, so it all depends on the tannin content and the wine grower's preference.

Their white Cassis is a blend of Marsanne, Clairette, Ugni Blanc, Sauvignon and Bourboulenc, which ferment together as they ripen. Usually they give the Marsanne some skin contact, provided the grapes are in good condition, and the wine undergoes a malolactic fermentation, which is usual for Cassis. They have experimented with blocking the malolactic fermentation, but now prefer it to take place. In accordance with the new regulations, they are planting more Marsanne and Clairette. Their 1996, with a high proportion of Marsanne, was full and rounded, with some backbone. Marsanne will give more structure to the wine and will also enable it to be kept longer, which François Paret sees as a future development. There is no strong tradition of a *vin de garde* in Provence, particularly for white wine, merely a few isolated examples, of which the most notable is Château Simone of Palette. In the tasting room there were old bottles from Vignobles Imbert – Imbert being Paret's mother's family name – including a Cassis Supérieure 1934 with the legend *authenticité garantie*.

DOMAINE DE FONTCREUSE

Jean-François Brando is the owner of Domaine de Fontcreuse and also president of the growers' *syndicat*. Whereas most of his fellow growers are men of the land, he is much more the businessman and was originally involved with a *négociant* business, as well as another property in the Côtes de Provence. The château dates back to 1687, apart from a tower that was added in the nineteenth century to make the building more imposing. It has been charmingly restored and elegantly furnished in the Provençal style of the eighteenth century. Much of the furniture is walnut from Haute Provence, with the painted wood that is traditional to Aix-en-Provence. At the end of the last century it was owned by a Colonel Teed, who chanced to stop at Cassis on his way home to England after service in India. Instead of returning home, he bought the property and planted vines. Virginia Woolf was a friend and the cottage where she stayed still stands in the middle of the vineyard. The next owner was Joseph Maffei, who served in the RAF during the war and came to Cassis in 1953 to take over the estate. It was he who sold the property to Jean-François Brando.

The cellars are the most modern of Cassis, with pristine, shining stainless steel vats and high-tech facilities for temperature control. A battery of tiny vats ranging from twelve to three hectolitres in size were described as the *cuves de la monnaie*, for the 'small change', or small lots of wine. Great care is taken to prevent any contact with air and the fermentation is slow and long, grape variety by grape variety. The final blend is usually about forty per cent Marsanne and thirty per cent each of Clairette and Ugni Blanc, which are put together in January and kept in vat over two winters. The wine is neither fined nor filtered, nor is there a malolactic fermentation or any skin contact. Brando described white Cassis as a *vin de bouche*. It is not aromatic and it should taste of the sea and develop some honey with age. You should find a balance between the acidity and the alcohol; if there is a malolactic fermentation, there is less acidity and then you become more aware of the alcohol.

Brando also makes some *rosé*, from one-third Cinsaut and two-thirds Grenache Noir, but no red wine. He is concerned about the rising demand for *rosé*. Each appellation has its reputation based on one colour, even if it makes the other, and 'white is our *couleur de notorieté*'. Certainly that is where the charm and originality of Cassis lies, with white wines that go so well with the local seafood, that are refreshingly unoaked, with a certain salty flavour from grapes that have been bathed by the sea mists.

Key facts

AC 1936, one of the earliest; red, white and pink, but reputation based on white; currently 180 hectares in production, entirely within the *commune* of Cassis; 40 hl/ha.

Grape varieties:

WHITE: Clairette and Marsanne, a minimum of forty per cent together, rising to sixty per cent by 2005, with thirty per cent minimum for Marsanne alone; also Ugni Blanc, Doucillon (the local name for Bourboulenc), Sauvignon.

RED: Grenache Noir, Cinsaut, Carignan and Mourvèdre, but no Syrah.

Limestone and clay soil.

Average annual rainfall 600 mm; average annual sunshine 3000 hours.

Vintages

Of less significance for white wines, but 1999 and 1998 were both very dry years, making quite full-bodied wines with a relatively high alcohol level. There was a very heavy rainstorm in August 1997, and fears of rot developing resulted in quite an early harvest, but nonetheless gave wines with good fruit and body.

Bandol

—

Bandol fully deserves its reputation as the leading red wine of Provence. Although the appellation also includes pink and white wine, and currently produces more pink than red, the best wines of the area are undoubtedly red. They are wines with stature and depth, with a potential for longevity that comes from the very successful expression of the Mourvèdre grape. Bandol is where the demanding Mourvèdre is at its very best – and yet fifty years ago the variety had almost disappeared from the vineyards there.

The wine takes its name from the port from which the production of the surrounding vineyards was shipped for some two hundred years. Today the port of Bandol is very much intended for pleasure, for the yachts of the wealthy who cruise the Mediterranean, and the broad bay is lined with cheerful restaurants offering copious plates of seafood, washed down with liberal quantities of Bandol *rosé*. The appellation covers the eight *communes* of Bandol itself: Sanary, La Cadière, Le Castellet, parts of Le Beauset, St Cyr-sur-Mer, Ollioules and Evenos. The area under vines is now fourteen hundred hectares and more vineyards could be planted, with the possibility of increasing the appellation by a further ten or even twenty per cent over the next twenty-five years. For the moment, about fifteen hectares of planting rights are granted each year, but in reality much of the land is more valuable for building and there is enormous pressure on it caused by the constant demand for holiday villas. Le Castellet and La Cadière are both old hilltop towns, dramatically perched on opposite peaks separated by the motorway. Le Castellet has retained some of its medieval charm and is home to several artists and craftsmen, while La Cadière has one of the appellation's better restaurants, the Hostellerie Bérard. The annual *fête du vin* or harvest festival takes place on the first Sunday in December, providing the local populace with an opportunity to taste the new wines.

Greeks from Phocaea first brought viticulture here when they founded their colony on the site of present-day Marseille around 600 BC. When the Romans arrived in 125 BC, they found the vineyards sufficiently well established for them to be able to send wine back to Italy. Roman amphorae have been found on the seabed between the Ile de Bendor and the coast of the mainland, indicating the existence of a lively export trade.

Archives illustrate the importance of viticulture in the Middle Ages, showing that in 1023 a certain Etienne gave vineyards at La Cadière to the monks of the nearby abbey of St Victor. Numerous documents from the fourteenth to the sixteenth century mention the sale and circulation of grapes and speak of vines and harvests. Until the harbour of Bandol was built in the eighteenth century, the barrels of wine were thrown into the sea to be taken on board by ships anchored off the coast. A local nobleman, M. de Boyer Bandol, wrote at the beginning of the seventeenth century that these wines kept well and even improved during long sea journeys. He had experience of this, for he exported them in large quantities to the Iles Françaises, as the French West Indies were called at the time. Louis XV favoured Bandol and was said to drink wine only from the Rouve district, which is within the village of Le Beausset and part of the present-day appellation.

The project of building a deep-water harbour at Bandol was first discussed in 1754 and finally concluded in 1765. This was to make a considerable difference to the reputation of the wine. During the Napoleonic Wars, when all shipping was escorted by convoys from Toulon, the town of Bandol obtained the privilege of marking barrels of its wine with the letter B in order to distinguish them from the other wines of the region. In the first half of the nineteenth century, Bandol was sent not only to Italy, northern Europe and America, but as far as India and Brazil. It was deemed to improve with a long sea voyage and could withstand the heat. During the last years of the Second Empire, the town of Bandol was a flourishing port with a thriving cooperage trade. Rendu, writing at the time, described Bandol as wine that was rich in colour, body and alcohol, coming from Beausset, La Cadière, Castellet and St Cyr, a total of eight *communes* about ten kilometres apart. The vines were grown on limestone slopes and Mourvèdre was almost the only grape variety. At first the wines were hard and coarse, but they improved with age and they could also withstand a sea voyage.

This prosperity vanished with the arrival of the phylloxera louse, which virtually destroyed the vineyards of Bandol in two short years between 1870 and 1872. Few had the heart to replant their vineyards, and those that did chose hybrid varieties, or possibly Grenache Noir, Carignan and Cinsaut. Bandol had to wait until the second half of the twentieth century for its renaissance. It was one of the earlier appellations, dating from 1941, but even then Mourvèdre only needed to account for a minimum of ten per cent in the red wine. Now, since 1986, fifty per cent is the absolute minimum, with the better wines containing much more, to the extent that some are even pure Mourvèdre. Then in 1989 the regulations were also modified to forbid the inclusion of vines under eight years old in the red wine; yields were limited to 40 hl/ha with no PLC, and the density of planting was increased to five thousand vines per hectare. In this context one vine provides one bottle of Bandol.

The story of the appellation of Bandol and of the vital part played by Lucien and Lucie Peyraud of Domaine Tempier is related in Richard Olney's *A Provençal Table*, and also in a small booklet, *Si Bandol AOC m'était conté*, by Lionel Heinic. Lucien Peyraud is seen by many as the father of the appellation of Bandol. He came from the industrial town of St Etienne in the department of the Loire and went to agricultural college in Aix-en-Provence. As he said, 'I liked this place so much that I stayed.' He met Lucie Tempier at Sanary in 1935 and married her the following year. Then in 1940 her father offered the young couple the family estate of Domaine Tempier, which at the time was producing more peaches than grapes, with vines that were Carignan for bulk wine rather than Mourvèdre for Bandol. However, moves were afoot, with a handful of like-minded estates, to raise the quality of Bandol.

André Roethlisberger, the Swiss proprietor of Château Milhière, played an important role in the creation in 1939 of the Syndicat des Anciens Vins de Bandol, with a group of some fifteen wine growers including the Comtesse Arlette de Portalis of Château Pradeaux, Bernard de Pissy of Chateau Frégate, Edouard Estienne of Château La Laidiere and Louis-François Férec of Domaine Lafran-Veyrolles. Lucien Peyraud was elected president of the wine growers' syndicat in 1945, a post he was to hold until his retirement in 1982. Sadly,

Château Milhière has since disappeared under tarmac and holiday villas, but the vineyards of the other supporters of the appellation still exist. They were the first to put their wine in bottle for the new appellation; the first bottling of Domaine Tempier was the 1942 vintage, just five thousand bottles of *rosé*, while their first red wine was not bottled until 1951.

Sadly, Lucien Peyraud died in 1996. I remember him from my very first visit to Bandol, when he took me on a bumpy ride in an elderly Citroën 2CV to see the vineyards. We went up a long dirt track to the viewpoint at Beausset-le-Vieux. There is an old chapel that has been restored by the villagers and the views across the valley to Mont de Ste Baume are breathtaking. The vineyards of Bandol seem to form an amphitheatre of terraces, locally called *restanques*, and indeed Bandol has been called 'the appellation of ten thousand terraces'. Some of them were actually built by the Phocaeans, but many were abandoned as the vineyards returned to scrub and woodland after the phylloxera crisis. They are, however, essential for preventing erosion on the steepest slopes. As well as vines, there are olive trees and some fruit trees, but little else will grow here.

The soil is very poor, a mixture of clay, limestone and sandstone with a stony, gravelly topsoil. The region is known to geologists for the Renversement du Beausset, a formation in which the geological layers have somersaulted, so that the older rocks lie above the later ones. The sand in the soil proves useful for retaining some water during the summer months of minimal rainfall.

The Mistral can blow hard here, even on an otherwise fine summer's day, but it provides one enormous advantage, a wonderful natural treatment against rot and any other problems caused by humidity. The growers consider it to be their best friend. The sea breezes can also bring humidity and dew, so while the Mourvèdre likes water as well as warmth, it obtains sufficient humidity from the proximity to the sea, even if there is no rain for months. The climate is generally very favourable to viticulture, for there are long hours of sunshine. Sea breezes also temper the heat of the day, while at night cooler air from the mountains helps to offset the daytime temperatures. Normally there is little rain, rarely more than 600 mm a year, but the south east wind coming from sea does bring rain, and when that happens a torrent of water can fall out of the sky.

Even though the appellation began with just ten per cent of Mourvèdre, it is indisputably Mourvèdre that gives red Bandol its intrinsic character. This is where Mourvèdre is at its very best. The grape probably originates from Spain, where it is called Monastrell, taking its name from Murviedro in the province of Valencia, and features in wines like Jumilla, Alicante and Almansa. In Australia it is called Mataro and is now being taken more seriously, while in California it is enjoying a resurgence of fashion in the hands of the so-called Rhône Rangers. As one of the *cépages améliorateurs* of the south of France, it appears in numerous appellations between Banyuls and Bellet, but it is really in Bandol that it comes into its own, though only in recent years.

Mourvèdre disappeared from Bandol after phylloxera, as it proved very difficult to graft on to American rootstock. It is a temperamental variety, really quite pernickety about its vineyard conditions. It wants its head in the sun and its roots in the damp, in cool soil. It likes to see the sea, for it enjoys the marine breezes, but it also demands hot Provençal sunshine and likes the clay soil that retains humidity. Its bud break comes late, making it a late ripener. The vintage in Bandol begins in late September, and Mourvèdre is always the last grape variety to be picked, often not until well into October. Under the dry conditions produced by the Mistral, it rarely suffers from rot, especially with its tough, thick-skinned berries.

It is difficult to control the yield with Mourvèdre, especially from young vines, and for this reason a vine has to be eight years old to contribute to red Bandol. Until it is a well-established, mature vine that is fifteen years old, it tends to lack balance, producing either too much or too little. In *rosé* wine, Mourvèdre not only provides structure but also has an anti-oxidant effect, making wines that will keep rather than fading after just one summer. Young vines often need a green harvest and some clonal selection has encouraged better yields, although some growers, such as Mme Jouve at Domaine Lafron-Veyrolle, prefer to replant using cuttings from their own vines. She explained that although the original vines of Mourvèdre may have been less resistant to disease, the berries were small and concentrated in flavour, unlike those from clonal selection. The Bunan family at Mas de la Rouvière are also conducting experiments with a dozen different clones, comparing their various characteristics and looking in particular for low yields and small berries. Neither Mourvèdre nor Grenache Noir likes to be trained on wires, so most are planted as bush vines, or *gobelet*, but there are also some experiments with *cordon royat*.

Pink Bandol comes from the same three grape varieties as red Bandol, namely Mourvèdre, Grenache Noir and Cinsaut. As the Mourvèdre for the red wine must come from vines with a minimum age of eight years, most Bandol *rosé* contains a high proportion of Mourvèdre. Although the appellation of Bandol firmly bases its reputation on red wine, the greater part of the production is in fact *rosé*. In 1998 it represented sixty per cent of the production, as opposed to thirty-five per cent of red wine, partly because so many recent plantings are not yet eligible for red wine. White Bandol, which usually accounts for between five and eight per cent of the appellation, is based on Clairette and Ugni Blanc and perhaps some Bourboulenc and Sauvignon.

DOMAINE TEMPIER, LE PLAN-DU-CASTELLET

Domaine Tempier is now run by Lucien Peyraud's two sons, François and Jean-Marie. We tasted in the cellars with Jean-Marie and his wife Catherine, for this is very much a family concern where everyone plays their part. Domaine Tempier now consists of thirty hectares of vines, including three specific vineyards, La Tourtine, Migoua and Cabassaou. In addition they make what they call a Cuvée Spéciale and a Cuvée Classique as well as some *rosé* and a tiny drop of white wine. Jean-Marie Peyraud explained how three things are absolutely forbidden in Bandol: irrigation, which is rarely allowed in a French appellation vineyard; chaptalisation – and he mentioned as an aside that in Châteauneuf-du-Pape, you may ask for permission to chaptalise, whereas in Bandol you are not even allowed to ask; and mechanical harvesting, which is any case would be totally impossible in vineyards planted on such narrow terraces.

Peyraud likened the vineyards of Bandol to *une petite Bourgogne*, for you have the same diversity of microclimate and soil, and he cited the example of other estates. At la Bastide Blanche the soil is white, whereas at Terrebrune it is indeed red. The soil in his vineyard of La Tourtine is a hundred million years old, whereas at Migoua it is two hundred million years old, which is all to do with the Renversement du Beausset. Peyraud makes his wines as naturally and simply as possible. They do not use artificial fertiliser, for if you add fertiliser to the soil you change its character, and he seeks to retain the individuality of each vineyard. The red grapes are destemmed to avoid any harsh tannins from the stalks, for he wants the noble tannins that come from the pips and skins. The length of the *cuvaison* depends upon the vintage. For the Cuvée Classique it might be ten days, and as long as three weeks for La Tourtine, all in stainless steel vats.

Their *cave d'élevage* is below ground, for the appellation regulations for Bandol demand a minium of eighteen months ageing in wood, traditionally in large *foudres*, which provide oxygenation for the Mourvèdre rather than any wood tannins. However, Cabassaou is given just a little *élevage* in small barrels. In 1995 they tried out *barriques* for the first time, and in 1996 they used *demi-muids* of five hundred litres for just one-sixth of the wine, as an experiment to see whether the oak influence would affect the typicity of the wine, but they are certainly not looking for a taste of new oak.

The distinction between the different wines has evolved gradually. Up to 1967 they simply made a Cuvée Classique, blending everything together. Then, in the difficult vintage of 1968 they had one *foudre* that was much better than the others, so they bottled it separately as a Cuvée Spéciale. Now it comes from a vineyard of Mourvèdre close to their cellar, where the soil is alluvial and clay, packed with tiny stones, blended with some Grenache Noir from the Mijoua vineyard. Then in 1979 they separated Mijoua and La Tourtine, as they seemed quite different from the other wines, and finally in 1987 they made Cabassaou, which comes from forty-year-old Mourvèdre vines planted on steep terraces in the lower part of the Tourtine vineyard. Peyraud described Mijoua as the warmest *cuvée*, for it only has fifty-five per cent Mourvèdre, with more Cinsaut than Grenache Noir. In the 1996 the fruit was warm and spicy, with firm tannins, hints of cedarwood, *garrigue* and red fruit. In contrast, La Tourtine was more substantial, powerful and solid, but with harmonious tannins, while in Cabassaou you could detect the effect of the small barrels and newer oak, with just a hint of vanilla. The structure of the wine was not the same, with less elegance and a different style of fruit. It was quite intriguing, but somehow not true Bandol.

Over the years the proportion of Mourvèdre in the Cuvée Classique has increased. Originally it was fifty per cent, but became seventy per cent in 1992 and finally eighty per cent in 1995. The 1995 had quite a cedary nose, with the characteristically meaty character, what the French called *viandé*, that Mourvèdre in Bandol takes on as it begins to age. The Cuvée Spéciale was undoubtedly more complex, with finesse, elegance and length. It would benefit from more bottle age, but nonetheless was drinking deliciously when it was only three years old. Best of all was the 1989 La Tourtine, with wonderful mature notes on the nose, hints of *sous bois*, or more prosaically in English, undergrowth, as well as truffles, ripe red fruit and layers of flavours, showing just how much fine Bandol benefits from bottle age.

Domaine Tempier has produced white wine since 1988, initially from Clairette and Ugni Blanc, with the addition of some Bourboulenc in 1996. Their *rosé* blend is half Mourvèdre with equal parts of Cinsaut and Grenache Noir, which are given a night of skin contact, resulting in a pretty rose-petal colour, with ripe, rounded fruit, conjuring up summer days in Provence. *Rosé* has enjoyed the favour of fashion over the last few years, but it can also have a beneficial effect on a grower's cash flow, alleviating some of the consequences of tying up stock in the cellar for eighteen months. Domaine Tempier has remained the benchmark of the appellation. It was a friendly visit, with Jean-Marie Peyraud taking the time to talk while engaged in work in the cellar, insisting on their philosophy that wine is to be shared.

CHATEAU PRADEAUX, ST CYR-SUR-MER

Château Pradeaux was another key estate in the creation of the appellation of Bandol, at a time when it was owned by the *grande dame* of the appellation, the Comtesse Arlette de Portalis. I met her in 1987 when she was a frail old lady with an air of eccentricity. She received us in her bedroom, with the words 'What can I tell you, my dears?' We encouraged her to reminisce and she talked about the old days, explaining that Mourvèdre was the only grape variety before phylloxera, but that the Provençaux were lazy and preferred to plant the easier Aramon and Carignan; however, even as a *vin de table* Bandol had a good reputation.

Today the estate is run by her nephew Cyrille de Portalis, who learnt his wine making at Beaune and Montpellier, followed by practical experience in the Médoc, the Loire valley and California. He is the eighth generation at the estate, which was created in 1750. An earlier Portalis had been one of Napoleon's ministers, and had a hand in the creation of the Code Civile. There used to be olive trees here too, but they suffered in the severe frosts of 1929 and 1956. Now they have twenty hectares of vines, including two in the appellation of Côtes de Provence, where the soil is sandier and therefore too rich for Bandol. The yields are accordingly different. Bandol allows for 40 hl/ha, although they rarely obtain more than about 30 hl/ha, whereas 55 hl/ha is the maximum for Côtes de Provence, but again that is rare. Mourvèdre is no good if it is allowed to overproduce. They make two qualities of red Bandol, L'Enclos des Pradeaux, from vines between eight and fifteen years old, and Château Pradeaux from the older vines, for it takes about fifteen years to obtain really good-quality grapes from the vines.

The two red wines are made in much the same way, the main difference being that L'Enclos is given two years of ageing in *foudres*, as opposed to four for Château Pradeaux. In lighter years such as 1986, it may be only three, and for more powerful vintages like 1985, as much as five years. For de Portalis, *barriques* are most certainly not suitable for Bandol; that would be a catastrophe. The *foudres*, old German beer barrels, soften the tannins with some gentle oxidation, and they are topped up every three or four weeks, for there is as much as three per cent evaporation each year. The wines have a high percentage of Mourvèdre, with some Grenache Noir and Cinsaut. These are very much seen as *vins de garde*. I have always found Pradeaux to have a very firm tannic backbone, for the grapes are not destalked and so perhaps the stems add extra astringency, but sometimes the flavours seems a little harsh, with the tannin jarring amongst the fruit. Older vintages have tasted rather dry, almost as though they have lost their fruit before the tannins softened.

Pradeaux does not produce any white wine, for the soil is not suitable, but like all Bandol estates they do make some *rosé*. De Portalis observed how fashionable *rosé* has become. Twenty years ago the appellation of Bandol was two-thirds red to one-third *rosé*, while today it is nearer the opposite, but at Pradeaux *rosé* accounts for just twenty per cent of their production. Their *rosé* has a high proportion of Cinsaut, as too much Mourvèdre makes the wine too heavy, while Grenache Noir renders it too alcoholic. The 1996 vintage was ripe and rounded, with a flavour of strawberries.

DOMAINE LAFRAN-VEYROLLES, LA CADIERE-D'AZUR

Mme Claude Jouve-Férec at Domaine Lafran-Veyrolles is a charming lady of a certain age, as the French so politely say. Her father was another of the creators of the appellation in the 1940s and had been a teacher as well as an artist. There are some of his paintings, including attractive views of the vineyards, in the tasting room, as well old pieces of equipment, including a rather antiquated *fouloir* and a minute press that M. Férec used to see if the grapes were ready to pick. Since her father's death, Mme Jouve has been responsible for the wine making at Lafran-Veyrolles with the help of her oenologist, who confirms what to do, though she said she essentially worked *au feeling*. She explained proudly that although her father had died just the day before the vintage began in 1965, she had none the less won a prize at Mâcon for her wine that year. Her husband runs another property, Château Rochebelle, near la Cadière, where the vines are on the valley floor and so produce Côtes de Provence and *vin de pays*, rather than Bandol. At Lafran-Veyrolles she has ten hectares.

There is a neat little cellar, with stainless steel tanks and *foudres*. A high proportion of the grapes are destalked, as the stalks can absorb too much colour if the juice is in contact with them for too long. However, they aid the extraction of flavours and also make *remontage* easier, as they create what could be called a drainage system. Mme Jouve's wines have a very high proportion of Mourvèdre. 'That is our originality,' she said. She remembered that at the beginning no one had really believed in Mourvèdre, with a few exceptions, and it was really only in the mid-1950s that the variety had taken off. As well as a small amount of white and *rosé*, she makes two qualities of red. There is a Cuvée Tradition, with seventy per cent Mourvèdre, some Grenache Noir and Cinsaut and just ·a drop of Carignan from fifty-year-old vines. Generally she considers Grenache Noir to be rather vulgar, but a tiny amount can add something to the wine. The Cuvée Spéciale, which is usually pure Mourvèdre, with its powerful tannins, is intended for even longer ageing. The 1993 had great concentration, but there was also an underlying elegance.

DOMAINE LA LAIDIERE, STE-ANNE-D'EVENOS

The Estienne family has been at Domaine la Laidière for several generations. Today it is the friendly Freddy Estienne who makes the wine, but his father and grandfather were also among those who supported the creation of the appellation in 1941. At that time they had just two and a half hectares of vines, but the estate has since been gradually extended, including the purchase of seven hectares of terraced hillside just behind the cellars, which have been replanted with two rows of vines per terrace. They now have twenty-four hectares of vines. In 1941 they made just six hundred litres of Bandol, but today by contrast their average production is eight hundred and fifty hectolitres.

Domaine La Laidière has a justified reputation for its white wine. Although it comes from two seemingly unexciting grape varieties, Clairette and Ugni Blanc, it has a fresh, pithy flavour, with good acidity. The vinification is quite simple, with both varieties fermenting together; there is no wood, no skin contact and no malolactic fermentation. It is not meant to age, but with just a year's development in bottle had become full and nutty, with a delicate dry finish. The *rosé* is half Mourvèdre, which gives structure and makes the wine a little longer lasting, with equal parts of Cinsaut, which provides elegance, and Grenache Noir for body. Bandol *rosé* is not what the French call a *vin de soif*, to quench your thirst, for it needs food and must have body as well as finesse.

There are two red wines, a Cuvée Tradition and in the best years a Cuvée Spéciale, with eighty per cent Mourvèdre, as well as some Grenache Noir and Cinsaut. Even though the appellation dictates a minimum of 11.5°, for really ripe Mourvèdre you need a minimum of 13° or even better 13.5°. Some of the earlier vintages of the 1990s were difficult, with rain at harvest time, while in contrast 1997 produced wonderfully concentrated wines. We tasted the 1995 Cuvée Tradition, with its slightly meaty berry flavours and some elegance. The 1993 Cuvée Spéciale was rounded and meaty, both solid and supple at the same time. Finally the 1982 Carte Noire, the previous name of the Cuvée Spéciale, was very elegant, balanced and long, with hints of old leather and tar.

DOMAINE FREGATE, BANDOL

Domaine Frégate is another of the old estates of Bandol, owned by the de Pissy family and run by a son-in-law, the genial Sebastian Thiollier. He explained that the estate is the lowest in altitude of the appellation, the closest to the sea and the only vineyard within the *commune* of Bandol itself. There are twenty-two hectares of vines, now attached to a golf course and conference centre. Commercial demands have made this more than just a wine estate, with an inevitable impact on the style of the wines. Thiollier said that their reds are less powerful, owing to the proximity to the sea, and that their aim is a wine for medium rather than long-term keeping. The grapes are destalked and they make two *cuvées*, what they call the *cuvée cave* with a high proportion of Mourvèdre, and the *cuvée restaurant*, with forty per cent of Grenache Noir. As well as *foudres*, they have had some *barriques* since 1991, *pour s'amuser*. The 1993, of which twenty per cent was aged in *barriques*, still had quite a strong vanilla bouquet, with some cedary pencil shavings on the palate. It was well made, but somehow not quite Bandol. The 1994, aged in *foudres* alone, was fruity and accessible with sufficient tannin, but no great depth of flavour.

CHATEAU DE PIBARNON, LA CADIERE-D'AZUR

As well as the old estates, there have been many newcomers to the appellation over the last twenty years or so. Some arrived here more by accident than design, such as the Comte Henri de St Victor at the Château de Pibarnon. He said that back in 1973 he hardly knew of the existence of Bandol. When he took the train to Nice he was vaguely aware of the loudspeaker calling *Bandol, deux minutes d'arrêt*, but no more. Then a few years later, when he was looking for a wine estate to buy, he did stop in Bandol. He had a lousy meal but the wine was wonderful, so the moral of the story is 'Beware of what you drink in restaurants – that's what led me here.'

After some searching he bought the Château de Pibarnon, which at three hundred metres is the highest estate of the appellation. You approach it along a series of dirt tracks from La Cadière, and on a fine day you can see La Ciotat and the coast. The estate was very run down, with five hectares of vines and some pigs. So from being a patent agent, M de St Victor turned wine grower.

His enthusiasm for Mourvèdre and Bandol is infectious, and his conversation wonderfully opinionated and stimulating. In contrast, his son Eric, who also works on the estate, is rather shy. They now have forty-eight hectares, half of them rented, all around the cellar. There is a multitude of different aspects and microclimates, so the grapes do not all ripen at once. The soil here, from the Triassic period, gives very tannic wines, but they are what the French describe as *tannins fondus*, or melted tannins. One vineyard includes what the geologists calls *marnes bleues*, or blue marl, which is particularly prized. The soil is blue when uncovered, but turns red once it is exposed to air.

Everything is done to obtain the maximum amount of concentration in the wines. The wine is left on the skins after fermentation for more extraction, and since 1982 they have experimented with *barriques*. The 1996, from barrel, was redolent of vanilla, while the 1993 had softened. The count said that it had not yet digested its oak, and the structure was certainly quite different from a wine aged in *foudres*. He considers that the wines of Pibarnon need at least six years to evolve some mature *arômes tertiaires*. Certainly the 1990, drunk in the autumn of 1997, had some attractive meaty, gamey notes. The *rosé*, from equal parts of Mourvèdre and Cinsaut, tasted of ripe strawberries, and the white, from Clairette and Bourboulenc with a little experimental Viognier and Roussanne, had some appealing fruit.

MOULIN DES COSTES AND MAS DE LA ROUVIERE, LA CADIERE-D'AZUR

The independence of Algeria bought an influx of newcomers into the area. The Bunan family, owners of Moulin des Costes and Mas de la Rouvière, originally had vineyards in Algeria. They bought their first estate in Bandol in 1962 and the second seven years later. Altogether they have eighty hectares of vines and are one of the most experimental estates of the area, making *vin de pays* as well as Bandol. The cellars had grown considerably since my previous visit, with new equipment, stainless steel galore and a Bucher press, and also what they call *la monnaie*, a room with smaller tanks of twenty hectolitres and less for experiments and leftovers, as well as a large *salle de vieillissement*, an attractive hall with two rows of *foudres*.

We were shown round by Laurent Bunan, who is responsible for the commercial side of things, but also helps his father Paul with the blending. He explained how at the beginning people never thought that pure Mourvèdre would be feasible, but now their best wine, labelled Château de la Rouvière, comes solely from a four-hectare vineyard of Mourvèdre at Le Castellet. These are their oldest vines, fifty years old or more, planted on south-facing terraces. Moulin des Costes includes five per cent of Syrah, which is unusual in Bandol. They like Syrah for its depth of colour and fruit, and Laurent compared it to the pepper on the steak.

In 1997 they began the harvest on 13 August with Sauvignon, but were not quite the first in the Midi, for someone in Frontignan had started the previous day. Sauvignon has always existed in the appellation, but can pose problems by being so precocious and therefore many people have pulled it up. The Bunans are also experimenting with Marsanne, which they have grafted on to older vines and are using for the local Vin de Pays du Mont Caume, for which they also have some Cabernet Sauvignon. Their Bandol tends towards the lighter, more accessible style, with less obvious tannins from destemmed grapes, but are none the worse for that, making for wines with instant appeal and more immediate fruit.

LA ROQUE, LA CADIÈRE-D'AZUR

Most appellations in the south of France could not function without a co-operative, and Bandol is no exception. In fact, a small vineyard holder has a choice of five different co-operatives, including that of La Roque, which is the only one to deal exclusively with Bandol. It was not created until 1950, significantly later than most, and purely as an ageing cellar, but is now responsible for the entire vinification process. The director, Olivier Maquard, is friendly and enthusiastic about his appellation. For him, Bandol means wood, Mourvèdre and *terroir*. He explained how they have been working to identify the different geological characteristics amongst their vineyards, so that they will eventually produce four red wines illustrating those differences, as well as wines of different qualities. For the moment the bulk of their production is *rosé*, involving fewer differences in *terroir*, and they also make a small amount of white wine. Several of their members have less than a hectare of vines, for there are a hundred and eighty members with two hundred and twenty hectares between them, so that twenty per cent of the membership, with their larger vineyard holdings of between seven and fifteen hectares, accounts for eighty per cent of the production.

The co-operative's cellars are well equipped. A pneumatic press, a recent investment, has improved the quality of both the white and the *rosé* wines, allowing them to give their white wines skin contact without any fear of oxidation and their *rosés* a gentle maceration. They make their *rosés* by *saignée*, even though *pressurage* is the traditional method of Bandol. Each grape variety is vinified separately as it is picked, first Grenache Noir, then Cinsaut and Carignan, and finally Mourvèdre. Their white wine is mainly Clairette with some Ugni Blanc, and since 1985 they have had a little Sauvignon. Although the appellation regulations decree a minimum of eighteen months ageing in wood, they do not specify the size of wood. Mostly the co-operative has fifty-hectolitre *foudres*, which they keep for fifteen or twenty years, as well as a few very large 100–120 hectolitre barrels, but these are essentially containers and do not really contribute anything to the *élevage*. They are also working with a few *barriques* and five hundred-litre *demi-muids*, to see if new wood adds anything to the wine.

The Grande Réserve white, a blend of Clairette and Sauvignon, is fermented in new barrels and given regular *bâtonnage* until bottling the following spring. The first, experimental vintage of 1996 certainly tasted of oak, but the vanilla flavours were attractive rather than coarse. The Cuvée Grande Sélection *rosé* also includes ten per cent of barrel-aged wine, which adds a little more structure compared with their Cuvée Sélection. The grapes for their red wines are now all destalked, which makes for more supple flavours. The 1993 Cuvée Grand Sélection, from Mourvèdre with just a token bunch of Grenache Noir – for in theory Bandol should include two grape varieties – includes ten per cent of wine aged for two years in *barriques*, while the rest is kept in *foudres*. It had an attractive cedary note, more reminiscent of *barriques* than *foudres*, with some tannin and an elegant finish. I was left with a feeling that this was a co-operative that was working well for its appellation and staying abreast of new trends.

DOMAINE LA SUFFRENE, LA CADIERE-D'AZUR

Domaine la Suffrène is a new producer. The vineyards belong to Simone Gravier's father and until the 1995 vintage the grapes were delivered to the co-operative. Then when her son Cédric finished his oenology studies, they decided to build a cellar, or more precisely, a modern efficient shed, and vinify their thirty hectares of Bandol themselves. The twelve hectares of *vin de pays*, of old Carignan on low-lying land, still go to the co-operative. Cédric said he would have found it frustrating not to be able to make his own wine, and he thought that the co-operative was much better for people with very small vineyard holdings. As a young wine maker, you can obtain some advantageous loans and subsidies, provided you are prepared to fill in all the necessary forms and cope with an obstacle course of bureaucratic hassle. One essential investment is the wood. A new *foudre* costs around FF 50–60,000, or often the price is quoted by the hectolitre, at FF 15–1800 per hectolitre, while second-hand *foudres* cost about FF 280–300 per hectolitre. You can find these, but you need to be confident about your source. Young Cédric has wisely bought from Domaine Tempier.

We tasted his first *rosé*, half from Mourvèdre with equal parts of Grenache Noir and Cinsaut, which had delicate fruit and good structure. The red 1996, tasted from *foudre*, with fifty-five per cent Mourvèdre, twenty per cent each of Grenache Noir and Cinsaut and just five per cent of Carignan, promised well, with ripe blackberry fruit, some spicy flavours and good structure. A second 1996, from eighty-five per cent Mourvèdre, some of which was planted in 1942, and fifteen per cent Carignan, including vines planted back in 1903, was firm and peppery with some hints of liquorice, again showing potential.

Madame Gravier is president of the Syndicat des Vins de Bandol and is also involved with the Association 50 ans d'AOC Provençales, which unites the four appellations of Provence that are over fifty years old, namely Bandol, Palette, Cassis and Bellet. She combines competence and businesslike efficiency with French charm, seeing her role as ensuring that the producers respect the appellation decree and care for its future evolution. It is very important for a small appellation to maintain its typicity and defend its reputation. The *terroir* is very particular and the climate very localised. Although efforts are being made to develop the red wine, there is still an enormous amount of *rosé* in the appellation. It all depends on the quality of the vintage and also on economic factors. However, Mourvèdre gives the *rosé* of Bandol a certain individuality and structure, making what she called a *rosé de bouche*, not a *rosé de nez*.

CHATEAU STE ANNE, STE-ANNE D'EVENOS

Château Ste Anne outside the village of Ste-Anne d'Evenos has been the property of the Dutheil de la Rochère family for five generations. They were military people and, as such, the absentee owners of a farm producing not only wine but flowers and vegetables too. The current generation took over and bottled their first wine in 1960. Gradually things have changed. Originally there was a lot of Carignan as well as Aramon in the vineyards, but no Mourvèdre. The replanting took about ten years, and they now have eighteen hectares in production, on the hillside behind the château and on the other side of the valley. The two vineyards have quite different soil structures. The land opposite is drier with more limestone, making for more concentrated wine, while that behind the château is also limestone, but drains better and has more sand, which gives some finesse. The two are blended together. You approach the château, which was built in 1840, along an alley of lime trees; the vineyards on either side, on flatter land classified as Côtes de Provence, here again could be worth even more as building land. There is great pressure to convert agricultural land into building land, although fortunately the pine forests are protected. Sometimes vineyards have to be sold to pay inheritance taxes and most of the construction is for unattractive holiday villas for northern Europeans.

At Château Ste Anne the Marquis François Dutheil de la Rochère follows strictly organic methods. In the vineyard the wind usually keeps everything dry and free of rot, though some plots are less aerated than others. Cinsaut is thin-skinned and particularly prone to rot, so that storms at the end of August can cause problems, necessitating treatment with Bordeaux mixture. Their pink wine could age for a year or two, for they look for length and body, not just fruity acidity. Grenache Noir and Cinsaut are the main varieties. The Cinsaut, with its large, juicy berries, gives richness, and they add a little Mourvèdre from young vines – but not too much, or else the wine will have too much character for a *rosé*.

They make two qualities of red wine. The Tradition, from fifty-five per cent Mourvèdre and equal parts of Grenache Noir and Cinsaut, spends eighteen months in *foudres*. All the grapes are destalked and given a ten to twelve-day *cuvaison*, resulting in some structured, peppery fruit, with an underlying elegance. Some *terroirs* give more concentration, but they do not want too much extraction and seek elegance in their wines. The Cuvée Collection, which is essentially pure Mourvèdre, give or take a bunch or two of Grenache Noir, is a fine balance of tannin and peppery fruit, with an elegant finish. They rack as little as possible during the *élevage* and the wines are not filtered. The 1992 Cuvée Collection had developed some of the smoky, meaty flavours characteristic of maturing Mourvèdre, while the 1989 was a wonderfully harmonious wine, which amply demonstrated the ageing ability of fine Bandol.

CHATEAU VANNIERES, LA CADIERE-D'AZUR

Château Vannières is one of the most attractive properties of the appellation. It is owned by the Boisseaux family, who used to have vineyards on the Côte de Beaune, but since 1990 Eric Boisseaux has settled in Bandol. The estate had its origins in the sixteenth century, with André de Lombard, Seigneur du Castellet. The present château was built by a Scotsman in about 1850 and then belonged to the family of the French minister Bénazet, whose heirs sold the estate to Eric Boisseaux's grandfather in 1957. The original vaulted cellar is now used as a tasting room; there are delightful gardens and a three hundred-year old pine tree in the courtyard. You enter the cellars from a magnificent sixteenth-century staircase.

There are thirty-two hectares of vines, with an average age of thirty years, all in one large plot, which is quite unusual for Bandol. Boisseaux concentrates on red wine and offers a range of older vintages. Not all the Mourvèdre is destalked and the *cuvaison* takes about twenty days, with a daily *pigeage* in open-top cement vats. Usually his wines spend about three years in *foudres*, but he is also trying out some *barriques*. The 1994, from ninety per cent Mourvèdre with some Grenache Noir, had tannin and structure, while the 1989 was quite dry and meaty, with a long finish, and the 1985 was again quite firm with some backbone. The wines were sound but for some reason did not really excite.

DOMAINE DE L'OLIVETTE, LE CASTELLET

Domaine de l'Olivette is an estate that has undergone quite a dramatic transformation in the last twenty years. The owners are an elderly couple who now live in Paris, and when his rental agreement expired in 1980 M. Dumoutier had a choice, to rent again or to run the estate himself. He decided on the second option and put a keen young manager, Yves Perga, in charge. In 1980 there were just three hectares of vines for Bandol, while the rest were hybrids. By 1988 they had replanted fifteen and now have twenty-two hectares, as well as renting another thirty-three. Perga explained that there is plenty of opportunity to rent vines from people who want to retain their land but are not interested in cultivating it themselves.

The most striking feature of the estate is a charming old dovecot, while by contrast the cellars are very functional. Perga vinifies each plot separately, which in 1997 meant twenty-five different vats of *rosé*, as well as fourteen vats of red, from vineyards all over the appellation. The variety makes for complexity and he produces four different wines, including Château de Sylvabelle and Domaine de Colombier as brand names for different customers, as well as Clos des Oliviers, a part of the estate that is kept separate. He also conducts experiments for the *syndicat* as part of their technical commission. At the moment they are working on Mourvèdre for *rosé*, with various experiments in *pressurage*, *saigné* and *maceration à froid*. They are also looking at the effects of the malolactic fermentation, blocking it in some instances, so that they can advise the growers on what to avoid and provide some general guidelines.

Perga favours post-fermentation maceration, but said that you had to taste the wine daily, as certain components will return into the skins if the wine is left in contact with them for too long. Done well, it rounds out the wine. In a year like 1993 the fermentation took between eight and fifteen days, but the juice stayed with the skins for a total of a month. It had some attractive spicy fruit, but was still very youthful. 1988 was the first vintage when, he said modestly, he did as he was told, and it won a gold medal at Mâcon. The wine was quite delicate, lightly meaty with a dry finish.

He explained how a *rosé* will evolve. In the wine for early drinking there is a higher proportion of Cinsaut and Grenache Noir, for the Grenache Noir has the most aroma in a young wine and is more flattering. In contrast, Mourvèdre needs more time and does not open out until the following summer, so wines later for later drinking will have a higher proportion of Mourvèdre, resulting in more structure and complexity. Their white Bandol, made for early drinking, is based on Clairette, with just five per cent of Sauvignon; any more and the Sauvignon takes over. Nor must the Clairette be too ripe, or else the wine becomes too alcoholic and fat. It grows in quite humid, deep soil, where it ripens slowly, making a wine that was honeyed and leafy, with acidity on the finish.

DOMAINE DES SALETTES, LA CADIERE-D'AZUR

Domaine des Salettes has belonged to the Ricard family for sixteen generations. The present incumbent is Madame Sabine Ricard, whose ex-husband Jean-Pierre Boyer makes the wine. His arrival on the property prompted their first bottling of Bandol in 1966. Before that, the wine had been sold in bulk to local merchants, and the earlier owners had been very much absentee landlords, of a farm that produced wheat and (until the great frost of 1956) oil, and also had flocks of sheep. They now have twenty-three hectares of Bandol in production, as well as some Vin de Pays du Mont Caume. Mme Ricard took us to see the vineyards, which have red, stony soil and several *restanques*, the retaining walls or terraces that prevent erosion. Wild boar and rabbits can be a problem. They found the remains of a Roman villa when they were replanting the vines.

M. Boyer showed us his cellar, which was built in 1984. He is very earnest, informative and opinionated – although the two dogs Estelle and Stephan introduced a note of frivolity into our visit. Boyer described the cellar as his mistress, for it demands so much of his time. However, it is also well organised and efficient, operating by gravity. Their white Bandol is made from Clairette, Ugni Blanc and Bourboulenc, while they have been experimenting with some more flavoursome grape varieties, such as Marsanne, Viognier and Rolle. Boyer considers Viognier to have too much character and flavour. Nor is he impressed by Marsanne, but he thought that Rolle could give some good results; for the moment, however, there is unlikely to be any modification to the appellation. I liked his white wine: the 1996 was lightly perfumed, with a hint of apricots, and the 1993 more leafy and herbal in flavour. As at Domaine de l'Olivette, the blend for the *rosé* varies during the year, with an increasing amount of Mourvèdre, up to as much as sixty per cent by the end of the season, making more of a food wine than a light aperitif.

The red wines at Domaine des Salettes have a supple elegance. The grapes are destalked and the wines aged for a couple of years in *foudres*, formerly Austrian beer barrels. The 1995 was peppery with red fruit and liquorice, while the 1990 was more full-bodied and meaty in character We also tried a 1986, an experimental pure Mourvèdre that had spent three months in *barriques*. Theoretically it is not Bandol, for you need two grape varieties for the appellation, nor did it taste of Bandol, with cedary oak, some fruit and a firm tannic finish.

Over the years Boyer has been very concerned about the development of Bandol and was involved with one of the two growers' *syndicats*. Happily these are now reunited, but the split had come about through a divergence of philosophies and objectives. There is concern over the future of the appellation, for people are tempted to sell their land for the more profitable purpose of building villas. You have to convince the wine growers that their land is a treasure chest of gold and that they should not sell it. The number of estates has doubled and there has been a considerable increase in production, from thirteen thousand hectolitres in

1968 to forty thousand hectolitres in 1997. Boyer considers that saturation point has been reached, leaving only limited opportunities for new plantings – but not everyone has the interests of the appellation at heart.

OTHER ESTATES

Of the growing number of producers in Bandol, there are several others whose wines are worthy of note. Michel Bronco at Domaine de la Bastide Blanche produces an elegant range of wines, notably a perfumed, full-bodied white from Clairette and Ugni Blanc with some Sauvignon. There were two contrasting red 1993s, one with sixty per cent Mourvèdre that was quite firm and cedary with supple tannins, and a pure Mourvèdre, made since 1990, that was more gamey and meaty in character.

Domaine Terrebrune at Ollioules also houses a friendly restaurant, La Table du Vigneron, that has a reputation for its barbecued meat. Georges Delille's first vintage here was 1975, but he only made white wine for the first time in 1996, from Ugni Blanc, Clairette and some Roussanne, Marsanne and Rolle that spent six months in *foudres*, making a ripe, almost *moelleux* wine. His red wine is usually seventy per cent Mourvèdre, with equal parts of Grenache Noir and Carignan, while the *rosé*, made by *pressurage* with a high proportion of Mourvèdre, is given six months of *élevage* in *foudres* to fill out the palate. A red 1992 was quite Burgundian in style, supple and gamey, a 1989 was delicate and smoky, while the 1985 was perfect with some barbecued lamb. Elegance is the hallmark of the wines of Terrebrune.

I have also enjoyed wines from Domaine de l'Hermitage, Château Ray-Jane, Domaine du Cagueloup and Domaine de la Noblesse. There are other new estates making their mark: a Burgundian, Luc Sorin, has been in Bandol since 1994 and a Bordelais, Guillaume Tari, produces pure Mourvèdre at Domaine la Bégude, from some of the highest vineyards of the appellation. The future looks good, with Mourvèdre grown on the sun-soaked terraces of Bandol making wines with structure, elegance and ageing potential that are among the most individual of the Midi.

Key facts

AC 1941 for red, white and pink; percentages vary, but in 1996 sixty per cent *rosé*, thirty-five per cent red and five per cent white; covers eight *communes*.

Grape varieties:

RED: fifty per cent Mourvèdre since 1986, plus Grenache Noir and Cinsaut; Syrah allowed but unusual.

WHITE: Clairette, Ugni Blanc, Bourboulenc and Sauvignon.

Since 1989 only vines older than eight years produce red wine; density five thousand vines per hectare. Reds must have minimum of eighteen months ageing in wood. No irrigation, chaptalisation or mechanical harvesting.

Clay and limestone soil: Le Renversement du Beausset.

Average annual rainfall 600 mm.

Vintages

1999: Very dry year. Good colour, concentration and tannin.
1998: Very dry weather, making wines of great concentration. Wines to age.
1997: Very similar to 1998. Wines to keep.
1996: Some rain, but ripe grapes and wines with good concentration.
1995: Again some rain, but a successful vintage, with ripe grapes and good fruit in the wines.

Côtes du Lubéron

The Côtes du Lubéron form the transition between the wines of the Rhône valley and those of Provence. They are part of both regions, for Provence stretches as far north as Montélimar, while for the purposes of vinous administration they are linked with Châteauneuf-du-Pape, the Côtes du Rhône and Côtes du Ventoux. But for me, they are psychologically very much part of the heart of Provence, more akin to the appellations of the Coteaux d'Aix-en-Provence and the Côtes de Provence. There is a difference between the two faces of the Montagne du Lubéron, as communications between the two are not that easy. The north looks to Avignon and does have more in common with the Côtes du Rhône, but the south faces firmly south towards the town of Aix-en-Provence and adjoins the Coteaux d'Aix-en-Provence.

The road from Cavaillon to Apt offers dramatic first impressions of the Montagne du Lubéron, which is a national park, and firmly separates the Côtes du Lubéron from the Côtes du Ventoux. Villages like Lacoste, Oppède and Ménerbes, the setting of Peter Mayle's infamous *A Year in Provence*, nestle in the folds of the hills. In the distance on the north side of the road there are views of the sombre grey summit of Mont Ventoux, which looks misleadingly snow-capped in a haze of sunshine. In spring the valley floor is filled with flowering orchards of cherries, peaches and apricots, with vineyards on the higher slopes. The principal road across the mountain twists and turns through the pretty village of Bonnieux and down into Loumarin. The slopes on the southern side are more gentle, and the vineyards are separated from the sprawling appellation of the Coteaux d'Aix-en-Provence by the broad Durance river, which flows into the Rhône at Avignon. Apt is an attractive town on the eastern edge of the mountain that provides the focus of the appellation. On market day it is lively and bustling, with its central square filled with stalls purveying succulent vegetables, numerous varieties of olives and colourful *provençal* fabrics, with the nearby cafés a throng of people drinking pastis and coffee.

Vines have grown on the Montagne du Lubéron since Roman times, but have had little historical significance. Grapes were but one crop amongst several in a region that is eminently suited to market gardening. The Côtes du Lubéron first became a VDQS in 1958, thereby acquiring a separate administrative identity from the Côtes du Rhône and Côtes du Ventoux, and in 1988 they graduated into an appellation, the area being delimited to include only the hillside vineyards, while those on the plain were declassified into the departmental Vin de Pays du Vaucluse. The appellation is dominated by fourteen village co-operatives, thirteen of which belong to the vast Cellier du Marrenon. The odd one out, the co-operative of Goult, produces mainly Côtes du Ventoux as it is situated in that appellation on the other side of the valley. Until recently, there were just a handful of private producers, with Château de l'Isolette and Château de Mille maintaining the traditional reputation of the appellation. However, over the last five or more years there has been a considerable increase in the number of private estates, so that they now number twenty-nine. There were four new producers for the 1998 vintage alone, including the Burgundian Jean-Marie Guffens at Château des Tourettes. As elsewhere, an appellation benefits enormously from an influx of new ideas and growers, from people with experiences in other vineyards or other fields of activity. None the less, the co-operatives still account for eighty-five per cent of the appellation.

In 1998 there were 3758 hectares of vines in production out of a total of six thousand delimited, with a greater concentration of vineyards on the south side of the Montagne de Lubéron. There are quite distinct climatic differences between the north and the south. The north is cooler but in fact more sheltered, with steeper slopes, while the south, though warmer, is subject to cooling winds from the Alps, which can blow hard down the valley of the Durance. Generally Syrah does better in the north and Grenache Noir in the south, but that also depends upon the particular *terroir*. The soil is limestone and clay, with varying amounts of *galets*. Altitude, which varies between two hundred and three hundred metres, also has an influence; the lower-lying vineyards are deemed to be inferior. The annual rainfall is about 500 mm, which apparently is less than it was twenty-odd years ago, when people remember as much as 700 or 800 mm during the year.

White wine accounts for between twenty and twenty-five per cent of the appellation, a higher proportion than for any other appellation of the Rhône Valley or Provence, with the exception of Cassis. *Rosé* comprises thirty to thirty-five per cent, which leaves forty to forty-five per cent for red wine. The principal grape varieties for red and pink wine are the usual five varieties of the Midi: Grenache Noir, Syrah, Cinsaut, Mourvèdre and Carignan. Syrah and Grenache Noir must account for at least sixty per cent of the blend, with Syrah representing a minimum of ten per cent, while Carignan and Cinsaut are each restricted to twenty per cent. Clairette dominates the white wines, along with other traditional varieties such as Grenache Blanc and Bourboulenc. These have been enlivened by increasing amounts of Marsanne and Roussanne, which have been allowed in the appellation since 1995, as well as Rolle or Vermentino, which was introduced in 1992. In common with the other appellations of the Midi, there has been a general move away from Carignan towards Syrah and Grenache Noir, while Ugni Blanc, which must not exceed fifty per cent, has been replaced by the more aromatic white varieties, as well as by Grenache Blanc. Grape varieties like Chardonnay, Viognier and Cabernet Sauvignon are strictly limited to the departmental Vin de Pays du Vaucluse.

CELLIER DE MARRENON, LA TOUR D'AIGUES

The Cellier de Marrenon was set up in 1965. The idea came from Amédée Giniès, the director of one of the co-operatives, and was considered very advanced, for there were very few *groupements de producteurs* in existence at the time, apart from the Vignerons Catalans in Perpignan and the Cellier du Dauphin in the Rhône Valley. The Cellier de Marrenon, named after a farm on the Montagne de Lubéron, groups the bottling and commercial activities of its thirteen co-operative members. Each co-operative makes its wines and the Cellier de Marrenon takes its requirements, usually about three-quarters of the production of each co-operative, provided the quality is appropriate, covering all categories: *vin de table*, *vin de pays*, Côtes du Lubéron and also a little Côtes du Ventoux. They blend wines as necessary and prepare them for bottling, with fining, filtering and cold stabilisation. For the moment there is no *élevage* in wood. Everything is centred on the large cellar and warehouse at La Tour d'Aigues. They produce various qualities of appellation wine, including what they call an *haut de gamme*, La Grande Toque, as well as some individual estates, such as Château La Tour d'Aigues. They have encouraged investment in the vineyards, changing the emphasis away from Carignan and Ugni Blanc and towards Syrah, Grenache Noir, Rolle and other more flavoursome varieties. They also produce a range of varietal wines: their first Chardonnay was in 1990, while Cabernet Sauvignon and Merlot were only planted as recently as 1994. A tasting of a selection of 1997s, when they were a year old, demonstrated a sound range that inevitably lacked the individuality that you will find in smaller private estates. That is where the interest really lies.

CHATEAU DE L'ISOLETTE, BONNIEUX

The original reputation of the Côtes du Lubéron lies with two estates, Château de l'Isolette and Château de Mille, which belong to the two Pinatel brothers, Luc and Conrad, who sadly have not spoken to each other for years. There are local rumours of a family feud over a question of inheritance. Luc Pinatel proudly tells you that his family have been *vignerons* from father to son since 1535 and that his eldest daughter is now working with him at Château de l'Isolette. This is an estate with one hundred and thirty hectares outside the village of Bonnieux, making it the second largest property in the Côtes du Lubéron after Château de Val Joannis. The château dates mainly from the eighteenth century, but there has been much restoration and renovation at various stages in its history. Pinatel is an older man, quite serious and confident in his opinions, but he has moved with the times and his cellar is well run and efficient, with concrete vats and several large *foudres*, the biggest holding 230 hectolitres. He began working in the family cellars at the age of twelve and took over the wine making on his father's death, when he was eighteen.

In the vineyard he prunes for a yield of 45 hl/ha and uses sheep manure to feed the vines. He favours a mechanical harvester, as it allows for flexibility in picking. His Chardonnay is harvested at the end of August. Then there is a pause before he picks the Syrah, another pause before the Grenache Noir and then, a few days later, everything else is harvested. Such delays would be impossible if you were employing pickers. He has had a mechanical harvester for twenty-five years and is now on his fourth model.

We tasted in an attractive room housing a small wine museum, with various pieces of defunct equipment. There is a *fouloir* going back to 1740, a decrepit corking machine and various antique pumps, but best of all was a splendid Fiat dating from 1924 with a barrel on the back. Pinatel's white Côtes du Lubéron is a blend of five varieties, with Clairette for freshness, Marsanne and Roussanne for their floral notes, Bourboulenc for acidity and Grenache Blanc for body. The wine had an appealing smoky fragrance, with a dry finish. A Chardonnay Vin de Pays du Vaucluse, of which a third was fermented in oak, with *bâtonnage* and fining with real egg whites, was firm and buttery, with obvious oaky characteristics that would doubtless tone down with bottle age. Pinatel would like to have Chardonnay included in the appellation, making a dry comment about 'the INAO blocking us in order to preserve the big appellations'.

Next came two contrasting *rosés*, one light and fresh and the other, bearing the name Aquarelle, more solid and substantial. Three qualities of red followed, first a Sélection from young vines for early drinking, and next a Cuvée Prestige with more substance, for the wine is given a three-week *cuvaison* and aged in old wood. It includes a small amount of Carignan, from vines planted in 1916 and 1922 that produce just 15 hl/ha. Finally there was Aquarelle, from the oldest vines of Syrah and Grenache Noir, aged first in *barriques* and then in *foudres*, so that it tasted solid and structured with some fruit.

CHATEAU DE MILLE, APT

Château de l'Isolette seems to have successfully moved with the times, unlike Château de Mille. I admit that I have not visited the property, but every time I have tasted the wines, they have struck me as unnecessarily dry and lacking in the fruit and warmth that you expect from the Côtes du Lubéron. Encountered over a tasting and lunch, Conrad de Pinatel proves to be as opinionated as his brother. He has some sixty-year-old 150-hectolitre *foudres*, in which he leaves his wine for seven or eight years, allowing for some slow oxygenation. '*C'est ça, la vieillissement*', he insisted. His white wine was more intriguing, again quite old fashioned in style, with tarry notes. He is even more damning of the INAO than his brother, resenting their refusal to allow Viognier, Chardonnay, Merlot or Gamay in the appellation. Gamay seems a surprising possibility for the south, but apparently it was permitted in the VDQS for *rosé*.

CHATEAU LA CANORGUE, BONNIEUX

For me, the pace-setter in the appellation is undoubtedly Jean-Pierre Margan at Château la Canorgue outside the village of Bonnieux. The original owner of the property was Méry de la Canorgue, but it has been in Margan's wife's family for four generations. He took over his father-in-law's neglected estate in 1979 and now has thirty hectares in production. Syrah forms the base of his red wine, with Grenache Noir and some Cinsaut. He used to have some Merlot, but found it unsatisfactory. As for white, there is some Viognier and Chardonnay for *vin de pays*. He does not like Chardonnay either, but it was already planted, and he has added some Roussanne and Marsanne.

We walked through the vineyards accompanied by a hound called Merlot. It was a sunny spring morning, and Margan talked about organic and biodynamic viticulture and his indignant reaction to a minister who accused French farmers of polluting the countryside. His vineyards are surrounded by pinewoods, giving them a healthy isolation so that he can maintain a balanced environment, while assiduously avoiding the pesticides that destroy the natural cycle. He has a questioning approach to biodynamic viticulture. Some aspects of it are very convincing, such as bottling during the waning moon – the pressure in the wine is affected by the moon – while others are completely far-fetched. Margan has also planted a hectare of olive trees. He admits to four passions in life: wine, olive oil, truffles and the wide-open spaces of the desert.

His cellar is well organised, with stainless steel and concrete vats and a pneumatic press that has made a marked impact on the quality of his white and *rosé* wines. He ages his wine in *foudres* rather than *barriques*, preferring to keep to the tradition of the Midi and regarding *barriques* as a phenomenon of fashion. He finds that forty or fifty-hectolitre *foudres*, allowing for an exchange of oxygen, suit the wine very much better than *barriques*, which can have a hardening effect on the wine, especially in the warm climate with its drying winds. Perhaps he will try out some five hundred-litre barrels, which are enjoying a certain popularity at the moment.

Our tasting began with a Viognier, which Margan first made in 1994. It had some convincing varietal character, while the Chardonnay was rounded and buttery, with well-integrated oak. A third of it is fermented in new oak, for he feels that Chardonnay needs some oak to express itself – though he admitted that he does not really like it. As for Côtes du Lubéron, he makes one *cuvée* of each colour. The white is a blend of Ugni Blanc, Clairette, Bourboulenc and Grenache Blanc, with a little Marsanne and Roussanne. The Clairette adds the acidity which the Grenache Blanc lacks, while the Marsanne and Roussanne provide a little more aroma to an understated, subtle flavour. The *rosé* is a blend of Grenache Noir and Cinsaut, pressed rather than *saignée*, which makes for a more delicate wine. The red is mainly Syrah, with some Grenache Noir and a little Mourvèdre, but Mourvèdre ripens with difficulty on the northern side of the Montagne du Lubéron and so Margan has pulled up some of it. As for the method of vinification, 'that is my secret', but the wine spends four or five months in *foudres*. The 1996 had some ripe berry fruit on the nose with a spicy, peppery palate and hints of liquorice, while the 1993, another good vintage, had developed some warm, meaty flavours, with a long finish.

DOMAINE DE LA CITADELLE, MENERBES

Domaine de la Citadelle outside Ménerbes *vaut le voyage*, as the Michelin guide would say, for its museum of corkscrews, which was created by Yves Rousset-Rouard. The collection was begun as recently as 1989 and contains some wonderful pieces. Some are elegant and ornate, while others are splendid examples of kitsch. There are delightful miniatures for perfume bottles and an extra-ordinary compression of corkscrews into a solid block of metal created by César. Rousset-Rouard made his money in films, of which *Emmanuelle* is his best-known, or perhaps most notorious, work, although he would prefer to be remembered for *Le Souper*. He bought a farm outside Ménerbes in 1989, built a state-of-the-art cellar and gradually began buying vineyards so that he now has a total of forty hectares. The estate takes its name from the old citadel in the village of Menerbes, which formed part of the papal defences during the Avignon papacy.

I met his son, Alexis Rousset-Rouard, who seemed charmingly unaffected by his father's wealth. We tasted in one of the more elegant tasting rooms of the appellation, looking out over rows of vineyards and lavender bushes. The first vintage at Domaine de la Citadelle was 1992 and since then the range has evolved to include three qualities of each colour of Côtes du Lubéron, as well as various varietal *vins de pays* from Chardonnay, Viognier and Cabernet Sauvignon. Cuvée le Châtaignerie is firmly unoaked, while Domaine de la Citadelle may include some oak ageing. The special *cuvée*, Réserve du Gouverneur, which is not made every year, is usually all given some *élevage* in barrel. Highlights included the white Domaine de la Citadelle, from equal parts of Grenache Blanc and Roussanne, with some fragrant fruit and harmonious layers of flavour. In contrast, the blend for Cuvée la Châtaignerie consists of Grenache Blanc, Clairette, Bourboulenc and Ugni Blanc, which are all fermented together, making for a broad, nutty-flavoured wine. The differences between the three *cuvées* are most apparent with red wine. The 1998 Cuvée la Châtaignerie, a blend of Carignan vinified by carbonic maceration, Grenache Noir and some Syrah, bottled during the winter for early drinking, was ripe and easy, with soft tannins and fresh fruit. 1996 Domaine de la Citadelle, a blend of thirty per cent Syrah and seventy per cent Grenache Noir, vinified together, of which half is kept in barrel and thirty-hectolitre *foudres* for six months, had a certain peppery character, discreetly filled out by the oak. In contrast, the 1995 Cuvée du Gouverneur, from two-thirds Syrah and one-third Grenache Noir, is given eighteen months *élevage* in *barriques*, of which one-third are new. In the young wine the oak was quite obvious, with vanilla overtones, firm fruit and tannins. None was made in 1996, for it was too light a year, but 1997, 1998 and 1999 have more than compensated for that by their quality.

DOMAINE DE LA ROYERE, OPPEDE

Anne Hugues was a museum curator at L'Isle-sur-Sorgues until the mid-1980s, when her husband Jean-Pierre inherited the family property of Domaine de la Royère outside Oppède. Thereupon she changed direction and did what is called a *formation adulte* in wine making. The vineyards, which had been left in the hands of managers for three generations, were retrieved from the co-operative and Hugues now runs a twenty-five hectare estate, producing *vin de pays* as well as Côtes du Lubéron. There was a neolithic site on their land, as well as a Roman tomb, and they have found numerous flints dated between 4000 and 2000 BC, coins and a bowl from the tomb, all of which are on display in their tasting room. The cellar is simple and functional, with a small barrel cellar for which she buys secondhand barrels from Domaine la Nerthe in Châteauneuf-du-Pape, while favouring François Frères and Seguin Moreau as coopers.

Her white wine is a blend of equal parts of Ugni Blanc, Clairette and Rolle, and was fresh and delicate, with leafy flavours. The *rosé* is a blend of Syrah and Cinsaut. Grenache Noir is not included, as it is simply too alcoholic to make delicate *rosé*, while Syrah adds structure and finesse to the Cinsaut, making an elegant wine with a slightly herbal taste. There are two red wines, one a blend of Syrah and Grenache Noir, while the second, first made in 1993, includes Mourvèdre as well as some older vines, with both the Syrah and Mourvèdre given some *élevage* in barrel. The development in wood is closely followed to ensure that the wines are not over-oaked, and the red wines tasted from vat and barrel showed promise. A Côtes du Ventoux, from Grenache Noir and Syrah – there should have been some Carignan too, but the wild boar had arrived before the harvesters – provided an interesting contrast, for it seemed warmer and more alcoholic than the more structured and elegant Côtes du Lubéron. Jean-Pierre Hugues is passionate about the art of distillation, and so they also produce a range of fruit-flavoured *eaux de vie*, as well as *marc*, which I tried after dinner later that evening.

The cassis was opulently redolent of blackcurrants, as all good cassis should be.

DOMAINE DE MAYOL, APT

Bernard Viguier of Domaine de Mayol has his cellars on a hill outside Apt, while his vineyards are a veritable jigsaw of different plots, totalling some twenty-five hectares, spread out as far as Bonnieux. Forty years ago his father had just five hectares, planted with the traditional varieties of Grenache Noir and Carignan, which he described as a Provençal plant. He talked of selling wine in bulk to both Bordeaux and Burgundy, and they started bottling when his son took over the estate in 1980. Although they make a little white wine, they do not consider that they are properly equipped for it and instead concentrate on red wine, making three different reds, one that is mainly Grenache Noir, another that is predominantly Syrah and a third that is also mainly Syrah and is given twelve months *élevage* in oak. The Syrah-based wine was deliciously peppery; the Grenache Noir was more rounded and a touch jammy; while the oak still dominated the 1994 *cuvée fût* in the spring of 1999. Best of all was the 1989 that Viguier opened to contradict the idea that Côtes du Lubéron does not age. It was almost ten years old and exuded a beautiful balance of warm fruit, sunshine and tannin. '*Moi, je trouve ça formidable!*' he exclaimed with enthusiasm, and I could not possibly have disagreed.

CHATEAU VAL JOANNIS, PERTUIS

The largest estate of the Côtes du Lubéron is Château Val Joannis near the village of Pertuis on the southern side of the mountain. The Chancel family came to wine from olive oil, and when they bought Val Joannis in 1978 there were just five hectares of vines adjoining the sixteenth-century château. The first thing they did was to bring in the bulldozers and clear the scrubland where there had been vines before phylloxera. They found the remains of crumbling terraces, but the bulldozers achieved more gentle slopes. In twenty years the estate has grown to one hundred and seventy-five hectares of vineyards, producing some 1.2 million bottles a year, both of *vins de pays* and Côtes du Lubéron. A back label on the *vin de pays* explains that the *savoir faire* and creativity of the wine maker sometimes conflict with the appellation rules relating to grape varieties, so the wine is labelled *vin de pays*, allowing you, the consumer, to decide on its quality. It sounds better in French than English, but I enjoyed general manager Christian Duport's observation that the INAO is an old lady who does not like to be jostled.

Essentially they make three versions of each colour at Val Joannis. There is a *vin de pays* that includes grape varieties planted in anticipation of their inclusion in the appellation. This did not happen, so the white *vin de pays* includes Chardonnay as well as Ugni Blanc and the red *vin de pays* some Merlot with the Syrah. The *rosé* is also Syrah, but blended with Gamay, which was originally allowed in the VDQS but was withdrawn from the appellation in 1988. Then there is a Cuvée Tradition and a Cuvée Prestige, which are both appellation wines.

The white Tradition is made from Ugni Blanc and Grenache Blanc, while the Cuvée Prestige Les Aubépines, includes an old plot of Grenache Blanc, as well as Clairette, making a ripe, honeyed mouthful of wine. The *rosé* Tradition is mainly Syrah and deep enough in colour to be almost a light red wine, while the *rosé* Prestige les Mérises, which is mainly Syrah, fermented in new wood for five or six weeks was, for me, too obviously oaky.

The red Tradition is mainly Syrah and Grenache Noir with some Carignan and Cinsaut, and also Mourvèdre, which has proved unsatisfactory, while the Cuvée Prestige, Les Griottes, made from Syrah with a little Grenache Noir, was solid and oaky after twelve months in wood. Perhaps it is a question of small is beautiful, but somehow the wines did not excite as much as they had on my previous visit twelve years earlier. Perhaps complacency crept in once their position in the appellation had been established. You are certainly much less aware of the energetic presence of the Chancel family.

The cellar is streamlined, with stainless steel galore, and they use *foudres*, for their oxidative effect, as well as *barriques*. An old jeepney (a larger and more brightly painted version of a jeep, which I have only ever encountered previously in the Philippines) in the courtyard seems idiosyncratically out of place, and the gardens, created by Cécile Chancel, are on every garden enthusiast's itinerary. There are three terraces with vegetables, flowers and orchards, as well as lemons and orange trees in pots. In summer and spring they must be a delight, but unfortunately I was there at the end of autumn when they looked sad and forlorn.

DOMAINE DE FONTENILLE, LAURIS

Domaine de Fontenille, outside the village of Lauris, is run by the two brothers Jean and Pierre Levèque. The name of the estate derives from springs near by. Their grandfather bought the property in 1949 and they took over from their father in 1991. Jean was a fireman in Paris for seventeen years and now handles the sales and administration, while his brother makes the wine. Their vaulted cellar dates back to 1530 and they even have three large stone vats that were built at the same time. Originally the family had fruit trees as well as vines, but when market gardening proved difficult, their father decided to concentrate on wine, with his first bottling in 1978. They now have twenty-one hectares of vines.

Their white wine is a blend of Ugni Blanc, Clairette and Bourboulenc, and they are planting Grenache Blanc. Clairette provides vivacity, Ugni Blanc, with its large bunches, some body and Bourboulenc, which they consider a *cépage améliorateur*, some aroma; the flavour was delicate and grassy, with fresh acidity. The *rosé* had slightly herbal notes, with some weight. Usually they produce only one red wine, although in the particularly good vintage of 1995 they made a Cuvée Vieilles Vignes that spent three years in vat. It includes forty-year-old Grenache Noir, some thirty-year-old Syrah planted by their grandfather and some almost centenarian Carignan; it was firm and peppery, with body and structure. A 1998 from Grenache Noir and Cinsaut for early drinking had some appealing ripe berry fruit, and a 1997, from the more usual blend of Grenache Noir and Syrah, was more structured, with pepper and spice. They have also made a Cuvée 2000 from the excellent 1997 vintage, which has been aged in a six hundred-litre *tonneau*. This is the first time they have used wood and the wine now needs some time in bottle, but it promises well for the millennium.

DOMAINE CONSTANTIN CHEVALLIER, LOUMARIN

My final visit in the Côtes du Lubéron was to Constantin Chevallier just outside the attractive village of Loumarin. The cherry orchard was in flower and a view of the pretty house was spoilt by the presence of a large mobile bottling line. Allen Chevallier explained that although he was born in England, he was brought up in France and worked in advertising. Then in 1990 he and his wife Maire-Laure were looking for a holiday home with a small garden. Instead they bought fifty hectares of land, including twenty of vines, as well as olive groves and cherry orchards.

Chevallier realised that he had two options. He could join the co-operative, but you do not make any money from that. Or else 'we could make wine and maybe lose a lot of money'. They fitted the cellar into the old building, squeezing in the stainless steel vats, and now everything works by gravity. The white wine is based on Rolle or Vermentino, with some Clairette and Ugni Blanc. Chevallier enthused about the white wine, made from Vermentino, from Clos Nicrosi in Corsica, which he had drunk while on holiday on the island. A proportion of each grape variety is fermented in barrel, with *bâtonnage*, and the wine had a certain weight and structure. In comparison, a white wine from vat was crisp and floral. There was a rounded, ripe *rosé*, from Syrah and Grenache Noir, and two reds: one is vinified in vat and the other, Cuvée des Fondateurs, spends twelve months in wood. The 1997, when it was eighteen months old, was firm and oaky, with a certain vanilla sweetness and structure, while the unoaked wine, from equal parts of Carignan, Grenache Noir and Syrah, was perfumed and appealing – a fitting note on which to leave the Côtes du Lubéron.

Key facts

VDQS 1958, AC 1988; red 40–45 per cent, white 20–25 per cent, pink 30–35 per cent; 3760 hectares planted out of six thousand delimited on either side of the Montagne du Lubéron; 55 hl/ha.

Grape varieties:

WHITE: Clairette, Grenache Blanc, Bourboulenc, Marsanne, Roussanne, Rolle, Ugni Blanc.

RED: Grenache Noir and Syrah must account for a minimum of sixty per cent; Syrah for a minimum of ten per cent, with Mourvèdre; also Carignan and Cinsaut, both restricted to twenty per cent. Usually more Syrah on northern slopes and more Grenache Noir in the south.

Vineyards at two to three hundred metres on clay and limestone soil.

Average annual rainfall 500 mm.

Vintages

1999: Generally fine weather; higher acidity levels than 1998, making for supple, balanced fruity reds. A few *vins de garde*.

1998: A very hot, dry summer gave some problems with stressed vines, which were solved by rain in September. Ripe, rounded wines with good fruit and flavour.

1997: A successful year, much more so than in the Languedoc or neighbouring appellations in the Rhône Valley. A hot summer and dry weather during the harvest. Wines to keep.

1996: Not an easy year; rain and a lack of sunshine resulted in wines that lacked colour and alcohol. Not for keeping.

1995: A more structured year than 1996; a hot summer without rain made for more tannic wines.

Coteaux de Pierrevert

The Coteaux de Pierrevert form a natural continuation of the Montagne de Lubéron, making a sleepy backwater in the department of the Alpes-de-Haute-Provence, far away from the mainstream of *provençal* viticulture. The pretty little hilltop village of Pierrevert lies at the centre of the appellation. From the terrace there is a view of the vineyards, with the Alps in the distance, and a wine museum has just opened in a turreted medieval house. I suspect that the village only really comes to life for the annual *fête du vin* at the end of May. Nearby Manosque, which has one claim to fame – it is the birthplace of the writer Jean Giono – is the only town of any size in the area.

The Coteaux de Pierrevert were first classified as a VDQS in 1959 and the overall area was defined to cover forty-two villages, many of which did not actually grow grapes at all. Consequently, when the Coteaux de Pierrevert were promoted to appellation status in 1998, the culmination of a process that had started ten years earlier, the vineyard area was reduced to cover just eleven villages concentrated around Pierrevert and Manosque, mostly on south-facing slopes overlooking the broad Durance river. These are some of the highest vineyards of the south of France, averaging 450–500 metres, and they feel the cooling influence of the nearby Alps. Altogether there are about a thousand hectares of vines, of which about three hundred and fifty produce the appellation wine. The rest is *vin de pays* for reasons of grape variety or yield. Eleven grape varieties are permitted in the appellation, allowing for quite a diversity of blends and flavours. Whereas the VDQS demanded only two grape varieties in the blend, without stipulating the precise proportions, the appellation regulations require more specific percentages. Red wines represent sixty per cent of the appellation, compared with thirty per cent of *rosé* and just ten per cent of white.

Ugni Blanc was once the main variety, but it is now disappearing, so that Rolle and Grenache Blanc are the principal white varieties. By 2006 they must account for a minimum of fifty per cent of the blend, while other varieties are allowed in a supporting role, namely Clairette, Roussanne, Marsanne and Picpoul, as well as Ugni Blanc. The key varieties for red wine are Syrah and Grenache Noir, while Cinsaut is allowed for *rosé*, and Carignan and Mourvèdre may also be included. Again, Carignan is tending to disappear, and as Mourvèdre does not ripen properly, apart from in exceptional years, it is only included under sufferance.

CAVE DES VIGNERONS DE PIERREVERT, PIERREVERT

For a long time the co-operative of Pierrevert dominated the appellation, although today there are now five private estates of varying importance. And where there were once four other village co-operatives in the area, at Manosque, Montfuron, Quinson and Villeneuve, these have all joined up now to form one co-operative at Pierrevert, although the old cellars are retained for pressing the grapes and a special *cuvée* is made for each village. The co-operative at Pierrevert was created in 1925. At that time the area had a reputation for sparkling wine called Clairet de Pierrevert, made from Ugni Blanc and Clairette, which won medals in the 1930s. Today the co-operative has three hundred members and is responsible for four hundred and fifty hectares all over the appellation; on average it produces 7,500 hectolitres, half the production of the appellation. The other 12,500 hectolitres are sold as *vin de pays*.

The director of the co-operative, Hubert Sylvestre, energetically defended the quality of his wines as we tasted, dipping into the tops of the concrete vats that are so typical of southern French wine co-operatives. There was a white, from Grenache Blanc and Roussanne, with some firm fruit. A blend of equal parts of Syrah and Grenache Noir had the peppery flavour of Syrah, with some weight from the Grenache Noir. Syrah is not an easy variety to grow here, as it tends to be very vigorous and really tests the talent of the wine grower.

593

Sylvestre also introduced me to a Pierrevert peculiarity, *rosé fruité*. This was a region that also grew table grapes, mainly Muscat Hamburg, but when the market for such grapes disappeared at the end of the 1970s, most of them arrived at the co-operative. 'What was I to do? I sorted something out.' The result was lightly sweet, fruity pink wine with a Muscaty flavour. It falls foul of European regulations, as you are not supposed to turn grapes specified as table grapes into wine. If you were to plant Muscat Hamburg in the future, you would not be allowed to use it for wine, and so it is gradually being replaced by a blend of Muscat *á petits grains* and Cinsaut. In some ways the taste is quite unlike that of any other wine, a curious combination of dry orange and rosewater, with an intense perfume. As Sylvestre said, the people who drink this are not wine drinkers, so it is not in competition with their other wines.

DOMAINE DE REGUSSE, PIERREVERT

The largest estate of the appellation is Domaine de Régusse, which was owned by the hyperactive Claude Dieudonné at the time of my visit. However, the estate changed hands in the spring of 2000, passing to two Canadian associates who were brewers in Vancouver. One of the associates, a Mr von Krosijk, has a son who has just completed oenology studies in Germany, so he is taking over the wine making at Domaine de Régusse.

From his two hundred and forty hectares of vines, Dieudonné produced Coteaux de Pierrevert, Côtes du Lubéron and a large quantity of *vin de pays*, that are mainly sold as *vin de cépage*, which he considered to be his speciality. It was almost a question of what didn't he make. We raced round his cellar, going from vat to barrel and then to bottles galore. The vineyards include Pinot Noir, Syrah, Cabernet Sauvignon, Merlot, Grenache Noir and Gamay, and for whites, Chardonnay, Viognier, Aligoté, Muscat *à petits grains*, Chenin Blanc, Ugni Blanc, Clairette, Picpoul, Rolle and Grenache Blanc. Dieudonné proudly proclaimed that '*l'entreprise, c'est la diversité*'. How true, but I could not help feeling that he had somewhat overstretched himself.

The wines that stood out in a haze of bottles and glasses and increasingly illegible tasting notes included an unoaked Coteaux de Pierrevert from Grenache Noir and Syrah that was firm and peppery, while the oaked Cuvée Prestige, with a preponderance of Syrah, was more tannic and structured. His daughter's vineyard, Bastide des Oliviers, also produced a firm, peppery red wine. Louis Latour, the Burgundian producer, advised on planting Pinot Noir back in 1978 and Dieudonné has continued to make creditable wine with some varietal character. There was also some barrel-fermented Chardonnay with buttery fruit, whereas the Viognier did not have very marked varietal character. Chenin Blanc has been used for a *vin de paille*, for which the grapes were left to dry from October until the end of January and were then fermented in wood until July. Five kilos of grapes will produce just one litre of wine, which had a markedly oaky, nutty flavour and firm acidity. There was also a late picked Muscat *moelleux*, as well as a dry Muscat and a sparkling Chardonnay, made in the *méthode traditionnelle*. Our tasting finished with some heady *ratafia* with a taste of prunes, from Grenache Noir. It remains to be seen what the new owners will achieve instead.

CHATEAU DE ROUSSET, GREOUX-LES-BAINS

If you drive over the Durance south of Manosque, you will see an imposing château with an orange-red facade on the opposite hillside. This is the Château de Rousset, which has been owned by the du Chaffaut family since 1830. It is the daughter of the family, Roseline, together with her husband Hubert Emery, who is responsible for the twenty-one hectares of vines on the estate. In all, the estate has some one thousand hectares, and other members of the family are responsible for other crops and the livestock. Their vineyards consist mainly of Syrah, with some Grenache Noir, Cinsaut and Carignan, for red Coteaux de Pierrevert, and a little Cabernet Sauvignon for a Vin de Pays des Alpes-de-Haute-Provence, while Rolle and Grenache Blanc are grown for white Coteaux de Pierrevert, and just half a hectare of Viognier for a *vin de pays*. Like most of the appellation, the vineyards are quite high, at 350–400 metres, with a south western aspect. They have also planted some olive trees.

The Emerys' first vintage was in 1987. Before that, Mme Emery's father and brother had made all their wine for sale in bulk, but by

1997 they were putting all their production in bottle. They started from scratch and are still very much learning, but they are enjoying what they called the *côté pionnier*, finding out which grape varieties will work well in the area. They make two qualities of white wine, Château du Rousset and a Cuvée du Château, which is a selection of the better grapes, mainly Rolle and Grenache Blanc, and is consequently finer and more perfumed. The red Château du Rousset, from equal parts of Grenache Noir and Syrah, spends at least twelve, if not eighteen, months in vat and had a green peppery flavour. The red Cuvée du Château, with a much higher proportion of Syrah, tasted sturdier and more tannic. Finally there is the Grand Jas, again from Grenache Noir and Syrah, but grown in one specific vineyard. The wine included some pressed juice and is aged in wood, for they began working with *barriques* about five years ago. The flavour seemed very thick and dense, and I wondered how it would age. Certainly it was not characteristic of the Coteaux de Pierrevert, the typicity of which Mme Emery described as '*nerveux et montagneux*'.

DOMAINE LA BLAQUE, PIERREVERT

Undoubtedly the most professional producer of the appellation is Domaine la Blaque. The land was first bought in 1963 by Charles Pons Mure, who also owned a property in Lirac in the southern Rhône, and he set about creating the first independent estate of the appellation. Since 1987 Domaine la Blaque has belonged to a German company and is now run by its very efficient manager Gilles Delsuc. They have vineyards in some of the best sites of the appellation, on very steep slopes at some 420 metres, outside the village of Pierrevert. The Germans also invested in Domaine Châteauneuf, which was not originally a wine estate, but they have planted vineyards and also built some functional cellars there. Altogether the two properties comprise fifty-four hectares of appellation vineyards, together with six hectares of Viognier, which they hope will eventually be allowed in the appellation.

The white Coteaux de Pierrevert, from equal proportions of Rolle, Grenache Blanc, Picpoul and Roussanne, was rounded, with some fragrant fruit. Weight comes from the Grenache Blanc and Roussanne, while Rolle provides some aroma and Picpoul a certain lemony character and freshness – but as it does not usually ripen sufficiently well, it is condemned to be pulled up. The young Viognier vines produced a delicate wine with some convincing varietal character; an oak-aged white, from Roussanne and Grenache Blanc, was heavier and more honeyed, and a *rosé* from Grenache Noir, Syrah, Mourvèdre and Cinsaut had some attractive raspberry fruit.

The red wines were more serious. Delsuc is very concerned about colour, for this can be the problem with Grenache Noir – it does not always provide sufficient colour and tannin in vineyards at such an altitude. In fact, he admits to a certain obsession with it, doing both *délestages* and *remontages* in order to extract the absolute maximum amount of colour. He also does carbonic maceration for Syrah and Carignan, again with colour in mind. A 1997 red, vinified in vat from Carignan and Grenache Noir with a little Syrah and Mourvèdre, had some pepper and spice, with a certain structure and rusticity. 1997 was a good year in the Coteaux de Pierrevert, much better than in the Rhône valley, for they had a drier harvest with very healthy grapes, while the quantity was reduced by a hard frost on 18 April. A vat sample of 1997 Syrah destined for some barrel ageing also promised well, with good body and tannins, while a 1994 Réserve, mainly from Syrah with some Grenache Noir, was quite cedary, with flavours more reminiscent of the northern than the southern Rhône. While plantings of Syrah are increasing, it has apparently always been grown in the area and was called La Petite Syrah (not to be confused with Petite Sirah, the Californian name for the Durif grape of the southern Rhône) because of its very low yields. Indeed, Delsuc find 35 hl/ha to be the average, although the appellation allows for 50 hl/ha. We finished with a 1989 that was beginning to dry out a little, but in an elegant way, with a cedary, dusty palate. The Coteaux de Pierrevert will never be great wines, but they have charm and character in a backwater of rural France.

Key facts

VDQS 1959; AC in 1998, covering eleven villages around Pierrevert and Manosque. Red (sixty per cent), white (ten per cent) and pink (thirty per cent); 450–500 metres; Three hundred and fifty hectares out of a thousand hectares planted are AC; 50 hl /ha.

Grenache Blanc and Rolle, a minimum of fifty per cent by 2006, plus Clairette, Roussanne, Marsanne, Picpoul, Ugni Blanc.

Syrah, Grenache Noir, Cinsaut, Carignan, Mourvèdre.

Vintages

1999: Attractive fruity wines, with less concentration than 1998. Quite a large crop.

1998: Average quantity; good fruity reds and elegant whites.

1997: Spring frosts; low yields and good concentration. A vintage to keep.

1996: Hail caused problems, and quality was rather mixed; whites did best.

1995: Small yields; a fine summer and an early harvest made some good wines.

Coteaux Varois

The Coteaux Varois are sandwiched between various parts of the much larger and more extended appellation of the Côtes de Provence, while the north eastern corner adjoins the Coteaux d'Aix-en-Provence. Brignoles is at its centre, surrounded by twenty-seven other villages or *communes*, including on the south eastern edge the more lively town of St Maximin-la-Ste-Baume, with its awe-inspiring medieval basilica. The skyline to the south is dominated by the Montagne de la Loube. However, the heart of this relatively new appellation is at La Celle, a small village just outside Brignoles, where an old oil mill adjoining the remains of the abbey of La Celle houses the Maison du Vin des Coteaux Varois. When I was there, not only was there a selection of wines on display for tasting and purchase, but also an exhibition by a local artist, a charming portrayal of the various bell-towers of the area – for each village, with the exception of Brignoles, has a metal *campanile* that is quite different from the others in design. Part of the cloisters of the abbey remain, with an old mulberry tree as a reminder of the other vocation of the area. Since my visit the renowned chef Alain Ducasse has opened a restaurant there, the Hostellerie de l'Abbaye. There is also a small vineyard within the abbey confines that was planted in 1995, with a total of eighty-eight different grape varieties representing some of the rarer vines of Provence. Some came from Château Simone in Palette and others from the INRA vineyard near Sète. There are also tiny plots of Syrah, Rolle, Cinsaut and Grenache Noir for experimental vinifications, and a third plot containing examples of secondary varieties that are not yet in production.

The Coteaux Varois were one of the very first *vins de pays*, created at the early stages of the classification back in 1973. In 1984 they were promoted to a VDQS for red and pink wine, but not white. That came five years later, in 1989, and the appellation for all three colours followed in 1993, making it the only wine to have made the logical progression through the hierarchy, from *vin de pays* to VDQS and then to appellation status. The reason for the distinction between the Côtes de Provence and Coteaux Varois is historical, although there are also distinct differences of climate and *terroir*. When the idea of a delimitation of the Côtes de Provence was first mooted after the Second World War, the market for *vin de table* was still buoyant. It was a case of people preferring easy cash, from vines yielding 150–200 hl/ha without any constraints of quality. Quite simply, to conform to any restrictive regulations would have been too much of a hassle, so as a consequence these villages were omitted from the Côtes de Provence. Now they are trying hard to catch up and maybe even overtake their larger neighbour.

The climatic differences from the Côtes de Provence are very apparent, for the northern edge of the Coteaux Varois is considerably cooler, with an average altitude of some three hundred and fifty metres, rising to five hundred metres at the highest point. You only have to compare harvest dates, which tend to be about a fortnight later in the Coteaux Varois than in the Côtes de Provence, starting in mid-September; in 1997 some people were still picking in early October. This means that the wines tend to be fresher, with a better alcohol and acidity balance, and also higher acidity, which makes them more suitable for ageing.

In 1997 the appellation consisted of seventeen hundred hectares, but not all is declared as an appellation. Often the wine is sold more easily under the label of the departmental Vin de Pays du Var. As a *vin de pays* the Coteaux Varois produced two hundred thousand hectolitres per year, while as an appellation it makes just seventy thousand hectolitres. Pink wine is the most important, accounting for two-thirds of the production, while red makes up one-third and white represents a tiny drop, at just three per cent.

Grape varieties are similar to those of the Côtes de Provence. Rolle is the dominant white variety, while Sémillon is limited to thirty per cent and Ugni Blanc to twenty-five per cent. Grenache Blanc is also allowed in the Coteaux Varois, but not in the Côtes de Provence. For pink wine, Grenache Noir and Cinsaut are the most usual, often a blend of forty per cent Grenache Noir, the minimum in the regulations, with sixty per cent Cinsaut. Together Cinsaut and Grenache Noir must make up seventy per cent of the blend, while the other thirty per cent may come from any of the other varieties allowed for red wine, namely Carignan, Cabernet Sauvignon, Mourvèdre and Syrah. The red wine must always be a blend, even if it is ninety-nine per cent of one variety and just one per cent of another. Syrah, Grenache Noir and Mourvèdre between them should not account for less than seventy per cent of a wine, while Carignan is limited to thirty per cent, as is Cinsaut, and Cabernet Sauvignon must not exceed twenty per cent. Mourvèdre is grown mainly in the southern part of the appellation, so it is really Syrah and Grenache Noir that are the principal red grape varieties.

Village co-operatives have in the past dominated the appellation and continue to do so in terms of volume, but they are diminishing in importance and shrinking in number. Where once they were twenty, there are now fifteen, and with further mergers they are likely to shrink to ten. Without doubt, the most interesting wines come from the private estates, which are growing in number and now total about sixty-five. New estates have been created as land that might once have been part of a co-operative has been returned to private vineyards. Perhaps a change of ownership has brought a renewed interest in the viticultural heritage of the property. Outsiders too play an important role in the area, with five estates belonging to foreigners.

CHATEAU DE MIRAVAL, LE VAL

I stayed at the beautiful Château de Miraval, which is the home of an American couple, Tom and Jane Bove. The château is built in soft yellow Provençal stone, with a backdrop of old terraces that have been painstakingly restored. Some of the old olive trees remain, and there are Roman remains on the property; the vineyards are further along the valley. Château de Miraval once belonged to a M. Lambot, who is credited with the invention of reinforced concrete, and later to Jacques Loussier, the pianist who developed *Bach en jazz*; there is a building that is still used for sound recordings. The large cellar was built at the beginning of the last century and has recently been extensively modernised, while a barrel cellar has been created in the oldest part of the château. Of their twenty-five hectares of vines, ten are for white wine, planted mainly with Rolle, with a little Grenache Blanc coming into production. There are also seven hectares of old Cinsaut and eight hectares of Syrah, Grenache Noir and Cabernet Sauvignon. The talented and amiable oenologist Emmanuel Gaujal oversees the wine making.

We tasted vintages of the white Coteaux Varois, mainly from Rolle, with Gaujal explaining how he achieves a very slow fermentation. In 1996 the Rolle was very ripe, with an intriguing flavour more reminiscent of Viognier. When the Grenache Blanc comes into production it will add structure. As the Château de Miraval is on the edge of the appellation, some of their vineyards are in the Côtes de Provence, so that they make both appellations in white wine and only Côtes de Provence for red wine. The difference in flavour between the two whites comes from the percentage of new wood, with 1996 being the first year that Gaujal tried fermentation, as opposed to just *élevage*, in oak.

CHATEAU DE ST JEAN-DE-VILLECROZE, TOURTOUR

Tom and Jane Bove also own the Château de St Jean-de-Villecroze. This was the estate that did much to establish the early reputation of the Coteaux Varois, when it was owned by another American, Alan Hirsh, and his French wife Denise. It is on the northern edge of the appellation, quite isolated from the other vineyards and near the pretty village of Tourtour, which describes itself as *le village dans le ciel*. They bought the property in 1974 and planted a vineyard from scratch, with a large proportion of Cabernet Sauvignon, as well as Syrah, Grenache Noir and some Cinsaut. Then in 1988 they sold it to the Shivdasana family, who are the owners of Château du Galoupet in the Côtes de Provence, and also briefly owned Château Vignelaure. Their ownership of St Jean-de-Villecroze was similarly brief, and the Boves bought the property with some Italian partners in 1993.

Three wines are made at St Jean: a red and a pink appellation wine and a Vin de Pays du Var, from Cabernet Sauvignon. Just one and a half hectares of white vines were planted in the early 1990s, for experiments with Sauvignon and Sémillon. Hirsh spared no expense in equipping the cellar and with his Californian wine makers was the first estate in the Var to use *barriques*. Now the

Cabernet Sauvignon is kept in *barriques* for nine to twelve months, while the Syrah in the appellation wine is aged in small *foudres* and blended with twenty per cent each of Grenache Noir and Cabernet Sauvignon. These are wines made to age, with a long *cuvaison* of a minimum of three weeks for each variety. The 1993 was warm and spicy with a firm structure, the 1988 Cabernet Sauvignon was elegant with a slightly vegetal nose and the 1989 was more obviously blackcurranty. I liked the 1991 best, which had a smoky, cedarwood character and firm tannins.

DOMAINE DES CHABERTS, GAREOULT

Betty Cundall, an Englishwoman, has lived in the Coteaux Varois for the past twenty years. She was a friend of the previous owner of Domaine des Chaberts, Mrs Pitt-Rivers, who was married to the grandson of the anthropologist after whom the Pitt-Rivers Museum in Oxford is named. When Mrs Pitt-Rivers was widowed, her children showed no interest in the property, so Mrs Cundall came out to help her friend with her estate and has simply stayed on. There are thirty hectares of vineyards planted with the usual varieties of the appellation. Cabernet Sauvignon was introduced in 1983 and Rolle and Sémillon are more recent. At least two, if not three, *cuvées* are made for each colour. Highlights included a white Cuvée Prestige, from Rolle, Sémillon and Clairette, with delicate herbal fruit; the pink Cuvée Bacchus from equal proportions of Cinsaut and Grenache Noir, which was rounded with fresh acidity; and the 1995 red Cuvée Prestige from Mourvèdre, Cabernet Sauvignon and Grenache Noir, which spends six months in ten-hectolitre *foudres*, and was rounded with some appealing fruit and just a hint of prunes.

CHATEAU ST ESTEVE, BRUE-AURIAC

Château St Estève belongs to Sven Arnerius, a jovial Swede. He ran a manufacturing company in Sweden for some twenty-five years, but had always dreamt of owning a vineyard. At the end of 1989, when his company changed hands, he decided that this was the moment to realise his dream. It was a toss-up between Provence and

Tuscany, but his Italian was not so good and he knew Provence well. It took eighteen months to find the right vineyard. Estève describes a spring on the property, the source of the Argens, which flows into the sea near Fréjus. There are twenty-eight hectares of wines, from which he makes, with the help of his Palestinian wine maker Sami Aburabi, several different wines, both appellation and varietal *vin de pays*. There was a delicate white from Rolle and Ugni Blanc, with a lightly herbal nose, and a lightly flavoured pink Cuvée Prestige from Syrah, Grenache Noir and Cinsaut, made by the *saignée* method. Both *vins de pays*, Cabernet Sauvignon and Merlot, had good varietal flavours, and a 1993 red Cuvée Prestige, from Grenache Noir, Syrah and Cabernet Sauvignon, was solid and ripe, with good body. The majority of the production is red, and Arnerius remembered how twenty-five years ago Provence had meant *rosé*, and mediocre *rosé* at that.

CHATEAU ROUTAS, BRAS

Philippe Bieler of Château Routas has done much to put the Coteaux Varois on the international wine map in the last few years. He is the son of German-Swiss parents and was educated in Geneva, but his father went to Canada, so Bieler also holds a Canadian passport, speaks English with a North American accent and divides his time between the two sides of the Atlantic. He is a welcoming extrovert with an infectious enthusiasm. Various cousins had inherited vineyards, such as Château Ripaille in Savoy, and he had always said to himself 'One of these days . . .' Meanwhile he took up a career in investment banking, pursued his enthusiasm for cooking and, after meeting various of the so-called Rhône Rangers, who introduced the grape varieties of the Rhône valley to California, began looking for a vineyard in the south of France, with the help of Luc Sorin, who had sold a family property in St Bris-le-Vineux in the Yonne and moved south to Provence.

Looking for good plots of old vines, Grenache Noir, Syrah and Cabernet Sauvignon, Bieler finally bought five small adjoining estates that have been amalgamated into Château Routas. We went for a bumpy but scenic drive through the vineyards. The soil is dry and so stony that sometimes, when vines were replaced, it was necessary to use a crowbar. One area called Le Trou de l'Infernet has an enormous cavern that may have been inhabited in prehistoric times, while local legend has it, for the benefit of naughty children, that Satan resides at the bottom of it. Another vineyard plot is called Le Théâtre, for it forms a small natural amphitheatre where plays are performed on summer evenings. The area is cooler than the northern Rhône valley, for it benefits from the cooling effect of the Alps, and this makes it very different from the southern part of the Coteaux Varois.

Luc Sorin helped Bieler to build a cellar, or as he put it, 'helped him to spend a lot of money', and made the first vintages. However, Sorin's style was very much classic French, producing wines that demanded to be aged, but for Bieler you cannot sell a Coteaux Varois that needs time. It must have an immediate drinkability, even if it will also benefit from further ageing in bottle. Consequently in 1996 he enlisted the help of Bob Lindquist from Qupé in Sante Bulbera, and as a result his wines have become much more accessible and consumer-friendly. A basic difference is that Lindquist prefers open-top metal tanks to closed stainless steel. He also favours less extracted wines and wants them to undergo some oxygenation, so most of the wines are given some *élevage* in barrel.

We sat in the dining room and tasted with a forest of glasses in front of us, while Bieler poured an eclectic range of wines, interspersed with serious comments and humourous observations. Not all his wines conform to the appellation as, with Lindquist's encouragement, he has extended his range to include some varietal wines. The 1996 Pyramus is a fragrant white, from Rolle, Ugni Blanc and Clairette. Coquelicot, a blend of Viognier and Chardonnay, is a Vin de Pays du Var, for neither grape variety features in the appellation. Amusingly, Qupé means poppy in North American Indian, as does *coquelicot* in French. Cuttings of Viognier from Condrieu were grafted on to thirty-five-year-old vines and both varieties are fermented in wood, so that the flavour has a toasted oakiness and an underlying streak of Viognier oiliness. A 1995 Ugni Blanc, Théâtre, is fermented in new wood, giving a firm oaky character, balanced with acidity, and providing an unusual dimension to an often unexciting grape variety. The 1996 Rouvière, a pink wine that was partly fermented in old wood, with a partial malolactic fermentation, was rounded and mouth filling.

The range of reds is even more varied. The 1992 Traditional from Cabernet Sauvignon, Cinsaut and Carignan was unoaked, with rounded berry fruit and some spice, whereas later vintages are now put in *foudres* for a few months. This was Bieler's first vintage, made by Luc Sorin, and the 1992 Infernet, from fifty per cent Grenache Noir with some Syrah, Cabernet Sauvignon, Carignan and Cinsaut, was peppery, with hints of cedarwood and the scents of the *garrigue*. In contrast, the 1996 was much more accessible, with peppery fruit and more immediate appeal, demonstrating the contrast between the French and the Californian wine making approaches. The 1992 Agrippa, from equal parts of Cabernet Sauvignon and Syrah, spent about ten months in oak, including a small amount of new wood, and was chunky and intense with firm meaty, cassis flavours. This blend is now called Mistral after the wind. Cyrano is a pure Syrah given eighteen months in barrel, and the 1994 was closed and peppery with structure and elegance. A pure Carignan is made from some forty-five-year-old vines that ripen late with a small yield. Part of the wine spends six months in small oak, resulting in some peppery flavours and cherry fruit, as well as more elegance than is usually associated with this often decried grape variety.

This is an estate where nothing is taken for granted. Bieler has a forceful personality and a strong sense of purpose; he is intent on obtaining the best from his grapes, caring little for appellation regulations and questioning everything. His enthusiasm carries him along on a tidal wave.

CHATEAU LA CALISSE, PONTEVES

Château la Calisse outside the village of Pontevès is another new estate, but of French origin. Once there had been mulberry trees for silk worms and subsequently vines were planted, but when Patricia Ortelli and her husband bought the estate, the vineyards were abandoned and they had to build a cellar, which was finished the day before their first harvest began in 1996. He is a Peugeot dealer for the region and she went back to college, to study oenology as a mature student at Hyères. You approach the cellars through an alley of lavender bushes. The vineyards, six stony hectares in all, lie at four hundred and fifty metres and face due south, with views of the village of Pontavès and the Mont Ste Victoire in the distance. The soil is very red and the vineyards are lined with rose bushes, white blooms for the red varieties and vice versa. They follow organic methods in the vineyards.

The cellar is neat and compact, operating by gravity, with stainless steel vats for the white wine and cement for the red. Patricia Ortelli's first vintage promised well. A white, from Rolle with twenty per cent Grenache Blanc and ten per cent Clairette, was quite full and biscuity. The pink, a Grenache Noir and Syrah blend, was redolent of ripe strawberries, and best of all was the red, made from equal parts of Syrah and Grenache Noir with ten per cent Cabernet Sauvignon; it showed soft, spicy fruit and tannin.

DOMAINE DE TRIANS, GAREOLES

Domaine de Trians, outside the village of Garéoles, was an abandoned property in 1990, when it was bought by Jean-Louis Masurel, a Parisian financier. There were twenty hectares of vines, half of which have been replanted and half severely pruned so that they could be trained on wires. The cellar is a recently constructed and elegant shed, well equipped for modern vinification methods. They produce two wines of each colour, labelled either château or domaine, vinifying each plot separately, differentiating not only grape varieties but also older vines. The white wines are made from Rolle, Ugni Blanc and Sémillon. The 1996 white Château de Trians was ripe and heavy, quite honeyed and full bodied, benefiting from some skin contact, but there was no domaine white that year as wild boar ate two and a half hectares of grapes. The domaine *rosé*, from Grenache Noir and Cinsaut, was ripe and rounded with some strawberry fruit, while the château wine, which includes a little Syrah, had more fruit and finesse.

Reds benefit from a period of cool maceration before fermentation and a few days of *maceration à chaud* afterwards, in order to extract maximum flavour from the grapes. The 1994 Domaine de Trians had blackberry flavours on both nose and palate, with soft tannins, while the 1995 Château de Trians was more concentrated and chunkier, with spicy, peppery flavours. It contains more Syrah than the domaine wine, along with Grenache Noir and Carignan. I was left with the impression of a well-run estate, despite the absentee owner.

DOMAINE DU LOOU, LA ROQUEBRUSSANNE

More traditional is Domaine du Loou at La Roquebrussanne. It is owned by Daniel de Placido, president of the growers' *syndicat* and mayor of the village. His brother-in-law, Jean-Claude Giamarchi, makes the wine and gave us a tasting in the spacious conventional Midi cellar, with its huge cement vats and large barrels. Loou is an old *provençal* word meaning to work the land, or in this context, a place where the land is cultivated, compared to some of the more rugged and inaccessible terrain of the Coteaux Varois. The origins of the estate are Gallo-Roman, and they have found the remains of tombs from that period when replanting the vineyards. Once there were almond trees, wheat and sheep as well as vines, and now they have about fifty-five hectares of vineyards in production, mainly of Syrah, as well as Grenache Noir and Cabernet Sauvignon.

The first Cabernet Sauvignon was planted about 1978 and Syrah followed in the early 1980s; Mourvèdre had already been planted after the Second World War. They are moving towards more structured wines, concentrating on Syrah, with less Grenache Noir. Longer macerations provide length and tannins, and the wine usually spends about eight to twelve months in wood, after blending fifteen months after the vintage. A 1996 pure Syrah promised well, while the 1994 red Coteaux Varois was disappointingly lacking in fruit. However, the 1983, a pre-appellation wine, demonstrated the ageing potential, with some mature cedary flavours. Rolle and Sémillon have been planted for white wine, while Grenache Noir and Cinsaut constitute the pink wine, which was pretty and fresh.

DOMAINE DU DEFFENDS, ST MAXIMIN-LA-STE-BAUME

Another very traditional estate is Domaine du Deffends, situated on a hillside offering wonderful views just outside St Maximin-la-Ste-Baume in the south western corner of the appellation. Its origins are Roman; a Roman coin was found in the vineyard and the Via Aurelia, which ran from Rome to Spain, passes close by. Suzel de Lanversin bought the abandoned property with her husband, a professor of law, back in 1963 and gradually they decided to do something with their land, first planting the vineyards and then making wine for the first time in 1981. The grapes were selling too cheaply, so they realised that they were faced with a choice, either to build their own cellar and make wine, or to pull up the vines – so they built a cellar.

Some Viognier was grafted for a first vintage in 1995, so that they now make a delicious blend of Viognier and Rolle as a Vin de Pays du Var. Originally they had thought to make two separate varietal wines, but find the blend more satisfying. In addition they have Clairette, Sémillon, Grenache Blanc and what M. de Lanversin called the 'ignoble' Ugni Blanc. They also had the idea to plant Chenin Blanc. They were told that they are mad, but none the less they have about five hundred vines, just to see, from which they have yet to make some wine. Their main red wine, Clos de la Truffière, is a blend of Syrah and Cabernet Sauvignon that spends about twelve to sixteen months in *foudres*. I was treated to a vertical tasting over dinner. The 1996 was rounded and spicy. The 1995 had more concentration of fruit and plenty of potential, while the 1994 was rounded, with sweet cassis flavours. Generally the vintages of the 1990s have been more difficult than those of the previous decade, with 1982, 1985 and 1990 being particular successes. We finished with the 1986, which was elegantly peppery and firm. Maybe it was drying very slightly on the finish in comparison with the younger wines, but was delicious none the less, especially with a truffle omelette made with truffles found on the property by Syrah, their keen-nosed teckel.

CHATEAU LA CURNIERE, TAVERNES

Michèle Pérignon explained that she and her husband were looking for an active retirement when they bought Château la Curnière some ten years ago. He originated from Champagne and she came from Vichy, which she described as a region of water. The property had been somewhat neglected by the previous owners, so they pulled up the Carignan and replanted Syrah and Cabernet Sauvignon, keeping the old Grenache Noir and Cinsaut. They have also added Rolle and Sémillon, as well as some Chardonnay for a *vin de pays*, and now have fifteen hectares in production. The vineyards are some of the most northern of the appellation, lying at three hundred metres, so that spring frost can be a problem, and yields tend to be low, around 35 hl/ha.

La Curnière is an elegant early eighteenth-century building with its own small chapel and a cellar at one end. Methods are quite simple, and the wine is made with the help of Elphège Bailly, another of the talented oenologists of Provence. They produce three varietal *vins de pays*, Chardonnay, Cabernet Sauvignon and Rolle, and one *cuvée* of each colour of the appellation, of which red is the most important. The white is mainly Rolle, with a little Sémillon. The Rolle is left almost to overripen so that it can be fermented with the later-ripening Sémillon, and the wine had a herbal, nutty character. The pink is a blend of Grenache Noir, which is pressed, and Cinsaut, which is *saignée*, making what Mme Pérignon called a *rosé vif des collines*. The Cinsaut gives suppleness and elegance, while the Grenache Noir provides weight, with some raspberry fruit and acidity. The red, from equal parts of Grenache Noir and Syrah with about fifteen per cent Cabernet Sauvignon, part of which spends six months in *barriques*, but is mainly aged in vat for a couple of years, in order to soften the tannins rather than provide any oaky flavour, had some appealing peppery, spicy fruit. The wines were supple and charming, with some easy, accessible flavours.

DOMAINE DES ALYSSES, PONTEVES

In contrast, the wines of Jean-Marc Etienne at Domaine des Alysses demand time and thought. His is a small property outside the village of Pontevès. Twenty years ago the grapes here went to the co-operative, until he bought the land in 1977, pulled up the old vines, replanted and built a small cellar on to the back of the house. This is now bursting at the seams with vats, *barriques* and *foudres*, and a new cellar is under construction. Etienne is one of the original thinkers of the area, indeed of the south. He explained how he had been a French teacher at the Institut Franco-Scandinave in Aix-en-Provence and had then worked on various estates until he had the opportunity to buy this land. He now has twelve hectares, mostly around his house with its large mulberry tree, of Cabernet Sauvignon, Grenache Noir, Syrah and some Merlot for *vin de pays*, and he has rented some vineyards of Chardonnay and Pinot Noir. The soil is red and stony, a mixture of clay and limestone, with traces of bauxite. The vineyards lie at an altitude of about 380 metres, making for more *nerveux* wine, with good ageing potential.

We sat in the kitchen and tasted. First was a Chardonnay. Etienne admitted that he would not have chosen Chardonnay, as he dislikes varietal wines and prefers the complexity of a blend, but it is part of a rented vineyard. The wine spends time on the lees, with some *bâtonnage*, in a small vat, and is bottled the following spring. From his own vineyard Etienne makes three wines. There is a pink, which he described as not being his *tasse de té*; it was fresh and fruity, but certainly did not have the interest of the red wines. The first, Cuvée Angélique, named after a great friend who helped him to sell his wine, is made mainly by carbonic maceration and is a blend of Grenache Noir, Cabernet Sauvignon and Carignan, making what Etienne called *un petit vin de paysan*. He explained that the carbonic maceration takes fifteen days, for if it is too short you obtain only primary fruit, whereas he wants a wine that will last longer. As the grapes are crushed, the classic fermentation takes over at the end and then the wine spends some time in *foudres* before bottling. There was some attractive spicy, plummy fruit, while the carbonic maceration gave a certain suppleness.

The Cuvée Prestige is quite different, a wine demanding time and patience. It is a blend of fifty per cent Grenache Noir, twenty per cent Cabernet Sauvignon and thirty per cent Syrah that undergoes as slow a vinification as possible and then a long post-fermentation maceration, leaving the cap in contact with the juice in a closed vat for three or four weeks. You have to take great care that the malolactic fermentation does not start; if it does, he runs the juice off immediately, into *barriques* of one wine, for eighteen months. The 1994, tasted in the spring of 1998, was deep in colour, with closed, concentrated flavours, structure and tannin. It was intense but elegant at the same time, promising great things in five or ten years' time. In fact it went very well with a casserole of *macassin*, or baby wild boar, at the friendly Chez Nous restaurant in St Maximin later that evening. Somehow the gutsy flavours of the boar softened the wine.

Etienne is a firm believer in organic viticulture. That is how he started, although he admitted that the organic image can be something of two-edged sword, a hindrance as well as a help. The two main diseases in the region are mildew and oidium, which can be treated with copper sulphate and sulphur dioxide. He uses no weedkiller, no insecticides and only organic fertilisers. Things are more complicated in the cellars, but if your wine is in balance, you do not need lots of sulphur dioxide.

It is not always easy to create a vineyard and cellar from scratch, for it demands capital. You can see the advantage enjoyed by the larger foreign investors compared with the small *vigneron*. The price of land has increased and now a hectare of good vines in the Coteaux Varois costs FF 100–150,000. I left with a feeling that Domaine des Alysses, like its appellation, deserved a much bigger reputation.

One of the problems with the Coteaux Varois is that the word Provence does not feature anywhere on the label. Even ardent lovers of all things Provençal can overlook the fact that the main department of Provence is the Var. The area is overshadowed by its bigger, but not necessarily better, neighbours, the Coteaux d'Aix-en-Provence and the Côtes de Provence. It is a compact, homogeneous area that is working hard to get itself better known, and thanks to the interest of foreign investors it should succeed. Certainly it has undergone dramatic changes. It was Emmanuel Gaujal who said that he had seen *la préhistoire* as far as hygiene was concerned twenty-five years ago. There has also been an enormous growth in the amount of wine sold in bottle, from ninety per cent in bulk twenty-five years ago to eighty per cent in bottle today. Gaujal observed that the Coteaux Varois today are where Bandol was twenty years ago – and look where Bandol is today.

Key facts

Vin de pays 1973, VDQS for red and pink wine in 1984 and for white in 1989, AC for all three colours in 1993.

Two-thirds pink, one-third red and just three per cent white.

Twenty-eight communes between Coteaux d'Aix-en-Provence and Côtes de Provence, with Brignoles at centre.

Seventeen hundred hectares planted, but not all producing AC.

Grape varieties:

RED: Grenache Noir, Syrah and Mourvèdre, combined minimum of seventy per cent; Carignan and Cinsaut, maximum of thirty per cent.

WHITE: Cabernet Sauvignon, maximum twenty per cent; Rolle, Grenache Blanc, Clairette and Semillon, maximum thirty per cent; Ugni blanc, maximum twenty-five per cent.

Vineyards average 350 metres in altitude, so are cooler than those of Côtes de Provence.

Vintages

Generally the decade finished better than it began, with the exception of the fine vintage of 1990.

1999: A hot, dry summer with some localised rain, followed by a sunny autumn, with a harvest in fine weather. Good quantity and quality, making for balanced wines with ripe fruit and soft tannins. Promises well.

1998: A year of excellent climatic conditions, making well-balanced wines with some staying power.

1997: Another excellent vintage, one of the best of the decade, with a fine summer. Small crop resulting from an April frost.

1996: A year that was marked by rain, giving some problems with rot. Saved by a fine October. Lighter wines than usual.

1995: A warm, dry year, making quite sturdy, tannic wines.

DOMAINE DE VALMOISSINE, AUPS

A postscript to the Coteaux Varois is provided by two nearby *vins de pays*. The first is Domaine de Valmoissine, just outside the town of Aups on the northern edge of the appellation. Here the Burgundian house of Louis Latour planted twenty hectares of Pinot Noir in 1989, employing their Burgundian expertise to make a varietal Pinot Noir sold as a Vin de Pays des Coteaux du Verdon, the regional *vin de pays* named after the dramatic gorges in the northern part of the department. The cooler climate seems to suit this fickle grape variety and Burgundian talent has produced some convincing silky flavours.

DOMAINE DE TRIENNES, ST MAXIMIN-LA-STE-BAUME

Burgundians are also responsible for the creation of Domaine de Triennes outside St Maximin-la-Ste-Baume. The vineyards were bought in 1990 by Jacques Seysses of Domaine Dujac and Aubert de Vilaine, who owns a family estate in the Côte Chalonnaise and is also part owner of Domaine de la Romanée Conti with a mutual friend, Michel Macaux. Why the Var? Jacques Seysses was looking to do something new, but the New World options are all so far away; however, the Var is just a five-hour drive from Burgundy and so it would be possible to be closely involved with both estates. However, he does admit that he failed to realise quite how demanding Domaine de Triennes would be. Seysses looked at about twenty different estates over a six-month period in 1989, seeking a cooler site to avoid the blistering summer heat of the Midi.

Estate manager Rémi Laugier explained that this was once a typical Midi estate, planted with Cinsaut, Ugni Blanc, Carignan and Alicante for high yields of bulk wine, but that it had now been completely transformed. There are forty-six hectares in one large plot, limited by the Aurélien hills to the north and the main road to the south. Extensive grafting has changed the composition of the vineyard. There was already some Cabernet Sauvignon and Syrah, but they have added Chardonnay, Merlot and Viognier, with the express objective of *vins de cépage*. In common with the Coteaux Varois the grapes ripen quite late here, so that in 1997, for example, the vintage lasted from 20 September to 11 October. Yields have been severely reduced, from 120 hl/ha down to 40 hl/ha. They decided against Pinot Noir. As Jacques Seysses rightly observed, with the combined reputations of Domaine de la Romanée Conti and Domaine Dujac, any Pinot Noir they produce has to be excellent, but with Cabernet Sauvignon and Syrah they are allowed to enjoy a learning process, finding out about their new *terroir*.

Although there was an existing cellar, it was not very satisfactory and they have invested in new vats as well as *barriques*. There are rotary vats for a shorter *cuvaison*, as well as traditional ones, and a Bucher pneumatic press, which is described as the Rolls Royce of wine presses. Some of the barrels come from Domaine Dujac, and are even still marked as Charmes-Chambertin and Morey-St-Denis.

We tasted from barrel. There was some delicate Viognier that was given just four hours of skin contact; this constituted a new challenge, as Viognier is difficult and he had not produced it before. An elegant Chardonnay was made very much in the Burgundian way, with lees stirring. Barrel samples of Syrah, Merlot and Cabernet Sauvignon followed, all showing potential. Laugier considers Cabernet Sauvignon to be more successful here than Merlot, as it is a later-ripening variety and its small berries resist any rot successfully. Asked about the principal differences between wine making here and in the Côte d'Or, Seysses talked about reduction. Pinot Noir is usually made in a very reductive way, while Syrah responds better to more oxidation, preferring *remontages* and *délestages* to *pigeage*. He also gives the wine a very much longer *cuvaison* than for Pinot Noir, maybe as long as thirty days, aiming for supple tannins, for at a certain moment there is a chemical change resulting in the softening of the tannins.

In bottle, the Viognier showed some delicate apricot fruit, but without any oily mouth feel. The Chardonnay, Le Clos Barry, which spends six to ten months in oak, was quite full and buttery, intended for relatively early drinking. Le Gris de Triennes, a *rosé* from Cinsaut, had a delicate colour, with a fresh strawberry fruit and elegance. As for reds, they make a pure Merlot, of which the 1995 was quite smoky and compared favourably with the 1995 Cabernet Sauvignon. Les Auréliens is a blend of equal parts of Syrah and Cabernet Sauvignon; the 1994 was quite cedary and the 1993 was more closed, with a note of austerity. It was a very dry year, making for wines with a long future. Finally, in the very best years they take the most successful vats of Cabernet Sauvignon and Syrah to blend them for a Cuvée Réserve. The 1995 was the first, from two-thirds Cabernet Sauvignon to one-third Syrah. It had a rounded, smoky nose, firm fruit and a long structured palate, with ageing potential, providing an exciting example of what outsiders can do in the region without regard for appellation regulations, for these are mere Vin de Pays du Var.

Côtes de Provence

Despite its name, the appellation of the Côtes de Provence covers a relatively small part of the former Provincia Romana. Vines have been grown here since the Greeks founded the city of Marseille in the sixth century BC. The Romans furthered the importance of viticulture: Julius Caesar created the port of Fréjus, formerly known as Forum Julii, and wrote in his *Commentaries* about the region's wines, which found their way to Rome.

In the early thirteenth century the marriage of Eleanor of Provence to the English king Henry III brought the wines of Provence to England. A couple of centuries later René of Anjou, the last Count of Provence, was a great ambassador of his country's wines. He was born in Angers and became titular king of Naples, Sicily and Jerusalem, and ceded Provence to Louis XI of France when he died without heirs in 1480. He was a man of letters who is also credited with the introduction of the Muscat grape to Provence, from whence it spread west. It was planted extensively around Cassis until phylloxera destroyed the vineyards, and today features in the various *vins doux* of the Languedoc. René of Anjou is also said to have invented the method of making *clairet*, a deeper-coloured pink wine, for until the fifteenth century, even wines made from red grapes were no more than pale pink in colour.

In the seventeenth century that indefatigable letter writer Madame de Sevigné often stayed at Entrecasteaux near Draguignan and enthused about the local wines. It was only in the nineteenth century that wine became the most important agricultural product of Provence, for until then it had been overshadowed by cereals, olives, fruit and vegetables. The vines grew on terraced hillsides, mixed with olive and fruit trees, and wheat was cultivated in the valleys.

None of the nineteenth-century authorities wrote about the wines of Provence with noticeable enthusiasm. Jullien tells us that 92,900 hectares produced 1,687,000 hectolitres in 1816, of which 889,000 were drunk locally. The most sought after were the Muscat wines and the *vins cuits* or cooked wines. He said that the variety of grapes grown was enormous, but the mixture gave no specific taste to the wine and took away all its qualities without giving it anything. No mention was made of any pink wine, only red and white, *vins cuits* and Muscats. For Rendu, the wines of Provence were mostly in the class of common wines for local consumption, and there was a lack of good grapes and careful vinification. Cavoleau wrote that the wines of Provence had little reputation and were only sought after in France when there was a small harvest in other vineyards. He thought that they had potential, with good grapes and a suitable climate, but that there was a lack of attention to the production process.

Phylloxera wrought havoc in the vineyards of Provence in the 1870s, and during the subsequent replanting the low-yielding Mourvèdre was abandoned in favour of the more prolific Carignan. Muscat too disappeared. However, the early years of the twentieth century saw the introduction of improving grape varieties from outside the region. Marcel Ott arrived from Alsace and bought Château de Selle near the village of Taradeau in 1912, and in the spirit of experimentation he planted the vineyards with all the principal grape varieties of France, including Gewürztraminer, Riesling, Cabernet Sauvignon, Sémillon, Sauvignon and so on. Others were to build upon his work, and the 1930s saw the first tentative efforts towards the recognition of a standard of quality, with the formation of an association dedicated to obtaining an appellation.

This ambition was not ultimately achieved until 1977, although a VDQS was granted for the Côtes de Provence in 1951. The issue was confused by the union of a group of *crus classés*, consisting of some twenty-three estates, which was formally recognised by the INAO in 1955. At the time these were considered to be the best estates, but in practice they were those that regularly bottled their own wines rather than selling in bulk to local merchants. Although the classification still exists, as the only system of *crus classés* outside Bordeaux, it is now of little significance and the fortunes of these twenty-odd properties have fluctuated. Some have disappeared altogether and only a handful merit a reputation today. There are other, newer estates that would merit inclusion in any modern classification, but the INAO, with its strong Bordelais influence, has forbidden the extension of the classification. Here for the record is the list of estates recognised in 1955: Domaine de Mauvanne, Coteaux des Ferrages, Domaine de la Source Ste-Marguerite, Castel Roubine, Domaine de l'Aumérade, Domaine de la Clapière, Clos du Relars, Domaine de Rimauresq, Château Ste Rosaline, Château de Selle, Clos Mireille, Château St Martin, Domaine de la Croix, Domaine de St Maur, Clos Gibonne, Domaine du Galoupet, Domaine de Bregançon, Château Minuty, Domaine de la Grande Loube, Domaine du Noyer and Domaine du Jas d'Esclans. Those worthy of note today include the two Ott properties, Clos Mireille and Château de Selle, Château Ste Rosaline, Château Minuty and a handful of the others. There is talk in some quarters about reviving the classification, which as yet has come to nothing.

The area of the Côtes de Provence was delimited to eighteen thousand hectares in eighty-three *communes* in 1951 and was not significantly altered with the introduction of the appellation in 1977. The vineyards cover a wide area, mainly in the department of the Var, including islands off the coast such as Porquerolles and Lérins, as well as a few villages in the Bouches-du-Rhône. The Massif des Maures separates the more maritime vineyards from those inland; on the west side the appellation adjoins the Coteaux Varois, while the sprawling city of Toulon interrupts the coastal vineyards. Finally there is just one isolated *commune*, Villars-sur-Var, in the department of the Alpes-Maritimes. The appellation covers a considerable variety of terrain and microclimate, leading to quite a diversity in the wines. The soil changes too, for clay and limestone are the dominant constituents inland, whereas shale with quartz is more common in the coastal vineyards. In either case the soil is poor and stony and lacking in humus, the type of soil that vines love but in which little else can grow.

As in other large appellations, there are moves to distinguish between the local variations in soil and climate, but as yet none of these delimitations has any official or legal weight. La Bordure Maritime covers the coastal area from St Raphael to Toulon, taking in the Presque 'Ile of St Tropez. The soil is granite and schist and the maritime influence is very marked. The Vallée Intérieure to the north of the Massif des Maures is the largest area, providing about half the production of the appellation, including the *communes* of Cuers, Pierrefeu, Vidauban and Les Arcs. The Collines du Haut Pays around Draguignan is a region of hills and valleys, with red iron soil and white pebbles. As it is nearer to the mountains, winters are harder and summers are hot, unmitigated by maritime breezes. The Bassin du Beausset is a small area squeezed between the appellations of Bandol and Cassis. Limestone is the main soil component here, with the white cliffs reflecting sun and heat and the sea bringing cooling breezes. Finally the area of the Massif Sainte Victoire covers the vineyards on the southern edge of the mountain, where the Mistral can blow hard; there is a more continental climate and the soil is a mixture of limestone and sandstone.

The average annual production totals some eight hundred thousand hectolitres, of which pink wines currently account for between seventy-five and eighty per cent. It was *rosé* that was responsible for the early popularity of Côtes de Provence and which today poses problems. When the Côte d'Azur became a popular holiday destination and tourists flocked to Provence, they wanted light, refreshing wines to quench their thirst in the warm sunshine. Pink Côtes de Provence was the ideal drink, perceived as a pretty, frivolous wine for holidays, picnics and barbecues. The production of white Côtes de Provence is very limited, just five cent, while the grapes that make red wine can equally well produce pink wine to satisfy the holidaymakers. However, the demand for *rosé* outside the tourist season is non-existent. For many Frenchmen, the first requirement of a wine is that it should be red, even when they are eating fish. Consequently in recent years there was been a gentle drift towards red wine among the more serious producers who are eager to establish a longer-lasting reputation for their wines.

The climate is Mediterranean, with hot, dry summers, cool winters and a small annual rainfall of 600–800 mm, which usually falls at the end of autumn and in the spring. The summer months are generally free of rain and the vines can suffer from drought. In some places where the water table is high, the vines' roots are able to tap underground sources of water. Provence is the region of the Mistral, the north east wind that comes down the corridor of the Rhône valley, reaching speeds of 100 kph and sometimes damaging the younger, more fragile vines. Generally though, it does more good than harm, for it prevents the humidity that causes rot and disease. For those who practise organic viticulture, and there are several in the appellation, life is made easier by the drying effects of the Mistral. Even for those who are not purely organic, treatments are less demanding than in damper regions.

Such a variety of soil and microclimates encourages a diversity of grape varieties. The tiny amount of white comes from Ugni Blanc, Clairette, Sémillon and Rolle. While Sauvignon is allowed in the appellation of Coteaux d'Aix-en-Provence, it does not feature in the Côtes de Provence, nor does Grenache Blanc. Red grape varieties account for ninety-five per cent of the vineyards, with considerable variations from one estate to another. A sharp drop in the percentage of Carignan has been balanced by an increase in Grenache Noir and growing interest in Syrah and Cabernet Sauvignon. When the appellation was first created, Carignan accounted for seventy per cent of the blend for red and pink wines, but is now limited to forty per cent. Cinsaut is popular for pink wines, and the soft-skinned Tibouren also makes some successful *rosé*. Mourvèdre performs very much better in Bandol than in any of the vineyards of the Côtes de Provence, especially those inland where it sometimes fails to ripen fully.

The two grape varieties that have attracted the most interest are Syrah and Cabernet Sauvignon. They can both enhance the sometimes bland wines of the Côtes de Provence, but neither must exceed thirty per cent in a blend. Indeed, the appellation regulations are littered with maximum and minimum percentages. They determine what is planted in a vineyard – but who is to say that a wine does or does not contain a certain percentage of a particular grape variety, provided it tastes 'typical' of the appellation? Cabernet Sauvignon arouses enthusiasm for its potential to enliven and refine the sometimes rugged flavours of the south. However, serious producers are adamant that it should not be allowed to overwhelm the true flavour of the appellation, for the last thing they want to produce is a *provençal* claret. Even so, it is undeniable that a small amount of Cabernet Sauvignon provides aroma and backbone to a wine, without changing the essential character of a Côtes de Provence. Syrah, as one of the *cépages améliorateurs* of the Languedoc, has also been encroaching on the vineyards of Provence. It certainly contributes flavour and fruit, without detracting from the true character of the appellation.

Vinification methods have improved dramatically, keeping pace with the modernisation of cellars all over the south of France.

Temperature control is now the norm in any well-equipped cellar. There are stainless steel vats for fermenting white and pink wines, but concrete vats, in which the temperature fluctuations are much less dramatic, are still favoured for red wines. Wine in stainless steel responds quickly to heat or cold, whereas in concrete the impact is much slower. Large *foudres* are still the traditional containers for the *élevage* of red wines, while *barriques* are also used by more adventurous estates, for red and white, and sometimes pink, wine.

The range of quality is still quite dramatic, both amongst private producers and the village co-operatives. Fifty-two co-operatives vinify just over half the annual production of the appellation, and there are some three hundred and fifty private estates. I was able to visit just a few, chosen partly by those whose reputation is well established on the international market and partly by the publicity arm of the energetic Comité Interprofessionnel, who responded well to my request to meet people who were articulate and thoughtful about their appellation. Inevitably, there are some obvious omissions.

The appellation has a fine showcase at the Maison des Vins, on the main road outside the village of Les Arcs. Each *vigneron* who belongs to the *syndicat* can exhibit his wines there. They encourage visitors to taste and buy, and there is a welcoming restaurant where you can enjoy bottles at greater leisure – all of which helps to develop the touristic aspect of the appellation's wines.

Much of the recent improvement in the Côtes de Provence has come from foreign investment and changes in ownership. About seventy of the private estates, some twenty per cent, have changed hands since the end of the 1980s, and as many as half of these have been bought by foreigners, not just for a holiday home in Provence, but also with the positive intention of doing something with their property. New estates have also been created by former co-operative members who have decided to take an independent route.

Bordure Maritime

DOMAINE DES PLANES, ROQUEBRUNE-SUR-ARGENS

Domaine des Planes, outside the attractive village of Roquebrune-sur-Argens with its lovely russet-coloured roofs, belongs to a Swiss-German couple, Christophe and Ilse Rieder. They met over studies at Geisenheim, which they completed in Montpellier. They then spent five years at La Croix Valmer, 'when it was still a serious estate', before buying Domaine des Planes in 1980. The vineyards were in good condition, but they needed to modernise the cellar, which is now more of a spacious insulated warehouse with stainless steel vats, Swiss *tonneaux* in the traditional oval form of German barrels, and a pneumatic press. Mme Rieder explained how suitable the microclimate is here, on the edge of the Massif des Maures. Many English people settled here at the beginning of the last century and created the first golf course in the region.

Their twenty-seven hectares includes Syrah, Grenache Noir, Mourvèdre, Cabernet Sauvignon, Tibouren, a little Carignan and Cinsaut, Sémillon, Rolle and some Clairette that was planted in 1902. They make an impressive range of wines with various *cuvées*, all illustrating thoughtful wine making and a perceptive appreciation of the different grape varieties. Cuvée Flamant Rosé, from Grenache Noir and Cinsaut, is partly *saignée* and partly given a cold maceration before pressing. A closed pneumatic press can be used almost like a vat, in an intermediate stage before pressing. Tibouren is a peculiarly Provençal grape variety, really only found in the Côtes de Provence, and even then mainly on the coastal area between Grimaud and Toulon rather than in the hinterland. It is particularly suitable for *rosé*, but can prove quite problematic in the vineyard. Bud break comes early, so it can suffer from spring frosts and needs attention. It produces a lot of buds and can be sensitive to the weather during flowering, resulting in *coulure*. Throughout the ripening season it can prove susceptible to rot, especially during the August storms. It produces small, very sweet grapes. They give it a cold maceration and no malolactic fermentation, resulting in a delicate floral flavour. The Cuvée Admirable comes from young Mourvèdre vines, the grapes of which, as in Bandol, are better for pink than for red wine. It was rounded and ripe. Quite simply, if something tastes good on its own, they do not blend it with anything else.

Their white Côtes de Provence comes from sixty per cent Sémillon and forty per cent Rolle, vines that they planted when they arrived on the property. The Sémillon provides the bouquet and body on the palate, while the Rolle contributes fruit and acidity on the finish. For me, it had a solid, rounded mouthful of flavour. Cuvée Elegance, made for the first time in 1990, consists of Sémillon aged in forty-hectolitre *tonneaux* for three or four months. The oak in the 1996 vintage was well integrated and the wine was not unlike a good Graves in character. Their red wines include a Cuvée Sanglier, named after the wild boar that abound in the area and made from Syrah and Grenache Noir, which spend nine to twelve months in *tonneaux*. It had some rounded berry fruit. The Cuvée Réserve, from sixty per cent Cabernet Sauvignon and forty per cent Mourvèdre, was more structured, again with some ripe berry fruit. In the best years they make a pure Mourvèdre, which spends up to two years in *tonneaux*; the 1995 had some sturdy fruit, with well-integrated tannins. Illogically, their Cuvée Tradition is a pure Cabernet Sauvignon, which gives regular yields and better quality than Mourvèdre. It spends two years in *tonneaux* and *barriques* and tasted quite rugged. Although varietal wines are in some ways contrary to the appellation, they are permitted provided that you have the correct varieties in the vineyards. However, their pure Muscat, with its fresh, pithy fruit, is labelled Vin de Pays du Var, as Muscat is not part of the appellation, even though it was once a traditional variety in Provence.

CHATEAU MINUTY, GASSIN

Château Minuty, outside the village of Gassin near St Tropez, is an old estate, going back to the eighteenth century. The present château was built under Napoleon III, with the addition a few years later of a tiny chapel in the grounds to commemorate a son killed in the Franco-Prussian War. A mass is said there every year for the grape pickers. Since 1936 the estate has belonged to the Farnet family, but there has been a change of name: Mlle Farnet married a M. Mattron, and it is their son François Mattron who is now responsible for the day-to-day running of the property, concentrating particularly on the vineyards. He is young and opinionated, not afraid to voice his ideas about the current situation in the appellation. You sense that he really wants to do well for his estate. Altogether they make four wines of each colour: a *vin de pays*, Cuvée du Bailly, from young vines; Domaine Farnet, which is a separate estate at Vidauban; Château Minuty, Cuvée l'Oratoire, from vines that are at least ten years old, and finally a Cuvée Prestige. The two estates have a total of ninety hectares.

I was given a comparative tasting of the Cuvée l'Oratoire and the Cuvée Prestige. Rolle and Sémillon are the main varieties for white wine, and in the Cuvée l'Oratoire the Rolle provides perfume and Ugni Blanc the volume. Here they are looking for fruit and elegance, and it had just that, with good acidity. In contrast, the Cuvée Prestige, made for the first time in 1987, is a blend of Rolle and Sémillon, providing length, with much more body and weight. They have also tried fermenting it in barrel, but found that the oak simply overwhelmed the fruit.

The blend for the two *rosés* is different. Cuvée l'Oratoire, mainly from Cinsaut, with some Tibouren and Grenache Noir, is very traditional, with fresh, delicate fruit and lively acidity, while the *rosé* Prestige includes Syrah and some Mourvèdre, and has more body and length, with layers of flavour. Both are pressed rather than *saignée*. The two red wines provide the same contrast. Cuvée l'Oratoire is an equal blend of Syrah and Grenache Noir, without any wood. It is very much a red for summer drinking, with a short fermentation giving fresh fruit and soft tannins, making it eminently *gouleyant*, while the Cuvée Prestige is a blend of Cabernet Sauvignon, Syrah and Mourvèdre, vinified by carbonic maceration. The Syrah is aged in *barriques* for a couple of years. Although their first white vinification in oak was in 1991, they did not start experimenting with *élevage* in small barrels for red wine until 1994. Now the large cellar of *foudres* that you can see from the tasting room is just for show, a striking visual reminder of old Provence.

CHATEAU DU GALOUPET, LA-LANDES-LES-MAURES

The heavens opened as I arrived at Château du Galoupet, and the pots of lemon trees and palm trees in the courtyard seemed quite out of place in the teeming rain. Since 1973 this has been the property of the Shivdasani family, who also owned Château St Jean-de-Villecroze and Château Vignelaure for a brief period in the early 1990s. Jean-Pierre Marty is the highly capable and well-informed manager who has been responsible for running the estate since 1993. He enthused about the potential for the development of viticulture in Provence with its soil variations and huge diversity of grape varieties, as well as the considerable scope for investment, all in sharp contrast to the conservatism of Bordeaux. There are seventy-two hectares of vines at Galoupet, and some of the older vineyards have been replanted, reducing the amount of Cinsaut. Grenache Noir is the main variety, but there is also Syrah, Tibouren and Mourvèdre for red wine, as well as Rolle and Sémillon for white wine, while Chardonnay and Cabernet Sauvignon are used for *vins de pays*. The Carignan has now all gone. They make two qualities of wine, Château du Galoupet and Les Charmettes du Galoupet.

Although there has been extensive modernisation, they have retained the wonderful sixteenth-century vaulted cellars. The estate was once the property of the Chartreux de la Verne at Cogolin, and the wine of Galoupet had a reputation at the time of Louis XIV. For red wines they believe in the traditions of Provence, which excludes Cabernet Sauvignon but includes Mourvèdre, even though it is the last to ripen. Nor do they want *barriques*, again because they are not typical of Provence, so the red wines are aged in *foudres*, with a new one purchased each year. However, as there is no real tradition for white wine in Provence, they are quite happy to use *barriques* for that. Everything is mechanically harvested, with different fermentation vats depending on grape variety, vineyard plot, different cultured yeast and so on.

Their white wine is a blend of one-third Sémillon to two-thirds Rolle, and a quarter of each is fermented in *barriques*, both old and new. Both are given skin contact and spend time on the lees for additional complexity. The wine was rounded, with good structure and mouth feel, and with balancing acidity. It will also age well, as the 1994 demonstrated with its elegantly complex, herbal flavours. The *rosé* is a blend of pressed and free-run juice, while a special *cuvée* is made from Tibouren, with some supple, elegant fruit. Red wine is a blend of Syrah, Grenache Noir and Mourvèdre aged in *foudres*, with some warm, spicy berry fruit and youthful appeal.

Marty spoke of moves to rejuvenate the Union des Crus Classés. Their formation coincided with the classifications of St Emilion and Graves in Bordeaux. At the time it was really those who put their wine in bottle. Today there is a self-imposed quality charter. There must be an actual château, and usually the estate makes all three colours – in other words, the only pink *cru classé* – while Clos Mireille is the exception in producing only white wine. Marty sees the *crus classés* as a real opportunity, a godsend, while others are not so sure.

CELLIER DES VIGNERONS DE RAMATUELLE, RAMATUELLE

Although the number of co-operatives has shrunk from sixty ten years ago to fifty-one today, they still account for fifty per cent of the production of the Côtes de Provence. In their own way, the more dynamic co-operatives are keeping abreast with viticultural developments and improvements in cellar technology. However, there is still a feeling that the co-operatives are above all producers of grapes, while it is the *vignerons* who actually make wine, even though some co-operatives are changing their image and improving their commercial attitudes. Nevertheless, I was told that members will refuse to attend an administration meeting on wild boar hunting days!

The Cellier des Vignerons at Ramatuelle is an example of a co-operative that works well for the appellation. They have 142 members in the *communes* of Ramatuelle, Gassin, la Croix Valmer and St Tropez, with 370 hectares of Côtes de Provence as well as seventy hectares of Vin de Pays des Maures. The holdings of members vary enormously in size, but you can earn a reasonable living with twelve hectares. The co-operative was not created until 1952, the penultimate co-operative of the department, and relatively late in the history of the co-operative movement. Inevitably, *rosé* dominates their production, with a very small amount of white and some red wine. Their members have been encouraged by bonuses to plant specific varieties such as Rolle, while Carignan has been pulled up and Merlot, which does well on the Presque Ile de St Tropez, has been planted for *vin de pays*.

They particularly favour Tibouren, paying the highest price for it, and their best *rosé*, Cuvée Antiboul, is a pure Tibouren. Antiboul was a sailor from St Tropez who is reputed to have brought Tibouren to the region in the nineteenth century. The wine was quite elegant, with structure and body, a vivid illustration of how co-operatives have progressed in the last ten years or so. They do not find Tibouren difficult to cultivate, but its yields are quite erratic. If it rains, the berries tend to burst, resulting in rot. Their best red, Cuvée l'Ormeau, after the old elm that dominates the square in the village of Ramatuelle, is a blend of Grenache Noir and a little Syrah, with some soft fruit, while the Cuvée Spéciale includes Mourvèdre as well as Grenache Noir and Syrah, with some meaty, perfumed fruit.

Ile de Porquerolles

A highlight in any tour of the Côtes de Provence must be a visit to the tiny island of Porquerolles, the largest of the Iles d'Hyères, where there are three wine estates. Vines have been encouraged on the island as they form an effective firebreak against forest fires, which are a considerable threat to the vegetation. Even the ferry ticket has a notice exhorting passengers to take care with matches and cigarettes. The boat leaves from La Tour Fondue, a ruined citadel on the point south of Hyères, and the crossing takes just twenty minutes across a calm sea. It was a beautiful spring morning, a sharp contrast with the previous day, when 30 mm of rain had fallen and we had almost paddled our way to dinner on the harbour at Hyères.

DOMAINE DE L'ILE

My first destination was the Domaine de l'Ile. Sebastian Ber's grandfather bought the island of Porquerolles in 1910 after he made his fortune in silver mines in Mexico. He left Mexico when the revolution broke out, and the island was said to have been a wedding present to his wife. They had five daughters, one of whom was Ber's mother, and it was she who planted vines. Most of the island now belongs to the French state and is protected as a national park, with collections of various Mediterranean plants, such as olive and bay trees. There are very few cars on the island, with dirt tracks for cyclists and pedestrians, and the small village of Porquerolles has just one hotel. The island is divided into four cultivated plains, namely the Village, La Courtade, Notre Dame and Brégançonnet. The green leaves of the trees on the shoreline made a vivid contrast with the azure sea and pale sand of the Plage de Notre-Dame, with views of the mainland in the distance. After the rain of the previous evening, the scent of the eucalyptus trees surrounding the vineyards was intoxicating, and I was enchanted, despite the cacophony of rowdy frogs croaking in a nearby pond.

Murielle Guillé makes the wine at Domaine de l'Ile. Their vineyards are in two parts: there are fifteen hectares in the western half of the island, on the plain of Brégançonnet, and in the eastern part they have rented sixteen hectares from the French government, including five hectares of olive trees. At Brégançonnet the soil is sandy and at Notre Dame it is schist, which particularly suits Syrah. In addition, they have plenty of Grenache Noir, as well as some Tibouren, Cinsaut, some very old Carignan and more recently planted Mourvèdre, with some Rolle for white wine. Mildew and oidium can be a problem, as the humidity is inevitably high, to the extent that people need dehumidifiers at home. The Mistral helps to protect the vines from rot and they try to aerate the vines as much as possible. The older vines are *en gobelet* and younger ones trained on wires. Deer can be a big problem as well as rabbits and pheasants, all of which are partial to young vine leaves, not to mention the odd grape or two. The salt in the wind can also burn the leaves.

1997 was a difficult vintage, as there was a huge storm in the middle of August, bringing problems with rot, so that they left a third of the grapes on the vines. That year was just their second vintage of white wine, made from Rolle that was given a few hours of skin contact, making for some delicate fruit. I found the *rosé*, made from a bit of everything, rather heavy, while the red, from Syrah and old Grenache Noir, was ripe, perfumed and fruity, with a peppery palate. It is intended to provide easy early drinking and does just that.

DOMAINE DE LA COURTADE

The more serious estate is Domaine de la Courtade, which is managed by Richard Auther, a talented Alsacien. He explained that Henri Vidal had originally bought the property in 1979 as a holiday home, but then decided to make more of his land. Auther was just finishing his studies at Dijon in 1985 when he was invited to submit a project for the estate. His was the one that was accepted, and he was given instructions to carry it out. He laughingly explained that Vidal's original intention had been to commission someone of about thirty-five with ten years' experience, whereas he was not yet twenty-five and had no experience. They began by clearing *garrigue* on the plain of La Courtade and planting Mourvèdre and Rolle, a little Grenache Noir, Tibouren for *rosé* and some Syrah. He believes that Mourvèdre has more character than Syrah here. It is quite capricious, with low yields, and you have to pay attention to disease, but it is very individual. He wanted something with character and that is what he has obtained, with Mourvèdre giving 'the best and the worst'. 1987 was the first real harvest at La Courtade.

We tasted our way around the cellar, with Auther explaining how he had created two levels, following the *bordelais* idea of a second wine, so that the Alicastre label includes all three colours and La Courtade just red and white. Alicastre is made from pure Rolle, for in Auther's opinion Sémillon is not *provençal* and Ugni Blanc is worse than rubbish. In fact, his description of Ugni Blanc enlarged my French vocabulary to include the expression to call a spade a spade, or in French, *un chat un chat*. The Rolle is given some skin contact but no malolactic fermentation and makes a wine with delicate, smoky fruit and good acidity. For a part of La Courtade Blanc he uses the system of *microbullage*, giving the wine an infinitesimal amount of oxygen, just 3 mgs/l per month, while it is kept on the lees. This provides richness without the effect of wood, and the lees, which prevent oxidation, are stirred every two weeks. Then the wine is blended in the early summer with some that has been in *barriques*. The best recent white vintage was 1995, which was quite full and buttery, but with an elegant finish. 1990 was a good year too, but the vines were still very young and so the flavour of the wine was masked by oak. Alicastre *rosé* is a blend of equal parts of Tibouren, Grenache Noir and Mourvèdre. The Grenache Noir is given a gentle maceration in the press, the Tibouren is pressed immediately and the Mourvèdre is free-run juice. Auther called it a *rosé de repas*, as it is quite full and solid, with a slow fermentation giving body and smoothness, enhanced by ten per cent from *barrique*. It was good, but I felt that it was made under sufferance to meet market demands.

More serious are the red wines. Red Alicastre is a blend of two-thirds Mourvèdre and one-third Grenache Noir. The 1995 had some perfumed fruit, with some of the meaty character of Mourvèdre and some tannin. It was what Auther called a *sympa*, or friendly, wine. La Courtade is rather more serious, made almost entirely from Mourvèdre with a drop of Syrah, which spend between twelve and eighteen months in older *barriques*. Several coopers are used, Radoux, Seguin Moreau and Saury, and usually medium toasted oak from the Vosges. The young 1995 had a ripe, rounded nose and palate, with body and tannin. The 1990 La Courtade showed just how well these wines age, with the warm flavours of the south, some meaty overtones, a structured backbone and an elegance originating from the schist soil.

DOMAINE PERZINKSY

Cyril Perzinksy is Richard Auther's brother-in-law, which is how he heard that land was available on Porquerolles for planting vines. He studied in Beaune and then moved south, working in Bandol at Pibarnon and Vannières, and has now been on Porquerolles for over ten years. His white wine is mainly Rolle with a drop of Sémillon, aged in second-hand Burgundian barrels from Bernard Michelot in Meursault. It was solid and rounded. His ten hectares include a lot of Mourvèdre, as well as some Grenache Noir and a little Syrah. The 1996 was firm and peppery and the 1995 had some tight fruit. It was not as supple as La Courtade – a difference attributed to *pigeage*, which makes for more tannin, whereas Auther only does *remontages*.

We finished with a conversation about Quarry Road, a New Zealand winery owned by Perzinksy's brother-in-law, which illustrates just how small the world of wine has become, and Auther opened a bottle of 1996 Porterolles, made from muted Mourvèdre. It was sweet and alcoholic, not unlike a ruby port, and went very well with chunks of Parmesan cheese. When I returned to the ferry, the sky was covered and the wind was beginning to blow, causing waves after the morning calm.

Collines du Haut Pays

DOMAINES OTT AT CHATEAU DE SELLE, TARADEAU

One of the best-known names in the Côtes de Provence is Domaines Ott. Altogether the family owns three estates, Clos Mireille and Château de Selle, both in the Côtes de Provence, and Château Romassan in Bandol, while their offices are on the coast in Antibes. Marcel Ott bought the run-down estate of Château de Selle near Taradeau in 1912. The land was used by the Counts of Provence for hunting wild boar, and the existing château was built in the eighteenth century. It is a beautiful old building with a façade of soft pink stone and terraced vineyards.

While Marcel Ott worked on his vineyards, establishing grape varieties such as Cabernet Sauvignon and Sémillon, his son concentrated on the commercial aspects of the business and created the distinctive Ott bottle, the design of which is based on the Provençal *jarre*, the large earthenware pot, or amphora, that today is so often filled with geraniums. His design was almost accepted as the standard Provence bottle, but instead there is a plethora of different shapes, including a *négociant's* bottle and a producer's bottle, as well as several special shapes for individual growers. Usually, however, the more serious wines are put in the tall-shouldered Bordeaux bottle.

Viticulture on the Ott estates is virtually organic and each property has its own flock of sheep to provide the vines with natural manure. They favour the lyre form of trellising for their vines, explaining that the problem with the traditional *cordon de royat* and *gobelet* of Provence is that the sun does not penetrate the canopy. With the lyre, all the branches go upwards, which is more logical for a growing plant. At Château de Selle they have mainly red grapes, Grenache Noir, Cinsaut, Syrah and Cabernet Sauvignon, but no Mourvèdre as it does not ripen here. The altitude is too high, and a cool spring brings a late bud burst. The international reputation of the Ott family rests on their pink wine, Coeur de Grain, made from pressed juice kept in *foudres* on the lees for four to six months. The wood is quite unobtrusive, providing body without affecting the flavour, so that it has delicate fruit and a rounded mouth feel.

The red wine at Château de Selle comes from the older vines on the property, the very oldest of which date from the 1940s. Cabernet Sauvignon usually accounts for about half the blend, providing tannin, structure and colour. About fifteen per cent of Grenache Noir gives the alcohol and equal amounts of Syrah and Cinsaut provide the fruit. Usually Grenache Noir and Syrah are fermented together, as they ripen at the same time, while Cabernet Sauvignon and Cinsaut come later. In an ideal world they would like to ferment all four varieties together, making for a more harmonious marriage. The wine spends about ten months in *foudres* and has considerable ageing potential in bottle. The 1996 was fresh and peppery. In the best years, mostly recently 1993, 1992, 1988, 1983 and 1982, they make what they call a Cuvée Longue Garde, which spends eighteen months in wood. The 1988, tasted when it was ten years old, had a certain warmth and vegetal sweetness. I also remember a 1950, drunk when it was about thirty-five years old, with some remarkable staying power – past its prime, yes, but still with life and flavour.

CLOS MIREILLE, LA-LANDE-LES MAURES

At Clos Mireille you can walk down to the Mediterranean from the vineyard, and this proximity to the sea means that the grapes are ripened by reflected heat and light from the water. The soil here is quite different from the limestone of Château de Selle, with mica-schist and quartz, and here they make white wine, from about two-thirds Sémillon to one-third Ugni Blanc, in two qualities: Blanc de Côte and Blanc de Blancs. Again, methods are very traditional, yet these are some of the most exciting white wines of Provence, with ageing potential and intriguing honeyed flavours reminiscent of a fine Graves.

CHATEAU DE RASQUE, TARADEAU

Château de Rasque, just down the road from Château de Selle, is an example of a completely new estate, for what you see today has been created out of nothing since 1981. It is an attractive spot in the hills outside the village of Taradeau. You pass an old Saracen lookout tower and approach the estate along a drive lined with olive trees and lavender bushes. The vineyards are quite high, at 180 metres, so the vintage starts later than in the valley below and the soil is very stony. The land belonged originally to the Rasque family, but had been greatly neglected. The current owner, Gérard Biancone, began with four hectares of old vines, two of which were pulled up, and he has cleared scrubland to plant a total of twenty-one hectares. This is no mean investment, for you pay FF 30–40,000 per hectare for scrubland and then it costs about FF 180–200,000 per hectare to clear the land and plant vines. It used to be much easier to obtain planting rights than it is today. Biancone admitted that he might have been courageous to embark on such a project, but more likely he was simply oblivious. For white wine he has only Rolle, which is allowed as a single varietal, and the white Cuvée Alexandra, named after his last daughter, was fragrant and lemony with a light herbal note. The *rosé*, from equal parts of Grenache Noir and Cinsaut, was ripe, rounded and mouth-filling, intended for drinking within the year. There are two red wines, Pièce Noble from Syrah and Grenache Noir, which spends at least twelve months in *foudres*, has warm berry fruit and a good tannic backbone, while the basic Château de Rasque, from mainly Grenache Noir, is less structured.

CHATEAU DE BERNES, LORGUES

Château de Bernes belongs to English investors who have radically transformed the estate since its purchase in 1985. It is an impressive showpiece, but rather overwhelming, with a flamboyance bordering on vulgarity. They encourage visitors, and the Salle de Bacchus provides an overall view of the different parts of the cellar, looking down on *barriques*, *foudres*, stainless steel vats and *pupitres* for sparkling wine. There is a large reception area for tastings and exhibitions; when I was there, the works of a rather garish local artist were on display. The winery is efficiently managed by Marc Petrequin, who has had a varied career, ranging from the co-operative in Uzès in the Gard to a winery in Atlanta that bought in grapes from California.

In 1985 there were twenty hectares of run-down vineyards, but now they now have sixty, with Cinsaut, Grenache Noir, Syrah, Cabernet Sauvignon, Ugni Blanc, Sémillon and Rolle, as well as some olive trees, making a total of five hundred hectares of land. They make three qualitites of wine, a special *cuvée* with some oak produced for the first time in 1990, a traditional *cuvée* with *foudres* and the Cuvée des Oliviers for young vines. There is also a sparkling wine called Wild Pig, after all the wild boar that roam the estate. The wines are sound and competent, but did not excite.

DOMAINE DE LA BERNARDE, FLASSANS

The Meulnart family bought Domaine de la Bernarde outside Flassans in 1974. Guy Meulnart's father had worked in industry, running a company that manufactured reels for fishing rods, but wine was his passion and with the purchase of Domaine de la Bernarde he fulfilled a lifelong ambition. Guy Meulnart himself first studied mechanical engineering and then trained and worked as an architect in Zurich, before settling on the estate in 1982. He has the thoughtful attitude of someone who has broader horizons than his vineyard, and his lively conversation is peppered with observations showing a perceptive understanding of the problems of the market for Provençal wine. He is aware of the enormous gap between the public's appreciation of Mediterranean cuisine and their appreciation of the wines of Provence; they make little distinction between the different appellations of the region. The problem with *rosé* is its short seasonal use, allied to the summer holiday mentality of the region. The market demand is very localised, with very few Provençal wines being drunk outside the region. And when I asked why his friendly spaniel was called Newton, I was told that he liked sleeping under apple trees!

In the Côtes de Provence, vinification methods for red wine tend to be traditional, but Guy Meulnart is a keen exponent of carbonic maceration, and his own particular variation of it is finely tuned to suit his grapes and his objectives, with at least a twelve-day if not a twenty-one day maceration. This means that the grapes are hand picked, so that the harvest takes about three weeks. His neat cellar contains concrete vats, but not a single *foudre* or *barrique*. He prefers his wines to develop in bottle rather than wood, and as a 1992 demonstrated when it was six years old, these are wines that will benefit from bottle age. Two qualities of each colour are produced, the domaine wine and the Clos Bernarde from a walled vineyard that is the best site of the estate. The white wines are a blend of Clairette, Ugni Blanc and Sémillon, for Meulnart dislikes the aniseed notes of Rolle, finding it too simple. The white Domaine Bernarde was fresh and peachy, while the Clos Bernarde had more substance and body, with lightly herbal fruit.

The two *rosés* provide a similar contrast, for the domaine wine had ripe strawberry fruit, while the Clos was more substantial. The red Domaine Bernarde had wonderfully appealing spicy fruit and was both supple and structured, ripe and easy to drink and peppered with the herbs of the *garrigue*, while Clos Bernarde, although you could taste the similarity, was more structured, with some length. The 1992 had some appealing meaty flavours with spicy vegetal notes on the nose.

Massif de la Sainte Victoire

The area of the Massif de la Sainte Victoire forms a very precise entity within the Côtes de Provence, for the area is delimited by natural boundaries such as the Mont Ste Victoire itself, the Monts Auréliens and the appellations of Palette and the Coteaux d'Aix en Provence. The wine growers in this area consequently have a very firm sense of local identity, much greater than elsewhere within the broad appellation, and very much favour what they call the regionalisation of the Côtes de Provence. They would ultimately like to see an appellation Côtes de Provence-Ste Victoire and the appropriate dossier has been submitted to the INAO. Producers number twenty-eight in total, including five co-operatives, and the region includes seven villages, with vineyards on either side of the valley of the Arc, their 2700 hectares accounting for fifteen per cent of the appellation.

There are distinct differences in climate and *terroir*: for example, there is much less maritime influence here than in other parts of the appellation, for the Massif de la Ste Baume and the Monts Auréliens form a barrier. This means that Mourvèdre does not ripen well here. Winters are also colder and summers can be warmer, with the more markedly continental climate making wines with more ageing potential. Rainfall averages 600–700 mm a year. Spring frost can be a problem, and a strong Mistral wind in May and June can cause a tremendous amount of damage to young vine shoots. The soil is based on sandstone, with some very red iron-rich soils.

The main grape varieties are Syrah, Grenache Noir, Cabernet Sauvignon and Cinsaut, with Rolle, Sémillon, Ugni Blanc and Clairette for white. Although Rolle has always been in the appellation, there has been a recent revival of interest in it, with new plantings; they would like a minimum of thirty per cent in the blend for their proposed appellation. Other restrictions would include a minimum of ten per cent of Syrah in the *rosé*, while red wines would consist mainly of Grenache Noir and Syrah, with Cabernet Sauvignon as a complementary variety. Yields would be restricted to 50 hl/ha, as opposed to 55 hl/ha for the main appellation; the white and pink wines would be not sold until March, and the red wine not before November.

The wine growers of the Mont Ste Victoire have an attractive showcase in the shape of a *vinothèque* in part of the old castle, adjoining the vestiges of the ramparts of the attractive little town of Trets. The Maison Ste Victoire at St Antonin on the foothills of the mountain provides tourist entertainment with a 3-D show about the dinosaurs that used to inhabit the area. This is apparently one of the original sources of the dinosaurs and remains of their eggs have been found in the vineyards. At Mas de Cadenet they have dinosaur eggs on display, as well as an enormous fossilised oyster shell from the Etang de Berre.

MAS DE CADENET, TRETS

Guy Négrel from Mas de Cadenet is president of the group and an articulate exponent of the characteristics of his region. His own vineyard consists of forty hectares lying at three hundred metres on the foothills of the Mont Ste Victoire, which dominates the skyline. The colours of the mountain change with the sunlight, for sometimes it can seem very grey and sombre and at other times quite gentle, with soft pink stone. The soil is a mixture of gravel and sandy clay, with good drainage. Originally Négrel sold all his wine in bulk to the *négociants*, but since his first bottling in 1974, he has expanded the sales to put all his production in bottle. He has barrels as well as three small *foudres* and has aged wines in oak since 1987. Most intriguing was a *rosé* that had spent six to eight months in wood after fermentation in barrel, with regular *bâtonnage*. Négrel is adamant that *rosé* should be taken seriously and his wine was rounded and full-bodied, with gentle oaky undertones. He aims to treat his *rosé* like a white Burgundy, making a wine that will age, and so he works on its richness and mouth feel. There is also a white wine that is fermented in wood, with a more obviously oaky flavour and a certain structure, but I preferred the unoaked pure Rolle, which was delicate and fragrant. The red is serious, a blend of Syrah, Grenache Noir and Cabernet Sauvignon, which was given fifteen months *élevage* in barrel. The 1990 showed the ageing potential of the region, with a warm, cedary character and perfectly integrated oak, with fruit, length and structure.

DOMAINE MAUVAN, PUYLOUBIER

Gaelle Maclou at Domaine Mauvan is the first member of her family to be a wine maker, for her grandfather bought the estate on his retirement for the sole purpose of hunting. Her grandfather and mother were both chemists and the grapes went to the co-operative. In 1990 she took the decision to build a cellar and now has a functional shed in which she makes a white, a *rosé* and two red wines. A *monocépage* for white wine is permitted, so that hers is pure Rolle, with fresh, delicate fruit. One red is mainly Cabernet Sauvignon, aged in wood for nine months, while the other, a blend of Carignan and Grenache Noir destined for early drinking, is fruity and supple with no pretensions. The soil is red and stony, giving wines with some firm tannins. This is the Bouches-du-Rhône, making for a comparison with the wines of the Var, which Maclou considers to be warmer and more alcoholic, whereas here there is more tannin, and more acidity in the *rosé* and white wines. She is also wondering about planting olive trees, for there is a project of an appellation Pays d'Aix for olive oil. Olive trees can suffer from frost here, and there were many more a century or two ago, but currently there is a revival of interest.

Vallée Intérieure

CHATEAU STE ROSALINE, LES ARCS

Château Ste Rosaline is another estate that has changed hands recently and consequently undergone something of a trans- formation. The father of the previous owner, Baron Henri de Rasque de Laval, was one of the original pioneers of the appellation, along with the Ott family. Four religious orders have been here, Templars, Cistercians, Carthusians and Observantines, but by 1750 there were just three nuns left, who transferred to another abbey. Then it became the secondary residence of the Bishop of Fréjus until the Revolution. As for Ste Rosaline, she was a prioress here for nearly thirty years at the beginning of the fourteenth century and was canonised by Pope John XXII. Pilgrims come here, particularly for Ste. Rosaline's birthday on 17 January. There are tranquil cloisters, a riot of roses in June, and a 140-year-old Carignan vine that still bears fruit; two plane trees planted in 1750 still stand in front of the château. The chapel is worth at least a detour, if not a voyage. There is an enchanting Chagall fresco, sculptures by Giacometti, including a lectern in the form of the tree of knowledge, and some beautiful modern stained-glass windows.

Just outside the pretty village of Les Arcs, with its picturesque old quarter and narrow cobbled streets, Ste Rosaline now belongs to Bernard Taillaud. His family had owned another estate nearby and when he sold a successful property business, he came here in 1996, since when he has been determinedly transforming the property, vineyards, cellar and château. He had pulled up thirty hectares of vines and is replanting forty, replacing the Aramon, Picpoul and other varieties not allowed in the appellation and at same time increasing the density from 3600 to five thousand plants per hectare, while training the vines on wires. The proportion of Syrah will rise significantly, with a greater concentration on red wine, and Carignan will disappear completely. Taillaud is convinced of the potential of red wine and considers that this is the way to establish the reputation of Ste Rosaline. The cellar has been dramatically modernised. From my previous visit I remembered a cellar of elderly oak casks and now there is stainless steel galore and newer wood, both *barriques* and *foudres*.

They now produce various *cuvées* of each colour. Le Cloître de Ste Rosaline is the simplest, a white, mainly from Rolle with some Ugni Blanc, that is light and fresh, while the red is a blend of Grenache Noir, Mourvèdre and Cabernet Sauvignon, with ripe, easy fruit for summer drinking. White Château Ste Rosaline comes from Rolle, Sémillon and Clairette, with a certain herbal character, while the *rosé* is a blend of Tibouren, Cinsaut and Mourvèdre. Taillaud admitted that he found Tibouren difficult, as it is so fragile and spoils easily, while the Mourvèdre still feels the effects of the Mediterranean here. The wine was delicate and fresh, perfect for summer drinking. The Syrah is not yet in production, so the red is currently a blend of Mourvèdre and Cabernet Sauvignon that have spent eighteen months in *foudre*. It had an appealing warmth, with some meaty Mourvèdre flavours. Finally, the Cuvée Prieuré benefits from some oak, of which they have still quite limited experience. In the white wine, the oak is quite obvious on the nose but well integrated on the palate. For the *rosé*, from Tibouren, Mourvèdre and Syrah, they use less new oak, so that there is no obvious taste of wood, just a certain feeling of weight and body. The red Cuvée Prieuré, for which Cabernet Sauvignon is the dominant variety, together with Mourvèdre, seemed much more international in flavour, with oak and some ripe cassis fruit.

CHATEAU DE RIMAURESQ, PIGNANS

Château de Rimauresq, outside Pignans, belonged to the Isnard family for three hundred years and was sold in 1989 to a Scottish company when the last member of the family died. Again, the investment here has been considerable, but on a much more human scale. The old cellar, which was under the house, still exists, offering a striking contrast with the new, streamlined cellar. Marc

Jacquet is the manager. As one of the new generation of producers who have brought about enormous improvements in the vineyards, he has a keen appreciation of the land. They now have thirty-five hectares on two types of soil, the *galets roulées* of Châteauneuf-du-Pape and the red granite of the nearby Massif des Maures. The vines are orientated north west, which provides a longer ripening period than a southern orientation and also protects the grapes from sunburn. They start the vintage on about 7 September, which is fifteen days later than in the village opposite. The reason for this particular aspect of the microclimate is quite simple. The highest point of the Massif des Maures takes an hour and a half of sunshine per day during the ripening period, which adds up to fifteen days.

Rimauresq was one of the original *crus classés*, with a reputation for red wine, and so, with that objective in mind, the vineyard is planted mainly with Syrah, Cabernet Sauvignon and Mourvèdre. They even have some eighty-year old Syrah and sixty-year-old Cabernet Sauvignon. They are unusual in making just one wine for each colour. The white is predominantly Rolle, which is given three or four hours of skin contact and a slow fermentation, resulting in some delicate fruit, with a good balance of acidity and alcohol. The *rosé* is a blend of five varieties, Cinsaut, Tibouren to provide elegance, a little Grenache Noir for alcohol, Mourvèdre for structure and Syrah for aroma. The result was very pleasing, with fruit, body and structure, and a hint of spice. The red, a blend of thirty per cent each of Syrah and Cabernet Sauvignon with twenty per cent Mourvèdre and a little Grenache Noir and Carignan, is aged in *foudres* for ten months, while a small part is kept in *barriques*. The wood is very understated and the wine elegantly structured, with good fruit. Rimauresq certainly merits its *cru classé* status.

Another part of the large Vallée Intérieure covers the vineyards around Pierrefeu and Cuers. My first introduction to some of these wines came at the Restaurant le Lingousto outside Cuers, where Alain Ryon is a talented chef and his English wife Jane a welcoming hostess. The dining room has frescos by Mentor, Picasso's last pupil, of colourful buxom ladies flaunting their assets. Domaine de l'Aumérade is the largest estate in the area, with a convincing range of wine: a perfumed white blend of Sémillon and Rolle and a ripe, fruity red, while the Cuvée Dame de Piegros was more solid and concentrated by comparison. Château la Moutète is the property of the Duffort family, who also own Domaine l'Hermitage in Bandol. Their white is delicate and herbal, while the red is warm and smoky. The red Vieilles Vignes includes Carignan that was planted in 1928. Alain Baccino at Domaine de Peirecèdes is a young grower who is beginning to make his mark: Cuvée La Règue des Botes, from Mourvèdre and Cabernet Sauvignon, was firm and structured with ageing potential, after eight months *élevage* in barrel, while his *rosé*, from Grenache Noir and Syrah, was ripe and rounded, with a delicate colour.

DOMAINE DE LA MAYONETTE, PIERREFEU

Henri Julian at Domaine de la Mayonette explained the characteristics of the *terroir* of the Vallee Intérieure around Pierrefeu. The valley runs north to south, attracting a lot of wind from both land and sea. This makes for very good sanitary conditions, preventing disease, but the winters can be hard and the summers hot. Frost can also be a problem. He remembered the very bad frost of 1991 when the temperature dropped to −8°C on 24 April. That year he produced just forty hectolitres, when the crop from his twenty-hectare estate is usually around seven hundred. The soil is very gravelly, with alluvium from the river of Le Réal Martin.

Part of his property, which he bought in 1987, comes within Vin de Pays des Maures. As for Côtes de Provence, he is unusual in making more red than anything else, with various different *cuvées* depending on the quality of the vintage. The Cuvée Jean-François, named after his son, is a blend of sixty per cent Grenache Noir with twenty per cent each of Cabernet Sauvignon and Carignan, making a rustic, peppery wine. Everyone is pulling up Carignan, but his is good and he is adamant that he wants to keep it. His Tradition, a blend of Syrah, Cabernet Sauvignon and Grenache Noir, was supple and spicy with appealing fruit. Most years he makes a Cuvée Prestige, for which the blend varies. In 1996 it was forty per cent Syrah with sixty per cent Cabernet Sauvignon, and in 1997 eighty per cent Syrah with twenty per cent Grenache Noir, given a longer *cuvaison* than for the Tradition, as well as twelve months ageing in vat. In 1998 he had some Syrah that he described as *extraordinaire*, which he may put in *barriques*, although in general he is not keen on wood. The use of oak must not be automatic, as it makes for very powerful wines with hard tannins and can overwhelm all the interesting flavours in a lighter wine. His delicate, fresh white wine is pure Rolle, destalked to avoid any bitterness. The *rosé*, mainly from Cinsaut, with a little Syrah and Grenache Noir, was ripe and full-bodied, with what the French would call *gras*, or fat, which Julian considers to be a characteristic of the area.

CHATEAU LA TOUR DE L'EVEQUE, PIERREFEU

Régine Sumeire divides her time between Château la Tour de l'Eveque, just up the road from Domaine de la Mayonette, and Château Barbeyrolles near Hyères, so that she sees a distinct difference between the two areas. Although both enjoy a strong maritime influence, there are striking variations in the soil. Here it is limestone and clay with gravel, giving more structured, full-bodied wines, while in contrast the vines at Château Barbeyrolles are on the schist of the hills of the Maures. Mourvèdre does better here than at Barbeyrolles, even though both are close to the sea.

Château La Tour l'Evêque belonged to the bishops of Toulon and like all ecclesiastical property was sold at the Revolution. It was bought by the Magnan family, who kept it until 1956, when they sold it to Sumeire's grandfather. There are the remains of an old tower at the entrance to the property, and a more modern tower forms part of the château, while an attractive courtyard has two large palm trees, with rose and lavender bushes. Sumeire laughingly explained that she had wanted to be a journalist and travel, for which she had first studied political science and Spanish, but then she had learned to make wine instead; her first vintage was in 1984. She makes more *rosé* than anything else, in particular a delicate Pétale Rose, a blend of Cinsaut, Grenache Noir, Mourvèdre and Syrah, which are pressed very slowly and gently, giving a pale orange-pink colour and a fresh, delicate palate, with some body. As for reds, she is working with *barriques*, especially for Syrah, and admits that she is still experimenting, finding out what works best. 1991 was her first attempt and she thought it too woody, so she gave up for a couple of years and then in 1996 tried again, with more satisfactory results. The oak was quite obvious on the palate, but balanced with some cedary fruit. There have been no really great vintages between 1990 and 1998, whereas the decade of the 1980s had several excellent vintages. Rather like Bordeaux, only 1984 and 1987 were less successful.

CHATEAU LA GORDONNE, PIERREFEU

The adjoining property is Château la Gordonne, which has been part of Domaines Listel since 1940. Today it is managed by Nicolas Julien, whose uncle Pierre Julien ran the wine arm of Les Salins du Midi after the Second World War. We went for a drive through the vineyards. It is a large estate of a hundred and eighty hectares, including eighty of woodland and olive trees. There were abundant bushes of white heather, with beehives carefully positioned nearby and resplendent Judas trees in brilliant purple flower. The cellar is fairly modern and functional, adjoining a château that was built at the beginning of the nineteenth century. The old cellar of the house provides an attractive tasting area, with mellow red bricks and a *foudres* in each vault. These are just for show, although they do make an oak-aged wine, Cuvée Marronniers Reserve, from Syrah and Cabernet Sauvignon. Their Cabernet vines are over thirty-five years old, for these were some of the earlier plantings of that variety in the Var. Only part of the wine goes into wood, and even then only for a couple of months, so the oak effect is minimal, with some soft fruit. *Rosé* is the main vocation of the estate, with the brand name of Billette, which they try to differentiate from the Listel Gris de Gris, making a wine with a deeper colour, ripe raspberry fruit and more body than the wine of the sands.

Villars-sur-Var

CLOS ST JOSEPH

The *commune* of Villars-sur-Var forms a curious outpost of the Côtes de Provence, for it is quite isolated from the rest of the appellation. Apparently, when there was first talk of an appellation, or rather a VDQS, for the area, the mayor of the village was staunchly in favour, unlike his colleagues in neighbouring villages, who preferred to take the easy route of quantity without any quality restraints. There is now just one small producer in the village, at Clos St Joseph, who has just four hectares, planted with Ugni Blanc, Clairette, Rolle, Sémillon, Cinsaut, Grenache Noir and Mourvèdre. The white wine is fermented in oak and is ripe and rounded, with well-integrated oak and satisfyingly ripe flavours and mouth feel. I have yet to taste the red.

OTHERS

There are other producers whose wines I have enjoyed, including some near the town of Hyères. At Château Maravenne, Jean-Louis Gourjon is making fragrant whites and structured reds. Domaine St André de Figuière is now the property of Alain and Gaby Combard, a couple from Chablis who have moved south, and Jean-Pierre Fayard is reviving the reputation of the *cru classé* Château Ste Marguerite with a delicate white wine and supple red. Near Flassans, Françoise Rigaud owns the historic property of Commanderie de Peyrassol, where the cellars date back to the twelfth century. A magnum of her 1986 Cuvée Marie Estelle was drinking beautifully when it was twelve years old. Nearby Domaine de la Bastide Neuve produces a pure Rolle with layers of flavour and a structured red, while Château des Crostes makes an attractive white from equal proportions of Rolle and Sémillon and a firm peppery red with a high proportion of Syrah.

François Millo, the dynamic director of the Syndicat des Côtes de Provence, should have the last word on this very diverse appellation. He previously spent eight years in Bordeaux and has a perceptive view of the problems and potential of the appellation. They want to escape from the pink image by insisting, with an appropriate logo, that Côtes de Provence is an appellation of three colours. Although it is one of the oldest wine regions of France, it has all the characteristics of a young appellation, with rapid evolution and disorder at the same time. There is a good market for pink wine in France and demand has increased, as production methods and flavours have improved, but this is none the less a three pronged appellation. Not only is there *rosé*, offering wines of sunny appeal, but there are whites with growing finesse, and above all serious reds with stature and originality.

Key facts

VDQS 1951 for red, white and *rosé*, AC 1977; twenty-three estates recognised as *crus classés* in 1955.

Eighteen thousand hectares in eighty-three *communes*, mainly in the Var; 55 hl/ha.

Grape varieties:

RED AND ROSÉ: Carignan, maximum of forty per cent; Mourvèdre, Syrah and Cabernet Sauvignon, maximum of thirty per cent each; Cinsaut and Tibouren, especially for *rosé*.

WHITE: Ugni Blanc, Clairette, Semillon and Rolle.

Very varied soils and climate, so there are moves towards differentiating the various areas:

La Bordure Maritime

La Vallée Intérieure

Les Collines du Haut Pays

Le Bassin du Beausset

Le Massif de la Sainte Victoire

Vintages

1999: A warm year made for very healthy grapes, combining a good yield and a fine quality. Promises well.

1998: A fine summer and generally good weather throughout the harvest made for ripe grapes, giving wines with good fruit and balanced tannins.

1997: Spring frosts affected some of the appellation; there was a warm July and early August, some storms in mid-August followed by a drying Mistral. An early harvest in exceptional weather. A smaller crop as a result of frost and some hail, but some good wines, more supple than 1996s, with ripe fruit and ageing potential.

1996: Less successful than 1997, but none the less wines with good fruit, with some reds that benefit from bottle age.

1995: A fine July promised an early harvest, but storms in August threatened to cause problems. Happily, the Mistral dried the grapes and a fine September made for a trouble-free harvest, giving some red wines with ageing potential.

Bellet

The vineyards of the tiny appellation of Bellet nestle amongst the suburbs of Nice, and there are many among the city's four hundred thousand inhabitants who fail to realise that there are vineyards within the city boundaries. Indeed, Nice is the only large town or city to have an appellation vineyard within its confines. There is the Clos de Montmartre in the heart of Paris, but that is not an appellation. None the less, if you ask for a bottle of Bellet in one of the open-air restaurants of the old town, your request is likely to be treated with sceptical disbelief as to the existence of Bellet. I was firmly told, '*Ça ne se fait plus.*'

If you leave behind the elegance of the Promenade des Anglais and the bustle of the city, and drive up into the hills to the outlying village of St Romain-de-Bellet, you come to vineyards that are often overlooked by suburban villas. In the nineteenth century the Alpes-Maritimes, which only became part of France in 1860, was an important viticultural department, with many vineyards of which barely any traces remain today. Vines have given way to carnations, which are now the main crop, housed in the enormous greenhouses that dominate the landscape.

The earliest historical reference I could find to the wines of Bellet was a letter from a certain Marshal de Catinat, who wrote to the governor of Nice on 26 August 1696 saying, 'You ask me for news of the wine from Bellet that you sent to me. I can assure you that it was found to be admirable and better than the wines of France that we have here, although they were well chosen.'

Two centuries later Guyot was rather less enthusiastic, saying that if the vineyards were well kept they would give delicious wine and that Bellet was good if it was well made, but often it was not. He mentioned Braquet as being a very fine and rich grape, accounting for a fifth of the vineyards, while Fuella, the present day Folle Noire, accounted for three-fifths and the rest were Roussanne, Négret, Pignerol and Clairette.

The appellation of Bellet was created in 1941 and six hundred and fifty hectares were delimited, of which only fifty are currently in production. This figure is unlikely to increase significantly, as any available land is greedily snapped up by building contractors. The appellation of Bellet had a rather chequered early career, and was nearly demoted in 1943 for its lack of quality. It really only began to emerge from the doldrums in the early 1960s. Today there are eleven producers, but some are tiny, making not even two thousand bottles a year, and the reputation of the appellation is maintained almost single-handedly by Ghislain de Charnacé at the Château de Bellet.

CHATEAU DE BELLET

The Château de Bellet is a charming building, situated in a large park with a private chapel. The oldest part dates from the sixteenth century, while the eighteenth-century façade consists of a magnificent *trompe-l'oeil*. Even close to, you would think that the walls were multi-faceted, and yet they are absolutely flat. A former owner, Pierre Roissard, was created Baron de Bellet by the Duke of Savoy in 1777 and the property has come to Ghislain de Charnacé through his mother, Rose de Bellet, whose family gave their name to the local wine.

The property comprises thirty hectares of which ten are planted with vines, partly on terraces, with views over the valley of the Var and towards the Alps. It had snowed the previous Easter weekend, and although it was a sunny afternoon, the distant mountains were snow covered and at seven that morning the temperature had been a chilly 3°C. The vineyards lie at about two hundred and fifty metres in altitude and their average temperature is 4°C lower than on the coast. It is hardly a Mediterranean climate, and with the open vistas they benefit from the influence of the prevailing winds, the Marin, which comes up the valley of Var, and the Tramontane, which can blow from the north. This means that there is a permanent breeze, but nothing stronger, and consequently the vines are rarely affected by problems of rot and humidity. The soil is poor and stony, but of sandy, alluvial origin.

Bellet can be red, white or pink and it is unusual for its grape varieties. The principal white variety is Rolle, and there is much discussion about whether this is synonymous with Vermentino. The ampelographer Galet maintained that they were two separate varieties, and Boubals agrees, but others in the Languedoc and Provence interchange the two names as though they were identical varieties. The Syndicat de Bellet recently carried out DNA testing on the wood of the two varieties, which showed that they do belong to the same family. So it does seem that the names are interchangeable, with Rolle coming more easily to the French tongue and Vermentino to the Italian. Chardonnay has also been allowed since 1955, thanks to the efforts of the Bagnis family, former owners of the other sizeable property, the Château de Crémat. Clairette is another option, but is rarely planted. The best white Bellet are made from Rolle.

As for pink and red wines, the most characteristic is Braquet, which I was firmly told is indigenous to this area and nothing at all to do with Brachetto from Piedmont, despite the Italian influence in the region. Then there is Folle Noire, or Fuella Nera in Niçoise, which is no relation to Folle Blanche. These two varieties must account for sixty per cent of a red Bellet, while the balance is made up with Grenache Noir and Cinsaut. De Charnacé considers Cinsaut to be a mistake for the appellation as it does not perform well, producing characterless wine. Grenache Noir gives alcohol and Folle Noir some colour, while it is Braquet that accounts for the typicity of Bellet.

He explained that when he took over the family property in 1970, the general view was that Braquet was much too difficult; the variety was in danger of disappearing, for it produced very low yields, averaging about 20 hl/ha. But he was intrigued, for he remembered his grandfather talking about Braquet, and so he concentrated his attention on it and has gradually increased his vineyard of Braquet to four hectares by *selection massale*, using his own cuttings and the best rootstock. Braquet also demands a particular type of pruning, with a longer shoot, as it only bears fruit furthest from the trunk.

We tasted the 1997 red from vat, a blend of fifty per cent Braquet with thirty per cent Folle Noire and twenty per cent Grenache Noir.

They ripen at quite different periods and are blended in vat once the fermentation is finished. When the wine was six months old, it was redolent of sour cherries, while a sample from a new barrel also had a firm cherry character over the oak. De Charnacé is the only producer to make his *rosé* from pure Braquet. The colour was an orange-pink, for Braquet never gives much colour, and the fruit was delicate, with floral notes – what de Charnacé described as 'a faded rose' – and with a certain texture and mouth feel, certainly making an unusual and not unattractive *rosé*.

For my taste buds, it is the white wines of Château de Bellet that were the most satisfying. There are two *cuvées*, one without wood and Baron G, which is fermented in oak. The unoaked 1997 was given twelve hours of skin contact and had a smoky nose, some fragrant fruit and good acidity, even though it underwent a malolactic fermentation and certainly had the potential to age well. 1997 was a particularly good vintage, with no climatic problems and a long ripening season.

De Charnacé began working with *barriques* in 1987. He wanted to show that, with low yields, good structure and sufficient ripeness, Rolle can age. Baron G spends twelve months in *barriques*. Originally they were all new, but now only two-thirds are and one-third are wood of one wine. He is experimenting with different origins and degrees of toasting. A 1997, from a light-toasted Allier barrel, was structured and elegantly buttery, balanced deceptively like a young Meursault. The same wine in a medium-toasted barrel had a tighter palate, with good fruit underneath. In the 1996 vintage, I preferred the unoaked wine, with its delicate, slightly nutty fruit, while the Baron G was quite oaky on the palate. It takes two years for the oak to integrate fully into the wine, and this was proved with the 1993, which had an attractive leafy character and the merest hint of oak in the background.

DOMAINE FOGALAR

The other two producers that I visited are very typical of the small scale of Bellet. Jean Spizo at Domaine Fogalar first bought land here in 1974. He looks Italian and teaches Italian, but was brought up in Alsace. He planted his first tiny vineyard in order to make some wine for his personal consumption, and then in 1986 bought another small plot of land, which had given him just over one hectare. On the day after my visit he was due to sign the purchase of a further three hectares, two within the appellation and one at the bottom of the valley, on which he was planning to plant olives trees. He explained that there is a regional appellation for oil, for the whole of the Alpes-Maritimes may produce *huile de Nice* from the tiny *caillette* variety. As for grapes, Spizo was planning Rolle, Braquet, Grenache Noir and a little Folle Noire, all of which he already has in tiny amounts, as well as some Cinsaut.

His are the vineyards nearest to the sea. They face south and you can see Cap d'Antibes on the horizon. His neighbours are market gardeners, growing carnations, and before he came here his vineyard was planted with lettuces. He has a neat little cellar under his house, with an old press, some stainless steel vats and a few *barriques* for both red and white wine. Altogether he makes about five thousand bottles. His white wine, of which a small proportion goes into wood, was quite delicate, slightly nutty with firm acidity and some intriguingly spicy fruit. The *rosé* is a blend of earlier-ripening Grenache Noir and Braquet, as well as Cinsaut and Folle Noire, made by *saignée*, and it had an intriguing rosewater flavour. Spizo began working with wood in 1993, first of all old wood for his red wine and then, in 1995, for his white wine. The red 1996, tasted from barrel, was not too oaky, but light and peppery; the same pepperiness was apparent in the 1995, while the unoaked 1992 was quite perfumed and vegetal. The wines are sold under the Collet de Bovis label.

CHATEAU DE CREMAT

Château de Crémat is the only other estate of any size, but it has had a rather unfortunate history in recent years. The previous owners, the Bagnis family, sold the bankrupted property to a M. Pisoni, whose cellarmaster apparently produces very oaky wines that are not typical of the appellation. When I went to taste, the place was deserted apart from a silent dog. As well as making wine from their own vineyards, the Bagnis family were *négociants* with the large Provençal brand L'Estandon, which now belongs to the Union des Caves Coopératives, and they used to buy grapes from various tiny producers who were often market gardeners, concentrating on carnations but with just a few vines as a sideline. These people suddenly found themselves without an outlet for their grapes.

DOMAINE AUGIER

One solution was to make your own wine and this is what Rose Augier and her husband Charles did. Sadly, she was widowed in 1997 and is struggling to run the vineyard on her own. She remembered her grandfather making wine in large barrels, but subsequently they sold their grapes to Bagnis until 1991. She has Rolle, Folle Noire, Grenache Noir, Braquet, Cinsaut, Clairette and Roussanne in her small vineyard, all of which are vinified in a tiny cellar in her basement. Her wines, a delicate *rosé* and a peppery red, were quite rustic, but not without a certain charm.

OTHER PRODUCERS

Among the other producers of Bellet there is a sculptor, Mascha Sosno. Robert Cohendet at Via Julia planted vines when he retired from IBM, while Jacques Dalmasso at Domaine de la Source and Jean Massa also grow carnations. A group of three producers make wine from five or six hectares under the label of Les Coteaux de Bellet, almost as a mini-cooperative. The new owner of Clos St Vincent used to run a pizzeria, but has turned to wine; and sadly, the vineyards of Domaine de Fontbellet lie abandoned.

VINS DES BAOUS

De Charnacé feels rather isolated in his task of single-handedly maintaining the reputation and tradition of Bellet. If you look at the wine map of Provence the appellation seems to stand alone, quite isolated from the Côtes de Provence, for the nearest vineyards of that appellation are a small enclave in the village of Villars-sur-Var. In fact, there are odd pockets of vineyard scattered around near by, grouped together in the Association des Vins des Baous, which was formed in the late 1980s and covers about ten hectares of vines. A *baou* is a particular type of hill, a foothill of the Alps; that of the village of St Jeannet is well known. There are also vines at St Jeannet and an old viticultural tradition, but no one had thought to ask for an appellation for the village. The best-known producer is a M. Race. Neighbouring La Gaude also has a vineyard and Guyot rated the wines there more highly than those of Bellet. At St Paul-de-Vence there is just one hectare run by Adrian Maeght of the famous Maeght collection. The villages around Grasse were also important for their viticulture, but the vines have long since disappeared.

Happily the de Charnacé family continue to maintain the viticultural traditions of Bellet, and they are joined by other small but committed producers. It would be sad to see them disappear, for they have an intriguing originality, deserving a greater appreciation in their home city. Asked about the future, de Charnacé admits to a hankering to try out Pinot Noir – and why not? The climate is much cooler than the coastal Mediterranean, but for the meantime he continues to maintain the tradition and flavour of Rolle and Braquet.

Key facts

Tiny appellation within the *commune* of Nice. AC 1941 for red, white and *rosé*; fifty hectares planted out of six hundred and fifty delimited.

Grape varieties:

WHITE: Rolle, Chardonnay and Clairette.

RED: Braquet, Folle Noire, Grenache Noir and Cinsaut.

Vintages

1999: A smaller yield than usual, following a hot summer and an early harvest. Promises well, completing the succession of good vintages since 1995. 1990 was another excellent year.

CORSICA

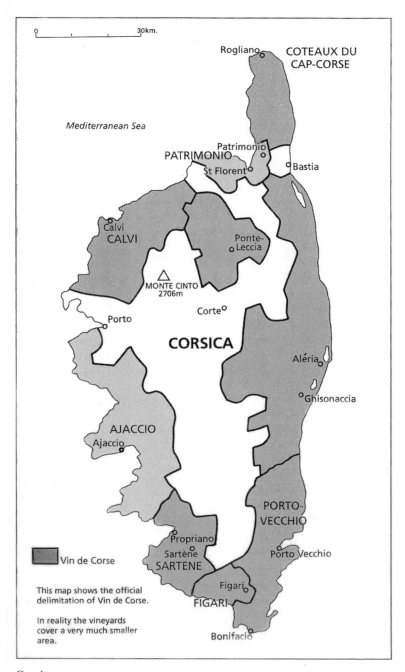

Scale: 0 — 30km.

Rogliano

COTEAUX DU
CAP-CORSE

Mediterranean Sea

Patrimonio

PATRIMONIO

St Florent

Bastia

Calvi

CALVI

Ponte-
Leccia

△
MONTE CINTO
2706m

Corte

Porto

CORSICA

Aléria

Ghisonaccia

AJACCIO

Ajaccio

PORTO-
VECCHIO

Propriano

Sartène

SARTENE

Porto Vecchio

Vin de Corse

Figari

FIGARI

This map shows the official
delimitation of Vin de Corse.

In reality the vineyards
cover a very much smaller
area.

Bonifacio

Corsica

I fell in love with Corsica at first sight. Maybe it was something to do with leaving London on a grey, sleety February morning and arriving in Ajaccio to find spring sunshine, a blue sky and flowering almond and mimosa trees. It was irresistible and I was enchanted. And my enthusiasm was not dampened on a subsequent visit, when the heavens opened in a torrential downpour as we landed at Ajaccio. The Greeks were right when they called Corsica Kallisté, which means the very beautiful. Later the name became Kersiké, for the rocky mountains that dominate the centre of the island, and finally Korsia for the extensive forests; this was to become Corsica in Latin, Corse in French.

The Greeks came here from Asia Minor in 565 BC and founded the town of Alaia, on the site of present-day Aléria, on the east coast of the island. It was around this time that they also settled in Marsalia, which was to become Marseille. Although there may have been wild vines on the island, there is no doubt that it was the Greeks who were responsible for the first fumbling steps of Corsican viticulture. In the museum at Aléria there are Greek artefacts depicting vintage scenes. After the Greeks came the Romans, described by the former *vigneron* François Mercury in his informative book *Vignes, Vins et Vignerons de Corse*, as the first professional wine makers of the island. In 35 BC Virgil wrote about the wine of La Balagne, the area around Calvi, describing the ruby-coloured wine that was agreeable to the palate. In Pompeii, an important centre for the wine trade of the time, there was a reference to Corsica and its wine of 'second quality'.

The Arabs followed the Romans, causing a hiatus in the development of viticulture, so that the next important influence came from the city state of Pisa, which had control of the island from 1077 until it was ousted by the Genoese in 1284. During the period of the 'Pax Pisana', viticulture prospered. Wine was sent to Tuscany, particularly from the northern part of the island, the regions of La Balagne and Cap Corse. Eight out of twenty-one Corsican wine merchants resident in Pisa in the late fourteenth century were members of the guild of wine merchants. The bishop of St Florent, Monsignor Agostino Giustiano, compiled a detailed description of the island's economy in 1531 in his *Dialogo nominato Corsica*, describing both dry and sweet white wines and referring to the excellent wines of Farinole, which today is part of the appellation of Patrimonio. In one of his short stories, Guy de Maupassant describes a medieval pope who wanted no other wine on his table than that of Cap Corse.

The Genoese also encouraged viticulture, along with other crops, olives, sweet chestnuts and figs. In 1572, when peace had been restored to the island after a period of conflict, every landowner was obliged to plant ten fruit trees and four vines or risk a fine. A description of the town of Ajaccio in the early seventeenth century mentions a green belt of gardens and vineyards, while a second decree in 1658 required the planting of six fruit or olive trees or twenty vines by every inhabitant over the age of twenty. However, many Corsicans were nomads at heart, taking their sheep to summer pastures in the mountains and only returning to their homes for the winter. Such a migratory life was not conducive to viticulture. But the Genoese persisted. Wheat, olive oil and wine were sent to Genoa and sales were strictly controlled by the issue of export licences.

At the end of the eighteenth century vines accounted for 3.82 per cent of all agricultural land, as opposed to 1.24 per cent for olive trees and 54 per cent for wheat. Vines took their place alongside other crops in a system of polyculture, and were often planted on the higher land, partly for fear of attack from the sea and partly because of the presence of malaria in the low-lying coastal areas. The northern part of the island was more populated and prosperous, so viticulture was more successful and widespread there. A *vigneron* made a decent living for his family from two hectares of vines, whereas in the south, it was subsistence viticulture that prevailed.

James Boswell travelled through Corsica in 1765 as part of his Grand Tour of Europe, with the aim of meeting the charismatic

Pasquale Paoli, who had championed the cause of Corsican freedom. He went from Leghorn in a Tuscan vessel that was going over to Cap Corso for wine and described a view of the mountains covered in vines and olive trees that made the most agreeable impression on him. He also enthused about the variety of wines that he enjoyed.

There were other kinds of comment on the quality of Corsican wine. De Roux, a French officer, categorically stated in a letter in 1772 that the wine was worthless and did not keep, and that it was difficult to find any good wine. Likewise the Abbé Gaudin was less than enthusiastic in 1787, saying that the grapes were delicious, but why could their juice not be of the same quality? None the less, viticulture continued to develop, and by the end of the eighteenth century the ownership of olive trees and vines was certainly seen as a sign of advancement in the social hierarchy.

Other nations had designs on Corsica, such as the Aragonese, who were just across the water on Sardinia, and of course the French. The Genoese had to work hard to maintain their hold on the island, and evidence of this remains today, for scattered along the coastline are the ruins of the numerous Genoese lookout towers. The French finally gained control of the island in May 1769, just three months before the birth of Napoleon Bonaparte in Ajaccio.

During the Napoleonic Wars Corsica was for a short period in the hands of the English, and the English consul Drummond observed that anyone with even the smallest plot of land automatically despised manual work and fiercely maintained their position as a landowner. In 1794 Horatio Nelson mentioned that the export of Corsican wines was almost completely forbidden, as they competed with French wines, and in 1796 he described the conquest of Corsica as one of the most important successes for Britain, adding that her wines were preferable to those from Italy.

The census of 1814 gave 11,304 hectares of vines, a marked increase from 9800 at the end of the previous century, broken down as follows: 1468 in Ajaccio, 6462 in Bastia, 2059 in Corte in the centre of the island (which today is of much less significance), 933 in Sartène and 382 in Calvi, also known as La Balagne.

Jullien, in his *Topographie de Tous Vignobles Connus*, recognised that certain vineyards produced wines of quality and mentioned all the areas that are appellations or *crus* today, as well as others that are now quite unknown. As for grape varieties, he makes no mention of Nielluccio or Sciacarello, the two mainstays of Corsican viticulture today, but refers to various Italian varieties, such as Angiola, Ambrostina and Pinzutello, and the more familiar Trebbiano, Malvasia and Moscadello.

Rendu, writing in 1856, said that Corsica enjoyed a magnificent climate, which could enable her to become one of the richest producers of dry wines and fortified wines, but that the grape varieties were badly chosen and there were insufficient cellars. The wines were manipulated without intelligence and they were strong but vulgar.

Dr Guyot described how beautifully the vines grew in Corsica, at Cap Corse, Bastia, Vescovato, Cervione, Corte and Ajaccio, observing that the vines were vigorous and only asked to bear fruit. The right grape varieties gave excellent results. It was the same at Calvi and Sartène. In 1855 Corsican wines were sent to Paris for the industrial exhibition and in 1862 they were at the London exhibition. Abbatucci in his *Enquête Agricole* of 1867 observed that enormous progress had been made with the introduction of new varieties from France, Spain, Italy and even Constantinople. Albitreccia, another observer, noted that the wine growers considered the cultivation of the vines to be so remunerative that the island's landowners set to work and achieved a progress in viticulture that justified all their hopes. The arrival of oidium in 1852 had only a slight impact on development.

In 1874 an official report cited viticulture as the principal resource of three-quarters of the population, and an official figure of forty thousand hectares was given in 1876, but that was to change dramatically when phylloxera arrived on the island two years later. It affected first Ajaccio and then Corte, and spread throughout the island in the 1880s. However, the first American rootstocks arrived in 1879 and Corsica was, for a short period, to benefit from the lack of wine on mainland France. In 1883 a *négociant* in the Faubourg St Honoré created the Societé des Grands Vignobles de Sartène, with the planting of four hundred hectares of vines. A wealthy Sartenais planted a hundred hectares of vines and postcards of the period apparently illustrated vast warehouses filled with presses, harvesting equipment and enormous barrels. However, this period of euphoria, with its high prices, was short-lived and after 1900, by which time the vineyards of mainland

France were largely replanted, prices dropped, as they did elsewhere in the Midi. The producers of Sartène were particularly affected when the price of their wine fell to just one sou per litre, so that companies went bankrupt and vineyards disappeared.

At the beginning of the twentieth century, Corsican viticulture was primarily based on auto-consumption. Everyone had his own vines, usually a small plot on a terraced hillside, and his own barrels, along with a pig and a goat. All the elements necessary for the disappearance of vineyards were in place. By 1914 the area under vines had fallen to six thousand hectares, and the First World War was to have an even greater effect because of its disastrous demographic impact. More than forty thousand men were killed out of a total population of 230,000, more than from any other department of France. After the war, many more preferred to remain 'on the continent', as Corsicans usually describe mainland France, or to emigrate further afield. The war left Corsica with a severe problem of rural depopulation, so that yet more vineyards disappeared. The Second World War had a much less dramatic effect on the island, but as Mercurey says in his book, peace brought the return of the island's two demons, the exodus and economic somnolence. People were content to cultivate the existing vineyards but had no sense of a future direction. In the post-war years Corsica remained in its island isolation.

This situation was not really solved until the independence of Algeria brought an enormous influx of *pieds noirs* in the 1960s. More than seventeen thousand people from North Africa settled on the island, bringing with them, for better or for worse, their own viticultural experiences, so that the years between 1960 to 1976 saw a veritable explosion in viticulture. There is no doubt that the arrival of the *pieds noirs* galvanised the economy of the island, but its own indigenous viticulture suffered badly at the hands of the newcomers. Many of them had grown grapes in Algeria and Morocco in conditions that gave generous quantities of *vin ordinaire* with minimal production costs. They expected to find these same circumstances on Corsica. Vast expanses of *maquis*, the scrubland that covers much of the interior of the island, were *démaquisé* or cleared without consideration of the suitability of the terrain. It was often impossible to assess this beforehand and no attempt was made to control the plantings. The eastern coastal plain, which the Americans had rid of malaria during the Second

World War, was the prime target of the new arrivals. They planted the same grape varieties that they had grown in North Africa, namely Grenache Noir, Cinsaut, Carignan and Alicante Bouschet. Quantity not quality was their objective, and they certainly succeeded in changing the face of Corsican viticulture to a dramatic extent. In 1960 indigenous Corsican grape varieties accounted for seventy per cent of the island's vineyards, but by 1968 that figure had dropped dramatically to just thirteen per cent. The extension of the vineyards, particularly on the eastern side of the island, was equally dramatic, rising from 9,000 hectares in 1958 to 32,000 in 1973. However, the *pieds noirs* were soon to realise that conditions on Corsica were simply not the same as in North Africa. Yields were very much lower and even the favourable financial terms given by the French government could not make viticulture as remunerative as it had been in Algeria. Wine scandals were the consequence. On an island that has no trouble in obtaining ripe grapes, nearly 8,000 tonnes of sugar were used for chaptalisation in 1971.

The swift growth in the vineyard area was followed by an equally abrupt decline. From 32,000 hectares, the vineyard area fell to less than 10,000 hectares by 1987 and to 8500 in 1997. The number of harvest declarations – in other words, producers – dropped from 1808 in 1976 to 724 in 1988. Production plummeted too, from an astronomical 2,200,000 hectolitres at its height to 428,351 hectolitres in 1989. The latest figures give a total of 332,000 hectolitres from 9,700 hectares, of which just 2576 are within an appellation. Where once subsidies had been available for planting new vineyards, there were *primes d'arrachage* for grubbing them up. Some vineyards were simply left to revert to *maquis* and others were converted to a new and equally fleeting fashion, kiwi fruit.

It is now firmly recognised that the future of Corsican viticulture lies with the traditional grape varieties of the island that form the backbone of her appellations. The result has been an intensive programme of what is called *restructuration*, replacing the likes of Carignan, Cinsaut and Ugni Blanc with Sciacarello, Nielluccio and Vermentino (the name used in preference to Rolle on the island). Corsica's first appellation, Patrimonio, was created in 1968, followed by the Coteaux d'Ajaccio in 1971, renamed Ajaccio in 1984. These two appellations remain separate from the all-embracing Vin de Corse, with the *crus* of Sartène, Figari, Porto-Vecchio, Coteaux du Cap Corse and Calvi. There is also some wine produced in the centre of the island near Ponte Leccia which is included in the area of Vin de Corse, while most the vineyards on the coastal plan south of Bastia are covered the evocative-sounding Vin de Pays de l'Ile de Beauté.

Native grape varieties now account for a substantial proportion of the appellation wines. There is Sciacarello, which in the Corsican language sounds much more like Italian than French, and means 'the grape that bursts under the teeth', for it does indeed have a hard skin and plenty of juice. It is at its best on the granite soils of Ajaccio and Sartène. Occasionally you find a pure Sciacarello, but its main defect is a lack of colour, and therefore it is usually blended with Nielluccio, or with Grenache Noir, which is sometimes called Alicante de Corse. Syrah is another possibility, for it is permitted in Vin de Corse but not in any of the *crus*, and Carignan or Cinsaut may also be used, but much less frequently now with the replanting of the vineyards.

Nielluccio, in contrast, is a tougher, more substantial and tannic grape, said to be related to the Sangiovese of central Italy. In Patrimonio it used to represent at least 75 per cent of the red wine, a proportion that was increased to ninety per cent with the 2000 vintage, and you can certainly find examples of pure Nielluccio. Elsewhere it is usually blended with other varieties.

The most important white grape variety is Vermentino, which confusingly is also known as Malvoisie de Corse, although it bears no relationship to any other of the grape varieties called Malvoisie. Vermentino is the Italian name for Rolle, which is grown in Provence, especially in Bellet, and in ever-increasing quantities throughout in the south of France. It also features in Sardinia, as Vermentino di Sardegna and the more flavoursome, Vermentino di Gallura, from the northern part of the island, closest to Corsica. There is also the occasional example on mainland Italy such as in the Colline Pisane. Muscat *à petits grains* is also important in the north western part of the island for the more recent appellation of Muscat de Cap Corse, of which more on page 688.

Corsica has been described as a veritable ampelographical reserve, and there are other indigenous island grape varieties with exotic-sounding names like Carcagiolu, Barbirossu, Montaccio, Pagadebit, Bianco Gentile and so on. Some of these are of little importance, but others are beginning to reappear in the vineyards in larger quantities. Corsica has lagged behind the rest of France in the field of viticultural research, but efforts are being made to make up the lost ground. A research station was established in 1981 under the auspices of CIVAM, the Centre d'Information et de Vulgarisation pour l'Agriculture et le Milieu Rural, the organisation that has been responsible for guiding much of the replanting of the vineyards. It has been working with some twenty-two different grape varieties altogether, with as many as seventy different clones, not only in its own three and a half hectare vineyard but also with some wine growers as well as the agricultural *lycée*. Different aspects of viticulture and cellar work are being examined. In the vineyard they have looked at different training methods. After each harvest they carry out as many as seventy different micro-vinifications, in hundred or two hundred-litre vats, and have a press that will operate with just fifty kilos of grapes. Yeast is a subject of particular interest. They have been working to establish whether Corsica has good natural yeast strains and have identified as many as ninety-one different varieties. The best have been isolated and became commercially available for the first time in 1998. So far, of the lesser-known native grape varieties, Bianco Gentile is showing the most potential.

Finally, there is a third strand to Corsican viticulture that causes some of the purists a certain amount of unease. This is the more recent introduction of grape varieties such as Cabernet Sauvignon, Merlot, Syrah, Chardonnay and Pinot Noir. Those who uphold the island's traditions are anxious that these more international varieties should not infiltrate the appellations. Syrah is allowed in Vin de Corse and there is some discussion about Mourvèdre, but for the moment the interlopers are planted only on the coastal plain south of Bastia, where they are included in Vin de Pays de l'Ile de Beauté.

Corsica has been described as a land of mountains in the sea, for mountains do indeed account for nearly half her land mass, and the average altitude of the island, 568 metres, is higher than that of any other Mediterranean island, particularly compared to neighbouring Sardinia, with its average of only 344 metres. Fifty-five per cent of the island lies at over 400 metres and twenty per cent is above 1,000 metres. One long chain of mountains dominates the centre of the island. In winter these are snowcapped and it is not unusual in February for roads to be impassable at Bavella while spring has already arrived in Porto-Vecchio on the coast.

Corsica enjoys mild winters and warm summers. Edmond About wrote in the middle of the nineteenth century that he had spent the winter in Corsica, which would give him two summers that year. The sunshine hours are longer than anywhere else in France, regularly reaching 2500 hours all over the island. Nor is there a shortage of rainfall, as I know to my discomfort on various occasions. Wind is another significant climatic factor. The Mistral, from Provence, is dry and fierce, while the Tramontane from the Alps is dry but cold. The Gregale from the Appenines brings rain, as does the most frequent wind, the Libeccio from Gibraltar, while the Sirocco from North Africa can carry the sand of the Sahara. The areas of Cap Corse and Bonifacio, the northern and southern tips of the island, are particularly exposed to the effects of wind.

Inevitably the sea is a dominant influence on the island's climate and viticulture. It lessens the contrasts between day and night time temperatures up to an altitude of about five hundred metres, ensuring that there is always a marked maritime influence, with refreshing humidity, particularly during the summer months. In short, it creates an ideal climate for viticulture.

As will be seen, Corsica also enjoys great geological diversity in her vineyards.

Ajaccio

━━━━━━

Ajaccio is the natural start for a visit to Corsica. This is the city of Napoleon, who was born here in August 1769 in the old quarter, in a substantial town house that is now a simple museum. The main square, the Place des Palmiers, has a statue of the French emperor emulating his Roman predecessors, with toga and laurel wreath. The northern side of the Gulf of Ajaccio ends in the Iles Sanguinaires, four islands of which the largest, La Grande Sanguinaire, was given by the Genoese in 1503 to the Ponte family on the condition that they planted eight hundred vines and six hundred fruit trees. Alphonse Daudet lived in the lighthouse at the end of the point for a short time in 1863 and described the island in one of the *Lettres de Mon Moulin*.

The appellation Ajaccio covers a wide area from Cargese in the north down as far as the Taravo valley in the south, but many of the vineyards are on the hillsides overlooking the Gulf of Ajaccio, with a concentration of producers around Ajaccio itself. Mountains dominate the skyline, with Corsica's highest peak, Monte Cinto, rising to three thousand metres, so that it is snowcapped even in the height of summer.

The individuality of the wines of Ajaccio derives from the combination of the Sciacarello grape and the granite soil. Sciacarello provides wines with a fine bouquet, but as mentioned earlier its main problem is lack of colour, and for this reason it is rare to find a pure Sciacarello. However, it does not lack body and will age well. Sciacarello must represent a minimum of forty per cent of any red Ajaccio, with a minimum twenty per cent of other Corsican varieties, which may effectively mean sixty per cent Sciacarello, plus Cinsaut, Grenache Noir and Carignan, which are each limited to fifteen per cent. Currently of the two hundred and five hectares of vines in the appellation, about a hundred are planted with Sciacarello.

DOMAINE PERALDI, MEZZAVIA

My first visit was to Domaine Peraldi in the hills just outside Ajaccio, which belongs to the de Poix family. It had been eleven years since my last visit there. The first time I had met Count Louis de Poix, an aristocratic elderly gentleman who had explained that Peraldi was the name of his mother's family, owners of the estate for some four hundred years. He has retired from active involvement and his son Guy is more interested in producing wine in Romania, so the wine making is now in the hands of the young oenologist Christophe George. He has a wider view of things than many other wine makers in Corsica, as he spent time at Petaluma in the Adelaide Hills of Southern Australia after his training at Bordeaux. He found it quite a culture shock after the classic oenology of Bordeaux. The Australians do not worry about tradition and they do things that would be completely aberrant in France

Domaine Peraldi is a fifty-hectare estate, with a further ten hectares rented in the neighbouring appellation of Sartène. Sciacarello accounts for sixty per cent of the vineyard, with equal plantings of Carignan, Grenache Noir, Cinsaut and Vermentino. The cellar is well equipped, with cooling equipment for controlling the fermentation temperatures, stainless steel vats in an insulated warehouse and an ageing cellar with *barriques*, which are still uncommon in Corsica. They are used for the estate's top wine Cuvée du Cardinal, which is made only in the best years, mainly from thirty-year-old low-yielding Sciacarello vines.

Their white wine is pure Vermentino and has some attractive herbal overtones. George is experimenting with barrel fermentation, but the flavour is still overwhelmed by oak. However, he feels that there is potential if the wine has sufficient body and is given time to recuperate from the oak influence. The pink wine, mainly from Sciacarello, has some delicate raspberry fruit and fresh acidity. The 1995 red, consisting of Sciacarello aged in wood for eight months and blended with Grenache Noir, Cinsaut and Carignan, was perfumed and spicy. Sciacarello never has much tannin, so the wood provided some backbone without being intrusive. It must also be fully ripe, for it is much more expressive with 13° than with 12° alcohol. George made the apt comparison that the difference between Sciacarello and Nielluccio is similar to the difference between Burgundy and Bordeaux, in that one is delicate and fragrant while the other more substantial and structured.

CLOS CAPITORO, PORTICCIO

A little further south is Clos Capitoro, a family estate created by Louis Bianchetti in 1856; the present head of the family is Jacques Bianchetti. Appropriately, the bull's head is the emblem of the property. The fifty-hectare estate consists of three distinct vineyards, Punta di Cuccu, Capitoro itself and Paviglia, which used to belong to François Mercury, the historian of the appellation, until he sold it on his retirement. They have Vermentino for white wine and for a sparkling wine, as well as Sciacarello and Grenache Noir for red wine, but no Cinsaut or Carignan. There is talk of including Syrah in the appellation of Ajaccio, and also Mourvèdre, to compensate for the colour deficiency of the Sciacarello. Syrah is allowed in the appellation Vin de Corse, but for the moment the prevailing view is that the potential of Sciacarello is still unexplored. It may not have enough colour or tannin, but they recognise the need to work on it, as the Burgundians did with Pinot Noir, for that too is light in colour and tannin but certainly not lacking in flavour. To prove his point, in the best vintages Bianchetti makes a Cuvée Réserve of pure Sciacarello from a selection of the best vines. It spends two years in vat rather than barrel before bottling. The 1993 vintage, when it was four years old, had some lovely herbal, spicy notes, flavours reminiscent of the Corsican *maquis*, balanced with a sufficient backbone of tannin.

DOMAINE PRATAVONE, PILA CANALE

The road to Domaine Pratavone in the Taravo valley is narrow and winding. Pratavone is the name of the hamlet and literally means a meadow in a hole. Isabelle Courrèges has been working here with her father Jean since 1992. She too has broad horizons, for after training in Bordeaux and Montpellier she worked for Stellenbosch

Wine Farmers in South Africa and then for Rosemount in Australia's Hunter Valley. First she took me on a tour of the vineyards. The scenery is dramatic and the gradients steep. There was evidence of a forest fire in the blackened trunks of cork trees. However, the *maquis* was quickly growing back, first cistus, then mastic and finally myrtle. We also admired her father's feijoa trees, which she laughingly described as his mistress. They look like olive trees in the distance, with silver-grey leaves, and have spectacular white and red flowers. The fruit makes delicious jam.

Courrèges explained that over the last ten years they had taken advantage of the *primes de restructuration* to replant eighteen of their thirty-one hectares with Corsican grape varieties. They now have a lot of Sciacarello, as well as two hectares of Barbirossu and some Vermentino, all to emphasise the typicity of the appellation. Her father had settled here from Algeria in 1963 and not unnaturally had at first planted the grape varieties with which he was familiar, namely Grenache Noir, Ugni Blanc, Carignan and Cinsaut. These are now disappearing. They do not have any Nielluccio, but they do have two hectares of Syrah as an experiment, on the advice of the CIVAM, and do find that ten to fifteen per cent blended with Sciacarello adds colour. However, it must not dominate the flavour. Barbirossu is a pink grape and makes good *rosé* with an attractive flavour, but without much acidity or alcohol.

Although they have invested in their vineyards and a new bottling line, the cellar remains the traditional building with the concrete vats that Jean Courrèges constructed in 1963. In her wine making, Isabelle Courrèges aims for minimal handling of the grapes and emphasises the importance of hygiene. The pure Vermentino, half of which is given some skin contact, was fresh and perfumed, while her red wine, made from sixty per cent Sciacarello and forty per cent Grenache Noir with two years ageing in vat, was warm and spicy.

Sartène

─────

From Pratavone I made a detour to admire the extraordinary neolithic *menhirs* of Filitosa, which had remained hidden in the *maquis* until as recently as 1954. From there the road led to the attractive seaside town of Propriano and then inland to Sartène. Sartène is one of the old towns of the island, perched on the side of a hill dominating the surrounding countryside. Tiny narrow streets lead to a central square. On my first visit one late February it seemed rather sombre, almost sinister, with its shuttered grey stone houses, but on a bright June morning it was bustling with people and traffic chaos. It is famous for its Easter festival, vividly described in Dorothy Carrington's evocative book about Corsica, *The Granite Island*.

DOMAINE FIUMICICOLI, SARTENE

The best producer of the *cru* of Sartène is Domaine Fiumicicoli, to the north of the town in the Fiumicicoli valley. Since my previous visit, the river had flooded dramatically, sweeping away the vegetation along its banks to reveal the elegant single-arched Genoese bridge that features on the estate's label. There had also been a change of generations in the Andreanni family, in that Simon Andreanni is now working with his father Félix. They have forty-five hectares of vines and they too have taken advantage of the *primes de restructuration* to convert fifteen hectares of Carignan, Cinsaut and Grenache Noir into Nielluccio, Sciacarello and Vermentino. In contrast with Ajaccio, Nielluccio performs well in Sartène, while Sciacarello enjoys the granite soil. They too have planted three hectares of Syrah as an experiment, but remain very anxious to preserve the typicity of Sartène. The subsidies for replanting have been available since the early 1980s, but came to an end in 1999. They were funded partly by the French government, partly by the region and partly by the European Union. In 1997 growers received FF 45,000 per hectare as an incentive to replant and to help tide them over the consequent loss of three or four years' crop.

Domaine Fiumicicoli also illustrates the various improvements in cellar equipment and wine making that have occurred over the last few years. They now have a reliable means of temperature control and a pneumatic press, while their wine making has become more precise as they ferment each grape variety separately rather than putting everything into the same vat. There is an insulated area in the cellar for storing bottles, but ideally they would like an under-ground cellar for storage; however, they nurse no ambitions to age wine in *barriques*. Andreanni is convinced of the ageing potential of his red wines and feels very strongly that the image of Corsica would be greatly enhanced if it were realised that the island can produce wines that benefit from bottle ageing. Certainly his 1990 blend of Nielluccio, Sciacarello and Grenache Noir, which I tasted in June 1997, had some attractive peppery fruit, even though it had not been stored in ideal conditions.

Andreanni's younger wines also showed potential. The Vermentino was quite rich and solid, with some spicy fruit. The *rosé* comes from a plot of fifty-year-old vines, with about twenty different grape varieties all mixed together. It had a very pale colour, with a delicate raspberry nose and some fruity acidity. Reds are usually a blend of the three varieties Nielluccio, Sciacarello and Grenache Noir, aged in vat for two years, giving some firm, peppery fruit and sufficient backbone, but not a lot of tannin. Andreanni explained that Sciacarello can sometimes have a *côté boisé*, so that people think it has been aged in barrel when in fact it has not been near a stave of wood. We finished with a 1992 pure Nielluccio, which tasted of the warmth of *maquis*, of herbs and sunshine.

DOMAINE SAN MICHELE, SARTENE

The soil changes at the Taravo Valley separating Ajaccio from Sartène, and the appellation of Sartène stretches as far south as

Roccapina, a dramatic rocky promontory on the coast that looks like a lion's head from a distance. The only other estate of any significance in Sartène is Domaine San Michele, well to the south of the town and so very much off the beaten track that Mme Phélip de Mazarin insisted that I met her in Sartène so that she could guide me to the estate. It was certainly worth the detour for the wonderful views of the mountains, the Omo de Cagna and the Rocher de la Fée, with the vineyards in rich red clay and granite soil. The rather primitive cellar was at the end of a long dirt track full of potholes. Mme Phélip has Vermentino, Sciacarello, Nielluccio, Barbirossu and a little Carignan and Cinsaut, but no Grenache Noir, as its stems prove too fragile in the strong winds. The vineyards have undergone a considerable amount of reorganisation, with each grape variety now in its own plot rather than all mixed up together, as was the traditional Corsican system.

The wines were somewhat rustic, a slightly bitter Vermentino, a *rosé* with light raspberry fruit and a rugged red, a blend of Sciacarello, Nielluccio and Carignan. I persuaded the *régisseur*, who was born on the estate in 1934, to reminisce about the changes he had seen. Mules used to pull the carts until tractors arrived in about 1960. The large old *foudres* disappeared in the mid-1970s. Pumps are now electric, where originally they had been manual and, following that, powered by diesel. Over lunch, looking at a wonderful view of the lion of Roccapina, Mme Phélip talked about her family, who had owned the estate since 1700 and were among the principal landowners of Sartène. We drank her 1993 Vermentino, which has some attractively mature herbal but dusty fruit, demonstrating that Vermentino could indeed age. I also learned a Corsican nursery rhyme about the mountains I had seen that morning:

> *Le lion de Roccapine*
> *disait au Omo de Cagne,*
> *Moi je surveille la marine*
> *Et toi tu surveilles la montagne.*

In other words, the lion of Roccapine said to the Omo de Cagne, I will look out over the sea and you look out over the mountain.

Sartène was once the most important wine region of Corsica, but in recent years it seems to have lost its way, with a sharp decline in the vineyard area to the present 190 hectares. Some of the old estates have disappeared and the town co-operative has gone out business, all since the first flush of enthusiasm of the *pied noirs* waned. Old people are retiring and few young people are interested in carrying on their parents' work. Yet on this poor soil vines are the only viable crop.

Figari

═══

The road to Figari continues along the coast, with spectacular views of a brilliant blue sea, a rocky coastline and in the distance Sardinia. Figari is in the southern corner of the island, near the historic town of Bonifacio. This is an area that was particularly affected by the influx of immigrants from North Africa. The co-operative of Figari was founded in 1962 to accommodate the new arrivals, but now, after a period of closure, it makes an insignificant amount of wine. At the height of the vineyard expansion in the mid-1960s, there had been as many as fourteen hundred hectares of vines, but now most of the vineyards have been pulled up, leaving just one hundred and twenty-five hectares.

DOMAINE DE TANELLA

There is only one estate of any significance: Domaine de Tanella, run by the energetic Jean-Baptiste de Peretti de la Rocca. He explained that his father had cleared a vast expanse of *maquis* and in mid-1980s had replanted forty-six hectares of vines, so that he now has fifty-seven hectares in one enormous plot, Sciacarello, Nielluccio, Vermentino, a little Grenache Noir, Syrah and forty-year-old Carignan, all overlooked by the rocky southern face of the Omo de Cagna. The typicity of Figari comes from the red soil and the wind that blows off the sea, which means that vineyard treatments are rarely necessary but that sometimes you can taste salt on the grapes.

De Peretti exudes enthusiasm. He more than anyone else I met is in favour of Syrah, describing himself as the ambassador of the variety, which he first planted in 1990. His basic Domaine de

Tanella includes ten per cent of Syrah, while his best red wine, Grande Réserve, has fifty per cent Syrah, thirty per cent Sciacarello, ten per cent Nielluccio and an assortment of other varieties for the remaining ten per cent. The 1996 vintage was indeed rather Rhônish in character, warm and spicy, with some tannin. De Peretti recognises that he is open to criticism from his more traditional colleagues, but he loves the wines of the Rhône Valley, especially Côte Rôtie. He has tried to make a pure Sciacarello, but found it simply too light in colour, although the flavour was good.

His cellars are vast, with some enormous concrete vats – one as big as fifteen hundred hectolitres – built in 1963 at the peak of the wine boom in Figari. He would like to experiment with barrels, but does wonder if the oak would mask the fruit, and he would also like to give his wines a longer period of bottle ageing. Altogether Peretti makes three red wines. The basic Domaine de Tanella is from younger vines, while the Cuvée Alexandre, named after his daughter, is made from several grape varieties and was spicy and rounded. There is also a white Cuvée Alexandre, a pure Vermentino with some attractive quince-like fruit, and a *rosé*, a mixture of Sciacarello and Nielluccio with a little Grenache Noir, that was a bit dusty. The best wines are labelled Cuvée Alexandre Grande Réserve, of which the red was full-bodied and Rhônish, and the *rosé*, from the free-run juice of Sciacarello and Nielluccio, delicate and herbal. De Peretti is also planning a late harvest sweet Vermentino. Sheep's cheese is another concern, and I went away with a *fromage de brebis* that survived my island tour and tasted delicious when it finally reached London.

Porto-Vecchio

―――

Overlooked by the old fortified town, Porto-Vecchio is an attractive port with a marina full of smart yachts belonging to the jet set. This area also experienced an influx of *pieds noirs*. Once there were numerous tiny vineyards around the port. People also grew wheat and olives and led a nomadic existence with their animals, moving between the coast and the mountains. Then the immigrants arrived and cleared the *maquis*, but found the soil to be poor and granitic, so that the excessive yields of North Africa could never be achieved here.

DOMAINE DE TORRACCIA, PORTO-VECCHIO

Today there is just one estate of any significance, Domaine de Torraccia, which was created by Christian Imbert. He told me that when he found Torraccia, he felt that he had found his refuge, like a hermit. He had been a trader in Africa, which he described as a great life but not when you are married, so he was looking for somewhere to settle and came to investigate Corsica. He gave a little old lady a lift, who said, 'If I'm not being indiscreet, may I ask why you are here?' He told her that, like Voltaire's Candide, he was looking for somewhere to cultivate his garden. 'Ah,' she said, 'I have a cousin who might be able to help.' That evening the cousin appeared at the hotel and the next day took him to see Torraccia, which at that time consisted of a ruined house with a spring and several hectares of *maquis*. And so he found his refuge. And the moral of this story is that you never know what might happen if you give an old lady a lift.

His neighbours treated him as the *fou du coin*, but he cleared the *maquis*, planted vines and olive trees, restored the house and built a cellar. His first vines were Grenache Noir, Syrah and Nielluccio, and then, after listening to the *pieds noirs*, he added Carignan and Cinsaut. Now he has forty-three hectares in production, including Vermentino and Sciacarello, but no longer any Carignan. The soil is decomposed granite and you could describe the vineyards as organic, but Imbert prefers the term *culture à l'ancienne*. Some are on steep slopes with dramatic views.

The cellars are functional, operating by gravity, and since my previous visit Imbert has built an underground cellar for storing wine in bottle, but not barrel. He is against wood. 'Our grape varieties have an original organoleptical quality and if you put them in wood, you eliminate the expression of the wine and they become banal, false Burgundies.' He makes a delicate raspberry-flavoured *rosé*, from Nielluccio, Sciacarello, Cinsaut and Grenache Noir. The Nielluccio is pressed immediately, as otherwise it gives too much colour, while the others are *saignée*. The white, made from Vermentino, had attractive herbal notes. A Nielluccio, made by carbonic maceration, was warm and raisiny, with some ripe spicy fruit and none of the astringency associated with Sangiovese. It was supple, but with backbone. The red Domaine de Torraccia comes from fifty per cent Nielluccio, thirty per cent Grenache Noir and ten per cent each of Sciacarello and Syrah, which are blended after the fermentation. It had the sun-soaked flavours of the *maquis*, with a firm backbone. Oriu, which Imbert described as *ma petite fierté*, is only made in the best years, mostly recently in 1998, and consists of eighty per cent Nielluccio and twenty per cent Sciacarello, blended in the spring following the vintage. It is the epitome of the flavours of Corsica, warm and spicy, with the scents and herbs of the *maquis* in a glass.

Imbert is the president of Uva Corse, an organisation formed by the leading independent producers with the object of promoting their wines. They are all people who make and bottle their own appellation wine from their own grapes and share a similar philosophy. The members use the special bottle of Uva Corse, which has the embossed motif of the Moor's head with two tritons and a crown. Legend has it that Corsica is guarded by tritons, or male mermaids, while the Moor's head is the island's emblem. There are all sorts of tales associated with the emblem, going back to the struggles between the Christians and the Saracens in the Middle Ages.

However, despite the efforts of Uva Corse, there is a feeling that sales are not as buoyant as they should be. They are very dependent on the tourist trade, which means that ninety per cent of all sales take place in the three peak summer months. There have been problems recently. The tourist trade is not flourishing as it was; there are fewer visitors, Italians in particular, coming to the island, as a result of the weak lire and Italy's political problems. The internal problems of Corsica, including the odd terrorist bomb and arson attack, have not helped either. Competition is also much greater, as there are now more individual wine producers. Consequently Uva Corse is working on promotions outside Corsica, mainly *sur le continent* of mainland France. But transport costs are prohibitive. To send wine from Figari to Paris costs FF 1 per bottle for a whole pallet of about fifty cases, but if you are just sending a couple of cases to an private customer the cost escalates to ten francs per bottle. As an outsider, Imbert is perceptive about the Corsican weaknesses and strengths. The problem is that the average Corsican has simply no idea how to sell his wine. He is not a salesman, but a shepherd or a warrior. The more dynamic emigrate, even if only as far as mainland France.

Plaine Orientale

North of Porto-Vecchio the coastline opens out into the vast Plaine Orientale. This is where most of the island's *vins de pays* are produced, mainly by co-operatives.

CAVE COOPERATIVE D'ALERIA

The co-operative of Aléria, where the Greeks settled so many centuries ago, is part of the Union des Vignerons de l'Ile de Beauté. There is an archaeological museum at Aléria, but little else to recommend the town. The co-operative is responsible for some two thousand hectares of vines – in other words, about a quarter of the wine production of Corsica – with vineyards stretching from Borgo, just south of Bastia, down as far as Ghisonnaccia, covering the whole of the Côte Orientale, or what is now more picturesquely called La Costa Serena. They have ninety members around Aléria, while the sister co-operative at Casinca, up the road, has a further sixty-five members, with vineyards ranging in size from half a hectare to one hundred and eighty hectares. You need between twenty-five and thirty hectares to make a satisfactory living from your vines.

The last fifteen years have seen a significant replanting of the vineyards as well as a shift away from *vin de table* and *vin de pays* to appellation wines. Hectares of Carignan, Alicante, Cinsaut and Ugni Blanc have been pulled up and replaced with Vermentino, Nielluccio, Syrah and (although it is less successful here than Nielluccio) Sciacarello, as well as *cépages améliorateurs* for varietal *vins de pays*, namely Cabernet Sauvignon, Merlot and Chardonnay. Although Carignan is still allowed in the appellation wine, Vin de

Corse, it is usually destined for *vin de table*. They also have aspirations towards a regional appellation, Coteaux d'Aléria, but for the moment the INAO is showing little enthusiasm for their request. With so many different grape varieties the vintage lasts from the end of August into the third week of October.

The co-operative buildings are surrounded by a sea of vines stretching down to the coast. The cellars are well equipped, with stainless steel vats as well as cement vats, five different *quais de réception*, pneumatic presses and efficient temperature control for fermentations. There is an insulated warehouse for storage, both for bottles and 130 small barrels. They work as much as possible by gravity and produce altogether some fifty different wines, with about two hundred different labels, of which I tasted a small selection. They are also responsible for bottling the wines of Clos d'Orlea, a private estate in the hills towards Corte, on the plateau of Pianiccia.

Their principal label is Réserve du Président, and there is a more select Prestige du Président. The white Prestige du Président comes from Vermentino that has spent three months on fine lees following a light skin contact, and twenty per cent of the wine is fermented in new barrels. I found it quite heavy and not very Corsican in flavour. The Réserve du Président, from Chardonnay kept on fine lees without any wood contact, was well made but lacked any distinctive character, while the *rosé* was fresh and fruity. The red Réserve du Président, from two parts Nielluccio to one part Syrah, spends twelve months in vat and was soft and fruity with a little tannin, but again without much Corsican typicity. The red Prestige du Président is made from the same varieties and in the same proportions, but from older vines, with sixty per cent of the wine spending eight months in wood. It is Nielluccio that provides the tannin and Syrah the fruit; the taste was quite chunky, with some spice, a hint of vanilla and some soft tannins. The wines are well made, but on the principle that small is beautiful, they failed to excite.

LES COTEAUX DE DIANA

North of Aléria is the Etang de Diana, which gave its name to Skalli's establishment Les Coteaux de Diana. A floating restaurant, aptly called Les Pieds dans l'Eau, is worth a detour for the fat, creamy oysters from the salt lake, the barbecued fish and the views across the water to Skalli's vineyards. Just by the turning that leads to Skalli's cellars is a sombre reminder of the political turmoil that lies under the surface of Corsican sunshine: a derelict cellar, once the property of a *pied noir*, that had been *plastiqué* by terrorists for political reasons. The Coteaux de Diana are run by M. and Mme Costa, who both trained at Montpellier. He makes the wine and she is responsible for the *cuverie*. The first vineyards were planted here in 1957 by a Dr Pietrelli from Morocco, who sold them to Skalli in 1970. Since then the vineyards have been enlarged to 120 hectares in one plot on the edge of the lake, and their composition has been changed to include more Chardonnay, Vermentino and Nielluccio, as well as Cabernet Sauvignon, Merlot, Grenache Noir, Syrah and Pinot Noir. Their objective is varietal wine, and the cellar has been improved accordingly, with modern heat exchangers and pneumatic presses.

All the harvesting is done at night, which is essential when the vintage begins on about 20 August. Cabernet Sauvignon is the one exception, for it has no flavour if the grapes are too cold. I tasted a selection of different vat samples. They have the only Sauvignon in Corsica, with some lemony fruit and that slightly sweaty Sauvignon flavour. There was a Chenin Blanc, which was fresh and grassy with a hint of saltiness, a delicate Chardonnay and a spicy Vermentino. The reds consisted of a plummy, easy-to-drink Merlot and a rather stalky Cabernet Sauvignon, all giving an impression of carefully made wines that are performing well on the export market.

CAVE DE LA MARANA

The other leading co-operative on the Côte Orientale is the Cave de la Marana, which is part of the Union des Vignerons Associés du Levant, or UVAL. Their primary aim is high-tech table wine, in the form of varietal *vins de pays* for the export market, but they have also begun to develop a range of appellation wines, based on the estates of some of their members. I was impressed when I first visited them in 1986. They had an appreciation of the economic facts of life that was rare on the island, as well as some of the most modern cellars, with highly sophisticated equipment. Back in the mid-1980s they used cultured yeast, centrifuged the must and controlled everything very closely, with rigorous attention to fermentation temperatures. Today their cellars are even more impressive, with new pneumatic presses, powerful chilling facilities, barrels in an air-conditioned cellar, a high-powered bottling line, and everything absolutely spotless. They are also planning a visitor centre, which will certainly be worth the detour.

The director, Alain Mazoyer, has always been very enthusiastic about the exceptional climate of Corsica, explaining that it is the equivalent on the coastal plain to the Californian climatic zone 3, which includes the top of the Napa Valley. There is no risk of frost and summer temperatures are never really excessive. There are 2500 hours of sunshine annually, and with 500 mm they have the same rainfall as Bordeaux. The rain usually comes in the autumn and winter months, while the mountains in the centre of the island provide a good contrast between day and night time temperatures.

UVAL's original range of varietal wines included a Blanc de Syrah, Cabernet Sauvignon, Nielluccio, Chardonnay and Chenin Blanc, but they are gradually extending the range, with Merlot, Vermentino and Sciacarello *rosé*. They are now much more selective in their choice of grapes, vinifying the fruit from particularly good vineyards separately, especially Chardonnay, Pinot Noir, Nielluccio, Vermentino and Muscat. Pinot Noir is the subject of considerable experimentation. Their first attempt was in 1987 and now they produce about ten thousand hectolitres, which makes them the largest producer of that variety in the whole of the south of France. Mazoyer is well aware of how difficult it is to vinify, for you need to develop its fruit and aroma while keeping its suppleness. I tasted a 1996 vat sample, which certainly showed some potential. They are also developing Muscat, making different styles such as a dry Muscat, a semi-sweet wine with 40 gm/l of residual sugar, and a *vin de liqueur*, which is like a *vin doux naturel* but cannot be called that because there is no category of *vin doux naturel* in the appellation Vin de Corse. Muscat is also blended with Chenin Blanc, combining the vivacity of the Chenin Blanc with the fruit of Muscat. They are considering other double varietals, now that these are allowed under the *vin de pays* regulations.

You will find the wines of Cave de la Marana under numerous different labels and estate names, including Le Corsican, with the slogan *le Corse un peu pirate*, for the supermarkets, as well as Vignerons des Pieves and Cuvée San Michele, with a label illustrating a carving of a grape-picking scene from the nearby Romanesque church of St Michel-de-Murato. I tasted a range of Chardonnays. There was Domaine de Lischetto, ten per cent of which had been fermented in wood, giving just a hint of oak. Mazoyer explained that they were working to develop more complex Chardonnay, for which the first vintage using barrels was 1990. In the 1994 Cuvée San Michele, twenty per cent of which was fermented in wood, the oak was quite marked, with some buttery fruit. Another example had spent six months in wood and had a little more body. Altogether they have four hundred hectares of Chardonnay in production. I also enjoyed a 1994 Cabernet Sauvignon Cuvée San Michele, which had spent six months in oak so that it was ripe and rounded, with some attractive vanilla and cassis flavours. Mazoyer considers that they had mastered Cabernet Sauvignon and I would not disagree with him. My tasting finished with their first vintage of Muscat from Clos de Rasignani, with some elegant orange-peel notes and floral fruit.

DOMAINE DE MUSOLEU, FOLELLI

On this part of the island there are a few individual estates producing Vin de Corse that do not come within the various *crus* of the appellation: for example, Domaine d'Orlea, which has a link with the co-operative at Aléria; Domaine de Vico, which is in the hills above Bastia; and Domaine de Musoleu at Folelli, on the coast below Bastia, which is the property of Charles Morazzani, president of the newly formed Comité Intersyndical des Vins de Corse that has the aim of promoting Corsican wine on mainland France and further afield.

The name Musoleu refers to the fact that there was a Roman cemetery near by. Folelli is opposite the small island of Monte Cristo, and records in the archives at Genoa show that monks from the island were cultivating vines in this area in the eighth century. Morazzani has sixteen hectares of vines in several plots, on a plateau where the soil is a mixture of clay, chalk and sand. They are planted with just four grape varieties, Nielluccio, Grenache Noir, Syrah and Vermentino. Both his grandfather and his father had made wine. His father had had seven hectares of vineyards where the different varieties were all mixed up together, and he produced other crops as well. Only since Morazzani took over in 1972 has the estate become dedicated to viticulture. He treated me to a splendid vertical tasting of red wines, but first we tried his Vermentino, which had the herbal notes of the *maquis*, with the flavour enhanced by a short period of skin contact. His *rosé*, a blend of Nielluccio and Grenache Noir, was redolent of ripe strawberries. The red wine, usually a blend of twenty per cent Syrah with forty per cent each of Nielluccio and Grenache Noir, depending on the vintage, spends a year in vat. He is tempted by wood, out of curiosity and because some consumers like it, but reckons that you lose flavour and typicity. The 1994 had a certain herbal character, the 1993 had more berry fruit, while the 1990, which included the mixture of different varieties from his father's vineyard, had some attractive herbal fruit and a cedary finish. Even the 1985 when it was twelve years old was showing some appealing herbal notes, with a long finish, quite contradicting the generalisation that Corsican wines do not age. In fact, Morazzani did not build an insulated warehouse until 1990, so initially it had been kept in far from ideal conditions, but none the less showed a distinctive character.

Morazzani also talked about the arrival of the *pieds noirs* and the harm that they have done to the traditional viticulture of Corsica. Hitherto nobody had chaptalised in Corsica. They did not need to, for the long hours of sunshine made the grapes ripe enough. However, the *pieds noirs* concentrated on Alicante for colour and Carignan for yield, and obtained between 200 and 300 hl/ha, but with a alcohol level of only 6.5–7°, which they boosted to 12–13° with liberal quantities of sugar. This went on for about ten years until the traditional Corsican wine growers asked for the use of sugar to be suppressed and the market collapsed, quite spoiling the image of Corsica in the process.

Today it is difficult to plant a new vineyard. You need planting rights, which could cost FF 7–10,000 per hectare. A bare hectare of land would cost about FF 20,000, going up to FF 80,000 in Patrimonio, and then you need to allow about FF 100,000 to cover the expense of planting and costs until it comes into production three years later. Existing growers were being offered FF 45,000 per hectare to replant their vineyards with the Corsican varieties, but the only viable way for a newcomer to set himself up as a wine producer was to find vines and a cellar for sale.

Cap Corse

The coastal plain ends at Bastia, which was the old capital of Corsica. For the brief two-year period during the Napoleonic Wars when Corsica belonged to Britain, the viceroy Sir Gilbert Elliot held his court there. There is a cheerful port with fishing and pleasure boats, overlooked by colourful, slightly shabby houses. From Bastia, I drove north on to Cap Corse. The road is narrow and winding, with more than its fair share of potholes. Before phylloxera there were eighteen hundred hectares of vines on Cap Corse and you can still see the remains of crumbling terraces. Today, the vineyards have almost disappeared, leaving not much more than forty hectares shared between the four producers of the appellation of Cap Corse. The villages of Morsiglia, Rogliano and Santa Severa are all that remain of a vineyard that once covered the whole of Cap Corse.

CLOS NICROSI, ROGLIANO

Clos Nicrosi is the leading estate of the area, run by Jean-Noël Luigi, a tall man with a dark beard. The ageing cellars are now in a rambling house above the village of Rogliano, which seems literally perched on the hillside and was just below the cloud line on the day I was there. The house was built in the 1870s by Luigi's great-grandfather and his brothers, who made their money in Alabama running a tearoom and later supermarkets. They were typical of the many Corsicans who left the island in the 1800s. Many went to Puerto Rico and to Peru, Brazil and Venezuela, returning home when they had made their fortune.

Luigi's twenty-eight hectares of vineyards are planted with

Vermentino, a little Nielluccio and Muscat. Originally the *cru* of Cap Corse consisted solely of dry white wine made from Vermentino, but in 1993 the INAO finally granted the appellation of Muscat de Cap Corse, after what Luigi described as a twelve-year struggle. The area for Muscat de Cap Corse includes not only the promontory of Cap Corse but also most of the appellation of Patrimonio, so that most of the wine growers there make it too.

The soil of Cap Corse is schist, unlike that of the rest of the island. Although it is unusual in traditional Corsican vineyards, the vines here are trained on wires, for the wind can be so strong that they need the extra support. In the summer the Libeccio blows from the south west and also the Sirocco; a strong wind at flowering can easily destroy two-thirds of the crop. However, they have less rain than the rest of the island – except on the two occasions I have visited.

Like all the dry white wines of Corsica, Vermentino is the variety for Cap Corse, producing particularly elegant, subtle flavours in the schist soil. Here it gives an average yield of 30 hl/ha. The juice is never given any skin contact and is fermented at 17–18°C, with no malolactic fermentation, and the wine is bottled the following spring. The 1996 when it had just been bottled had delicate, herbal notes on the nose, with an attractive weight in the mouth. It was ripe and rounded, with a touch of ginger and an ageing potential of three or four years. I greatly enjoyed the white wines from Clos Nicrosi when I visited them in 1985, and now, although there are other contenders, they still deserve their reputation as some of the best whites of Corsica.

Muscat de Cap Corse is vinified like any other *vin doux naturel* from the south of France. However, after the grapes have been carefully picked to eliminate any rotten ones, they are left in boxes to dry in the wind for about eight days, which has the effect of giving more weight, concentration and perfume to the wine, as well as extra potential alcohol, which rises from 14–15° to 18–19°. At the same time it lowers the yield to about 20 hl /ha, with a twenty-five per cent reduction in volume. The 1996 was quite honeyed, but the alcohol was still quite apparent on the finish, while the 1994 had benefited from some bottle age and was more concentrated in flavour, very honeyed and almost Sauternes-like in character. Clos Nicrosi also produces a *rosé*, mainly from Nielluccio, but no red wine.

DOMAINE PIERETTI, SANTA SEVERA

Happily, Clos Nicrosi no longer stands alone as the only estate of note on Cap Corse. An energetic and enthusiastic young woman, Lina Venturi, is now running her family estate of Domaine Pieretti in the village of Santa Severa. She has built a neat new cellar with shining stainless steel vats and efficient cooling systems, which was first used for the 1993 vintage. Before that, things were very rustic. Her father reminisced about how he had used a manual press and *fouloir*, and had trodden the grapes in a shallow concrete vat. His wine was kept in barrels of varying sizes. Friends helped you to pick your grapes and everyone brought something to share for lunch, but water was traditionally forbidden at the table for the harvest festival. He said that the new cellar had cost more money than he had ever spent. Was he shocked? No, very pleased and proud. His family had been making wine since 1720, but after he lost a substantial portion of his vines in one of the fires that can do so much damage to the *maquis*, he had felt discouraged. However, he was delighted when his daughter said she wanted to take over. Fire can be a severe hazard, especially when combined with a strong wind, and insurance for vineyard damage is not accepted in the departments most at risk, namely those of Corsica and the Midi.

Venturi has planted more vines and will soon have a total of six hectares in production, consisting of Vermentino, Nielluccio, a little Grenache Noir and a variety she called Alicante that is peculiar to Cap Corse and can withstand the strong winds. As well as Muscat, they have some other curious white Corsican varieties, such as Codiverta, which is named after the green tip at the end of the bunch, even when it is ripe; up to ten per cent is allowed in the white wine of Cap Corse. There is another variety called Giunizella, which used to be mixed with Muscat and Vermentino and is the subject of research by the CIVAM. Venturi's white Coteaux du Cap Corse includes a drop of Codiverta as well as Vermentino, which is picked at varying degrees of ripeness in order to add an extra dimension of flavour. It was quite full and rounded, with a touch of acidity.

The *rosé*, from Grenache Noir, Nielluccio and a little Alicante, was a light orange-pink, with a touch of strawberry on the nose and quite a full herbal mouthful of fruit, reminiscent of the scent of the *maquis*. The red, from equal parts of Alicante and Nielluccio, had tannin and herbal fruit, and was a touch rustic on the finish. At the time of my visit the Muscat was not yet in production. While we tasted, the father entertained me with local legends of knights in the nearby tower of Luri, one of the many lookout towers scattered along the coast. He showed me a conch shell and explained that they were used to sound the alarm for an invasion. The wines showed promise, and Venturi deserves to do well.

DOMAINE GIOIELLI, ROGLIANO

My final visit on Cap Corse was to Domaine Gioielli, where Michel Angeli runs a ten-hectare family vineyard outside the village of Rogliano. He is an elderly man, friendly but quite taciturn, who makes his wines in a large shabby shed that is none the less equipped with a cooling system and barrels. In his vineyards he has Vermentino, Nielluccio, Codiverta and Aleatico (also found on the island of Elba), as well as Grenache Noir and Muscat. His white Coteaux de Cap Corse consists of Vermentino with twenty per cent of Codiverta, which he said added finesse to the wine. It had some delicate fruit, with herbal notes. His *rosé* was delicate and pretty. The 1995 red, a blend of three parts Grenache Noir to one part Nielluccio, with eight months ageing in new and one-year-old barrels, had some ripe fruit and firm tannin, but because of the oak lacked the original flavour of Corsica.

The Muscat *à petits grains* is grown on south-facing slopes and the grapes are left to become overripe, with a potential of 16–17°, resulting in a ripe, full-flavoured and honeyed wine. Angeli is also unusual in making Rappu, an old Corsican tradition. Grenache Noir and Aleatico grapes are left to dry on the vines and the fermenting juice is muted with alcohol, like the Muscat, then aged for eight years in old *foudres*. The end result is not unlike a rich, sweet, raisiny Rivesaltes.

Patrimonio

From there I took the less winding road down the east side of Cap Corse and drove over the Col de Teghine just below the cloud line. The clouds did not completely spoil the views of the Etang de Bigulia and the plain of Bastia. The road then descended through the village of Patrimonio. Mont St Angelo dominates the skyline, with terraces of vineyards covering the steep hillsides, and in the village numerous growers' cellars advertise their wines. I stayed in nearby St Florent, a lively fishing town dominated by an old citadel, the harbour lined with restaurants offering fish that probably came out of the sea only that morning.

Patrimonio is the oldest appellation of Corsica, dating from 1968, but the reputation of the area goes back to the Middle Ages, when the monks of the abbey of Farinolle cultivated vines and sent their wine to the papal court in Rome. The appellation now covers seven villages, for as well as Patrimonio itself and St Florent, there are Oletta, Poggio d'Oletta, Barbaggio and Santo Pietro di Tenda. Forty years ago the appellation was even more extensive, with some six hundred hectares cultivated by two hundred and fifty growers, mostly people with other crops who sent their grapes to the local co-operative. Then in August 1960 disaster struck, in the form of a severe hailstorm that completely wiped out the crop for that year and destroyed many of the vineyards. The older people with only a few vines were reluctant to replant, and others left the area, abandoning their vines. Today, happily, you have the impression of a lively appellation, with twenty-four producers including a small co-operative, which is more than for any other *cru* or appellation of Corsica. However, the variation in quality is considerable: some are working hard for their reputation and their appellation, and some are content to rest on their laurels, taking advantage of the tourist industry.

Patrimonio is the appellation where Nielluccio comes into its own, for it thrives on the limestone and clay soil that you find nowhere else on the island. You used to be able to blend Nielluccio with a small amount of Grenache Noir, but as the vineyards have been replanted under the *restructuration* programme, the percentage of Grenache Noir has diminished, and from 2000 red Patrimonio has had to be a minimum of ninety per cent Nielluccio. Whether the wine should be aged in wood or not is another matter of debate, and opinions are sharply divided.

DOMAINE GENTILE, ST FLORENT

First I went to see Jean-Paul Gentile, who works with his father Dominique. They have a thirty-hectare estate and since my last visit in 1989 they have considerably enlarged their cellars, which are now well equipped with cooling equipment and their own bottling line. There is not an oak barrel in sight. Gentile is adamant that wood deforms Corsican wine. An appellation depends on its quality, typicity and tradition. Above all, it must be Corsican, but if it smells and tastes of wood, it is not. By wood he means of course Bordelais *barriques*. He would, on the other hand, like to try out the large *foudres* that were once traditional to the island, but that would be a question of controlled oxidation, not of wood contact.

We tried a range of his wines in his small tasting room, chatting as we tasted. First there was a young white Patrimonio, made from Malvoisie, the name he prefers to Vermentino. It was fresh and delicate, with herbal notes and a definite flinty, stony flavour that came from the chalk soil. Gentile wants his white wines to age, and demonstrated just how well they do with a 1983. It had turned an attractive golden colour, had a wonderful herbal aroma and some honey on the palate, with layers of nutty, tarry flavours, and was long and complex. They take great care to pick at just the right moment so as to have the best level of acidity, correcting it if necessary with the juice of less ripe grapes; nor does the wine undergo a malolactic fermentation. The *rosé*, made from Nielluccio, was quite full bodied, with a flavour of strawberries, and was intended for consumption during the year. Since 1993 they have produced two reds in the best vintages; one from the 1996 vintage, with only a four or five-day maceration, had the flavour of red fruit, with some peppery tannins. In contrast, the Sélection Noble 1994 from selected vineyards and grapes, made with a long maceration to obtain more extract, had a solid, meaty nose, with the warmth and herbs of the *maquis* on the palate and a depth of concentration. It had spent a couple of years in vat before bottling.

All the producers of Patrimonio, except for the three estates south of the river Aliso outside St Florent, come within the appellation of Muscat de Cap Corse. At Domaine Gentile they make two styles of Muscat with different sugar levels, one that conforms to the appellation and the other with a lower sugar level of 70 gm/l; the minimum for the appellation of Muscat de Cap Corse is 95 gm/l. The appellation wine is given twenty-four hours of skin contact, and because it has more sugar is heavier and richer in the mouth than the wine called simply Muscat Gentile, which has thirty-six hours skin contact and is redolent of honey and apricots. The Muscat de Cap Corse is classified as a *vin doux naturel*, whereas Muscat Gentile is simply a *vin de liqueur* as the term *vin doux naturel* is reserved for appellations. The final wine in the range is Rappu, which comes from a blend of Muscat and Nielluccio with a little Grenache Noir. According to Gentile, Rappu was the traditional way of using up any leftover grapes. The fermentation is stopped in the same way as for a *vin doux*, but these days they are much more selective, only making Rappu when the grapes are healthy and have overripened on the vines. The wine is then left in wood for four or five years to oxidise gently, although the barrels are occasionally topped up.

ORENGA DE GAFFORY, PATRIMONIO

The largest producer is Orenga de Gaffory, which has a fifty-five hectare estate and in 1991 took over the thirty-five hectare estate of San Quilico, which is vinified separately and kept as a separate label. Henri de Orenga is the man in charge, with the confidence that goes with being one of Corsica's larger producers. He explained how his grandfather used to produce Mattie, the most popular blend of the typical Corsican aperitif called Cap Corse, which is a mixture of herbs and wine. Then his father began planting vineyards in Patrimonio in the 1970s and built his first cellar in 1974. They now have a large streamlined cellar and warehouse outside the village of Patrimonio.

In contrast to Gentile, Orenga is in favour of wood, and he has been using *barriques* consistently since the 1987 vintage for red wine and since 1992 for white. He usually makes two versions of the same wine, one with wood called Réserve du Gouverneur, and one without. He considers that Nielluccio marries well with oak, for it is a grape variety that gives structure and tannin and the combination of two is very harmonious. His Patrimonio undergoes a twenty-day maceration at fermentation, and the wine is put into new wood for about nine months. When I tasted the 1996 just before bottling, it was full of sweet vanilla on the nose and palate, with a firm tannic finish. In older vintages the oak had toned down a little, but I was not convinced. Although the wines were well made, to my taste buds they simply did not taste of Corsica, for the oak gave them an international flavour that destroyed their regional typicity. The white Réserve du Gouverneur is fermented in *barrique* and remains there for four months. Again, I found the flavour overwhelmingly oaky and much preferred the wine that had seen no wood, retaining the light, lemony taste of Vermentino.

The most successful oaked wine was, to my surprise, the Muscat de Cap Corse. The 1996 Muscat du Gouverneur was fermented and muted in wood, spending four months in barrel altogether. In a curious way it was quite Sauternes-like in character, while the 1994 was intensely sweet and honeyed, with some toasted apricots. Orenga criticised the INAO for forcing the producers of Muscat de Cap Corse to increase the sugar level in their wines so that they conform to the other French *vins doux naturels*, for he considers that a lower level of 85 gm/l would make for a far more balanced wine.

DOMAINE ANTOINE ARENA PATRIMONIO

It is in Antoine Arena's cellars that Vermentino really comes into its own. He achieves a complexity and depth of flavour in his white wines that are unequalled in Patrimonio or anywhere else on the island. He makes three dry Vermentinos, one that he calls his basic wine and two from selected vineyards. The basic wine enjoys a standard vinification: he uses a pneumatic press, gives the wine a gentle *débourbage* and the fermentation, controlled between 18° and 20°C, with natural yeast, takes about three weeks without a malolactic fermentation. The flavour of the 1996 vintage was quite delicious, with a salty, almost mineral character and some attractive herbal fruit on the nose and palate.

The first vineyard, Grotte di Sole, was planted in 1991 and faces due south, giving very low yields. It had wonderfully rich fruit on the nose, with a firm, smoky, mineral character. The fermentation takes as long as six to eight weeks, which is made possible because Arena does not use cultured yeast and the wine is racked only once, so that it stays on the fine lees for several months until bottling in early summer. He is considering *bâtonnage* but has not tried it yet. The wine of the second vineyard, Le Carco, is made in the same way and tasted more like Viognier than Vermentino, with a flavour of apricots and weight in the mouth.

Arena has also experimented with late picked Vermentino. I tried a 1996 Moelleux Vendange Tardive, for which the grapes had been picked towards the end of October. From twenty-five hectares of vines he obtained two hundred litres of juice. The taste of the wine the following June was rounded and honeyed, but still had the edges of youth, while the first vintage, the 1993, which had spent two years in wood, had a nose more reminiscent of sherry, with an intriguing taste of bitter oranges and marmalade. Another fascinating taste comparison was between two different Muscats de Cap Corse, one muted with neutral alcohol and the other with Marc de Muscat. The first was quite classic Muscat, with honey and bitter oranges, while the second was more subtle, with a softer, herbal character and less obvious sweetness.

As for red wines, Arena makes just one. His 1995 Patrimonio had some solid fruit with a dry cherry taste, while his *rosé*, made principally by pressing, which he finds gives greater vivacity, with just twenty per cent *saignée*, which in contrast provides body, was ripe and fruity. It was the white wines that really stood out, however, and the conversation moved on to our mutual enthusiasm for Chablis and a comparison of our favourite producers.

DOMAINE LECCIA, POGGIO D'OLETTA

Since my previous visit to Yves Leccia, he has moved out of his tiny, cramped cellar in the middle of the village of Poggio d'Oletta to a modern building, filled with stainless steel vats, on the narrow road from St Florent. You drive past the old cathedral dating from the twelfth century, which is considered to be a fine example of Pisan architecture. Sadly it was firmly locked, but I enjoyed the Romanesque exterior with its carvings and round-arched doorway, as well as the remnants of columns, vestiges of the former cloisters, that now stand in the middle of a small vineyard.

Leccia has a total of twenty-two hectares of vineyards, which he has gradually been replanting. The training system has been changed from *gobelet* to *cordon de royat*, with four thousand rather than five thousand plants to the hectare. There has also been a distinct shift in the composition of the vineyards, towards pure Nielluccio for red wine and pure Vermentino for whites. Ugni Blanc has disappeared completely from the vineyards of Patrimonio and there is very little Grenache Noir left either. Leccia's Vermentino is fresh and minerally, while his *rosé* is quite rounded and full-bodied. He makes two reds, a Cuvée Classique and a selection of his best vines called Petra Bianca after the white limestone. The Cuvée Classique, which undergoes a six or seven-day maceration and ageing in vat over two winters, is quite deep in colour, with an enticing smoky character combined with the warmth of the *maquis*. Pietra Bianca enjoys a longer maceration, and with better-quality grapes has more substance and tannin, so that it needs more bottle age. The 1993 was the first vintage of Pietra Bianca, which proved a difficult year – Leccia described it as a 'poker game' – with storms during the harvest that even caused flooding on 22 September, but the red grapes picked after the storms made some good wine. Leccia experimented with barrels for the 1993 vintage, putting part of Pietra Bianca into Vosges oak for eight months. It had some cedary notes with vanilla overtones, but was not Corsican. Maybe *foudres* would be more successful.

The final wine in Leccia's repertoire is Muscat de Cap Corse. He explained that there are really three ways of making Muscat. You can dry the grapes, as they do at Clos Nicrosi, which makes for a very solid, substantial wine. You can avoid skin contact, which gives a lemony, honeyed style for an aperitif. Or you can do as he does and macerate the grapes for two or three days, running the juice off the skins once the fermentation starts. His wine had a rich, honeyed, orange flavour, with 100 gms/l of residual sugar.

DOMAINE DE CATARELLI, PATRIMONIO

My final visit in Patrimonio was to Roger le Stunff at Domaine de Catarelli. His surname is Breton in origin, but his vineyards come from his mother's side and have been in the family since 1880. They are in a breathtaking position right by the sea at Marina de Farinole, and you can see the ruined abbey of Farinole on the hill opposite his cellar. Le Stunff is one of the newer producers of Patrimonio. He trained in Montpellier and has been making wine here since 1990. A new cellar was built partially underground in 1992. One wall is bare earth and provides a perfect illustration of the *terroir* of Patrimonio, with fossilised oysters in the limestone and layers of clay. Le Stunff makes just one wine of each colour, a delicately fragrant Vermentino and a rounded, raspberry-flavoured *rosé*, from Nielluccio and a little Grenache Noir as well as a drop of Sciacarello, which was planted as an experiment. His red wine is almost pure Nielluccio, which spends eighteen months in vat and is quite solid and fruity. Occasionally he uses *passerillés* grapes for his Muscat de Cap Corse, provided they are very healthy. They were not in 1996, but nonetheless the wine had delicate honeyed fruit, providing a good note on which to drive south to Calvi.

Calvi

The road takes you across the Désert des Agriates, a desert not so much because of its aridity but because of the lack of all human habitation or even sheep. It is now a nature reserve and home to numerous wild ducks. Although the road has improved considerably since my last visit to the island, you will hardly meet another car. The coastline remains unspoilt and the film *The Longest Day* was made on the isolated beaches near St Florent, as well as on the cliffs of Cap Corse.

The first thing you notice as you drive into Calvi is a large sign proudly proclaiming the town as the birthplace of Christopher Columbus, a claim that may be substantiated, for Calvi belonged to the Genoese in 1441. However, there are other contenders. A marble plaque marks the spot, but only a few stones remain of the house. Today Calvi is an animated seaside resort, with a bustling old town dominated by the Genoese citadel. It lies at the centre of the area known as the Balagne, which stretches from Ile Rousse nearly as far south as Porto, but most of the vineyards are relatively close to Calvi itself.

CLOS CULOMBU, ST PIERRE-LUMIO

There has been progress in Calvi since my last visit. Some new estates have come to the fore, established ones have consolidated their work and the co-operative of Calenzana has ceased to operate. Clos Culombu is an example of a family estate that has moved on in a very satisfactory way. Etienne Suzzoni took it over from his brother Paul in 1986. Their father had planted the vineyards originally with the aim of delivering his grapes to the co-operative, but he soon realised that this was not a viable financial proposition so he built a cellar ready for their first vintage in 1976. There are now thirty-four hectares in eleven plots within a two-kilometre radius of their cellar outside the village of St Pierre-Lumio. They are planted with Nielluccio, Sciacarello, Grenache Noir and Vermentino, as well as a little Muscat, Syrah and Cinsaut. The name of their estate is open to debate. The French *colombe* means a dove, but in Corsican *culombu* also describes a conch shell, and that is the interpretation that they prefer, as it is depicted on their label. Conch shells were traditionally used to sound the alarm against the many invaders of the island.

Suzzoni is one of the thinkers of the appellation, taking nothing for granted and questioning everything. The appellation needs to define its objectives. Are we making wines for early drinking or wines to age? And how much of each? We risk doing neither one thing nor the other well. He explained that, in contrast to Patrimonio, which is very much an area of monoculture – in other words, viticulture – the farmers of the Balagne have other crops, olive trees and cereals as well as animals, so that vines are not necessarily the main source of revenue on a farm. At the end of the nineteenth century there were nine hundred hectares of vines in the area, with the different grape varieties all mixed up together. Today, by contrast, there are only three hundred hectares, but there is a positive move towards a vineyard of quality. The typicity of Calvi is defined by the mountains and the sea, which determine the microclimate. It is the mountain of Monte Grosso, rising to two thousand seven hundred metres, that separates Calvi from the rest of the island. The soil is granite, as in Ajaccio and Sartène; it is a poor soil but rich in minerals, so that the vines extract a lot of flavour.

Suzzoni feels that the light soil is very good for white wine, but does not consider that he has got his red wines right yet. They are either too hard or have too much fruit, so they need *élevage*, a year or two in an insulated cellar, which he has yet to build. The summer is the problem. From October to April the temperature is a fairly constant 11–16°, but then in May it begins to rise inexorably. He is perceptive about the characteristics of the different grape varieties. He would not plant Syrah again. It is all too easy to correct the flavour of a wine by blending Syrah, but it spoils the typicity of the flavour. It is much more difficult, but also much more interesting and rewarding, to keep to the Corsican varieties. More work should be done on those varieties so that they can find an alternative to Syrah. Nielluccio is not very regular in Calvi, as it is a very fickle variety demanding great attention in the vineyard. It needs a minimum of 13° or else it will be green and tannic. Acidity is also a key factor in Nielluccio, as a lower level makes for more rounded tannins, while too much acidity makes the tannins too dry. Nor is Nielluccio a good variety for early drinking; however, it does complement Sciacarello very well, and that is the tradition of Calvi, to blend several varieties together. Sciacarello is more regular in its yields and does well in years of drought, but there is the problem of lack of colour. As for white wines, he feels there is potential in Bianco Gentile, which is the subject of experimentation by the CIVAM.

For each colour Suzzoni makes two qualities of wine, a basic Tradition and a more selected Prestige. His red Tradition is made from five grape varieties, Nielluccio, Sciacarello, Grenache Noir, Syrah and Cinsaut, and has some easy, peppery berry fruit with a backbone of tannin. His Prestige, a blend of eighty per cent Nielluccio and twenty per cent Sciacarello, is more complex, a *pot pourri* of Corsican flavours typical of the herbs and scents of the *maquis*, with a firm, peppery finish. He has also experimented with pure Nielluccio, for the first time in 1993, the last really dry vintage, putting part of it into *barriques* for six months after a long *cuvaison*. Since 1993 rain has hindered his efforts. You need sufficient extract, as the wood must not toughen the wine but on the contrary make it more open in flavour. *Foudres* may be another option. Corsican wine makers tend to avoid *élevage*, but if the grape varieties are suitable, the yields smaller and the *cuvaisons* longer, why not? You cannot say that wood does not have a place in Corsica.

Suzzoni has worked with wood for his white wines too. The Tradition was quite full and floral, but was intended for early drinking. The Prestige comes from grapes that will provide more structure and depth, and for these he has also tried a fermentation in *barrique*, choosing wines with more acidity. His aim was not to obtain an oaky, toasted flavour, but to see if *bâtonnage* would give more depth of flavour without destroying the character of the wine, and also to see whether the *barriques* would enhance its ageing potential. He was frank in his assessment of this first experiment, considering that he had made a mess of the *bâtonnage* and had left the wine a month too long in wood. It was undoubtedly very oaky, and only time will tell how it will develop in bottle. None the less it demonstrates the curious, enquiring mind that will advance the cause of Corsican viticulture.

Our tasting finished with Dolcebiancu, a Muscat Vin de Liqueur that is not eligible for an appellation. It is made from raisined grapes and the fermentation is stopped by the addition of alcohol in the usual way. The 1996 was ripe and redolent of apricots, with a firm finish. Suzzoni would like to see an appellation for Muscat Vin de Corse and feels that this style of wine should not be the sole prerogative of Cap Corse and Patrimonio.

DOMAINE ALZIPRATU, CALENZANA

More food for thought was provided by Pierre Acquaviva at Domaine Alzipratu outside the village of Calenzana. He too has a broader view of things, having studied history and economics. He came to wine later and has now been running the family estate for six years. The estate had originally been created in the mid-1960s by Baron Henri-Louis de la Grange in association with Pierre's father Maurice. Opposite is the convent of Alzipratu, with its medieval frescoes, that was once also the property of the Baron de la Grange but now belongs to Giovanni Agnelli. When I visited, Acquaviva was struggling valiantly with the problems of working in the middle of a building site, as a new cellar was being constructed for the 1997 vintage.

Acquaviva believes firmly in the typicity of Corsican wine and its grape varieties, so all the original Carignan, Alicante and Ugni Blanc have been removed from his vineyards. There is still a little Grenache Noir and Cinsaut, but otherwise they are firmly Corsican in composition. The old vines are still pruned in *gobelet*, as bush vines, while the new vineyards are trained in *double guyot*. They are on south-facing hillsides on very stony granitic soil, with excellent drainage. The climate of Calvi is influenced strongly by both the sea, which is five kilometres away, and the nearby mountains, which rise to nearly two thousand metres.

We tasted as we talked. Acquaviva said he thought that there were two approaches to Vermentino. Some people pick their grapes when they are not fully ripe, which does not make for a lot of aroma but because of the greater acidity allows the wine to age. People are only just beginning to realise the ageing potential of Vermentino. Or you could choose a ripe, very aromatic style with much less acidity, which will not last. He makes his Vermentino in a very straight-forward way, in stainless steel vats and without any skin contact, taking the flavour of the *terroir* and the grape variety. It was slightly herbal with some fresh acidity.

In 1996 he made two *rosés*, a Cuvée Tradition and a Rosé Gris, Cuvée Prestige, which comes from two hectares of old vines, some at least fifty years old, which give more concentration. As it was so good, he decided to separate it from the other *rosé*. This style of pale orange-pink, or *gris*, wine is quite characteristic of the *rosé* wines of Calvi.

Acquaviva's red wine comes mainly from Nielluccio with some Sciacarello and Grenache Noir, which are usually fermented together. It is like making a soup, in that you often get better flavours if you cook all your vegetables together rather than separately. The wine then spends two years in vat before bottling. It had some attractive sweet pepper and liquorice fruit. Acquaviva is experimenting with the length of macerations, trying some shorter and some longer, but above all he wants to make wines to age, for that is how they will establish their reputation as a serious viticultural region. There is not a long tradition of private estates and cellars on Corsica, so they have a lot to learn, which will take time.

DOMAINE ORSINI, CALENZANA

The most ostentatious estate in Calvi is without doubt Domaine Orsini. The property of Tony Orsini, it is an amalgamation of two properties, Domaine de Rochebelle, a family estate that goes back six generations, and a newer addition, Domaine de Pietralba. Altogether there are sixty hectares of vineyards. It is off the road to Calenzana, with breathtaking views over the bay towards Calvi. The tasting room, or what the French might call *bar au vin*, is breathtaking for other reasons: one wall is taken up by a brilliantly coloured and perfectly hideous mural, depicting I was not quite sure what; and although the tables cunningly have a spittoon incorporated into their design, you are offered wines to taste out of the most inappropriate glasses. Orsini is a slick talker and he presented some of his wines. There was a 1996 Malvoisie, the name he prefers to Vermentino, which was light and fresh, but had no great flavour. He is working on a base wine from Vermentino for sparkling wine, and he too has experimented with fermenting a small amount of Vermentino in new barrels, but just for fifteen days, as he was anxious to avoid making what he called a *vin de menuiserie*, or carpenter's wine. It has to be seen whether oak will add to the ageing potential of Corsican whites.

Next came a Gris de gris, from Malvoisie and Sciacarello fermented together, giving a very delicate colour with light fruit and acidity. Apparently *rosé* was not made in Corsica until the mid-1960s. Previously the choice was red or white, but then the tourist demand came and now a substantial part of the island's production is *rosé*. A *rosé* Tradition from equal parts of Sciacarello, Grenache Noir, Cinsaut and Nielluccio had a certain peppery, herbal character, while a red Tradition from the same varieties but less Cinsaut, had quite a distinctive minty flavour with some rounded fruit. Orsini first began using *barriques* in 1993, and his 1995 Prestige red, a pure Nielluccio, spent a year in new wood. The oak was not too marked and it had some attractive herbal fruit. Orsini trained at Hyères, but is adamant that it is experience that counts. The ten-year-old cellar seemed well run; gravity is used as much as possible and the *barriques* are kept in an insulated environment.

CLOS LANDRY, CALENZANA

In complete contrast was Clos Landry, just down the road at the end of a drive lined with mimosa trees. I first visited this estate in 1986, when it was one of the leading properties of Calvi, with a reputation for *vin gris*. Today Fabien Paolini has been joined by his daughter Catty. Their twenty-six hectares are planted with Corsican varieties and the cellar has been slightly modernised to include a pneumatic press and more efficient cooling equipment, but M. Paolini seemed less energetic and communicative. I tasted the wines with Catty at their tasting booth on the main road outside Calvi: a soft, biscuity white and a smoky red that has been kept in vat, made from Sciacarello, Nielluccio and Grenache Noir, as well as a pale *rosé* made from the same varieties by direct pressing. We had a wonderful view of the citadel of Calvi, and there was a bird's nest in the rafters above our heads.

CLOS REGINU, MURO

My last taste of Corsica came from Michel Raoust at Clos Reginu, outside the village of Muro in the hills above Calvi. His estate seems to be in the middle of nowhere, down a winding road along which you travel optimistically – in this case, however, you are well rewarded for your patience. His twenty-eight hectares are planted with the principal Corsican varieties as well as Grenache Noir, a very small amount of Mourvèdre, some Syrah and a little Barbarosa, Ugni Blanc, Carignan and Cinsaut. He also has some olive trees.

His cellar is simple and functional – and also insulated, which is important in the Corsican summer – with stainless steel vats and second-hand *foudres*. He would very much like to try new wood, but then the wine would have to be aged for six or seven years in bottle, and he does not yet have the customers prepared to wait for that. His first experiments with *foudres* were in 1984 and he now makes two red wines, one with and one without wood.

For Raoust, the typicity of Calvi comes from the mixture of grape varieties, with each one doing something slightly different to add to the diversity, and also from the soil, which is variations upon clay and granite, making about five different soil types. He makes two qualities of each colour, of which the best is called E Prove. The white E Prove, from free-run Vermentino juice, is delicate and subtle, while the pink E Prove, mainly from pressed Sciacarello and Nielluccio, has a delicate herbal flavour. Sciacarello gives aroma to *rosé*, but lacks structure and colour.

As for reds, Raoust makes his Clos Reginu with less extract for early drinking. It is bottled after six months in vat, and the 1996 had softer tannins and a peppery finish. More interesting is E Prove, from Grenache Noir and Nielluccio with a little Syrah and Sciacarello. It enjoys a longer maceration and part is put into *foudres* for twelve months. He likes the addition of Syrah, as he enjoys the wines of the Rhône, and the tiny drop of Mourvèdre from just half a hectare, which is difficult to vinify separately, makes an insignificant contribution to the flavour. The 1994 E Prove was long and spicy, quite rich, with some sweet fruit and tannins.

And there my tour of the island ended. I headed back to the airport at Bastia, over the hills that run down the centre of the island. The views from the plane the next morning were breathtaking. The highest peaks were snow-covered, even in June, and the sea was a brilliant turquoise colour. The appeal of Corsica to outsiders is all too easy to understand, but none the less Corsica suffers from its insularity. No one produces bottles, corks or capsules on the island, so these all have to be brought from mainland France. The tourists provide a ready sale for the wines in the summer, but they form a limited market that confirms Corsica's insularity. Too often, although the island is part of France, its wines are neglected or simply ignored in a survey of French wines. Yet there are wines of great character and individuality, with the original flavours of the indigenous grape varieties. Progress has been made in the last ten years, but to give the last word to Pierre Acquaviva, 'we will make even greater progress in the next ten'. There is everything to achieve, with the splendid trump card of originality.

Key facts

First AC was Patrimonio in 1968; now a minimum of ninety per cent Nielluccio.

Coteaux d'Ajaccio 1971, became Ajaccio in 1984: Sciacarello, minimum of forty per cent; other Corsican varieties, minimum of twenty per cent; Grenache Noir, Cinsaut and Carignan, maximum of fifteen per cent each.

Vin de Corse 1976, with five *crus*: Sartène, Figari, Porto-Vecchio, Coteaux du Cap Corse, Calvi.

Muscat de Cap Corse 1993, including most of Patrimonio. A *vin doux naturel* with 95 gm/l residual sugar.

Vin de Pays de l'Ile de Beauté covers whole island.

Three strands to Corsican viticulture:

Indigenous varieties, such as Nielluccio, Sciacarello, Vermentino and others.

Varieties introduced from Algeria by *pieds noirs*, such as Carignan, Cinsaut and Grenache Noir.

International varieties used for *vins de pays*, such as Syrah (also allowed in Vin de Corse), Cabernet Sauvignon, Merlot and Chardonnay.

Vintages

1999: A drought in Patrimonio gave yields thirty per cent lower than average. A dry year, with some welcome rain in mid-August elsewhere, giving a good yield as well as good quality.

1998: Drought in Calvi reduced the crop. Otherwise good quality, with balanced wines.

1997: No climatic problems, making for some good wines throughout the island.

1996: Rain at harvest time caused some problems. Lighter wines than usual.

1995: A very good year, the reds with good colour and concentration.

1990: Described by Christian Imbert as 'the best year ever'.

Heat summation figures

St Martin-de-Londres (Pic St Loup) 1450
St Christol (Coteaux du Languedoc) 1596
Nîmes 1785
St Gilles (Costières de Nimes) 1813
Montpeyroux (Coteaux du Languedoc) 1693
Gignac (Coteaux du Languedoc) 1675
Marseillan (Picpoul de Pinet) 1665
Roquebrun (St Chinian) 1819
Béziers 1641
Carcassonne 1556
Maury 1746
Limoux 1345
Perpignan 1883

Figures are for degree days.
Data provided by Philippe Tolleret from Skalli.

Vins de Pays *for the region*

A new *vin de pays*, **des Portes de la Méditerranée**, was created in 1999, covering the departments of Alpes-de-Haute Provence, Hautes-Alpes, Alpes-Maritimes, Ardèche, Drome, Var and Vaucluse. However, the Drome, Ardèche and Hautes-Alpes are outside the scope of this book.

d'Oc, see page 434

des Alpes-de-Haute Provence

des Alpes-Maritimes

de l'Aude:
    de la Cité de Carcassonne
    des Coteaux de la Cabrerisse
    des Coteaux de Miramont
    des Coteaux de Peyriac (also in Hérault)
    des Coteaux de Narbonne
    des Coteaux du Littoral Audois
    des Côtes de Lastours
    des Côtes de Pérignan
    des Côtes de Prouilhe
    de Cucugnan
    d'Hauterive
    de la Haute Vallée de l'Aude
    des Hauts de Badens
    du Torgan
    du Val de Cesse
    du Val de Dagne
    de la Vallée du Paradis

des Bouches-du-Rhone:
de la Petite Crau

du Gard:
des Cévennes
des Coteaux Flaviens
des Côtes du Vidourle
des Sables du Golfe du Lion (also in the Hérault)
de la Vaunage
de la Vistrenque

de l'Hérault:
de l'Ardailhou
de la Bénovie
de Bérange
de Bessan
de Cassan
de Caux
de Cessenon
des Collines de la Moure
des Coteaux de Bessilles
des Coteaux de Fontcaude
des Coteaux de Laurens
des Coteaux de Murviel
des Coteaux de Peyriac (also in the Aude)
des Coteaux du Salagou
des Coteaux d'Ensérune
des Coteaux du Libron
des Côtes du Brian
des Côtes du Céréssou
des Côtes de Thau
des Côtes de Thongue
des Gorges de l'Hérault
de la Haute Vallée de l'Orb
du Mont Baudile
des Monts de la Grage
de Pézenas
des Sables du Golfe du Lion (also in the Gard)
du Val de Montferrand
de la Vicomte d'Aumélas

Corsica:
de l'Ile de Beauté

des Pyrenées-Orientales:
Catalan
de la Côte Vermeille
des Côtes Catalanes
des Coteaux des Fenouillèdes
des Vals d'Agly

du Vaucluse:
d'Aigues

du Var:
d'Argens
des Maures
du Mont-Caume
des Coteaux du Verdon

Glossary

Agrément – approval – refers to the official approval of a wine for its appellation.

Assemblage – blend of grape varieties.

Barrel of one wine/two wines – barrel that is not new but has already matured one or two wines.

Barrique – the Bordeaux barrel of 225 litres.

Ban de vendange – proclamation allowing the commencement of the harvest.

Bâtonnage – lees stirring.

Capitelle – old stone shelter for shepherds.

Carbonic maceration – see pp. 50–1 for a detailed description; a process of fermenting whole bunches of grapes in a vat filled with carbon dioxide.

Cave particulière – a private cellar, belonging to an independent producer, not a co-operative member.

Cépage – grape variety, so a *vin de cépage* is a varietal wine.

Cépage améliorateur – literally an 'improving grape variety', such as Syrah or Mourvèdre; these have been planted extensively in order to improve the traditional blends of Carignan, Cinsaut and so on.

Climat – term for a specific vineyard.

Commune – a French administrative unit, ranging in size from a small village to a city as large as Nice. Appellation regulations always list the permitted *communes*.

Cordon de Royat – a method of pruning, with one or two branches trained along wire horizontal to the ground.

Coulure – a disorder of the vine caused by flowering in unsatisfactory climatic conditions. The small berries fail to develop, so that the crop is greatly reduced.

Cuvaison – the period of time the juice spends in the vat, on the grape skins, irrespective of whether it is actually fermenting or not.

Débourbage – the process of allowing the juice of a potential white wine to fall clear, usually by chilling before fermentation.

Délestage – means of extracting flavour and colour for wine, described at greater length on pages 52–3.

Demi-muid – a barrel bigger than a *barrique*, usually 500–600 litres in size.

Egrappage – the removal of grape stalks, done by an *égrappoir*. Interchangeable with *éraflage*.

Elevage – discussed at greater length on pages 53–5, but essentially the ageing of wine in the cellar before bottling.

Encépagement – blend of grape varieties.

Eraflage – Destalking or destemming, done by an *érafloir*. Interchangeable with *égrappage*.

Etang – inland salt-water lake, of which there are many along the Mediterranean coast.

Etat sanitaire – literally the state of health of the grapes, particularly with regard to rot or disease. A quality criterion for all co-operatives these days.

Flottateur – a piece of equipment designed to facilitate debourbage. The juice is put in a broad vat, into which gas is injected under pressure. Little bubbles of air rise to the surface, at the same time bringing the suspended lees to the top, where they can be removed by suction.

Foudre – the traditional large barrel of the Midi. Their size varies considerably, but they are usually about 40–50 hectolitres.

Fouloir – machine that gently breaks the grape skins in order to release juice.

Garrigue – the typical scrubland of the Midi, with plants such as bay, sistus, rosemary and so on. Known as *maquis* in Corsica.

Giropalette – a large metal frame used for mechanical riddling or *remuage*.

Gobelet – a method of pruning best described as 'bush vines'.

Groupement de producteurs – a producers' union or group, such as Les Vignerons Catalans.

Heat exchanger – equipment for heating or cooling grape juice.

Hydric stress – water stress, a factor in ripening grapes. Too much rain makes the grapes swell excessively, but too little water can stop the ripening process – a little water stress does no harm.

ICV – Institut Coopératif du Vin.

INAO – Institut National des Appellations d'Origine, the body responsible for the implementation of the French laws of appellation, which has to agree to any changes proposed by the relevant producers.

Labelle – the official tasting that checks that a wine is typical of its appellation.

Lieu-dit – literally a placename, a mention on the vineyard map.

Lutte raisonnée – integrated or sustained viticulture. Not organic, but implying a detailed consideration of when and how to treat the vines.

Lyre training – the vine canopy is divided into two in the form of a V, allowing for better aeration and exposure of the grapes to sunlight.

Macération à chaud – a warm maceration of the grape skins and juice, in order to extract yet more flavour and colour from the grapes.

Malolactic fermentation – a second fermentation that converts malic acid, as in apples, into softer lactic acid, as in milk.

Microbullage – micro-oxygenation, as discussed on pages 55–6; it involves injecting a minute amount of air into a vat of wine.

Moelleux – a lightly, but not lusciously, sweet wine.

Mustimeter – measures sugar in grape juice, giving an indication of ripeness and potential alcohol.

Mutage – the act of stopping the fermentation of grape juice by the addition of alcohol. An essential part of the process of making *vin doux naturel*.

Négoce – collective term for the activity of *négociants*.

Négociant – a traditional merchant. Their role is discussed on page 24.

Nouaison – the setting of the grapes, after flowering.

PLC – Plafonde Limite de Classement, literally a classification ceiling, allowing an extra percentage, usually twenty per cent, on top of the annual permitted yield for an appellation.

Passerillage (noun), *passerillé* (adjective) – refers to grapes that have been left on the vines in the autumn sunshine and wind, to dry and dehydrate so that they become almost raisin-like.

Pièce – a small barrel, similar in size to a *barrique*.

Pieds noirs – French nationals born in Algeria, who returned to France when they were expelled at the time of Algerian independence.

Pigeage – Originally described the traditional treading of the grapes, but is now usually a mechanical pressing-down of the skins in order to extract colour and flavour.

Pneumatic press – the newest type of press. The grapes are pressed very gently by a large bladder that is usually filled with air, but occasionally water.

Pressurage directe – a way of making *rosé* wine, in which the grapes are pressed immediately so that any colour is extracted during the pressing. Wines made this way tend to be lighter in colour than those made by *saignée*.

Primes d'arrachage – subsidies paid for pulling up vineyards.

Pupitre – wooden stand used for riddling sparkling wine.

Quai de réception – facility for the reception of grapes.

Rancio – a *vin doux naturel* that has been aged in contact with air, in barrel or glass jar.

Ratafia – drink made in Champagne and Chablis from grape juice and the previous year's grape brandy.

Régisseur – vineyard and cellar manager.

Remontage – for red wine, the pumping over of the juice to extract more colour and flavour.

SAFER – Societé d'Aménagement Foncier d'Etablissement Rural, the organisation responsible for the development of rural France, which exercises considerable authority over the ownership and changing hands of vineyards.

Saignée – method of making pink wine whereby juice is run off, or bled, from the fermenting vat.

Sélection massale – mass selection of vine wood, usually from the grower's own vineyard. A means of maintaining the characteristics of a particular vineyard.

Sélection parcellaire – vineyard selection; an important consideration in the choice of wines for blending.

Skin contact – a process used in making white wine to extract more flavour from the grape skins by macerating the juice and skins for a few hours at a cool temperature before fermentation begins.

Stage – a period of apprenticeship in a grower's cellar or vineyard.

Syndicat – growers' union; each appellation has one, and sometimes two.

T-budding – a method of grafting the bud of one variety on to the established vine of another; a time-saving way of changing the composition of a vineyard, entailing the loss of only one year's crop.

Terroir – not just soil, but the whole environment in which the vines grow – microclimate, aspect and altitude, as well as soil.

Triage – the picking of grapes for sweet wines, when a meticulous selection of the grapes, entailing several pickings or *tris*, is necessary.

VDQS – Vin Delimité de Qualité Supérieure – the quality category between *appellation contrôlée* and *vin de pays*.

Vendange verte – green harvesting, or picking of unripe grapes, usually in July, to reduce the crop.

Vendange tardive – late harvest; the use of this term on a label is carefully controlled by the INAO, despite the growing number of these wines produced in the Midi.

Véraison – moment at which the grapes begin to change colour, from youthful green to reddish-purple or yellowish-green.

Viandé – literally meaty; often used to describe Mourvèdre in the Bandol.

Vigneron – a wine producer, making wine as well as growing grapes.

Vin de presse – wine from pressed grapes, as opposed to free-run juice.

Vin de primeur – a young wine, which can be released for sale as early as the middle of October following the harvest.

Viticulteur – a grape grower and usually a co-operative member.

Vrac, as in *en vrac* – the sale of wine in bulk rather than bottle.

Bibliography

Asher, Gerald, *On Wine*, Jill Norman and Hobhouse, London 1983.

Atkin, Tim, *Vins de Pays d'Oc*, Gilbert & Gaillard, Bailly 1994.

Baillaud, Robert, and Clavel, Jean, *Histoire et Avenir des Vins en Languedoc*, Privat, Toulouse 1985.

Bedot, Pierre, *Guide des Vins du Var*, Editions Jeanne Laffitte, Marseille 1987.

Berry, Liz, *The Wines of Languedoc-Roussillon*, Ebury Press, London 1992.

Boissieu, Jean et al, *Les Vins du Rhône et de la Mediterranée*, Editions Montalba, Paris 1978

Casamayor, Pierre, and Monteilhet, Hubert, *Vignes et Vignerons du Soleil*, Editions de Fallois, Paris 1994.

Cavoleau, Jean-Alexandre, *Oenologie Française*, Paris 1927.

Clavel, Jean, *Le 21ème siècle des Vins du Languedoc*, Editons Causse, St Georges d'Orques 1999.

Dion, Roger, *Histoire de la Vigne et du Vin en France des Origines au XIX ème siecle*, Flammarion, Paris 1959.

Dovas, Michel; Lecouty, Chantal; Martini, Michel; and Spurrier, Steven, *Encyclopédie des Vins de Corse*, Editions de Fallois, Paris 1990.

Duyker, Hubrecht, *Grands Vins du Rhône et du Midi*, Nathan, Paris 1985.

Ferré, Georges, *1907 La Guerre du Vin*, Editions Loubatières, Portet-sur-Garonne 1997.

Guyot, Jules, *Etudes des Vignobles de France*, Paris 1868.

Heinic, Lionel, *Si Bandol AOC m'était conté*, Editions Scriba, Avignon 1992.

Imbert, Christian, *Historique de la Vigne en Corse*, 1984.

Johnson, Hugh, *The Story of Wine*, Mitchell Beazley, London 1989.

Jullien, André, *Topographie des Vins de France*, Paris 1816.

Laborieux, Alain, *Muscats, Des vins, des terroirs, une histoire*, Editions Espace Sud, Montpellier 1997.

Lachiver, Marcel, *Vins, Vignes et Vignerons: Histoire du vignoble français*, Fayard, Lille 1988.

Lichine, Alexis, *The Wines of France*, Cassell, London 1952.

Guide to the Wines and Vineyards of France, third edn, Papermac, London 1985.

Luret, Nicolas, *Guide des Vins de Provence*, Editions Jeanne Laffitte, Marseille 1994.

Marcillaud, Laurent, and Rivière, Pascale, *Grands Vins du Languedoc-Roussillon*, Editions Climats, Castelnau-le-Lez 1997.

MacKenzie, Alastair, *Daumas Gassac: The Birth of Grand Cru*, Segrave-Foulkes, London 1995.

Millo, Francois, *Vignobles et l'Art de Vivre en Provence*, Editions Bopca, Le Cannet 1996.

Mercury, François-Noël, *Vignes, Vins et Vignerons de Corse*, Editions Alain Piazzola, Ajaccio 1991.

Mouillefert, *Les Vignobles et les Vins de France*, 1891.

Norman, Remington, *Rhône Renaissance*, Mitchell Beazley, London 1995.

Paul, Harry W, *Science, Vines and Wine in Modern France*, Cambridge University Press, Cambridge 1996.

Olney, Richard, *A Provençal Table*, Pavilion, London 1995.

Pomerol, Charles (ed.), *Terroirs et Vins de France*, Total-Edition-Presse, Paris 1984.

Redding, Cyrus, *A History and Description of Modern Wines*, Whittaker, Treacher and Arnot, London 1833.

Rendu, Victor, *Ampélographie Française*, Paris 1857.

Renault, Georges, *Méditerranée Vignerons du Soleil*, Editions Georges Renault, Cap d'Agde 1996.

Robinson, Jancis, *Vines, Grapes and Wines*, Mitchell Beazley, London 1986.

Sagnes, Jean; Pech, Monique, and Rémy, 1907 en Languedoc et Roussillon, Espace Editions, Montpellier 1997.

Shand, P. Morton, revised and edited by Cyril Ray, *A Book of French Wines*, Penguin, Harmondsworth 1968.

Smith, Michel, *Corbières*, Editions Jacques Legrand, Paris 1996.

Tovey, Charles, *Wine and Wine Countries*, Whittaker & Co, London 1877.

Vizetelly, Henry, *The Wines of France*, 1908.

Wilson, James, *Terroir*, Mitchell Beazley, London 1998.

Woon, Basil, *The Big and Little Wines of France*, Wine & Spirit Publications, London 1974.

Index

How to use this index

Wines, winemakers and estates are listed in alphabetical order, but may appear in different places in the index depending on what the first word of the entry is. Remember that the entry you are looking for may begin with:
(i)   'Cave', 'Château', 'Clos', 'Cuvée', or 'Domaine', sometimes followed by 'de', 'de la' or 'du', followed by the name you know;
(ii) 'Le', 'La', 'L'', or 'Les', followed by the word you know,
(iii) 'St' or 'Ste', followed by the word you know.

717